DICTIONARY OF
CAPE BRETON ENGLISH

Biff and whiff, baker's fog and lu'sknikn, pie social, and milling frolic – these are just a few examples of the distinctive language of Cape Breton Island, where a puck is a forceful blow and a Cape Breton pork pie is filled with dates, not pork.

The first regional dictionary devoted to the island's linguistic and cultural history, the *Dictionary of Cape Breton English* is a fascinating record of the island's rich vocabulary. Dictionary entries include supporting quotations culled from extensive interviews with Cape Bretoners and considerable study of regional variation, as well as definitions, selected pronunciations, parts of speech, variant forms, related words, sources, and notes, giving the reader in-depth information on every aspect of Cape Breton culture.

A substantial and long-awaited work of linguistic research that captures Cape Breton's social, economic, and cultural life through the island's language, the *Dictionary of Cape Breton English* can be read with interest by Backlanders, Bay byes, and those from away alike.

WILLIAM J. DAVEY is a senior scholar in the Department of Languages and Letters at Cape Breton University.

RICHARD MACKINNON is a professor of Folklore and director of the Centre for Cape Breton Studies at Cape Breton University.

DICTIONARY OF
CAPE BRETON ENGLISH

WILLIAM J. DAVEY
AND RICHARD MACKINNON

UNIVERSITY OF TORONTO PRESS
Toronto Buffalo London

© University of Toronto Press 2016
Toronto Buffalo London
www.utppublishing.com

ISBN 978-1-4426-4790-9 (cloth)   ISBN 978-1-4426-1599-1 (paper)

Library and Archives Canada Cataloguing in Publication
Davey, William J., 1944–, compiler, editor
Dictionary of Cape Breton English / William J. Davey and Richard
MacKinnon.

Includes bibliographical references.
ISBN 978-1-4426-4790-9 (cloth)   ISBN 978-1-4426-1599-1 (paper)

1. English language – Dialects – Nova Scotia – Cape Breton Island –
Glossaries, vocabularies, etc. 2. English language – Nova Scotia – Cape
Breton Island – Dictionaries. 3. Canadianisms (English) – Nova Scotia –
Cape Breton Island – Dictionaries. 4. Popular culture – Nova Scotia –
Cape Breton Island – Dictionaries. 5. Cape Breton Island (N.S.) –
Languages – Dictionaries. I. MacKinnon, Richard Paul, 1957–, compiler,
editor II. Title.

PE3245.N6D39 2016   427'.97169   C2016-902471-7

University of Toronto Press acknowledges the financial assistance to its publishing
program of the Canada Council for the Arts and the Ontario Arts Council, an agency of
the Government of Ontario.

Canada Council   Conseil des Arts
for the Arts   du Canada

ONTARIO ARTS COUNCIL
CONSEIL DES ARTS DE L'ONTARIO
an Ontario government agency
un organisme du gouvernement de l'Ontario

Funded by the   Financé par le
Government   gouvernement
of Canada   du Canada   Canada

Contents

Acknowledgments

After so many years, it is a great pleasure to acknowledge and thank those who have shown interest in the progress of the dictionary and offered help in various ways. If it takes a village to raise a child, this adage is also true of this project.

Special thanks to Heather Davey, proofreader extraordinaire, and to those who assisted with the pronunciation of loanwords: Stephanie Inglis, Jim St. Clair, Heather Sparling, Ronald Labelle, and Carmen MacArthur. We are also grateful for the long-term support and contributions to the dictionary from Jim St. Clair and the late Bob Morgan, and for advice and encouragement from lexicographers Terry Pratt, Katherine Barber, and Joan Houston Hall. Thanks are also due for the many useful comments from the two peer reviewers of the manuscript, and the mentoring and direction from Siobhan McMenemy, Acquisitions Editor, University of Toronto Press. The *Dictionary of Newfoundland English* and the *Dictionary of Prince Edward Island English* provided inspiration and models to follow.

The work of the student research assistants at Cape Breton University was invaluable during the collection stage of the project. Many of these students worked several terms on the dictionary before going on to postgraduate studies: Patricia Babin, Kevin Kearney, the late Moira Ross, Tammy Quinn, Donelda MacDonald, Melissa Grant, Maureen Flynn, Jennifer Gardiner, Tammy MacNeil, Maureen McDonald, Laura Schella, Mary Vickers, and Nicole MacDougall.

We are also grateful to those who generously volunteered their time and knowledge to complete the surveys (Pilot Survey, Survey I, and Survey II) or be tape recorded for the dictionary (the *DCBE* Tapes). The names of these people are listed in the Works Consulted. In addition, those sending emails and offering oral comments also made an important contribution, as many words that they suggested are used in conversation but do not frequently appear in published materials.

Many others, especially colleagues at Cape Breton University, also shared their expertise in fields like marine biology and music. Many people have suggested words or helped finding informants: Jane Arnold, Elizabeth Beaton, Walter Bond, Sam Boutilier, Lee-Anne Broadhead, Mickey Campbell, Diane Chisholm, Peyton Chisholm, Jan Curtis, Jeri Doucette, Bill Doyle, David Frank, Barry Gabriel, Johnny Gillis, Patrick and Lee Gillis, Barb Glassey, George Hussey, John Johnson, Chris Jones, Katherine Jones, Charles MacDonald, Donald MacGillivray, Sheldon MacInnes, John and Laureen MacKenzie, Greg

MacLeod, Mary K. MacLeod, Anne Marie MacNeil, Richard Marchand, David Muise, Joyce Rankin, Heather Sparling, Laura Syms, Brian Tennyson, Janice Tulk, Joan Weeks, and Carla White. The members of the word-a-day coffee gathering (Derrick Hayes, Allan Fraser, Glenn MacDonald, George MacLeod, and Richard Watuwa) were both cheerful and helpful in testing Cape Breton usage.

We are also grateful for administration provided by Arthur Tucker, Mary K. MacLeod, Robert Campbell, Joanne Gallivan, Harvey Johnstone, Rod Nicholls, Dale Keefe, Mary Keating, Arja Vainio-Mattila, and Sander Taylor. We are also thankful for the office space for the dictionary research from 2009 to 2015.

Library and Archives

We are extremely grateful to the library and archival staff members for their expertise and the kindness extended to both the editors and the student research assistants during the years of compiling material. The dictionary could not have been completed without their help and the library and archival resources available: the Beaton Institute, the Archive of Cape Breton University and community at large, Cape Breton University's main library, the Mi'kmaq Resource Centre at Cape Breton University, and the Cape Breton Regional Library, especially the Cape Breton Room at the James McConnell Memorial Library, Sydney.

Financial Support

We gratefully acknowledge the many funding agencies that allowed us to hire student research assistants to gather citations for the dictionary. The research grants from Cape Breton University's research committees provided a foundation from which we could apply for other funds. This funding was essential to the completion of the dictionary and also contributed to the academic development of the students working on the project.

Cape Breton University, 1997–2009, 2013
SSHRC, Assistance to Small Universities Program, 1993–5
Enterprise Cape Breton Corporation, 1993–5, 1998–9
Nova Scotia Economic Renewal Agency, 1994, 1996–7
Human Resources Development Canada, 1994–2001, 2003–4, 2007
Canadian Museums Association, 1997–8
Canada Research Chair, Intangible Heritage, 2007–10, 2013

A Sample *DCBE* Entry

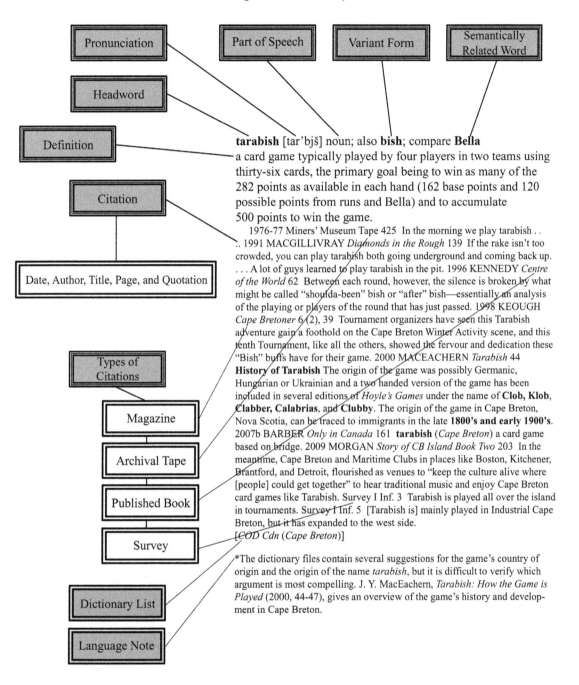

Pronunciation

Part of Speech

Variant Form

Semantically Related Word

Headword

Definition

Citation

Date, Author, Title, Page, and Quotation

Types of Citations

Magazine

Archival Tape

Published Book

Survey

Dictionary List

Language Note

tarabish [tar'bjš] noun; also **bish**; compare **Bella**
a card game typically played by four players in two teams using thirty-six cards, the primary goal being to win as many of the 282 points as available in each hand (162 base points and 120 possible points from runs and Bella) and to accumulate 500 points to win the game.
1976-77 Miners' Museum Tape 425 In the morning we play tarabish . . .. 1991 MACGILLIVRAY *Diamonds in the Rough* 139 If the rake isn't too crowded, you can play tarabish both going underground and coming back up. . . . A lot of guys learned to play tarabish in the pit. 1996 KENNEDY *Centre of the World* 62 Between each round, however, the silence is broken by what might be called "shoulda-been" bish or "after" bish—essentially an analysis of the playing or players of the round that has just passed. 1998 KEOUGH *Cape Bretoner* 6 (2), 39 Tournament organizers have seen this Tarabish adventure gain a foothold on the Cape Breton Winter Activity scene, and this tenth Tournament, like all the others, showed the fervour and dedication these "Bish" buffs have for their game. 2000 MACEACHERN *Tarabish* 44 **History of Tarabish** The origin of the game was possibly Germanic, Hungarian or Ukrainian and a two handed version of the game has been included in several editions of *Hoyle's Games* under the name of **Clob, Klob, Clabber, Calabrias,** and **Clubby**. The origin of the game in Cape Breton, Nova Scotia, can be traced to immigrants in the late **1800's and early 1900's.** 2007b BARBER *Only in Canada* 161 **tarabish** (*Cape Breton*) a card game based on bridge. 2009 MORGAN *Story of CB Island Book Two* 203 In the meantime, Cape Breton and Maritime Clubs in places like Boston, Kitchener, Brantford, and Detroit, flourished as venues to "keep the culture alive where [people] could get together" to hear traditional music and enjoy Cape Breton card games like Tarabish. Survey I Inf. 3 Tarabish is played all over the island in tournaments. Survey I Inf. 5 [Tarabish is] mainly played in Industrial Cape Breton, but it has expanded to the west side.
[*COD Cdn* (*Cape Breton*)]

*The dictionary files contain several suggestions for the game's country of origin and the origin of the name *tarabish*, but it is difficult to verify which argument is most compelling. J. Y. MacEachern, *Tarabish: How the Game is Played* (2000, 44-47), gives an overview of the game's history and development in Cape Breton.

Introduction

The Scope of the Dictionary

James Murray, the primary editor of what became the *Oxford English Dictionary* (first edition, 1884–1928), began his address *The Evolution of English Lexicography* (1900) by referring to an exchange that occurred in the House of Commons in 1887. When a member questioned the meaning of *allotment* in a government act, the minister in charge of the bill brushed off the query with "look in the Dictionary" and, in response to a subsequent question, answered, "Johnson's Dictionary! Johnson's Dictionary!" (5). Murray used the incident to illustrate that many people "habitually speak of 'the Dictionary,' just as they do of 'the Bible'" (6).[1] Far from being a single work written by one author, "the dictionary" as it existed when Murray gave his address was continuing its "evolution" as he and others were shaping the future direction of dictionaries. Murray and his staff were labouring on their monumental historical dictionary of the English language, Joseph Wright was editing his six-volume *English Dialect Dictionary* (1898–1905), and in North America Noah Webster had long since published *An American Dictionary of the English Language* (1828).

A century after Murray's address, most people are well aware that there are several editions of the Bible and a great variety of dictionaries available. In addition to the many general-purpose dictionaries meant for university, business, and government use, publishers produce specialized dictionaries for second-language learners; technical dictionaries for those working in specific disciplines such as geography, linguistics, literary studies, and psychology; and dictionaries for those interested in regional language.[2] Each of these dictionaries has a specific audience in mind and objectives that determine the selection of the words to be defined and the style of definitions. What then is a regional dictionary and what type of words should an editor include?

As the name suggests, regional dictionaries focus on the words and senses in a particular geographical area, but this range varies greatly. As *The Oxford Companion to the English Language* points out, regional dictionaries of English "list and define words as used in a particular country ... or part of a country" (McArthur 1992, 857). *A Dictionary of Canadianisms* (1967), the *English Dialect Dictionary* (1898–1905) and the *Dictionary of American Regional English* (1985–2013) have a national scope as their range is countrywide, but they are also regional, or, "exclusive" (Görlach 1990, 1477), as they collect terms used in a specific locality.

Others consider smaller regions such as the *Dictionary of Newfoundland English* (1990) and the *Dictionary of Prince Edward Island English* (1988). Like these two island dictionaries, the *Dictionary of Cape Breton English* seeks to collect and define the words that have particular meaning on Cape Breton Island, words and senses that many people outside the Atlantic Region would not know. These regional dictionaries are also historical in the sense that they give dated quotations, or citations, that illustrate the earliest and latest examples of the words defined, and record the words that were important to the early history and culture of the region as well as those currently used. Although regional dictionaries do not have the historical development of the regional words as a main purpose, they function in part as historical dictionaries too.[3]

Each regional dictionary follows principles for excluding and including words. The *Dictionary of Cape Breton English* (hereafter *DCBE*) does not include slang, which tends to be short-lived, confined to a particular in-group, and difficult to identify.[4] Jonathon Green, editor of *Cassell's Dictionary of Slang*, defines slang as the "counter-language ... the language of the outlaw, the despised, the marginal, the young" (1998, v). By contrast, regional language is often rural, conservative, limited to certain areas, and reflective of older speakers and practices. For example, the choice of informants for the questionnaire used in the *Dictionary of American Regional English* has "a deliberate weighting toward older people. Folk language is traditional, and older people remember many things that young ones have never heard of" (Cassidy 1985, xiv). In addition, regional words are distinguished from what might be called general or common vocabulary that appears without usage labels in general-purpose dictionaries like the *Canadian Oxford Dictionary* (2004) and the *Merriam-Webster Collegiate Dictionary* (2009). This type of vocabulary is widely known, not limited to specific localities, and used in official writing and addresses. As one would expect, the border between regional and other types of vocabulary are not impervious, as some words may change from general usage to regional. As the *Dictionary of American Regional Dictionary* indicates, *widow woman* for "widow" was once widespread but is now restricted to certain regions (1985, xxxvi). For the most part this dictionary has also omitted encyclopedic terms for people and places. A few generic terms like *miners' row* (a line of company owned houses) have been included, as well as some widely known encyclopedic terms that have cultural and historical importance such as *Davis Day*, the *Boston States*, and the *quatorze vieux*.[5] The editors have not been able to include the many informal names for Cape Breton places like *Senator's Corner* in Glace Bay, *the Shipyard* in Sydney, and *Phillip's Nose* (a prominent turn on the road climbing Cape Smokey). This is an area of research worthy of its own book.

Following the general principles outlined by Walter Avis in his introduction to *A Dictionary of Canadianisms*, the *DCBE* includes two types of words: those that are "native" to a region, and those that are "distinctively characteristic" (1967, xiii). The first type is the *-ism* words that originate in a particular area. Terms like *suête* (a strong south-east wind), *tarabish* (a card game), *Fat Archies* (soft molasses cookies), and *Cape Breton Pork Pies* (a small tart with date filling) are some of the terms that appear to be Cape Bretonisms according to our research. However, in the *DCBE*, and typically in other regional dictionaries, the more frequent type of word is not exclusive to an area, but regional in nature; these are distinctive, but did not originate in the geographical region, nor are they exclusively found there. As Atkins and Rundell note, "A regional label indicates that *the item is mainly but not exclusively used*" (2008, 227) in a particular area or country. Further to this, because of the many factors connecting Canada and the United States, Avis concludes, "the problem of identifying many terms as specifically 'American' or 'Canadian' is virtually impossible of solution" (1967, xiii). There is corresponding challenge to identify the provenance of words in Atlantic Canada because of the similar climates, geography, and occupations. An example of this second type of word is the specialized sense of *breeze*. Most English speakers understand this as a gentle movement of air, whereas to eastern commercial fishers it is a strong wind, often at gale force. The verb *to junk*, having the local meaning "to cut logs, meat, or other things into pieces or chunks," is recorded in the *Dictionary of Newfoundland English*, the *Dictionary of Prince Edward Island English*, *A Dictionary of Canadianisms*, and beyond the Atlantic Region in the *Oxford English Dictionary Online* (2000–, www.oed.com), the *Dictionary of American Regional English*, and *Maine Lingo* (1975). As a regional word, this sense is not recorded in general-purpose dictionaries but is mainly found in Atlantic Canada and parts of the United States.

Avis's general criteria serve as a useful first screening process, but to represent the regional vocabulary of Cape Breton more comprehensively, the editors have also included a limited number of words and senses that are more widely known. These words appear frequently in the *DCBE* collection of evidence discussed below and record the activities or things central to the historical or cultural development of the island. This type of term is similar to what Stefan Dollinger, Laurel J. Brinton, and Margery Fee, editors working on the second edition of the *Dictionary of Canadianisms*, describe as "'culturally' significant terms." They explain that this broader approach allows "for the inclusion of terms which are of greater significance to Canadians than to those of other nationalities" and is similar to national dictionaries from Australia and South Africa (2012, 171–2). On Cape Breton Island, the commercial fishery is one of these significant factors that shaped the development of the island. Thus, the dictionary includes words like *codline* (a light line employed in the ground fishery and for other purposes requiring a light, sturdy line) and other fishing terms that were used along the Atlantic coast where fish were prepared for export to Europe and the Caribbean islands. In the same way, industrial terms from mining and steel making that have made their way into the wider Cape Breton community are regional in Cape Breton but also found in other areas where these industries exist. Other mining communities would know terms like *pan shovel* (a short-handled shovel with a large circular blade), and a town with a steel plant that made coke for steel making would probably know the term *quenching car* (a railway car that transports hot coke from the coke ovens to be quickly cooled with water). Other less technical terms like *crumb* (extra working time, either a shift or part of one) would probably not be as widely known outside of Cape Breton Island. The cultural term *ceilidh*, originally a Gaelic noun meaning an informal visit or gathering, occurs in several dictionaries and was used widely in this sense during the early settlement of Cape Breton Island. Its range of meaning has extended from a noun indicating informal gatherings with food, music, and storytelling in homes to one that identifies public concerts held in halls, to its use as an adjective and verb, to its growing popularity as a personal name with several creative spellings. Because of its central importance in the social life of Cape Bretoners, the editors have included it and selected citations from over 250 attestations that illustrate its meanings.

Collection

The collection stage of the project began in 1993 and could not have been completed without the long-term support of grants from the Research Committee of Cape Breton University and external funds from several sources. These funds allowed the editors to hire student research assistants to help with the collection of quotations illustrating Cape Breton English from a variety of sources. The Beaton Institute, the archive at Cape Breton University, has been an invaluable resource with its extensive collection of published works about Cape Breton, an audiotape collection made with informants from all four counties of Cape Breton Island, and archival records of diaries and documents. Since many regional terms do not appear in published works, our collection has emphasized oral and unpublished sources. The research assistants excerpted quotations from 454 audiotapes: 384 tapes from the Beaton Institute, 59 from the Glace Bay Miners' Museum, 6 from the Sydney and Louisbourg Railway Museum, and 5 identified as *DCBE* Tapes. The audiotapes from the Beaton Institute were particularly useful with informants discussing topics like local histories, biographies, family histories, Christmas traditions, children's games, folk medicine, milling and weaving, beliefs (such as ghosts, forerunners, legends), music (violin styles, concerts, festivals, etc.) and personal recollections of events like the 1929 earthquake. Of the five *DCBE* Tapes, four are interviews with those having expertise in various areas, and the fifth records a local CBC radio program in which listeners called the station to offer their suggestions for Cape Breton words. The research assistants also excerpted quotations from the Beaton Institute's collection of diaries, correspondence, family papers, and business records. The dates range from the early 1800s (with over 30 in the nineteenth century) to recent acquisitions, including a large collection of transcribed tapes from the "Steel Project" made in the early 1990s under the direction of Elizabeth Beaton.

In addition, the reading program covered published materials written about Cape Breton such as academic journals, books, brochures, and selected articles from magazines and newspapers. Other records have been accessed through *Early Canadiana Online* (1998–2013), a digital collection of early Canadian print heritage. Brian Tennyson's *Cape Bretoniana: An Annotated Bibliography* (2005) was particularly helpful in tracking down published works. Along with the academic books and journals, the local histories and memoirs were productive sources for regional words. Ronald Caplan's *Cape Breton's Magazine* (1972–99) was another valuable source for regional language. The majority of these articles are transcribed interviews made with Cape Bretoners from all parts of the island who discuss their beliefs, work, leisure activities, and the events of their lives in their own voices. Consequently, some *DCBE* entries have more than one citation from this magazine as the person being interviewed and the perspective change in each article. Over 15,000 citations collected from this research were recorded in the database program *FileMaker Pro*, using fields for items like the headword, author, title, date, page, and the excerpted quotation, and having the capacity to sort and retrieve data in a number of ways.

In addition, three surveys have collected evidence for selected words. The first, identified as the Pilot Survey (1996), investigated 89 words with similar meanings in the *Dictionary of Newfoundland English* and the *Dictionary of Prince Edward Island English*. Because of the similar weather, ice conditions, occupations (especially the commercial fishery), and coastal features, one would expect that the Atlantic Provinces would have words in common, a shared Atlantic vocabulary. To test whether these regional terms were also found in Cape Breton English, the editors conducted tape-recorded interviews with five informants who were asked if they were familiar with the words. The informants were selected because of their different backgrounds (farming, fishing, logging, and music) and their interest in Cape Breton language and history. A detailed analysis of this survey is found in *Proceedings of the Annual 26th Meeting of the Atlantic Provinces Linguistic Association* (Davey and MacKinnon 2002), but in general the informants indicated that nearly all these terms are also used in Cape Breton English.

To investigate these 89 words further, the editors created Survey I (2002–4) and added words for which clarification or more evidence was needed. After nearly ten years of collecting from published, archival, and tape-recorded materials, the editors discovered that several words known to be widespread on Cape Breton Island were not showing up in the collection. *Puck*, meaning "a forceful blow" as a noun and "to hit or strike forcefully" as a verb, is a typical example. Despite its wide oral usage, the dictionary's data had only three citations for the word: two were part of the impolite Gaelic phrase, popularized in English as *puck ma thon* (kiss my rear), and the third citation was a metaphorical reference to a personal loss as a "tough puck," rather than the usual sense of a physical blow. Consequently, another 38 terms were added to the shared regional words of the Pilot Survey, giving a total of 127, including a general question asking for other distinctive words or senses not mentioned in the survey. Following the example of a questionnaire employed by T. K. Pratt while collecting material for the *Dictionary of Prince Edward Island English*, Survey I used a direct method of investigation. Fifty-five informants completed the survey, indicating if they "used," "knew," or "did not know" the words with suggested meanings. Several terms had further questions to clarify meanings. *Scoff*, an abundant meal of delicious food, for instance, had related queries about the time for the meal and about the menu (one food such as lobster or a variety of foods). Participants were also invited to give their own understanding of the terms. A nearly equal number of male and female informants completed the questionnaire, and their ages ranged from twenty to over seventy. They were all natives or residents of Cape Breton and were from the four counties of Cape Breton, with the largest representation from Cape Breton County because it has the largest population.[6] Survey I provided information about the frequency of occurrence of words, geographical distribution, and varying senses. Since there were too few respondents for statistical analysis, in the few instances in which the editors comment in the Language Notes (see below) that a term is used in a particular geographical area, the decision is based on all the *DCBE* evidence. For example, the word *dairy* (meaning a convenience store, as opposed to a business where milk is processed) is found frequently in Cape Breton County but less so in the other three counties as indicated by results from surveys, *DCBE* tapes, and the citation file.

The editors also designed a shorter version of Survey I, designated as Survey II (2002), to learn more about the vocabulary of the commercial fishery. This questionnaire repeated 26 terms from Survey I that referred to things like weather, ice, and water features, and added another 37 questions to gather information on things such as fishing equipment, giving 63 terms in total. This survey was prompted by the importance of the fishery on Cape Breton Island. Similar to the results found in Rose Mary Babitch's study *Le Vocabulaire des pêches* (1996), Survey II found that usage of Cape Breton fishers varied for terms for things like the parts of a lobster trap. For instance, the section of the lobster trap that holds, or traps, the lobster after it leaves the baited section (the *kitchen*) is called the *parlour*, *jail*, or *prison*. The editors interviewed eight fishermen, all over the age of fifty, from the east coast of Cape Breton (five from Cape Breton County and three from Victoria County) and took notes on their responses.

In order to concentrate on defining the words, the editors ended the collection stage in 2007, with the exception of one further *DCBE* interview, some email and web inquiries, and a few works published after this date.

Selection: Evidence and Distinctiveness

Although it is a truism that the collection stage of any dictionary is never complete, it is necessary to move to the second stage to select and define the words that fit the criteria for inclusion: "native" words, those that are "distinctively characteristic," and those that are culturally and historically significant to the region. To select a word, the editors must first determine if sufficient evidence exists in the collection of data to consider it "characteristic" of Cape Breton English. The basic criterion for including a term in this dictionary is a minimum of three citations or survey evidence.[7] This minimum is extended to five citations if the term is a loanword that has been naturalized from a foreign language. Occasionally, the editors have included terms for which survey results indicate that the word or meaning is used frequently but for which there are no suitable quotations in the citation file. In this situation, the Pilot Survey, Survey I, or Survey II designate the source(s) of evidence.

If the evidence for a term or sense meets the criteria, the next step is to determine if it is native, distinctive, or historically and culturally significant. To do this, the editors check each potential headword (the word or phrase to be defined) in what the editors have informally called the "dictionary list." This list has eighteen dictionaries from three countries: Canada, the United Kingdom, and the United States. Table 1 lists these dictionaries with their abbreviations.

Table 1. Dictionary List and Abbreviations

COD *Canadian Oxford Dictionary. 2nd ed. 2004.*	**FWCCD** *Funk and Wagnalls Canadian College Dictionary.* 1989.
COED *Concise Oxford English Dictionary.* 11th ed. 2009.	**GCD** *Gage Canadian Dictionary.* 1998.
DA *Dictionary of Americanisms on Historical Principles.* 2 vols. 1951.	**ML** *Maine Lingo: Boiled Owls, Billdads, and Wazzats.* 1975.
DAE *A Dictionary of American English on Historical Principles.* 4 vols. 1938–44.	**MWCD** *Merriam-Webster's Collegiate Dictionary.* 11th ed. 2009.
DARE *Dictionary of American Regional English.* 6 vols. 1985–2013.	**NCD** *ITP Nelson Canadian Dictionary of the English Language.* 1997.
DC *A Dictionary of Canadianisms on Historical Principles.* 1967. Reprinted 1991.	**NOAD** *The New Oxford American Dictionary.* 2nd ed. 2005.
DNE *Dictionary of Newfoundland English.* 2nd ed. 1990.	**OED3** *The Oxford English Dictionary Online.* 3rd ed. 2000–. www.oed.com
DPEIE *Dictionary of Prince Edward Island English.* 1988.	**SSPB** *The South Shore Phrase Book.* 2nd ed. 1988.
EDD *The English Dialect Dictionary.* 6 vols. 1898–1905. Reprinted 1986.	**W3** *Webster's Third New International Dictionary of the English Language Unabridged.* 1961. Reprinted 1993.

The dictionary list has seven general-purpose dictionaries to evaluate how widespread the geographical distribution of a word or particular meaning is. The nine regional dictionaries in the list provide further information about the geographical area where the words are used.[8] The two unabridged dictionaries, *The Oxford English Dictionary Online* and *Webster's Third New International Dictionary of the English Language Unabridged* (hereafter *OED3* and *W3*), give information about the words that are often excluded from smaller dictionaries. The usage and regional labels in these dictionaries have been included to give further insight into the status of the terms. Although not part of the list of eighteen dictionaries routinely checked for each potential headword, other dictionaries are also consulted as appropriate, such as foreign language dictionaries. The list entitled Abbreviations of Dictionaries Cited in the *Dictionary of Cape Breton English*, following the introduction, provides the total list of dictionaries cited and the abbreviations used in the dictionary.[9]

The editors have emphasized the dictionaries of the Oxford University Press and Merriam-Webster because of their extensive databases and their long and distinguished records. Using both general-purpose dictionaries and the unabridged dictionaries from the same publisher does result in duplication, but it has the benefit of providing useful information about the distribution of certain words. If a word is defined in the *OED3* or *W3* but not in these publishers' general-purpose dictionaries, it is a good indicator that the word is rarely used. Clearly, strong arguments can be made for including different or additional dictionaries in this list as each dictionary publisher brings valuable perspectives and also draws on extensive databases. For reasons of practicality, it was not possible to do so in this case.

Having searched these eighteen dictionaries for the potential headword and sense appropriate for the dictionary, the editors used the dictionary list as another piece of information to guide their judgment in determining the distinctiveness of the potential headword. The results from the dictionary search may indicate that the potential headword is too widespread for inclusion. As a general principle, if the headword appears in more than six dictionaries without a usage label, it is excluded. For instance, our research has several citations for *backlog* as it refers to a large log placed at the back of a fireplace to keep the fire going. This sheds light on the historical origin of the word but was excluded as this sense is also found in ten dictionaries: four Canadian, five American, and the *OED3*. *Bannock* was the predominant bread of the immigrants to Cape Breton, especially during the nineteenth century, but since it is known across Canada and is defined in thirteen of the eighteen dictionaries of the dictionary list, it was omitted. One of the meanings of the verb *to coast* is to slide down a snow-covered hill on a sled or toboggan; although this meaning is widespread in Cape Breton English, it was excluded as this sense is found in thirteen dictionaries. The dictionary list provides direction in determining the distinctiveness of words and winnows out those that are widespread, but because it is limited to eighteen dictionaries, it is not conclusive. The results of the dictionary searches are recorded as part of the dictionary entry and broaden the perspective beyond the usage found in Cape Breton English.

Since this dictionary does not specifically identify terms as "native," "distinctive," or "culturally important," some typical examples might best illustrate what is possible to learn from the dictionary lists. At times, a short dictionary list may indicate that the word is a Cape Bretonism. *Cape Breton pork pie* (a small tart with date filling) is recorded only in the *Canadian Oxford Dictionary* (2004) and is a likely candidate. The strong southeastern wind along the northwest coast of Cape Breton, *suête*, is another such example and is recorded by the *Canadian Oxford Dictionary* (labelled "Cdn (Cape Breton)") and the *Dictionnaire du français Acadien* (1999). Other words like *tarabish* (a card game), the *order* (groceries), and those beginning with *Cape Breton* (e.g., *Cape Breton fiddler*) are possible candidates.

On the one hand, the length of the dictionary list, or the absence of one, does not necessarily indicate a Cape Bretonism. The *Dictionary of Canadianisms* is the only dictionary of the eighteen to define *backlander*, and its sole citation is from an 1869 history of Cape Breton, thereby suggesting it may be a Cape Bretonism. On the other hand, it may also be that other dictionary editors decided not to record this derivative of *backland* or that a regional dictionary as yet unwritten may find this form in its research, as *backland* is not exclusive to Cape Breton English. The *DCBE* dictionary list for *barachois* is medium length: "*COD Cdn (Nfld. & Maritimes)*; similar definitions are found in *DNE*, *DC Atlantic Provinces* (1760), *NCD Atlantic Canada*; compare *DPEIE*, *GCD Cdn*." The list reveals that 1760 is the earliest known date in English sources for the word, and the geographical labels limit the area primarily to the Atlantic Provinces. Although the earliest extant source recorded in the dictionary list is from Thomas Pichon's ... *History of the Islands of Cape Breton and Saint John* (1760, 21), it is unlikely that the word originated in Cape Breton. Both Alan Rayburn (2010, 19) and William

Hamilton (1996, 291) point out the frequent use of this generic in Atlantic Canada place names. Further, William J. Kirwin's article (2011) exploring the occurrence of *Barachois* (and the variant *Barasway*) in place names in Newfoundland and Labrador leaves little doubt about the word's widespread use beyond the coasts of Cape Breton. Citing French documents, Kirwin notes 1662 as the earliest known date for the form *barachois* from the Dépôt de la Marine 128/2/6 (2011, 26; also see Cormier, *Dictionnaire du français acadien* 1999).

Other dictionary lists have required prolonged searches and further judgment about the words' suitability for inclusion. *Time* is one of those words with a surprisingly large number of related meanings, ranging from the time of day to serving time in jail. Even the modestly sized *Nelson's Canadian Dictionary* (1997) has fifteen senses, and *OED3* has thirty-five main categories with numerous subcategories, phrases and compounds. The regional meaning of a "house party or community celebration at a hall" is found in several dictionaries that indicate that the word is used most frequently in Atlantic Canada. The *DCBE* dictionary list records the six dictionaries (of the eighteen routinely checked) that have this definition: "*DNE* (1878), *DPEIE*, *DC Esp. Atlantic Provinces*, *COD Cdn (Maritimes & Nfld)*, *NCD Atlantic Canada*, *OED3 N. Amer. regional* (chiefly *New England* and *Newfoundland*) (1878)." The dictionary list reveals that this sense of *time* is distinctive but not native. Similarly, the hard-working verb *to make* has 222 senses recorded in the *English Dialect Dictionary* and has an average of ten to fifteen separate meanings in the general-purpose dictionaries. Among these many senses, the regional meaning is "to preserve fish by cleaning, salting and drying." Six dictionaries indicate this sense is a regional word in Atlantic Canada, especially Newfoundland, and three American dictionaries indicate it is also found in the United States: "*DNE*, *DPEIE*, *DC Esp. Nfld*, *COD Cdn (esp. Nfld)*, *SSPB*, *OED3* Now *N. Amer. regional* (chiefly *Newfoundland*) (1503), *DARE*, *DAE*, *W3 dial*." Here, the dictionary list reveals that this meaning has a geographical range that extends beyond Atlantic Canada to the Atlantic coast. In addition, the appearance of this sense in *W3*, but not its general-purpose dictionary (*MWCD*), suggests this meaning is rarely used in the United States.

In addition to the geographical range, the dictionary list also indicates the "chronological range" of the headword—how long the word has existed according to the date of the earliest attestation (a dated quotation) found in the historical and regional dictionaries. While the noun *puck*, denoting a blow, may appear to have an unusual local meaning, the dictionary list "*DNE*, *EDD*, *OED3* Chiefly *Irish English* (1855), *W3 dial chiefly Brit*" demonstrates that this sense is also alive and well in Newfoundland and Irish English, and its history dates back to the mid-nineteenth century as the *OED3* indicates. Its presence in *W3*, but not other American dictionaries, suggests that this meaning is rare in the United States. While the usual meaning of *button* is widely known in standard English, the dictionary list "*DNE*, *DPEIE*, *OED3* (1867), *W3*" reveals that the meaning of "an oblong door fastener rotating on a nail or screw" is used in Newfoundland, Prince Edward Island, and rarely in the United States. The 1867 citation indicates the earliest date of this now regional meaning.

As mentioned in the section on the scope of the dictionary, the *DCBE* also includes some words with wider use than just Atlantic Canada. *Flake* (a raised wooden frame covered with boughs and used to dry salted fish) is one of these. Essential in the dry fishery from the early settlement of Cape Breton, flakes were used on the island until the mid-twentieth century. Because both Canadian and American fishers employed similar curing processes to provide fish for the European markets, the word's geographical range is the Atlantic coast, and, consequently, the *DCBE* dictionary list is long: "*DNE* (1578), *DPEIE, DC Atlantic Provinces, EDD, OED3, DARE, DAE, DA, ML*" and several general-purpose dictionaries." The dating is interesting here as the *Dictionary of Newfoundland English* has the earliest documented record of 1578, earlier than the 1623 citation in the *OED3* (as available on the online version when accessed on January 8, 2014). The *OED* editors are revising the online third edition and will no doubt update their entry to include the 1578 citation as its earliest attestation, but this circumstance demonstrates how regional dictionaries can contribute to larger ones. It is also worthwhile to record that the word is used in Atlantic Canada, given that it appears as an Americanism in Mathew's *Dictionary of Americanisms* (1951), and as a regional word in *Dictionary of American Regional English* and *Maine Lingo*. In this instance, the regional home of *flake* is wider than the dictionary's usual range of Cape Breton and the Atlantic Provinces, but because of the central importance of the commercial fishery to Cape Breton, the editors included it.

Semantic Domains of the Terms Defined

The terms defined in this dictionary come from several semantic domains. A context for these domains is found in the "Settlement History of Cape Breton Island" (page xxxix), which provides an overview of the island's settlement and industrial development. Like the *Dictionary of Newfoundland English* and the *Dictionary of Prince Edward Island English*, some of these terms derive from important occupations in which the terms have moved from the workplace to the regional idiom, especially in localities close to the work areas. The two largest sources for the *DCBE* terms are mining and fishing. Mining has contributed words like *gob* (the area in a mine where the coal has been removed), a *bob-tail paysheet* (a miner's pay slip with little or no money left after deductions), and *pit socks* (grey woolen work socks, whether worn by a miner or not). Several terms from the commercial fishery also occur, such as *sticker* (a harpooner on a boat fishing for sword fish) and *dummy rock* (a stone placed in a wooden lobster trap as temporary ballast until the trap becomes waterlogged). Other related nautical terms refer to the various boats such as a *smack* (used to transport live lobsters), and practices like *coasting* (sailing to ports along the coast to deliver and trade cargo). The terms from steel making are not as numerous as those from the two previous sources, but among these terms is the *soaking pit*, identifying the oven in the steel plant used to heat steel ingots to a uniform temperature before being reshaped and rolled.

Other productive sources are food terms like a *bun of bread*, designating a loaf of bread, and terms for social gatherings such as *milling frolics* where woolen cloth was thickened, and fund-raising events like *box socials* where decorated boxes with food were auctioned off. The domains of religion and beliefs, and of music and dance have also generated groups of related terms: *forerunners* are omens foretelling a death or other events, *close to the floor* characterizes step-dancing performed with a minimum of movement of the upper body and in a limited space on the dance floor. Cape Breton's climate and maritime location have contributed over a dozen ice terms such as *red ice* (reddish ice appearing along the Cape Breton coasts in early spring) and *barricade* (ice piled on the shore creating a barrier), and water features such as *tittle* (a narrow, dangerous seawater passage). Weather, farming, and lumbering have also contributed regional words: *to spill* (to rain hard), *society bull* (a bull owned by an agricultural society for breeding cows belonging to its members), and *to snig* (to drag timber from the woods). There are several references to alcohol, especially to its illegal production, such as the *black pot* used in distilling moonshine. Fewer terms come from references to domestic items like a *summer kitchen* used for cooking during the hot weather and others referring to vehicles, health and disease, personal characteristics, and miscellaneous sources.

Some of the terms cut across semantic boundaries. For example, humour includes terms like the *flying axe handles* (diarrhea) from health and disease, and the old-fashioned word for commercially baked bread, scornfully called *baker's fog*, comes from the food domain. Because of the island's settlement history and ethnic diversity, several loanwords (i.e., words borrowed from foreign languages and used in English contexts) occur in the domains mentioned above. Gaelic provides *bochdan*, an evil spirit or a ghost, and is often used in the phrase *bochdan stories*; French has generated *mi-carême*, a mid-Lent celebration; and Mi'kmaq is the source of *waltes*, an ancient Mi'kmaw game in which players bump a shallow wooden bowl on a flat surface to raise and overturn six coin-shaped disks.

While some terms from these domains reflect current usage, many others are traditional, and a few are both traditional and current in usage. Thus, some occupational terms recall the earliest fishing practices of drying salted fish and mining techniques using a pickaxe and shovel, while other terms attest to modern developments in these industries. Similarly, words like *ceilidh* reflect both the original and current meanings (an informal visit and a concert in a public venue), as mentioned above. *Milling frolic* and *kitchen party* are undergoing a similar widening of meaning from a private to a public gathering. Other terms, however, are historical in nature: many older people remember terms like *ton timber* (a measure of squared logs for shipping) and *statute labour* (legislated work on public roads in lieu of taxes), but these words are used to refer to earlier practices.

Presentation of Dictionary Entries

In its simplest form, each *DCBE* entry contains a headnote, definition, and supporting evidence in the form of citations or in rare instances survey evidence alone (as noted above). In most entries, a dictionary list follows the citations, and, occasionally, a language note appears as a final element. See the sample entry on page ix. Each of these components is explained to assist the reader's understanding of the dictionary and the principles underlying them.

Headnote

The headnote always contains a headword (the word or phrase being defined) and the part of speech. If needed, the headnote also gives information about pronunciation, variant spellings, synonyms, and an invitation to "see" or "compare" words that are semantically related to the headword. Like the *Dictionary of Newfoundland English*, the *DCBE* does include usage and regional labels.[10] Many headwords identified as "historical" or "obsolete" in other dictionaries are still used in Cape Breton English. *Glib*, used to identify ice as slippery, is one such example; three dictionaries identify it as *archaic* and another two label it as *rare*, despite being recognized by nearly half of the respondents to Survey I and found in the *Dictionary of Prince Edward Island English* and *Canadian Oxford Dictionary*.

The headwords are in alphabetical order; compound words and phrases are considered as one continuous word for the purpose of alphabetizing. To simplify the reader's search, the editors have alphabetized compounds and phrases by the first word, so *August Gale* appears at *A* rather than *G*. In most instances, the spelling of the headword is standard, and where it is not, it is because the editors have selected the most frequently used spelling in the citation file. Since regional dictionaries draw on a variety of sources as well as published works, the spelling poses challenges as William J. Kirwin (2006) discusses in his article on the spelling conventions in the *Dictionary of Newfoundland English*. The word *skooshin* (moving quickly and nimbly on pans of ice) is an example of this in the *DCBE*. While the citation file has several attestations for this word, the *Cape Bretoner* is the only published source (1994 and 2002) and prints *skooshin*. Consequently, this is the *DCBE* headword. Unfortunately, the spelling looks like eye-dialect[11] and, in addition, the alternative spelling of *skushing* is needed to reflect an alternative pronunciation given orally for the word. So, *skooshin* is the headword and *skushing* is listed as a variant spelling.

Occasionally, two or more headwords are homonyms—the same spelling, pronunciation, and part of speech, but different in meaning. For example, the regional term *stripper* means "a crane with an apparatus to remove molds or casing from cooled ingots" and also "a cow capable of producing milk throughout the winter." To distinguish these, the more frequently used term is designated with a superscripted "1" and the less frequent term has a superscripted "2".

The part of speech, or word class, follows the headword, six of which are found in this dictionary: noun, adjective, verb, adverb, preposition, and interjection. Nouns that are usually plural are identified, and compound and phrasal nouns are labelled simply as nouns. Most nouns can be used as an adjective, and so are not identified as an attributive. Verbs are identified as transitive or intransitive, and *verb phrase* identifies a verb plus particle and fixed expressions in which a verb governs a particular object, such as *stand the gaff*. Verbal adjectives and verbal nouns are also labelled. Adjective and prepositional phrases are labelled as such.

Phonetic respellings are provided only for headwords for which the pronunciation may be in doubt, such as loanwords from Gaelic and Mi'kmaq and words that may be unfamiliar such as *tarabish*. This respelling is a broad transcription, presented between square brackets, and appears before the part of speech, if needed. The phonetic symbols are listed in the Pronunciation Guide given below.

Next, variant spellings of the headword are listed in order of frequency. Thus, the headword *killick* (a homemade anchor) is followed by "also spelled *kellick* and less frequently *kelleck, kellic, killack*." The alternative spellings provide indications of different pronunciations, especially of loanwords, which frequently have several variants.

Synonyms, different words with the same meaning, are listed according to frequency in the citation file. For example, since there are more citations for a game called *peggy* than its synonym *tiddly*, *peggy* is the headword, and the latter is listed as a variant and noted in a cross reference, "*tiddly*: see *peggy*." On the other hand, if the words are not exact synonyms and are strongly represented in the dictionary's citation file, then they have their own entry. With over 110 citations, *milling frolic* was and is currently one of the most popular of the gatherings at which a particular task was performed, and so is defined separately from *frolic* where it appears as a variant, along with twenty-three other variants, such as *chopping* and *stumping frolics*.[12] Not all variant forms or spellings listed in the headnote appear in the citations given after the definition, as some of these variant spellings and forms appear in citations that add little or no new information about the word being illustrated. Similarly, the variant forms in the headnote that are not strongly represented in the citation file are not cross-referenced.

The word *see* directs the reader to near synonyms when they are defined in separate entries: e.g., at *wall face* (the vertical surface of the coal seam where miners excavate coal), the reader is directed to "see *coal face*." *Compare* directs the reader to a related (but not synonymous) dictionary entry that is in the same semantic field or subject area. At *box social*, the reader is invited to "compare *pie social*." Both of these socials are fundraisers but use different procedures. The verb *compare* is not used for semantically related words that are adjacent headwords, such as *bush* and *bushline*. The headnote for *milling board* illustrates several of the features mentioned above and demonstrates the bolding format used in the dictionary: "**milling board** noun; also spelled **milling-board**; also **milling table**; see **harrow**."

Definition

After the headnote comes the definition, the element that most readers associate with a dictionary.[13] In the early 1970s, Ladislav Zgusta expressed his regret about the lack of published resources on theory and practice of lexicography (1971, 12). More recently, several handbooks, collections of articles, and journals have been published giving guidance on lexicography in general and on defining principles and procedures, such as the recent books by Béjoint (2000, 2010), Landau (2001), H. Jackson (2002), Sterkenburg (2003), Atkins and Rundell

(2008), and others. These books provide useful defining principles, some of which Béjoint (2000, 189–208) and Landau (2001, 152–89) note that even the large commercial dictionaries do not always follow. Not all of these principles, however, apply to a regional dictionary. A general-purpose dictionary should define each word used in the definitions of its headwords to avoid circularity. On the other hand, regional dictionaries do not require this feature. All editors face the challenge of finding the essential qualities of the word being defined, but unlike the style of "telegraphese" made famous by the Fowler brothers' edition of the *Concise Oxford Dictionary* in 1911 (Béjoint 2000, 200), editors defining regional words try to record the distinctive characteristics of the word that distinguish it from other regions. So, *backlanders* were not merely settlers "in the back country" as indicated in *A Dictionary of Canadianisms*, but they were also settlers on inferior land who were often economically and socially deprived in contrast to their frontland neighbours. Somehow this needs to be conveyed. *Skooshin* is not just moving from one pan of ice to another but also suggests the skill and challenge of moving nimbly over pieces of ice that may or may not be large enough to support the person's weight. The editor strives to express these ideas concisely while distinguishing the local sense.

The *DCBE* uses numbered senses to define headwords that have related but different meanings, and these senses are listed with the more frequently used meaning(s) given first. For instance, *snood,* meaning a short, light line attaching a hook to a main line, appears before the second meaning, in which *snood* indicates the line that attaches a lobster trap to a buoy. However, where the meanings are more closely related, a semicolon divides the senses. So, the fishing term *bait box* has two numbered senses, one referring to a small, baited container placed in a lobster trap, the other to a large container that stores bait used in longline fishing; a *bun of bread* combines two related senses: "a loaf of bread; one section of a double loaf." These different senses are listed in order of decreasing frequency.

Occasionally, in place of the editors' definition, "see quotation at (a stated year)" directs the reader to a particular citation that provides a clear definition of the headword.

Citations

The primary function of the citations, dated quotations from the dictionary files, is to illustrate the meaning(s) and context of the headword. In addition, to indicate the timeline of the word in Cape Breton English, the dictionary gives the earliest and latest citations in the *DCBE* files. Other citations are selected that lead the reader to events important to individuals or to the history of Cape Breton Island. One citation for *clamper* (a pan of ice) comes from a newspaper article published on Christmas Eve, 1919, as it reports the deaths of two young brothers who apparently stopped to play on the clampers, fell beneath the ice, and drowned. A citation for the word *flake* used in drying fish records the wreckage caused by the famous August Gale in 1873. The diary of the wife of the lighthouse keeper on Gabarus Island describes the events of their isolated lives and comments on of the types of ice that prevented ships from moving between the island and the mainland. A citation referring to *killick* tells of the heroic rescue by a local fisherman who "fastened a *killick* in the frozen ground above, and attaching a rope thereto, lowered himself to the wave-swept deck of the brig" (Knight 1913, 104). The dictionary's citations record the format, spelling, and punctuation of the original as closely as possible with two exceptions. Dashes have been normalized and three dots with no spaces between the dots represent ellipses. Occasionally, an unusual spelling or form is followed by "[*sic*]," but in early documents or diaries in which spelling variants obviously differ from modern usage, [*sic*] is not used.

Citations also clarify the meaning of the words that are understood differently. Thomas Pichon concisely describes the water feature *barachois* as "small ponds near the sea from which they are separated by a kind of causeway" (1760, 21). This presents an accurate view of a barachois, but other citations indicate that the "causeway" may be open to the larger body of water, thus making the *pond* a lagoon. Both understandings are equally valid, and both differ from how the word is understood on Prince Edward Island: "A backwater near the mouth of a river; a marsh" (Pratt 1988). The citations and comments in the surveys have helped clarify the meanings of some of these words that are understood in various ways both on Cape Breton Island and in Atlantic Canada.

As discussed in the section on collection, the sources for the citations are varied and, consequently, so is the format used to record the citations. The editors have tried to make these as accessible as possible while meeting the demands for economy of space. The abbreviations used in the dictionary (for instance, *n.p.* for "no page" and *trans.* for "translator") are kept to a minimum and listed under Abbreviations Used in the *Dictionary of Cape Breton English* at the end of the introduction. The abbreviations that appear in the eighteen dictionaries cited in the *DCBE* dictionary lists account for the largest number. As recommended by *The Chicago Manual of Style* (2010), italics indicate titles of published books, journals, newspapers, magazines, and movies; quotation marks identify titles of published short works or unpublished manuscripts, reports, theses and dissertations; and titles of other unpublished works such as letters or diaries have neither italics nor quotation marks. For economy of space, short titles are formed with key words from longer titles; for example, Charles Dunn's *Highland Settler: A Portrait of the Scottish Gael in Nova Scotia* (1953) is shortened to *Highland Settler*. The following format is used to introduce the citations.

(i) The format of published works varies according to the type of publication. Books and journal articles begin with the year of publication, followed by the author's last name,[14] the title of the book or journal, the journal's volume number and issue number (if available), and finally the page number: e.g., 1973 MACPHAIL *Girl from Loch Bras d'Or* 130 (a novel), or 1988 BITTERMANN *Acadiensis* 18 (1), 43 (a journal article). Newspapers and magazines begin with the year of publication, followed by the name of the author for magazines (but not newspapers), the title of the work, the day, month or season (varying with the publication schedule), and the page number: e.g. 1977 *Inverness Oran* 28 Oct. 1 (a daily newspaper), 1925 MACLELLAN *Maclean's* 15 Jan. 20 (a weekly magazine), or 1994 LEBLANC *Equinox* Sept./Oct. 63 (a magazine published every two months). Since *Cape Breton's Magazine* uses volume numbers instead of months, the volume number precedes the page number, e.g., 1987 *CB's Magazine* 44, 16. The magazine *The Cape Bretoner* varied its use of month/season during its the publication, and so the volume and issue number are used for clarity, e.g., 1996 BEDFORD *Cape Bretoner* 4 (3), 12.

(ii) The format for a manuscript, such as a diary, begins with the year of writing, then the location of the work (such as the Beaton Institute), MG (Manuscript Group), accession number assigned by the archive or museum, the date and month (if available), and finally the page number: e.g., 1890 Beaton Institute MG 12 45, 27 Jan. 6, and 1914 Beaton Institute MG 12 59, 4 May n.p. A comma separates the accession number from the number indicating the date or page. The accession numbers given before the citations in the dictionary are often more specific than those in the Works Consulted to assist future researchers.

(iii) The format for a tape held by an archive or museum begins with the year it was recorded, then the location of the tape, and the accession number assigned to the tape, e.g., 1970 Beaton Institute Tape 145, and 1976–7 Miners' Museum Tape 128.

(iv) The format for a tape made for the *DCBE* begins with the year it was recorded, then its description (*DCBE* Tape), the informant's name, and the page number of the transcription of the tape: e.g., 2008 *DCBE* Tape CURRIE 8. The recorded radio program devoted to the dictionary is identified as 2002 *DCBE* Tape *Information Morning* 27 Feb. 10.

(v) The format for a documentary or movie begins with the year it was released, then its title, e.g., 1992 *Making Steel*.

(vi) The format for the three surveys made for the dictionary begins with the name of the survey followed by the abbreviation "Inf." and the number assigned to the informant: e.g., Pilot Survey Inf. 3, Survey I Inf. 25, and Survey II Inf. 8.

Occasionally, a citation begins with two years, for example, "1858 in 1984"; this indicates that the quotation was written or published earlier (1858) than the work (1984) in which the citation is found. To avoid excessive detail, the editors have used "et al." when more than two authors or editors have contributed to the work. Full details for all sources are given in the dictionary's Works Consulted.

Dictionary List

Following the citations, the dictionary list records the abbreviation(s) from any of the eighteen routinely checked dictionaries that have similar definitions to that in the *DCBE*. These abbreviations are given in Table 1 (page xvii). Set off by square brackets, the abbreviations are arranged in national groups (Canada, the United Kingdom, and the United States). Within these groups the dialect dictionaries precede the other dictionaries, with the two descriptive dictionaries (*South Shore Phrase Book* and *Maine Lingo*) last in their respective national group. If needed, abbreviations of other relevant dictionaries are cited, such as the *DSL* (*Dictionary of Scots Language* 2004) for a word of Scottish origin, and are placed in the appropriate national group. Foreign language dictionaries appear last. The cumulative list of all the dictionaries consulted is found in Abbreviations of Dictionaries Cited in the *Dictionary of Cape Breton English* after the introduction.

Usage and regional labels are recorded as they appear in the consulted dictionaries and therefore vary in form.[15] Many of these labels are abbreviated and are listed in Abbreviations Cited in the *Dictionary of Cape Breton English* (page xxxi). When available, the date of the earliest citation in an individual dictionary list appears in round brackets after the abbreviation of the dictionary.[16] An invitation to *compare* an alternative definition is made to indicate a different but related meaning or form than that in the *DCBE*. Thus, the dictionary list may be brief, as that for *pit sock* (a grey woolen work sock, not worn exclusively by miners): [*COD Cdn (Cape Breton)*], or *frontland* (land with access to the sea, a lake, or a river): [*DARE* (1941)]. It may be longer, as for *gib* (to clean (fish), removing the gills and entrails): [*DNE* (1862), *DPEIE*, *OED3*; compare the earlier form *gip*: *OED3* (1603), *EDD*, *W3* (with *gib* as a variant)].

Language Notes

In some instances the dictionary entry concludes with a "Language Note." These notes are identified by an asterisk and comment on some aspect of the word's usage or meaning. For instance, when *after* follows the verb *to be* and precedes a present participle in sentences like "I *was after doing* that" (I *had done* that), the construction has been informally called the "after perfect." As several dictionaries acknowledge, the structure is widely used in Irish English, but the note in the *DCBE* suggests there is reason to consider the structure more generally characteristic of Gaelic speaking areas. The note on *baker's fog*, a scornful reference to commercially baked bread, explains that this sense is current only among older speakers, and another note on *kitchen racket* (an informal house party) explains that the more widely known *kitchen dance* is rare in our citation file. The verbs *biff* and *whiff* mean to throw an object, but the note on *biff* explains that survey respondents differ in how they interpret the force of the throw: some see the verbs as close synonyms while others consider one to be a more forceful throw than the other. Finally, it is beyond the scope of this dictionary to provide etymologies for the terms defined, but where the evidence is clear that a term is a loanword from Scottish Gaelic, Acadian French, or Mi'kmaq, a language note indicates that the term is taken from one of these languages and lists a relevant dictionary from the source language. For example, the note for *beag* reads: "*A loanword from Scottish Gaelic, see *beag* 'light (of import), little, minor, petty, slender, slight, small, trifling, wee' *GED*." Loanwords from standard French and other languages are not noted. These notes are kept to a minimum but the editors hope they will be useful.

Intended Audience

The intended audience for the dictionary is paradoxically both the general reader and the specialist interested in regional language for various professional and academic pursuits. Although the *DCBE* uses a limited number of the lexicographical conventions that some readers find challenging (see Béjoint 2000, 189–208), the aim has been to follow recent trends in dictionary editing to make the dictionary accessible to all who consult it. Consequently, parenthetical explanations often follow technical terms in the definitions, rather than expecting the reader to search for technical words among the defined words. Other features also try to make the dictionary more easily accessible, such as a reduction in the number of abbreviations and suiting the vocabulary of the definitions to the general reader.

In addition, various features of the dictionary will appeal to linguists, historians and others interested in matters connected to Cape Breton and the Atlantic region. As in other regional dictionaries, the citations provide a broader context for the defined word than is possible in the definition, and they illuminate and enliven the definition. As noted above, the dictionary list places the *DCBE* headword or sense in a chronological frame and helps to locate it in a wider geographical context. Researchers from many fields will draw on the book to clarify the meaning of terms defined.

While the national scope of the *Dictionary of American Regional English* is obviously much larger than this dictionary, Joan Houston Hall, chief editor for its final three volumes, has outlined the surprisingly broad range of inquiries her staff received about the regional vocabulary in their files. In addition to expected questions from historians, reference librarians, linguists, lexicographers, and literary scholars, other researchers sought information on topics such as architecture, biology, gambling, logging, weather conditions and details helpful in criminal investigations (2010). Despite the much smaller scope of the *DCBE*, the editors hope it will be useful to those working in Atlantic studies of various kinds with interests discussed in the previous section on semantic domains, ranging from industrial terms to entertainment and social activities, music, food, beliefs, types of ice, and other domains.

NOTES

1 Later scholars have noted that the use of the definite article before *dictionary* and *bible* also indicates the authority that many people place in both works. Millward in her *A Biography of the English Language* (1996, 240) is one of these. In a study examining a selection of MA theses, PhD dissertations, and scholarly journal articles, Ammon Shea found that 11% of theses, 8% of dissertations, and 16% of published articles identified the source for a definition with the general term "the dictionary" without further citation (Shea 2012, 109–10).

2 Sidney Landau in his *Dictionaries: The Art and Craft of Lexicography* (2001, 456–63) has eight pages listing the dictionaries "from Johnson (1755) to present." The list of abbreviations for selected modern dictionaries (and their editions) runs to five and a half pages in Henri Béjoint's *The Lexicography of English: From Origins to Present* (2010, xix–xxiv).

3 In the introduction to the *Dictionary of American Regional English*, Frederic Cassidy comments on this purpose referring to *"DARE's* function as a historical dictionary"

(1985, xvii), and *The Oxford Companion to the English Language* lists the *Dictionary of Newfoundland* under the heading of "Historical Dictionaries" (McArthur 1992, 178; see "regional dictionary," Hartmann and James 1998, 118).

4   The identification of slang is challenging. John Ayto, editor of *The Oxford Dictionary of Slang*, comments that many words exist in "that uncertain borderland between slang and colloquial usage. One person's slang is another's colloquialism" (2003, v), and *The Oxford Companion to the English Language* states slang "is widely used without precision" (McArthur 1992, 940). Similarly, Frederic Cassidy concludes, "Attempts to define it [slang] are as numerous as their attempters, and while there is some core of agreement, the word remains so imprecise that its use as a scientific term has been challenged" (1985, xvii), and so *DARE* does not use *slang* as a register label.

5   The parenthetical definitions given in the introduction are often abbreviated forms of the more detailed versions in the dictionary.

6   The distribution of the 55 informants by county is: 42 from Cape Breton County, 5 from Inverness County, 4 from Richmond County, and 4 from Victoria County. The 2011 census gives the population of Cape Breton Island as 135,974 with roughly 75% living in Cape Breton County; 76% of the informants in this survey were from Cape Breton County.

7   This requirement of at least "three attestations or survey evidence" has resulted in holding back many interesting terms from the dictionary such as milk leg, stump potatoes, sham marriages, splash dam, sock social, stretch day, water horse, and many others.

8   Two of these regional dictionaries (*The South Shore Phrase Book* and *Maine Lingo*) provide useful insights into regional meanings as the editors discuss, rather than define, the meanings of headwords, and so they might be called descriptive dictionaries.

9   Other dictionaries are used as needed, such as the online *Dictionary of the Scots Language* (2004) and foreign-language dictionaries. Colin Mark's *The Gaelic-English Dictionary* (2004) is the first choice for naturalized, or borrowed, Gaelic words, but occasionally when the word is not recorded there, the editors cite Malcolm MacLennan's useful but earlier work, *A Pronouncing and Etymological Dictionary of the Gaelic Language* (1925, rpt. 1979). Similarly, the *Mi'kmaw-English Lexicon* ([2007]) is the first choice for Mi'kmaw loanwords, as it best represents usage in Cape Breton, but Albert DeBlois's *Micmac Dictionary* (1996) is used once as a supplement in an instance in which the *Mi'kmaw-English Lexicon* does not define the word *saqmaw* (chief).

10 In the absence of usage labels, the editors have occasionally clarified definitions by referring to cultural values (*bungalow*), humour (*Cape Breton steak*), or derogatory intent (*baker's fog*) in instances in which these connotations may not be clear to the reader. Other dictionaries do this occasionally, such as *DARE*'s definition of *bug*: "used in jocular place-names for presumed insect-infested small settlements." In one of the many definitions for *string*, the *OED3* has "In 16th–18th c. applied jocularly to the hangman's rope. *Obs.*" (at I.1.a.). T. K. Pratt defines *buggerlugs* as "An insult, sometimes affectionate, sometimes contemptuous" (*DPEIE*). In addition, occupational or domain labels are not used in the *DCBE*, as the editors have written definitions to identify the industry or occupation. As Atkins and Rundell state, domain labels "nowadays tend to be used sparingly" (2008, 227). For a thorough and systematic discussion of usage and regional labels, see Atkins and Rundell's *The*

Oxford Guide to Practical Lexicography (2008, 226–35). The verb *jig* is an example of a regional sense now considered obsolete elsewhere. The *DCBE* defines *jig* as "to sing vocables (syllables that do not express words), and occasionally Gaelic, that imitate bagpipe or fiddle music; less frequently to imitate the rhythm of a tune by tapping feet or sticks." The *OED3* labels this sense as *obsolete* and gives Shakespeare's *Love's Labour's Lost* iii.i.10 as the earliest citation (1598): "To ligge off a tune at the tongues ende, canarie to it with your feete, humour it with turning vp your eylids." The sense is still widely used in Cape Breton English as indicated by seventeen citations for the verb *to jig* and another twelve for the verbal noun *jigging* in the citation files.

11 Frederic Cassidy in his introduction to volume one of *DARE* gives a succinct definition of eye-dialect: "*Eye-dialect spellings* are those which an author uses intentionally to suggest that a character's speech is substandard and that the person is illiterate, even though those spellings correspond to pronunciations that are perfectly standard" (1985, xix). Speaking informally, many North Americans do not pronounce the final *g* in the suffix -*ing*.

12 Another example of near-synonyms being defined separately is *jigging, mouth music, puirt-a-buel* and *canntaireachd*. All designate the singing of vocables (syllables that do not express words), and occasionally Gaelic, that imitate fiddle and bagpipe music, but they are defined separately because of the high frequency in the citations file and especially since *canntaireachd* has its own particular musical tradition.

13 Béjoint's *Modern Lexicography: An Introduction* (2000, 140–7) summarizes research on what readers look for when consulting a monolingual general-purpose dictionary, and Atkins and Rundell note, "Explaining what words mean is the central function of a monolingual dictionary" (2008, 405).

14 Occasionally, the editor or compiler of a book has been given instead of the author and designated with "ed." or "comp."

15 The dictionary list does not include the regional references in the *DPEIE* (such as "From British and Irish") as they are "merely a brief indication of which dialect or language possessed the word immediately before its use on Prince Edward Island, and was the probable source" (Pratt 1988, xxvii).

16 In the dictionary lists, square brackets around a year within round brackets, e.g., ([1875]), indicate that the year of the quotation is earlier than the work in which the citation is found. The dates given in *MWCD* are not recorded in the dictionary list because, as a general-purpose dictionary, it does not give citations so it is difficult to know to which of the multiple meanings the date refers. Rarely, if two dictionaries cite the same source but give different dates for the source, then the two dates are given, as occurs at *fig of tobacco*, in which editors assign different dates for Thomas Haliburton's *Clockmaker*.

Abbreviations

Abbreviations of Dictionaries Cited in the *Dictionary of Cape Breton English*

CDS *Cassell's Dictionary of Slang*. 1998. Edited by Jonathon Green. London: Cassell.

COD *Canadian Oxford Dictionary*. 2nd ed. 2004. Edited by Katherine Barber. Don Mills: Oxford University Press.

COED *Concise Oxford English Dictionary*. 11th ed. 2009. Edited by Catherine Soanes and Angus Stevenson. New York: Oxford University Press.

DA *A Dictionary of Americanisms on Historical Principles*. 2 vols. 1951. Edited by Mitford M. Mathews. Chicago: University of Chicago Press.

DAE *A Dictionary of American English on Historical Principles*. 4 vols. 1938–44. Edited by William A. Craigie and James R. Hulbert. Chicago: University of Chicago Press.

DARE *Dictionary of American Regional English*. 6 vols. 1985–2013. Edited by Frederic G. Cassidy [vol. 1], Frederic G. Cassidy and Joan Houston Hall [vols. 2–3], Joan Houston Hall [vols. 4–5], and Joan Houston Hall with Luanne von Schneidemesser [vol. 6]. Cambridge, MA: Belknap Press of Harvard University Press.

DC *A Dictionary of Canadianisms on Historical Principles*. 1967. Reprinted 1991. Edited by Walter S. Avis, Charles Crate, Patrick Drysdale, Douglas Leechman, Matthew H. Scargill, and Charles J. Lovell. Toronto: Gage.

DFA *Dictionnaire du français acadien*. 1999. Edited by Yves Cormier. [Saint-Laurent, QC]: Éditions Fides.

DNE *Dictionary of Newfoundland English. Second Edition with Supplement*. 1990. Edited by G. M. Story, W. J. Kirwin, and J. D. A. Widdowson. Toronto: University of Toronto Press. http://www.heritage.nf.ca/dictionary/

DPEIE *Dictionary of Prince Edward Island English*. 1988. Edited by T. K. Pratt. Toronto: University of Toronto Press.

DSL *Dictionary of the Scots Language Dictionar o the Scots Leid*. 2004. Edited by Susan C. Rennie. Dundee, Scotland: University of Dundee. http://www.dsl.ac.uk/

EDD	*The English Dialect Dictionary.* 6 vols. 1898–1905. Reprinted 1986. Edited by Joseph Wright. Oxford: Oxford University Press.
FWCCD	*Funk and Wagnalls Canadian College Dictionary.* 1989. Edited by Walter S. Avis (Canadian Edition) and Sidney I. Landau (Editor in Chief). Toronto: Fitzhenry and Whiteside.
GCD	*Gage Canadian Dictionary.* 1998. Edited by Gaelan Dodds de Wolf, Robert J. Gregg, Barbara P. Harris, and Matthew H. Scargill. Vancouver: Gage.
GD	*A Pronouncing and Etymological Dictionary of the Gaelic Language: Gaelic-English, English-Gaelic.* 1925. Reprinted 1979. Edited by Malcolm MacLennan. Aberdeen: Acair and Aberdeen University Press.
GED	*The Gaelic-English Dictionary.* 2004. Edited by Colin Mark. London: Routledge.
MEL	*Mi'kmaw-English Lexicon. L'nui'sultinej.* [2007]. Edited by Mi'kmaw Kina'matnewey Board of Directors. Eskasoni, NS: Eskasoni Centre of Excellence.
MD	*Micmac Dictionary.* 1996. Edited by Albert D. DeBlois. Mercury Series Canadian Ethnology Service, Paper 131. Hull, QC: Canadian Museum of Civilization.
ML	*Maine Lingo: Boiled Owls, Billdads, and Wazzats.* 1975. Edited by John Gould. Camden, ME: Down East Books.
MWCD	*Merriam-Webster's Collegiate Dictionary.* 11th ed. 2009. Edited by Frederick C. Mish. Springfield, MA: Merriam-Webster. http://www.merriam-webster.com/
NCD	*ITP Nelson Canadian Dictionary of the English Language: An Encyclopedic Reference.* 1997. Edited by Susan Green, Jan Harkness, David Friend, Julia Keeler, Dan Liebman, and Fraser Sutherland. Toronto: ITP Nelson.
NOAD	*The New Oxford American Dictionary.* 2nd ed. 2005. Edited by Elizabeth J. Jewell, Frank Abate, and Erin McKean. New York: Oxford University Press.
OED3	*The Oxford English Dictionary Online.* 3rd ed. 2000–. Edited by John A. Simpson. Oxford: Oxford University Press. http://www.oed.com
SOED	*Shorter Oxford English Dictionary on Historical Principles.* 5th ed. 2 vols. 2003. Edited by William R. Trumble and Angus Stevenson. New York: Oxford University Press.
SSPB	*The South Shore Phrase Book.* 2nd ed. 1988. Edited by Lewis J. Poteet. Hantsport, NS: Lancelot Press.
W3	*Webster's Third New International Dictionary of the English Language Unabridged.* 1961. Reprinted 1993. Edited by Philip Babcock Gove. Springfield, MA: Merriam-Webster. http://unabridged.merriam-webster.com/
WGUS	*A Word Geography of the Eastern United States.* 1949. Edited by Hans Kurath. Ann Arbor, MI: University of Michigan Press.

Abbreviations Used in the Dictionary of Cape Breton English

The abbreviated dictionary titles are listed separately above, and well-known abbreviations such as those for the days of the week, the names of the months, Canadian Provinces, and parts of speech are not listed. The editors have tried to limit the number of abbreviations as much as possible, but they have recorded the abbreviations for usage labels displayed in the various dictionaries cited in the dictionary lists that appear at the end of most entries. These cited dictionaries use different conventions for their abbreviations (such as using or not employing: initial capitals, italics, bolding, and periods after the abbreviation). These conventions have been retained in the dictionary lists, but this list of abbreviations gives one form rather than listing all the possible forms (such as *Dial.*, Dial., dial., and *dial*). The detailed geographical labels used in the *Dictionary of American Regional English* are explained on page xxxii of the first volume (Cassidy 1985); for instance, *NEng* indicates *New England* and includes the states of Connecticut, Massachusetts, Maine, New Hampshire, Rhode Island, and Vermont.

a	ante (before a date)
AK	Arkansas
Anon.	Anonymous
arch.	archaic
attrib.	attributive
Austral.	Australia(n)
Brit.	British
c / ca	circa ("about" before dates)
Canad.	Canadian
C Atl	Central Atlantic
CB	Cape Breton
Cdn	Canada
Cent	Central
colloq.	colloquial(ly)
comp.	compiler
DCBE	Dictionary of Cape Breton English
Derog.	Derogatory
dial.	dialect
ed.	Editor, edition
e.g.	for example (*exempli gratia*)
eNEng	east(ern) New England
Eng.	England, English
esp.	especially
et al.	and others (*et alii* [people] or *et alia* [things])
exc.	except
fig.	figurative(ly)
Geol.	Geology, geologic(al)
hist.	historical
Inf.	Informant

intr.	intransitive (verb)
Irel.	Ireland
Lab.	Labrador
MA	Massachusetts
MB	a reel of microfilm
ME	Maine
Metall.	metallurgy
MG	Manuscript Group
MI	Michigan
Midl	Midland
Missip	Mississippi
N. Amer.	North America
N Atl	North Atlantic
naut.	nautical
N Cent	North Central
n.d.	no date
NEast	North East
NEng	New England
NewEng	New England
N Midl	North Midlands
north.	northern (dialect)
n.p.	no page [given in the work cited]
Nth	North
NW	Northwest
NY	New York
N.Z.	New Zealand
obs.	obsolete
Obsol.	Obsolete
old-fash	old-fashioned
orig.	origin(al)(ly)
PA	Pennsylvania
S. Afr.	South Africa
Sc.	Scottish, Scotts
Scot.	Scottish
SE	Southeast
s.l.	without place [of a publisher] *sine loco*
S Midl	South Midland
s.n.	without name [of a publisher] *sine nomine*
spec.	specifically
Sth	South
SW	Southwest
trans.	translator
U.S.	United States
usu.	usually
wInland	western Inland

Pronunciation Guide

Consonants

b	bub
č	church
d	dad
f	few
g	rig, rag
h	ho
ǰ	judge, jug
k	kick
l	lily
m	mom
n	none
ŋ	sing
p	pip
r	rip
s	sip
š	ship
t	tip
θ	thin
ð	then
v	view
w	we
y	yet
z	zip
ž	treasure

Additional Consonants for Loanwords

x	Scottish loch (voiceless velar fricative)
ç	German ich (voiceless palatal fricative)
ł	Mi'kmaq lnu (velarized or pharyngealized lateral)

Vowels

	FRONT	CENTRAL	BACK
HIGH	i eat		u pooh
	ɪ it		ʊ put
MID	e they	ə putt, pert, sofa	o toe
	ɛ pet		ɔ port
LOW	æ pat	a art	ɑ ought, spa

Diphthongs

aɪ bite	aʊ how	ɔɪ boy

Additional Diphthongs for Loanwords

iə Dhia	uɛ suête	uə fuarag

Diacritics

′ stressed syllable (placed before the syllable)
: long vowel (placed after the vowel)

Note: Because most of the citations for the headwords come from written sources, the transcription is by necessity broad, and pronunciation will differ among individuals. In addition, the sounds may change within certain phonetic environments. Stress markers are not needed in Mi'kmaq (Inglis Email 24 February 2014).

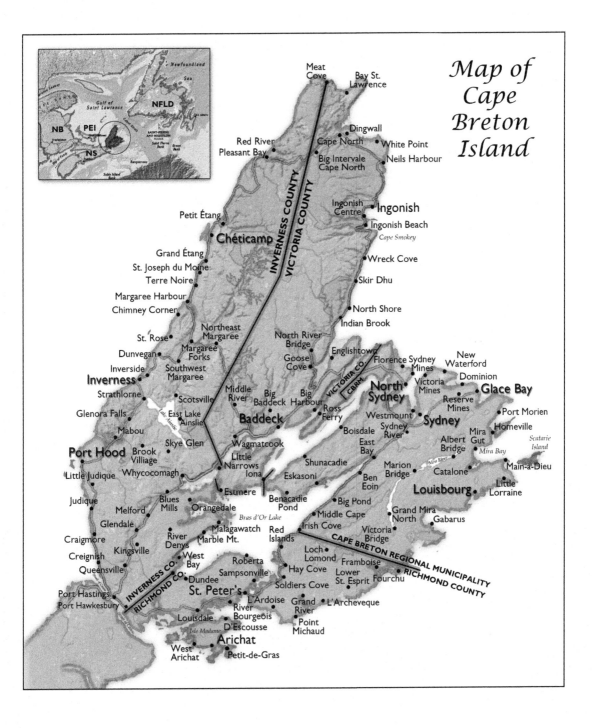

Map of
Cape
Breton
Island

Settlement History of Cape Breton Island

Throughout Cape Breton's history, various peoples have been drawn to the island to exploit its material resources. Originally the Mi'kmaq lived off the land and sea and call the place "Unama'ki, the foggy land," one of seven Mi'kmaw districts (Morgan 2008, 10). According to Silas Rand: "They divided it into seven districts, each district having its own chief, but the chief of Cape Breton, which comprised one district, was looked upon as head of the whole. As marked on the 'wampum belt,' C. B. is at the head" (Rand 1875, 81). The Mi'kmaw understanding of the geography and land is illustrated by many of their place names that are full of deeper meanings than appear at the outset. For example, Sable and Francis summarize: "Place names tell of where to find resources, features of the landscapes, or where particular events took place. These legends, in turn, provide geographical information ... and acted as oral maps of the landscape Mi'kmaq continue to call home" (Sable and Francis 2012, 53). Currently, archaeological work at Debert, Nova Scotia, highlights "approximately 11,000 years of Mi'kmaw ancestral presence in Eastern North America" (Sable and Francis 2012, 19). These original inhabitants met immigrants who came from afar to settle on Cape Breton Island. These new people learned much about how to survive the climate and landscape from their aboriginal counterparts.

International wars and treaties resulted in French and English immigration. The eighteenth and nineteenth-century flow of immigrants was also caused by an economic impetus that continued in waves as Europeans came to fish and farm, engage in shipping and shipbuilding, and to mine and make steel. The nature of the island industries caused interaction between people and cultures, creating a separate Cape Breton Island identity. In addition, these groups of immigrants helped develop the island and have contributed much to the diversity of Cape Breton English and its lexicon.

The fishery was the first industry to draw Europeans to the island. As early as the 1500s, the migratory fishery was prosecuted by the Spanish, Basques, Portuguese, French and English off the shores of Cape Breton Island. As geographer Stephen Hornsby points out, "Cabot's discovery of the cod-rich waters of the northwest Atlantic in the late fifteenth century led to the incorporation of the inshore fishing grounds of Cape Breton, along with those of Labrador, Newfoundland, and Nova Scotia, into a massive, European-based fishery" (Hornsby 1992, xxiv). These early migratory fishers left their mark through the small, scattered coastal communities that caught, dried, shipped, and sold codfish to ports throughout Europe and the Caribbean. During the sixteenth and seventeenth centuries this important industry was dominated by the French, who constructed fishing stations for the summer cod fishery and returned to Europe with dried and salted cod in the fall. These fishing villages were most numerous on the east coast during the French regime, but with time the commercial fishery spread to the Bras d'Or Lake and around the coast where suitable harbours made fishing more achievable. By the early eighteenth century the French established Louisbourg as a major fishing station and built a substantial fortress to protect French interests in fishing and trading along the east coast.

By the mid-eighteenth century, Acadian French families lived and fished in many Cape Breton coastal communities and traded and sold their fish at Louisbourg. Conflicts between England and France continued at this time creating a climate of tension throughout the region. Acadian settlers were asked to sign an oath of allegiance to the British crown by the governing Legislative Council in Halifax. Refusing to sign, Acadians experienced Le Grand Dérangement known as the Expulsion of the Acadians in 1755 when British Governor Lawrence decided to deport them from mainland Nova Scotia Acadian communities (Daigle 1982, 45–6). In Cape Breton, however, deportations followed the 1758 siege of Louisbourg when British forces took the French city. As Morgan says, "After the fall of Louisbourg, Cape Breton was practically depopulated. When word reached Acadians at places like Port Toulouse (St. Peter's) and Isle Madame that their settlements might once again be pillaged by the British and they could be banished like their brethren on the mainland, many fled to the woods in places like the interior of Isle Madame. Others simply left Cape Breton for St. Pierre and Miquelon or even France" (Morgan 2008, 55).

The Cape Breton fishery shifted to the control of the English with the Treaty of Paris in 1763 when Cape Breton and Upper Canada were ceded to England. Between 1763 and 1784 land ownership was not allowed on the island (Brown 1869, 352). Jersey merchants, however, were permitted to establish fishing stations and premises in some coastal Cape Breton areas by 1865 (Brown 1869, 381). The fishery was gradually taken over by English speaking settlers, although French settlers survived particularly in the Isle Madame, Margaree, and Chéticamp regions. Other Acadian families came to Cape Breton in the mid-1780s from Prince Edward Island and St. Pierre and Miquelon settling in and around the Chéticamp area (Chiasson 1986, 24). A group of Acadians known as *"Les Quatorze Vieux"* – the fourteen original settlers – were granted 700 acres of land in 1790 in which they, in turn, parceled out to their fellow Chéticamp settlers (Morgan 2008, 109).

As a result of this important foundational industry, many words concerning the material culture of fishing have become part of the general vocabulary. Furthermore, the small, isolated, self-reliant communities that were created along the coast helped preserve some older words and expressions in Cape Breton English.

Gaels migrated to British North America beginning in the late eighteenth and early nineteenth century, in search of land to call their own. Bringing their rich Gaelic traditions, culture, and language to the island, they established farms in coastal areas, beside the Bras d'Or Lake and along rivers such as the Margaree,

Middle River, Mira, and River Inhabitants. As Hornsby says, "At the height of the migration, during the late 1820s and early 1830s, more Highland Scots were moving to Cape Breton than to anywhere else in North America. The effect on the Island was dramatic. The population increased from fewer than 3,000 in 1801 to almost 55,000 in 1851, and the ethnic composition [of the island] changed greatly" (Hornsby 1992, 31).

Nevertheless, the short growing season and rocky land forced many to engage in a variety of work, on the farm, in the fishery, and in the coal mines that began developing on a large-scale early in the nineteenth century. During the winter, farmers at the time often cut forest timber to use in the burgeoning coal mines as "pit props" (Vernon 1903, 135). Other groups who worked the land include the Irish, Acadian French, and United Empire Loyalists. The so-called frontland farmers settled in the fertile river valleys and along the coastal areas of the Bras d'Or Lake and the coasts where the land was arable. These farmers often employed the "backland" farmers, whose land was poor and rocky, as labourers (Bittermann 1990, 84). Many of these workers from the back regions migrated to coal mining communities in search of wage labour.

Some nineteenth-century migrants such as the Archibalds of North Sydney, Charles Campbell of Victoria County, and J. S. Christie of George's River, became merchants and engaged in the shipping, trading, and shipbuilding industries throughout the island. As Morgan says, "At St. Ann's John Munro – first at Munro's Point, later at Shipyard Point – built a variety of ships, purchasing local lumber, employing settlers, and shipping timber to Britain and butter, farm produce, and cattle to Newfoundland" (Morgan 2008, 138). At this time, the most common form of transportation was by sea. The largely forested island of nearly four thousand square miles (10,360 km^2) provided the raw materials to construct sailing vessels. MacKenzie points out that in the mid-nineteenth century, "At least 600 vessels were built in Cape Breton, from twenty-ton schooners to one thousand-ton-full-rigged ships. Every creek mouth and foreshore with level land enough for stocks and cribwork, echoed to the tap of the caulking hammer and rasp of the pitsaw" (MacKenzie 1979, 18). Farming, shipping, and shipbuilding have supplied Cape Breton English with many characteristic words.

Lowland Scots and English settlers from the British Isles coal fields came to develop Cape Breton mines between 1827 and 1857 when a British based company, the General Mining Association (GMA), held a monopoly on Cape Breton coal. Mines, railways, and wharves were built for the new production processes of large-scale, industrial coal mining. Hornsby describes the typical mining town: "Like those in GMA rows, most houses had a garden where miners kept a pig, some chickens, perhaps a cow, and grew potatoes and vegetables. The rest of a typical mining village comprised pit buildings, manager's house, company store, school, several churches, and, off company land, bars and independent stores" (Hornsby 1992, 178). These workers introduced many British terms for mining practices.

During the nineteenth century, coal mines were located in the western side of the island in Mabou Mines and Broad Cove (now Inverness) and in what is called the Sydney Coal Field including communities such as Sydney Mines,

Port Morien, Bridgeport, Glace Bay, Victoria Mines, Florence and New Waterford. One scholar describes Cape Breton just before the industrial boom in the 1890s as "poor, underdeveloped, primitive and isolated" (MacKenzie 1979, 15). At the end of the century and turn of the twentieth century, steel mills in Sydney Mines and Sydney added to the emerging industrial landscape, making Cape Breton Island one of the most important coal and steel regions in Canada. This period saw the arrival of Eastern Europeans, Chinese, Italians, Ukrainians, Czechoslovakians, Polish, and Barbadian/West Indian Blacks to work the steel mills and mines. Two large corporations controlled this end-of-the-nineteenth century development: Dominion Coal and Nova Scotia Steel and Coal.

By the 1920's, another large company, British Empire Steel and Coal Corporation (BESCO) controlled all the coal mines and steel mills on the island. These large corporations, managed from outside the region, created the climate for the growth of a strong, militant working class tradition that supported the development of unions. As Manley notes, "The peculiar intensity of class conflict in Cape Breton's coal districts, David Frank has argued, grew out of the intersection of 'two historical cycles': the coal miners' embrace of the heightened aspirations and class consciousness that swept the European and North American working class following the Bolshevik Revolution and the end of World War I; and the arrival of BESCO, a new and particularly aggressive industrial landlord eager to exploit coal holdings that formed the most profitable part of its operations but which were becoming increasingly vulnerable to extra-provincial competitive pressures" (Manley 1992, 66). The rapid growth of the steel and coal companies encouraged immigrants and many Gaelic speaking Cape Bretoners (backlanders) working on marginal farms, to seek jobs in the coal and steel communities. This, in turn, created language contact between several nationalities, particularly Gaelic and English, resulting in many Gaelic loanwords and numerous words and expressions deriving from these primary occupations becoming part of the common vocabulary of the areas near these industries.

Cape Breton Island is indeed a distinctive place in contemporary Canada. As well as being a major contributor to the commercial fisheries, it was also one of the main industrial centres of Atlantic Canada by the early 1900s. Over the last few centuries its landscape has been inextricably shaped by aboriginal inhabitants, colonial expansion, immigration, and the powers of unbridled industrial capitalism. The regional variety of English that has emerged from these industrial influences, the Mi'kmaw people, and immigrant cultures has its own particular qualities. The *DCBE* records and preserves many of the island's distinctive and characteristic words and senses.

DICTIONARY OF
CAPE BRETON ENGLISH

DICTIONARY OF CAPE BRETON ENGLISH

A

ach: see **och**

after preposition, following a form of *to be* and preceding a present participle in the phrase *to be after* (*doing*)
to have (done) or have recently (done)
   1932 Beaton Institute MG 12 134, 22 I am just after having supper. 1933 Beaton Institute MG 12 43 D2 f5 Box 2, 152 I was after leaving the house ... 1973 MACPHAIL *Girl from Loch Bras d'Or* 130 They are after making the road so good since the railroad came your way, Millie and Sadie can walk to school on the tracks. 1975 *CB's Magazine* 10, 32 You're after frightening a lot here but you're not frightening me tonight. 1981 ACKERMAN *Black around the Eyes* 96 I guess you'll be after thinking about how you will both spend your days now [in retirement] ... 1984 Beaton Institute Tape 2144 It's so long ago. I'm after forgetting. 1988 MACGILLIVRAY and MACGILLIVRAY *CB Ceilidh* 111 By this time I was after learning four or five steps. 2007 *DCBE* Tape SHERRINGTON 19 He was after leaving ... he had just left. 2007 MACDONALD *Lauchlin of the Bad Heart* 167 "Malkie, I'm after forgetting what night it is, boy!" Survey I Inf. 5 I'm after hearing from her three times this month. The expression might be derived from the Gaelic adverb for *after*. Survey I Inf. 41 I

was after mopping the floor when you walked over it with your boots on.
   [*DNE, DPEIE, COD dialect, EDD, OED3* Chiefly *Irish English* (1682), *COED Irish, DARE, DAE Anglo-Irish, W3 chiefly Irish, MWCD chiefly Irish*]

*Informally called the "*after*-perfect," this construction may be expressed in formal English by the perfect verb forms using the auxiliaries *have, had, will have*. Its wide use in Cape Breton English can be attributed to the influence of speakers of Anglo-Irish and Scottish Gaelic. The *OED3* analyzes the history of this phrase and concludes: "The construction is found in Irish English and in varieties of English in other parts of the world (especially North America), which were influenced by Irish English. It is also found in the English of the Highlands and Islands of Scotland, where it reflects the equivalent construction in Scottish Gaelic" (at *after* Phrases 5b). David Crystal notes this construction is also used in Wales (1991, 6), suggesting that contact with Gaelic may be one of the primary influences. See Sandra Clarke (2012) for a thorough analysis of the *after*-perfect and other perfect forms used in Newfoundland and Labrador English.

ahide verbal adjective; also spelled **a-hide**
hidden, concealed (from public scrutiny)
   1992 GILLIS *Promised Land* 14 I have to keep her ahide, or she'd be gone. 1996 GILLIS *Stories From the Woman From Away* 106 To put a man such as Dave "a-hide"

as if he were some penance cast upon his parents and family seemed inhuman to Mary. 2008 *DCBE* Tape CURRIE 10 She was at our place and she was talking about something that was ahide up behind the barn. Hidden.

Anderton shearer: see **shearer**

angashore, angishore: see **hangashore**

artist noun
someone who draws government money such as employment insurance, social assistance, etc.
    Survey I Inf. 13 Yup, he's an artist for the government. Survey I Inf. 22 I have a job. I'm an artist for the government.

[*Artist* is a humorous pun on the idea of "drawing" government money and can occasionally suggest disapprobation by association with the term *con artist*. Compare *government man DPEIE*]

Associated Loyalist noun, usually plural
a United Empire Loyalist who affiliated with others to resettle in Canada, some of whom came to Cape Breton Island
    1903 VERNON *CB Canada* 57 It was about the end of October, 1784, that the first considerable influx of settlers came to Cape Breton. Three vessels then arrived, having on board about one hundred and forty persons known as the "Associated Loyalists." 1967 PARKER *CB Ships and Men* 60 There were always Indian settlements at Baddeck and about 1782 settlers who called themselves the Associated Loyalists, arrived from New England and were given grants in the vicinity. 1980 MORGAN *CB Historical Essays* 19 Lord Sydney wrote Haldimand to allow the Associated Loyalists to leave Quebec for Louisbourg.

August Gale noun; also **Lord's Day Gale**

historically a destructive storm on August 24, 1873, now any late summer storm and a nickname for someone known for prodigious activity
    1874 WHITMAN *New Dominion Monthly* Mar. 129 Indeed, the sad effects of the great August gale were still visible: anchors, chains, rigging, numerous heavy bars of iron were piled up pell-mell, and mixed with the rocks and waters, as a pile of jack-straws might be with the hand on a tea table of Jack. 1967 PARKER *CB Ships and Men* 38 During August 23rd and 24th, 1873, a very severe storm took place over Nova Scotia ... At Cow Bay (Port Morien), which at this date and season was very busy shipping coal, the breakwater and loading facilities were badly damaged and thirty-seven vessels were driven ashore. Ever since, a late summer storm over this Island has been known as "The August Gale". 1974 LOTZ and LOTZ *CB Island* 30 This 'August Gale' (originally known as the Lord's Day Gale) was probably the tail end of a tropical hurricane ... 1978 *CB's Magazine* 19, 8 He was a MacDonald. He had a nickname – poor old fellow – they called him August Gale. 1981 Beaton Institute Tape 2046 Jim O'Donnell, he was a man about six foot three, and his nickname, they used to call him the August Gale. He was one of the greatest woodcutters ... 1992 *CB's Magazine* 59, 36 So there was a violent August gale came on. And many, many boats were lost that time. There was a whole month I didn't know where he was. You couldn't phone. It wasn't like today – you wouldn't hear of ships that were lost.
    [*DPEIE* (1982)]

[*The 1979 citation at *breeze* in the *DNE* equates *breeze* ("A strong wind, gale") with an *August Gale*.

away adverb; often used as a noun in the phrases **from away, come from away**; compare **CFA**

an indefinite locality other than Cape Breton; occasionally a place on Cape Breton Island other than one's home locality

1975 Beaton Institute Tape 1017 They were bringing in rams from away even back in the 20s. 1982 MERTZ "No Burden to Carry" 115 In describing relatives who left Cape Breton during the early twentieth century, informants often spoke of their return from "away," of visits made to them "away," or of their spouses who were people from "away." 1987 *Inverness Oran* 2 Sept. 3 We must strive to open these events more and more to the tourist who is not "home from away." 1993 CB CONNECTION *Retiring to CB* 58 Ingonish is rather isolated, and the community is very family oriented. We are foreigners, everyone from away is and anyone from the other side of the mountain is from away. 1999 DOUCET and DERRY *Looking for Henry: A Poem* 103 From away, a good down-home / expression / which means / the ether of existence / beyond Cape Breton. 2005 MACDONALD *Forest for Calum* 120 I saw Taurus standing with some home-from-away relatives ... 2007 *DCBE* Tape SHERRINGTON 2 He and I were here in town working in Mabou, and he said, "Well, I'm from away," and I said, "You're from Inverness." And he said, "Here [in Mabou], that's from away." 2007b BARBER *Only in Canada* 8 **come from away / CFA** (*Atlantic Canada*) a person who is not from the Atlantic region generally. 2009 MORGAN *Story of CB Island Book Two* 203 With the growing affordability of the automobile and improved roads, people returning home from "away" came to perform at the summer concerts. Pilot Survey Inf. 2 Anywheres that's not here is *away*. Survey I Inf. 5 *From away* is older and preferred; *CFA* is more recent and has a pejorative quality – she is come from away. It can also be apologetic – I am a come from away; how would I be expected to know that? Survey I Inf. 10 I always

thought it [away] referred to places other than the Maritimes, or sometimes places other than Isle Madame.

[*DPEIE, COD Cdn* (*Nfld & Maritimes*), *SSPB, DARE* (1888), *DAE* (1888), *DA* (1888), *ML*; at *from*: *NCD Atlantic Canada & Maine, OED3* (1888)]

*Respondents to Survey I preferred *from away* to *come from away*, and considered the latter to be more pejorative (see citation from Survey I Inf. 5). The majority of respondents understood *away* to be outside of Cape Breton, but a few use the phrase to indicate areas of Cape Breton other than their own home locality. Occasionally, *from away* becomes a phrasal noun (referring to people rather than location), for example, "the from aways" (Survey I Inf. 22) and "a come from away." See notes by Pratt (*DPEIE*, 6–7) and Poteet (*SSPB*, 16) for a discussion of the indefinite nature of *away*.

B

baccalao [bækə'leo] noun; also spelled **baccala**
historically codfish, currently salted codfish

1855 in 1869 BROWN *History of the Island of CB* 10 [quoting Tytler's *Historical View* ...] ... there are soles also above an ell in length; but especially great abundance of that kind of fish called in the vulgar tongue baccalaos. 1855 in 1869 BROWN *History of the Island of CB* 13 [quoting Tytler's *Historical View* ...] ... in the seas thereabouts he found such an immense multitude of large fish like tunnies, called Baccalaos ... 1892 BOURINOT *Historical and Descriptive Account of ... CB* 8 It is not often that we find evidence more conclusive in support of early exploration than that which connects the name of Baccalaos, the Basque for cod, with the countries in the gulf where that fish is found in such abundance. 1999a MIGLIORE and DIPIERRO eds. *Italian Lives* 265 The prize at the top was ten dollars, a chicken, a couple of salami, two bottles of wine, and *baccala* (salt cod).

[*DNE* (c1504), *DC Hist.*, *GCD Cdn.*; at *bacalao*: *NCD*, *OED3*, *W3*, *NOAD*; at *baccala COD*]

Baccalaos noun; also spelled **Bacaillos** an historical designation for the lands adjacent to the Atlantic cod fishery; occasionally Cape Breton Island specifically

1555 in 1869 BROWN *History of the Island of CB* 12–13 [quoting Peter Martyr, *Decades of the New Worlde or West India*] But consyderynge the could and the strangeness of the unknowne lande, he turned his course from thence to the Weste, folowynge the coaste of the lande of Baccalaos unto the 38 degrees, from whense he returned to Englande. 1609 LESCARBOT *Figvre de la Terre Nevve, Grande Rivière de Canada, et Côtes de l'Ocean en la Novvelle France* Bacaillos [on a map designating Cape Breton Island]. 1869 BROWN *History of the Island of CB* 15 Immediately after the discovery of the Baccalaos, which embraced Nova Scotia, Cape Breton, and Newfoundland, the fishermen of Normandy, Brittany, and the Basque Provinces, began to frequent the coasts to take cod. 1903 VERNON *CB Canada* 19 Certain it is that the name Baccalaos, applied in the earliest maps to this island (sometimes with and sometimes without the adjoining mainland), was the Basque word for cod, which abounded in the waters around the island.

[*DNE* ([1555]), *DC Hist.* ([1555]), *NCD*]

back brushing: see **brushing**

back kitchen noun; compare **summer kitchen**
a room in an older home off the kitchen, often an extension, typically used for

cooking in the summer, kitchen chores, storage, etc.; rarely a pantry

1984 CUMMING et al. *Story of Framboise* 28 In the back kitchen, the winter supplies would be kept, like the barrels of flour, sugar, meal and things like that. 1986 LATREMOUILLE et al. *Pride of Home* 59 *The back kitchen came as a godsend to the miner's wife who could be called upon to prepare up to six meals a day in a family of shift workers.* Pilot Survey Inf. 1 The term I've used to refer to a pantry is the back kitchen ... a room off the kitchen, a small little room – almost like a walk-in cupboard sort of thing. We used to refer to that as the back kitchen. Survey I Inf. 5 It was generally disconnected from the house so the main house would not get too hot. It was used for storage during the winter. At times it was a small room in addition to the pantry. Survey I Inf. 22 The back kitchen was attached to the main house and used in the summer. Survey I Inf. 34 They used to separate the cream from the milk in this room.

[*DNE*, *DPEIE*, *COD*, *OED3* (at *back* and spelled *back-kitchen*), *DARE* **chiefly NEng**, *DAE* (1708 in a citation at *back*)]

backland noun, usually plural; also spelled **back land(s)**; compare **frontland**, **rear**
1. a sparsely populated area, often of inferior agricultural land, situated behind properties fronting on water

1829 HALIBURTON *Historical and Statistical Account of N-S* vol. 2, 258 The greatest body of fertile land not yet occupied, lies in the interior ... the back land at St. Anne's, between Cape North and Cape St. Lawrence ... 1878 Beaton Institute MG 12 247 [page A2] He lived at back lands Baddeck. 1933 MORRISON *Collections of the NS Historical Society* 22, 92 ... those who arrived, after the McLeod hegira [exodus] ... had been obliged to content themselves with the "back land"

settlements. 1984 CUMMING et al. *Story of Framboise* 17 First, the best lands fronting lakes, rivers, and seacoasts were settled. (Water provided the only "roads" and a bountiful food supply as well.) Then the "backlands" were settled ... 1987 BITTERMANN "Middle River: Social Structure" 115 While some "backland" farms were isolated as single holdings behind front properties, large clusters of these holdings began to develop in the 1830's and 1840's. 1990 HORNSBY *Island: New Perspectives on CB* 57 Much of this "backland" was wretchedly bad, but by mid-century [19th] it was home to most of the island's population. 1992 MACLEOD and ST. CLAIR *No Place like Home* 7 Fearing further exploitation and expulsion, they did not settle directly along the coast; instead they settled in the backlands of the coastal communities of Cheticamp, Grand Etang and St. Joseph du Moine. 1999 ANDERSON *Broughton: CB's Ghost Town* 10 ... *to connect with what they call backlands, another name for what we used to call in P.E.I. the 'back settlements.'* 2007 MACDONALD *Lauchlin of the Bad Heart* 16 ... the high backland farms where the living was a hard scratch, the soil thin, the rock often too great to move even after the trees were downed. 2008 MORGAN *Story of CB Island Book One* 117 Whether it was pride or reality, there were also those who were so grateful for the land that the backlands were their heaven.
2. an area behind a developed portion of a property
 1975 Beaton Institute Tape 1017 Each farmer pastured his own sheep, but usually they had backlands, you know. There was pasture in the back of the property and they would band together, you know, three or four flocks in one spot. 1996 *CB's Magazine* 71, 26 On returning to my home I left my chum at the wagon road and took a short cut across the backlands over a small footpath.

[Sense 1: *COED, DA* (1681), *W3, NOAD, MWCD*; at *backlands*: *DC, COD*; at *back-land OED3*; at *back land(s) DAE* (1681). Sense 2: "The back portion of a piece of ground" *OED Sc.* (1488), *COED, NOAD, DSL*]

*In addition to backlands being sparsely populated, a characteristic mentioned in several dictionaries, the Cape Breton sense frequently implies the inland area has inferior soil. Occasionally, however, some of the backland farms did have good farmland.

Backlander noun, usually plural; also spelled **backlander(s)**
typically, a settler who struggled to survive on inferior agricultural land without frontage on a lake, river, or ocean
 1869 BROWN *History of the Island of CB* 425 All the best lands fronting on the lakes, rivers, and sea-coast, were taken up previous to the year 1820; since that period the lands in the rear of front lots have been occupied by the later immigrants, who are in consequence distinguished by the name of 'Backlanders.' 1988 BITTERMANN *Acadiensis* 18 (1), 43 The geographical epithet adhering to this group of settlers, "Backlander", came to indicate not just the location of their holdings, or chronology of arrival, but, more importantly, their status and position in rural society. 1994 BYERS and MCBURNEY *Atlantic Hearth* 299 Those who were impoverished when they came had to settle for what, if any, land they could get, and so became part of a relentless cycle. Their poor, rocky, and hilly land could not support a farm. These, then, were the 'backlanders' – a term that referred not only to the location of their lands but to their poverty. 2008 MORGAN *Story of CB Island Book One* 117 While not strictly backlanders, the North Shore settlers overcame poor soil with a combination of farming and fishing.
 [*DC Hist.* (1869)]

backline noun; compare **bridle, snood, trawl**
1. a long rope with baited hooks attached by short, light lines (snoods), with a buoy and anchor at each end
    1984 *CB's Magazine* 36, 65 (One fellow rowed.) And the other kept setting the gear till you came to the end of the tub ... You hook one backline onto the next backline. Survey II Inf. 4 In cod fishing the backline is connected to two anchors ... Survey II Inf. 6 The backline or main line – it is heavier than other lines. Survey II Inf. 7 Backline is used for cod fishing. Other terms are mooring line or main line.
2. a hauling rope with lobster traps attached by connecting lines with either anchors at each end or with enough ballast to hold the traps on the ocean bottom
    1979 *CB's Magazine* 23, 46 But now the way we fish (with a buoy on each end of the backline and no anchoring at all, four traps to a swing), if they float they're gone. So we try to make them so they won't float, the ballast can't get out. 1988 MACDONALD *Eyestone* 55 He had started out young hauling by hand, setting out his swings in the old method, the backlines anchored with kellicks ... Survey II Inf. 8 The backline is used to haul up the trap.
    [Sense 2: *DPEIE* (1903)]

bain wagon noun
a horse-drawn wagon used for heavy loads
    1984 CUMMING et al. *Story of Framboise* 172 An express wagon or "Bain" wagon was used for heavy loads. 1990 *CB's Magazine* 54, 66 ... I got a little bain wagon that Allen Gwinn had. So I started to haul (the wood) up to Duncan MacDonald's. 1996 *CB's Magazine* 71, 78 And every Friday of each week he would go – he'd have his big bain wagon they called them, you know, and he'd pack his meat in that.
    [at *Bain wagon DC Hist.* (1897), *GCD Cdn.*]

*While the *DC* and *GCD* state the wagon was probably named after its maker (hence, the initial capital for *Bain*) and was "widely used in the West in the late 19th and early 20th centuries," the *DCBE* evidence indicates *bain* is primarily a generic term in Cape Breton English.

bait box noun; compare **spindle**
1. a large container to store bait for longline or lobster fishing
    1988 MACDONALD *Eyestone* 62 In the turns of wind he smelled the mackerel in the bait box, the fumes of the engine. Pilot Survey Inf. 4 It [bait box] would be on land where you would store bait for the trawl line or baiting lobster traps. You would probably have a bait box on a lobster fishing boat for baiting traps. Survey II Inf. 2 Now they use plastic boxes ... they used to have a wooden-type box. Survey II Inf. 3 The size varied; they were homemade and usually about 100 pounds so two men could lift it.
2. a small receptacle to hold bait in the first section (or kitchen) of a lobster trap
    1957 WILDER *Canada's Lobster Fishery* 16 The traps are baited with readily available fresh or salt fish which are skewered whole on the bait spindle or placed in mesh bait bags or wooden bait boxes. Pilot Survey Inf. 2 Then there's a little box that you use inside of your lobster trap, and they're called bait boxes and that's what you put your bait in, inside of the trap ... The tide, it rips the bait off the spindle. Survey II Inf. 4 The bait box is four inches by six inches and held in the trap by a bungee cord.
    [Sense 1: *DNE, DPEIE*; at *bait-barrel DAE* (with *bait box* as a variant) (*a*1841). Sense 2: *DPEIE* (1957)]

bait shed noun
a small outbuilding used for storing bait and fishing gear, salting bait, and baiting hooks

Pilot Survey Inf. 2 We have a bait shed down on the wharf. That's where you keep your gear and ... during trawling season you'd be putting your bait and gear inside. It's ... usually a rickety old shed. Pilot Survey Inf. 4 The bait shed would be where people would go to bait the hook and line, and then they would wind it up in boxes. Survey II Inf. 2 [We] use freezers now, very little bait is salted now. Everyone had a bait shed where they salted the bait.
[*DNE, DPEIE* (1984)]

bakeapple noun; also spelled **bake-apple, bake apple**
the plant and edible amber berry of the *Rubus chamaemorus* (cloudberry) that grows in bogs
1829 HALIBURTON *Historical and Statistical Account of N-S* vol. 2, 216 The surface of the bog itself [adjacent to the Fortress of Louisbourg] is covered with a fruit bearing plant, resembling a dwarf raspberry, the berry being nearly the size and appearance of the yellow Antwerp raspberry, and is termed by the inhabitants, "bake-apple." 1865 in 1958 UNIACKE *Uniacke's Sketches of CB* 99 The *Bake-Apple* is another peculiar plant which grows abundantly in some parts of the Island of Cape Breton ... It bears a fruit not unlike the raspberry in shape, but of a yellow amber colour, growing to the height of five or six inches. 1899 CANADA *Sessional Papers of the Dominion of Canada: Vol. 11*, 199 "The 'bake-apple barrens' are great bogs covered chiefly with *Rubus Chamoemorus* [sic] (the bake-apple) and a few ericaceous shrubs." 1984 CAMERON *CB Collection* 37 "... you ever see bakeapples growin' wild? They look like a little orange hat on a green spike, just one to a bush, the swamps was full of 'em." 1985 Beaton Institute Tape 2328 ... we'd give them ... a nice bakeapple drink. 2007b BARBER

Only in Canada 115 **bake apple / baked-apple berry** (*Atlantic Canada*) a low-growing plant of the raspberry family with an edible amber fruit; a cloudberry. Origin: corruption of Inuktitut *appik* + "apple". Pilot Survey Inf. 4 They're fairly valuable as well; a gallon of bakeapples can possibly fetch twenty or thirty dollars ... it requires a lot of work walking through the woods and through the marshes to pick them.
[*DNE* (1775), *DPEIE, DC Esp. Atlantic Provinces* (1775), *COD N Amer.* (esp. *Nfld & Maritimes*), *FWCCD Canadian, NCD Canadian, GCD Cdn., esp. Atlantic Provinces*; at *bake-apple*: SSPB, OED3 *Canadian* (1775), DA; at *baked-apple*: DC (1778), W3; at *baked-apple berry*: DC *Atlantic Provinces* (1818), GCD, DARE]

*Three dictionaries (*DC, COD, GCD*) indicate the *bakeapple* is found especially in the Atlantic Provinces, and three others (*FWCCD, NCD, OED3*) apply the more general label of Canadian. The dictionary files indicate the word is used widely in Cape Breton English, but less frequently in Inverness County.

baker's fog noun; also **fog, cotton batting**
commercially baked white bread, used disparagingly
1976 Beaton Institute Tape 535 They [the company stores] gave them lots of what was known as baker's fog. Pilot Survey Inf. 1 Any time ... my mother wasn't feeling well enough to make bread and you had to buy a bun at the store, my father would say, "Oh, not that baker's fog again." Pilot Survey Inf. 5 That's what my dad used to call it. He used to get mad at my mother if there was no homemade bread: "All you got is the g. d. baker's fog." Survey I Inf. 5 They also used cotton batting. Survey I Inf. 23 If my mother ran out of homemade bread, she might say "Go for a couple of loaves of fog at the store."

[*DNE* (1972); at *fog*: *DPEIE* (also *baker's fog*), *DARE* (1966)]

*Respondents to Survey I indicate equal familiarity with *baker's fog* and *fog*, and several noted their parents used the phrase more so than their generation.

balance noun; compare **level**
a passage or tunnel cut into a coal seam at right angles from a main level; also one of a pair of passages used for moving air to or from the surface of the mine
1918 Beaton Institute MG 12 46 A9 n.p. Balance onsetters [$2.95 per day]. 1976 *Oran Inbhirnis* 6 Aug. 6 Staying within the seam of coal smaller tunnels or 'balances' were now dug in an up-hill direction at right angles to the level. It was in these 'balances' that the actual commercial coal-mining took place. 1983 SHEDDEN et al. *Mining Photographs* 269 **Balance** – An inclined passage running up at right angles from a main level, into the coal seam, normally tracked, with boxes drawn up and lowered by balance gravity; the term generally refers to a pair of passages connected at the top, one of which is upcast and the other downcast for ventilation. 1983 MELLOR *Company Store* 85 A huge ventilation fan mounted on one of the back deep shafts forced great volumes of air down through all the workings of the mine, where it was evenly distributed using a variety of devices known as ... lower balance tunnels.

banjo noun; see **pan shovel**
a short handled shovel with a large circular blade used to load coal, a pan shovel
1978 *CB's Magazine* 21, 38 There he'd pass out a rainbow / And then a banjo, / Then he'd stand there behind us / And watch every blow. 2001 MACKENZIE *In the Pit* 70 The pan shovel was also known as the "banjo."

[*OED3* Chiefly *Austral.* and N.Z. (1918), *DARE* **chiefly Nth, West, W3**]

bankhead noun; also spelled **bank-head, bank head;** compare **pit head**
a large, multi-storeyed building near the entrance to a coal pit, to which coal cars are drawn to be emptied
1894 Anon. *The Canadian Mining Review* 13 (12), 250 New bank head and pit frame have been erected and new screening machinery put in operation [at the Old Bridgeport Colliery]. 1905 DAVIDSON and MACKENZIE *The Canadian Mining Review* 24 (3), 50 The bankhead consists of a steel structure containing modern appliances for picking and screening coal and delivering it to the railway cars. 1929 *North Sydney Herald* 27 Feb. 6 Gangs of men cleaned [the snow] out the switches and branch lines leading into the bankheads, and by Thursday night the pits were again ready for hoisting. 1951 MACLENNAN *Each Man's Son* 241 ... [he] saw the black mass of the bankhead loom against the lighter mass of the sky ... 1978 *Oran Inbhirnis* 2 Feb. 19 The complex [at Inverness] consisted of two mines, no.1 and no.2, a bank-head 350 ft. by 18 ft. ... 1983 MELLOR *Company Store* 86 Above ground, the bankhead was the largest and most important of the many buildings scattered throughout the compound. Three storeys high, it towered above the rest. Coal boxes brought to the surface ... were pulled to the top floor of the bankhead to be checked and weighed. 1996 MACMILLAN *Boy from Port Hood* 52 ... I went [to work] on the bankhead. That's where the coal cars were brought up from down in the pits, and the coal was then dumped in the chutes for sale. The bankhead was the structure at the head of the slope.

*Compare the different meaning in the *OED3* at *bank-head* (at *bank*, sense 10) "in *Mining*, the surface of the ground at the pit-mouth, or top of the shaft" and *W3* at *bank head* "the mouth and immediate environs of a coalmine."

barachois [berə'šwɑ, barə'šwɑ] noun; also spelled **barrachois, barrasoi, Barrasoi** a coastal pond, separated from a larger body of water by a bar of sand or gravel; a lagoon partially open to the larger body of water; used in place names
1760 PICHON *Genuine Letters ... CB* 21 They give the name of *barachois* in this country to small ponds near the sea, from which they are separated by a kind of causeway. There is no possibility of travelling even the distance of a league along the coast without meeting with some of these pieces of water. 1829 HALIBURTON *Historical and Statistical Account of N-S* vol. 2, 232 The settlers here [at Aspy Bay] are scattered round the lagunes, or as they are termed, barrasois. 1832 BOUCHETTE *British Dominions in North America* vol. 2, 75 ... it [East Bay] makes a course of thirty-one miles to the head of East Bay, or St. Andrew's Channel, terminating in the Barrasoi ... 1869 BROWN *History of the Island of CB* 309 On the morning of July 1 [1758], a large party, which left the town and approached the Barachois, were attacked by Wolfe with a corps of Light Infantry, and driven back into the town. 1885 in 1978 PATTERSON *History of Victoria County* 3 The beach [at Aspy Bay] we have referred to forms three large lagoons, or as they are called, barrasois ... 1974 LOTZ and LOTZ *CB Island* 151 At least one word coined by the Acadians has passed into ordinary usage in Cape Breton. *Barachois* is used to describe a lagoon or pond cut off from a larger body of water by a neck of land or a sand bar. 1994 LAWLEY *Guide to CB's Cabot Trail* 51–2 Called barachois ponds, these unusual water bodies are formed by a stream gradually eroding a small seawater cove at the ocean's edge. A combination of strong ocean waves and longshore ocean currents then begin to deposit sand, gravel and boulders across the mouth of the cove. Finally, as the cove is completely closed off, it fills with fresh water, creating the pond you see today. 2007b BARBER *Only in Canada* 24 **barachois / barrasway** (*Atlantic Canada*) a shallow coastal lagoon or pond created by the formation of a sandbar a short distance offshore from a beach. Survey I Inf. 5 It is a salt-water pond, landlocked by a sandbar ... for example, the barachois at Barachois Mountain. Survey II Inf. 4 It is an inland pond along the shoreline with a brook going to the ocean, a mixture of fresh and salt water.
[*COD Cdn* (*Nfld* & *Maritimes*); similar definitions are found in *DNE, DC Atlantic Provinces* (1760), *NCD Atlantic Canada*; compare *DPEIE, GCD Cdn.*]

Barachois is popular element in toponyms in the Atlantic Provinces, with over thirty occurrences in Nova Scotia alone (Hamilton 1996, 291). The term, however, is understood differently in various locations. Alan Rayburn emphasizes two elements: a water feature, "a pond enclosed by a bar at sea level," and a coastal feature "with its original application applying to a gravel bar" (2010, 19). *GCD* stresses only the coastal element ("a narrow strip of sand or gravel ... [a] causeway"), and the *DPEIE* emphasizes only the water feature ("a backwater near the mouth of a river; a marsh"). Other dictionaries note both the water and coastal features. *DNE* defines it as an openwater feature, an "estuary, lagoon or harbour ... sheltered from the sea by a sand-bar or a low strip of land." *DC* gives a two-part definition as an enclosed water feature (a pond) and a causeway, and *NCD* has "a tidal pond partly obstructed by a bar" and "a sand or gravel causeway." *COD* and *DCBE* define it as either an enclosed or open water feature (a pond or lagoon), separated or partially protected from the larger body of water by a sand or gravel bar. For discussion of the Basque origin of the word, see Miren Egana Goya (1992, 65) and William Hamilton (1996, 159–60, 291). Yves Cormier discusses the French usage in Quebec and the Atlantic region (1999, 80–1).

bar harbour noun
a harbour or bay with a bar of sand or gravel partially blocking its mouth
Pilot Survey and Survey II.
[*DNE, DC Maritimes* (1830), *COD N Amer.*; at *bar harbor DPEIE*]

*Most of the respondents to Survey II reported using this word, but the *Gazetteer of Canada / Répertoire Géographique du Canada: Nova Scotia / Nouvelle-Écosse* (1993) lists only one official occurrence of this name (*Bar Harbour Lake*) in Nova Scotia. It seems that *barachois* is the preferred term for this sort of water feature.

barachois and barrasoi(s): see barachois

barrack noun, usually plural; also **hay barrack, hay-barrack**; compare **longer**
a rough structure with an adjustable roof supported by four poles (or longers), used to protect hay, and occasionally dried fish, from wet weather
1865 in 1958 UNIACKE *Uniacke's Sketches of CB* 66 ... good crops of hay, which are well stacked in "hay-barracks" (a roof moving up and down upon four poles). 1885–6 FARNHAM *Harper's New Monthly Magazine* 72 Dec.–Mar. 615 ... carts passed to and fro between the fields and the barns, or the "barracks" ... 1979 MACKENZIE *Irish in CB* 60 Stacking hay, so common in Ireland, was successful in Cape Breton if "barracks" were employed. (These movable wooden stack covers set on four poles were apparently a borrowing from the continent of Europe by way of New England and Newfoundland.) 1984 *CB's Magazine* 36, 68 They had flakes all over the beach, and faggots, barracks that came down over their pile of dry fish. 1984 CUMMING et al. *Story of*

Framboise 65 Barracks were four poles put into the ground with a roof on top of it. There were holes in the poles so that you could pick the roof up however high you wanted it. 1992 HORNSBY *Nineteenth-Century CB* 18 During the summer men were accommodated in ... sheds and stables, and a hay "barrack." Survey I Inf. 5 ... four poles with a movable roof, called hay barracks. In old deeds it might be part of the sale, seen in one deed from the 1840's.
[*DNE, DPEIE, COD Cdn* (Maritimes), *OED3, DARE* **chiefly NY, C Atl** (1697), *DAE, DA* (1697), *W3 Northeast*; at *hay barrack*: *OED3, DARE* **chiefly NEast, C Atl**, *DAE, DA* (1767), *WGUS*]

Barraman noun, usually plural; also spelled **Barra-man, Barra man**
immigrant from Barra
1932 CONNOR *Arm of Gold* 133 Those Barra men are a wild lot, and Ranald has a temper. 1937 in 1991 *CB's Magazine* 57, 59 ... settlers living around the Bras d'Or lake [*sic*] (in Gaelic called Loch Mór nam Barrach, 'the Big Loch of the Barramen,' from this fact) knew old waulking songs that were unknown around Lake Ainslie or Whycocomagh. 1976 MACLEAN *God and the Devil* 7 ... the people of the adjoining county of Victoria were mostly Catholics from Skye and Barra – we knew them all as Barra-men.

barren noun, frequently plural in sense 2; often modified by the berry found there, e.g., **blueberry barren**
1. a flat tract of land, often marshy and known for supporting edible berries
1829 HALIBURTON *Historical and Statistical Account of N-S* vol. 2, 244 Yet even its finest lands are not exempt from a mixture of swampy and barren spots, with which the whole face of the country is dotted. 1899 CANADA *Sessional Papers of the Dominion of Canada: Vol. 11*, 199

"The 'barrens' themselves are classified by the fruits they produce, as, blue-berry barrens, bake-apple barrens, etc., but the cause of all is the same. The soil is but a light covering and of a peaty nature." 1951 MACLENNAN *Each Man's Son* 227 The train swerved away from the lake and ran through more spruce, then it came out of the woods into a blueberry barren. 1990 PEACH *Memories of a CB Childhood* 67 Then came the annual pilgrimage to the "bakeapple barren," ... this square mile of steamy peat bog ... 2007b BARBER *Only in Canada* 25 **barren** (*New Brunswick & Nova Scotia*) an expanse of marsh or muskeg. **2.** an elevated area of rocky terrain with thin soil supporting mosses and low-growing vegetation

1922 MACDOUGALL *History of Inverness County* 59–60 Where the summit is of large extent on these highlands, "barrens" occur on which rockcrops appear in places with the vegetation varying from moss and marsh grasses, through low shrubs into stunted trees around the margin. 1948 WALWORTH *CB Isle of Romance* 112 Down the spine of the rawboned northern peninsula runs a strip of land that is known as "the Barrens." This region is covered with semi-Arctic tundra ... 1977 *CB's Magazine* 16, 2 They used to call it the Everlasting Barren back there ... That's the highest place in Cape Breton.

[Sense 1: *DNE* ([1776]), *DC N.B.*, *COD Cdn* (NB & NS), *SSPB*, *OED3* in Nova Scotia and New Brunswick. Sense 2: *DNE* ([1770]), *DC* "In the Atlantic Provinces" ([1770]), *COD* "in eastern N America," *OED3 spec.* applied in N. America]

barricade noun; compare **rafting**
ice piled on the shore creating a barrier, formed by spray and ice being driven ashore

Survey II Inf. 2 Build up of ice on the shore is a barricade – as high as a single-storey house. Survey II Inf. 7 A barricade is a wall of ice on shore. Survey II Inf. 8 Barricades are caused by drift ice on shore and spray builds up a barricade.

[*DC* (1909), *GCD Cdn.*; compare *ice barricade*: *DC*, *OED3* (1853), and *barricade* used as a verb in *DNE* in this sense (1775)]

*This ice feature is also known in other regions as a *ballicatter* (variously spelled in *DNE*, *DC*, *COD*, and *OED3*) and a *barricado* (*DNE*, *DC*, and *GCD*).

Bay bye noun; also **Bay Boy**; compare **b'y**
an inhabitant of Glace Bay

1953 MACINTYRE *CB Mirror* 2 May 9 ... they never visited the coal town's [Glace Bay's] famed Senator's Corner on the weekend, where the 'Bay Boys' played around on pay night and spent their money. 1964 ROBINSON *Canadian Geographical Journal* 69, 93 Men of the town [Glace Bay] are still often called "Bay Byes". 1985 MACGILLIVRAY and O'DONNELL *CB Song Collection* 18 You might say us little Bay Byes were into Heavy Metal long before it became fashionable. 2002 *CB Post* 7 Oct. B1 Did the Bay byes meet the Pier dears?

*Although the spelling "b'y" is slightly more frequent in our files than "bye," the phrase identifying a person from Glace Bay is consistently spelled either "Bay bye" or "Bay boy."

beach noun
a shore with rounded stones suitable for drying salted cod

1981 *CB's Magazine* 29, 4 And before the vessel would come to load it [the salted cod], you'd dry it all – just give it a day's sun on the beach or on the flakes again, whatever you'd have. 1984 BALCOM *Cod Fishery of Isle Royale* 26 Three types of drying apparatus (beaches, flakes, and *rances*) were used in France's North American cod fishery. Beaches were gravel beaches, either man-made or natural, which were relatively level and devoid of large rocks, sand, soil, or vegetation. 1992 HORNSBY *Nineteenth-Century CB* 154 Even in the late 1880's, the Robin company recruited some 20 shoremen – agents, clerks, beach-masters, and foreman – in the Channel Islands each year to staff its fishing stations at Arichat and Chéticamp. 2001 JOHNSTON *Colonial Louisbourg* 97 The priority was for fishing proprietors to establish themselves close to the harbor with direct access to the water and with enough land for fish flakes, cobbled beaches, and required buildings.

[*DNE* (1613), *COD Cdn* (*Nfld*); compare *beach lot DC*]

beag [bɛk] adjective; also spelled **beagh, bheag**; compare **tea bheag**
small, little, light; when used as a nickname, young, small
1952 MACLEOD *CB Mirror* 1 July 5 Ceòl Beag, or Ceòl Aotrom, meaning The Small or Light Music, is comprised of Marches, Strathspeys, Reels and Jigs, and is the most popular form of bagpipe music known to us at the present time. 1976 PRINGLE *Pringle's Mountain* 15 The older folks had gruel or bread and *tea beag* (veck) a Gaelic word for *small tea* ... 1977 Beaton Institute Tape 900 So to differentiate, one [son] was Rory and the other was Rory Beag, and beag in Gaelic means small. 1981 MACGILLIVRAY *CB Fiddler* 17 Belief in the "daoine beaga" or "little men" was common among pioneer Cape Bretoners. 2007 ST. CLAIR Email 24 Mar. The warming oven on the upper part of a wood cook stove has been called both "oven beag" with the English oven and the Gaelic word for small.

*A loanword from Scottish Gaelic, see *beag* "light (of import), little, minor, petty, slender, slight, small, trifling, wee" *GED*.

Bella noun; also **Bells**; compare **tarabish**
in the card game tarabish, the king and queen of the trump suit held in one hand;
the oral signal given before playing the second of these cards
1996 KENNEDY *Centre of the World* 66 Bella, also known as "bells," is the king and queen in trump ... Bella is worth 20 points. 2000 YORK *Tarabish* 20 Any hand that contains the "**King**" and "**Queen**" (known as the Bella) of the **trump suit** will earn any team 20 points if proper procedure is followed. Simply announce the **second part** of this feature by saying "Bella" before the card is played to the trick on the table. 2003 CRANE Email 23 Feb. 3 ... if they periodically shout out "Bella" you know the game is tarabish. 2003 MARCONI-MACASKILL *Cape Bretoner* 11 (3), 17 I got the name Bella – well, think about it. It's Cape Breton right? The day I was born ... Ma was waiting her chance to play the other part of Bella, when her water broke. No way would she leave till the game was over.

[Compare *bella* "the king and queen of trumps given a special scoring value in European card games" *W3*]

biff transitive verb; compare **whiff**
to throw (something), occasionally to throw out
1997 GABRIEL Oral Communication 16 July To throw hard, they biffed stones at the dead seal. 2002 *DCBE* Tape *Information Morning* 27 Feb. 11 I said "he biffed it out the window." 2003 MUISE Email 3 July "... biff" – to throw – "He was biffin' rocks at the cat." Survey II Inf. 8 Biff means to toss or throw away. Survey I Inf. 41 Biff implies a harder throw [than whiff].

[*OED3* Also *intr. Austral. and N.Z.* (1941), *W3 chiefly Austral*]

*Many respondents to Survey I considered *biff* and *whiff* to be synonyms, while others thought one verb indicated a harder or more violent throw than the other. This sense is also found in Australia (*OED3*, *W3*) and New Zealand (*OED3*), which were settled during the same period as Nova Scotia and where Cape Breton emigrants migrated in the mid-nineteenth century.

big ice noun, usually with **the**; compare **shore ice**

extensive, tightly packed drift ice, typically stretching out from the coast

1891 Beaton Institute MG 12 45, 27 Jan. 6 Harriet said that there is no crossing over Port Hood Harbour the big ice hasnot [*sic*] come in yet. 1922 MACDOUGALL *History of Inverness County* 250 In February 1789, Captain David and three of his sons went out sealing on the "Big Ice" north of their Island home. 1977 *Inverness Oran* 28 Oct. 1 What the pirates were unaware of when they buried their loot was the violence of a Cape Breton winter and the capacity of the 'big ice' to alter the face of the shoreline. 1986 MACLEOD *As Birds Bring Forth the Sun* 46 The "big ice," which was what we called the major pack of drift ice, was in solidly against the shore and stretched out beyond the range of vision. 2003 ELLISON *Cape Bretoner* 11 (3), 11 Sometime around mid-January, "slob ice" (slush) and then "ice pans" begin to appear. Soon they merge and interfreeze and "the big ice" settles in along the west coast. Sometimes this floe ice hangs around until late into the spring ... With shifting wind patterns the ice begins to move into the Cabot Strait and out into the Atlantic, towards Sydney Harbour and the eastern side of Cape Breton. 2007 DANIELSON *CB Weather Watching* 158 ... the building carried out on the big ice. Survey I Inf. 5 Big ice refers to ice that packs the west coast of this island from the Causeway to Cape North. The ice drifts from the St. Lawrence and the Arctic.

[*DNE* (1924)]

*The phrase primarily indicates the sea ice on the western side of the island, but it occasionally refers to drift ice on the Bras d'Or Lake.

bingo noun

inexpensive wine

Survey I.

[*DC Slang* (1963); compare "A slang term for brandy" *OED3* (1699)]

bish: see **tarabish**

black forest noun; also **black wood(s)**; see **burnt land**

soil made fertile from the ashes of wood burnt on it

1953 DUNN *Highland Settler* 29 Fortunately for the Highland settler, the newly cleared ground, the *coille dhubh* (black forest) or *coille loisgte* (burnt forest) as they called it, was magnificently fertile. 1963 Beaton Institute Tape 7 They cut down the trees and cut them up fine, you know, all they could, and then they burnt the ground. Then they put potatoes in them black woods and put oats in them. 1987 WATSON and ROBERTSON *Oral Tradition ... CB Gaels* 11 We had our own burnt wood. They called it a black forest.

Black Friday noun; see **Parade of Concern**

see quotations

1967 *Chronicle Herald* 16 Oct. 1 On Black Friday, Oct. 13, the people of Nova Scotia were informed of the intended close down of the steel plant of the Dominion Steel and Coal Corporation on April 30, 1968, and if it was not done, the Trenton ... and the Halifax Shipyards, employing nearly 1,100, would be closed sooner than might be the case otherwise. 1967 *CB Highlander* 18 Oct. 2 The ill winds of that dreadful Black Friday, October 13, [1967] for the Sydney community may have blown some good if lessons are learned from that chilling experience. 1974 LOTZ and LOTZ *CB Island* 109 Black Friday – 13 October 1967 – marked the turning point in the history of economic development on Cape Breton Island. On that day the Dominion

Steel and Coal Corporation (DOSCO) announced that it would close its steel plant ... 1991 *CB's Magazine* 58, 38 And shortly after G. I. Smith took over (as premier of Nova Scotia), we had Black Friday. So, we had the politicians on our side. Because they claimed they had no idea it was going to happen. 1993 WHITNEY PIER HISTORICAL SOCIETY *From the Pier Dear* 6 On "Black Friday," October 13, 1967, Hawker-Siddeley announced that it was closing the plant. 2003 SLAVEN sydneysteelmuseum.com/history/blackfriday.htm Thus [through the establishment of the Sydney Steel Corporation, SYSCO, as a crown corporation] ended the crisis of October the 13th of 1967, the day that became known as "Black Friday."

[Compare the general sense of *Black Friday* as a calamity on any Friday, typically associated with the financial collapse in the US on September 24, 1869: *GCD, DA, OED3 U.S.* (1869)]

black lung noun
a lung disease, pneumoconiosis, common among coal miners as a result of long-term inhalation of coal dust

2000 BARLOW and MAY *Frederick Street* 39 In fact, the men could claim compensation for only one condition: pneumoconiosis, or "black lung." 2004 MACKENZIE *Bloody CB Coal* 137 Coal dust becomes imbedded in the lungs, and causes them to harden, a condition known as black lung. 2006 MACISAAC *Better Life* 108 ... miners developed black lung disease from the coal dust and poor ventilation in the mines.

[*COD, NCD, GCD, OED3* (1837), *NOAD, MWCD*]

black pot noun; also spelled **blackpot**; also **pot**
a still; the pot, blackened by wood fires, used in distilling moonshine

1964 CREIGHTON and MACLEOD *Gaelic Songs in NS* 75 I am the son of Black

Pot (i.e., the Still), and I am sitting at the fire-hearth. 1976 *CB's Magazine* 14, 2 He could time from the time he left home till he ran a pot or two pots and came home ... 1996 MACMILLAN *Boy from Port Hood* 45 They brought their moonshine stills with them to Nova Scotia. When they came from the Scottish Highlands, if they didn't bring the "black pot" – that's what they used to call it – to make their moonshine in, they built one. 1996 MACMILLAN *Boy from Port Hood* 46 "Worms," or coils of brass, were inserted into the black pot. And they would put ice around that to distil it. As the brew boiled, it would go through the worm or coil and into a jug. 1998 GILLIS *John R. and Son* 14 ... it was generally believed that Father had made a vow to hunt out all blackpots and put them out of business as part of his atonement.

[at *pot*: *OED3* (1799), *EDD, DARE* **esp S Midl**]

blank end: see **head**

blueberry buckle noun; also **buckle**
see quotation at 2007b

1970 CANADA, DEPARTMENT OF AGRICULTURE *Food – à la canadienne* 73 *Blueberry buckle: A popular dessert in the Maritime Provinces, old-time blueberry buckle has a spicy crumb crust.* 2007b BARBER *Only in Canada* 125 **blueberry buckle** (*Maritimes*) a cake topped with blueberries and a crumbly topping. 2008 ROBIN HOOD http://www.robinhood.ca/recipe.details Summer Fruit Buckle: This cake is called a fruit buckle because as it bakes it 'buckles' under from the weight of the fruit inside and the streusel topping. Survey I.

[*COD Cdn* (*Maritimes*); at *buckle*: *DARE* (1959), *W3, MWCD*]

blueberry grunt noun
cooked blueberries with or without a dough topping

1976 BRUCE *Axiom* 3 Dec. 13 The Waipu Highlanders have laid on a lunch of dainty sandwiches ... and blueberry grunt. 2007b BARBER *Only in Canada* 126 **blueberry grunt** (*Maritimes*) a dessert of blueberries cooked in a saucepan with a dumpling-like topping. Survey I Inf. 23 A dough on top of the boiling blueberries. Survey I.

[at *grunt*: *DPEIE, DC Maritimes* (1894), *COD N Amer., NCD Atlantic Canada & New England, DARE* **chiefly NEng** (1896), *W3 New Eng, NOAD, MWCD*]

*The description of *grunt* differs in various dictionaries: some have the steamed berries with or without a topping, and the berries differ.

board noun
a table used for eating meals
1933 MORRISON *Collections of the NS Historical Society* 22, 76–7 The household furniture was scanty and rough, consisting of a table or "the Board" as it was called. 1962 MCPHERSON *Watchman against the World* 128 The tables on which the food was served were rough structures, hand-made with poor tools, but, however awkward its appearance, the family table was given the title of "the board". 1978 *CB's Magazine* 21, 38 Then we dashed to the cookhouse / Our breakfast to eat. / On the board there was plenty / Of cold beans and meat. Survey I Inf. 14 Kitchen table known as a "board."

[*NCD, GCD, EDD, OED3* (1200), *W3 archaic, MWCD archaic*; compare "A table used for meals; now, always, a table spread for a repast" *OED3*]

board(s): see **cooling board**

bobtail paysheet noun; also **bob-tail(ed) sheet, bobtail, bob-tail pay**; compare **pluck-me**

a miner's payslip with little or no money left after deductions; the pay after deductions
1953 MACINTYRE *CB Mirror* 2 May 9 Because of these deductions on the paysheet, the company stores became known as the "pluck-me" stores. Through this, some miners' pays became known as bob-tail pays. 1988 CURRIE *Company Store* 70 Another bobtail paysheet next week. 1990 WILLISTON *Johnny Miles* 13 Credit was extended to all coal-company employees. Weekly purchases were deducted from a miner's wages, along with his rent, coal, light, water, medical, church, and blasting-powder charges – all neatly recorded on a "bobtailed sheet." The miners' pay sheets were so dubbed because of the system of cutting off the bottom to show that the employee had no wages coming to him. 1992 O'DONNELL *Coal Mining Songs* 84 ... so they would take the whole works (a miner's pay) and you draw a bobtail. 2006 MACISAAC *Better Life* 101–2 Because of these deductions, some miners referred to their pay cheques as the "bob-tail sheet," that is, the pay cheque with the tail end cut off because the miner had no wage coming to him.

bochdan ['bɑxkən] noun; also spelled **Bochdan, bochan, bocan,** and rarely **bochain, Bochin, boccan**
an evil spirit or ghost, occasionally a bogeyman, the devil
[ca. 1955] Beaton Institute MG 12 103 2C n.p. The Bochin's gone to his defeat / Beneth [*sic*] the tides of Canso. 1969 Beaton Institute Tape 165 From MacMillan's Point to Porcupine, it's the Bocan Bridge of Canso. It glimmers in the moonlight and you can see it any night, provided you have second sight. 1979 THOMAS *Songs and Stories from Deep Cove* 31 We used to tell bochdan stories and everything like that. Some nights, if I were alone,

after hearing a lot of them, I'd be afraid
to go home. 1982 MACLELLAN *The Glen*
49 There were in the Glen and in the
wider neighborhood visitors whose forte
was telling ghost stories and all about
bochdans – the bochdan was the Gaelic
for an evil spirit – and for the old devil
himself. 2005 MACKENZIE *Neighbours are
Watching* 18 The "bochdans" appeared in
a variety of forms, and frightened the Irish
settlers even more than did the bears. 2006
MACINTYRE *Causeway* 38 He talks about
the *bocan*, which means ghost ... Survey
I Inf. 5 A bochdan is a ghost or spirit,
always malevolent or eerie – evil spirits
that spook horses.
   [at *bocan* "A bogeyman" *DPEIE*
([1939])]

*A loanword from Scottish Gaelic, see *bòcan*
"apparition, bogeyman, ghost, goblin, hobgoblin, sprite, spectre" *GED*; compare *bockie* "A
hobgoblin" *EDD*.

boiled dinner noun
a meal of meat, vegetables, and water,
simmered in one pot
   1996 *CB's Magazine* 71, 7 And we
had everything to eat. We had boiled
dinners. 1997 MACDONALD *Fall on
Your Knees* 516 She filled ... the bone
china plates with what we called boiled
dinner down home. Potatoes, carrots,
pork hocks (she calls them "pig's feet"),
doughboys, but instead of cabbage there
were green leaves of some kind. 2003
PRINCE *Cape Bretoner* 11 (1), 64 I eat
boiled dinner, not jigs dinner. 2007b
BARBER *Only in Canada* 117 **boiled
dinner** (*Atlantic Canada*) a dish of meat
and vegetables, especially beef brisket,
potatoes, cabbage and root vegetables,
stewed together in water.
   [*COD N Amer.* (*Maritimes, Nfld, US
North & US North Midlands*), *DARE* **chiefly
Nth, N Midl**, *W3*; at *boiled*: *OED3* (orig.
U.S.), *DAE* (1805), *DA* (1805)]

books, the noun; also spelled **Books**;
often in the phrases **say (the) books, take
the books**
the Bible, read or precented during family
worship
   1933 MACDONALD *Cape North and
Vicinity* 31 It was a common custom to
"take the books" morning and evening,
and have family worship observed in
some suitable form. 1940 MORRISON
Dalhousie Review 20, 181 The only exception to the universal observance of formal-
ity, while "the Books were being taken,"
was furnished by the toddling baby ...
1973 MACPHAIL *Girl from Loch Bras d'Or*
13 ... Mama "said books" (that is what the
activity of family worship was called) ...
1984 CUMMING et al. *Story of Framboise*
53 After breakfast (and again after supper), Father or Grandfather would take
out the Gaelic Bible and say "The Books"
(family worship). Scripture would be
read, Gaelic psalms precented, and the
family would pray together. 1991 *CB's
Magazine* 56, 20 Papa'd say books – that's
what we'd call it. He'd read a piece in the
Bible, a chapter in the Bible. And then
we'd all go on our knees ...

*The use of *the (good) book* identifying the Bible
(*OED3* c. 1200) and *the books* referring to an
account book is widespread, in contrast to *the
books* referring to the Bible.

bootleg adjective; often in the phrases
such as **bootleg pit, mine, coal, miner**;
compare **crop pit**
of mining coal, illegal, illicit
   1976–7 Miners' Museum Tape 128 I
went to a couple of bootleg pits – nearly
lost the horse in the holes. 1986b FRANK
On the Job 117 Along the shores, at
abandoned mine sites and even on the
ballfields, miners opened shallow "bootleg" pits to mine coal from the outcrop-
pings of the coal seams in violation of
coal company leases. 1988 MILLWARD

Geographical Perspectives 76 Though the effect of each pit was slight, there were a great many of them, particularly when the scores of bootleg pits are included. 2007 MACKENZIE *CB Coal Mine Disasters* 60 A lot of small mine operators sprang up, but they all failed, leaving the coal to bootleg miners.

*While most dictionaries associate *bootleg* with illicit alcohol, music recordings or software, only W3 refers to coal as a product illegally procured and sold.

bord: see **room**

Boston States, the noun, plural
1. New England, occasionally Boston
1927 ARCHIBALD *The Token* 11 Well, Angus man, the sealin' trip may be dangerous, but it's not so dangerous as the trip to the Boston States whateffer! 1948 MACNEIL *Highland Heart* 23 ... Rory had a daughter who some years before had gone to Boston, often known in Cape Breton as the Boston States. Boston in those days was the Valhalla of all ambitious Washabuckt boys and girls who ventured out into the world to better themselves. 1951 MACLENNAN *Each Man's Son* 161 "... once when he wass buying a suit of clothes in the Boston States the man in the store asked wass they too loose, so Captain Livingstone swelled out the muscles of hiss back and shoulders and burst every seam in them just to show a little of what he could do." 1975 BIRD *NS Historical Quarterly* 5 (4), 326 Many of them [visitors] were from the Boston States (as the New England States used to be called). 1988 MACDONALD *Eyestone* 34 I *left* Boston, left that place your kin fled to over the generations, the Boston States, land of plenty. 1994 GILLIS *Travels* 106 She taught school in Port Hood for a few years and then moved to 'The Boston States' in the early 1920s. Aunt Mary

worked in Boston as a domestic (maid), at a salary that was more than double what she had made as a teacher in Cape Breton. 1994 MACLEOD and ST. CLAIR *Pride of Place* 59 Work in the "Boston States" was akin to a finishing school. 2007 ST. CLAIR and LEVERT *Nancy's Wedding Feast* 14 *She determined that the best thing for her fatherless children was for her to leave them with their grandparents and go to work in Boston, Massachusetts, "The Boston States," as many still refer to New England.* 2007b BARBER *Only in Canada* 95 **Boston States** (Maritimes & Nfld) New England.
2. United States
1951 MACLENNAN *Saturday Night* 3 July 11 People no longer refer to the great republic as "the Boston States." 1974 LOTZ and LOTZ *CB Island* 103 They left for the 'Boston States' – the Cape Bretoner's term for the United States ... 2006 MACISAAC *Better Life* 124 Women who were good letter writers would sometimes embellish the wonders of their life in the "Boston States," a name given to all the American states by the Highland Scots of eastern Nova Scotia. Survey I Inf. 2 ... down in the States. Survey I Inf. 20 The States.
[Sense 1: *DPEIE, DC Maritimes* (1948), *COD Cdn* (Maritimes & Nfld), *NCD Maritimes, SSPB*. Sense 2: *DPEIE* (1939); compare "In Nova Scotia, the United States of America are the *Boston* states ..." *ML*]

*Respondents to Survey I indicate that the first sense is more widely known and used.

bow [bo] noun; compare **sill**
1. a semicircular branch or small tree serving as part of the upper frame of a lobster trap and set into the sills
1957 WILDER *Canada's Lobster Fishery* 15 Basically the popular trap is in the form of a half cylinder with three or four curved wooden bows fitted into a rectangular wooden base. 1987 Beaton Institute

Tape 2324 [Tape 1] You went to the marsh then, cut those little black spruce. They're about an inch [wide] and forty-one, forty-two inches long ... you get your bows, you bring them home, you clean all the knots and everything off them, smooth them out good ... I bend my bows over an old truck rim ... as soon as I get them. I never steam them. 1993 Beaton Institute Tape 3229 B The bows would come from branches of trees and they'd probably be about three quarters of an inch in diameter ... Most people would like to get black spruce for this because it was really good for the traps. It would last a long time. Pilot Survey Inf. 2 The framework of your lobster trap. You cut bows in the woods ... a half-moon shape.
2. a unit of measure indicating the size of the lobster trap, either a three or four-bow trap

　1979 *CB's Magazine* 23, 46 There were a lot more big traps then – 4-bow instead of 3-bow traps. Survey II Inf. 7 There's a three-bow trap and a four-bow trap with offsetting headings for the parlour.

　[Sense 1: *DNE, DPEIE* (1895). Sense 2: at *bow trap DPEIE* (1978)]

*Respondents to Survey II indicated that the three-bow trap has two compartments (one with bait and the second to trap the lobster after it has taken the bait) and the four-bow trap has three sections (one with bait and another two to trap the lobster). The larger trap is preferred only if the ocean floor is suitably level and the lobsters are plentiful.

box social noun; compare **pie social**
a fundraiser and dance, where women bring food in decorated boxes for auction and share the food and evening with the successful bidders

　1917 Beaton Institute MG 12 93, 17 Jan. 397 A Box Social in LOC hall. 1972 Beaton Institute Tape 548 They also had pie socials and later it became box socials.

The box was homemade and was quite fancy. Crepe paper of different colors cut up in different ways representing flowers and ribbing was pasted to the box. The box was filled with some cake, cookies, tea biscuits and candies. The ladies brought the boxes to the social, and the men did the bidding. The highest bidder won the box and the lady for the evening. Then a dance followed. 1978 *Oran Inbhirnis* 13 July 19 There will be a box social and dance at the Ainslie-Upper Margaree Firehall, Scotsville, Friday, July 14th, 9:00 p.m.–1:00 a.m., admission $2.00. The ladies who bring a "box lunch" to be auctioned, will not be charged admission. 1985 Beaton Institute Tape 3080 We used it [box social] as a fund-raiser. If there was somebody in the community needed help or they wanted something for the school or the church or whatever, it was always for some sort of charity. 2007 *DCBE* Tape SHERRINGTON 36 There was a school just up the road from us, and the women would all make a little box lunch and put it in [a box], and then you wouldn't know whose it was and you would bid on that. And then you ate the lunch with whomever's you won. And that was a box social. The money went to the school.

　[*DPEIE, DC, COD N Amer., GCD Cdn., OED3 N. Amer.* (now chiefly *hist.*) (1882), *DARE* **chiefly Nth, N Midl, West**, *DA, W3, NOAD, MWCD*; compare *box supper DA*]

boxy adjective
of trees and logs, tough, gnarled, difficult to cut

　Pilot Survey Inf. 3 You could be cutting a tree, of course with a crosscut saw ... and you can hardly move the saw because the wood is boxy ... I think what's happening is that the wood starts to push in against the saw ... The colour of the wood can be white, but this boxy part will be kind of

reddish. The gum or resin has a tendency to push down against the saw. Survey I.
[*DNE* (1915), *DPEIE*]

brath [bræh] noun; also spelled **brad, bradh**
a hand-operated mill for grinding oats and other grain into flour
[1940] MACNEIL *History of Iona-Washabuck* 81 In these early times every family used a hand mill to grind their oats and flour. This primitive hand mill was known to the early pioneers as "brath". 1953 DUNN *Highland Settler* 30 The harvest was ... ground in a stone hand-mill (*brath*). 1965 Beaton Institute MG 12 79, 4 The hand machine called a "Bradh" (Gaelic for 'Querl'), consisted of two chiseled slabs of freestone of about 24 inches in diameter, the bottom one stationary, with a plug in the center holding the top slab in position as it revolved – a wooden handle by the side and a depression in the center completed the outfit. 1984 CUMMING et al. *Story of Framboise* 66 The early settlers had [a] **brad** (or "grinders"), hand querns for grinding grain into flour.

*A loanword from Scottish Gaelic, see *bràth* "quern, handmill" *GD*.

break (the) road verb phrase
to open a track through heavy snow on a rural road
1976 Beaton Institute Tape 255 No snow ploughs, you had to go out breaking roads – we had three miles of a section to break. Everybody was assigned a section of the road to break. That's how they kept the roads open. 1976 PILLAR *Aunt Peggy* 51 After a storm abated, Alex arranged a 'frolic' for breaking roads. All those who had horses would make their way to the main road where those who had no horses would arrive with shovels to dig out banks of snow. Horses would attempt to go as far as possible before being shoveled out to continue to tramp back and forth until the road was passable. 1984 Beaton Institute Tape 2113 [Tape 4] There'd be snow up to your hips sometimes. But all the people made the – you know – they broke the road. 1993 *CB's Magazine* 62, 18 I had to be at all the houses, get the men out with their shovels. If they had horses, take their horse; if they had an ox, take their ox. And break the road and get it open. And this is the system that was carried on in these days.
[*DC*, *DARE* **Nth** (1779), *DAE* (1779); compare *road-breaking DPEIE*]

breeze noun
typically among commercial fishers, a strong wind, often at gale force
1986 *CB's Magazine* 43, 76 But I knew there was a kind of a breeze or a storm coming in. So I said to him, "I think it would be just as good for us to stay in, the way it's looking." 1990 *CB's Magazine* 53, 19 They'll [dories] float, but you can't hang onto her – a breeze of wind, when it's rough, you'll wash off of them ... Pilot Survey Inf. 3 If it was a gale, they still might refer to it as a big breeze. That term is [used] quite often, not just for sailing. Survey I Inf. 5 I heard it used in Port Hawkesbury for a gale. Survey I Inf. 22 They are calling for a breeze, a gale along the coast. Survey II Inf. 3 [A breeze is] a gale of wind.
[*DNE* (1842), *DPEIE*; at *breeze of wind DARE* (1842), *WGUS*]

*The noun is well known on Cape Breton Island, but the verb *breeze up*, which has a North American range meaning "to increase to gale force" (for example, see *DNE*, *DPEIE* in a note, *COD*, *SSPB*, *DARE*, and at *breezen ML*), is not found in the *DCBE* records.

breillon [brɛ'yɔn] noun, usually plural
a rag, often associated with hooked rugs

1986 CHIASSON and LE BLANC trans. *History and Acadian Traditions of Chéticamp* 87 These were very simple rugs, most often made with old rags called *breillons*. There were ... the *tapis à breillons* (mats hooked with old rags) ... 1988 CHIASSON ed. *History of Hooked Rugs of Chéticamp* 17 "Breillons" rugs were made as follows: used garments of fabrics other than wool were cut into long strips of about one half inch in width. These "breillons", as they were called, were set by means of a hook into a canvas made from burlap bags ... a strip of "breillon" was held under the canvas with the left hand ... 1990 *Inverness Oran* 8 Aug. 9 At first the rugs were very simple articles, used at home and made with old rags called "breillons."

*A loanword from French, see *breillon,* which has a cross reference to *brayon* (*Tapis de brayons*), "confectionné à partir de vieux morceaux d'étoffe tressés" *DFA MARITIMES.*

bridle noun; compare **backline, snood**
a short rope tied in two places at one end of a lobster trap and used to attach the trap to the rope that secures, raises, and lowers the trap (the backline or snood)
1979 *CB's Magazine* 23, 42 Along this backline four traps are attached with a rope bridle. 1993 Beaton Institute Tape 3229 B Then you make your bridle [for] which you bore two holes [into the sill of the trap] and you put a knot in each end of the rope and then you tie your rope onto the trap. Survey II Inf. 1 The bridle is a rope attached to the trap, a 5/16 rope, on the kitchen. Survey II Inf. 2 The bridle is on the kitchen end to stop the lobster from getting out when the traps are hauled up. Survey II Inf. 3 The buoy has a snood that attaches to the bridle on the trap. Survey II Inf. 6 The bridle stays with the trap.
[*DPEIE* (n.d.); compare *bridle,* defined in general terms as a piece of rope or cable fixed to an object for pulling: *OED3, COD, W3, NOAD, MWCD*]

bridle end noun; also **front end, kitchen end**
the end of a lobster trap to which the bridle is tied, usually the baited section of the trap (the kitchen)
1987 Beaton Institute Tape 2324 [Tape 1] There's going to be some [lobsters] up in the kitchen end that are not going to go back into there [the parlour or more secure section]. Survey II Inf. 1 The bridle [is attached to] the front end of the trap, called the bridle end. Survey II Inf. 4 The bridle is tied to the bow or sill – the bridle end or front end. Survey II Inf. 8 It is usually front end.
[compare *snood end DPEIE*]

brin bag noun
a sack made of burlap or a coarse fabric
1992 *CB's Magazine* 61, 67 My wife used to go down to the shore with a brine [*sic*] bag and an ax, cut driftwood up, fill up the bag and carry it home. 2002 MUISE Email 25 Mar. "Brin bag" is used here for burlap bag or any large sack. As kids we searched for brin bags to make hockey nets. They were also used to carry coal or kindling.
[*DC Lab. and Eastern Arctic* (1924); at *brin*: *DNE* (1924), *COD Cdn* (*Nfld*); compare *brin* "strong linen" *EDD Obsol.*]

brush transitive and intransitive verb, often used as a verbal noun; also **back brushing**; compare **pack**
to enlarge (haulage tunnels) in a mine by removing stone, building roof-bearing walls (packs) and installing various roof supports
1972 Beaton Institute Tape 537 The last five years I've been brushing. Well we'd take down powder and you'd blast your stone ... And the shotfirer would come and shoot that, blast it, and break up all

the stone for us. And we'd start shovelling one to another, seven of us in the row passing the stone down. 1974 Beaton Institute Tape 878 When I stopped working as a miner, I went what you call brushing, on the main deep for to make the height properly. We arch railed it. The arch rail was spread about ten feet ... and from the center of that arch rail to the pavement was about five foot six. 1980 Beaton Institute Tape 763 After you brush it once, probably in six or eight months, it gets too low again, so you have to shoot the roof again. That's what you call back brushing; you do the same thing again. 1983 SHEDDEN et al. *Mining Photos* 269 **Brushing** – keeping the roof, sides and pavement of a passage in repair and clear of any loose ore. 1999a MIGLIORE and DIPIERRO eds. *Italian Lives* 65 So I went loading and brushing [extracting stone to enlarge the haulage tunnel] and things like that.
[at *brushing* OED3 (1883)]

brusher noun; often in the phrase **brusher(s) pack**; compare **pack**
a miner who enlarges haulage tunnels, builds roof-bearing walls (packs), and installs various roof supports
1939 Beaton Institute MG 12 43 E4 Box 4, 101 I would not say it was as good as the pack we built because we made an extra good job that night; being a brusher and used to stowing rock you know how to go about it. 1999a MIGLIORE and DIPIERRO eds. *Italian Lives* 330 To enlarge the tunnels for coal transport and ventilation, "brushers" removed stone from the roof and/or floor. 2004 MACKENZIE *Bloody CB Coal* 73 The brushers were responsible for removing the overhead stone at the very end of the level after the coal had been removed from under it. They shot this stone down, and used it to build a roof-supporting "pack" at the side of the level and part way down the wall. 2007 MACKENZIE *CB Coal Mine Disasters* 168

Loss of ventilating air in and around these brushers packs, or "chocks," was the focus of much attention at the inquiry into the explosion.

buckle: see **blueberry buckle**

buddy noun; also spelled **buttie**, **butty**, **buddie**
one of a pair of workers responsible for each other's safety and the completion of a job
1922 Beaton Institute MG 12 88 A 1e f2, 2–3 ... do they leave the cutting down to Jack the Overman who gives you and your Butty as high as 30 to 40 cents per week consideration. 1976 *Oran Inbhirnis* 6 Aug. 8 Being a 'miner' was not easy ... Even then [after passing an examination] a man would have to find a 'buddie' to work with and to do this you had to be a safe worker, and a hard worker, since one man's negligence could jeopardize the lives of everyone and since the miners were paid according to the amount of coal they loaded. 1990 Beaton Institute MG 14 206 Box 6 C. iii b) File 84, 19 It [the furnace] worked 24 hours a day and we had a buddy system. When your buddy came out, you went home. 2000 MACGILLIVRAY *Men of the Deeps* 149 For instance, my father and his buddy worked together for thirty years in No. 24 Colliery ... They were afraid that if a stranger was working with them, an accident was more likely to happen. 2003 SAINT AGNES ELEMENTARY SCHOOL *Coal Miners' Stories* 45 When my buddy and I heard this [an announcement of a runaway trip] we jumped in holes on either side of the track.
[*COD* N Amer., *NCD*, *EDD* (at *butty*), *OED3* (1917), *DARE* (1917), *DAE* (1917), *DA*, *W3*, *NOAD*]

bug row noun; also spelled **Bug Row**; compare **row**
shabby company row houses

1981 STEPHENSON *Dominion, Nova Scotia* n.p. The coal company built long rows of buildings ... on Station Street it was "Bug Row". 1981 Beaton Institute Tape 2110 "Do you remember the bug row in Dominion [interviewer]?" "Not very well but I know it was there – a lot of liquor there." 1999a MIGLIORE and DIPIERRO eds. *Italian Lives* 18 In response to the need [for housing], the company built long rows of buildings such as those erected on Henry and Station Streets in Dominion in 1910 – on Henry Street, they came to be called the "Shacks;" and, on Station Street, "Bug Row."

[Compare *bug* (sense 8): "used in jocular place-names for presumed insect-infested small settlements" with examples such as *Bugtown, Bughill, Bug Hollow DARE* **chiefly Sth, S Midl** (1960)]

buidseachd ['bučʊk] noun
witchcraft, an evil spell

1986 MACLEOD *As Birds Bring Forth the Sun* 142 It was felt she might have been some part of a buidseachd or evil spell cast on the man by some mysterious enemy. 1999 THURGOOD "Storytelling on the Gabarus-Framboise Coast" 409 ... [the mail carrier] uses *uisge-airgaid* (silver water), a traditional remedy known to counteract the effects of *buidseachd* (witchcraft) and *an droch suil* (the evil eye). 2006 MACINTYRE *Causeway* 263 The curse is called the *buidseachd*. And it always seems to be women with the power to put it on or take it off.

*A loanword from Scottish Gaelic, see *buidseachd* "witchcraft, witchery, wizardry" *GED*.

bull beer noun; compare **seed beer**
strong, homemade beer, often sold illegally

1982 Beaton Institute Tape 2068 [In] 1946 ... liquor was hard to get. We used to make what we call bull beer. 1989 Beaton Institute Tape 2400 If he could give him five dollars, he could give him two gallons of bull beer. 1992 *Inverness Oran* 23 Sept. 9 ... Archie Neil got into a particularly potent patch of bull beer and having drunk too much, felt that he was on his last legs so he sent for Father Chisholm. Archie Neil thought there was a frog in his stomach because he pulled the bull beer cask from a swamp so Father Chisholm planned to use this to cure Archie Neil. He sent a young fellow to get a frog and then mixed a horrible concoction for Archie Neil to drink to help him bring up the frog. Father Chisholm hid the frog in his pocket and dropped it in the vomit that Archie Neil deposited on the floor after downing the mixture. Archie Neil never took another drink. 2000 CHISHOLM comp. *As True as I'm Sittin' Here* 79 The country was dry at that time but they told him, "We'll have all kinds of bull beer and some bush whiskey."

bull wheel noun; compare **endless haulage**
a large wheel or drum around which a cable is wound, typically used for haulage in a mine

1900 Anon. *The Canadian Mining Review* 19 (9), 206 These branch lines were operated by endless cables driven by bull wheels at the central station which received their motion from a shaft driven by a bull wheel on the main cable. 1939 Beaton Institute MG 12 43 E4 Box 4, 140 ... stone dust placed in the grease cup of the bull wheel ... 1990 PEACH *Memories of a CB Childhood* 116 Powered by a huge electric haulage engine on the surface, an endless steel cable, two inches in diameter and five miles in length, passed around a "bullwheel" at the extreme end of the mine. This served to bring down the empty one-ton coal cars (boxes) and take up the full ones. 2004 MACKENZIE

Bloody CB Coal 94 Cyril lost his toes in a "bullwheel," a spoked steel wheel about three feet in diameter, part of what is called an "endless haulage."
    [*OED3* at *bull-wheel*, *DA* (1874), *W3*]

bump noun
a sudden shift in the underground strata, often causing cave-ins and roof falls in a mine
    1985 CALDER *Coal in NS* 40 ... the phenomenon of rock bursts or "bumps" claimed many lives ... 1999a MIGLIORE and DIPIERRO eds. *Italian Lives* 330 A "bump" is a sudden shifting of the strata, underground. The infamous 1958 mine disaster in Springhill, Nova Scotia, was caused by a series of major bumps. 2007 MACKENZIE *CB Coal Mine Disasters* 98 ... a "bump" – an incident where the tunnel closes and the floor meets the ceiling, crushing everything between.
    [*GCD, OED3* (1883), *W3*]

bungalow noun
a summer cottage, typically, modestly built but highly valued as a family retreat
    1918 Beaton Institute MG 12 147, 15 Sept. n.p. Lovely Day – Went to Bungalow ... 1938 Beaton Institute MG 12 43, 16 June [a letter] Mrs. Salter was away to the New Harris bungelow [*sic*] for a few days, but see she has returned home now. 1996 MACLEOD *Centre of the World* 29 Although there are many stylishly constructed, well-maintained summer homes in Cape Breton, there are also many rustic, somewhat dilapidated bungalows, built with an eclectic mix of old, new, and borrowed elements. What is interesting about this fact is that even the most humble of bungalows is not ridiculed or scorned. It seems we rate these possessions more for their sentimental value than for their material or resale worth. 1997 MACINNES *Journey in Celtic Music* 100 Playing my pipes at the square dances in the old

parish hall in Big Pond, for the "bungalow" people and for the local teenagers, in the mid 1960's, was exciting. 2002 MUISE Email 2 Apr. Capers call a summer cottage a "bungalow" and a bungalow style house is just a "small house". 2007b BARBER *Only in Canada* 90 **bungalow** (*Cape Breton*) a summer cottage, especially a modest one.
    [*COD Cdn* (*Cape Breton*), *FWCCD, NCD, OED3* (1676), *W3*]

bunk noun
a heavy beam extending across a logging sleigh or wagon to support the logs
    1977 *CB's Magazine* 16, 3 There were 3 beams into it and the beams (the bunk) were on standards (the posts). 1981 *CB's Magazine* 30, 33 The front wheels – they were [the] truck wagon. Then there were poles put on the bunk – and this is what they put the stuff on, on the rack. Pilot Survey Inf. 3 Yeah, [the beam would go] from one runner to the other. Most of the bunks' runners would be more like six feet long. There'd be two of them.
    [*DPEIE, COD, OED3* (1770), *DAE, DA* (1770), *W3, ML*; compare *bunk sled DARE*]

bun of bread noun; also **bun**; compare **loaf bread**
a loaf of bread; one section of a double loaf
    1972 Beaton Institute Tape 551 When it would come to a day when I would have to bake, I'd take a bun of bread out of their batch. 1976–7 Miners' Museum Tape 124 Anyway I went to the bakery for a few buns of bread. 1996 *CB Post* 22 June 3A I used expressions such as "a bun of bread," and "I got in a hook with him" and "I biffed it" – expressions that I was compelled to explain endlessly. 2002 MUISE Email 2 Apr. A loaf of bread is a "bun" of bread. Survey I Inf. 23 A bun of bread is also a double loaf of bread.
    [at *bun*: *DNE, OED3* (1371)]

*The *OED3* notes at *bun,* "In some places, as in the north of Ireland, it means a round loaf of ordinary bread," and the *EDD* defines *bun* as "A dinner-roll, a small loaf of bread" (n.d.).

buoy line: see **haul-up**

burnt land noun, often plural; also **burnt wood, burnt ground**; see **black forest, black wood**
soil prepared for cultivation by burning wood and stumps
[1818] DESBARRES *Description of the Island of CB* 43 ... potatoes and turnips produce well on the new burnt lands, and require no other manure. 1922 MAC-DOUGALL *History of Inverness County* 4 The second year wheat was sown in the plot which grew the potatoes of the previous year, and a new piece of burnt ground was made ready for the second season's potato yield. 1974 MACLEOD *Stories from NS* 10 This "black wood," or "burnt wood," as the settlers called it in Gaelic, was the most productive soil ever seen. 1977 Beaton Institute Tape 900 But the rest of the stumps and so on were burnt out, and they called that the burnt land, and they kept that for just potato growing, and in the spring they seeded the potato. 2005 A Sign at the Highland Village Museum, Iona, 25 July The garden you see before you is referred to as "A' Choille Dhubh," Gaelic for "burnt wood," and serves as an example of the method of planting used by early settlers. Faced with the immense task of clearing the forest in order to plant, the early settlers simply cut the trees, burned the stumps and then planted among them. The ash created by the burning of the stumps created ideal growing conditions for potatoes.
[*DC, DAE* (1811), *DA* (1811); compare: *burnt land savages SSPB, burnt piece DARE, burned piece DA*]

bush transitive verb; often in the phrase **bush the ice**
to set (a line of small evergreen trees or branches) into the ice to mark a safe crossing and give direction during a storm
1869 Beaton Institute MG 12 155 B2, 2 In winter travelling on ice offered advantages. The ice was "bushed" by setting tops of small trees indicating a safe ice surface. 1871 in [1969] ELMSLY *Elmsly: Diary* 84 ... bushed ice to Boulardarie. 1889 LOCKETT *CB Hand Book* 29 ... small spruces, set about as far apart as telegraph poles and in a beeline. This is called "bushing the ice" and serves as a guide by which the traveller may find his way over the trackless ice in a snow storm. 1985 *CB's Magazine* 2, 7 ... the way was marked from the Englishtown shore to Raymond's Beach with about 125 seven-foot Spruce trees. I used to help my father bush the ice. 1985 *CB's Magazine* 39, 16 ... the county used to pay a fellow to take some little spruce trees, you know, chop a hole down in the ice, and put the trees there for markers. Oh, about a hundred feet apart, so even in a storm you could follow from tree to tree, as a rule. What they called "bushing the ice." 2002 MACDONALD *All the Men Are Sleeping* 141 The ice has been bushed, he told her back in his office, we'll have markers to follow.
[*DPEIE* (1838), *DC, GCD, W3*; compare *MWCD*]

bushline noun
a row of small evergreen trees or branches set in the ice, marking a safe crossing
1975 MACMILLAN *Memoirs of a CB Doctor* 37 We went out on Nyanza Bay, and followed the bushline to what we called Long Point. 1994 MACDONALD *Underlying Reverence* 32 The men had not laid down a bushline yet but someone was crossing the new ice anyway ... 2000 MACDONALD *CB Road* 29 Lord, yes, he

put out the bushline on the ice until he
was too old to stand.

button noun
an oblong door fastener, rotating on a nail
or screw, used to latch doors of barns,
sheds, lobster or crab traps, etc.
   1980 *CB's Magazine* 25, 17 We had two
doors: one had a big button on it at that
time, the other door had just a latch. 1996
CB's Magazine 70 Inside Front Cover The
inside wooden button was no match for
bull moose's strength. Pilot Survey Inf.
2 On your lobster trap where your door
is, they used to have what they called a
button, and there'd be a double latch and
you'd put the button down between the
two latches to kept the door shut ... but
they're not used much any more. Pilot
Survey Inf. 3 We put buttons on doors
around here; any barn door would have
a button on it. Survey II Inf. 4 We used
to use buttons [on the lobster traps], but
now we use bungee cords to outsmart the
seals.
   [*DNE, DPEIE, OED3* (1867), *W3*; compare *snap lath DPEIE*]

b'y noun; also spelled **bye**; compare **Bay
bye**
buddy, friend, [my] boy; a term of friendly
address to a male of any age, and occasionally to a group
   1925 REILLY *Maclean's* 15 Jan. 20
"Come over to dinner with us on Sunday,
bye, and spend the evening." 1985 ROB-
ERTSON *Cranberry Head* 46 "It's rough,
b'y, rough." 2004 MCNEIL Email 12 Mar.
1 Just as a conversation can begin with
"What's going on B'y." Survey I Inf. 42 As
in "How's she goin', bye?" 2008 CREWE
Ava Comes Home 185 "How's she goin',
b'y?" Johnnie nodded at them.
   [at *boy*, in the sense of familiar term
of address: *DNE* (with *b'y* as a variant),
FWCCD, OED3 (1532), *NOAD*]

b'y interjection; also **bye, b'ye**
encouraging agreement, eh, right
   1988 MACGILLIVRAY and MACGIL-
LIVRAY *CB Ceilidh* 114 I'd have her hands
and she'd be looking at my feet, and she
picked it up right quick, bye. 1993 *CB's
Magazine* 64, 91 He said, "Fadder, I'll
pay you back, b'y, as soon as I get my
cheque." 2003 CRANE Email 23 Feb. 2
There's a very popular way of communi-
cating here, referred to by some as "Cape-
bretonese". For example, if you want to
talk this language, you must omit the
ubiquitous "eh" used by almost all other
Canadians, and replace it with "b'ye".

C

cabanne [kə'bæn] noun; also spelled
cabane, cabban
a shack or hut, typically one used by commercial fishers
   1952 ALMON *CB Mirror* 1 June 4
Before night time on the 25th of August
of that year [1725] the inhabitants of
the hamlets around Baleine, some six
or eight score of them, took refuge in
their rude huts, called Cabbans, from
the oncoming fury of the southeast gale.
1984 BALCOM *Cod Fishery of Isle Royale*
20 ... living quarters such as *cabannes*
... were also erected near the work
areas. 1994 *CB's Magazine* 65, 41 Their
first house was a log "cabban." 2000
BOUDREAU and CHIASSON *Chéticamp
Memoirs* 138 When I was young, nothing pleased me more than staying in the
fishing huts and eating a meal of cod-fish
cooked "cabane" style.
   [at *cabane DC Cdn French* (1843); compare: *caban, cabane,* "earliest forms of
CABIN *n*. Still sometimes used for the
sake of local colouring (French or Canadian)" *OED3* (1866)]

cailleach ['kælyəx] noun; also spelled
caileah, cailliach, caleach
an old woman, occasionally a witch or
crone

1897 *MacTalla* 24 Sept. 2 ... among all
the activities that were there, it was the
"cailleach-dubh" (black old lady), at
which they were throwing darts, that I
preferred. If you hit her on the nose, a
little bell on the back of her head would
ring, and this was an indication that you
had won a prize ... 1973 MACPHAIL *Girl
from Loch Bras d'Or* 124 ... he wouldn't take
a cailleach (an old woman) like me. 1993
CB's Magazine 63, 62 ... there was an old
woman – *a cailleach* – almost like a witch –
in those days they called that a cailleach
in Gaelic. 1999 MACINTYRE *Long Stretch*
93 Grandpa used to talk about the *cailleach
oidhche*, the old woman of the night. She'll
creep into your dreams, he'd say.
    [*DPEIE, EDD* Sc. Irel. (1814), *OED3*
(1814), *W3 Irish & Scot, DSL*]

*A loanword from Scottish Gaelic, see *cail-
leach* "hag, old woman; the meaning of 'hag' is
seldom found now" *GED*.

cake: see **ice cake**

Candy Day: see **grading day**

canner noun; also **canner lobster**; compare **market lobster**
a lobster of legal catchable size, but too
small to be sold in stores, restaurants, etc.
and thus sold to canneries and by fishers
to local residents

1957 WILDER *Canada's Lobster Fishery*
16 In some areas the legal-sized lobsters
are divided into two categories – the
"canners", about seven to nine inches
long which are canned or prepared
as chilled, fresh lobster meat, and the
"markets" over nine inches long that are
shipped to market alive. 1978 *CB's Magazine* 20, 8 and 11 All what we call canners

today are boiled and put into a freezer –
for sandwiches and so forth ... The term
canner is used today – they are below the
size of the market lobster – but they aren't
usually canned ... [page 11] And I believe
[around 1929] we were getting three
cents a pound for the canner lobsters and
ten cents each for a ten-inch lobster and
over. 1993 Beaton Institute Tape 3229 B
They've upped the size for the canner lobster. 2007b BARBER *Only in Canada* 120
canner (*Maritimes*) a lobster designated
for canning because it is too small for the
market.
    [*DPEIE* (1957), *COD Cdn* (*Maritimes*);
compare "A beast fit only for canning":
OED3 Chiefly *U.S.* (1890), *DAE, DA, W3*]

*Originally, the "legal catchable size" for a lob-
ster was determined by its total length (Wilder
1957, 16, 22), but now the size is determined
by the length of its carapace, the hard shell
covering the lobster's upper body. This length
is established in each "Lobster Fishing Area"
(*Strategic Lobster Framework* 2006), and most
areas recommend releasing female lobsters
bearing eggs (berried lobsters). The average
consumer is more likely to measure the size of
a lobster by its weight: roughly, three quarters
of a pound for a *canner* and a pound or more
for a *market lobster*.

canntaireachd ['kaʊntərəxk] noun; also
spelled **Canntaireachd**; compare **jigging,
mouth music, puirt-a-beul**
the vocal representation of instrumental
music, particularly of bagpipe tunes, typically using a formal system of vocables
(syllables that do not express words)

1952 MACLEOD *CB Mirror* 1 July 5 ...
the most intricate and most beautiful
bagpipe scores having as their basis a
traditional verbal notation, or vocable
syllabic scale called in Scottish Gaelic,
Canntaireachd. 1981 MACGILLIVRAY
CB Fiddler 5 The overall flavour suggests the inflections of piping and

Gaelic music, such as puirt-a-beul and canntaireachd. 1988 MACGILLIVRAY and MACGILLIVRAY *CB Ceilidh* 152 A lot of the old tunes had Gaelic words to them, and quite a few of the stepdancers learned to dance by the canntaireachd – the old people singing the words of the tune. 1989 *CB's Magazine* 52, 43 ... they used to sing the tunes to each other. And that was called the *canntaireachd*. And some people in Scotland wrote down the actual syllables for pibroch. 2013 SPAR-LING Email 8 Aug. ... "canntaireachd" (pronounced "COUNT-er-ukhk") which, like jigging, is the vocal rendition of instrumental tunes – in this case, pipe tunes in particular – through the use of vocables. However, unlike jigging, canntaireachd uses a formal system of vocables ... 2013 DOHERTY Email 23 Oct. 1 Canntaireachd – this is *specifically* related to bagpiping and is a complex system of vocables which related to melodic pitches and ornaments; used in the transmission (i.e. the passing on) of piping; complex and fixed (compared with other forms such as puirt-a-beul and jigging which are much more flexible in terms of the actual vocables being used) – associated with ceol mor/piobraichead.

*A loanword from Scottish Gaelic, see *canntaireachd* "humming a tune; chanting, singing; warbling" *GD*. Mouth music, jigging, puirt-a-beul, and canntaireachd all render instrumental music vocally, but canntaireachd particularly represents bagpipe tunes and uses a formal system of notation that may be written. It is more difficult to distinguish the other three terms because of overlapping usage. Frank Rhodes explains: "'Jigging' was the English word used on the island for a form of canntaireachd or mouth-music. This [canntaireachd] was originally a method of representing the notes and grace-notes of bagpipe music by vocable syllables" (1996, 188). Mouth music, jigging, and puirt-a-beul typically all use vocables, and occasionally Gaelic words, to imitate bagpipe and fiddle music, especially dance music; all are less formalized than canntaireachd. Heather Sparling's research has recently indicated that puirt-a-beul uses Gaelic words more than vocables and has less improvisation than jigging (2014, 50).

Cape Bretoner noun; compare **Caper**, **Cape Bretonian**
a long-term resident of Cape Breton
    1926 MACKENZIE *Travel* 47 (2) June 42 One needs a keen sense of rhythm and perfect muscular development to compete with Cape Bretoners at a milling party. 1978 *Oran Inbhirnis* 29 June 3 Last week I was again reminded of how proud I am to be a Cape Bretoner and in particular a resident of Inverness County being able to live among some of the most gifted people in the world. 1991 PEACH *My CB* 70 ... a Cape Bretoner is one who when he steps off the late jet from Toronto is certain to feel like a celebrity surrounded by a crowd of hero worshippers ... 1993 MACDONNELL *Cape Bretoner* 1 (3), 6 One distinctive thing about Cape Bretoners is their music. 1993 *Inverness Oran* 10 Nov. 24–5 I am so used to being a Cape Bretoner now. I am used to the different sayings, nicknames, geography and climate. In the early years I used to get a great kick out of all the different names ... I feel that I am a Cape Bretoner because I have fallen into all the Cape Breton ways. For the past forty-seven years I have lived as a Cape Bretoner, but I will always be known as a war bride ... 2001 DORNADIC *Cape Bretoner* 9 (2), 63 ... the True Cape Bretoner has managed to keep his identity intact. He still goes *down* north instead of *up* like the rest of the world; he still carries stuff in *Sobey's bags* no matter where the bag came from; and he still calls everyone *dear*, regardless of age, social status and sometimes even gender.

Cape Breton fiddler noun
a fiddler who plays Scottish music characterized by rapid cuts of the bow, grace notes, and a strong rhythm

1978 *Oran Inbhirnis* 20 Apr. 6 Every Saturday night a gypsy Cape Breton fiddler who had ferried across the Strait of Canso would rosin his bow there [in Brookline, MA] and the Capers would stomp louder than they ever did in Glencoe, Margaree or Mabou. 1981 *CB's Magazine* 29, 40 A Cape Breton fiddler, of course, is a complex creature, so you have all different types of personalities and all different styles of fiddling. 1997 MACINNES *Journey in Celtic Music* 57 This [bowing technique] allowed him to generate the sounds which he believed were unique to the music of the Cape Breton fiddler, sounds that have been nurtured by the individual fiddlers and passed on through several generations. For Dan Joe, the art of bowing included highlighting rapid cuts and accenting grace notes, that is the use of additional subtle fingering between notes. 1999 *CB's Magazine* 74 Inside Back Cover August 20–2, 1999 The Cape Breton Fiddlers' Association celebrates its 26th festival with concerts, square dances and workshops. 2005 MACDONALD *Forest for Calum* 316 Once, in John Alex's barn I heard Johnny Rosin say how it's not how sparsely or ornamentally a Cape Breton fiddler plays a tune that he will be judged by, but whether or not he slurs his timing ... He went on to say that the best Cape Breton fiddlers prefer dancers to audiences.

Cape Breton fiddling verbal noun; also **Cape Breton fiddle**, occasionally **Cape Breton violin**
a tradition of playing the fiddle characterized by rapid bow cuts, grace notes, and strong rhythm

1972 *CB's Magazine* 1, 4 Cape Breton Fiddling is really quite hard, perhaps harder than any other. I would say it's coming from the bow ... You shiver that bow at the end, try to get that dadadadum. 1978 *Oran Inbhirnis* 23 Feb. 6 Most loved and authentic, however, is the music of the "Cape Breton violin" and the dancing that accompanies it ... for those who are of the area it forms perhaps one of the most dominant threads in the fabric of their lives. For years it was part and parcel of almost every household and those who are not musicians or dancers were highly appreciative listeners. Today it still accompanies most major events from weddings to funerals, being present almost literally from conception to the grave. 1989 *CB's Magazine* 50, 90 ... this 3-part traditional setting [of "The Grey Old Lady of Raasay"] appears to be unique to the Cape Breton fiddle repertoire. 1993 *Inverness Oran* 1 Dec. 28 "My first love [is] in Cape Breton fiddling," says the native of Troy, N.S. [Natalie MacMaster], "and that's where I always want to stay focused."

Cape Bretonian noun; compare **Cape Bretoner**
a Cape Bretoner, especially as designated in the late nineteenth century

1883 *North Sydney Herald* 14 Nov. n.p. Will you allow a short space in your journal for the following account of an accident which occurred to a Cape Bretonian in one of mines here [Leadville, Col.]? A few days ago Mr. James Murphy, a native of Grand Narrows, Cape Breton, was killed by the falling of a cave [in] while at his work in the mine. 1887 in 1992 HORNSBY *Nineteenth-Century CB* 199 "A SUCCESSFUL CAPE BRETONIAN VISITS HIS FRIENDS," proclaimed the [*North Sydney*] *Herald* in May 1887 ... 1899 in 1985 *CB's Magazine* 39, 35 [quoting *Island Reporter* Feb. 1899] "Let every Cape Bretonian lay that fact to heart ..." 1976 *Oran Inbhirnis* 13 Aug. 8 ... it may be said that two Cape Bretonians, a Neil MacDonald, of West Ainslie, and a John J. MacFarlane, of Upper Margaree (both of them untrained), did something tough too. 2011 DOYLE *CB Facts and Folklore* 163 In 1830, Charles W. Ward founded the *Cape Bretonian*, the island's first newspaper, as a platform to fight for separation from Nova Scotia

Cape Breton pork pie noun, usually plural; also **pork pie**
a small tart with date filling, often with maple-flavoured icing, traditionally served at Christmas
1956 *Kitchen Karnival of Kooking* 49 PORK PIES Roll [the pastry] in little balls and press in small muffin tin. Bake in 325 degree oven about 15 minutes. Fill with date filling and put a dab of maple icing on each. "I love these, Pauline." 1989 NIGHTINGALE *Out of Old NS Kitchens* 164 *How these little tarts got their name remains a mystery to us. It could be that pork fat was once used as the shortening, or it might just be a reflection of the wonderful Cape Breton sense of humour.* CAPE BRETON PORK PIES ... Ice with butter icing. 1992 CATHOLIC WOMEN'S LEAGUE *Serving Family and Friends Cookbook* 114 Cape Breton Pork Pies: shell: butter, flour, cornstarch, icing sugar; filling: dates, water, lemon juice. Ice with maple icing. 2006 SYMS Email 24 Feb. 1 In the North America hogs were plentiful. It is quite likely the original Cape Breton pork pies employed lard from these animals. This fact can be verified by using something like Early Canadiana Online which has a cookbook published in Montreal in 1895 in which "pork pie" is pie pastry made from pork suet. Now butter and other shortenings are used, thus rendering the name "pork pies" a relic of times past ... Cape Breton pork pies are actually small date-filled tarts, or tartlets, with a maple-flavoured icing. 2007b BARBER *Only in*

Canada 126 **Cape Breton pork pie** a date-filled tart with short pastry.
[*COD Cdn*]

Cape Breton Silver noun; also spelled **Cape Breton silver**; also **silver**; compare **shine**
moonshine; an alcoholic drink made by the Glenora Distillery ©, Inverness County
1979 MACGILLIVRAY *Song for the Mira* 46 I coined the term "Cape Breton Silver" to symbolize "moonshine," one of the least publicized of our local products. 1992 O'DONNELL *Coal Mining Songs* 163 Sing hurrah and hurrah for the pure and the sweet, / The Cape Breton silver ... The pride of our island. 1993 *Inverness Oran* 8 Sept. 3 ... in the past, and some say even today, the hills and valleys of Cape Breton have seen many a still producing moonshine or Cape Breton silver. 1995 *CB's Magazine* 68, 34 Come take a tour of our distillery and sample Glenora's own products: **Smuggler's Cove Rum, Kenloch Scotch, and Cape Breton Silver**. 1995 BRUNEAU *Angel Mill* 23 After supper the mob got bigger, full of men drunk on rum and moonshine – silver, as they called it ... 2002 MACDONALD *All the Men Are Sleeping* 214 Do you have a still, Murdock, are you moonshining? I mine a little silver, he'd told her ... 2005 MACKENZIE *Neighbours are Watching* 102 But "Silver Dan" and some other manufacturers turned out an acceptable product ...

*As the citations indicate, the term *Cape Breton Silver* was coined by Allister MacGillivray and later adopted by the Glenora Distillery.

Cape Breton steak noun
humorous reference to baloney
1997 MACDONALD *Fall on Your Knees* 355 Cape Breton steak – take a pound and a half of baloney; slice it; now scorch it. 1998 CURTIS Oral Communication 17

May Cape Breton steak, that's baloney.
2005 KENDALL *Cape Bretoner* 13 (1), 7
Cape Breton steak is just bo-lo-neeeeeee.

Caper noun; also spelled **caper**; compare
Cape Bretoner
1. a long-term resident of Cape Breton,
especially used informally
    1977 *Oran Inbhirnis* 3 Feb. 10 But
"Capers" who've arrived [in Alberta] over
the past six months estimate their numbers to be close to 600. 1989 MLECZKO
My Book of Memories [PART II] 58 Striving
to become a real Caper, and to talk like
they did, seemed to be an impossible task
for me. 1995 MACDONELL *Cape Bretoner*
3 (7), 5 Although I left Judique over forty
years ago, I still am part of the fabric of
being a Caper. 2002 MUISE Email 1 March
Capers are always "turning around" ex ...
"I was talking to him and he turns around
and says ..." 2005 MACINTYRE and
WALLS *NS Book of Everything* 36 **Caper:**
Someone from Cape Breton.
2. a varsity-team member at Cape Breton
University, formerly University College of Cape Breton and College of Cape
Breton
    1987 *CB's Magazine* 44, 5 [Caption]
Lynn Crawford, Whitney Pier, mem-
ber of N. S. Core Team, and centre with
U.C.C.B. Capers. 1994 MORGAN et al.
*University College of CB Alumni Directory
1994* xi Caper teams have won 42 confer-
ence championships and 177 individual
athletes have won awards [in 43 years].
2004 MORGAN *Story of CB's University
College* 88 Meanwhile, in March 1976, the
college colours of white, Kelly green, and
Texas orange were adopted, along with
the appropriately predictable team name
"Capers." 2004 MORGAN *Story of CB's
University College* 187 As for the name
"Capers", other possibilities, such as
"Highlanders" have been suggested, but
rejected as too ethnic or exclusive.
    [Sense 1: COD]

carry the bag verb phrase
to pick up and live on donated food during a strike
    1925 Beaton Institute MG 12 37, 27 Apr.
14 deside to picket and carrie the Bag.
1967 Beaton Institute Tape 28 Everybody
carried a bag to the relief depot and got
his order every day. Sometimes there may
be a big cod or herring, a few potatoes
and some flour ... that carried on through
the whole strike. 1980 *CB's Magazine* 27, 3
And we [striking steel workers] had to go
to City Hall and "carry the bag." We had
to ... register for the relief, and we had to
go there every Wednesday, go pick up our
groceries. Give you the codfish, turnips,
two loaves of bread – a dollar's worth.
1981 AKERMAN *Black around the Eyes* 77
The local unions set up relief stations ...
Another household expression was born:
"carrying the bag." 1984 Beaton Institute
Tape 2137 As they say, "carrying the bag"
during the 1925 strike. You went down
the road with a potato bag or a gunny
sack and got what they wanted to give
you, and that's what you lived on.

*The phrase was used during the 1925 coal
mining strike but as the 1980 citation indicates,
it continued to be used during other strikes.

cas chrom [kæs xraum] noun; also spelled
cas-chrom, cas crom, caschrom
a hand or foot plow consisting of a long
handle with footrest above the crook near
its base to which a narrow metal blade is
attached and used to till rocky ground or
around stumps
    [1940] MACNEIL *Iona-Washabuck Area*
80 ... one of the first implements that they
used to break the ground was a crooked
or bent stick generally made of hard
wood. This was called "Cas Chrom". 1953
DUNN *Highland Settler* 29 Their principal
instrument was the *cas chrom* (crooked
leg), a simple hand plough something
like a narrow, elongated spade. 1978

CB's Magazine 19, 41 They [early Scottish immigrants to Cape Breton] brought the caschrom (foot plow) and the quern ... 2000 MORGAN *Early CB* 138–9 The new settlers had learned little in Scotland of scientific agricultural methods. They simply cleared the trees, burnt the wood for fertilizer, and with a *cas-chrom* – a homemade hand plough – planted their potatoes or some wheat among the stumps.

[at *cascrom*: EDD, DARE; at *caschrom*: OED3 (1803), DSL]

*A loanword from Scottish Gaelic, see *cas-chrom* "a long-handled delving-crook" GD; *crom* "bent, crooked, hooked" GED.

ceilidh ['keli] noun; also spelled **célidh, Ceilidh**; also in the phrases **kitchen ceilidh, reading Ceilidh**; compare **kitchen racket**
1. an informal gathering or visit of family and neighbours at a home, typically to share conversation, storytelling, music, singing, dancing, and food
 1921 MURRAY *History of the Presbyterian Church in CB* 264 They were also accustomed to exchange social visits between neighboring homes, especially in the long winter and fall evenings, after the day's work was done. The Gaelic name for those social visits was *Ceilidh*. 1975 RETSON *Atlantic Advocate* 65 Feb. 19 A favorite of [John Allan] Cameron's in those early days was the community "ceilidh" (Gaelic for get-together) where neighbours would tell stories, sing songs, or perform mouth music ... 1982 MACLELLAN *The Glen* 47 More peaceful and cosier than the pie-social or the haying frolic was the traditional Scottish gathering, the Ceilidh, of authentic Celtic heritage. It varied from a personal visit by a neighbor or friend to a more or less formal gathering of friends, relatives and neighbors for an evening of entertainment ... A principal feature of the Ceilidh was the lunch which consisted of

bonnach, oaten bread or *aran coirc*, homemade cheese, preserves, wild strawberries or raspberries and a strong cup of Cape Breton tea. 1988 MACGILLIVRAY and MACGILLIVRAY *CB Ceilidh* 5 On our Island, a * céilidh* has come to mean any event where people and music (traditional "Scotch") are present: a house party, a festival or even a few avid musicians jamming in the tuning room at Glendale. To have a good céilidh you need a fiddler and an accompanist. 2006 GRAHAM *CB Fiddle* 46 While to this day, people's kitchens and homes remain as lively gathering places for stories, music and dancing, it is only in recent years that the céilidh – Gaelic for visit – has had much attention from the wider world.
2. a gathering or concert at a public venue, such as a hall, with Scottish or Irish music, dancing, and other elements of a ceilidh
 1979 *Inverness Oran* 17 May 26 This aspect [Handcraft and Historical Exhibit] of the Ceilidh is organized this year by Mr. James St. Clair who was one of the originators of the Mabou Ceilidh. 1988 MACDONALD *Culture and Tradition* 12, 76 In Nova Scotia, the term *ceilidh* has been used in recent years, notably in tourist literature, to indicate a pre-arranged concert or dance featuring Scottish or Cape Breton music. 1998b CAMERON *Canadian Living* May 42 Reading ceilidhs are MacNeil's own spin, featuring Cape Breton writers reading from their works, with Celtic musicians performing in the breaks between. Afterward, everyone retires for tea, sandwiches and talk. 2000c O'NEIL *Cape Bretoner* 8 (2), 31 Cape Breton's Route 19, better known as The Ceilidh Trail, probably has more fiddlers, stepdancers, guitar players and singers per kilometre than any other stretch of roadway on the planet.

[Sense 1: *DPEIE, COD, NCD, GCD, OED3* (1875), *COED, DSL, W3, NOAD*. Sense 2: *COD, OED3* (1959), *DSL, W3*]

*A loanword from Scottish Gaelic, see *cèilidh* "visit" *GED*. *Ceilidh* is one of the culturally salient terms that has widened its meaning from an informal visit with neighbors to a formal gathering at a public venue. Some of the citations (1982 and 1988) supporting sense 1 reflect this transition. A similar, but less prevalent, widening is occurring with a *kitchen party* (see *kitchen racket* below).

ceilidh ['keli] intransitive verb
to attend a ceilidh, a social gathering with entertainment at a home or public venue
1966 Beaton Institute Tape 202 When you got to the house that you were ceilidhing, there'd be a group of friends or neighbors in there and they would start violin music and sing songs and tell stories, and some step dance and we'd be there until 12 o'clock at night. 1976 PILLAR *Aunt Peggy* 37 ... he loved to *ceilidh* with his friends. 1996 *CB's Magazine* 70, 44 Alec was going up to ceilidh at their house, and who met him, but Father MacPherson and Christopher O'Henly.
[*DPEIE* (1884), *DSL*]

ceilidh house ['keli həʊs] noun; also spelled **céilidh house**
a home known in the community as a popular setting for a ceilidh
1994 BYERS and MCBURNEY *Atlantic Hearth* 301 Some communities had 'ceilidh houses' in the middle of the settlement. 2000 SHAW and ORNSTEIN *Brìgh an Òrain: A Story in Every Song* 15 In each Gaelic settlement the *céilidh* houses (*taighean céilidh*), though not formally designated, were known to all. A particular *céilidh* house could be regarded as excelling in a certain form of entertainment, and was often the home of a highly regarded performer. 2007 ST. CLAIR and LEVERT *Nancy's Wedding Feast* 28 *Remember when, in rural areas, one house in each area seemed to be a "ceilidh house," a home where the neighbours gathered spontaneously to share stories and music – a gathering known in Scottish Gaelic as a "ceilidh"?*
[*DSL* (1940)]

Ceist [kešč] noun; also spelled **ceist, cesid, Kest, kestch**; also in the phrases **Ciest day, La Ceist**; compare **Question Day, open-air communion, men**
a question derived from a scripture passage, discussed chiefly by the laymen throughout the second day of a five-day Presbyterian communion service; by extension, question day (La Ceist)
1913 CAMPBELL *CB Worthies* 5 Friday was known as the Question Day, "La Ceist." 1953 MACDONALD *CB Mirror* 2 Jan. 5, 24 Thursday was the day of fasting; Friday, the *Ceist* or question day ... Of the *Ceist* (question), I shall speak briefly. The Minister, at this service, would give out a text in the Gaelic tongue. This verse of Scripture would then be thoroughly discussed, in turn, by the elders or any man of the congregation who was well-versed in the teachings of the Book, and would put their own interpretation on it. 1984 CUMMING et al. *Story of Framboise* 114 ... Friday there would be the **ceist** (**Question Day**). 1992 PRINGLE *Pringle's Mountain* 57 They left home on Thursday, took part in the church service on Friday (which was carried on mostly by the elders). The 'Kest' they called it. 2006 STANLEY-BLACKWELL *Tokens of Grace* 30 The balance of the Ceist, however, was given over to discussion of the "Question" proposed by one of Na Daoine (the people), noted "old Christian inquirers." The "Question" was based on some passage of scripture that was read or quoted and then dissected by members of this special brotherhood of godly laymen. Their commentary invariably hinged on identifying the "marks" or "tokens" of genuine grace.

*A loanword from Scottish Gaelic, see *ceist* "enquiry, issue (of law), problem, query, question" *GED*.

chain runner

Ceòl [kyul] noun; also spelled **ceòl**; also in the phrases **Ceòl Beag, Ceòl Mor, Ceòl Meadonach**, and others
music

1952 MACLEOD *CB Mirror* 1 July 5 In the first category, Ceòl Mór (The Big Music), we find the most intricate and most beautiful bagpipe scores having as their basis a traditional verbal notation, or vocable syllabic scale called in Scottish Gaelic, Canntaireachd. Ceòl Meadhonach (The Middle Music), contains mostly bagpipe adaptations of Gaelic melodies ... Ceòl Beag or Ceòl Aotrom, meaning The Small or Light Music, is comprised of Marches, Strathspeys, Reels and Jigs, and is the most popular form of bagpipe music known to us at the present time. 1988 MACGILLIVRAY and MACGIL-LIVRAY *CB Ceilidh* 214 He's what we call "a finished piper", which means you play everything: Ceòl Mór [big] and Ceòl Meadhonach [middle]. 1992 DUCHARME *Archie Neil* 11 There were pleasant days, when Momma had time to rock him for an hour in the afternoon, singing "ceòl beòil," a humming mouth music, simple musical rhythms and melodies ... 2006 GRAHAM *CB Fiddle* 16 After a presentation of the views of his informants, Shaw concluded: "In the light of the foregoing comments by traditional Gaels, the younger, non-Gaelic speaking generation of fiddle players may be understood to practise a post-Gaelic style, rather than being situated within the traditional Gaelic realm of *ceòl ceart*." (*Ceòl ceart* is a Gaelic phrase for correct playing.)

*A loanword from Scottish Gaelic, see *ceòl* "music" *GED*.

CFA initialism; compare **away**
Come From Away, a person not from Cape Breton or the Atlantic Provinces

2001 CURRIE *Sculptures from Jagged Ore* 56 A large portion of serious literature coming from Cape Breton is produced by displaced Cape Bretoners and by, as they say, CFA's, (come from aways) like Tessie Gillis. 2005 MACINTYRE and WALLS *NS Book of Everything* 36 Someone from anywhere but Nova Scotia, especially from outside the Maritimes. (CFA for short.) 2007b BARBER *Only in Canada* 8 **come from away / CFA** (*Atlantic Canada*) a person who is not from the Atlantic region generally. Survey I Inf. 5 *CFA* is more recent and has a pejorative quality – she is come from away. It can also be apologetic – I am a come from away; how would I be expected to know that?

[*COD Cdn* (*Maritimes* & *Nfld*), *GCD Cdn., Nfld.* & *P.E.I.*]

chain runner noun; also spelled **chain-runner**; compare **rake**
a miner in charge of the haulage of coal boxes and mine cars transporting miners (rakes)

1939 MG 12 43 E4 Box 3, 144 ... he merely told the chain runner it was getting late ... 1984 Beaton Institute Tape 2151 I worked at that for a while, what they called chain runner. I used to bring the trip of empties. There'd be 20 boxes on the trip or 25 ... Then take 25 full ones out ... You'd run about three or four hundred boxes a day. 1990 [MACNEIL] *History of Sydney Mines* 89 ... it was the chain runner's duty to check the carrying capacity of each box, and then rap the trip away. 1995 *DCBE* Tape NICHOLSON 14–15 We get in a rake; this is the regular rake what we used to drive in ... It would have twelve or fifteen boxes on it. Your chain runner would lower you down. When you're ready, all the men are in, he'll rap her down. 2007 MACKENZIE *CB Coal Mine Disasters* 42 The miners filled the box with coal, and another man, called a "chain runner," signaled the hoist operator on the surface to haul the full box back up.

chaloupe [šæ'lup] noun; also spelled
chaloup; compare **shallop**
a small boat powered by oars or sails and
used in the inshore fishery
  1740 in 1869 BROWN *History of the
Island of CB* 175 In the year 1740, according to a report sent to the Lords Commissioners of Trade ... 48 schooners and 393
chaloups were employed in the cod fisheries of Cape Breton ... 1984 CUMMING et
al. *Story of Framboise* 10 Fishing was done
from **chaloupes** (shallops, small boats
that employed five men – three on board,
two on land). 1991 LAVERY and LAVERY
Gabarus and Vicinity 4 ... the chaloupe, or
'shallop' as it is called in English, was by
far the main craft used by the fishermen of
Cape Breton throughout the 18th and 19th
centuries.
  [*OED3* (1680), *W3*]

Chandeleur noun; also spelled **chandeleur**; compare **Escaouette**
the feast of the blessing of candles on Candlemas (Feb. 2), and a community party
with a festive meal and dancing at a local
home
  1975 *CB's Magazine* 10, 1 ... and something else they used to celebrate which
they don't now is something they called
the Chandeleur, when they bless the candles. Oh, it used to be a great feast. 1991
Inverness Oran 24 July 31 La Chandeleur
(candlemas), the feast of the Purification
of Saint Mary on February 2nd, was celebrated in Acadian circles with a special
dance and lots of food. The religious
aspect has been somewhat obscured and
the food emphasized ... 1992 DOUCET
Priest's Boy 42 The Chandeleur began
with the women making the candles for
the priest to bless. 1993 *CB's Magazine*
63, 38 The war started in 1939, and then
there was not (enough) people, to make
the Chandeleur. They used to start making the Chandeleur a week before the
Chandeleur – before February the 2nd.

They used to pass with the horses and [at]
every house somebody would furnish the
flour, and molasses, and sugar, and salt,
you know. Every house you passed. And
then you had a place to make the Chandeleur. And then they were preparing
that (house) for February the 2nd. 1999
DOUCET *Notes from Exile* 23 At bottom,
La Chandeleur belonged to Bacchus; the
priest had good reason to be suspicious of
it as an "occasion for sin" and the people
good reason to love it.

*For a discussion of the *Chandeleur* traditions in
the Maritimes, Quebec, and France, see *DFA* at
Chandeleur, courir la.

checkers noun, plural; compare **run**[1]
a lattice of bricks in a tunnel through
which hot gas passes to the open-hearth
furnace
  1980 *CB's Magazine* 27, 5 Gas goes
through the checkers to melt the steel,
coming from the gas producers. 1990
Beaton Institute MG 14 206 BOX 6 C. iii c)
File 19, 1 ... I had to go down the open-
hearth checkers. We have to clean the
checkers out with a chain. That sort of
helps the draft for the furnace when it's
in operation. It's a dirty, messy job.1993
CB's Magazine 64, 53 The checkers were
a latticework of brick under the stacks in
the Open Hearth. They had to be replaced
often. 2001 MACKINNON *Cape Bretoner* 9
(2), 15 Who will describe what it was like
to work in the checkers ...?

check number noun
an employee number used for company
business, such as indicating when a miner
was working underground or obtaining
credit at the company store; by extension,
the brass tag with the number on it, used
by miners and steel workers
  1973 MACKINNON *CB's Magazine* 3,
3 But the trouble with the stores was that
when you were hired on you were given

a check number, a brass check number – and you could get credit on that number at the store. 1984 Beaton Institute Tape 2146 In the morning when they took out the lamp, they put in their check number. When they came up in the evening they took the check number out. 1992 *CB's Magazine* 60, 14 But he gave me my clock card, and best of all, he gave me my check number – 1057. 2008 *DCBE* Tape CURRIE 10 When you went to work, if you were loading coal, you got a check number.

check-off noun; also spelled **check off**; often in the phrase **check-off system**; see **off tax**
an authorized deduction by the company for dues, services, and purchases
    1926 DUNCAN *Royal Commission ... Coal Mines of NS 1925* 45–6 **Check-Off System** ... This system has been used in the main for the following purposes: Rents of Company-owned houses; Supplies from Company-owned stores; Coal; Checkweighmen; Supplies, such as Powder and Tools; Doctor; Hospital; Benefit Societies; Church; U.M.W.A.; and even Town Taxes in some cases; the operators making the necessary deductions from the workers' pay and handing over the funds to the appropriate channels. 1934 in 1999 FRANK *J. B. McLachlan* 489 [quoting McLachlan in the *NS Miner*] "The check-off, in our view, is bad in any form, and nothing more nor less than an attempt of the boss to gain certain control over union affairs." 1971 Beaton Institute Tape 217 It is amazing to some people when you tell them this story that men had lived and worked so hard, and at the same time did not see money because of the fact that it was deducted through the check-off system. 1996 MACMILLAN *Boy from Port Hood* 58 We [NS miners] had a check-off on our union dues long before any other province did. 2002 *CB Post* 14 Jan. B1 No less a man than Justice Emmett Hall, the

author of the Royal Commission Report on Health Care in Canada, acknowledged that the miners' check-off system was the "precursor of Medicare." 2006 MACISAAC *Better Life* 101 The miners' salaries and company-provided expenses were allocated through the check-off system, which was established in 1880.
    [at *checkoff* W3, *MWCD*]

*The *OED3* (1911), *FWCCD*, *NCD*, and *GCD* define *check-off* as limited to union dues only.

checkweighman noun; also spelled **check weighman**, **check-weighman**
a miner, elected and paid by the union, to ensure that the company weighman accurately records the tonnage of coal sent to the surface by the miners
    1889 CANADA *Report ... Labor and Capital in Canada: Evidence, NS* 452 In June, 1887, the gross amount of my work was $29.75 Q. How much was deducted from that? A. Powder and oil, $2.84; sundries, $1.90; store, $20.23; check weighman, 35 cents; cash, $5. (That was in advance.) There was a balance of $4.18. 1926 DUNCAN *Royal Commission ... Coal Mines of NS 1925* 45 This system has been used in the main for the following purposes: Rents of Company-owned houses ... Checkweighmen ... 1984 Beaton Institute Tape 2134 "It [the coal] was taken to the surface ... then it was weighed by your check weighman and by the company weighman, and at the end of the week you checked the tally of the boxes you loaded, and he gave you your tonnage for the week. You were paid so much a ton for every ton you had. 1999 FRANK *J. B. McLachlan* 144 ... checkweighman – the miners' elected representative at the surface of each mine ... 2008 *DCBE* Tape CURRIE 10 And a checkweighman ... there were two: there was somebody who represented the company and someone who represented the union, and they would weigh the coal so that the

union guy would be there to make sure the mine wasn't cheap.

[*EDD* (1849), *OED3*, *W3*]

chicken fricot: see **fricot**

chuck noun; also spelled **chock**; also **chuck block**; compare **pack, brusher**
a squared block of hardwood, typically two feet long, used chiefly to make a frame filled with stone (a pack) to support the mine roof; by extension, a pack made in this manner

1928 HAY *Coal Mining Operations in the Sydney Coal Field* 36 Three lines of hardwood chocks made up of 6″ x 6″ x 30″ squared hardwood were erected parallel to the face ... 1939 MCARTHUR commissioner "Inquiry into Conditions at Florence Colliery" 2–3 Hardwood chocks are built up, hardwood blocks 2 ft. long and 6 in. square built in the form of a crib ... The interior is filled with stone packed as tightly as possible against the roof so that the amount of immediate settlement will be as little as possible. 1984 Beaton Institute Tape 2143 That is, where the coal has been excavated and back from the coal face, back probably a distance of 20 feet has to be held up by those, what we call chucks. 1984 Beaton Institute Tape 2156 As soon as the coal is out, there is men there to put up what we call the chuck, that is, put up hardwood blocks crossways. And that was put there on the other side of the conveyor to protect the roof conditions. 2003 SAINT AGNES ELEMENTARY SCHOOL *Coal Miners' Stories* 12 Another time we nailed Neil's lunch can to a chock block and when it was time to go, Neil grabbed his can and the top came right off. 2007 MACKENZIE *CB Coal Mine Disasters* 168 Loss of ventilating air in and around these brushers packs, or "chocks," was the focus of much attention at the inquiry into the explosion.

[at *chock*: *EDD*, *OED3* (1708)]

chuck drawer noun; also spelled **chuck-drawer**; compare **draw chucks**
a miner who removes the chuck blocks for reuse in a frame packed with stone (a pack) once the roof support is no longer needed where the coal has been removed (the gob)

1972 Beaton Institute Tape 537 Then when I went in the, its called the gob, drawing the chucks, I was the chuck drawer's helper. 1984 Beaton Institute Tape 2143 I was a chuck drawer, drawing chucks in the longwall ... the chucks are drawn out, retrieved, saved, as the coal is taken out, and the waste, the gob, is allowed to come in. 2000 MACGILLIVRAY *Men of the Deeps* 71 At first he was classed as a chuckdrawer's helper ...

ciad mile failte [kɪt milə faulʲə] interjection; also spelled **cead mille failte**
a hundred thousand welcomes, a traditional greeting and now a tourism slogan

1948 WALWORTH *CB Isle of Romance* 56 A banner over the rustic gate proclaimed "Ciad Mile Failte" – a hundred thousand welcomes ... 1948 MACNEIL *Highland Heart in NS* 141 The largest figure that I had heard mentioned in Washabuckt Gaelic was 100,000 and that was in the salutation "cead mille failte," literally "100,000 greetings," a figure that was felt to approach infinity in a greeting that was considered the ultimate in welcomes. 1993 *Inverness Oran* 9 June 24 Stop for a ceilidh. CIAD MILE FAILTE! 1998 Anon. *Cape Bretoner* 6 (1), 10 October will be here before you can say "Ciad mìle fàilte"!

[at *cead mile failte*: *OED3* orig. and chiefly *Irish English* (1825); compare Scottish Gaelic, *fàilte* "greeting, salutation, welcome" *GED*]

clamper noun, usually plural; also **ice clamper, clamper of ice**; compare **skooshin, ice pan**

a pan of floating ice, large enough, or nearly so, to support one or more people; also a large pan of floating ice

1914 Beaton Institute MG 12 59, 4 May n.p. The Drift ice is grounded down by North Sydney and can't get up on a few clampers. 1919 *North Sydney Herald* 24 Dec. 8 ... when the searchers went to the place they discovered a clamper of ice which had stood on its side. Six feet below the bodies of the two brothers, each holding the other's hand, were found. 1932 *Teachdaire nan Gaidheal* [*Gaelic Herald*] Dec. 11 ... the clamper on which they stood drifted towards the open water, and the young men were never seen afterwards. 1987 *CB's Magazine* 45, 49 Every once in awhile you'd see a great big sheet of ice, which would be an ice clamper. And we used to go off and we'd skate on that. 1987 MANN *Memories of Harbour Point, Gabarus* 12 Every spring huge ice clampers creaked and groaned as they piled up on the rocks and beaches near our house. 2007 ST. CLAIR and LEVERT *Nancy's Wedding Feast* 185 The ice cakes, or clampers as some call them, hold the land tightly in their grip. 2008 *DCBE* Tape CURRIE 8 Clampers, the ice, people used to go out and jump from ice to ice ... kind of a dangerous sport. Survey II Inf. 8 Jumping ice clampers – run over them as quickly as possible to avoid sinking.

[Compare the similar meaning but variant forms: *clumper DNE* (with *clamper* as a variant), *COD Cdn* (*Maritimes & Nfld*), and *clumpet DNE, DPEIE*]

*Although the *DC* (1960) records the form *clamper*, it defines the term as it is understood in Saskatchewan: "one of the large chunks of ice that pile up on the shore, especially during spring break-up."

clanny noun; also spelled **Clanny, glennie, glanny**; also **clanny lamp**; compare **pit lamp**

a generic term for a flame safety lamp, named for Dr. William Reid Clanny and used to prevent the explosion of mine gases while providing a dim light for working underground

1969 Beaton Institute Tape 78 Using the same technique as the Davy safety lamp, Dr. Clanny invented the Clanny lamp which was a glass cylinder that sat on the bottom of the lamp and surrounded the flame and upon which the gauzes were set. Now this glass cylinder allowed the light to illuminate the place. 1979 *Inverness Oran* 8 Mar. 1 The three couples carried a piece-can, a pit-helmet and a glennie to the altar along with the bread and wine. 1980 MCINTYRE *Collier's Tattletale* 87 Doctor Clanny ... improved his mine lamps during his lifetime, and for many years, in mining districts all over the world, all of the flame safety lamps used by the miners were known as "the Clannys". 1981 Beaton Institute Tape 2037 When the clannies came in first, they ... would go out. You have to take it out to the door where a young fellow called a trapper had to put it in a machine, what they call a boiter, with light. 1984 Beaton Institute Tape 2159 The only thing that I find hard, we used to have a little glanny and the light was too small. Right small light ... You had to hold it by the handle. 1996 *CB's Magazine* 70, 65 ... the lamps were called a clanny lamp – their purpose was for testing for gas and also provided the minimum amount of light for them to work ... Any vibration and they went out. 2013 FRANK Email 9 Aug. I have heard men in Cape Breton use the term "clanny lamp", which I take to be a generic reference to the safety lamps.

[at *clannylamp EDD* (1888)]

*By extension, the term *clanny blink* was used to describe an eye ailment suffered by miners: "I wonder what he thinks caused the deformed legs, the drawn-up shoulders, the fallen-in chest and the 'clanny blinks' on the workers of such a town?" (McLachlan 1906, quoted in Frank J. B. McLachlan 1999, 56).

clever adjective
of a person, hospitable, pleasant, kind
    1991 *CB's Magazine* 57, 20 The wives would come and tell my mother. Mother was very clever like that. She listened to them. And then the husband would come and tell her why he beat the wife up, and so on! This is the way it used to go on. 2008 *DCBE* Tape CURRIE 17 A hospitable, agreeable person. Survey I Inf. 23 Hospitable, some clever.
    [*DPEIE, FWCCD U.S. Dial., GCD Informal, EDD* (1682), *OED3 U.S. colloq., DARE* **formerly NEng, now chiefly Sth, S Mdl,** *DAE*]

clò [klo] noun; compare **milling frolic**
homespun woolen cloth, especially a heavy material for garments such as a jacket or pants
    1974 MACPHAIL *Bride of Loch Bras d'Or* 23 ... he wouldn't wear homespun 'clo', which is Gaelic for this type of cloth. 1976 PILLAR *Aunt Peggy* 40-1 In *clo* (Gaelic for all wool homespun, pronounced "claw") the warp threaded in the loom is also wool, finely spun and twisted, and when woven looks like serge or twill ... Margaret also made a heavy pair of work trousers from homespun *clo* for Alex. These proved to be almost indestructible, as he wore them lumbering. 1991 *CB's Magazine* 56, 23 And they made some of our clothes in the loom. She'd make skirts. Jackets. And she'd make the clò (heavier woolen cloth) – when they go milling? 1991 *CB's Magazine* 57, 42 There were a lot of milling frolics ... Because they'd have to mill the cloth that they'd make – the clò – the homespun, and the blankets.
    [at *cloa: EDD* Sc.]

*A loanword from Scottish Gaelic, see *clò* "cloth, tweed" *GED*.

close to the floor adjective phrase
characterized by step-dancing performed with a minimum of movement of the upper body and in a limited space on the dance floor
    1988 MACGILLIVRAY and MACGILLIVRAY *CB Ceilidh* 63 ... people used to remark "He looked so beautiful when he danced and he was so close to the floor that you could hardly see his feet moving!" 1991 *Inverness Oran* 25 Sept. 22 ... lively jigs, reels and strathspeys played on fiddle and guitar complimented by some very close-to-the-floor steps. 2005 MACDONALD *Forest for Calum* 316 Every eye in the hall was riveted on Catherine's feet, trained in the Cape Breton tradition of staying close to the floor while the music swirled around them ... Catherine, arms relaxed and motionless by her side, standing erect, staring into the music, was dancing with little movement or motion above her feet where the energy of the dance should be focused. 2006 GRAHAM *CB Fiddle* 187 Step-dancing is "close-to-the-floor," (done neatly within a couple of square feet of space), the best dancers moving mainly from the knees down to the feet ...

coal company house: see **company house**

coal company store: see **company store**

coal face noun; also **face**; compare **wall face**
the vertical surface of the coal seam where the miners excavate coal
    1954 MACDONALD *Maclean's* 18 Mar. 25 Mine Trains take him to the coal face, a long ride. In some cases his work is ninety minutes away. 1988 *CB's Magazine* 49, 81 The miners down in the pit sit with their back against the coal face and eat

their sandwich, and then leave part of the sandwich for the rats. 1995 MACDON-ALD *Port Morien* 19 The coal was hauled directly from the working area (coal face) by a forty-five horse power engine, and loaded on ships waiting at the wharf. 1997 *CB's Magazine* 72, 5 And it's continuous mining in the true sense of the word, because you just cut down (along the coal face), move over, cut up again – you get six or seven cuts in the one shift.

[*COD*; at *coalface OED3* (1771), *COED*]

coal trimmer noun; also **trimmer**
a worker who balances (trims) the coal in the hatches and bunkers of a ship

1918 Beaton Institute MG 12 46 A9 n.p. Coal Trimmers [3.11 per day]. 1978 *CB's Magazine* 19, 13 The train carried coal to the pier at Port Hastings, and men like those above served as trimmers as the coal was loaded aboard vessels. 1987 *CB's Magazine* 44, 27 ... coal trimmers – when (the coal shippers would) load the coal into the boats, the trimmers had to level off all the coal in the hatches, and fill up every corner to make sure that the ship was safe for sailing ... [to] make sure the ship would have enough bunker to sail to her next port. 1988 Beaton Institute Tape 2371 Old Bab Lewis and a bunch from Point Edward, they were coal-trimmers. They worked in the coal piers and they used to have these great big pan shovels ...

[at *coal-trimmer OED3* now chiefly *hist.* (1828); at *trimmer*: *EDD*, *OED3* (1836), *W3*, *MWCD*]

*Compare *COD*, *FWCCD*, *COED*, and *NOAD* that define *trimmer* as a person who balances or adjusts cargo in a ship.

coasting verbal noun and adjective
sailing to ports along the coast to deliver and trade cargo

1829 HALIBURTON *Historical and Statistical Account of N-S* vol. 2, 255 The registered vessels belonging to the Island are three hundred and forty, principally employed in the coasting and carrying trade, the greater number being owned in Isle Madame ... 1832 BOUCHETTE *British Dominions in North America* vol. 2, 77–8 Beyond Miray Bay lies the small harbour of Menadon, or Main-à-dieu, on which is a settlement of active fishermen, who are also engaged in the coal and coasting trade from Sydney to Halifax. 1858 HAMILTON *N-S Considered as a Field for Emigration* 88 These dimensions [for the lock at St. Peter's] are expected to be sufficient to accommodate any coasting or fishing vessel frequenting the neighbouring waters. 1978 Beaton Institute Tape 1154 Well, they used to go coasting. They'd carry freight; like in the spring of the year they'd go to Halifax ... Coasting vessels they'd call them. 1991 LAVERY and LAVERY *Gabarus and Vicinity* 97 She was considered a very good vessel for "coasting" (hauling freight) and was stable even when empty. 1996 *CB's Magazine* 71, 12 Along in the afternoon this coasting vessel was coming down, a schooner.

[*DNE*, *COD*, *OED3* (1679), *COED*, *NOAD*]

cobble noun
a twisted piece of steel, typically a rail, less frequently wire, malformed during the manufacturing process

1989 *CB's Magazine* 52, 18 Now, you could buy scrap barbed wire. Like, for instance, when it was going through the machine, she'd have a cobble, she'd catch, and you'd only get a half a roll. 1990 Beaton Institute MG 14 206 Box 5 C. iii b) File 22, 16 ... you had to cut the piece of steel coming through the trumpet of the shears ... You had to be quick, and if you cut it too fast or too slow you made a "cobble". If you made a cobble, you had to run, because it just looped around ... 1990 Beaton Institute MG 14

206 Box 7 C. iii c) File 60, 5 Scrap yard, [I] was a burner, and these rails that were "cobbles," we used to call them; they weren't any good. 1991 Beaton Institute MG 14 206 Box 6 C. iii b) File 87, 5–6 Now if that [hot pieces of steel] went through the machine and went through the cutter, they came out perfect. But if they didn't they were like a worm ... A cobble, that's just what it was.

[W3; compare *cobble* verb "To entangle, become entangled" *EDD* n.d.]

*The documentary depicting steel production at the Sydney steel plant, *Making Steel: Technology, History, Culture of Work* (1992), shows a hot steel rail twisting out of control, making a "cobble."

cod flake: see **flake**

codline noun; also spelled **cod line** an 18-thread line used in the ground fishery and for other purposes requiring a light, sturdy line
  1869 BROWN *History of the Island of CB* 198 The land force 'was composed of fishermen, who in time of war could no longer use the hook and line on the Grand Bank, but with prudent forethought took with them their codlines ...' 1996 *CB's Magazine* 70, 30 [I] kept pulling the cod line until I got a rope over the bar, then put a running knot on the rope, and away I goes.
  [DC; at *cod-line*: DNE, OED3 (1634); at *cod line*: DAE (1634), W3]

cold board(s): see **cooling board**

come from away: see **away, CFA**

communion token: see **token**

company house noun; also **coal company house**; see **double house**; compare **miners' row**

typically, a company-owned duplex, divided by a central wall and rented to mine or steel employees; less frequently, a company-owned tenement or detached house
  1889 CANADA *Report ... Labor and Capital in Canada: Evidence, NS* xiii Rents one of [the] company's houses and pays 50 cents a month; two rooms upstairs, two down; that is the average rent. Not very comfortable, but wells are handy. 1890 Beaton Institute MG 12 43 C1 1–19 Box 2 n.p. I have got a Company house now ... 1940 ARNOLD *Story of Thompkinsville* 4 Then there are the deductions ... And back rent if you have gotten behind with a "Company" house. 1952 WISDOM *CB Mirror* 1 Apr. 5 ... [Bridgeport] where the first "Company Houses" were built about 1865. 1978 *Oran Inbhirnis* 13 July 11 In 1901 a large mining operation was started by the Mabou and Gulf Coal Company ... There were at least nine duplex company houses ... 1980 SUNDERLAND *Still Standing* n.p. At the turn of the century, the Inverness Railway and Coal Company ... built about eighty divided tenements, or 'company houses', for the miners ... Because each house is divided down the middle and occupied by two families, most develop a characteristic 'split-personality'. Each half of this house is painted a different colour and the roof is finished in two different ways. Houses of this kind can be seen in any Cape Breton coal-mining town. 1986 LATREMOUILLE et al. *Pride of Home* 57 The early company houses were attached units built in rows much like the workers' rows in the potteries or the black country of England. Sydney Mines once boasted eleven rows, although only the last, the brick and timber Red Row is still standing. 2006 MACISAAC *Better Life* 99 Eighty per cent of mining families lived in the company houses that were built in large numbers in the Pictou and Sydney fields.

2011 DOYLE *CB Facts and Folklore* 213 … company house: A dwelling that coal operators built for their workers all over Cape Breton. They were duplex design.

[at *company DA* (1935); compare *company tenement OED3* (1907)]

company store noun; also **coal company store**; compare **pluck-me**
a general store owned by the coal and steel company and known for extending credit to employees

1889 CANADA *Report … Labor and Capital in Canada: Evidence, NS* xiii Store in connection with mine, but not compelled to go there … Some articles as cheap in company's store as in others. 1969 Beaton Institute Tape 118 I don't think the company ever sold rum in the company store. 1976 MACEWAN *Miners and Steelworkers* 42 "Now, my brethren, let us figure a little bit and see if we cannot find out why so many of us are in such a hell of a fix at the pluck-me company store." 1983 MELLOR *Company Store* 11 All company stores were constructed alike – two storeys high, complete with basement and loading dock at the rear – and, like the company houses, built of wood. 1986 FITZGERALD *CB: A Changing Scene* 73 Company stores, so-called because they were operated by mining companies, date from the 1790's in Cape Breton. Workers bought their goods there, becoming indebted to the companies. 1988 MCKAY *Essays in Canadian Historical Sociology* 31 The G[eneral] M[ining] A[ssociation] inherited both this tradition of the company store and brought its own schemes for company housing directly from England … 2007 DCBE Tape SHERRINGTON 28 So they referred to that [a co-op store] as the company store, partly I think cause you had credit; you could have credit for the whole season there.

[*COD N Amer.*, W3; at *company: OED3* (U.S.) (1872), *DAE* (1872), *DA* (1872)]

continuous miner noun; also **Dosco Continuous Miner, Dosco miner**; compare **shearer**
a machine that breaks the coal with tapered metal teeth on a rotating track and transfers it to a pan line or conveyor belt in a single process

1982 *CB's Magazine* 32 Inside Front Cover … mining methods (and thus the use of labour) were radically changing with the introduction of the Dosco Continuous Miner. 1983 SHEDDEN et al. *Mining Photographs* 269 **Continuous Miner** – A machine which fractures coal from the face of the seam and loads it onto a conveyer in a single step. 1986 *CB's Magazine* 72, 7 *The Dosco Miner was a rare instance of a coal company's trying to develop new machinery rather than purchase it from a manufacturer. Tried out in the workplace, its preliminary flaws were exposed – and while it was the main coal getter for years before the Anderton Shearer, it rarely had a good name with the work force.* 2003 SAINT AGNES ELEMENTARY SCHOOL *Coal Miners' Stories* 57 In the mid 1940's, they put a machine in the mines called the continuous miner. This machine saved a lot of backbreaking work. The continuous miner put the coal on a pan line down at the bottom of the wall, where there was a belt line that took the coal and it was dumped into one-ton boxes.

[W3, *OED3* (1958)]

contract work noun; see **task work**
piecework where a worker is paid for a job completed

1984 Beaton Institute Tape 2134 Well, if you can do the job in an hour, you're back up on the surface … We never used to call it task work; we used to call it contract work. 1997 *CB's Magazine* 72, 3 If you didn't get your coal, all you made was the cost-of-living bonus, for being down there. That was what you call contract work. 1999a MIGLIORE and DIPIERRO eds. *Italian Lives* 77 "Contract work" was piecework, where a loader was paid for each ton he shovelled into "boxes" to be hauled from the mine.

[*OED3 attrib.* and *Comb.* (no quotation recorded for this compound)]

cookhouse noun; also spelled
cook-house, cook house
a building with a kitchen and dining area for workers in camps or those fishing or processing fish
1978 *CB's Magazine* 21, 38 Then we dashed to the cookhouse / Our breakfast to eat. 1981 *CB's Magazine* 30, 42 After this material made its way to the mines, the same carpenter was hired to reconstruct it at Gold Brook, where he also erected an office, bunkhouse, cookhouse, and living quarters. 1992 HORNSBY *Nineteenth-Century CB* 93 This "valuable fishing establishment" consisted of ... a one-and-a-half-storey cookhouse, a blacksmith's forge and a stable ...
[*DC, DARE* (1831)]

cooling board noun; also **board(s), cold board(s)**
one or more planks on which a corpse is laid out while the coffin is being made
1966 Beaton Institute Tape 202 ... they were carrying on at the wake ... they even went outside and put a stick ... between the logs, and tried to move the cooling board which they used in them days, just laying them out on a board. 1975 *CB's Magazine*12, 3 ... they used to put them on what they called the cold boards. They used to put them between two chairs in a room and lay the remains out on that until they'd build a casket. There'd be a sheet put over the boards. 1982 MACLELLAN *The Glen* 44 While the coffin was being constructed, the body of the deceased was laid out on a stretcher-like arrangement, known as "the boards". 2000 BOUDREAU and CHIASSON *Chéticamp: Memoirs* 109

The deceased was dressed in his best clothes, then placed "sur les planches" (on his boards), as we used to say.
[*OED3 U.S. regional* (1839), *DARE* **Sth, Midl**, *DAE, DA, W3 chiefly South*]

cope transitive and intransitive verb; often in the phrase **cope over**
to turn, tip (something)
1976 *Oran Inbhirnis* 9 Dec. 16 "She'll [the train, the Judique Flyer] ram into everything and cope over," he said again in a hushed whisper. 1977 Beaton Institute Tape 235 The top of the place [where the miners load the coal], we take the empty box off, cope it to one side and push the full box on and [it] would have to run back to the bottom. 1977 *CB's Magazine* 18, 39 The head [of the corpse] was stuck out ahead of me – it coped down. Survey I Inf. 31 Cope – to tip over. Survey I Inf. 35 Will the boat cope over?

cork noun, usually plural; also **ice-cork, shoe-cork**
a tapered metal projection on the bottom of a horseshoe to give traction on ice, a calk
1978 *CB's Magazine* 19, 15 My brother was a blacksmith in Portland, Maine, and he made me a set of shoes – oh, they were light and the corks were all quite long. [1986?] HUNTINGTON *Looking Around* 9 Just in case anyone's asking, "What's a sharpshod horse?", it's one that's wearing shoes with sharp calks (we called them "corks") that cut into the ice. 1994 SAMSON *River Bourgeois* 223 During harness racing on ice, horses were sometimes fitted with shoe-corks affixed to the normal horse shoe to improve their footing. 1999 MACLEOD *No Great Mischief* 175 He borrowed a team of horses and had them shod with 'ice-corks' in their shoes and came across.
[*EDD, OED3* (1806), *DARE* (1806), *DAE* (1806), *DA, W3*]

*The dictionaries listed indicate that *cork* is a variant pronunciation of *calk*, and only the *EDD*, *OED3*, and *W3* refer to projections on horseshoes, rather than projections on boots.

cottage meeting noun; compare **house church**

a gathering in a private home for religious services

n.d. HUNTINGTON *Huntington Heritage* 9 For many years the Baptists held "cottage meetings" at the homes of the members. 1987 MANN *Memories of Harbour Point, Gabarus* 2 "Cottage meetings" were gatherings held in connection with the Methodist Church and there was usually a lot of singing which included favourite hymns. 1991 LAVERY and LAVERY *Gabarus and Vicinity* 116 There were also mid-week prayer services, sometimes held in private homes, where they were known as "cottage meetings".

[*DNE*]

cotton batting: see **baker's fog**

cracker noun

a worker in a lobster cannery who cuts open lobster claws and removes the meat

1977 Beaton Institute Tape 712 There was two crackers and five or six arm pickers all at the same table getting the meat out of the shells. 1978 *CB's Magazine* 20, 2 They, they'd take the box of claws to a fellow there called the cracker. Every one in the factory had their job. That fellow, the cracker, he had a block on a counter and struck that claw with a cleaver, to get the meat from the claw. 1995 MACDONALD *Port Morien* 59 One person would break the lobsters apart into sections, while the crackers used a cleaver with a 15 cm. blade to crack the claws on a block of wood.

[*DPEIE* (1982)]

crane chaser: see **rigger**

crazy rock: see **dummy rock**

creek noun

a saltwater inlet or an estuary into which a freshwater stream runs; retained in certain names such as Balls Creek and Leitches Creek

1829 HALIBURTON *Historical and Statistical Account of N-S* vol. 2, 207 This [north west] arm extends four miles to its head, where it is entered by two small rivers, Leitch's creek and Ball's creek ... 1864 CALKIN *Geography and History of NS* 104 CREEK. A small inlet of the sea; a brook. 1832 BOUCHETTE *British Dominions in North America* vol. 2, 88 At the north-east side of this cove [on St. Paul Island] there is a small creek, large enough for a line-of-battle ship's launch (a vessel about 10 tons), to lie well sheltered ... 1914 ARCHIBALD *Early Scottish Settlers in CB* 77–8 The scenery opening up to the view of the observer as he sails upon these [Bras d'Or] Lakes is most enchanting with its creeks, bays, inlets ... 1979 MCCONNELL *Our Own Voice* 146 Generally in North America, *creek* (often pronounced *crick*) has lost its present British meaning of a 'tidal estuary or saltwater inlet' and has become the name of a freshwater stream smaller than a river ... But in the Atlantic Provinces and on the British Columbia coast, areas which both face the sea and have much British contact, the older sense is occasionally retained, especially in place names. 1994 *CB's Magazine* 67, 41 A unique environmental project involving the removal of approximately 700,000 tons of waste sludge from a tidal estuary known as Muggah Creek. Sludge is dredged from the creek and transferred ...

[*COD Brit.*, *FWCCD Chiefly Brit.*, *NCD*, *GCD*, *OED3* (*c*1250), *COED chiefly Brit.*, *DARE* **Atlantic, esp Mid and N Atl**, *DAE*, *W3 chiefly Brit*, *NOAD*, *MWCD chiefly Brit*]

*The editors of the *OED3* suggest how the earlier sense of *creek* as an "inlet" extended to designate a stream or brook in North America: "creek **2. b.** In U.S., Canada, Australia, New Zealand, etc.: A branch of a main river, a tributary river; a rivulet, brook, small stream, or run. Probably the name was originally given by the explorers of a river to the various inlets or arms observed to run out of it, and of which only the mouths were seen in passing; when at a later period these 'creeks' were explored, they were often found to be tributaries of great length; but they retained the designation originally given, and 'creek' thus received an application entirely unknown in Great Britain."

crimco: see **Krim-Ko**

crop pit noun; compare **bootleg**
a small coal mine near the surface, usually mined illegally, a bootleg pit
　1939 MCMULLAN Letter to Mary Arnold, Radcliffe College Archives, Boston, Mass. A122–7 n.p. Some of the boys are working a crop pit and getting there [*sic*] own coal so I hope to dig enough for the winter as soon as I get strong enough. 1976–7 Miners' Museum Tape 124 I worked in the crop pit as we called it up until about 1934. 1992 MACKENZIE *Memories Recalled* 30 Knowing that the towns of Glace Bay, New Waterford and Sydney Mines were full of company coal mines, as well as crop pits commonly called 'bootleg mines' ... 1999a MIGLIORE and DIPIERRO eds. *Italian Lives* 156 My brothers worked the crop pits, digging and hauling coal.

crotal ['krɑhtəl] noun; also spelled **crotol**
a lichen found on hardwood trees, formerly used to make a brown dye
　1952 GRANT *CB Mirror* 1 Jan. 9 Brown dye was obtained from lichens or "crotal" as they call it in Gaelic ... 1984 CUMMING et al. *Story of Framboise* 49 Dye for

the wool was made from **crotal**, a lichen on hardwood trees. **Crotal** made a brown dye. [1991?] MACLEAN *Story of Canoe Lake, CB* 31 The moss was called crotal and they made a beautiful brown dye from it.
　[*EDD*, *OED3* (1778), *W3 Scot*; at *crottle*: *DPEIE, NOAD, DSL*]

*A loanword from Scottish Gaelic, see *crotal* "lichen" *GED*.

crowdie noun
a porridge of oatmeal and cream
　1899 GILLIS *Cape Breton Giant* 44 After the age of eight years until he arrived at maturity he always ate a bowl of a palatable mixture of cream and oatmeal, sometimes called crowdie, after each meal.1948 WALWORTH *CB Isle of Romance* 49 He ate good Scotch fare, topping off each meal with a bowl of crowdie (cream & oatmeal). 1990 LANGILLE *Giants: Angus McAskill and Anna Swan* 8 Some people said it was the marvelous climate of Cape Breton which had caused Angus to grow so tall; others said maybe it was the bowl of oatmeal and cream called *crowdie*, which he ate after every meal from the age of eight until maturity.
　[*FWCCD Scot.*, *EDD*, *OED3 Sc.* and *north. Eng.* (1668), *DSL*; at *crowdy W3 chiefly Scot*]

crumb noun
extra working time, either a shift or part of one
　2001 SMITH-PIOVESAN *Sculptures from Jagged Ore* 185 Words such as "crumbs" (staying behind after the shift to work a little overtime) ... are common. 2002 MUISE Email 26 Aug. "... crumb" – this means a small amount of overtime worked in the pit – not quite a full shift but a few extra hours – miners who do this are said to be "crumbing" (or more likely "crummin").

cut noun, usually plural; also **cutting**
a fiddle bowing technique where a single
note is replaced by two or three shorter
ones

1981 MACGILLIVRAY *CB Fiddler* 5 ...
the right hand supplies the all-important
"cuts" (called "doodles" or "gearraid-
hean"). These consist of rapid and suc-
cessive notes of the same pitch, which
are usually employed at the discretion of
the player in an attempt to add a degree
of complexity to simpler aspects of the
melody line. 1981 *CB's Magazine* 29,
38 This is really a typical part of Cape
Breton playing. Instead of say, holding a
long note, you'd break that up into 2 or
3 notes. I suppose that's where the word
"cutting" sort of comes from – instead of
a sustained single note, you'd break that
note up into a quick series of three. 1984
Beaton Institute Tape 2133 ... we call them
cuts [or] ... bow cuttings here, but over
in Scotland they call them a birl. 2006
GRAHAM *CB Fiddle* 63 Cuts are three
notes applied with bowing to mimic the
same sounding digital (finger) ornamen-
tation on the pipes. 2007 MACINNES
Buddy MacMaster 107 "Accents are also
produced by bowed triplets, called 'cuts'
or 'cuttings' ..."

cut transitive verb; also **undercut**; often in
the phrase **cut, shoot, load**; compare **mining, undercutter, shoot**
to make (a narrow channel) along the side
or bottom of the coal being excavated (the
coal face) to allow space for the coal to
break after the explosive (the shot) is fired

1889 CANADA *Report ... Labor and Capital in Canada: Evidence, NS* 414 Q. How do
they learn to become coal cutters? A. They
generally go in it [with] a man who knows
how to cut coal. 1977 Beaton Institute
Tape 993 You had to cut the coal. You had
to bore the coal. You had to shoot the coal
down and you had to load the coal into
boxes. 1984 Beaton Institute Tape 2134

You and your partner went down and
you were cutting, shooting, and loading in
a room or a level. You'd set your machine
up and you'd cut your coal on the face.
1986 *CB's Magazine* 42, 17 At that time that
I came to Cape Breton, they had already
a number of what we call "coal cutters,"
which were really like big chain saws.
And these undercut the longwall face.
2007 MACKENZIE *CB Coal Mine Disasters*
151 It was "cut, shoot and load" for those
working room and pillar. This meant that
the men working the room had to "cut"
the wall face with a radial machine. This
put a six-inch-wide, six-foot-deep cut into
the coal midway between the pavement
and roof of the seam.

[at *undercut OED3* (1883), *W3, NOAD,
MWCD*]

cut boat noun; compare **fish trap**
an open boat used with a fish trap where
fishers raise, or cut, the trap net to force
the fish into one section of the net

1977 *CB's Magazine* 17, 5 ... all but one
man leave and get into the cut boat – and
they are going to cut all this twine [net]
right around ... They keep cutting as far as
they can get twine, pulling it – driving the
fish to the corner where the collecting boat
is. 1993 Beaton Institute Tape 3229 B When
you had the door hauled up – it just takes
any chance away from the fish getting
out – then all the men would switch to the
cut boat. You would keep on the turn so
that the fish would have to move ahead
of you. You would finally get them in one
section – the far end of the trap – then
there was a big boat would come and take
our fish from us.

D

dairy noun
a convenience store, open 7 to 11

1972 *CB's Magazine* 1, 15 [Advertisement] GEORGE'S DAIRY Baddeck "Famous for nothing." 1978 *CB's Magazine* 23, 34 [Advertisement] Town Dairy "The Biggest Little Store in Town!" Groceries Confectionaries Ice Ice Cream ... Louisbourg. 2002 MUISE Email 2 Apr. And speaking of stores – corner or convenience stores are called "dairies" here. I think it comes from an old bylaw dealing with Sunday closings which exempted dairies since the farmers still had to milk on Sunday, so these stores were set up to sell milk and over time other products were introduced. 2007 SHERRINGTON Email 4 Sept. On the west side of the island, we call corner stores either corner stores (mostly) or convenience stores (less often) but never dairies – the only time I hear that usage is on CBC, referring to a store in the Sydney area. 2007b BARBER *Only in Canada* 131 **dairy** (*Cape Breton*) a convenience store. 2008–9 *Bell-Aliant: Cape Breton Phone Book*, [Yellow Pages for convenience store] Al's Dairy (Dominion), Madonna's Dairy (Sydney), Pierce Street Dairy (North Sydney), Poulettes [*sic*] Dairy (Eskasoni), Station Dairy (Sydney Mines), Terry's McKeen Street Dairy (Glace Bay), William Street Dairy (North Sydney), Young's Dairy (Eskasoni). Survey I Inf. 5 [Dairy is] not used any more on the west side, gone for twenty years.

[*COD Cdn* (*Cape Breton*), *SOED NZ* (M[iddle] E[nglish]); compare *OED3* "Sometimes in towns the name is assumed by a shop in which milk, cream, etc. are sold" (*c*1290)]

*This meaning is widely known in Cape Breton County, but less so in the other three counties. *SOED* (the *Shorter Oxford English Dictionary*, as one of the dictionaries occasionally consulted) is cited here as it lists New Zealand as another region where this meaning occurs. This is of interest to Cape Breton historians because both islands were settled during the same period

and a large number of Cape Bretoners immigrated to New Zealand in the mid-1800s.

darg: see **wee darg**

datal noun, but mainly used attributively; in the phrases such as **datal man**, **pay**, **rate** a day's work at a fixed rate
    1905–20 Beaton Institute MG 12 93, 12 $1.00 per day for datal. 1920 Beaton Institute MG 12 46 A9 n.p. Schedule of Datal Rates for the Different classification of Labor as of 1st July, 1918. 1926 DUNCAN *Royal Commission ... Coal Mines of NS 1925* 24 The wage rates – both datal and contract – payable in the various pits are provided for in a schedule of rates for each colliery. 1979 FRANK "CB Coal Miners, 1917–1926" 239 ... transferring pit drivers from tonnage to datal rates ... 1989 EARLE *Workers and the State* 118 In the 1937 contract there was a six percent increase for the contract miners and most of the daily paid (datal) men, leaving wages still below 1931 rates. 1999a MIGLIORE and DIPIERRO eds. *Italian Lives* 77 A "day's pay" or "datal" man received, instead, a fixed rate for the shift, regardless of his productivity.
    [at *daytal EDD*; at *day-tale OED3* Chiefly *attrib.* (1560); at *daytale W3 dial Eng*]

Davis Day noun
a memorial day and miners' holiday recalling the death of William Davis (11 June 1925) and the coal miners who died as a result of mining accidents
    1973 *CB's Magazine* 3, 4 The violence broke out at Waterford. A fellow named Davis was shot. For years we had a holiday, Davis Day, June 11th. He was shot when rioting started after pickets tried to stop officials from running the plant. 1992 *CB's Magazine* 60, 45 June 11th is Davis Day/Miners Memorial Day. Besides bringing to mind all miners who have died in the mines, Davis Day recalls the

death of William Davis, shot during the 1925 coal miners' strike. [1996] UNITED MINE WORKERS OF AMERICA DISTRICT 26 "Davis Day" District 26 records show that Davis Day was observed until 1938 when it was renamed District Memorial Day ... At the District 26 Convention held in 1974, a resolution was passed to once again use the name Davis Day; it shall remain unchanged. 2003 SAINT AGNES ELEMENTARY SCHOOL *Coal Miners' Stories* 52 ... June 11th has been known in Cape Breton as Davis Day. It is observed as a holiday in the mining towns and no mine has ever produced coal on that date.

Day of Questioning: see **Question Day, Ceist**

deep noun, often plural; compare **men of the deeps, slope, headway**
a tunnel that follows the downward slope of the coal seam and from which other tunnels lead, used chiefly for travel, haulage, or ventilation
1893 Anon. *Canadian Mining & Mechanical Review* 12 (1), 9 Last year Mr. Charles Archibald extended his deep 300 yards, and drove a new level east of the deep [in the Gowrie Mine]. 1901 Anon. *The Canadian Mining Review* 20 (1), 17 Sydney Coal Co. ... As the workings go to the deep the coal improves, the seam now averaging 4 ft. 6 inches. 1918 Beaton Institute MG 12 46 A9 n.p. Deep Boss $3.58 [per day]. 1925 MCCAWLEY *Standing the Gaff* 17 If the pumps are not manned, the water will fill up the deeps ... 1999a MIGLIORE and DIPIERRO eds. *Italian Lives* 330 By the early 1920s, that mine's main tunnel ("deep") ran about two and a half kilometres towards the ocean's edge on the near side of Glace Bay, at Bridgeport. 1999 CALABRESE *Cape Bretoner* 7 (4), 36 The deep is the passage into the mine. Some mines went straight down a vertical shaft

first, but they always ended up in a deep because a seam of coal lies at an angle, not flat. 1999 MELLOR *Company Store* 89 Long "trips" of coal boxes were pulled by the ponies ... before hooking them onto the main deep haulage system to be brought to the surface. 2004 MACKENZIE *Bloody CB Coal* 133 ... the deep being the sloped tunnel that follows the coal seam down, and which keeps going well below the spot where the level is started.
[Compare: "The lower portion of a vein; used in the phrase **to the deep**, i.e. downward upon the vein" *OED3 Cornish Mining* (1881), and "The part of the mine where coal or ironstone strikes below the general level or the work" *EDD*]

deputy noun; also **deputy inspector, (mine) examiner**
an official who inspects the mine for excessive gas, poor ventilation, and other dangers
1936 *NS Miner* 271, 2 A poor horse hooked to a box, and the examiner passed it – believe it or not. He never examined the place, that is why he did not see it. 1978 *CB's Magazine* 21, 8 Frank Burke, a deputy, was called and sworn. He stated that his section extended from Nos. 2 to 6 west side of the colliery. He visited the mine on the morning of the explosion and found gas in several cross cuts and reported the conditions in his regular report book. He considered the mine in its usually safe condition. 1983 SHEDDEN et al. *Mining Photographs* 270 **Examiner or inspector** – An official who patrols a mine section to examine the workings for accumulation of gas and other hazards. 1983 MELLOR *Company Store* 87–8 Before miners were allowed to enter a section of the mine at the commencement of a shift, a deputy (often known as a mine examiner) was responsible for testing for the presence of gas ... 1990 [MACNEIL] *History of Sydney*

Mines 66 The next shift went down early, and without waiting to see the deputy, walked into the face with their naked lights and fired the gas. 2007 MACKEN-ZIE *CB Coal Mine Disasters* 72 The deputies' job was to travel the coal mine and check it out for gas, water, roof collapses, or anything else out of order.
[*EDD* (1843), *OED3*, *W3*]

Dhia [yiə] noun, used as an interjection; also spelled **Dhe'a**
God
1970 MACPHAIL *Loch Bras d'Or* 6 He took the hot mug in his hands as he raised his agonized eyes to her he faltered, "Dhe'a! Dhe'a! What happened?" 1996 *CB's Magazine* 70, 52 Dhia, Dhia, he took one look at me, he threw the (pitch) fork and it pretty near went in me! 2000 CHISHOLM comp. *As True as I'm Sittin' Here* 5 "Dhia, dhia," the old fellow said. "What an awful choice I have. Will I go to hell by way of St. Peters or to heaven by way of Antigonish?"

*A loanword from Scottish Gaelic, see *Dia / dia* "deity, God / god" *GED*.

dileag ['ʃɪlɪk, 'ʃilɛk] noun; also spelled **gillick, jillick, deleag**
a small drink of liquor; liquor, moonshine
1977 Beaton Institute Tape 900 ... the first thing that you got when you walked in the door was a dileag. Now the dileag would be a little drink ... and that was homemade, homemade booze ... The man of the house was the one who gave the dileag. 1982 Beaton Institute Tape 2069 We always had something to eat and a little shot of dileag too. 2001 *Am Bràigh* 9 Summer 6 Dileag, you may recognize is the word for a little drop and is sometimes used for a wee drink or dram. Survey I Inf. 2 Dileag from Gaelic means a drink of booze. 2011 DOYLE *CB Facts and Folklore* 214 ... deleag (pronounced

"jillick"): a Highland Scots Gaelic word for any alcoholic beverage.
[at *gillock*: *DPEIE*, *EDD* (1857).

*A loanword from Scottish Gaelic, see *dileag* "a small drop, droplet" *GED*.

dip net noun; also spelled **dipnet**
a small-meshed fishing net with a long handle, used to scoop fish from the water
1899 CANADA *Sessional Papers of the Dominion of Canada: Vol. 9*, 358 In Cape Breton an instrument called a dip-net is used. It consists of a circular or oblong band of iron about 8 inches in diameter, and when oblong will have a depth of 12 inches by 8; at the back or bottom of this is attached a small net, made either of wire or twine, and fixed to a pole about 10 or 12 feet long for a handle; when an oyster is seen from the boat it is scooped into the dip-net. 1976 *CB's Magazine* 14, 8 Stephen Googoo has invented a new trap of steel and wire. No dipnet is used. The entire trap-box comes out of the river, dumping the gaspereaux. [1991?] MACLEAN *Story of Canoe Lake*, CB 56–7 There would be seven or eight of them each carrying a dip net [to catch capelin] over his shoulder. Pilot Survey Inf. 1 We used to use ... a dip net, usually for smelting. Pilot Survey Inf. 3 If you think the fish is going to get away, you get the dip net underneath, used more so around here for fishing gaspereaux in the channels. Survey II Inf. 2 [We] ... used the dip net to gather bait from the brooks.
[*DPEIE*, *COD*, *EDD*, *DAE* (1820), *W3*, *NOAD*, *MWCD*; at *dip-net*: *DNE* (*dip-net*), (*dipnet*), *OED3* (*dip-net*)]

dipper noun
a small saucepan used for cooking
1979 *CB's Magazine* 24, 34 I always had a dipper of that [cough medicine] on the back of the stove. 1998 *CB's Magazine* 73, 87 ... she poured the porridge in the

bowls, because I can't hang on to the dipper to do that, you see. 2007 ST. CLAIR Email 15 Mar. I have heard people say, "move the dipper with the potatoes to the back of the stove" as one cooked on a wood stove ... a sauce pan is indeed a use found here. Pilot Survey Inf. 3 Sure, we cooked in the dipper. Survey I Inf. 23 Take the dipper and boil some eggs.

[*DNE* (1976), *DPEIE* (1976), *COD Cdn* (esp. *Nfld* & *PEI*)]

*While the widespread meaning of a *dipper* is a ladle, the sense of a small cooking pot was known or used by half of the respondents to Survey I.

dirt noun
typically, cold, windy weather with either snow or rain

2008 *DCBE* Tape CURRIE 17–18 We're going to get some dirty weather; we're going to get some dirt. Pilot Survey Inf. 5 There's dirt in the air; there's dirt coming. Survey I Inf. 22 There's dirt coming; I can feel it in my bones. Survey II Inf. 6 [Dirt indicates] rain or snow – often windy and rainy, anything falling. Survey II Inf. 8 Dirt could be snow or rain – anything that is wet and cold.

[*DPEIE, EDD, OED3 dial.* (1836), *W3*]

*The adjective *dirty* referring to weather, which the *OED3* records as early as 1660, is widespread.

dit adjective
dressed elegantly

2008 MUISE Email 21 June The word "dit" comes up in certain areas to describe a well dressed or "big feeling" person. Survey I Inf. 7 Always used for women, "Isn't she dit!" Survey I Inf. 20 I would use dit only to those who frequently use this word.

door boat noun; compare **fish trap**

an open boat used by fishers with a fish trap to raise or lower the section of the net that functions as the entrance to the trap

1977 *CB's Magazine* 17, 3 Then they bring the ropes from the door around the bow and the stern so they can haul the door bar up on the inside of the trap. You get that up and tie it in the door boat. Then you're ready to purse your trap. 1993 Beaton Institute Tape 3229 B Then everybody would get into the door boat; there was six men ... Then, when there was fish in, you'd go to the door and you had ropes to haul them up.

Dosco miner: see **continuous miner**

double house noun; also spelled **double-house**; see **company house**
originally, a company-owned duplex, divided by a central wall and rented to mine or steel employees

1925 GOLD *Social Welfare* 7 (11), 221 Each house is of eight or nine rooms, divided by a thin wooden partition into two parts, and is called a "double" house. 1966 PEARSON *Town of Glace Bay* 35 Of the 1066 single [and] attached houses, some 980 are in double houses, the remainder being in various rows and blocks, frequently 100 to 140 years old. 1978 *Oran Inbhirnis* 26 Jan. 18 The construction of the houses was contracted out to an Amherst firm, Rhodes and Curry, and over the early years more than 84 double houses were built along with a row of single homes to accommodate the mining officials in town. All the houses were painted red, probably for economic reasons and the rows of uni-cloured houses frequently led to humourous confusion. 1992 ROBERTSON *Birds on a Rock* 154 Built as a duplex, or "double-house," as we called them, it was tight to one side of the property and allowed for a large garden.

[*W3*; compare *double house* with the meaning of a house with rooms on either side of a central entrance, rather than a duplex: *DARE* (1707), *DAE* (1707), *DA* (1707), *W3* (sense 1)]

double parlour noun; also **double trap**; compare **kitchen**, **parlour**
a lobster trap with three compartments, one baited (the kitchen) and the other two (the parlours) that trap the lobster after it leaves the kitchen
Survey II Inf. 1 A double trap has a kitchen in the middle and a prison on either end. Survey II Inf. 4 Double parlour may have a kitchen and two parlours beside it or the kitchen between two parlours – a four bow trap. Survey II Inf. 8 Wire traps have no bows and are described in lengths 36", 42", 48", a double parlour.

double sled noun; also **double sleigh**
a sled for hauling heavy loads, *double* indicating either two horses or two joined sleds
1975 *CB's Magazine* 10 Inside Front Cover ... the double sleds and the chains, it would make a road just like the floor here ... 1987 *CB's Magazine* 44, 63 And then we'd fix up that lumber [pit props] – double sleighs, you know – we'd haul it in to where the train was. Pilot Survey Inf. 3 This is one where there are two horses in the sleigh. Double horse, double sleigh, double wagon – fitted with a pole in the centre, a horse on either side. Pilot Survey Inf. 5 They used to use those for hauling long timber. Survey I Inf. 14 ... drawn by two horses. Survey I Inf. 22 Two sleds to haul wood out. Survey I Inf. 34 Two linked sections.
[*double sled*: DNE (with *sleigh* as a variant), *DPEIE* (with *sleigh* as a variant) (1895), *DARE* **chiefly NEng**; at *double sleigh*: DC Hist., DARE (1737)]

*The understanding of *double sled* varies. Roughly half the respondents to Survey I who knew this term indicated *double* designated

two horses, and the other half considered the *double* to be two joined sleds. The *DNE* and *DARE* define the term as two horses and two sleds while the *DPEIE* defines it as two horses and the *DC* as two sleds.

down home prepositional phrase
back home; to, or at, one's native community
1899 CANADA *Official Report of the Debates of the House of Commons* 231 Mr. TAYLOR. I might refer to a case down home that was called to my attention, in which a brother-in-law of mine sent a parcel prepaid, and which was returned. 1939 Beaton Institute MG 12 220, 18 She got sick about a week ago and decided to come down home until she got better. 1999a MIGLIORE and DIPIERRO eds. *Italian Lives* 173 Cape Breton is always down home. 2000 MACDONALD *CB Road* 29 ... "down home" belonged to his parents, to their time and their past, not to his ... 2007 MACINNES *Buddy MacMaster* 69 He did make occasional visits to Halifax where the resident Cape Breton population were interested in "down home" dances.
[*OED3* (1828), *DARE*]

down north prepositional phrase; compare **up south**
up north, northward, in northern Cape Breton; northern Cape Breton
1900 MORLEY *Down-North and up Along* 175–6 ... we had received such contradictory information concerning the resources for travellers "down north" that we determined to take with us the necessaries of life. 1903 VERNON *CB Canada* 296 To the old resident at the Sydneys or at Baddeck, "down north" is a well-known expression used to denote the northern part of Victoria County ... 1983 *CB's Magazine* 35 Inside Front Cover Then there was an old Gillis, down north of Inverness here. 2001 DORNADIC *Cape Bretoner* 9 (2), 63 ... the True Cape Bretoner

has managed to keep his identity in tact. He still goes *down* north instead of *up* like the rest of the world ...

DNE, *DC*, *COD*, and *NCD* define *down north* as "Northward along the coast of Newfoundland and Labrador" (*DNE*), and *DC* and *NCD* indicate that the phrase is also used in Northern Canada. *DARE* has some interesting explanations for the phrase's meaning in the United States such as the direction of the wind or water currents, movement to or from a main centre, and others. Several of the *DCBE* citations indicate that sailing "down wind" is the source for *down north*.

down the road prepositional phrase; often with the verb **go**
away from Cape Breton (to find work)
   1970 *Goin' Down the Road* www.imdb.com/title/tt0065788/ Story of desolation as two friends travel from Nova Scotia to Toronto in hope of finding a better life. 1994 O'NEIL *Explore CB* 99 And the descendants of the workers have long since left the place, "gone down" the road to better days. 2000 BARRATT *August Prelude* 12 ... they seemed like bland, unremarkable young men, two of the thousands in Cape Breton who would have to "go down the road," somewhere out west, in search of work. 2007 ST. CLAIR and LEVERT *Nancy's Wedding Feast* 14 *For generations, young people went "down the road" to work as housemaids and cooks and gardeners or in factories.* 2007 *DCBE* Tape SHERRINGTON 4 Well going down the road ... meaning to leave to find work; that is fairly common.

draegerman noun; also spelled **dragerman**
see quotation at 1988
   1978 *CB's Magazine* 21, 4 The draegermen had canaries in cages and had their masks on – and they wouldn't go down where I came up through,

through the smoke. 1982 *CB's Magazine* 31, 47 Throughout this article, the words "dragerman" and "mine rescue team" are used interchangeably. They mean the same thing, although drager is the older term. It comes from Draeger, which is the name of a German company that still makes mine rescue breathing and testing apparatus. 1988 SHEDDEN et al. *Mining Photographs* 270 **Draegerman** – A mine workman, or official, engaged in mine rescue while wearing a self-contained breathing apparatus. 2001 MACNEIL *Cape Bretoner* 9 (2), 22 The draegermen gathered their / crew for the journey below / could some have survived such a / force? God only knows! 2004 MACKENZIE *Bloody CB Coal* 114 Wilfred saw action as a draegerman during the Springhill "bump" of 1958.
   [*DC Maritimes* (1918), *COD N Amer.*, *NCD Maritimes*, *GCD Cdn.*, especially in the Maritimes, *OED3 N. Amer.* (1918), *W3*]

drag noun; also **tail drag**
a sled used year-round to haul heavy loads, a stoneboat; also a sled that drags the load behind it
   1968 ROWE "Linguistic Study of Lake Ainslie Area" 41 The term stone boat (21.8) is not common. After a description, ten informants said that I was describing a drag. 1971 JACKSON *CB and Jackson Kith and Kin* 26 Oxen ... hauled sleds in winter and contrivances known as drags in summer. The latter consisted of two long spruce poles, one end of each fastened to the ox's yoke, and the other dragging on the ground, the ends held apart by a box fastened to them in which was carried oats, potatoes, or whatever constituted the load. 1988 PRINGLE *Look to the Harbour* 157 The tail drag meant that the hind bob was unchained and the load was dragged behind the front bob and so the horse didn't have to *hold back* nearly so much on the steep hills or mountains. 1993

FARRELL *History of River Denys* 240 She
went up to the barn and harnessed the
horse to the stone-boat, or drag, as it was
called, and drove it to the shore for Peter.

[*DPEIE* (at *drag sled*), *NCD*, *GCD*, *OED3*
(1576), *DARE* **formerly chiefly eNEng,
now widespread**, *DAE*, *W3 chiefly New
Eng*, *MWCD*]

draw chucks verb phrase; also spelled
draw chocks; compare **chuck, chuck
drawer**
to remove the hardwood blocks (chuck
blocks supporting the roof) from the
area in a mine where the coal has been
removed (the gob) to reuse the blocks and
allow the roof to collapse

1939 MCARTHUR commissioner
"Inquiry into Conditions at Florence Colliery" 3 Then the second row of chocks
will be drawn out ... 1972 Beaton Institute
Tape 537 It was a different type of work
called drawing chucks. 1999a MIGLIORE
and DIPIERRO eds. *Italian Lives* 65 I went
on longwall to draw chucks for quite
awhile (that is, removing temporary supports, to allow the roof to cave in where
coal has been excavated, after the "longwall" system replaced "room-and-pillar"
mining). 2004 MACKENZIE *Bloody CB
Coal* 37 It wasn't long, however, before Joe
caught on and was permitted to "draw,"
or take down, the chucks himself.

[*EDD* n.d.]

draw the pillar: see **rob the pillar**

dress transitive verb; in the phrase **dress
a bed**
to make (a bed)

Pilot Survey Inf. 2 I've never used it
[dress], but I have heard it. Survey I Inf. 7
Grandmother would use "dress the bed"
and also use "dress clothes" for the sheets.
Survey I Inf. 23 [To dress a bed means]
just make the bed.

[*DNE* (1888), *DPEIE*, *DARE*]

drift ice noun; also spelled **drift-ice**
large fragments of floating ice driven by
wind and currents

1829 HALIBURTON *Historical and
Statistical Account of N-S* vol. 2, 245–6 The
ice seldom breaks up in the harbour of
Sydney, until after the middle of April,
and from that time to the middle of June,
the coast is subject to the visitations of the
drift ice from the Gulf of St. Lawrence, a
great impediment both to navigation and
vegetation. 1869 BROWN *History of the
Island of CB* 201 ... the south coast of Cape
Breton was blocked up by drift-ice, and
that it was impossible to effect a landing
any where near Louisbourg. 1914 Beaton
Institute MG 12 93, 191 Drift ice Clear of
the Harbour May 18/14. 1958 DOUCETTE
Notes of Ingonish 86 Now that the drift ice
has disappeared the fishermen are busy
setting their lobster traps and getting
other gear ready. 2008 MORGAN *Story of
CB Island Book One* 67 In May, when the
drift ice was likely just out of the harbour,
a permanent settlement was established
on the peninsula on the south side of the
harbour, to be called "Sydney" in honour
of Lord Sydney, the home secretary. 2011
DOYLE *CB Facts and Folklore* 91 1832 was
an unusually cold year in Cape Breton.
Drift ice clogged the shoreline until late
July and disrupted the fishery.

[*DPEIE*, *COD*, *COED*, *W3*, *NOAD*; at
drift-ice: *DNE*, *DC*, *NCD Atlantic Canada*,
GCD Cdn., *OED3* (1578)]

drive noun
a strong beat and liveliness in musical
performance

1986 *CB's Magazine* 43, 31 Like, we'll
single out Mary MacDonald. Her music
excited me. It is Gaelic expression – she
had a terrific lift, and a terrific drive to her
music. 1997 MACINNES *Journey in Celtic
Music* 96 Like Joe Hughie MacIntyre, these
pipers also had a distinct sound in music
and, like Joe Hughie, the drive in their

strathspeys and reels were always suited to dancing. 2006 GRAHAM *CB Fiddle* 75 *Good* for sure when the piano players add more "drive"/"life" to a performance but *bad* if the piano player is too dominant and takes away from the focus of the fiddler and his/her performance.

[*W3*; compare *drive* verb "To play music energetically or with strong rhythm" *OED3 colloq.* (1952)]

drive transitive verb; often in the phrases **drive'er, drive her**
to perform (an activity) with energy and enthusiasm, especially work, music, and dancing
1975 *CB's Magazine* 10, 2 They'd step [dance] for a while standing one opposite the other ... and then they'd stop again and drive her again at stepping. 1987 FRANK *Canadian Labour History* 142 The miners are noted for doing things with a vim ... 'They drive her' as the saying goes. 1990 Beaton Institute Tape 3008 So she got up and she tuned and she played ... When she got to the bass part of that ... driving her. 1997 MACINNES *Journey in Celtic Music* 84 ... Kyle ventured into a beautiful slow air despite the likely temptation to open with spirited strathspeys and reels to please the general audience who had gathered in Iona that day and who were encouraging the young performers to "drive'er."

[*NCD, OED3 fig.* (1835), *DAE* (1835), *W3, MWCD*]

droke noun; also spelled **drogue**; compare **forerunner, taibhs**
an omen, heard or seen, that foretells a death
1991 CAPLAN ed. *CB Book of the Night* 131–2 And I don't know how long it was before he died, before this happened – it might have been three weeks – that he saw his own droke. He saw the light ... He said, "A light. A light gave me that fright.

I was coming home and there was a light ahead of me." He said, "It passed over me. It kept going." Now that's what you call a droke. 1997 CLARK *Night on Kelly's Mountain* 14 Roddie was the oldest of three children of Highland Scottish stock and he was a wealth of information on old Celtic Folklore, especially those stories of ghosts, spirits, drogues, etc.

dry fish noun; compare **green fish**
fish, usually cod, dried on flakes or beaches after being cleaned and salted
1816 in 1989 *CB's Magazine* 51, 60 A vessel with four hands in general kills about 400 Quintals of dry fish in the season. These are cured by the wife and children of the owner. 1852 GREAT BRITAIN COLONIAL OFFICE *Papers Relative to the Fisheries of British North America* 357 ... the custom-house returns from Arichat and Sydney in the island of Cape Breton show the exportation 41,328 quintals dry fish ... 1974 MACKEEN *Cruise CB* 109 **Fish & Brewis** Soak dry cod fish in water overnight. 1992 HORNSBY *Nineteenth-Century CB* 93 This valuable fishing establishment consisted of a two-storey residence, a three-storey dry fish store ...

[*DNE* ([1577–8]), *DC Maritimes, OED3* at *dry* adjective, *DARE* **AK**, *DAE*]

dry fishery noun; also **dry cod fishery**; compare **green fishery**
the commercial fishery where shore workers dry fish, usually cod, on flakes or beaches after cleaning and salting them
1968 CLARK *Acadia: Geography of Early NS* 267 As early as the middle of the sixteenth century the "dry" fishery (chiefly shore-based with the fish cured under the sun, with less salt, on beaches and platforms) was of major importance, and the beaches and coves of Newfoundland, the Gulf, and Cape Breton were in great demand for preparing the higher quality

product. 1984 BALCOM *Cod Fishery of Isle Royale* 12 ... the dry fishery, at least in its North American context, referred to a technique by which the fish were first salted and then dried. 1996 PRINS *Accommodation, and Cultural Survival* 56 In addition to 4,000 green cod fishermen, some 2,500 men worked in the "dry" cod fisheries, drying the cod on shore stages before shipping it to Europe (N. Denys, 258–70). 2001 JOHNSTON *French Colonial Louisbourg* 97 Île Royale was in the "dry" not the "wet" fishery, so large stretches of shoreline were needed to land, process and store the cod before it could be exported.
[*DC Nfld* (1960)]

dubh [du] adjective; also spelled **Dhu, dhubh**
black or dark, often used in nicknames
1897 *MacTalla* 24 Sept. 2 ... among all the activities that were there, it was the "cailleach-dubh" (black old lady), at which they were throwing darts ... 1948 MACNEIL *Highland Heart* 23 Take for instance the sad case of Little Rory Donald Dhu. 1989 *CB's Magazine* 50, 102 Visit displays of early architecture, including the only known replica of a "Taigh Dubh" (Black House) in North America. 1992 MACLEAN *State of Mind* 57 Jimmy "Dubh" (black or dark), as our subject was familiarly known in Cape Breton ... 1996 HAMILTON *Place Names of Atlantic Canada* 403 **Skir Dhu** (Victoria) On the Cabot Trail, north of Breton Cove. The name is a Gaelic descriptive for 'black rock.' 2000 SHAW and ORNSTEIN *Brìgh an Òrain: A Story in Every Song* 7 ... helping to run off a commercial batch of poit dhubh ["black pot," part of a still] (illegal whiskey) for a friend ... 2011 DOYLE *CB Facts and Folklore* 102 *Marag dubh* is a black pudding.

*A loanword from Scottish Gaelic, see *dubh* "black, inky, profound" *GED*.

duff noun
small pieces of coal and coal dust
1897 ARCHIBALD *The Canadian Mining Review* 16 (10), 292 To utilize the unsaleable [*sic*] duff was what induced me to start the first, and I think the only patent fuel plant, now in the Dominion of Canada. 1934 *NS Miner* 4 (167), 4 The miners working in rooms or narrow works are compelled to load or clear away all the duff or fine coal before the place is considered safe to shoot. 1984 Beaton Institute Tape 2139 ... in the morning when the duff was getting loaded you couldn't see your buddy working along side of you – the dust was that thick. 1990 PEACH *Memories of a CB Childhood* 104 At the old wash plant, a mile from home, lay thousands and thousands of tons of "duff," the washings from coal brought there thirty years earlier. 2000 MACKENZIE *Cape Bretoner* 7 (6), 24–5 Adding to the clutter was a good two feet of mining duff all the way up the coal face where the pans had to be set up again. 2004 MACKENZIE *Bloody CB Coal* 29 Bobby is alive today only because there was some "duff" – just a few deep inches of fine coal cuttings left by the mining machine that undercut the wall face – under Bobby's head.
[*FWCCD, NCD, EDD* (1849), *OED3, W3, NOAD Mining, MWCD*]

duff transitive and intransitive verb; often in the phrase **duff out**
to remove (the dust and small particles of coal) near the coal face
1939 MCARTHUR commissioner "Inquiry into Conditions at Florence Colliery" 45 A. I was taken away duffin' for a while ... Q. You went duffing before you went packing? 1981 *Highlander* 22 Apr. 8 It was seven fifteen a.m. with his gob loaded, and his section duffed out, Rocky yells for the shotfire. 1984 Beaton Institute Tape 2139 ... you'd go down and

go to your place, and you'd first duff your section out ... that means cleaning out the mining at the bottom of the coal. 1990 [MACNEIL] *History of Sydney Mines* 107 1 – Duffing shovel ...

duine ['dunyə] noun; often used in the plural form **daoine**, especially in **daoine beaga**, the little men or people
man, person
1970 MACPHAIL *Loch Bras d'Or* 40 Oh Duine! Duine! (Man o Man) It done me goot to see Danny Ross piled in the corner. 1978 CAMPBELL *Highland Community on the Bras d'Or* 72 The belief in fairies, or the "Daoine Beaga," [Little Men], for instance, didn't infringe upon or desecrate in any way their religious beliefs ... 1981 MACGILLIVRAY *CB Fiddler* 17 Belief in the "daoine beaga" or "little men" was common among pioneer Cape Bretoners. 2006 STANLEY-BLACK-WELL *Tokens of Grace* 30 The balance of the Ceist, however, was given over to discussion of the "Question" proposed by one of Na Daoine (the people), noted "old Christian inquirers."

*A loanword from Scottish Gaelic, see *duine* "anyone, man, man (=husband), mankind" *GED*.

dummy rock noun; also **dummy stone**, **sinker (rock)**, **crazy rock**
a stone placed in a wooden lobster trap as temporary ballast until the trap becomes waterlogged enough to sit on the ocean floor
Survey II Inf. 2 Wooden traps have dummy rocks, crazy rocks, loose ballast to sink the traps early in the season before they are waterlogged. Survey II Inf. 4 The sinkers or dummy stones give extra ballast. Survey II Inf. 8 Sinker rocks are used in the Big Bras d'Or area – normally used at the beginning of the season ... Also called dummy rocks.

dump cart noun
a sturdy cart with a short box that tilts to empty its load, typically coal
1974 CALDER *All Aboard* 11 ... high wheeled dump cart to carry coal from a schooner. 1978 *CB's Magazine* 20 Inside Front Cover ... I used to make a lot of boxes for dump carts and you needed boards about 12 inches wide for that, for the sides of the dump cart boxes. 1981 *CB's Magazine* 30, 27 ... the horse and coal wagon, the dump cart they called it ... 2008 *DCBE* Tape CURRIE 12 I remember when they were hauling bootleg coal they had dump carts ... they probably had them on farms and things. A dump cart was a fairly short cart with sides and a tailgate you could take off, and you could dump it just like a dump truck.
[*DPEIE*, *OED3* (1868), *DAE* (1868), *DA* (1868); at *dumpcart FWCCD*, *W3*]

E

eight hand reel noun; also **eight(s)**, **huit**
a reel with four couples of dancers, an eightsome
1921 MURRAY *History of the Presbyterian Church in CB* 264 These frolics were frequently followed by a forenight of dancing, four and eight hand, Scotch reels, to the music of the fiddle or the bagpipe. 1975 *CB's Magazine* 10, 2 And the other one – they used to call them in French Une Huit – An Eight –something similar to the square sets they dance today ... And the ones that could dance those Eights – they'd get almost the best there – four couples. 1987 WATSON and ROBERTSON *Oral Tradition ... CB Gaels* 28 The eight hand reel was very fashionable too. 1988 MACGILLIVRAY and MACGILLIVRAY *CB Ceilidh* 24 He [Frank Rhodes] discusses The Scotch Four (four-handed reel), the eight hand reel, and solo stepdances such

as the *Flowers of Edinburgh* ... 1989 *CB's Magazine* 51, 43 It might have been, in Cheticamp, the first picnics might have been the eights – "Le Reel à Huit."

[Compare *eightsome EDD, OED3* Now chiefly *Sc. (c*1400)]

endless haulage noun; compare **bull wheel**
a hauling system in a mine consisting of a long steel cable joined to form a loop, driven by a large drum (the bull wheel), and used to pull coal boxes, etc.

1894 BLAKEMORE *The Canadian Mining Review* 13 (8), 151 The third system, "Endless Haulage," succeeds just where the other two fail, distance presents no difficulty ... so far as practical working is concerned it is as easy to haul 1000 tons of coal per day along a road of 5 miles by this system ... 1969 Beaton Institute Tape 160 I was down, must be ten, twelve years now, when they put the new belt line in, instead of the endless haulage. 2004 MACKENZIE *Bloody CB Coal* 94 Cyril lost his toes in a "bullwheel," a spoked steel wheel about three feet in diameter, part of what is called an "endless haulage." 2007 MACKENZIE *CB Coal Mine Disasters* 105 The haulage system in No.11 level was what is called an "endless haulage." This is the same idea as a pulley clothesline, only hundreds of times larger.

*The adjective *endless* is found in several dictionaries, but not the compound *endless haulage*.

engagé noun
a fisher contracted by the French government to spend three years in French colonial North America

1869 BROWN *History of Island of CB* 173 To prevent the fishermen who came out every spring from returning to France, an ordonnance was promulgated, which compelled the master of every ship going to America to take out a certain number of men ... bound to remain there for a term of three years. These men, who were called 'Engagés,' generally remained in the colony after their term of service had expired. 1893–5 EDWARDS *Collections of the NS Historical Society* 9, 147 ... the measure which had most effect in augmenting the number of residents was one which legally ordained that every vessel which sailed from France for the island should carry a certain number of men known as "*engagés*," who had agreed to remain there at least three years. 1903 VERNON *CB Canada* 36 Most of the men engaged in the fisheries were what was known as "engagés" ... who were bound to remain there for at least three years.

*Compare this definition for *engagé* as a fisher with several Canadian dictionaries (*DC, COD, GCD*) "a worker hired by a trader, explorer, or fur company for inland service" and with the American dictionaries *DAE* and *DAE* that have "canoeman or boatman, voyageur."

Escaouette [ɛskæ'wɛt] noun; also **L'Escaouette**; compare **Chandeleur**
originally, a lively dance and song performed in the homes of those contributing food for the celebration of Chandeleur (the feast of Candlemas); now, the name of a summer festival held at Chéticamp

1986 CHIASSON and LE BLANC trans. *History and Acadian Traditions of Chéticamp* 191 At these homes [of those providing food for the Chandeleur] the group was invited to enter and dance the Escaouette dance. One behind the other and hands on the shoulders of one another, everyone danced in a circle around the leader while jumping with both feet at the same time. The leader, in the middle, hitting the floor with his cane in time to the music, sang: **L'Escaouette**. 1975 *CB's Magazine* 10, 3 And you had a dance that they called L'Escaouette – the leader up front with his cane and you were dancing in a circle going around in the kitchen ... and when it came to the chorus of the song, then you'd start stepping away. 1991 *Inverness Oran* 24 July 31 Parades, music, arts and crafts display and a deep sea fishing contest are just a few activities planned for "Le Festival de L'Escaouette 1991" to be held during the first weekend of August in Chéticamp, Inverness County. 1999 DOUCET *Notes from Exile* 23 The leader danced with a beribboned cane at each house and sang an old song called "L'Escaouette," the words of which came from both the Mi'kmaq language and the exile. When the song was over, the leader asked for contributions for the party. It was a rare house that did not donate a pie, a loaf of bread, something to fill the Chandeleur tables.

*A loanword from French, see *escaouette* "Danse exécutée par les quêteurs de la Chandeleur. *La danse de l'escouette*" DFA *RÉGION* et *VIEUX*.

escape hatch noun
an opening in a lobster or crab trap to release undersized lobsters and crabs
1993 Beaton Institute Tape 3229 B And there's something new that's come out this year. You have to put escape hatches in ... and that's quite good too. Survey II Inf. 1 The escape hatch on metal traps is to let the little lobster out. Survey II Inf. 3 The escape hatch is on the metal lobster traps and round holes on traps for rock crab. Survey II Inf. 4 The escape hatch is one and a half inches high and five inches long and could be plastic or wooden, or could be two-inch plastic rings and required to be a certain distance from the bottom of the trap.
[at *escape ring DPEIE* (with *escape hatch* as a variant) (1985)]

evening noun
the afternoon, typically before supper

1815 in 1991 *CB's Magazine* 56, 54 Around 3 or 4 o'clock in the evening they decided to head for the shore. 1972 STAEBLER *CB Harbour* 86 "You was too late," the fisherman said, "evening is after noon." 1983 *CB's Magazine* 34 Inside Front Cover And then you go out at noontime, about 11 o'clock. And then again in the evening, about 4 o'clock. Three purses a day. Pilot Survey Inf. 3 I think that would be quite common here anyway ... once past one o'clock, if we were to meet, "Good evening to you." Pilot Survey Inf. 5 Anything after dinner was evening to my grandmother. After you had your dinner at noon, that was evening time. Survey I Inf. 5 Afternoon is derived from the Gaelic *feasgar*, meaning 1:00 or 1:30, but it is dying out. People would say "See you in the evening," meaning from 2:30 to dark.
[*DNE, DPEIE, FWCCD Dial., EDD, OED3 dial.* and *U.S. local.* (1788), *DARE* **chiefly Sth, Sth Midl**, *DAE, W3 chiefly South & Midland, MWCD chiefly Southern & Midland*]

examiner: see **deputy**

eyestone noun; also spelled **Eyestone**
the tip of a conch shell, placed under the eyelid to remove foreign matter and believed to be alive and require feeding
1973 *CB's Magazine* 4, 23 We have now seen two Eyestones on Cape Breton ... They are the color of flesh and about the size of half a pea. And they are said to be the tip of a conch shell. The Eyestone is alive, and has to eat – and both men keep theirs in about an inch and a half of sugar ... When the first Highland Settlers came to Cape Breton, they brought the Eyestone with them. It was used extensively here, and passed along from father to son ... In the eye, the Eyestone would move round and round the eyeball, searching for the speck. When it came out it would have the speck, and the eye would be clear – and the

Eyestone would be returned to the sugar. "Years ago," said John A., "there was a man who wanted to say just how awful a certain woman was, so he said of her she was so mean she wouldn't feed the Eyestone." 1998 MACDONALD *Eyestone* 38–9 It looks like a tiny white pebble. "You've come to where the eyestone is," she says. It cannot travel but in the eye ... "Tell me what this is, Mrs. Corbett." ... "The very tip of a conch" ...

[*FWCCD, SSPB, OED3* at *eye-stone* (1828), *DARE*]

F

face: see **coal face, wall face**

faggot noun; also spelled **frigget**
a pile of salted, drying fish, typically cod, stacked to protect them from rain
1974 *CB's Magazine* 8, 6 If it look[ed] like rain you'd gather them [fish] up – friggets. That's what the old fellows used to call it anyway. A frigget of fish – when they'd have so many piled up, see? 1984 *CB's Magazine* 36, 68 They had flakes all over the beach, and faggots, barracks that came down over their pile of dry fish. 1992 *CB's Magazine* 59, 33 He'd bring the fish in, and he would cure them. And then he would put them in puncheon tubs ... then wash them out of the pickle – make them up in small (piles), what they called "faggots." 1993 Beaton Institute Tape 3229 A There's the things we covered them [dry haddock] in the night with – called faggots

[*DNE* (1663), *DC Nfld*, *COD Cdn (Nfld)*, *DAE* at *fagot*; compare "A 'bundle', collection (of things not forming any genuine unity) *OED3* (1489)]

fair adverb
exactly; completely; straight, directly

1980 *CB's Magazine* 25, 18 Fair 3 o'clock this woman came. 1981 *CB's Magazine* 28, 11 He had been drinking, and he laid fair across the rail, face down. 1983 *CB's Magazine* 34, 47 I cast it [the fishing line] fair across the stream ... 1984 *CB's Magazine* 36, 69 ... setting trawl gear fair off of the Bird Islands. 1989 *CB's Magazine* 52, 69 They saw the glow of it. Dead ahead. My father said, "Fair ahead. As fair as if there was a line on him drawing it to that light."

[exactly: *COD, COED, EDD, OED3* Now *rare* (c1225); completely: *COD, COED, OED3* Now chiefly *colloq.* and *regional* (a1325), *DARE, W3, MWCD*; straight, directly: *FWCCD, NCD, GCD, EDD, OED3* Chiefly *Sc.* and *Engl. regional (north.)* in later use. Now *rare* (1490), *W3*]

*See the *OED3* for a thorough analysis of these various senses, at *fair, adv.,* sections 7 and 8, and Sandra Clarke (2010, 119) for a discussion of *fair* meaning "even, straight" in Newfoundland English.

Fairy Hole noun; also **Fairy Holes**
a cave on the shore, the most famous being at Cape Dauphin, St. Anns Bay, where the deity Kluskap retired from the world
1867 PROVINCE OF NOVA SCOTIA *The Statutes of N-S* 119 District number twelve shall be included within the following limits, that is to say: Commencing at Cape Dolphin to include the settlers at Fairy Hole; thence by a line along the ridge of Kelly's Mountain ... 1960 TOWARD *Baddeck and CB Island* 12 ... you will see the Baddeck River emptying into the Bras d'Or Lakes ... If there are children with you, they should look for the "Fairy Hole," and if they find it they should place a coin under the rock, make a wish, and it is sure to come true. 1974 *CB's Magazine* 9, 31 The tale ["Gluskap's Journey"] also includes mention of Fairy Holes, caves well-known by fisherman

in St. Ann's Bay ... 1990 *CB's Magazine* 53, 20 Gluscap's home was at Fairy Holes. 1999 HAYNES *Hiking Trails of CB* 145 Long a popular walk for local residents, the path to the Fairy Hole is known as "the trail of the Little People" by the Mi'kmaq. The cave itself is reputed to be *Kukmijnawe'nuk*, or "the place of my grandmother," where Glooscap, the man-god, retired from the outside world.

Fat Archie noun, usually plural
a soft molasses cookie
   n.d. *4-H Heritage Leaders Resource Manual* 33 www.novascotia.ca/agri/documents/4h/manuals/RGheritage.pdf Soft molasses cookies were often referred to as Long Johns or Fat Archies (on Cape Breton Island). 1993 LEVERT *CB Pictorial Cookbook* 34 [recipe]. 2008 CREWE *Ava Comes Home* 193 "Now, there are date squares in this one and Fat Archies in this one." 2008 STEWART *Anita Stewart's Canada* 18 Fat Archies are puffy spice cookies (Kevin [MacLeod from Boular-derie Island] thinks of them as "biscuits") that are best "spread with butter while they're hot." 2009 CAMERON *MyTown* 22 Feb. 4 ... [the Dancing Goat Bakery and Café] offers assorted breads, "old fashioned cookies including Cape Breton 'Fat Archies' ..." Survey I Inf. 23 Keigan's Bakery wrote Fat Archies on the package. [They were] soft molasses cookies as opposed to molasses cookies that were hard like a ginger snap.

feis [feš] noun
a festival celebrating Gaelic language and culture held in various communities
   1993 *Inverness Oran* 18 Aug. 32 From August 18–22 the community of Christmas Island will host the third annual Feis an Eilein, a Gaelic Cultural Festival dedicated to the promotion of the Gaelic language and culture of Cape Breton. 1996 *CB Post* 29 July 26 In 1990, Jim

Watson, of the Gaelic Council of Nova Scotia, approached residents of the community of Christmas Island interested in promoting Gaelic language, music and culture. The result was the first feis (festival) held outside Scotland in August of that year. 1997 *CB Post* 6 Oct. 20 The fifth annual Feis Mhabu will be held Thanksgiving weekend, (Oct. 11–13) at the Mabou Renewal Centre. 1999 *CB's Magazine* 74, 60 Schedule of Summer Events ... Feis an Eilean. 2011 DOYLE *CB Facts and Folklore* 215 ... *feis*: Scottish Gaelic word for a community-based festival that encourages the preservation of language and culture with a program of education and social events for children and adults.
   [*W3*, *OED3* (1896)]

*A loanword from Scottish Gaelic, see *feis* "feast, festival" *GED*.

fencing verbal noun; often in **fencing of the table(s)**; compare **open-air communion**, **token**
a minister's sermon to potential communicants at an open-air communion service outlining the characteristics of those worthy and unworthy to receive communion; deterring those unworthy from receiving communion
   1942 DENNIS *CB Over* 227 "Fencing of the tables" followed the "action sermon." The fencing was simply a description of the character of such as were worthy, or were not worthy to approach the Lord's table and partake of His supper. 1983 STANLEY *Well-Watered Garden* 145 Following the practice of their Free Church counterparts in Scotland, the Cape Breton ministers exercised stiff fencing procedures ... 2006 STANLEY-BLACKWELL *Tokens of Grace* 73 The Ceist expositions on genuine "tokens" of grace, the examinations for admission, the "fencing of the tables" and the pre- and post-Communion

addresses cumulatively heightened this
anxiety.
　　[*EDD* (1891)]

feu follet noun
a fire that hovers on the water, will-o'-the-
wisp, ignus fatuus
　　1920 SMITH and WIARD *CB Tales* 37
Now you must know that the *feu follet* is
of all objects whatever in the world the
most mysterious ... It is more like a ball
of fire than any other mortal thing, now
large, now small, and always moving.
1980 BEATON "Sorcery Beliefs ... Cheticamp" 92 The "chaudières de feu" which
frightened the fishermen were commonly
called the feux-follets or "pots of fire".
1992 SAMSON et al. *Island of Ghosts* 31 ...
when suddenly a strange ball of fire, the
feu follet, appeared before him.
　　[*OED3* (1832)]

field bed noun; also **seid**
a makeshift bed placed on the floor
　　1976 PRINGLE *Pringle's Mountain* 58
If there were not enough beds, then beds
were made on the floor ('Field beds' they
were called). 1984 CUMMING et al. *Story
of Framboise* 113 Guests would sleep on
a **seid**, a bed made on the floor. 2006
STANLEY-BLACKWELL *Tokens of Grace*
27 The elderly visitors and couples slept
in beds, while the parlour floor was allocated to the young girls who improvised
with *seids* or "field beds."
　　[*OED3* (1567), *DARE* old-fash, *DAE*, *DA*]

*The variant *seid* is a loanword from Scottish Gaelic, "pallet" *GED*.

field ice noun
an expanse of flat, floating ice
　　1874 Anon. *The Canadian Monthly and
National Review* 5 (2), 98 ... Oceanward
[from the Gut of Canso] its approaches are
blocked with field-ice from the Gulf of St.
Lawrence for six or eight weeks each winter

and spring, during which time vessels cannot enter or leave the harbour. Survey II Inf.
2 ... a big area, level. Survey II Inf. 4 ... flat ice
that would cover a bay. Survey II Inf. 6 ... a
field of ice, [you] would not see any water.
　　[*DNE* (at *field-ice*) ([1766]), *DPEIE*, *DC*,
COD N Amer., *FWCCD*, *NCD Atlantic
Canada*, *OED3*, *DA*, *W3*]

fig of tobacco noun; also **fig**
chewing tobacco pressed into a small
rectangular bar, similar in appearance to
dried figs
　　1885 in 1978 PATTERSON *History of
Victoria County* 69 A canoe immediately
left the island shore, and returned with
the customer, who would perhaps require
a fig of tobacco. 1900 CANADA *Official
Report of the Debates of the House of Commons* 1505 Under the Foster tariff the
fisherman, when he went in for his plug
or fig of tobacco in the store in his district,
paid 5 cents for it, but the moment the
present government came in and they
increased the price, he had to pay 6 cents
for the same plug under the Fielding tariff. 1976 MACDONALD *Bread & Molasses*
43 MacDonald's Twist was his favourite.
It was about six inches long, a half-inch
wide, and a half-inch thick. Some of the
figs were a red colour, dry and not juicy.
The others were black and juicy. 1989
CB's Magazine 50, 100 Fig of tobacco –
what I chew today – [was] 10 cents. Now
I'm paying over 2 dollars for it. 2005
MACKENZIE *Neighbours are Watching* 22
"Figgy" [McLaren] raised tobacco and
sold it in the form of "figs" – little bars or
cakes – hence the name.
　　[*DC* (*a*1836), *SSPB*; at *fig*: *OED3* (1838),
DARE (1837–40), *DAE*, *DA* (1837–40), *W3*]

*The *DC*, *OED3*, *DARE*, and *DA* all cite the
Clockmaker by Nova Scotia's Thomas Haliburton as the earliest recorded attestation. Coal
miners would often chew tobacco in mine to
cut dust and to compensate for not smoking.

fish belly noun; often in the phrase **fish-belly (iron) rail**
an iron rail with a curved underside having the middle lower than its ends, like the shape of a fish's belly
    1848 PROVINCE OF NOVA SCOTIA *Journal and Votes of the House of Assembly* A14–88 ... they [cheaper rails] have invariably been replaced by solid T or fish-belly Rail. 1971 JACKSON *CB and Jackson Kith and Kin* 65 In 1832, work was begun on the piers there [at Sydney Mines], and, by 1834, a railway, about three miles in length, with "fish belly" iron rails brought from England, was built from the mine to the wharf. 1984 NEWTON *CB Book of Days* n.p. **August 4, 1832** The "S. S. Cape Breton" ... arrives at North Sydney with a load of pig iron, machinery and rolled rails of the "fish belly" type to replace the old rails of the tracks for the Sydney Mines train tracks.
    [*OED3* (1888); *W3* at *fish belly rail*]

*The *EDD* does not have *fish belly* as a headword but does record "fishbellied rails" in a citation at *fish*; its 1848 citation parallels that of *DCBE* for the earliest recorded evidence for this word.

fish flake: see **flake**

fish gad: see **gad**

fish stage, fishing stage: see **stage**

fishing station noun
a commercial fishing camp near the shore to accommodate fish workers, with facilities to land, process, and store fish
    1837 PROVINCE OF NOVA SCOTIA *Journal and Votes of the House of Assembly* A75–368 ... the most important Fishing Stations, are from Canso Point up through Chedabucto Bay, and the Gut of Canso northwards. 1869 BROWN *History of the Island of CB* 147 ... St. Anne's was situated

at no great distance from Niganiche, the two entrances of the Labrador Lakes, and the baie des Espagnols, all noted fishing stations. 1934 in 1986 *CB's Magazine* 43, 21 Many of the isolated fishing stations are in small coves or beaches below cliffs from 200 to 400 feet high. 1981 *CB's Magazine* 30, 14 He [Charles Robin] establishes a fishing station at Arichat, and at first takes some fishermen from there to work each season at The Point, Cheticamp Island. 1992 HORNSBY *Nineteenth-Century CB* 93 Typical of a medium-sized Channel Island fishing station was the property belonging to Thoume Moullin & Co. at Port Hawkesbury. This "valuable fishing establishment" consisted of a two-storey residence, a three-storey dry fish store, a two-storey dry goods store, a cooper shop, a one-and-a-half-storey cookhouse, a blacksmith's forge and stable, a 120-foot-long wharf, flakes covering an acre of land, and a shipyard. The whole establishment stood on six acres of enclosed pasture land. More typical of the smaller fishing premises was a property sold at River Bourgeois that comprised a three-and-a-half-storey store (divided into areas for storing dry fish and goods), an 80-foot-long wharf, and an acre of fish flakes.
    [*DC, OED3* at *station* (1637), *DAE*; compare "a harbour or sheltered place ..." *DNE*, and "a small sheltered cove ..." *COD*]

fish trap noun; also **trap**; compare **cut boat, door boat, keg, purse**
a large, box-shaped net, anchored and buoyed, with a net between the shore and trap to direct fish along the shore and in rivers into the trap where a crew raises the door net and purses the trap
    1892 CANADA *Sessional Papers of the Dominion of Canada: Vol. 9*, 11A–10 The squid fishery was fairly good at Englishtown Bay and Harbour and fishing vessels

were quickly baited, although no fish trap exists at that place to aid fishermen in procuring this valuable bait. 1977 *CB's Magazine* 17, 7 Two fish traps for the first two weeks, if things go right and you get the right kind of weather and wind, you could easily land 100,000 [of fish in a day]. 1983 *CB's Magazine* 43, 33 And today, you can't get a haddock. That's my idea: what you were catching and keeping, and then those smaller ones – millions and millions of them were chucked overboard and went to waste. Not a trap down there today. Not in North Bay. 1993 Beaton Institute Tape 3229 A They had fish traps they used to call them ... It was a big square room set out about a hundred yards from the shore and then they put a leader on and that run to the shore attached to a stone or a tree and when the fish hit that leader they'd swim into that big box. It used to hold a hundred thousand pounds. 1996 *CB's Magazine* 72, 58 "I'm going to grab that fish trap site from old man Burke. "

[*DAE, DA* (1813), *W3*; at *trap*: *DNE* (1863), *COD Cdn* (*Nfld*); at *trap net*: *OED3* (1865), *DAE, DA, W3*]

five-day communion: see **open-air communion**

flake noun, usually plural; also **fish flake**, **cod flake**; compare **make**
a long, raised wooden frame, covered with spaced boughs and used to dry salted fish, typically cod
    1858 in 1984 *CB's Magazine* 36, 24 The fish are cured on flakes, or high platforms, raised upon poles from the beach ... 1873 *North Sydney Herald* 10 Sept. n.p. ... all the wharf and store lumber is where the little flake used to be. 1960 TOWARD *Baddeck and CB Island* 10 Here [at Neils Harbour] the Basque fishermen dried their fish on flakes similar to those you will see today ... 1984 BALCOM *Cod Fishery of Isle Royale*

26 Flakes were long, narrow, drying platforms made of two parallel lines of short upright poles, joined by stringers at the top with closely spaced cross-pieces covered with conifer branches stripped of their vegetation. 1985 MACGILLIVRAY et al. *History of Fourchu* 15 The flakes were lattice-work platforms made of "flake-brush" which was the new growth of fir, approximately 1 1/2 to 1 3/4 inches at the base. Some flakes were built sturdier so that they could be walked on when tending to the fish. 1987 MANN *Memories of Harbour Point, Gabarus* 3 Across the road grandfather had a good-sized barn and a long fish-flake where he dried cod and haddock. 1992 HORNSBY *Nineteenth-Century CB* 9 A day or two later, providing the weather was fine, the fish were laid out, again flesh side up, on flakes (raised timber platforms) for the third drying process. 2002 DONOVAN *Acadiensis* 32 (1), 3 The work associated with fishing properties seemed endless ... preparing stages, erecting flakes ... Survey II Inf. 3 Put the fish on the flakes, and turn them every four hours and take them in a night for three to four days.

[*DNE* ([1578]), *DPEIE, DC Atlantic Provinces, EDD, OED3, DARE* **NEng**, *DAE, DA* (at *fish-flake*), *W3, ML*, and several general-purpose dictionaries]

*The word is widely known along the Atlantic coast and was especially important in the Cape Breton fishery.

flat noun
a flat-bottomed rowboat used in shallow water along the coast or in a harbour
    1980 Beaton Institute MG 12 224 B14 (a) Box 2, 11 Apr. n.p. ... my cousin from Gabarous John was looking for a small row boat (a flat) ... 1985 MACGILLIVRAY et al. *History of Fourchu* 15 ... the fish were transferred to small boats called "flats" and taken to the landwash or wharf

where the splitting table was set up. 1993
CB's Magazine 62, 41 ... then I swum out
and got the boat – the flat I was rowing
around into.

[*DNE* ([1774]), *DC Maritimes*, *EDD*]

*Compare *DARE* ([1696]) **chiefly Missip and
Ohio R Valleys, SE coast** and *DAE* (1724) that
designate the river, instead of the coast, as the
place of use; the *OED3* gives a general definition, "A broad, flat-bottomed boat."

flying axe handles, the noun, plural
diarrhea

2005 CREW *Relative Happiness* 282 Lexie
sniffed. "Tell him I had the flying axe handles and had to go home." "The what?"
"The runs ... the trots ... oh forget it."
Survey I Inf. 5 [*Flying axe handles* is] used
by people over 40.

[*DPEIE* (at *flying axehandles*), *DARE* (at
ax-handle) **Nth** (1965–70)]

flyting verbal noun
a satiric debate in song or poetry, often
composed in Gaelic

1953 DUNN *Highland Settler* 67 ... his
bantering tone suggests that he is willing to accept a retort; and this retort was
provided, in the traditional manner of
a medieval flyting, by Duncan MacLellan in a song ... 1985 *CB's Magazine* 38, 38
This tradition is called "flyting" – where
one bard will answer another ... And
it's very common in Gaelic poetry. 2000
SHAW and ORNSTEIN *Brìgh an Òrain:
A Story in Every Song* 14 Likewise, the
accompanying narrative could be essential for explaining the basis for flytings
(bardic contests) between local song
makers ...

[*OED3* Now *dial.* (1568), *MWCD*; compare this sense with other dictionaries that
define this as quarreling (*FWCCD Dial.*) or
scolding (*EDD*, *W3 archaic*)]

fog: see **baker's fog**

forerunner noun; compare **droke, taibhs**
an omen, heard or seen, foretelling a death
and occasionally other events

1953 DUNN *Highland Settler* 47 Even
those who were not normally endowed
with this power might occasionally see
a "forerunner" (*taibhs*) of something
that would later come to pass ... 1957
CREIGHTON *Bluenose Ghosts* 1 Forerunners are supernatural warnings of
approaching events and are usually
connected with impending death. 1979
Beaton Institute Tape 1185 We could hear
big trucks going up the hill, but we never
saw any. They claim it was the forerunner
of the diesel trucks when the pulp mill
started. 1980 *CB's Magazine* 25, 15 No, I
never saw a ghost. But I have seen a forerunner of a living person. 1982 MACLEL-
LAN *The Glen* 50 Noises and unusual
sounds at night, like dogs howling or
roosters crowing, were also regarded as
forerunners ... 1999 MACLEOD *No Great
Mischief* 54 Others told stories of forerunners; of how they had seen "lights" out on
the ice "at the exact spot" [of the drown-
ing] years before, and of how such har-
bingers could now be seen as prophecies
fulfilled. 2001 LEWIS *Sculptures from Jagged Ore* 102 ... the people in Main-a-Dieu
believed that the sound of the moving
lumber at night down by the coffin-house
was a sure fore-runner [*sic*] of a death in
the community.

[*DNE*, *FWCCD*, *NCD*, *GCD*, *OED3*
(1589), *DARE*, *W3*, *NOAD*, *MWCD*]

*Of the dictionaries listed, only *DNE* and
DARE indicate a warning of death.

forty-five noun, often plural
a card game in which the first player scoring forty-five points wins the hand

1975 CURRIE *Antigonish Review* 24,
47 Only thing you can do different
from a pit pony is drink rum and play
forty-five. 1980 MCINTYRE *Collier's*

Tattletale 153 During the winter tournaments [forty-fives] many articles and animals were played for in the halls and homes; generally the prize was a horse, a side of beef, "spring pigs", fighting dogs or roosters. 2000 BOUDREAU and CHIASSON *Chéticamp Memoirs* 197 The most popular card game in Chéticamp has been **forty-five**. 2006a MACADAM *Big Cy* 21 Friends congregated to play cards – forty-fives – and to smack their lips over one (or two or more) of Paul's "hot ones," hot toddies concocted with moonshine.

[*COD N Amer.* (*Maritimes & New England*), *OED3* (1875), *DARE* **NEast**, *DAE*, *W3*; compare "FORTY-FIVE [was] ... introduced from the Maritimes. They have tournaments that go on and on." *ML*]

foulerie [ful'ri] noun; compare **milling frolic**
see the quotation at 1986
1975 CREIGHTON *Life in Folklore* 145 These occasions are known as Milling Frolics and today are a tourist attraction ... The Acadian French do it too but call theirs *une foulerie* ... 1986 CHIASSON and LE BLANC trans. *History and Acadian Traditions of Chéticamp* 227–8 To do this a *foulerie* was organized. Friends were invited for that evening. In the largest room of the house tables were installed end to end. On these tables was placed the length of material to be fulled, with both ends of it sewn together. Men and women placed themselves around the table. The first operation consisted in soaking the material in soapy water. Then the fulling began. To the rhythm of a song the material was raised to arms' length and slapped down on the table to the beat of the music. While those on one side of the table lifted the material, the other side slapped the material down in a circular motion. 2000 BOUDREAU and CHIASSON *Chéticamp Memoirs* 118 The fouleries (fulling parties) were well before my time. The material was slapped onto the table, where four men or four women sat on each side, with one at each end who held onto the end of the material and kept it turning around. In my younger days, the fulling parties were given up because a mill did this work.

*A loanword from French, see *foulerie* "Réunion ou corvée organisée pour fouler des étoffes, avant de les tailler et d'en confectionner des vêtements ou d'autres articles" *DFA SPORADIQUE OU VIELLI*.

fourteen: see **quatorze**

fricot [fri'ko] noun; also **chicken fricot**
an Acadian stew or hearty soup made with potatoes and meat, typically chicken
1980 DOUCET *Grandfather's CB* 18 "Have you ever had *fricot*?" asked Aunt Germaine as she ladled out a steaming spoonful of thick soup from the china basin into my bowl ... "*Fricot* is a potato and chicken soup." 1992 *Inverness Oran* 8 Apr. 8 More often, they gathered at each other's house for a "veillee" where they sang French Acadian songs and ate Acadian dishes, not pizza, but French delicacies such as meat pie and chicken fricot. 1996 CHIASSON ed. *Seven Headed Beast* 50 The others – the rich ones – told him, "If you can find three rabbits" (there were rabbits in that country) "to make a fricot, we will give you five hundred dollars." 2007b BARBER *Only in Canada* 118 **fricot** (*Maritimes*) a hearty Acadian stew containing potatoes and meat, fish, or seafood. 2007 ST. CLAIR and LEVERT *Nancy's Wedding Feast* 20 **Fricot au poulet** (Chicken Fricot) NOTE This wonderful stew soup was a staple in Acadian homes and can be served as an appetizer or served in large bowls as a main course with crusty bread.

[*COD Cdn* (*Maritimes*)]

*A loanword from French, see *fricot* "Ragoût traditionnel composé de volaille ou de boeuf, de pommes de terre ..." *DFA GÉNÉRAL.*

frolic noun; often preceded by a modifier: **barn, carding, chopping, cutting, digging, fulling, haying, hooking, house, milling, mowing, planting, ploughing, quilting, reaping, rolling, spinning, stumping, tucking, waulking, weaving, wood**; and by extension, **cockfighting** and **ferret frolic**; compare **milling frolic** formerly, a gathering of neighbours to work voluntarily on a specific task, frequently followed by a meal and entertainment, a bee

1897 *MacTalla* 24 Sept. 2 The young people got enough music and dancing anyway, and I should think they wouldn't want another "frolic" for at least a few weeks. 1915 Beaton Institute MG 12 156, 22 Aug. 2 I hope you will get the crops harvested alright but I know it will be hard on father try and get all the help you can even if you made a frolic there are quite a lot of boys left there yet while in other places they are getting scarce. 1921 MURRAY *History of the Presbyterian Church in CB* 264 When anything more difficult than usual was to be done, they called their neighbors to their assistance. In other words they made a frolic, as they called it. The men had their chopping, rolling, house or barn raising frolics ... 1982 MACLELLAN *The Glen* 46 There was, for instance, the frolic at Hay's River, some four miles from the Glen, where a certain hard-luck farmer decided to have the hay cut, dried, raked and gathered into the barn by means of a one-day frolic. The frolic was quite successful, and it was decided to celebrate with a night of music and dancing and of course something to drink. 1988 PRINGLE *Look to the Harbour* 127 The winter moved on and we had a chopping frolic for Sarah. Some chopped down the hardwood for firewood, and

some brought their teams and hauled it to the door, and some there sawed it up and split it. 1999 DOUCET *Notes from Exile* 122 In the days of my grandfather, a frolic was something between a party and communal work. The most spectacular frolics were for barn building, but most were for smaller things, to card wool, cut wood, or finish a project before winter closed in. Afterwards there would be a party. The party was the way people were paid back for their work. 2006 GRAHAM *CB Fiddle* 45 But the ceilidh was not the only occasion for dance: wives with an abundance of wool or flax to spin invited other women to a spinning frolic where they would "remain all day at work" and then "remain to dance for some part of the night." In the evening, men turned up – likewise the women would join the men for dancing after "chopping frolics." 2007 MACDONALD *Lauchlin of the Bad Heart* 257 ... at chopping frolics where lumbermen competed he'd excelled.
[*DPEIE* Historical, *DC, GCD, OED3* U.S., *DARE* (1775), *DAE Obs., DA Obs.* (1775)]

from away: see **away**

front end: see **bridle end**

frontland noun; also spelled **front land**; compare **backland**, **rear**
land fronting on water, typically fertile land with access to the sea, a lake, or a river

1989 HORNSBY *Annals of the Association of American Geographers* 79 (3), 421 The early arrivals, relatively well-off tenant farmers and crofters, had settled the frontlands of Cape Breton and, after a generation of effort, had created substantial farms. 1994 BYERS and MCBURNEY *Atlantic Hearth* 295–6 Those who received these first grants – the best land – became known as 'frontlanders.' This was not

because they had 'front' land by the sea
(for some land on the coast was rocky and
barren) but because they had land suitable
for good crops, whether by the sea or in
a river valley. 1998 DAVEY *Onomastica
Canadiana* 80 (1), 12 Known as the frontlands and the frontland settlements, these
areas had several practical advantages.
Not only were the frontlands more fertile,
they also provided access to the water,
an advantage which aided transportation
during a time when few roads existed
on the island and which allowed farmers to supplement their income and food
supply by fishing. 2008 MORGAN *Story
of CB Island Book One* 127 They [settlers on
backlands] often depended on working
for the more affluent settlers living on the
frontlands, generally near the water or
closer to denser settlements.
    [*DARE* (1941)]

fuarag ['furæk] noun; also spelled **furrag,
fouragh, furach, furag, forac,** and other
spellings
a dish of cream, usually whipped, and
oatmeal, traditionally served at Halloween often with small prizes hidden in it
    1974 MACLEOD *Stories from NS* 97 She
[Queen Victoria] began to question him
[Angus MacAskill] about his livelihood,
and the bowl of oatmeal and cream fuarag
that he used to take after his food. 1984
CUMMING et al. *Story of Framboise* 160
The **treat** was **forac**, raw oatmeal covered
with thick, rich cream and perhaps brown
sugar. Inside the bowl of **forac** was hidden treasure: whoever got the ring would
be the next to be married, whoever got
the button would be poor (or a bachelor),
and whoever got the money would be
rich (children were cautioned not to bite
into it). 1993 FARRELL *History of River
Denys* 399 The traditional Halloween Scottish delicacy furrag was served. Oatmeal
poured slowly over cream as it is being
whipped provides this treat. A custom in

days gone by was to drop into the frothy
mixture a ring, thimble, coin, button
or other small object. 2007 ST. CLAIR
and LEVERT *Nancy's Wedding Feast* 29
After all had arrived and real identities
were revealed, it was time for the major
event of the evening – bringing out the
big bowl of "fuarag." ... This night [Hal-
loween], it was filled with heavy cream
fresh from the milk separator. Having
beaten the cream until it was almost stiff,
Edith stirred in two cups of oatmeal; the
adults nodded their approval that it was
the "old-fashioned kind," ground very
fine. 2010 ST. CLAIR Email 27 Oct. 1 You
may be interested to know that the Inv.
Co. Consolidated Hospital serves the dish
[fuarag] to all its patients who wish it as a
special treat at this season.

*Compare the Scottish Gaelic *fuarag*, with a different meaning: "brose / gruel made with cold
water, cold water brose" *GED*.

full adjective; often modified by such
words as **pretty, extremely, half,** etc.
drunk, intoxicated, overcharged with
alcohol
    1920 Beaton Institute MG 12 59 Box
1, 29 Feb. n.p. Bob came in pretty full
last night. Started singing "Darling I am
Growing Old" about three in the morning. 1930 Beaton Institute MG 12 43 D2 f3,
23 He says on *page 251, line* 15, that when
he gets pretty full it takes his senses away
from him, and his memory, and he does
not know what he is doing ... 1978 Beaton
Institute Tape 2174 They drank then to get
drunk. It was not take a drink and leave
it alone or get half full or anything. They
got what they called it then stewed. 1985
Beaton Institute Tape 2411 [Tape 1] And
he was, as they used to say, three parts
full. 1996 GILLIS *Stories From the Woman
From Away* 114 In the Glen, there were
three stages in drinking – "wasn't sufferin'
any," "feelin' good," and "full." Lauchie

wasn't sufferin' any. 2000 CHISHOLM comp. *As True as I'm Sittin' Here* 125 John was extremely full and he fell in a snow bank and he wasn't getting up from there.

[*OED3* Now *arch.* (and *vulgar*) (*c*1000), *COED Austral./N.Z. & Scottish informal*, *DSL*, *DAE slang*; at *as full as* ...: *EDD* (1822), *OED3 Austral.* and *N.Z. slang, CDS*]

G

gad noun; also **fish gad**
a Y-shaped stick passed through the gills of a fish and out the mouth to secure and carry it; a catch of fish so held

1898 *MacTalla* 17 June 1 I saw an old man going home from the store and he had a "gad" with herring on it. [1940] MACNEIL *History of Iona-Washabuck* 64 When nothing else presented itself they would find employment in making fish gads or splitting shingles. 1986 *CB's Magazine* 43, 64 ... we used alder gads. It's a bush with two branches on it ... you slip the head of the trout on that. 2005 MACDONALD *Forest for Calum* 7–8 Ripping it from the hook, I snapped its head against an exposed stone, leaving a dark stain, then worked one side of my forked branch through the smelt's gill and out its mouth, pushing it down to the "V" of the gad. Pilot Survey Inf. 3 Make it like a "Y". Stick it through the gills and carry your fish home like that. Survey II Inf. 2 You had a gad of fish – a stick with a "Y" in it.

[*DNE* ([1894]), *DPEIE*, *COD Cdn (Maritimes & Nfld)*, *DARE*, *ML*; compare the senses "a stick" or "fishing rod": *DNE*, *EDD*, *OED3*, *DARE*, *W3 dial*, *MWCD chiefly dial*]

Gaelic Mod noun; also **Nova Scotia Gaelic Mod, Mod, Scottish Mod**
an annual festival celebrating Gaelic language, music, dance, and cultural activities, now held at the Gaelic College, St. Anns, with competitions in Highland games and cultural performances

1935 MCDONALD *Sydney's 150th Anniversary ... 1935 Official Souvenir Program* [57] PRELIMINARIES SCOTTISH MOD. This is the first event of this kind to be held in Canada. Cape Breton is the center of the Gaelic culture of the North American continent. Out of 31,012 Gaelic-speaking people in Canada in 1931, 21,976 were resident in Cape Breton Island ... **Sword Dance** ... **Highland Fling** ... **Band Selection** ... **Step Dance** ... 1950 WUORIO *Maclean's* 1 July 30 Scottish Canadians from other provinces also turn up for the annual Gaelic *Mod* (*Mod* means a meeting for Highland games), a gathering of the clans to be held for the 13th consecutive year this month. 1988 *CB's Magazine* 49 Inside Back Cover [Advertisement] TRADITION CONTINUES AT THE 50TH NOVA SCOTIA GAELIC MOD *St. Ann's, Nova Scotia August 7–13, 1988* Don't miss this week long festival of events including competitions in solo piping and drumming, pipe bands, Gaelic language and song, and Highland dance. 1996 *CB Post* 19 Aug. 1 The first Highland Scottish Gathering at St. Ann's Gaelic College dates back to 1938. The second Highland Gathering July 26, 1939 was held in conjunction with the first annual Gaelic Mod. Classes in the Gaelic College started the following day. In the following years these events were combined to be named the Nova Scotia Gaelic Mod amalgamating Highland games and competitions and the traditional Mod. In 1995 college officials decided to revert to the original format with all of the music, song, dance, competitions, displays, workshops and camaraderie that surrounds the Gathering. 2000 MACDONALD *CB Road* 231 Listen, I'd like to go over to the Gaelic Mod.

*A loanword from Scottish Gaelic, see *mòd, am mòd* "the Mod, the annual festival of Gaelic music and culture" *GED*. Compare *mod*: *COD*, *COED*, *OED3* (1891), *W3*.

gaff: see **stand the gaff**

gaff transitive verb; also spelled **gaffe**
to seize or grapple with (someone), to take hold of (something) with a hook attached to a pole; to steal (something)
 1977 *CB's Magazine* 17, 4 [Caption] Men on the door boat gaff the strongback rope – then haul up the door-bar, closing the trap. 1986 MACLEOD *As Birds Bring Forth the Sun* 16 Sometimes the older men miss the toss and the white cylindrical bottles fall into the sea ... until they are gaffed by someone in the boat ... 1991 *Inverness Oran* 3 July 6 I drive the boat, gaffe the buoys and band the lobsters. Survey I Inf. 5 "To grab or grapple with someone" is the more usual meaning. Survey I Inf. 22 He gaffed it, picked up the buoy with the gaff. Survey I Inf. 23 He gaffed him. Survey I.
 [in the sense "to seize": *DPEIE, OED3* (1844), *DARE, ML*; in the sense "to steal": *DNE, DPEIE* (1980)]

*Respondents to Survey I recognized both meanings (to seize and steal), but some were more familiar with one than the other. The sense of using a gaff hook to land a fish is widespread.

gaffle transitive verb
to grasp or seize (someone or something) forcefully
 Pilot Survey Inf. 3 Gaffled him – you grabbed him and roughed him up, causing a disturbance. Pilot Survey Inf. 5 [To gaffle is] to grapple onto. Survey I Inf. 22 I gaffled him (catch hold of him). Survey I.
 [*DNE, DPEIE, DARE* **chiefly NEng** (1900), *ML*]

ganging [gæn'ʃɪn, gen'ʃɪn] noun; also spelled **gengen**; compare **snood, backline**
in longline fishing, a short line that attaches a hook to the main line (or back-line) at regular intervals, a snood
 1988 *CB's Magazine* 49, 70 If a big hook is down his throat, you put that (a stick with a V notch the end) down his throat and you turn it around the gengin, they call it – where the hooks hung on – and you twist it out of his throat, like that. Survey II Inf. 4 Ganging attaches the baited hook to the trawl. Survey II Inf. 6 Snood is the most commonly used but also ganging. Survey II Inf. 8 Ganging is a snood, used on a codfish trawl.
 [*DNE* ([1819]), *OED3, DARE, DAE*; at *gangion W3*; compare "the twine from which a fishing line is made" *ML*]

gansey noun; also spelled **Gansey**
a heavy, homemade sweater; a person wearing this
 2005 ST. CLAIR Email 6 Mar. I just pondered whether or not anybody gave you the name Gansey for a person living in Margaree – and Gansey Town for a section of Margaree at the edge of Phillips Mt. – "he is a Gansey" is a term of derision for a Margaree-er. Coming from Gansey cloth which really was quite good cloth, but others thought wearing homemade Gansey cloth was a sign of poverty and a rural background. Pilot Survey Inf. 3 Yeah, that [gansey] is the Gaelic for sweater. Survey II Inf. 7 Nothing but a gansey.
 [*DNE* ([1843]), *DPEIE, SSPB, EDD, OED3, DSL, DARE, W3 dial Brit*]

*The *OED3*, *W3* and *DARE* note that *gansey* is a "variant of *Guernsey*."

gib transitive verb
to clean (fish), typically removing the gills and entrails
 1877 HALIFAX COMMISSION *Halifax Commission, Appendix G* 9 When we used to gib the mackerel on the fishing ground

and throw the gibs and refuse over, we always found that the fish left the place ... 1891 CANADA *Sessional Papers of the Dominion of Canada: Vol. 8*, 8–105 The method employed by them to put up good fish is, to "gib" the herring as soon as possible after being taken from the nets ... Survey II Inf. 2 Gib the mackerel. Survey II Inf. 3 Gib is an older term, use gut them now. Survey II Inf. 4 Gib means to take the gills out. [It was] done for four or five years to improve the quality. Survey II Inf. 7 Done for herring and put [them] in salt and sent to the West Indies.

[*DNE* (1862), *DPEIE*, *OED3*; compare the earlier form *gip*: *OED3* (1603), *EDD*, *W3* (with *gib* as a variant)]

gille [gɪlə] noun
a boy, lad, often used in nicknames
1970 BLAKELY *NS's Two Remarkable Giants* 28 At 14 he became known as St. Ann's Big Boy or Gille Mor ... 1970 CREIGHTON *Folklore in Action* 73 Of course Gaelic patronymics are common in Cape Breton, and are used glibly by those who haven't the slightest idea of their meaning. These are some examples of Gaelic names: Angus Mór, Angus Gille Bàn ... 1999 MACLEOD *No Great Mischief* 18 Still the *gille beag ruadh*. The phrase means "the little red boy" or "the little red-haired boy" ...

*A loanword from Scottish Gaelic, see *gille* "boy, fellow, lad, loon" *GED*.

gillick: see **dileag**

gimp noun
spirit or life, especially in musical composition or song performance; courage
1979 *CB's Magazine* 23, 9 Oh, songs were our entertainment. Indeed they were. And there was a great deal of singing in that home. Oh, my dear man. And you know, people don't do this anymore. There's not the gimp enough in them anymore. What I call gimp, well, you've got to be full of life. 1981 MACGILLIVRAY *CB Fiddler* 91 "I wanted to write a tune with a lot of 'gimp' to it ..." 2004 CURRIE *Lauchie, Liza & Rory* 14 Rory: You got no gimp, Lauchie. No gimp. Anne: Rory, on the other hand, had gimp galore.

[*DPEIE*, *NCD*, *GCD slang*, *OED3* (1901), *DARE* **chiefly NEng** (1901), *W3*, *MWCD*]

glanny, glennie: see **clanny**

glib noun; usually in the phrase **glib of ice**
an extremely slippery layer, a sheet (of ice)
2002 MUISE Email 1 Mar. He also refers to icy roads as being "a glib of ice." Survey I Inf. 2 The road is glib of ice. Survey I Inf. 23 It's nothing but a big glib of ice out there – like a sheet of glass.

glib adjective; usually in the phrase **glib ice**
of ice, extremely slippery
1974 CALDER *All Aboard* 60 Severe snow storms; silver thaws and alternating weather might produce deep cuts hardpacked with snow, or tracks of glib ice frosted rails, more effective than grease in causing the tall driving wheels to spin in aggravated fury. 1981 *CB's Magazine* 28, 5 But it wasn't so nice in the winter though, when it was ice, glib ice. 1999 CAMPBELL Oral Communication 22 Nov. It was glib ice. Survey I Inf. 5 I am not going anywhere today because of the glib ice. The ice is too glib.

[*DPEIE*, *COD Cdn* (esp. *PEI*), *EDD*, *OED3* Now *rare* exc. *dial.* (1594), *COED archaic*, *DSL*, *W3 archaic*, *MWCD archaic*; at *glib ice*: *DC* Now *Rare*, *NCD*]

*Although this meaning is described as *archaic* or *rare* by several of the dictionaries, nearly half of the respondents to Survey I knew or used this meaning.

glitter storm noun; compare **silver thaw**
a storm with freezing rain

1981 *CB's Magazine* 28, 10 And you take
after a silver thaw or a glitter storm ...
There'd be ice on the trains, even over the
coal, and the lumpy coal would be frozen.
1993 *CB's Magazine* 62, 18 There was a big
snowstorm, and then a glitter storm came
onto the top of it.

[*DNE* (1855), *COD* (*Nfld*); compare *glitter ice*: *FWCCD Canadian*, and *glitter DC
Nfld, NCD Newfoundland, GCD Cdn.*]

go ahead noun
nonsense, foolishness, confusing information; sound and fury signifying nothing

1978 *Oran Inbhirnis* 5 Jan. 9 At any rate
a great many people believe that all of this
'go ahead' [a television program warning
of the end of the world] was on the level.
1993 *Inverness Oran* 22 Dec. 13 Unfortunately, this go ahead with the league and
the go ahead with us is destroying the
league. 2007 *DCBE* Tape SHERRINGTON
23 All that go ahead, it's a crazy go ahead –
a lot of confusion, a lot of noise. 2008 *DCBE*
Tape CURRIE 14 You still hear this, "a go
ahead." All that go ahead, as a kind of ... a
mild derogatory thing ... All that stuff.

gob noun
the area in a mine where the coal has been
removed and where the roof is allowed to
collapse; also, the waste material, such as
stone or clay, left in this area

1897 ARCHIBALD *The Canadian Mining
Review* 16 (10), 292 ... every miner knows
that the danger of gob fires from slack
coal remaining in the rooms is always to
be dreaded. 1928 HAY *Coal Mining Operations in the Sydney Coal Field* 35 Two roads
were constructed in the gob, one being
the haulage level and the other the intake
airway. 1976 *Oran Inbhirnis* 6 Aug. 7 It
was then the job of the miner to load the
coal into one-ton boxes, store the clay in
the 'gob' (the already cleared area in the
room) and 'shore' the roof with wooden
props. 1983 SHEDDEN et al. *Mining
Photographs* 270 **Gob** – The void resulting
from the excavation of coal; also called
"crush" or "waste" and also meaning the
area where the coal has been excavated
and the roof is permitted to fall in. 1985
FITZGERALD *Atlantic Advocate* 75 Apr.
46 ... leaving a thousand-foot-long span of
ceiling behind, unsupported. The miners call this the gob. 1992 O'DONNELL
Coal Mining Songs 214 GOB is coal refuse
left on the mine floor. 2007 MACKENZIE
CB Coal Mine Disasters 26 Under normal
conditions, a combination of atmospheric
and ventilating air pressure works to hold
methane in the fallen stone of the "gob" –
that place in the mine where the roof has
been allowed to fall after the supporting
coal has been removed. 2008 *DCBE* Tape
CURRIE 18 ... a gob, a mining term too, a
sloppy place.

[both senses: *EDD, OED3* (1839),
DARE, W3]

gob stick noun
a stick with a V-notch in one end, used
to remove a hook embedded in a fish's
throat, or gob

1981 *CB's Magazine* 29, 9 And if the
hook got down their throat, you'd shove
down the "gob stick" – flat on one end
and a little V onto it – catch the hook in
that V and push down, haul it out. 1988
CB's Magazine 49, 70 You carry a stick,
they call it a gob stick – about that long –
of hardwood. Right in one end of it is a V,
like that. If a big hook is down his throat,
you put that down his throat and you turn
it around the gengin, they call it – where
the hooks hung on – and you twist it out
of his throat, like that.

[at *gob-stick*: *DNE, OED3* (1883); at *gob-
stick W3*]

goelette noun; also spelled **goêlette**
a schooner–sized boat used for fishing

1760 PICHON *Genuine Letters ... CB* 221 ... they likewise sell to our merchants a kind of boats, called *goelettes*, which come cheaper than if they were made in the country, and are far more durable, being of much better wood than those of Cape Breton. 1978 Beaton Institute Tape 1157 The sailing boat they call them the goelette schooners. They'd be bigger than a schooner [interviewer]? Oh yes. 1984 BALCOM *Cod Fishery of Isle Royale* 13 The prosecution of a dry bank fishery necessitated the use of an intermediate-sized vessel. The fore-and-aft rigged schooner or *goêlette*, averaging some 35–50 tons (1 ton = 0.907 tonne), proved large enough for the successful exploitation of the bank fishery yet small enough to make the relatively frequent trips to shore without under utilization of cargo space.
[*OED3* Now *hist.* and *rare* (1760); compare the later use: "a flat bottomed, motor–driven vessel used to carry freight" *DC, GCD Cdn.*]

gomach ['gɑmək, 'gɑməx] noun; also spelled **gomag, gammach**; compare **omadhaun**
a foolish person, often used to refer to a young person
1997 ROBERTSON *The Last Gael* 65 "Buying a beer, Tom? Jesus, you're turning into a friggin' gomach. You're nineteen, boy." 2007 *DCBE* Tape SHERRINGTON 24 And then the rest is just some Gaelic words ... fool and gammachs. 2011 DOYLE *CB Facts and Folklore* 215 gomach: Scots Gaelic for fool. 2014 SPARLING Email 18 Mar. I'm not clear whether it's "gomag" or "gomach" in Cape Breton Gaelic, but the "ag" ending means "little one" and can get added on to a noun. Adding it to "gom" would make it, "little fool," such as might be used when speaking to a child (I was thinking – does it ever get used to refer to an adult? I've only

ever heard people say that they heard it used to refer to themselves when they were kids). The "ach" ending can be used to refer to a person, such as "Caneidianach" (Canadian).
[*DSL* (1837 in 1842); at *gommie DPEIE* (with *gomaug* and *gommach* as variants)]; at *gommoch* Sc. Irel. Also Cor., *EDD* (with *gomach* Sc. Ir. as one variant)]

*The *EDD* and *DSL* indicate that *gomach* is used in both Ireland and Scotland with the sense of a fool or simpleton. Several dictionaries record the root *gom* and *gaum* with related derogatory meanings: at *gom DNE* ("a stupid person") and *OED3 Ireland* ("A poor silly fellow"); at *gaum EDD* ("A lout; a gaping idle fellow"), *DARE* ("A clumsy person; a lout"), and *W3 dial* ("an awkward lout : a stupid doltish person : CLOWN"). The *OED3* also defines the related form *gammock*: Chiefly *Eng. regional*. Now *Rare*: "**1.** A piece of fun; a game, a jest; a frolic. **2.** As mass noun: fun, sport; foolery."

good to (verb) adjective phrase
skilled or proficient at (doing some activity)
1974 *CB's Magazine* 7, 20 Donald Garrett MacDonald told us of a Sandy MacLeod, a man good to cure a toothache. He would write out a verse from the Bible on a sheet of paper ... [It was folded and] sewn in cloth and affixed to a cord to be worn about the neck. 1981 *CB's Magazine* 28, 22 He said to the old man. "Are you good to tell a story?" – "No, but my daughter here, she is a good story-teller." 1984 Beaton Institute Tape 960 Well, I was pretty smart on my feet when I was young. I was good to run. 2007 *DCBE* Tape SHERRINGTON 1 And the next one is *good to play the piano* [interviewer]. Oh and good to sing, good to read, good to – meaning to be "good at it" is how I would say it from where I come from, but here you are "good to." And he's good to talk – proficient.

government store noun; also spelled **Government Store**
a provincial liquor outlet, operated by the Nova Scotia Liquor Commission, where beer, wine, and various liquors are sold

1935 MACDONALD comp. *CB Songster* 20 Come all you bold miners of New Aberdeen, / ... And I'll make your hearts glad though they're now sad and sore, / When I'll sing you the song of the Government Store ... *This song was composed by two school boys of New Aberdeen after erection of a Government Liquor Store at that place.* 1976–7 Miners' Museum Tape 16 The only exercise I get now is I walk up to the government store and I walk up to the bank four times a month with my cheque. 1978 *Oran Inbhirnis* 9 Mar. 3 Come all ye miners of Inverness. / They say you are boozers, but never the less. / I'll sing you a song that will make your heart soar. / They call it the Inverness Government Store. 1986 Beaton Institute Tape 2311 The theatre was up where the government store is now – the Nova Scotia Liquor Commission. 1992 O'DONNELL *Coal Mining Songs* 68 Drink as much as would fill the big lakes of Bras d'Or, / Singing hip hip hurray for the government store. Survey I Inf. 33 Liquor store is still referred to as the government store by many.

[Compare *government liquor store* DC (1938)]

*The song "The Government Store" has many versions and is adapted to reflect specific locations.

grade intransitive verb
to pass from one grade to another in elementary and secondary school; less frequently, to graduate from school

1940 *Sydney Post Record* 28 June 3 "D'ya grade?" was the universal query, as youngsters raced away from the city schools about 9:30 o'clock this morning. Around the streets knots of excited and enthusiastic children could be seen checking over their grading cards. 1968 ROWE "Linguistic Study of Lake Ainslie Area" 47 ... the common question at the end of a school year is "Did you grade?" Only two [of 15] informants in the Lake Ainslie area used a form of pass. 1975 MACMILLAN *Memoirs of a CB Doctor* 172 In my spare time, which would be two to three months a year, I attended school, but never graded any year. 1995 *CB's Magazine* 68, 47 I graded from the Glace Bay High School. 1997 *CB's Magazine* 72, 95 They got ... bicycles for them when they graded. 2006 WALSH *CB's Lillian Crewe Walsh* 36 "The Boy Who Didn't Grade" ... His joy in life had faded – / His name was not upon the list / Of boys and girls who graded. 2007 DCBE Tape SHERRINGTON 39 That was new to me here ... to grade ... you passed where I came from; you didn't grade.

*As Murray Wanamaker records in his "The Language of Kings County, Nova Scotia," Kings County was one of the areas on mainland Nova Scotia where this meaning of *grade* was current (1965, 54). FWCCD and NCD list "to graduate" as one of the meanings of *grade*.

grading day noun; also **Candy Day**
the final day of the school year on which students learn whether they have passed the academic year or not, often celebrated by family, neighborhood, and community parties

1992 *Inverness Oran* 29 July 19 On grading day, often called "Candy Day," younger brothers and sisters were brought along. Apparently in 1932, twelve members from the MacDonnell family in Glengarry attended "Candy Day." 2007 *CB Post* 28 June B9 Glace Bay Grading Day Celebration ... Prizes, Giveaways, Cotton Candy, Hot Dogs and Pop. 2007 DCBE Tape SHERRINGTON 39 I don't know if it's Cape Breton or not and that's grading day ... But here you get grading presents, and it's grading day, the last day of school.

Grand March noun
a ceremonial promenade of graduating high school students with their dates moving in varied patterns before an admiring audience of family and friends

2007 *DCBE* Tape SHERRINGTON 39–40 Do they have the Grand March here for graduation [interviewer]? Yes, they do ... as part of the festivities of the graduation, not the actual giving of documents, but later [at] the party. 2008 CREWE *Ava Comes Home* 151 There was the Grand March to get to ... she and Lola sat like all the others, soaking up the sight of young people in their finery. As Vicky, Emily, and Samantha went by at regular intervals with their dates, they threw her big smiles and she gave them a little wave.

[*GCD, W3, MWCD*; at *march OED3* (1928)]

granny noun
a midwife

1975 MACMILLAN *Memoirs of a CB Doctor* viii In every little community in rural Cape Breton there was a dedicated body of women known as grannies or midwives. 1985 NICHOLSON et al. *Middle River* 23 Babies came into the world with a mid-wife or granny assisting. Every community had a "granny". 1987 *CB's Magazine* 46, 75 All my children were born in the house. But I was lucky I had a doctor and a nurse. But in those days, they had nobody but a granny. No doctor or nurse, just a granny.

[*DNE, FWCCD Southern U.S., OED3 U.S. local* (1794), *DARE* **chiefly Sth, S Midl** (1794), *DAE* (1794), *DA* (1794), *W3 South & Midland, MWCD chiefly Southern & south Midland*]

green fish noun; also **green cod**; compare **dry fish**

fish, typically cod, cleaned and salted, often aboard a fishing vessel, but not dried

1597 in 1962 HAKLUYT ed. *Voyages* vol. 6 107 [quoting M. Charles Leigh] ... the same day we tooke three hogsheads and an halfe of traine, and some 300 of greene fish. 1877 HALIFAX COMMISSION *Halifax Commission, Appendix G* 94 Each vessel makes from two to three trips each season, and catch each on an average one hundred thousand pounds of green fish. 1889 in 1992 HORNSBY *Nineteenth-Century CB* 167 We drove in the afternoon to Cheticamp and in the evening the fishermen congregated on the Room to know the price of Green fish. 1922 in 1997 *CB's Magazine* 72, 58 Therefore, commencing this date, we will pay one and three quarters cent [*sic*] (.01 3/4c.) per pound, green fish at the wharf, instead of one cent as formerly. 1984 BALCOM *Cod Fishery of Isle Royale* 12 The reason for the French interest in the dry fishery was the better preservative qualities in warm climates of dried over green cod. 1985 MACGILLIVRAY et al. *History of Fourchu* 15 ... the "green" fish would be placed outside on flakes to dry ... 1996 PRINS *Mi'kmaq Resistance* 56 Barrels of "green" cod (gutted and packed with salt on shipboard) were destined for the market in Paris.

[*DNE* (1623), *DC Nfd, NCD Newfoundland*; compare *wet* [fish] *OED3* (1580)]

green fishery noun; also **wet fishery**; compare **dry fishery**

the commercial fishery where mariners clean and salt the fish, typically cod, aboard the fishing vessel

1976 MORGAN *Journal of the Council on Abandoned Military Posts* 8 (2), 5 The wet or green fishery was practiced whereby fish was caught and salted aboard ship and carried immediately to France where it enjoyed wide sale. 1984 BALCOM *Cod Fishery of Isle Royale* 13 As no contact with land was needed, the green fishery supported fishing trips of several months duration to the offshore banks until the requisite amount of fish was caught. 1997 BIAGI *Louisbourg* 10 In this "green" fishery, the cod was simply packed in layers of salt and carried back to Europe in time for Lent. 2001 JOHNSTON *French Colonial Louisbourg* 97 Île Royale was in the "dry" not the "wet" fishery ... 2008 MORGAN *Story of CB Island Book One* 18 This wet or green fishery was practiced particularly by the Portuguese and Spaniards, people who brought their salt with them ...

[*DC Esp. Nfld, Hist.* (1960); compare *wet*: *DNE* ([1578]), *DC Esp. Nfld*, *OED3*]

gum rubber noun, usually plural; also spelled **gum-rubber**
a rubber boot, typically reaching to just below the knee

1971 PROTHEROE *CB Memories in Verse* 36 Oh, I'm telling you, friends, if it's travel you like, / Put on your gum-rubbers, and go for a hike! 1988 PRINGLE *Look to the Harbour* 18 When we were good and tired we slipped off our strap skates from our gum rubbers ... 1990 MACDONALD *'Tis me Again, B'y* 40 ... Teedy [*sic*] wasn't long slipping his pants and gum rubbers on and lightly following Billy down the stairs.

[at *gum boot* Also *gum (rubber) DARE somewhat old-fash* (1979)]

gumshoe noun, usually plural; also spelled **gum-shoe, gum shoe**
a low-cut rubber boot, a rubber shoe

1972 Beaton Institute Tape 344 He used to be in the wagon – a gumshoe on one foot and a big grey sock on the other. 1982 MACLELLAN *The Glen* 34 The arrival of the gum-shoe on the scene turned out to be a most popular piece of footwear during the early years of the century. In the gum-shoe one wore several pairs of heavily knit woolen socks and with the

heat that came from being shod all day with the gum-shoe, the odor of sweat was mighty powerful. The gum-shoe and its taller cousin the rubber boot were standard foot equipment during those lean years and they were well worth the money. 1988 Beaton Institute Tape 2424 ... we had gumshoes for working in the garden. We used to wear them when we were kids going to school – they were rubber shoes. 1998 GILLIS *John R. and Son* 11 Next morning John R. rose before dawn, put on a flannel shirt, gumshoes and a long-billed cap.

[*FWCCD, DARE* (1863), *DAE* (1863)]

gurdy noun; also **gurdy hauler**
a winch on a commercial fishing boat used to haul aboard lobster traps, trawl lines, and nets

Pilot Survey Inf. 5 ... I have heard the term ... from old fishermen. Survey II Inf. 2 [They] used to use "gurdy haulers," but "hauler" is used more frequently now.

[*DNE* (1924), *DPEIE, DC, COD N Amer.*, *W3*; compare the earlier form *hurdy-gurdy*, *OED3* (1883)]

guzzle transitive verb
to grab (someone) by the throat, to throttle or choke

Survey I Inf. 23 Wouldn't you like to guzzle that thing? Survey I Inf. 25 My brother used to say "I will guzzle you."

[*DNE, DPEIE, EDD* (1885), *OED3 slang* and *dial.* (1885), *DSL*; compare *guzzle* used as a noun meaning "throat" *OED3* (1659), *DSL*]

H

habit noun
a burial garment

1976 *CB's Magazine* 14, 29 So I turned around to look. Seen a brown shadow.

Fade like that. And that's what they used to bury them in – brown habits. The Catholic people. Just like a shroud, you know. 1993 Beaton Institute Tape 3219 E And those two ladies were always – in them days they made the dresses for the people – they made the habits and that went on them in the coffin.

[*DNE* (1971)]

habitant-pêcheur noun
formerly, a fishing proprietor, who employs others to catch and process fish
1984 BALCOM *Cod Fishery of Isle Royale* 3–4 ... the resident *habitant-pêcheurs* or fishing proprietors had a production capacity considerably greater than their numbers indicated at some points in the year. 1989 JOHNSTON *NS Historical Review* 9 (1), 63 It also reveals the degree to which the people employed in the fishery – owners ("habitant-pêcheurs"), fishermen, and shore-workers – dominated the resident population on the island, at least during the first period of French occupation, from 1713 to 1745. 2001 JOHNSTON *French Colonial Louisbourg* 251 The only authority figures in those settlements were the major employers, the *habitants-pêcheurs*.

handline noun; by extension **hand-liner**, **handliner**
a long fishing line with a sinker and baited hooks attached used without a rod to catch ground fish
1929b MCCAWLEY *CB Humour* 63 The politician scatters his promises as the hand-liner scatters his "pogey," and the poor fish rise to the bait and get the hook. 1942 DENNIS *CB Over* 2 The fishing was done by hand-lines and the men got the proceeds of half the fish caught. 1974 *CB's Magazine* 8, 6 ... there'd be two hooks on it, see? about a foot long from the main line. Handline ... You'd put your line over the side and just hold it. You'd let your line down till you'd touch the bottom;

then you'd pull it up a piece – say about half a fathom or around there. 1992 *CB's Magazine* 59, 66 It was handline, they call it. Seventy-five fathom of line with a lead at the end of it, weighed three pounds and a half. We used to have two lines like that, one at each side of the boat. 1993 *CB's Magazine* 62, 41 Twelve o'clock I had 1200 pound of fish in the boat. Alone. (And how were you fishing that – was it trawl?) A handline and bait.

[*COD, GCD, EDD, OED3* (1417), *W3, ML*]

hand loading verbal noun; also spelled **handloading**
loading coal using shovels as opposed to a mechanized method
1969 Beaton Institute Tape 160 There was no hand loading at all [in the wash plant]. 1994 SAMSON *Contested Countryside* 131 Inverness mine, like most of the mines in Nova Scotia until the 1920s, operated essentially as mines had operated for decades in what was known as "the hand-loading era". 1997 *CB's Magazine* 72, 4 But when we went to the mechanization, and the true mechanization, and we eliminated the handloading – we eliminated the contract work, too. 2004 MACKENZIE *Bloody CB Coal* 123 Hand loading had been a thing of the past for five or six years, and the Dosco Miner was in use here in the "Half."

hand pick noun; also spelled **handpick**; frequently before **miner, longwall, mining**
a pickaxe; a method of mining coal manually as opposed to a mechanized method
1897 BLAKEMORE *The Canadian Mining Review* 16 (1), 10 In the case of hand pick-work, the workman performs all the processes of cutting, shearing, blasting, loading, and timbering. 1967 MACDONALD *Atlantic Advocate* 57 Aug. 21 After a while I was put to work on the coal face.

There were then two methods used to get the coal out. One was by hand pick – that is, you dug the coal out ... and then there was the puncher machine. 1974 *CB's Magazine* 8, 9 We went in the old French Slope, the old East Slope – it was all handpick mining. And as true as I'm here, you see that wall there, it was just as straight and just as smooth as that. They took pride in their work those handpick men. 1990 [MACNEIL] *History of Sydney Mines* 74 The first attempt at successful pillar drawing at Princess Colliery was made in 1895, and continued with varied success until hand pick long wall work was introduced in the South side of the mine in 1903. 1993 Beaton Institute Tape 3191 It was hand-pick mining, see – they would make three ... dollars a day. The hand-pick miners that you would be hauling coal from – they would get [paid for the] work they do.

handy adverb
close by; nearly
    1877 HALIFAX COMMISSION *Halifax Commission, Appendix G* 21 ... the spring codfish are right in handy the shore .... 1973 *CB's Magazine* 2, 15 Take the tied Bows across your knee, have boiling water handy and a tub to catch it. 1983 Beaton Institute Tape 2113 [Tape 1] ... handy the highway. [1991?] MACLEAN *Story of Canoe Lake, CB* 68 The nurse stayed on to look after me for handy two weeks. 1995 CAPLAN ed. *Another Night* 53 The horse would sense when he was getting handy the stable ... 1996 *CB's Magazine* 71, 12 There were no boats around them, you see – no other boats handy. 2007 *DCBE* Tape SHERRINGTON 19 ... *handy* meaning close in time ... Pilot Survey Inf. 1 One of the reasons we bought our house was because it was handy town. Survey I Inf. 5 ... handy me, handy the store. Survey I Inf. 26 The house is handy the corner.
    [*DNE* (1792), *DPEIE, FWCCD, EDD*; at *handy* to *DARE*]

hangashore noun and by extension a verb; also spelled **angashore, angishore**
person who refuses to fish for a living
    2007b BARBER *Only in Canada* 76 **hangashore** (*Atlantic Canada*) **1** a weak or sickly person. **2** an idle person, especially one regarded as too lazy to fish. **Origin:** Irish Gaelic *aindeiseoir* "weak, sickly person". Pilot Survey Inf. 1 I've heard it [hangashore] out in Main-á-Dieu. Survey I Inf. 25 He's a real hangashore. Survey II Inf. 3 If sons do not want to follow their fathers as a fisherman ... they hangashore and get a job on land.
    [*COD Cdn* (*Nfld & Maritimes*); at *angishore DNE* (1924), *DPEIE*; compare *angish* "Hence *Angishore* "a poverty-stricken creature" *EDD*]

*"... this Irish loan *angishore* is often pronounced and spelled *hangashore*, and this in turn has been re-interpreted by folk etymology" (*DNE* 7). The word is not as pejorative on Cape Breton Island as on Newfoundland: "a man regarded as too lazy to fish; a worthless fellow, a sluggard; a rascal" (*DNE*).

hank noun, usually plural
a gallon container holding moonshine
    1979 CURRIE *Glace Bay Miner's Museum* 119 When they got there they found four hanks of colorless liquid. 1983 MELLOR *Company Store* 285 *The stuff [moonshine] was then poured into one-gallon vinegar jugs known as "Hanks" and sold to the bootleggers as pure alcohol.* 2008 *DCBE* Tape CURRIE 13 [A hank] would be like a gallon jug with a finger holder ...
    [Compare *hank* "The handle of a jug or pot. *dial.*" *OED3* (1530)]

harrow noun; see **milling board**
a long board used for milling (thickening homespun cloth) with lengthwise grooves to catch the water from the wet cloth and increase friction for thickening the cloth

1978 *CB's Magazine* 21, 40 Then when people in the harrow were getting tired the others would come down and go in the harrow for awhile ... [the] harrow's long and the cloth was long – 24 people, 12 on a side. 1978 *CB's Magazine* 21, 41 [Caption] ... the early portion of the milling, singing, gently passing, brushing [the] blanket along the grooves in the harrow. 1991 Beaton Institute Tape [no acquisition number assigned] ... there was a board made for the purpose of milling. It was made something like a washboard and it was about ... fourteen feet long, I guess. We put the cloth on that and went to it singing Gaelic songs ... They went around the harrow; they milled the wool until it got thick enough, fluffy enough. So the harrow that's the milling board [interviewer]? Yes, that's the milling board, the harrow ...

Harvest Train noun; also spelled **harvest train**; also **Harvest Excursion train**, **Harvest Special**
formerly, a seasonally scheduled railway trip taking Maritime workers to the prairie grain harvest
    1905 in 1984 NEWTON *CB Book of Days* n.p. **16 August 1905 Howling Mob** – The Westward "Harvest Train" leaves Sydney. About six hundred men going west for work are on the train by the time it departs New Glasgow. The car, with ladies in it, is cleaner and quieter than the others which are "filled with a howling, swearing, singing mob." 1924 Beaton Institute MG 12 46 A9 n.p. I don't know what the devil to do[;] the harvest train leaves next Sunday night. 1942 Beaton Institute MG 12 18 6a n.p. One of the big features of life in the first quarter of this century was the annual Harvest Excursion train. I think every boy in the Maritimes looked forward eagerly to the day when he was big enough to announce to the family in a big careless voice – Well

I guess I'll hit the harvest this year. 1984 CUMMING et al. *Story of Framboise* 102 In the 1920's, some paid $18 or $20 to go on the "Harvest Train" to work on the harvest on the Canadian Prairies. 1989 JACKSON *Fivescore and More* 56 ... in 1903 I went on a Harvest Excursion ... many adventurous Cape Breton young men went at least once to Western Canada for a few weeks ... to work for prairie farmers ... 1992 HORNSBY *Nineteenth-Century CB* 193 In the summer of 1892, the CPR inaugurated its first "Harvest Specials," running three trains from Halifax to prairie destinations. 2006a MACADAM *Big Cy* 16 He rode the "Harvest Trains" out west for the grain harvest.
    [*DC Hist.* (1954); at *harvest excursion*: *DC Hist.* (1925), *COD Cdn hist.*, *GCD*; at *harvest special*: *DC Hist.* (1964), *GCD Cdn.*]

haul-up noun; also **buoy line**; compare **snood**
a rope attaching a buoy to a lobster trap, used to lower and raise the trap in the sea; a rope to pull or raise other objects; by extension, the place where a boat is hauled
    1977 *CB's Magazine* 17, 2 ... you have a haul-up, a rope with a big ball float onto the end of it. Pilot Survey Inf. 3 I've heard that [haul-up] often enough ... used anytime you had to do some hauling. Survey II Inf. 1 The haul-up pulls the trap up; [also called the] buoy line, the buoy to the trap. Survey II Inf. 2 Buoy line or haul-up. Survey II Inf. 4 I use a snood or haul-up to raise the trap – also the rope used to haul the boat and the place where the boat is brought up. Survey II Inf. 7 Lobster fishermen use haul-up or haul line.

*The meaning of *haul-up* varies in other provinces: "rope used to raise a cod-trap to the surface" *DNE*, and "Synonym for 'snood': in lobster fishing, the rope that connects a lobster trap to the 'backline,' or main fishing line" *DPEIE*]

hay barrack: see **barrack**

head noun; also **heading, blank end;** compare **side head, kitchen, parlour, knit, nozzle**
a funnel-shaped mesh entry on a lobster trap, giving access to the baited chamber (the kitchen) or the adjacent chamber (the parlour); a flat piece of mesh used on each end of the lobster trap, also called a blank end
  1958 DOUCETTE *Notes of Ingonish* 16 George Whitty and Russell are already knitting heads for their traps. 1987 Beaton Institute Tape 2324 [Tape 1] After you get your lattice on, you get your five heads, your two blank ends, this one here – the fishermen calls it the parlour head. 1987 Beaton Institute Tape 2324 [Tape 2] You put a heading in here [interviewer]? Yeah, five per trap ... all nylon, one on each end, two on the side here, and one in the parlour. 1992 *CB's Magazine* 61, 61 The girls had to take their turn every morning doing this work besides knitting heads and blank ends to put on the lobster traps. 1997 COX "Engineered Consent" 216 Or he'd help them with the lobster gear and knitting heads and everything. Survey II Inf. 2 Headings or heads are the funnel shaped netting ... The opening is six inches long, called the side head. Survey II Inf. 3 This heading has a ring or nozzle bow.
  [*DNE, DPEIE* (1896), *NCD Atlantic Canada, DARE* **ME**; at *heading DNE*; compare *pothead* "The twine mesh funnel in the lobsterpot (trap)" *SSPB*, and *blank head DPEIE* (1972)]

*Many of the respondents to Survey II use *head* and *heading* interchangeably. These terms are often modified to indicate their location (*side head*) or the direction to which they lead (*kitchen head, parlour head*). Flat pieces of mesh cover the ends of the trap, variously called a *head(ing), blank end, blank,* and *blank head*.

header noun
a worker who removes the heads of fish, as a member of a team processing fish
  1981 *CB's Magazine* 29, 10 The header will cut the head and throw him in and the gutter will take the gut out ... 1984 BALCOM *Cod Fishery of Isle Royale* 37 The act of 1743 regulating the fishery specified a crew of 11 – a *maître* (master), a header, six companion fishermen, a salter, a *trancheur* (splitter), and a boy. 1992 HORNSBY *Nineteenth-Century CB* 12 ... others were engaged on shore, either as cut-throats, headers ... 2000 WILLIAMS *Cape Bretoner* 8 (5), 30 I heard the captain was looking for a "header" – someone to take the heads off the fish.
  [*DNE* (1623 [same source as the *OED3*]), *DC, OED3* (1622)]

headway noun; compare **deep**
a passage that follows the slope of the coal seam, often parallel to the main deep, typically used for haulage underground
  1928 HAY *Coal Mining Operations in the Sydney Coal Field* 20 Three headway trips, or fifty-one cars, constitute a normal main haulage trip. 1974 *CB's Magazine* 8, 9 The driver was going up this headway and the box come down and hit the horse. Killed the horse and broke the driver, pretty bad. 1983 MELLOR *Company Store* 86 ... each landing was then intersected every twelve hundred feet by headway tunnels ... corresponding to that of the slope shaft, which carried coal to the surface. 2007 MACKENZIE *CB Coal Mine Disasters* 152 A headway is almost the same as a main deep. It differs in that it does not go to the surface and the bottom of the mine.
  [*OED3* (1708)]

hobo noun; also spelled **Hobo;** also **hobo train, man train**
the Sydney and Louisbourg Railway train that transported miners to and from work

1946 Beaton Institute MG 12 107, 25 Jan. n.p. One of the "Hobo" cars was found burning yesterday at 1B, but the fire was put out before much damage was done. 1981 *CB's Magazine* 28, 2 And when Donkin [mine] closed up in 1926, they ran a train there back and forth, each shift, three times a day, keeping the men employed in the other mines. That's what they called the man trains. 1986 Beaton Institute Tape 2217 The train that carried the miners to and from the coal mines in Glace Bay during the late thirties 'til the early fifties was called affectionately the hobo. 1991 MACEOD *Place Called Donkin* n.p. The workmen's train or Hobo as it was more commonly known, was part of a transportation service provided by the S & L Railway. 1995 CAMPBELL *Tracks across the Landscape* 71 By comparison with the regular passenger service, the hobos or "man trains" as they were called, were considerably less comfortable. These were 50-foot long box cars with high windows and wooden bench seats stretched like church pews along either side. 2000 MACGILLIVRAY *Men of the Deeps* 144 *On day shift, you'd go to work around six o'clock in the morning on what we called "the hobo train"*.

home boy noun, usually plural; also **home girl**, **home child**
a child sent from an institution or "home" to a family to perform farm chores or domestic work
1982 MACLELLAN *The Glen* 69–70 The end result was that the Glen people raised a fair number of adopted children or, as they were called, "home boys or home girls" since they usually came from "the home", actually an orphanage in Halifax or London. A few of the home children came all the way from England but this was the exception ... 2003 SAWLOR http://canadianbritishhomechildren. weebly.com There were at least five

Home Children raised in Kennington Cove ... They were a tiny part of a much larger picture. In all, over 100,000 children arrived in Canada between 1869 and 1930, from the British Isles, to be placed in homes with people who were in no way related to them. In legal terms, the heads of these households were not referred to as the "adoptive parents" of the children, but rather as their "employers". 2009 ST. CLAIR *Information Morning* 14 Oct. n.p. Year of the British Home Child in Canada – 140 years of history ... During the years, at least six thousand children were brought to the Maritimes with over four hundred to Cape Breton. Survey I Inf. 7 Young orphans who worked on the farms.
[*DPEIE, DC Hist., NCD*; at *home child COD Cdn*; at *homeboy OED3* Chiefly *N. Amer.* (1885)]

*OED3 has 1864 for the first citation for *homeboy*, but it is not clear whether the citation refers to a "resettled" orphan or an orphan residing in an institution, and so the later date of the 1885 citation has been chosen.

horn noun
a drink of liquor, a dram
Pilot Survey Inf. 5 I am quite familiar with that term, "a horn of rum." Survey I.
[*DNE, DPEIE, EDD, OED3* (1682 for this sense), *DSL, DARE, W3*]

*DARE notes this sense is "By ext[ension] from *horn* a drinking vessel."

hot car: see **quenching car**

house church noun; compare **cottage meeting**
a private home used by family and friends for prayer, reading scripture, and singing psalms
1983 STANLEY *Well-Watered Garden* 59 The almost complete absence of pastoral attention in Cape Breton gave a

compensatory stimulus to family worship. In fact, many settlers in Cape Breton
developed a taste for this kind of worship
in the familiarity and warmth of "house
churches," with simple scripture reading,
extempore prayer and unskilled singing.
1992 HORNSBY *Nineteenth-Century CB*
78 ... as well as informal "house
churches," where families congregated to
worship, sing psalms, and read scripture.
[*OED3* (1644)]

COD, COED, and *NOAD* define *house church*
as a "meeting ..." for religious activities.

house racket: see **kitchen racket**

huit: see **eight hand reel**

hum noun
an offensive smell
2000 MACDONALD Oral Communica-
tion 27 Jan. An offensive smell, B.O.; that
fellow has a wicked hum off him. 2003
GABRIEL Email 15 Jan. Hum – a stink.
[*DPEIE, COD* esp. *Brit. informal, OED3*
slang (1906), *COED Brit. informal, CDS*]

Hunk(e)y Town: see **Kolonia**

hurdy gurdy noun
a small crane used to lift scrap steel
1989 BI MG 14 206 Box 6 C. iii c) File
10, 1 Well, the crane job was what they
called the "hurdy gurdy." It was a little
crane that was up – I'd say about twenty
thirty feet up in the cast house – like a
little box. It had forward and reverse
on it and it had what they call "fric-
tions," levers that would lower your
boom down and that's what you used
to clean up your cast house. You picked
your scrap up and tied it with chains
and take it and put it in the scrap bucket.
1991 BEATON *Scientia Canadensis* 15, 65
He learned to operate a crane called the
'hurdy-gurdy' ...

I

ice cake noun; also **cake**
1. a large piece of floating ice, typically
detached from the shore
1875 Anon. *The Canadian Gentleman's
Journal and Sporting Times* 4 (202), 3 Seven
wolves were seen to float over on an ice
cake from Cape Breton to Newfoundland
recently. 1935 Beaton Institute MG 12 59,
12 May n.p. From where I lay I could see
the ice cakes drifting ... 1986 *Inverness Oran*
30 July 17 At last they touched the shore
ice. By leaping from cake to cake they all
reached shore in safety. 2007 ST. CLAIR
and LEVERT *Nancy's Wedding Feast* 184–5
A sudden squall of snow came from the
north and the ice cake on which they were
standing broke in two with a loud crack.
2. a large block of ice used for
refrigeration
1973 *CB's Magazine* 5, 9 And I've seen
ice coming in from out there when one
horse could only haul four cakes. 1994
SAMSON *River Bourgeois* 127 The neatly
stacked ice cakes were covered with saw-
dust to reduce heat loss and to prevent
them from freezing together. 2004 AYERS
Cape Bretoner 12 (6), 26 "It was cut in
blocks 24 by 24 inches, commonly known
as a cake of ice," says Pat. "Some of them
cakes weighed 200 pounds."
[Sense 1: *DPEIE, DC, COD, GCD Cdn.,
OED3* (1683)]

ice clamper: see **clamper**

ice-cork: see **cork**

ice pan noun; also **pan of ice**; compare
clamper
a fragment of floating ice, typically flat
and large
1921 MURRAY *History of the Presbyterian Church in CB* 81 While thus engaged,

the current moved the pan of ice upon
which they were away from the land. 1987
MANN *Memories of Harbour Point, Gabarus*
12 Often the Barachois was filled with
floating ice pans and the children, myself
included, spent our spare time "jumping
clampers" propelling them around with
a long pole. 1997 *CB Post* 13 May 21 ...
there is a big pan of ice on the Inverness
side of the island. Although it is melting
rapidly it still has to come out around
Cape North. 2003 ELLISON *Cape Bretoner*
11 (3), 11 Sometime around mid-January,
'slob ice' (slush) and then 'ice pans' begin
to appear.
   [*COD, GCD Cdn., OED3* Chiefly *N.
Amer.* (orig. *Canad.*) (1842); at *ice-pan*:
DNE, DC]

ignorant adjective
rude, lacking civility, showing bad manners, crude
   1858 in 1984 *CB's Magazine* 36, 28 The
French soldiers were very much frightened
when the Highland men climbed up on
the rocks; they called them "English savages." "That showed," said Bruce, "what
a dommed [*sic*] ignorant set they were!"
Pilot Survey Inf. 1 These two brothers
were there, and one fellow was very full
and he was being kind of rude, and the
other fellow gave him a slap on the back
of the head, and he said "I told you a
tousand times bye, don't be igorant." Pilot
Survey Inf. 4 Someone is ignorant, as in
rude or very rough or crude.
   [*DNE, DPEIE, COD informal, NCD Informal, SSPB, EDD* ([1847]), *OED3* dial. and
colloq, *COED informal, DSL, DARE, NOAD
informal*]

Indian pear noun
a small tree with white blossoms and
red berries, of the genus *Amelanchier
canadiensis*
   1889 MACKAY *Canadian Record of
Science* 8 (2), 80 Indian Pear [observed in

Cape Breton]. 1998 MACNEIL *Personal
Note* 3 Some trees, like the pin cherries
and the Indian pear, were white with
blossoms ... 2000 MACDONALD *CB Road*
131 He nosed the fading blossoms on
a tree he didn't know, white and spicy
against the thick dark spruce. Was this the
Indian pear Starr had mentioned?
   [*DNE, DPEIE, DC Esp. Eastern Canada,
COD, OED3* (1796), *DARE, DA, W3*]

inside adverb and adjective; compare
outside
1. among commercial fishers, near the
shore, inshore
   1877 HALIFAX COMMISSION *Halifax
Commission, Appendix G* 98 The mackerel
are taken inshore, and the best grounds
for fishing mackerel are inside the heads
in this Bay. 1979 *CB's Magazine* 23, 47 If
you set them inside, they roll a lot more
than they do in deep water anyhow – you
have to have heavier traps to fish inside,
even after they soak the water. Pilot
Survey Inf. 2 Inside would be closer to
the shore; the water wouldn't be deep.
Pilot Survey Inf. 5 ... close to the shore, an
inside fisherman. Survey II Inf. 4 Inside
fishing is when you're fishing close to the
shore, a relative term.
2. among commercial fishers, on the lee or
protected side of an island, cape, or bar
   1992 *CB's Magazine* 59, 57 There was
another one [dead body] picked up in
Ingonish, went ashore in what they call
Bear Cove there, you know, just inside
Ingonish Island. Survey II Inf. 1 Inside is
where you're laying up in a storm. Survey
II Inf. 2 Inside is in behind an island.
   [Sense 1: *DPEIE* (1910), *DARE.* Sense 2:
DNE Supplement (1966)]

*The citation from 1877 illustrates both senses.

intervale [ɪntər'vʊl] noun
flat, fertile land at the bottom of a valley,
often beside a river; used in place names

1829 HALIBURTON *Historical and Statistical Account of N-S* vol. 2, 242 The rivers flowing into the Bras d'Or, are streams of sixty or one hundred feet wide, extremely winding, with a great number of short turns, and descending through flat land between ranges of hills. The flats are denominated intervales by the inhabitants, and often present scenes of uncommon beauty ... 1843 PROVINCE OF NOVA SCOTIA *Journal and Votes of the House of Assembly* A69–223 Mr. Turbull presented to the House the Petition of Alexander McLeod and others, of Broad Cove Intervale, Cape Breton, in the County of Inverness, praying aid for a Road in that Settlement. 1968 CLARK *Acadia: Geography of Early NS* 21 A descriptive term for the lower valleys of the short rivers was "intervale" or "interval." 1977–96 *Cape Breton's Magazine.com* [as noted in various articles] Big Intervale, Finlayson's Intervale, Whitty Intervale, Framboise Intervale, Aspy River Intervale, Ingonish Intervale, Intervale Bridge, Judique Intervale. 1988 *CB's Magazine* 49, 11 That was intervale land. You'd go down that deep and you wouldn't get a stone ... all pure leaf mould. 2007 *DCBE* Tape SHERRINGTON 28 Intervale ... pronounced ... "intervul," not "intervale." That area around a creek, sort of the level area, around the sides of a creek – a small creek valley, if you will.

[DC Esp. *Atlantic Provinces,* COD N Amer. (*Maritimes, Nfld & New England*), FWCCD *U.S. & Canadian,* NCD *Chiefly Maritimes & New England,* GCD *Cdn., esp. Atlantic Provinces,* OED3 *Now N. Amer.* ([1632]), DARE **chiefly NEng**, DAE, DA, W3 *chiefly NewEng,* MWCD, *chiefly NewEng*]

*As the dictionary list indicates, both American and Canadian dictionaries make regional claims for *intervale*; the *OED3* comments on the spread of the word, "Orig. in New England, but now used in other parts of U.S. and in Canada."

isbean ['išbɪn, 'išpɪn] noun; also spelled **iosban, isbeann, isban, Eespean, isoban** homemade sausage, containing meat, suet, oatmeal, onions, and seasoning, and traditionally encased in intestines

1953 DUNN *Highland Settler* 156 Others have unaccountably become very rare, such as the meat sausage known as *iosban* ... 1982 MACLELLAN *The Glen* 73–4 The isban was made from choice cuts of meat mixed with suet, oatmeal and elegantly spiced. It was a delicacy reserved for Christmas, New Year's and Easter. 1992 LELIEVRE *Belle Côte Story* [chapter] 4, 2 The Scottish and Irish seemed to prefer Eespean, made of suet, oatmeal and onions and put in calves intestines, which had been soaked, scrubbed, washed and turned inside out. It was then filled with the mixture and hung in the attic for several weeks, to dry and be ready for consumption. 2006 MACISAAC *Better Life* 78 Climaxing the achievement of the old farm kitchen were black and white puddings (*maragan*), a sausage (*isbean*) and haggis. Survey I Inf. 7 Isbean – usually [served] at Christmas and Easter, made with hamburger meat, with onions, salt and pepper, put in casings (sausage skins), cured and boiled.

*A loanword from Scottish Gaelic, see *isbean* "sausage" GED.

J

jack, jack boat: see **Newfoundland jack**

jail: see **parlour**

Jerseyman noun; also **Jerseys, Jersey people**

a seasonal worker in the fishery or settler from the Channel Islands (Jersey and
Guernsey), typically brought to Cape
Breton by the Robin Company; used in
place names

1873 CANADA *Sessional Papers of the
Dominion of Canada: Vol. 4*, 8–63 ... a fixed
red light, shown from the tower of a
square white building, 28 feet high, and
is situated at the north end of Jerseyman's Island, near Arichat. 1942 DEN-
NIS *CB Over* 8 I meet with more than
one old Jerseyman who in his youth was
brought over from Jersey to Arichat by
the Robin firm. 1981 *CB's Magazine* 30, 17
And I suspect that a lot of these stories of
sorcery were put out to keep the people
away from the Jerseys. Intermixing. It
was a barrier. 1988 LEBLANC *History of
Margaree* 3 ... the Jerseymen – people from
the English Channel Islands of Jersey who
spoke French but were English – Protes-
tants ... 1992 ROSS and DEVEAU *Acadians
of NS* 109 From the 1770s to the 1890s the
financial lifeline of Chéticamp was controlled and dominated by the "Jerseys" or
the Charles Robin Company.

[at *jersey man DNE* (1832)]

jig transitive verb; often in the phrase **jig
a tune**
to sing vocables (syllables that do not
express words), and occasionally Gaelic,
that imitate bagpipe or fiddle music; less
frequently to imitate the rhythm of a tune
by tapping feet or sticks

1972 Beaton Institute Tape 548 The
mother would jig a tune for the children
to dance. 1975 Beaton Institute Tape 210
He could jig a tune. You swear to God
it's coming right out of a violin. 1988
MACGILLIVRAY and MACGILLIVRAY
CB Ceilidh 109 He was jigging the tune
with his feet! 1994 LEBLANC *Equinox*
Sept./Oct. 63 ... then going to bed jigging (mouthing) tunes to himself. 1995
CAPLAN ed. *Another Night* 192 He came

in one day, and this Brown was jigging a
tune with two sticks. 2007 MACINNES
Buddy MacMaster 36 John Duncan was a
fiddler and Sarah was a noted "jigger" – a
form of mouth music. She could render or
"jig" a slew of tunes that would keep feet
tapping for hours. Buddy learned many
of the old Gaelic airs from the way his
mother would jig the tunes.

[*OED3 Obs.* (1598)]

*The sense of *jig* meaning to sing is 400 years
old. The *OED3* labels this sense as *obsolete* and
gives Shakespeare's *Love's Labour's Lost* iii. i.
10 as the earliest citation (1598): "To Iigge off
a tune at the tongues ende, canarie to it with
your feete, humour it with turning vp your
eylids." The sense is still widely used in Cape
Breton English as indicated by the seventeen
citations for the verb *jig* and another twelve for
the verbal noun *jigging* in the *DCBE* data.

jigging verbal noun; compare **mouth music, puirt-a-beul, canntaireachd**
singing that imitates bagpipe or fiddle
music using vocables (syllables that do
not express words) and occasionally
Gaelic, mouth music

1992 BEATON and PEDERSEN *Maritime Music Greats* 95 As often as not,
beginners learned to play by "jigging" the
tunes – singing the tunes with nonsense
syllables in order to learn the correct
notes and rhythms and pitches before
they had acquired their fiddle technique.
1996 DOHERTY "CB Fiddle Tradition"
80 Women were often noted for their
jigging of tunes, basically performing
the tunes vocally in a combination of
Gaelic words and nonsense syllables.
1996 RHODES *Traditional Step-Dancing
in Scotland* 188 'Jigging' was the English
word used on the island [Cape Breton] for
a form of canntaireachd or mouth-music.
2007 MACINNES *Buddy MacMaster* 160
In Cape Breton, transmitting the music
from fiddler to fiddler from community to

community through the aural tradition – including songs and *Puirt a Beul* (mouth music/jigging) and through the style of playing maintained within the bagpiping tradition – had remained the primary means of sharing and preserving the music.

[at *jigging* used as an adjective *OED3* (1590)]

jig wheel noun; also **jig wheel system**
a large wheel around which a cable is wound to raise or lower coal boxes using the force of gravity; a haulage system using such a wheel
1980 MCINTYRE *Collier's Tattletale* 168–9 Later a "jig wheel" was installed to shorten the horse haulage. A "jig" is a device which pulled mine cars by the acceleration of its own weight ... 1986 Beaton Institute Tape 2217 Archibald's wharf. The coal cars ran under a bridge and down on the wharf on the jig wheel system. That is, where the full cars of coal would go down while at the same time pulling the empty cars back up. 1995 MACDONALD *Port Morien* 26–7 A full box of coal would be transported to the wharf, and at the same time pull the empty car back up. This was what was known as the jig wheel system. The weight of the full car countered the empty car, which formed a string to go back to the mine for more coal.

Judique on the floor noun; compare **step dance**
skillful and energetic step dancing associated with Judique, Inverness County; a challenge to fight
1927 LIVESAY *Saturday Night* 11 Nov. 5 For even as far as "The Main" (Nova Scotia), the Judique men are famous for their fighting spirit, on land or sea. Such indeed is their fame that they have a slogan all their own: "Judique on the floor, Just once more!" 1935 MACDONALD *CB Songster*

13 There's MacDonald from Bras d'Or, / Perhaps you heard of him before. / There'll be Judique on the floor, / When we get to Flanders! 1978 *Inverness Oran* 24 Aug. 7 The place to be on September first & second is Judique Recreation Centre on Route 19 for "Judique on the Floor Days" ... So, take up the Judiquer's friendly challenge of "Judique on the Floor" and plan to be with us on September first and second. 1981 HAMILTON *NS Traveller* 112 There is, however, no connection between the origin of the name and the famous rallying cry of the locals: "Judique on the floor. Who'll put him off?" Today the phrase is a challenge to fight, but originally it had to do with the skill and dexterity of the Judiquers on the dance floor. Over the years Judique has become famous as the home of an intricate type of stepdance and this, in turn, gave rise to the cry. 1988 MACGILLIVRAY and MACGILLIVRAY *CB Ceilidh* 73–4 I asked my [Alex A. Graham's] brother how "Judique on the floor" originated. He said that in his opinion it was through the stepdancing. And he said, "When this Ronald Angus Ronald used to come to a picnic, he'd go on the floor early in the morning and he'd be on there about dusk, still dancing."

juggler noun
a medicine man, shaman, used derisively to suggest deception or fraud
1758 in 1891 Anon. "Beavers" *Folk-Lore* 2 (2), 248 The following quotation from "An Account of the Micmakis and Maricheets, dependent on the Government of Cape Breton" (1758), pp. 37–8, mentions the superstitious use made by native jugglers of river-water in which beavers built their huts. "The great secret of these jugglers consists in having a great *oorakin* [bowl] full of water, from any river in which it was known there were beavers huts." 1795 WINTERBOTHAM

Historical, Geographical, Commercial, and Philosophical View ... of the European Settlements in America 104 But these Spirits are extremely simple in their system of physic, and, in almost every disease, direct the juggler to the same remedy. 1961 HUTTON "Micmac Indians of NS to 1834" 29 Maillard relates ... the procession approached the campsite, the head juggler would come forward to meet them, and taking the young man by the hand would guide him to the bride's tent. 1974 MARTIN *William and Mary Quarterly* 31, 5 The seventeenth-century French, who typically labelled the shamans (or *buowin*) frauds and jugglers in league with the devil, were repeatedly amazed at the respect accorded them by the natives.

[*DC Obs.* (1748); compare *juggler* "One who deceives by trickery" *OED3* (*a*1340)]

junk noun
a piece or chunk, typically of wood (stove length) or meat, but also other things
1988 CURRIE *Company Store* 64 She drained the beans that had been soaking all night, put in some junks of fat and Pat shoved them in the oven. Pilot Survey Inf. 4 A junk of wood or a junk of anything else is a piece. Survey I Inf. 10 Anything cut up into chunks. Survey I Inf. 20 I've heard only junk of wood. Survey I Inf. 21 A junk of something, a big piece. Survey I Inf. 31 I heard of a junk of ham. Survey I Inf. 43 A junk of seal.

[*DNE, DPEIE, DC Esp. East, COD Cdn* (esp. *Maritimes & Nfld*), *EDD, OED3* (1726), *DSL, DARE* **chiefly NEng, esp ME**, *W3 chiefly Brit, ML*]

junk transitive verb; also **junk (something) up, junk up (something)**
to cut (logs, meat, or other things) into pieces or chunks
2007 *DCBE* Tape SHERRINGTON 24 A junk of firewood, you junk up your wood. You don't chunk it, you junk it. Pilot

Survey Inf. 3 They junked it up, cut the wood for the stove, to cut it up in stove lengths. Survey I Inf. 23 Junk the meat, a big junk or chunk. Survey I Inf. 33 The neighbour junked up the deer.

[*DNE* also *junk up* ([1776]), *DPEIE* also with *up, DC Obs., OED3, DARE* also with *up* **ME**, **ML**]

*The dictionaries vary as to what is cut: from wood or meat (*DNE* and *ML*), to wood or trees only (*DPEIE, DC, DARE*), and to cutting, dividing, or chopping in general (*OED3*).

K

keeler noun; also occasionally **keeled tub**
a shallow wooden dish often used to hold milk, especially to separate cream from milk
1839 in 1986 *CB's Magazine* 42, 25–6 Their [Mi'kmaw] camping ground was a perfect bee-hive – they caught and smoked lovely large trout at Middle River, as well as speared eels, made ... oil tanks, baskets, keeled tubs, ox yokes ... 1899 Anon. *Journal of Agriculture and Horticulture* 3 (7), 167 ... [equipment for churning milk] a keeler, (1) thermometer, and a supply of clean muslin for straining. 1970 MACPHAIL *Loch Bras d'Or* 30 Milk was placed in wooden keelers, made by Mic Mac [*sic*] Indians. After the cream rose to the top, and the milk clabbered, it was carefully skimmed to be churned into butter. 1977 *CB's Magazine* 17, 24 They [Mi'kmaq] used to come around selling baskets the women made and butter tubs and kealers [*sic*] (shallow tubs for setting the milk in) ... 1984 CUMMING et al. *Story of Framboise* 41 At first, cream was separated from the milk for butter in "**missies**" or keelers – staves of wood kept together with a couple of hoops. These would be placed in a cool place, usually in or above

a spring or stream. [1991?] MACLEAN *Story of Canoe Lake, CB* 32 In the early days the milk was strained and poured into round wooden dishes they called keelers or "mishrichean" as they said in Gaelic.

[*EDD, OED3 Obs. exc. dial.* (c1440), *DARE* **chiefly NEast, Mid Atl**, *DAE Obs.* or *local*, *W3 now chiefly dial*]

keeper noun
the crew leader of the cast-house workers who maintain the blast furnace in the steel plant

1989 Beaton Institute Tape 2347 Your keeper is your more lead hand in the cast house. He tells you what to do. Now, usually if he needs anybody helping him, they do that first. 1990 Beaton Institute MG 14 206 Box 5 C. iii b) File 55, 2 We had six jobs leading from the entrance in the furnace section ... The keeper was the gang leader in the section. 1995 BEATON *Acadiensis* 24 (2), 73 For instance, a 'keeper' was paid $2.25 per 12 hour day by MacGilvray, but was offered $2.75 by Means as of August 1901.

keg noun; compare **fish trap**
a small wooden barrel used by commercial fishers as a float for fish traps, trawl lines, etc.

1977 *CB's Magazine* 17, 2 Each anchor [holding the fish trap] has a keg and a haul-up [line] ... We call the keg ropes the moorings. So there's a keg at every corner, centre kegs and a main keg. 1984 *CB's Magazine* 36, 65 And then you had a trawl keg, a 5-gallon keg, and the first thing you did was fire that over [board]. 1991 CAMERON *Wind, Whales and Whisky* 210 The "iron" [used in sword fishing] is tied to a stout line with several wooden kegs on it.

[*DNE* ([1888]), *COD Cdn* (*Nfld*), *EDD Supplement*; at *keg-buoy OED3* (1883)]

keg: see **on the keg**

keptin [kɛpdɪn] noun; compare **kji**
a captain of the Mi'kmaw Grand Council

1992 MANNETTE ed. *Elusive Justice* n.p. **Alex Denny** is Kjikeptin (Grand Captain) of the Santé Mawi'omi Wijit Mi'kmaq (the Grand Council of the Mi'kmaq Nation). 1996 PRINS *Mi'kmaq Resistance* 203 Traditionally, Grand Council members (known as *keptins*/captains) are respected Catholic laymen known for their religious commitment. 1997 MCMILLAN "Mi'kmaq Grand Council" 111 Keptins would make funeral arrangements, conduct the salite, an auction to raise funds for the funeral costs, and generally be available for the grieving family; they would also lead prayers and inform other communities about the death. 2008 MORGAN *Story of CB Island Book One* 104–5 Without priests, the Mi'kmaq relied on their keptins – captains or local chiefs – for religious guidance, and for leading the prayers Abbé Maillard had left them in ideographic writing based on an orthography that priests had earlier noted in use among the Mi'kmaq.

*A Mi'kmaw loanword, see *keptin* "captain" *MEL.*

killick noun; also spelled **kellick** and less frequently **kelleck, kellic, killack**
a homemade anchor made with a stone bound in flexible wood and used to anchor small boats, nets, and lobster traps

1886 Beaton Institute MG 12 17, 18 Feb. n.p. Will commence trawl tonight, but must look around for killack stones after school. 1888 ENDLICE *American Magazine* Jan. 275 At most of the fishing villages of Cape Breton, the traveler will be reminded of the time when iron was a somewhat rarer commodity than it now is, by seeing a peculiar kind of anchor, known as a "killick." 1913 KNIGHT *Incidentally* 104 Archibald McLean (God bless him!) fastened a *killick* in the frozen ground above, and, attaching a rope thereto, lowered himself to the wave-swept deck of the brig. 1972 Beaton Institute Tape 515 The mackerel fishing starts. Kellicks and nets are out. 1988 *CB's Magazine* 49, 4 ... which I call "The Kellick (Calaich) Stone." (Note: "calaich" is Gaelic for moor or anchor, commonly called kellick in English.) 1992 MCLEOD *CB Captain* 6 Kelleck is a common word in Cape Breton fishing communities, referring to a homemade anchor fashioned by fixing a heavy flat stone into the fork of a branch. 2011 ST. CLAIR Email 28 June And how about "killick" as in the Lismer painting "Killick Anchor, Cape Breton Island." [Lismer 1945]. Pilot Survey Inf. 3 A big stone in the center and then usually hardwood that was kind of flexible it would be tied on the top. Then on the bottom there would be a fairly strong piece of hardwood that would hook on the ground. Survey II Inf. 4 Used as a net anchor.

[*DNE, DC Esp. East Coast, COD, FW-CCD, NCD Naut., GCD* "especially in the Maritimes and New England," *OED3* (1630), *COED, DARE* **chiefly NEng** (1630), *W3, NOAD, ML*; at *kellick DPEIE*; at *killock DAE*; several dictionaries give variant spellings in addition to those listed.]

*Compare *kelk* "A large detached stone or rock" *EDD*, and the Scottish Gaelic *calaich v.* "moor, anchor" *GD*.

King noun

see the quotation at 1988

1985 MACGILLIVRAY et al. *History of Fourchu* 55 Arthur Severance tells of playing a game called "king" (a variation of tag) ... 1988 MANN *School Days at Gabarus* 10 To play "King" all players were lined up on opposite sides of the level ground below the hill in front of the school. Each team had a captain and when "King" was called, the game was to catch and hold

prisoners. The side getting the most prisoners won the game. This game may be known as "Red Line" in city schools.

[Compare similar games described in the *EDD* (1824) and *OED3* (1849)]

kitchen noun; compare **double parlour**

the baited chamber of the lobster trap

1957 WILDER *Canada's Lobster Fishery* 15 The trap is usually divided into two compartments, the "kitchen", where the bait is fastened to a cord or wooden spindle, and the "parlour" or "bedroom". 1987 Beaton Institute Tape 2324 [Tape 2] There's going to be some [lobsters] up in the kitchen end that are not going to go back into there. 1993 Beaton Institute Tape 3229 B You need two kitchen heads and one parlour [head] per trap. Pilot Survey Inf. 2 The kitchen or the parlour ... they mean the same thing. It depends on the area. Sometimes the kitchen is where the bait is when they first crawl in, and then they move into the parlour, which is where they're kept. Survey II Inf. 1 A double trap has a kitchen in the middle and a prison on either end. Survey II Inf. 2 The bridle is on the kitchen end to stop the lobster from getting out when the traps are hauled.

[*DPEIE* (1957), *DARE* (1957) **ME**; compare *kitchen parlour DNE Sup.*]

kitchen end: see **bridle end**

kitchen meeting noun

a small gathering in a home to study, discuss, and solve a particular problem

1978 *CB's Magazine* 20, 12 Father Coady came here [Main-à-Dieu]. He made many trips here. He sent his squad in first to organize the kitchen meetings. We'd gather to study the cooperative principles in somebody's home. 1987 *Inverness Oran* 24 June 1 He said there were people in Port Hood who "grasped a good thing" and following "kitchen meetings", they decided to organize a Credit Union in the Port Hood area. 1993 *Inverness Oran* 30 June 18 Kitchen meetings will be held in communities in Inverness County and Richmond County in order for women to identify their needs and the needs will be evaluated by Leonard and Warner who will also organize and conduct a series of workshops. 2011 DOYLE *CB Fact and Folklore* 106–7 In 1938, Cape Breton coal miners [in Reserve Mines] launched the first co-op housing project in North America ... They began with "kitchen meetings" where they discussed everything from taking out a joint mortgage to the installation of plumbing.

kitchen racket noun; also **kitchen party, house racket, racket**; compare **ceilidh** noun
an informal and often impromptu house party, usually in the kitchen, with live music, singing, dancing, etc.
    1971 Beaton Institute Tape 306 My father was a violinist. He used to play at all the dances. We used to call them kitchen rackets. The dances in the houses, you know. 1981 MACGILLIVRAY *CB Fiddler* 141 I'd play at weddings, house rackets and at any little ceilidh, as well as at dances in Baddeck. 1996 BEDFORD *Cape Bretoner* 4 (3), 12 Saturday afternoons at the Black Diamond Bar & Grill have taken on the spirit and sound of a kitchen party. 1996 DOHERTY "CB Fiddle Tradition" 237 Archie Neil Chisholm remembers this: "when we were growing up, the social occasions would be just what we'd call house-parties. Kitchen rackets we would have called them." 1996 RHODES *Traditional Step-Dancing in Scotland* 190 The main venue for dances was in peoples' houses. They had their 'kitchen rackets' and 'milling frolics'. 2000 MACDONALD *CB Road* 149 ... a kitchen racket or any sort of drop-in fun ... 2007 MACINNES *Buddy MacMaster* 111 I would play all night ... It

was quite a racket, you know. 2007b BARBER *Only in Canada* 155 **kitchen party / kitchen racket** *Atlantic Canada* an informal entertainment held in a person's home, at which participants play music, sing, dance, etc. Survey I Inf. 5 [They were] spontaneous, never invited to a kitchen party.
    [*COD Cdn* (*Nlfd & Cape Breton*); at *kitchen party COD Cdn* (*Maritimes*); at *racket*: *DNE*, *OED3* (1745); at *kitchen dance DPEIE* (with *kitchen party* as a variant)]

*The regional phrase "kitchen dance," recorded in *DPEIE*, *DARE*, *DAE*, and *DA*, is rare in dictionary data for Cape Breton. *Kitchen party* is now being used to advertize a musical entertainment at public venues, undergoing a widening of meaning similar to that of *ceilidh* (see above).

kji [kəʝi] adjective; compare **keptin** grand
    1992 MANNETTE ed. *Elusive Justice* 11 We spoke of his father, the Kjisakamow (Grand Chief), who had died in August. 1996 PRINS *Mi'kmaq Resistance* 203 Other ranking members in the Grand Council include the *kji keptin* (grand captain). 1996 MCMILLAN "Mi'kmaq Grand Council" 100 Gabriel Sylliboy, renowned religious leader in Whycocomagh and a kji keptin, representing Whycocomagh on the Grand Council won the election ...

*A Mi'kmaw loanword, see *kji* "prefix, emphasis something" *MEL*.

knit transitive verb; compare **head, twine needle**
to knot (twine) into mesh to make heads (funnel-shaped mesh entries) for lobster traps, and make and repair nets
    1957 WILDER *Canada's Lobster Fishery* 15 One or both ends of the [lobster] trap are closed in with laths or hand-knitted cotton or nylon netting. 1992

CB's Magazine 61, 61 They [the girls] were
paid 2 1/2 C[ents] for each head. The most
money they could make knitting heads
would be about seventy cents a day. 1996
CB's Magazine 71, 82 He (had) worked all
winter long to (knit) those nets. And he
set them, for the herring. Pilot Survey Inf.
1 I remember my neighbour; he would
knit the entrance to the traps. He would
refer to that as knitting them. Pilot Survey
Inf. 2 You knit them [heads for lobster
traps] with a needle. Survey II Inf. 1 Knit
two balls of twine a day.
   [*DNE, DPEIE, OED3* Obs. (*c*1290); at
knitting: *SSPB, ML*]

*ML and this study found the mesh was used
for traps and nets, while the *DNE* and *OED3*
limit the knitted mesh to nets only, and the
DPEIE and *SSPB* designate mesh for lobster
traps only.

knitting needle: see **twine needle**

Kolonia noun; also the **Valley, Hunk(e)y
Town**
a nickname for an area in Whitney
Pier adjacent to the steel plant where
immigrants from Eastern Europe lived,
especially workers from Poland and the
Ukraine
   1991 *CB's Magazine* 57, 34 It is difficult
to determine whether the first immigrant
workers moved to Kolonia of their own
volition or whether these houses were all
that was available at the time. The fact
that the immigrants did not speak English made them vulnerable to the English
speaking community and probably was
the main reason for them to found their
own Kolonia. 1993 WHITNEY PIER
HISTORICAL SOCIETY *From the Pier
Dear* 21-2 About 40 "cottage residences"
of various shapes and sizes resulted from
the dismantling of the Breton Hotel. A
few years later the same cluster of buildings became the rented homes of a large

number of Slavic peoples who continued
their traditions of gardening and even
kept a few animals such as cows, geese,
and chickens. Thus this area became
known as "Kolonia" or "The Valley." It
was also known pejoratively as "Hunky
Town." The name remains as a proud
acknowledgement of the neighbourhood's
history. 1994 MACLEOD and ST. CLAIR
Pride of Place 149 Ferris Street is part of the
area of Whitney Pier known as "Hun-
key Town," "the Valley," or "Kolonia."
Bounded by Roberts Street to the east,
Ferris Street to the south, Byron Street
to the north, and the steel plant fence on
the west, "Hunkey Town" became home
to thousands of European settlers, first
from England and Scotland and then
from Eastern Europe, especially Poland
and the Ukraine. By 1914 the community
had become exclusively Slavic ... While
the term "Hunkey Town" was at first
pejorative, the people of the community
reversed the association to one of pride.

Krim-Ko noun; also spelled **krimco,
crimco**
chocolate milk
   1986 Beaton Institute Tape 2390 After I
finished my run, I had to go to Cape Breton Dairymen on the Esplanade and pick
up some milk and Krim-Ko and bring it
back to South Bar. 1992 DONCASTER *So
Tiny* 49–50 ... we shoveled the snow / 'til
up the driveway cars could go ... / for one
seven ounce bottle of this ~ / and Krimko
was what it is. 2009 Kerfoot Email 20 Aug.
I have looked through various materials, and can only find that Krim-Ko was
a chocolate drink, seemingly bottled by
various dairies in Canada, and certainly
having a patent in the US. Survey I Inf.
23 ... the bottle stopper would have Krim-
Ko written on it.

*Several respondents from Cape Breton
County answering Survey I use Krim-Ko as

a generic term for chocolate milk, which the Cape Breton Dairymen distributed in Cape Breton County. Chocolate milk bearing this name was produced by the Chicago based company, Krim-Ko Co., as early as the 1940s (Watson 2007, 56).

L

lamphouse noun; also spelled **lamp house, lamp-house**; also **lamp cabin**; compare **pit lamp, check number** formerly, a building where miners left their check numbers (brass tags with employee numbers) and received their pit lamps

1969 Beaton Institute Tape 118 Dorsey came out of the lamphouse. 1978 *Oran Inbhirnis* 5 Jan. 7 They picked up their lights at the lamp cabins and walked down the slope to the waiting head. 1983 MELLOR *Company Store* 87 Adjacent to the bankhead was the lamphouse, where the oncoming shift of miners received their safety lamps. 2000 MACGILLIVRAY *Men of the Deeps* 144 *Then you'd go out to the lamp house, put in your check number, and get a lamp and strap it on.*

landing noun; compare **level, deep** an area at the mouth of a mine passage (or level) near a haulage way (or deep) where full coal boxes are coupled to be taken to the surface and empty ones returned to be filled

1889 GILPIN *Canadian Mining Review* 8 (6), 77 ... horses are used only to collect and distribute the tubs from the landings and working falls [walls?] ... 1934 *NS Miner* 4 (188), 1 From No.19 landing to the pit bottom is a hard walk up-hill of one hour and a half. 1969 Beaton Institute Tape 118 ... working on the landing – coupling boxes and spragging boxes. 1982 *CB's Magazine* 32, 39 You hooked your

horse on and hauled it [coal box] out to the landing, where the trip hauled it up the deep. You took your empty boxes and the chain [runner] dropped them in off the landing, off the deep. 1990 PEACH *Memories of a CB Childhood* 116 ... a high degree of agility and skill was required of "landing tenders," who "put on" and "took off" the full and empty boxes ... 2003 SAINT AGNES ELEMENTARY SCHOOL *Coal Miners' Stories* 57 ... there was a belt line that took the coal and it was dumped into one-ton boxes. Then the diesel would take the coal out the level and put it on the landing.

[*OED3* (1883)]

landwash noun the shore between the high and low water marks; occasionally the wave action in this area

1977 *CB's Magazine* 16, 14 This ship was hard aground, in the very landwash, lashed by towering surf. 1983 Beaton Institute Tape 2048 The keg was there rolling back and forth in the landwash we called it, eh. This is where the water meets the shore. 1985 MACGILLIVRAY et al. *History of Fourchu* 15 ... the fish were transferred to small boats called "flats" and taken to the landwash or wharf where the splitting table was set up. 1987 MANN *Memories of the Harbour Point, Gabarus* 12 It [eel grass] drifted ashore and was to be found on the landwash, moving back and forth with the tide.

[*DNE* ([1770]), *COD Cdn* (*Nfld*), *OED3* at *land-wash* orig. and chiefly *N. Amer.* (1770), *W3*]

lap work adjective; also spelled **lapwork** of boats, built with overlapping exterior boards, clinker-built

1978 *CB's Magazine* 20, 33 The boats I build now are lap work, they call them clinker built – but the boats father was building had a crack between the planks

that had to be caulked. 1992 *CB's Magazine*
60, 62 See she's what they call lapwork
dory ... It wasn't smooth at all – lapwork –
one [board] would lap over the other, you
know.

[at *lap-work* OED3 (1868); compare *lap
seam DNE* and the more common *lapstrake*
(*GCD, COED, NOAD, ML*) and *lapstreak*
(*DAE, DA, W3*)]

large day noun
a fine, sunny, pleasant day, full of
potential

2002 *DCBE* Tape *Information Morning* 27
Feb. 2 It was not a large day. 2007 DAN-
IELSON *CB Weather Watching* 73 Cape
Breton skies are most intensely blue when
a flow of fresh, cool air arrives from the
west or north, a "large day" in the words
of some, a day with room for anything
and everything. Survey I Inf. 5 [A large
day is] sunny, low humidity, like a prairie day, see forever and feel expansive.
Derived from the Gaelic *latha mhor*. Survey I Inf. 23 A fine large day – everything
is the way you wanted it to be.

[*DPEIE*; at *large DARE* (1896)]

last ice: see **red ice**

lazy stick noun; also spelled **lazi-stick**
a game in which two players sit on the
floor facing each other with the soles of
their feet touching and pull on a stick to
lift the opponent from the floor; a stick
used in the game

1982 Beaton Institute Tape 2069 Yeah,
I pull on the lazy stick and you pull on
it ... And sometimes there'd be a bunch
around them and they'd have a basin
full of water or something and when you
were going to let me down, they'd slip the
basin under you and you'd come down
in it. 1985 MACGILLIVRAY et al. *History
of Fourchu* 54 For the game of lazy stick
you would get a stick of wood or a broom
handle and two fellows sitting on the floor

would pull on the stick to see which was
the stronger and he would win the game.
1990 MACQUEEN *Memory is my Diary*
24 Another interest was the Lazi-stick.
Two people sit on the floor facing each
other with the soles of their feet touching. A broom handle or strong round stick
is placed between the soles of their feet.
Each person takes hold of the stick and
pulls for all he is worth. Whoever can
keep his seat and bring the other up and
to him wins the match.

[at *lazy-stick DNE* (1981)]

level noun; compare **deep, coal face, balance, room**
an almost horizontal passage driven off
the main haulage way (or deep) through
the coal seam and used primarily to transport coal from the working area (or coal
face)

1871 BROWN *Coal Trade of the Island of
CB* 61 Under Desbarres' administration,
from 1784 to 1787 inclusive, the mines
were worked on Government account
by means of a level driven into the seam
from the foot of the cliff, where a wharf
was constructed for the shipment of the
coal. 1889 CANADA *Report ... Labor and
Capital in Canada: Evidence, NS* 296 ...
we are making these holes [man holes]
now in the tunnels; they are in the levels.
1976 *Oran Inbhirnis* 6 Aug. 6 As the slope
reached roughly four hundred feet in
length a 'level' was 'opened'. This means
that a tunnel was dug through the seam at
right angles to the slope. 1983 SHEDDEN
et al. *Mining Photographs* 270 **Level** – An
excavation or passageway driven in the
coal, establishing a base from which other
workings begin, e.g. from a level balances
are driven off at right angles and from
balances bords are driven off at right
angles into the coal. The coal is moved
from the bord via the balance to the level,
then from the level to the pit bottom, then
to the surface. Notwithstanding the name,

a colliery "level" does not mean a passage excavated on a horizontal plane. A level is generally driven in one or more slight (inclines). 1999a MIGLIORE and DIPIERRO eds. *Italian Lives* 66 *A "level" was a major coal-transportation tunnel, running from the coal-extraction area to the main haulage slope.* 2007 MACKENZIE *CB Coal Mine Disasters* 103–4 It happened on No.11 level. Levels are driven off the slope at right angles from the slope.

[*COD, EDD, OED3* (1721), *DAE* (1721), *W3, MWCD*]

lift noun
a lively, energetic style of playing music, especially dance music
1981 MACGILLIVRAY *CB Fiddler* 5 The local terms "lift" and "lively bow" are generally used to describe that aspect of a fiddler's playing which encourages dancing. 1986 *CB's Magazine* 43, 31 It is [a] Gaelic expression – she had a terrific lift, and a terrific drive to her music. 1988 MACGILLIVRAY and MACGILLIVRAY *CB Ceilidh* 198 ... the late Alex Gillis of The Inverness Serenaders who was a very lively, snappy fiddler – lots of lift to *his* playing. 1991 *CB's Magazine* 58, 65 Nowadays, keeping a steady rhythm with the beat of the hands is all important, the percussive accompaniment to the [milling] song – giving it an exciting lift, and the cloth is either constantly moving, or not moving at all. 1997 MACINNES *Journey in Celtic Music* 100 The current generations of Cape Breton pipers who play their music with the same drive and lift of the early Gaelic pipers include John Morrison ...

lift: see **on the lift**

link and pin noun; also spelled **link-and-pin**
a coupling device in which a rod (or pin) is manually inserted to connect and removed to disconnect a wagon, railway car, etc.
1979 *CB's Magazine* 23, 35 I remember when we tried to get automatic couplings. You know, we drank a whole bottle of Bobby Burns whiskey before we went to get automatic couplings instead of the old link and pin. 1980 *CB's Magazine* 27, 10 Cars were coupled up, you know, with link and pin. You had to put the link in and drop the pin, and sometimes you'd get caught – pinched. It was common. 1987 MACEACHERN *George MacEachern* 78 "... we went to get automatic couplings instead of the old link and pin."

l'nu [ɬːnu] noun; also spelled **ulnoo, Ulnoo, l'nu'k, l'nu'l**
see quotation at 1987
1888 RAND *Dictionary of the Language of the Micmac Indians* 164 **Man,** ulnoo (This is now the term for *Indian*, but its original meaning was the same as the Latin *homo* ... and signified *a man* as distinguished from all other animals or objects). 1892 FRAME *A List of Micmac Names of Places, Rivers, etc., in Nova Scotia* 10 **Ulnoo,** a man, as distinguished from all other animals. **Ulnooe,** to be a man, an Indian. 1972 *Micmac News* Nov. 27 I believe that Clarence is one of the few white men who has found the wisdom that is in the loneliness of the land of the "Ulnooe." 1976b JOE *Tawow* 5 (2), 23 History tells us about migrations to North America via the Bering Straight before the year 10,000. Evidence is found that man came to Nova Scotia at that time. This was ulnoo, as the Micmacs call themselves. 1987 WHITEHEAD *Spirit Sings* 20 The Micmac and Maliseet word *lnu'k*, meaning "people," is used today to designate a native person only. 1994 WICKEN "Mi'kmaq Society, 1500–1760" 1 The name which the Mi'kmaq use to describe themselves is not Mi'kmaq but lnu'k which means "the People." Mi'kmaq actually means

"my kin-relations" and may have come into use after the European invasion. 1996 PRINS *Mi'kmaq: Resistance, Accommodation, and Cultural Survival* 2 Traditionally Mi'kmaqs called themselves *L'nu'k* (or *Ulnoo*), meaning "humans" or "people" (Rand 1888:143). Today this Mi'kmaq word connotes native people in general.

*A Mi'kmaw loanword, see *l'nu* "native person, Canadian or American Indian, North American Aboriginal; people" *MEL*.

load of wood noun; also **load of hay** informal showcases to promote and develop Cape Breton musicians, singers, comedians, and writers

1996 MACDONALD *Centre of the World* 50 "Load of wood" or "load of hay": Semi-professional and professional musicians perform solo or together on stage as a showcase for Cape Breton's up and coming local talent. 1997 *CB Post* 31 Oct. 25 If you've never been to a Load of Wood or Load of Hay – check it out. You never know who's going to pop by to perform, and you're guaranteed to be treated to a variety of musical styles. 1998 BEDFORD *Cape Bretoner* 6 (1), 26 Started in 1986, the [Gaidheal] co-op sponsors regular "Loads of Wood" – workshops where performers can showcase new material, work together with other performers, receive audience feedback, and enjoy socializing with others. 1998 APPLEBY *Cape Bretoner* 6 (4), 38 On Dec. 6th, 1986, we opened the doors to Cape Breton's first Load of Wood, and Bob Bennett paid the first "three dollars at the door". It's now going on twelve years and the Load of Wood is still going strong. Ronnie MacEachern had come up with the name "Load of Wood" when he compared the variety of musicians on stage to the variety of wood in an armload – many differences and yet it's all wood, or in our case, performers.

loaf bread noun; compare **bun of bread** unsliced, yeast bread in the shape of a loaf as distinguished from rolls, biscuits, etc.

1986 *CB's Magazine* 41 Inside Front Cover They took bread, loaf bread – bread and butter, like – didn't make sandwiches – the bread that was in the [lunch] can, in the mine all day ... 1996 GILLIS *Stories From the Woman From Away* 44 What a tea! There was loaf bread, biscuits, pie, two kinds of cookies and shortbread. Pilot Survey Inf. 3 Yeast bread was considered loaf bread. Loaf bread was used just as much as loaf of bread. Survey I Inf. 5 Homemade bread or like homemade bread – unsliced baker's bread when it is like homemade bread. "She makes good loaf bread" is a compliment. Survey I Inf. 7 Loaf bread is unsliced.

[*DPEIE*, *DARE* **chiefly Sth, S Midl**, *DAE local*; at *loaf-bread*: *DNE*, *OED3* Now *dial.* (1559), *DSL*; at *loafbread EDD*]

lobster smack: see **smack**

loch [lɑk, lɒx] noun
a lake, occasionally a partially enclosed arm of water; used in place names

1845 PROVINCE OF NOVA SCOTIA *Journal and Votes of the House of Assembly* A83–258 ... Loch Lomond to Loch Uist 10 [miles]. 1894 BOLLES *Blomidon to Smoky* 20 Next day, August 5, we drove from Loch Ainslie to Whycocomagh ... 1974 MACLEOD *Stories from NS* 72 Once upon a time there lived at the head of a loch in Cape Breton, a farmer's wife who was also a midwife for women who were living near her. 1977 *CB's Magazine* 17, 38 ... by then they were so close to the edge of the loch that when the egg went out of the wild duck, down into the water it went and straight to the bottom of the loch. 1998 MACNEIL *Personal Note* 12 It was that natural lagoon that gave Big Pond – or Loch Mor, in Gaelic – its name.

[*COD Scot., FWCCD Scot., NCD Scots., GCD Scottish, EDD Sc. Irel., OED3 Sc. (c1480), COED Scottish, W3 Scot, NOAD Scottish, MWCD Scot*]

*A loanword from Scottish Gaelic, see *loch* "loch, lake" *GED*. Margaret MacPhail uses *Loch Bras d'Or* in the tiles of several of her books.

lolly noun; also **lollie ice**; compare **slob ice**
thick slush with broken bits of ice floating in sea water
1893 Beaton Institute MG 12 167, 29 Jan. n.p. Thick Lolly made last night. 1973 Beaton Institute MG 12 224 A6 ... the harbour was full of chunks of broken up, moving, wet ice, known locally as "lolly" ... 2001 *CB Post* 26 Apr. 25 Lolly ice is pack ice that is mostly slush. 2007b BARBER *Only in Canada* 20 **lolly** (*Atlantic Canada*) slush consisting of small ice crystals formed in water too turbulent to freeze over; frazil. **Origin**: British dialect "loblolly" = "thick soup or porridge". 2007 ST. CLAIR Email 19 May Do you have the word "lolly" for slush ice formed locally on harbours and bays? Used in Port Hood but apparently not in Inverness town – word shared with me by people in their eighties from Port Hood Island. Survey I Inf. 22 Lolly is snow and ice, slush over the water. Survey II Inf. 2 Lolly is not ice – it is cold water just before it freezes in a muck, cannot row through it. Survey II Inf. 4 Lolly forms in the fall – prevents small boats from moving. Like quicksand [it] forms along the shoreline and may freeze ... inches to feet thick. Survey II Inf. 8 Lolly is new ice, salt water ice as it is just forming.
[*DNE* ([1771]), *DPEIE, DC Orig. Nfld* ([1771]), *COD Cdn* (*Nfld & Maritimes*), *NCD, OED3 Canad., W3* (with *lolly ice* as a variant)]

longer noun; compare **barrack**
an unfinished wooden pole used in outdoor structures, especially fences
Survey I.
[*DNE* ([1772]), *DPEIE, DC Atlantic Provinces* ([1772]), *COD Cdn* (*Nfld & Maritimes*), *SSPB, OED3 Canad.* (*Atlantic Provinces*) (1772)]

longer fence noun; also **long fence**
a fence made with unfinished poles or longers
Survey I
[*DNE, DPEIE, DC Atlantic Provinces* (1832)]

longwall noun; also spelled **long wall**; also **hand pick longwall**; compare **wall face**
a method of excavating coal along an extended wall (or coal face), either by manual labour (hand pick mining) or with an automated coal cutter and loader (a continuous miner)
1892 Anon. *Canadian Mining & Mechanical Review* 11 (1), 1 There can be no doubt that the general adoption of mechanical coal cutters will lead to the introduction of long-wall methods of working, to the saving of coal and its improved quality when shipped. 1934 *NS Miner* 4 (167), 4 There is a system of longwall mining in operation at this mine, No. 2. There is a wall 330 feet long ... 1983 SHEDDEN et al. *Mining Photographs* 270 **Long wall** – A mining operation at a long coal face (wall), between parallel passages (levels), the face being from fifty to more than one hundred feet in length ... 1986 *CB's Magazine* 42, 17 And also, longwall does have the advantage that you take out all the coal. 1990 [MACNEIL] *History of Sydney Mines* 74 ... hand pick long wall work was introduced in the South side of the mine [Princess Colliery] in 1903. 1997 *CB's Magazine* 72, 6 Lingan mine broke every conceivable record that was known in world history in longwall mining. 1999a MIGLIORE and DIPIERRO eds. *Italian*

Lives 330 In the "longwall" system, two parallel tunnels were driven across the sloping layer of "seam" of coal.

[*EDD*, *OED3* at *long-wall* (1839); at *long-wall system* W3]

lop noun
short, choppy wave action, caused by strong winds

1975 *CB's Magazine* 10, 24 The water was coming in over her – a little lop that night. We were all soaking wet. 1982 *CB's Magazine* 32, 26 Rip tides are common. A lop tide forms under the southeast wind off Money Point which sets up great pyramidal waves through which a fisherman travels with caution. 1983 *CB's Magazine* 34, 34 … you could hear the wind on the mountains down there, you know, roaring over the mountains. And by and by, the lop struck in, heavy lop, and then the snow struck. 1996 *CB's Magazine* 71, 42 And you'd see a lop of wave go over a rock and fall away.

[*DNE*, *COD*, *OED3* (1829); compare *loppy* SSPB, *OED3* (1833)]

lumberman's rubbers noun, usually plural; also **lumbermen rubbers**
ankle-high rubber boots

1925 GOLD *Social Welfare* 7 (11), 223 He has no boots; he was given that week a huge pair of lumberman's rubbers by the Relief Committee, together with an old coat. 1976 CURTIS *Atlantic Advocate* 69 Mar. 42 These latter items [work socks] were worn rolled down to cover the tops of lumberman's rubbers, the ankle-high "gum boots". 1985 *CB's Magazine* 39, 84 You were going to school with lumbermen rubbers on. And you'd get to school, you'd have to dump the snow out of them, and the snow was still melting on your socks.

[*DPEIE*; compare *lumbermen's overs* "thick felt boots contained with heavy rubber arctics" W3]

lunch noun
traditionally, a large meal reflecting one's hospitality, especially served at an evening social gathering

1975 *CB's Magazine* 10, 4 Till about 11–11:30 [p.m.]. Then there was another big lunch: meat sandwiches and sweets of all kinds … 1981 Beaton Institute Tape 2039 [Tape 1] … then the lunch was made … oh we'd have every kind of sweet you could think and sandwiches. I always made the homemade cheese so they all went for the homemade cheese … they say I was the best. Did the women compete in making the lunches [interviewer]? Oh yes, I did pretty good. 1982 MACLELLAN *The Glen* 47 A principal feature of the Ceilidh was the lunch which consisted of *bonnach*, oaten bread or *aran coirc*, homemade cheese, preserves, wild strawberries or raspberries and a strong cup of Cape Breton tea. 1994 *CB's Magazine* 67, 67 Then they'd gather at night to visit, and they'd tell stories, and – making lunch. Everybody would have their cup of tea and their big lunch, and go home. 2006 MACISAAC *Better Life* 41 In the 1920s and 1930s in Inverness County, the typical lunch included bannock, oat bread, wild strawberry or raspberry preserves, homemade cheese and strong tea.

[*DNE* (1969), *SSPB*; compare "a light meal at any time": *COD*, *NCD*, *GCD*, *OED3* (1829), *DARE*, W3]

lu'sknikn [lu:skɪnɛgɪn] noun; also spelled **loosekaneegan, loose-kn-e-gn, loose-kinne-gan, luskinnikin**
a bread made with baking powder and preferred by the Mi'kmaq, bannock

1976 *Micmac News* Jan. 19 The Cremo family is a happy family and, like all native people, Lee likes his loose-kn-e-gn (Indian bread), so Nellie has learned to make it the way he likes it. 1977 *Micmac News* Feb. 8 The Loosekaneegan was more everyday fare. "It's like Irish bread only it's made with baking powder instead of soda and doesn't have any raisins in it." 1988 BATTISTE *Work, Ethnicity and Oral History* 64 It is easy here to lose the sense of historical drama and daily poverty, to become enmeshed completely in the casual pace of neighbourhood visiting, tea and luskinnikin, laughing children, endless gossip, and tales. 1999 JOE *We Are the Dreamers* 25 My older sister cooking at bonfire, the lu'sknikn tasting better than in the oven.

*A Mi'kmaw loanword, see *lu'sknikn* "bannock; bread" *MEL*.

lutin noun
the little people, often mischievous
    1931 FRASER *Folklore of NS* 71 At night the "lutin" would come and make braids in the horses' manes and drive or ride those horses that were best and swiftest. 1978 Beaton Institute Tape 1144 They [the lutins] were little men. It was only at night they did this. No one really saw them. 1980 BEATON "Sorcery Beliefs ... Cheticamp" 97 ... "little people" which the Acadians called "les lutins". 1992 SAMSON et al. *Island of Ghosts* 31 Now, there were little people, the *lutins*, who stole the horses if you didn't braid the mane and tail ...

M

Mackie Retarded Cooling noun; also **retarded cooling**
a process of slowly cooling hot steel rails by placing them in a confined area to reduce the number of internal cracks
    1981 *CB's Magazine* 28, 46 And as for rails, we made the best rails in the world – no question about that. And all rails made in the world today are made according to the process we developed right here: the

Mackie Retarded Cooling Process – either that or something that came out of it. 1990 Beaton Institute MG 14 206 Box 5 C. iii b) File 38, 25 What were the different jobs that you've done [interviewer]? Mostly hooking, hooking things up at the Mackie tanks where they cool the rails ... A slow, retarded cooling, they call it.

*As Bill Doyle points out, in 1931 the Sydney metallurgist Irwin Mackie discovered that slowing the rate at which hot rails cooled would prevent dangerous internal cracks from forming. "His innovation changed the way rails were made all over the world" (Doyle 2011, 197).

mail driver noun; also spelled **maildriver**
a postal worker who delivered mail in rural areas by wagon or sleigh
    1975 *CB's Magazine* 12, 3 He was a mail driver ... 1986 *Inverness Oran* 17 Sept. 38 It was not unusual for the mail driver to require some warming by the kitchen stove ... 1988 *CB's Magazine* 47, 63–4 And I'd have to come around from Meat Cove in a lobster smack over to Pleasant Bay, and then go with the mail driver from there up to Margaree, and then from there with another mail driver to Inverness. 1992 *Inverness Oran* 16 Dec. 21 ... mail drivers and postal workers sort and deliver cards, letters and oddly shaped packages to homes in small communities and in scattered rural areas ...

mainland noun; also spelled **main land**; by extension **mainlander**
usually peninsular Nova Scotia; less frequently Cape Breton Island itself from the perspective of nearby islands
    1832 BOUCHETTE *British Dominions in North America* vol. 2, 78 The Isle Madame, separated from the main land of Cape Breton by St. Peter's Bay and Lennox Passage, is about sixteen miles in length. 1973 *CB's Magazine* 5, 17 ... for six months

you'd never get a cold on St. Paul's Island. Unless somebody came from the mainland to bring it. 1976 *CB's Magazine* 14, 27 Main-a-Dieu Passage – that's the space between Scatari [Island] and the mainland – the Ciss sank there. 1985 *CB's Magazine* 40, 40 During the Mission, small boats go back and forth all day between the mainland and Chapel Island. 1998 COADY *Strange Heaven* 14 The problem was that this priest had been from the mainland, and ... somebody had spotted him with a flask. 2000 GILLIS *Bard's Tour of CB* x Above all, this is an attempt to distil the Cape Breton experience into a book that will bring happy memories to former Cape Bretoners, and entice others to visit a very special island that even mainlanders (reluctantly) admit is "Nova Scotia's Masterpiece."

[*COD Cdn* (*Cape Breton*); compare "the mainland of Canada as opposed to Newfoundland, Cape Breton, and Prince Edward Island" *OED3* (n.d.)]

make transitive verb; often in the phrase **make fish**; compare **flake**
to preserve (fish) by splitting and salting them, and then typically drying them on flakes or beach stones

1718 in 1980 CHARD *Seafaring in Colonial Massachusetts* 52, 137 [quoting Governor Shute of Massachusetts] There is a ship from France in the harbour and more dayly expected, they have seized the best places for making fish, and threaten the English with a removal, pretending that they act by the advice and direction of the Governor of Cape Breton. 1984 *CB's Magazine* 36, 68 They used to make all their fish on the beach. They'd take them and wash them out, and then they'd dry them along the beach and spread them. Spread them generally first on the stones, till the years we got the wire flakes. 1994 SAMSON *River Bourgeois* 26 Maria purchased codfish from the fisherman, employed local

ladies to *make fish* on flakes which were stored in the old lobster factory building. Survey I Inf. 22 [Making fish:] Put [the fish] in salt for a week or ten days. When they were "struck" (salty enough to dry – the salt had done its work), then washed and put on the flakes to dry. Dry for an hour before turning ... Fish will keep up to a year. Survey II Inf. 8 [Making fish:] Clean and wash [the fish], salt curing for ten to fourteen days in salt pickle or brine, washed [again], drying process on flakes. At night piled the fish at the end of the flake and covered. Wife and kids spread the fish out in good weather.

[*DNE, DPEIE, DC Esp. Nfld, COD Cdn* (esp. *Nfld*), *SSPB, OED3* Now *N. Amer. regional* (chiefly *Newfoundland*) (1503), *DARE, DAE Obs.*, *W3 dial*]

*Most respondents to Survey I and II indicated that *making* involved both salting and drying fish, but some indicated either drying or salting.

make-and-break engine noun; also **make and break**; compare **one-lunger**
a gasoline motor with one or two cylinders, called this because of the closing and opening of the electrical circuit, formerly widely used in fishing boats and for other work

1991 CAMERON *Wind, Whales and Whisky* 14 The make-and-break is an antique form of two-cycle gasoline engine ... 1998 PEACH *Inlets of the Heart* 59 Make-and-break engines / Drumming the sacred dawn. / Boats playing hide and seek / In coastal swells. Survey II Inf. 2 Make-and-break, one piston, a single cylinder. Survey II Inf. 4 Called make-and-break or put-puts.

[*DPEIE* (1983), *SSPB*; compare *make-and-break* referring to the electrical circuit only: *OED3, NOAD*]

manhole noun; also spelled **man-hole, man hole**; also **pigeon hole**

one of a series of small recesses dug into the wall of a haulage passage (a deep or level) to allow miners to avoid being hit by passing coal cars

1975 Beaton Institute Tape 210 There was what they call a manhole ... a little hole about the size of the freezer, for an escape. 1985 FITZGERALD *Atlantic Advocate* 75 Apr. 46 Every hundred feet or so along the deep are small dug-out areas in the wall called "man holes", big enough for one or two men to duck into in case of a runaway cable car. 1990 [MACNEIL] *History of Sydney Mines* 85 Some managed to time their escape well, and landed in the alcoves (man-holes) which stud the railway. 2001 MACKENZIE *In the Pit* 145 Pigeon holes were dug into the rib at several places along the level ... 2007 MACKENZIE *CB Coal Mine Disasters* 84 Joseph was sitting in a "manhole" dug in the side of the rib, and thus was spared.

[*EDD, OED3* (n.d.)]

man rake: see **rake**

man train: see **hobo**

marag ['merik, 'mæræk] noun, recorded plural forms **maragan(s)**, **marags**; also spelled **maracan, marak, madacan, maragh(an), marragan, marrigan, marrachain**; compare **white pudding**
a traditional sausage or pudding, either black (with blood) or white (without blood), made with oatmeal, suet, onion, salt, and pepper, and originally encased in an animal's intestine

1953 DUNN *Highland Settler* 156 Others have become unaccountably very rare ... the oatmeal sausage known as *marag gheal* [white], or the blood sausage known as *marag dhubh* [black]. 1973 MACPHAIL *Girl from Loch Bras d'Or* 25 ... marags, (this is a sausage of oatmeal, onions, suet, salt and pepper) ... 1986 MACLEOD *As Birds Bring Forth the Sun* 76 As the blood gushed

from the slashed throats, we would gather it in pans so that it might later be used for blood puddings – *maragan*, they were called in Gaelic. [1986?] HUNTINGTON *Looking Around* 38 To clear up a bit of confusion ... maragan are puddings, and one pudding is a marag. 2001 *CB Post* 21 Mar. 1 Marrigans – referred to by some as The Marragh – is a Gaelic dish consisting of oats, onions, suet from the kidney area of an animal and salt and pepper, tied in an animal intestine casing, usually of a cow or a hog. The marrigan is boiled, then fried or baked. Today marrigan is part of a meal, often served with potatoes and turnips, but years ago for many families marrigans were a necessity. 2006 MACISAAC *Better Life* 78 Climaxing the achievement of the old farm kitchen were black and white puddings (*maragan*) ... 2011 DOYLE *CB Facts and Folklore* 102 Highland Scots brought recipes for two traditional foods, *marg* and *marag dubh*, that are still eaten in Cape Breton. Survey I Inf. 5 The recipe [for marag] varied according to the locality.

[*DSL* (1957); at *marak* (with variant spellings) *DPEIE*]

*A loanword from Scottish Gaelic, see *marag* "pudding" *GED*.

market lobster noun; also **market**; compare **canner**
a lobster of a legal catchable size, larger than a canner, typically sold at stores, restaurants, etc.

1978 *CB's Magazine* 20, 8 The term canner is used today – they are below the size of the market lobster ... 1979 *CB's Magazine* 23, 43 Then there is a crate for the canners (lobsters measuring 2 3/4 inches) and a crate for the market lobsters (anything over 3 3/16 inches). These measurements ... indicate the length of the carapace, the solid shell covering the head and thoracic area. 1993 Beaton Institute Tape 3229 B At that time we were taking everything.

There was no small, no markets, no medium. [1996] BRAY *Our CB Lobster* 24 Fifty years ago, smacks or well boats, transported market lobsters from Port Morien to Boston.

[*NCD Atlantic Canada*; at *market DPEIE* (1957)]

*See **canner** above for a discussion of the "legal catchable size."

mauzy [mauzi] adjective; also **mosach** of weather, damp, misty, wet, dull

2002 *DCBE* Tape *Information Morning* 27 Feb. 2 I found it pretty mosach coming in. Survey I Inf. 5 Mauzy perhaps comes from Gaelic *mosach*, meaning gloomy, wet, cold. Survey II Inf. 4 [Mauzy means] foggy and light drizzle.

[*DNE* (1897), *COD Cdn* (*Nfld*); at *mosey*: *EDD*, *OED3* regional (now chiefly *New-foundland*)]

*The variant *mosach* is a Scottish Gaelic loan-word; compare *Là mosach*, "a 'dirty' day, a raw day" *GD*]

melter noun; compare **second helper** a steel worker in charge of an open-hearth furnace

1980 *CB's Magazine* 27, 15 For instance, I started as third helper, and it was my job to break those tests, and I'd have to take them to the first helper, the melter – he'd judge the carbon according to the grain and I'd ask him questions. That's where I learned. 1989 *CB's Magazine* 52, 9 When you ran your furnace, they considered you a melter. You were in charge of your furnace. You made the heat. 1990 Beaton Institute Tape 2600 E My father was a melter in the open hearth ...

[*EDD*, *OED3* (1511-1512), *W3*]

men, the noun, plural; also spelled **the Men**; compare **Ceist**, **Question Day**, **open-air communion**

devout Presbyterian laymen, prominent in prayer meetings and on Friday of the open-air communion (Ceist Day or the men's day)

1913 CAMPBELL *CB Worthies* 15 Mal-colm MacLeod, of River Dennis, [Denys] occupied a prominent place among the "men" of Cape Breton during a great part of the 19th century. 1983 STANLEY *Well-Watered Garden* 141 The individuals who monopolized the Friday Fellowship meetings, with their expositions on per-sonal saving grace, saturated with biblical allusions from their store of scriptural knowledge, were called "the Men." 1993 FARRELL *History of River Denys* 299 Log cabins became the locations for their first prayer meetings, led by elder laymen locally referred to as 'The Men'. 2006 STANLEY-BLACKWELL *Tokens of Grace* 39–40 Shortly after MacLennan's death in 1913, one admirer noted: "it was a rare treat to listen to him (always in Gaelic of course) either lecturing on a passage of scripture when conducting a prayer meet-ing or speaking at the fellowship meeting on the "Ceist day" – the men's day of the Communion season.

[referring to *the men* in Scotland: *EDD*, *OED3* (1835)]

men of the deeps noun, plural; also spelled **Men of the Deeps**; compare **deep** coal miners; the celebrated Cape Breton choir of retired and working coal miners

1989 MLECZKO *My Book of Memo-ries* [Part II] 88 Many Cape Breton mines extend miles under the ocean or the 'deeps', as they are termed, hence the name 'Men of the Deeps'. 1992 O'DONNELL *Coal Mining Songs* 211 THE Men of the Deeps are a choir of working and retired coal miners from the island of Cape Breton in Nova Scotia, Canada. Organized in 1966 as part of Cape Bre-ton's contribution to Canada's centennial year (1967), their inception was an effort by the people of Cape Breton to preserve in song some of the rich folklore of that island's coal mining communities. 1993 LEBLANC *Equinox* June 56 I grew up in southern Ontario hearing only vague tales of the faraway miners whose own lore describes them as the "men of the deeps" who choke down the "devil's dust" in a lifelong sweat after "buried sunshine." 2000 MACGILLIVRAY *Men of the Deeps* 19 [quoting Jack O'Donnell] *"And one of the miners ... said, 'Why don't we use something that mentions the deeps?' Then someone else called out, 'The Men of the Deeps'. Nina [Cohen] immediately exclaimed, 'The Men of the Deeps – it's a wonderful name! We'll use it.'"* 2005 MACINTYRE and WALLS *NS Book of Everything* 41 **Men of the Deeps:** Generically, miners who toil in Cape Breton Coal mines, and also a world-renowned choir consisting of the same. 2011 DOYLE *CB Facts and Folklore* 96 The Men of the Deeps are North America's only coal miners' choir.

M'eudail ['meʃəl, 'metəl] noun; also spelled **m'eudail**
darling, literally my darling or dear
  1997 MACDONALD *Fall on Your Knees* 419 ... she speaks to him, calling him by his Gaelic name, *Hello, Seamus. Mo ghraidh. M'eudail.* 1999 MACINTYRE *Long Stretch* 84 *M'eudail*, he called her. Darling. And it just seemed natural. When she was little. A lot of old people called kids *M'eudail*. 2001 *Am Bràigh* 9 Summer 6 Then there are the phrases m'eudail bheag (little darling), m'eudail air do chridhe (darling on your heart), which have gone into English here in traditional Gaelic-speaking areas.

*A loanword from Scottish Gaelic, *eudail* "darling, dear (usually in the vocative case)" GED.

mi-carême [mika'rɛːm] noun; also spelled **mi-careme**, **Mi-Carême**, **Mi-carême**, **mi-Carême**, **Micareme**

a mid-Lent celebration where disguised and masked visitors try to hide their identity from family and neighbours, formerly a one-day event and now several days; also the disguised visitor
  1978 Beaton Institute Tape 1077 Every time that a small mi-carême comes, I always have candies and sometimes cookies or apples. 1978 CAMPBELL *Highland Community on the Bras d'Or* 73 ... the season when most swains (and sometimes members of the fair sex) really went overboard in fun and merriment was at Micareme time, or mid-Lent. 1986 CHIASSON and LE BLANC trans. *History and Acadian Traditions of Chéticamp* 193–4 The Thursday of the third week in Lent is called *mi-carême* (mid-Lent). The children and the youth of the parish, boys especially, though often the girls too, run the mi-carême ... especially in the evening after supper, alone or in small groups, one left home all dressed up to visit the neighbouring families in the district. It was the task of the people in each family to guess the identity of the mi-carêmes and for these to try to hide it by changing their voices and their mannerisms so as to mystify the hosts. The success and the pleasure were that much greater when the mi-carêmes succeeded in chatting, dancing and making many gestures without being recognized by their close relatives or friends. 1992 *Inverness Oran* 25 Mar. 23 While many Acadian communities in the Maritimes have revived the mi-Careme, in Cheticamp it is a tradition that has never been lost during the more than 200 years that the village has existed. 1996 ROSS *Centre of the World* 175 Mary also refers to the Irish participation on mi-careme, a mid-lent festival, celebrated by the Acadians – similar to the Christmas mumming tradition of Ireland and Newfoundland. 2005 MACINTYRE and WALLS *NS Book of Everything* 41 **Mi-Carême:** This Cape Breton mid-Lent celebration, adapted from ancient French

custom, is designed to ease the drudgery of Lenten sacrifice. During Mi-Carême, people don costumes and visit their friends and families, who have to guess the identities of those in disguise. 2011 DOYLE *CB Facts and Folklore* 154 Inhabitants of the Cheticamp region are Nova Scotia's most enthusiastic *Mi-carême* celebrators. Some *Mi-Carêmes*, as they are known, change their disguises as often as four times a day. They keep the party going for a week ...
[at *mickeram*, also *Mi-Carême DPEIE* (1981)]

*Mi-carême is a French loanword, and Cormier's *DFA* defines the phrase *mi-carême, courir la*, "Aller de maison en maison au jour de la mi-carême pour chanter, danser et parfois déguster la nourriture (douceurs, pâtisseries) qu'offrent les hôtes *MARITIMES*."

milling board noun; also spelled **milling-board**; also **milling table**; see **harrow** typically planks arranged in a rectangle for milling (thickening homespun cloth), and less frequently a board with lengthwise grooves made specifically for milling cloth
1953 DUNN *Highland Settler* 153 Girls of the kindest courtesy will raise a melody true and even; when they sit at the milling-board, who wouldn't listen to their happy song? 1977 Beaton Institute Tape 2249 They had a web of cloth, so many yards into it, and then they had what they called milling boards. That was a table about 15 feet long or perhaps 20 feet with a bench on each side of it ... 1991 Beaton Institute Tape [no acquisition number assigned] They had a milling board ... some of them were just boards that they put together, but there was a board made for the purpose of milling. It was made something like a washboard and it was about ... from fourteen feet long I guess. 2001 MACGILLIVRAY *Cape Bretoner*

9 (1), 38 ... I remember on my sixth birthday they had a milling frolic at our house. The neighbours came in and they sang the old songs around the milling table.

milling frolic noun; also **waulking, fulling, tucking frolic**, and occasionally **milling party**; compare **foulerie, frolic, tucking, waulking, tucker**[2] formerly, a gathering of neighbours at one's home to shrink and tighten homespun cloth, by pounding the wet cloth on a table to the rhythm of Gaelic milling songs, frequently followed by a meal and entertainment; now, a re-enactment in a public venue of the traditional actions and songs
1921 MURRAY *History of the Presbyterian Church in CB* 264 The men and women together, had their planting, reaping, and fulling frolics. These frolics were frequently followed by a forenight of dancing ... 1927 ARCHIBALD *The Token* Foreword n.p. At these "Milling" or "Tucking Parties" as they were called, certain songs peculiar to the occasion were always sung, and even to the present day they still survive, although homespun as the general wear has passed into oblivion. 1933 MORRISON *Collections of the NS Historical Society* 22, 78 Before the cloth was ready to be made into garments it was subjected to more or less severe manipulation known as the "Louah" or the "tucking" and the occasion was called the "tucking frolic." 1936 BRINLEY *Away to CB* 199 Here in Baddeck it is called "A Milling Frolic." When the Scotch Highland housewives of this countryside have woven thirty or forty yards of woolen cloth ... and they want to get it "milled" (shrunk and the hard-twisted threads of the surface rubbed to yield a nap) the word goes 'round that there is to be a Milling Frolic. 1953 DUNN *Highland Settler* 38 No event made greater demand on the repertoire of folk-songs

than the milling frolic, when the home woven blankets were waulked or fulled – that is, worked until a nap was raised on the surface of the home-spun yarn. 1970 MACPHAIL *Loch Bras d'Or* 30 Many yards of all wool blanket were woven. This was thickened at a waulking or milling frolic. 1975 CREIGHTON *Life in Folklore* 144–5 As late as the depression of the thirties, many Cape Breton Scots wove the wool that made their clothing, and for the milling, or shrinking, they would gather at one another's homes and sit around a table. Songs were familiar, but the leader who sang the verses would often make them up as he went along; then all would join in the chorus much as sailors did in chanty singing. As they sang to a strongly marked rhythm they would thump the wet cloth on the table and pass it from one to another until it was dry ... These occasions are known as Milling Frolics and today are a tourist attraction. 2006 MACISAAC *Better Life* 39 Long after the milling frolic ceased to be used to full the cloth, it was held in Cape Breton for the purpose of perpetuating the tradition. 2007b BARBER *Only in Canada* 155 **milling frolic** (*Nova Scotia*) **1** *historical* a gathering at which participants pound new wool to raise the nap, usually with singing, dancing, etc. **2** a cultural event at which songs traditionally sung at these are performed. [*DC Cape Breton* (N.S.), *COD Cdn* (NS), *OED3 Canad.* (in Nova Scotia) (1936)]

milling song noun; compare **pairing song, putting up song**
a lively, rhythmic song, sung in Gaelic at a milling frolic
1976 MACGREGOR *Days That I Remember* 12 Young and old with sleeves rolled up, pounded the cloth and kept passing it around, keeping time to old Gaelic songs. The songs sung were milling songs and were mostly love songs and many a romance begun at the Frolic led to a

wedding later. 1986 MACLEOD *As Birds Bring Forth the Sun* 113 You're singing it like a milling song. It's supposed to be a lament ... 1994 *CB's Magazine* 65, 65 It was sort of a slow tune. It wasn't a milling song at all – it wasn't a lively song.

mind transitive verb
to remember, recall
1830 in 1982 *CB's Magazine* 32, 33 ... indeed I would be very happy if you could come but if you come mind to bring what I mention, otherwise you will find it a want. 1858 in 1984 *CB's Magazine* 36, 28 I remember grandfather telling us ... And now I mind me of his telling that when they landed at Gabarus, they had a hard fight with the French and Indians ... Pilot Survey Inf. 2 My parents used to say that all the time. SI 23 Grandmother would say "I nay mind," meaning "I cannot remember." Survey Inf. 25 "I minds when I went away that time." That means "I remember."
[*DNE, DPEIE, COD, FWCCD Dial.*, *NCD, GCD Archaic or dialect, EDD* Dial. uses, *OED3* Now *regional* (c1384), *COED, DSL, DARE* Now *arch.* and *dial.* **esp Sth, Midl**, *W3 chiefly dial, NOAD Scottish, MWCD chiefly dial, ML*]

mine examiner: see **deputy**

miners' row noun; also spelled **miner's row**; compare **company house, row**
a line of company houses, either attached or duplexes, built along a single street and rented to miners
1940 WISDOM *Glace Bay Looks Ahead* 8 Acquaintance with the Town's early history as a mining community will account for the number of "miner's rows" still in evidence in the colliery districts ... 1951 MACLENNAN *Each Man's Son* 7 Between the bridge and the colliery, for a distance of two hundred and fifty yards, crowded so close together they looked like a single downward-slanting building with a single

downward-slanting roof, were the houses of the miners' row. 1952 WISDOM *CB Mirror* 1 Apr. 5 The story is that of Bridgeport, an old residential section of one colliery district in the Town of Glace Bay, practically one street [Row Street], a so-called "miners' row" where the first "Company Houses" were build about 1865. 1976 PILLAR *Aunt Peggy* 16 As the years passed, the gritty, grimy life on "miner's row" did not appeal to either of them.

mining verbal noun; also **undercut, undermining**; compare: **cut** verb, **puncher, radial machine, undercutter**
digging a narrow, horizontal channel in the coal being excavated (the coal face), or along both sides, to allow the coal to break after the explosive charge (the shot) is fired
   1971 Beaton Institute MG 12 129, 10 ... in those days coal was dug from the coal face by the miners using hand picks, the miner would dig a trench (which they referred to as mining) along the bottom of the seam, some of the miners choose another method and would dig trenches or (minings) from the floor to the roof in the two ribs or (sides) of their working place. 1974 *CB's Magazine* 8, 9 An old handpick miner he'd ... lie on his side. He'd have to lie under a cut of coal. He'd dig a trench in the bottom of the seam. There could be perhaps seven feet above him. And he'd work his way in until all you could see sticking out from under the mining as they called it, was his heels. Solid coal was above him. He was taking a chance of being crushed. 1984 Beaton Institute Tape 2164 It was hand pick mining. When you got down on your side and you cut a channel into the face of the coal – about four feet in. It was pretty [hard] work. They called it the mining.

*Originally, the miner made this channel (mining) using a pickaxe by working his way under

the block of coal or along side the face. With mechanization, this task was accomplished with a "punching machine" (that worked like an pneumatic hammer) and later a "coal cutter" (which worked like a large chain saw). With the continuous miner, it was no longer necessary to "cut, shoot, and load" the coal (compare *cut* and *continuous miner*).

Mod: see **Gaelic Mod**

moggan noun; also spelled **mogan, moccan, mocan**
a woolen stocking with a cloth-reinforced sole, used indoors and outdoors in dry snow
   1953 DUNN *Highland Settler* 32 The *mogan* is a sort of knitted slipper strengthened with several thick layers of cloth sewed onto the sole. 1962 MCPHERSON *Watchman Against the World* 131 Another type of shoe which they had worn in Scotland and still found comfortable in dry snow was called the "mogan." 1976 MACGREGOR *Days That I Remember* 14 Now, the other kind of footwear which was used was the 'moggan'. They were only used in dry, cold weather and were of no use in wet snow. Thick yarn was spun and a short sock knitted a little larger so it could be pulled on over socks. Soles of heavy homespun in several layers were then sewn on the sole. This was the warmest of all and used mostly by the children and men who worked out in the woods in cold weather. 1982 MACLELLAN *The Glen* 34 Auntie used to make the moccans for us, a very long stocking with the sole heavily reinforced with huge patches of cloth. 2006 MACISAAC *Better Life* 79–80 I remember how the old women sat beside the stove and spent most of the day knitting socks, stockings, underwear, *mocans* [a form of footwear made out of wool] mitts, sweaters and coats.
   [at *moccan* DPEIE (1975)]

*Compare *moggan* meaning "a footless stocking": *EDD, OED3 Sc.* and *Irish English (north.)* (1754), and *W3 Scot.* The variant *mogan* is also found in Scottish Gaelic "stocking" *GED.*

monkey man noun; also **slag man**
a steel worker responsible for removing slag (waste product from steel making) from the blast furnace using an apparatus, with the nickname *monkey*, that controlled the slag flowing into a ladle
1989 Beaton Institute MG 14 206 Box 6 C. iii c) File 10, 1 But years before I got there, the monkey man's job was more hard because they had to flush the furnace out. 1990 Beaton Institute MG 14 206 Box 5 C. iii b) File 36, 3 ... the first six years after I started, I was on the slag, "monkey man," that's the name of the position. It's called "slag man" now ... When I was there, two hours after cast, you have to open your monkey and push maybe two, three, four [ladles] – if it was foamy slag, you'd have six ladles of slag off before they tapped the furnace. 1990 Beaton Institute MG 14 206 Box 6 C. iii b) File 79, 7 Then you go up to the "monkey man" and he was a slag man but he used to flush the monkey all the time. We called it the monkey. What's that [interviewer]? The reason why they got a nickname "monkey" on it, because it had a small "monkey" like [indicating round shape] as a brass cooler, water cooled.

moose shank: see **shank**

mor [mɔr] adjective; also spelled **mòr, mór**
big, large; often used in nicknames
1901 *MacTalla* 5 Mar. 283 He and his brother, Alexander "Mor" came out to Cape Breton in 1829. 1952 MACLEOD *CB Mirror* 1 July 5 In the first category, Ceòl Mór (The Big Music), we find the most intricate and most beautiful bagpipe scores ... 1970 CREIGHTON *Folklore in*

Action 73 Of course Gaelic patronymics are common in Cape Breton, and are used glibly by those who haven't the slightest idea of their meaning. These are some examples of Gaelic names: Angus Mór ... 1970 BLAKELY *NS's Two Remarkable Giants* 28 At 14 he became known as St. Ann's Big Boy or Gille Mor ... 1981 Beaton Institute Tape 2035 ... there was lot of people here on the Margarees that died of appendicitis. They called it in Gaelic cradh mor – the big [pain]. They really didn't know what it was. 1998 MACNEIL *Personal Note* 12 It was that natural lagoon that gave Big Pond – or Loch Mor, in Gaelic – its name.

*A loanword from Scottish Gaelic, see *mòr* "ample, big, bulky, grand, great, high, large, lofty, spacious, strapping, tall" *GED.*

mother-in-law's breath: see **stepmother's breath**

mosach: see **mauzy**

moufle noun; also spelled **Moufle**
the upper lip and soft part of a moose's nose, formerly considered a delicacy
1865 in 1958 UNIACKE *Uniacke's Sketches of CB* 87 They are always accompanied by strong dogs; and these running easily upon the surface at length overtake the exhausted animal [moose] and seize him by the nose or *moufle*, and thus hold him fast until the hunters come up ... 1865 in 1958 UNIACKE *Uniacke's Sketches of CB* 88 But the nose of the Moose called *Moufle*, which is very large and prominent is thought a great delicacy, and is sent sometimes from one part of the Province to another ... The moufle is usually made into soup, which is esteemed almost as much as turtle. 1975 LAMB *Hidden Heritage ... at St. Anns* 31 This was used to make a soup, called Moufle, which was considered a great delicacy in Europe ...

[*DC* (1791), *GCD Cdn.*; at *mouffle*: *NCD Canadian*, *OED3 Canad.* (1791); compare *muffle*, a general term for the upper lip and nose of ruminants and certain other animals: *COD, FWCCD, NCD, GCD, OED3* (1601), *W3*]

mouth music noun; also spelled **mouth-music**; compare **jigging, puirt-a-beul, canntaireachd**
singing that imitates bagpipe or fiddle music using vocables (syllables that do not express words) and occasionally Gaelic, jigging
1975 RETSON *Atlantic Advocate* 65 Feb. 19 ... neighbours would tell stories, sing songs, or perform mouth music – imitating pipes and fifes to the accompaniment of spoons, handclapping and footstomping. 1992–3 SHAW *Scottish Language* 11–12, 44 ... but a more direct and productive channel between language and music has been the 'mouth music' (*puirt-à-beul*), consisting of words and vocables sung to a fiddle or pipe tune. 2000 MACDONALD *Fiddler Magazine* 27 A practice also common in English and Gaelic, mouth music helped in remembering the tunes – a primitive melodic index. 2000 MURPHY *Cape Bretoner* 8 (4), 38 As a small boy Buddy started making music ... and, like his mother, would mimic the fiddle tunes using mouth music (jigging the tunes). 2007 MACINNES *Buddy MacMaster* 160 In Cape Breton, transmitting the music from fiddler to fiddler from community to community through the aural tradition – including songs and Puirt a Beul (mouth music/jigging) ... had remained the primary means of sharing and preserving the music.
[*DNE, COD, OED3* (1872)]

muck transitive and intransitive verb; often with **out**
to shovel and load (small pieces of coal and coal dust) from the bottom of the mine passage (pavement)

1973 Beaton Institute Tape 795 I started out ... behind the miner, either mucking or standing behind the miner. 2004 MACKENZIE *Bloody CB Coal* 85 ... sometimes he would be "mucking" – loading powdery coal duff that was soaked with water, which made it quite heavy.
[*FWCCD, NCD, GCD Mining, OED3 Mining* (chiefly *Canad.*) (1910), *DARE* **chiefly West**, *W3, MWCD*]

mucking verbal noun
shovelling and loading (small pieces of coal and coal dust) from the bottom of the mine passage (pavement)
1997 *CB's Magazine* 72, 5 You couldn't find a shovel down there now – you don't even need any mucking behind the machine or anything like that ... 1999 MACINTYRE *Long Stretch* 198 Sometimes he'd even grab a shovel and help with the hand-mucking. 2004 MACKENZIE *Bloody CB Coal* 65 Mucking was one of the hardest jobs in the pit, and it was also one of the lowest paid. As it cut a five-foot slice of coal off the 500-foot-long wall, the Dosco Miner left behind about a foot of duff (fine coal particles). That duff had to be shoveled off the pavement (bottom) and onto the pan line.
[*OED3 N. Amer.* (1918), *DARE* **chiefly West** (1918)]

mussel mud noun: also spelled **mussel-mud, muzzle mud**
sea mud taken from mollusk beds and used as fertilizer
1883 in 1992 HORNSBY *Nineteenth-Century CB* 163 It ... will obviate any necessity on my part to gather kelp or muzzle mud for manure. 2005 MACKENZIE *Neighbours are Watching* 92 The only worse labour was handling the mussel-mud – wet, smelly stuff, heavy as lead, that was dredged from the harbour floor through the ice and shovelled from pung sleds onto the land, always on fierce

cold winter days. 2007b BARBER *Only in Canada* 31 **mussel mud** (*Maritimes*) thick sea mud, rich in lime from the remains of mussels etc., used as fertilizer.

[*DPEIE, DC Maritimes, COD Cdn (Maritimes), NCD Maritimes, OED3* Chiefly *N. Amer.* (1774), *DA* (1774)]

N

Newfoundland jack noun; also **jack, jack boat**
a small, two masted schooner typical of a type built in Newfoundland and used in the Cape Breton fishery and occasionally to transport coal
1948 STAEBLER *Maclean's* 15 July 47 I pondered the gambling spirit of these men who follow the swordfish, the fishermen who come in their schooners and jacks ... 1988 POTEET *South Shore Phrase Book* 62 "... the 'jack schooners' or 'jack boats' so-called in Cape Breton, or 'two-spar boats' as they are known in Newfoundland, were 40 or 50 feet from stemhead to taffrail. They were gaff-rigged on both masts and they usually carried a longish bowsprit." 1985 MACGILLIVRAY and O'DONNELL *CB Song Collection* 19 Newfoundland Jack: a small schooner often used for sword fishing off Glace Bay. 1993 Beaton Institute Tape 3229 B They were called Newfoundland Jacks – two spar boats – and they used to have five or six men. We used to go up on the mast and look for them [sword fish]. It was quite a thing. 1995 CAMPBELL *Tracks across the Landscape* 54 Fishing boats from Newfoundland, called "jacks", came frequently to Louisbourg, especially in the fall of year. They would take the coal and deliver it to outports along the Newfoundland coast. 1995 *CB's Magazine* 69, 82 ... when I first started – [and] before me, all the fish that were

landed at these North Sydney plants were basically landed from what they used to call Newfoundland jack boats.

[at *jack: DNE* (1845), *DC Nfld, COD Cdn (Nfld hist.), OED3*; at *jack boat: COD Cdn (Nfld hist.), SSPB*; at *jack-boat DNE*; at *jack-boat DC Nfld*]

Nickel noun; also spelled **nickel**
formerly, a nickname for a movie theatre, or the movie itself, because of the price of admission
1919 in 1998 *CB's Magazine* 73, 50 Oh my you must be having one great time at the nickle [*sic*] and dancing school. Thats wat I call life. 1974 JACKSON *Windows on the Past* 162 The first moving picture theatre in town, the Bijou, was in the lower floor of a three-storey wooden building ... Because the cost of admission was five cents, it was called the "Nickel" ... 1986 PETRIE *Bay Boy* 22 DIANA "It's not called 'nickel' because it **costs** a nickel. It's short for 'nickelodeon.'" 1991 MACLEOD *Place Called Donkin* n.p. In fact, this mainly explains why the early theater or show was better known as the "nickel", since this was the general admission price. 2000 KEOUGH *Cape Bretoner* 8 (2), 29 Going to the "nickel", meant the Saturday matinees, which might be featuring, as John Hugh Edwards remembers, "Roman" movies or the latest instalment of a popular cliffhanger.

[*DNE* (1916); compare *nickel theater DA*]

nipper noun
a glove without fingers used to protect the hands of a fisher from a moving fishing line
1972 STAEBLER *CB Harbour* 112 "What are nippers?" "Gloves without fingers so you won't git blisters from handline. 1985 MACGILLIVRAY et al. *History of Fourchu* 20 The notion that any mittens other than white were unlucky was a commonly held one among the older fishermen ... Charlie

even insisted that the "nippers" used in handlining be made of white wool. 2007b BARBER *Only in Canada* 107 **nipper** (*Atlantic Canada*) a glove worn while handling lines to protect the hands from friction.

[*DNE, DC Maritimes, COD Cdn* (*Maritimes & Nfld*), *OED3 Naut.* (1840), *DARE* **NEng** (1840), *DAE* (1840), *DA* (1840), *W3, ML*]

Niskam [nɪsgəm] noun; also spelled **Nisgam**
God, Maker, Spirit
1976b JOE *Tawow* 5 (2), 24 This great respect for the dead is in keeping with the honourable rule that no matter what the person was like in life, he has gone to his maker – Niskam. 1993 *CB's Magazine* 62, 62 I knew then that Frank is at peace / ... He is working with Niskam now I know ... Note: *Niskam – God*. 1999 JOE *We Are the Dreamers* 4 She spoke of ... weji-uli-Niskam. [Note:] weji-uli-Niskam – Holy Spirit.

*A Mi'kmaw loanword, see *Niskam* "god" *MEL*.

Normanite noun
a follower of Norman McLeod, the charismatic religious leader at St. Anns, Cape Breton, and later of Waipu, New Zealand
1881 in 2007 ST. CLAIR and LEVERT *Nancy's Wedding Feast* 169 [quoting Hector Sutherland] And so it was that after thirty-one years in Cape Breton, we faithful, who were called "Normanites" by some, gathered on the hillside beside the Big Church. 1921 MURRAY *History of the Presbyterian Church in CB* 25 His friends and admirers in the county came to be known as "Normanites." 1949 FLEWWELLING *Collections of the NS Historical Society* 28, 104 This was the beginning of a migration which was to cause nearly

900 "Normanites" to leave Cape Breton during the 1850's. 1962 MCPHERSON *Watchman against the World* 52 The name [*Ark*, for their boat] was good-naturedly adopted by Norman's followers who were also winning their own distinctive name of "Normanites". 1974 CAMPBELL and MACLEAN *Beyond the Atlantic Roar* 198 The best-known pioneer minister to Cape Breton was the Reverend Norman MacLeod ... his followers were sometimes referred to as Normanites. 1999 *CB's Magazine* 74, 73 My grandfather, Samuel McInnes, a Gaelic scholar and Normanite, translated his [McLeod's] final words as, "You must support this young community now, as this earthly journey is stormeil (rough, uneven, unbalanced)."

note noun, usually plural
a maxim of spiritual instruction learned from ministers and catechists
1921 MURRAY *History of the Presbyterian Church in CB* 264 If piously inclined, as many of them were, they would recite "notes" from the lips of the ministers or catechists that they heard on certain occasions in the old land. 1953 DUNN *Highland Settler* 94 Presbyterian settlers brought with them in their minds short pieces of exhortation, spiritual advice, and biblical interpretation which they had heard from ministers and catechists in Scotland and had treasured up in their hearts. These "notes," as they called them, they could recite from memory whenever a conversation called for spiritual edification. 1983 STANLEY *Well-Watered Garden* 59 These "notes," as they were called, were "treasured like jewels only produced on special occasions and in the hearing of those who could appreciate them." 2006 STANLEY-BLACKWELL *Tokens of Grace* 126 According to Dunn, the Presbyterian settlers referred to these memorable words of spiritual wisdom as "notes."

[Compare "An interesting or noteworthy observation or remark. Now *rare* (*Sc* and *U.S.* in later use)" *OED3* (1577)]

Nova Scotia Gaelic Mod; see **Gaelic Mod**

nozzle bow noun; also **nozzle**; compare **head, kitchen, parlour**
on a lobster trap, a ring attached to the funnel-shaped mesh (the head) that allows entry into the baited section (the kitchen) and the section that traps the lobster (the parlour)
  Survey II Inf. 3 A nozzle bow is a ring that allows the lobster or crab into the trap. Survey II Inf. 4 The ring is called a nozzle bow or heading bow. Survey II Inf. 4 The parlour heading leads from the kitchen into the parlour. It may have a flap or nozzle.

nut bar noun
a generic term for a chocolate bar, with or without nuts
  1994 GAUM *Belarus to CB* 157 In the evening, when the store was closed, they would go back to their small room and sometimes they would treat themselves to an orange, or if things were really good, a chocolate bar. I recall Mom would refer to it as a "nut bar," even if it didn't have any nuts. 2008 DCBE Tape CURRIE 15 And, of course, ... we called chocolate bars, nut bars.

*Informants in their fifties recall using this as children.

nut coal noun; also **nut coke, nut**
a grade of coal or coke resembling nuts or marbles in size
  1897 ARCHIBALD *The Canadian Mining Review* 16 (10), 293 ... the coal in the Cape Breton seams made so much fine that when the nut was taken out considerably more than fifty per cent of unsalable coal was left. 1981 *CB's Magazine* 28, 6 You

know the way it was in those days, a boat came in, she had 6 hatches – she wanted one kind of coal in this hatch, another kind in the next hatch – "slacked," "screened," perhaps "nut" or something. 1987 *CB's Magazine* 44, 33 We were loading a boat once with nut coal. Nut coal is like marbles. And we buried two of them [coal trimmers] one time. But we got them out in 5 minutes. 1989 Beaton Institute Tape 2600 A The nut coke was ideal for Warm Mornings and Quebec Heaters. Everybody in the Pier, even [those] that used coal, they always tried to get a load of coke or two for the winter. 1992 HORNSBY *Nineteenth-Century CB* 100 Large coal was stored or "banked" ready for sale, while slack was divided into nut coal for the miner's domestic use ...
  [*OED3* (1861), *W3*; at *nut*: *COD* esp. *Brit.*, *OED3* (1857)]

O

och interjection; also spelled **ach**
alas, oh, chiefly expressing regret but also surprise, anger, and other responses
  1927 LIVESAY *Saturday Night* 11 Nov. 5 Ach, yes, terrible were the accidents ... 1970 MACPHAIL *Loch Bras d'Or* 6 Och! Och! I can't get along without Morag! 1974 MACLEOD *Stories from NS* 43 Och of ochs, my tragic tale, / Whilst you are stretched out in the seaweed. 1975 CALDER *Uncle Angus and the Causeway* 9 "Och, it's out of your head you are. 2000 COADY *Play the Monster Blind* 87 Ach, she said at him.
  [*COD Scot. & Irish, EDD, OED3* Chiefly *Sc.* and *Irish English* (1522), *COED Scottish & Irish, DSL, W3 Irish & Scot, GED*; at *ach*: *OED3* (1481), *DSL*]

*The variant *ach* has an equivalent in Scottish Gaelic "oh! alas!" *GD*.

off tax noun; also spelled **off-tax**; see **check-off**
an authorized deduction by the company for dues, services, and purchases
   1925 MCCAWLEY *Standing the Gaff* 20 If he was paid in cash, and had to pay all the services represented by the "off tax," in cash, the "off tax" would cost him a lot more than at present ... 1984 Beaton Institute Tape 2136 Well, there was the doctor, hospital, your union dues which was only about fifty cents a week or so, your relief society donation which was about thirty cents, that was if you were off sick you got so much a week, and your church. That's about all your off taxes. 1995 *DCBE* Tape NICHOLSON 14 When we got paid, got cash at that time, all our off taxes would be off it ... doctor, hospital ... warehouse supplies .... You get a pair of gloves or that, that'd be all off your pay. All the wages, all gone like that. 2001 DAVEY and MACKINNON *Acadiensis* 30 (2), 80 A widely known nickname, the *Big Pay MacDonalds*, ironically comments on the small pay resulting after the company store, or "pluck-me store", had taken all the deductions or "off-taxes" from the miner's pay.

og [ɑk] adjective
young; also understood as "the younger" in nicknames
   1901 *MacTalla* 30 Nov. n.p. ... John "Og" Campbell ... 1942 DENNIS *CB Over* 297 ... the new-born son was named Donald Og – Donald the Younger. 1979 MACDONALD *Story of the CB-New Zealanders* 15 "No, no, I said 'caileag og' – young girl." 1988 MACDONALD *Culture and Tradition* 12, 79 The main character [of the song] was a Scot, and the discussion about him led to several tales of Donald Og MacNeil, a man from the Isle of Barra who first spotted the Iona Peninsula and urged his sons to settle there.

*A loanword from Scottish Gaelic, see *òg* "young, youthful" *GED*.

omadhaun [ˈɑmətən] noun; compare **gomach**
a foolish or stupid person
   Pilot Survey and Survey I.
   [*DNE, COD, EDD, OED3* Chiefly *Irish English, Manx English,* and *Newfoundland* (1818), *DARE,* W3 *chiefly Irish*; at *omadan DPEIE*]

*As several of the dictionaries listed above indicate, *omadhaun* is borrowed from the Irish Gaelic *amadan* but is also found in Scottish Gaelic *amadan* "clown, fool" *GED*.

one-lunger noun; also spelled **one lunger**; compare **make-and-break engine**
an early engine with one cylinder; a boat using such an engine
   1994 SAMSON *River Bourgeois* 36 George DeRoche recalls that the mill was operated by a 10-horse power *Fairbanks Morris* motor. This engine was unique in that it had a magneto and was primed with gasoline, however it could operate on either gasoline or kerosene. Fred Digout called it a "one lunger", it was huge. 2000 MACKINNON *Cape Bretoner* 8 (1), 52 The Dan B. was a twenty-two-foot open craft with an old Acadia engine, often referred to as a "one lunger". Pilot Survey Inf. 3 A very reliable engine too. Survey II Inf. 8 As a youth, I worked one season with a man who used a one-lunger. He had a compass for navigation.
   [engine and boat *DPEIE*; boat only *DNE*; engine only: *SSPB, ML*; engine, boat and vehicle: *OED3 slang* (1908), *W3 slang, NOAD informal*]

*Most respondents to the Pilot Survey and Survey II reported that *one-lunger* applies to the engine, and nearly half of these indicated it also applies to the boat using the engine.

on the keg prepositional phrase
on the wagon, refraining from alcohol,
often for a specific time

1987 *CB's Magazine* 46, 16 And we had
no liquor, no rum. Little Jack was on the
keg. 1987 MACEACHERN *George Mac-
Eachern* 90 ... I was set up after being on
the keg for six months. I never recovered
from that for a long while. I hadn't had a
drink in six months ... 1990 Beaton Institute Tape 3012 ... I don't know how many
years we had him, but he had been on the
keg for years.

[Compare *keg* as a verb, meaning to ab-
stain from alcohol for a stated time: *DNE,
EDD, DAE* (1789)]

on the lift prepositional phrase; also **on
the liftens**
ill or weak, requiring help to stand up;
convalescing

2005 MACKENZIE *Neighbours are
Watching* 57 No priest, but old Doctor
Murray was at the bedside when another
Gulf Shore man was "on the liftens." 2010
ST. CLAIR Email 23 May ... having been
"on the lift" i.e. unwell for the past several
weeks, I have been wondering if you have
that expression – very common hereabouts – refers to the need to lift up sick
cows which were not able to rise on their
own – to be on the lift means ailing or sick
enough so as to curtail activities.

[*DPEIE, OED3* (*Southern U.S.*), *DARE*
chiefly Sth, Midl (1888); at *lift* W3 *South &
Midlands*]

open-air communion noun; often spelled
with initial capitals; also **five-day communion, sacrament**; compare **ceist, Sàcramaid, tent, token**
a Presbyterian communion service, held
out of doors to accommodate the large
congregation and originally spanning five
days (Thursday to Monday afternoon):
Day of Fasting (*La Traisg*), Question Day
(*La Ceist*), Preparation Day, Communion

Day, and Day of Thanksgiving (also the
Sad Day)

1913 CAMPBELL *CB Worthies* 19 At
the open air communion his place was
in front of the "tent" and he was often
the leading precentor ... 1921 MURRAY
History of the Presbyterian Church in CB
265–6 ... another custom which our pious
ancestors brought from the old land,
demands attention, and that was the
Annual Open Air Communion Season.
1940 MORRISON *Dalhousie Review* 20,
184 But the great event in their religious
life was the Open Air Communion, held
once a year, and known in the vernacular as "the Sacrament." 1976 MACLEAN
God and the Devil 48 This was the Sabbath of the "sacrament" Season. Once
a year in mid-June services began on
Thursday ... 1984 CUMMING et al. *Story
of Framboise* 113 Special five-day communion services (the **Comanachadh** or
sacrament), usually held in August, were
the outstanding event of the church year
in Framboise as in other Presbyterian
communities in Cape Breton. People
from as far as forty and fifty miles away
walked to these services, staying for the
five days with friends who had prepared
an abundance of food beforehand. 2006
STANLEY-BLACKWELL *Tokens of Grace*
7 For these staunch believers, few rituals
were as important as the open-air communion which became a central landmark
in their spiritual lives. This sacramental
event ... was transported from Scotland
to Cape Breton in the early 19th century
with little dilution. It retained, against all
odds, many of its original characteristics
for almost three-quarters of a century ...
By the early 20th century, Cape Breton's
open-air communion was only a shadow
of its former self, increasingly at odds
with the changing spirit of the times.

oran ['oræn] noun, plural form **orain**
a song

1953 DUNN *Highland Settler* 72 In Gaelic, he would never say "Sgriobh mi oran," "I *wrote* a song," but rather "Rinn mi oran," "I *made* a song." 1978 *Oran Inbhirnis* 6 Apr. 3 Dear "Oran Inbhirnis" people, I enjoyed the writeup in your very interesting paper ... 1978 *CB's Magazine* 21, 45 Then [a singer would] name one of the girls at the milling board, that she'd go with him ... We used to call them Oran Leannanachd (Courtship Song). I remember when there were two or three of those kinds of songs. 1984 CUMMING et al. *Story of Framboise* 168 Perhaps his most famous song is **Òran do Cheap Breatainn** (Song to Cape Breton) which has been recorded numerous times and is sometimes known as the "the Gaelic national anthem of Cape Breton." 1999 *CB's Magazine* 74 Back Cover Òran an Eich / The Horse Song. 2007 *DCBE* Tape SHERRINGTON 2 Like Rankin MacDonald who works at the *Oran* was here when I used to be at the paper, newspaper ...

*A loanword from Scottish Gaelic, see *oran* "song" *GED*.

order, the noun
groceries

1983 MELLOR *Company Store* 282 *I used to go up for the rations and the old feller serving them out would yell "Order for ten!"* 1999 MACNEIL Oral Communication 20 Sept. "The order" was used by my mother for groceries. Survey I Inf. 7 Mother would say "Pick up the order." Survey I Inf. 31 People used to order their groceries, and they would be delivered by cart (later by truck); now we pick up our own order. Survey I Inf. 34 Isolated communities would send in your order and it comes in a boat, etc. Survey I Inf. 38 You say, you're going to get the grocery order, which probably came from miners' wives going to company stores to get what they asked for, and consequently became shortened to "the order."

*Although "grocery order" is widely used (see for example, *GCD*, definition 8), many middle-aged and older Cape Bretoners routinely refer to groceries with the shortened *the order* and refer to grocery shopping as "going for the order."

ouragan noun
a water-tight platter, dish or bowl made of birch bark

1760 PICHON *Genuine Letters ... CB* 130 The guests bring with them each man a large bason [*sic*] made of the bark of a tree, which bason they call an *ouragan*. Then they carve the meat, and the portions being equally divided, they add another lesser *ouragan* filled with sea-wolf's oil. 1760 PICHON *Genuine Letters ... CB* 154 The bridegroom being seated among the lads, and the bride among the girls, each waited for their respective dish of meat. This was brought to them in two *ouragans* of equal bigness, which were placed in the middle of the cottage. 1975 MARTIN *Ethnohistory* 22 (2), 124 ... Lescarbot made a curious distinction between a "cauldron" and a "platter, or dish." The Micmac word for the former was "aouau, or astikov"; the word for "dish" (as in birchbark dish, described above) was "ouragan."

[at *ourogan DC* ([1693]); compare *rogan*: *DC* (1743), *OED3 Canad*. Now chiefly *hist*. (1743), *DA*]

outport noun
a small, remote fishing community along the coast

1886 CANADA *Official Report of the Debates of the House of Commons* 1178 I suggested that the outports be joined, and the large port of Sydney be independent ... 1968 CLARK *Acadia: Geography of Early NS* 282 Although it [St. Ann during the mid 1700s] never rivaled Louisburg in trading activity, it may have had more than any other outport; more ships visited it to pick up fish or sell supplies, and its residents usually had some sloops or schooners in the coastal trade (cabotage). 1984 BAL-COM *Cod Fishery of Isle Royale* 6–7 Distance and market size slightly weakened its [Louisbourg's] trading monopoly over the outports; Niganich (Ingonish) and Petit Degrat, both relatively large and distant centres, were the only outports that regularly received trading vessels from abroad. 1992 HORNSBY *Nineteenth-Century CB* 93 The outports were still dominated by the merchant premises. 1985 *CB's Magazine* 39, 3 And there was a little coastal motor vessel, called the Josephine K. She used to run from Halifax with freight for all the little outports.

[*DC Maritimes* (1835), *COD Maritimes*, *GCD Cdn*.]

*Contrast the regional usage in Cape Breton with that in Newfoundland: "a coastal settlement other than the port of St. John's" *DNE* (1810), *DC Nfld*, *COD Cdn* (*Nfld*), *NCD Newfoundland*, and a remote port found exclusively or especially in Newfoundland *FWCCD Canadian*, *OED3 Canad.* (1810), *COED*, *W3*, and *MWCD*.

outside adverb and preposition; compare **inside**
among commercial fishers, beyond the harbour; offshore in the open sea
1877 HALIFAX COMMISSION *Halifax Fisheries Commission, Appendix M* 1 Occasionally they find it advantageous to fish in-shore for mackerel, but they can usually do better outside, even for mackerel ... 1972 *CB's Magazine* 1, 1 Ten, fifteen fathoms for the harbour. Outside, they made them [ropes for anchoring nets] twenty-five fathoms long. 1993 Beaton Institute Tape 3229 B You would put in some long hours when you were going outside to fish. You would probably leave

at two in the morning, two a.m. If you got home at seven or eight o'clock in the evening, sometimes even later – this is when you were going outside – you'd put in the really long hours. 1996 *CB's Magazine* 70, 91 He was one of the king fishermen there. He'd go outside, perhaps 10 miles or so, and they used to fish and ship their fish to New York ... Pilot Survey Inf. 1 I've heard fishermen talking about "outside the harbour." They wouldn't say they're going "beyond the harbour"; they'd say I'm going "outside the harbour." Pilot Survey Inf. 5 Outside – there's two meanings: one means beyond the harbour, and the other one refers to a fishing area away from shore ... Well, I've often heard the term she's blowing bad outside, that'll be away from the harbour, and guys that are jigging cod or catching crabs they call it outside. So, it's a double meaning. Survey II Inf. 3 Outside – a relative term – out farther from the shoreline.

[*DNE* (1812), *DPEIE*, *SSPB*, *DARE*]

overman noun
a coal company official responsible for supervision of miners and safety underground
1905 DAVIDSON and MACKENZIE *The Canadian Mining Review* 24 (3), 51 He gave the alarm to the underground manager, who, with an overman, immediately travelled directly towards the fire, through the smoke on the Back Deep. 1936 *NS Miner* 271, 2 The big overman on 8 Landing refused to pay the men for work but told them they could work one idle day if they would load 30 boxes of dirt to pay him for the shift he lost. 1978 *Oran Inbhirnis* 9 Feb. 18 ... a commission was sent in to study the accident ... and reported that "The existence of this fault was known to the overman, but it did not appear serious to him." 1978 *CB's Magazine* 21, 4 When I got back out the overman was there. He said, "Listen, boy,

there's an explosion. How about going back in after those loaders?" 1999 KELLY *Cape Bretoner* 7 (4), 37 After I got my mine examiner's papers, I went to night school and got my overman's papers. You hear them called supervisor's papers today, but in the Mine Regulations Act it's overman's papers. 2007 MACKENZIE *CB Coal Mine Disasters* 15 The underground manager and the overman had entered some unexamined idle deeps with the goal of arranging a plan to begin working the area again.

[Although several dictionaries define *overman* as an overseer or foreman in general, the following stress the connection to coal mining: *EDD*, *OED3* Chiefly *Brit.* (1606), *COED*)]

over town prepositional phrase
down town, across town, to the other side of town

1975 *CB's Magazine* 10, 14 And in a week's time he sold every head he had with him over town or where he was selling it. 1993 *Inverness Oran* 18 July 5 [If Mary's Hill Home closes] Could John A. Chisholm still "go over town" and get the local newspaper? 1993 WHITNEY PIER HISTORICAL SOCIETY *From the Pier Dear* 1 The only connection with the rest of Sydney ("over town") is a huge overpass which travels over the railway tracks between the steel plant and the now defunct Coke Ovens. 1994 JESSOME *Murder at McDonald's* 13 Kids growing up in the Pier often find themselves on the defensive when they head "over town" to high school, perhaps because of the perception of the area as the "wrong side of the tracks." 2000 BLOOMER *Cape Bretoner* 8 (1), 54 I was born in Whitney Pier in 1928 at 105 Henry Street, where my family lived for thirteen years before moving "over town".

[at *overtown DARE* **chiefly NEast, N Cent** (1901)]

P

pack noun; also **brusher(s) pack, pack-wall**; compare **chuck, brusher**
a roof-bearing wall in a coal mine built with stone packed inside a frame of wooden blocks (chuck blocks), typically used along haulage ways and in long-wall mining

1928 HAY *Coal Mining Operations in the Sydney Coal Field* 25 Stone packwalls were built along both ribs of the haulageway ... The packwalls were given a coat of gunite, 1 cement, 3 1/2 sand. This bonded the walls, closed the crevices and reduced to a minimum irregularities where coal dust might lodge. 1972 Beaton Institute Tape 570 That was secured with timber and the regular security process of long-wall work – which is to build packs out of the waste material and what they call chuck blocks. 2004 MACKENZIE *Bloody CB Coal* 73 They shot this stone down, and used it to build a roof-supporting "pack" at the side of the level and part way down the wall. This pack would be about six feet wide, reaching 17 feet down the wall. 2007 MACKENZIE *CB Coal Mine Disasters* 3 But there were always those of us who pieced and patched, tossed rubbish and oil cans into the mix in the "brusher packs" to fill them more quickly, to keep things moving, to get the coal out – using methods "good enough for the pit."

[*OED3 Mining* (1867); at *packwall EDD* (1888)]

pairing song noun; compare **putting up song, milling frolic, milling song**
an impromptu song matching single men and women at the conclusion of a milling frolic

1953 DUNN *Highland Settler* 40 The more knowing matrons would pair off the various girls present with the men who were destined to be their husbands. There were many forms of this "pairing" song and many ingenious impromptu modifications of each form. 1991 LAVERY and LAVERY *Gabarus and Vicinity* 79 Since it was often late in the evening, the tone of this song [putting up song] was inclined to be "playful" in keeping with the spirits of the guests. It was also called a "pairing" song, because during the singing the girls were paired off with the men who would become their husbands.

pan line noun; also spelled **pan-line**, **panline**; also **pan**, **shaker pan**
a series of sloped metal pans that vibrate to move coal from the face (the area where coal is excavated) to coal boxes or conveyor belts for haulage to the surface
   1939 Beaton Institute MG 12 43 E4 Box 3, 111 ... from loading [coal] boxes they changed to shaker pans. 1997 *CB's Magazine* 72, 2 And you loaded that on a panline. The panline was shaker pans. (They ran the length of the wall?) That's right. And the coal went the length of the wall, and it was loaded in probably 18-box (car) trips, on the bottom of the wall ... 1999a MIGLIORE and DIPIERRO eds. *Italian Lives* 330 In the early years of longwall, loaders manually shovelled the mined coal onto a conveyer system ("pan line" or "shaker pans") which spilled the coal into boxes at the low end of the wall, for haulage out of the mine. 2003 SAINT AGNES ELEMENTARY SCHOOL *Coal Miners' Stories* 57 The continuous miner put the coal on a pan line down at the bottom of the wall, where there was a belt line that took the coal and it was dumped into one-ton boxes. 2004 MACKENZIE *Bloody CB Coal* 44 All the walls then were using what were called shaker pans to convey the coal from the wall face to the level below. Each pan was seven feet long and about three feet wide. It looked like

a huge bread pan with sides but no ends, the sides tilted outward, and made with a tapered "step" in them for strength. About 20 to 25 of these pans were bolted together to make one pan line. 2010 MCNEIL *Pit Talk* 108 The panline, the thing that took the coal, was right up tight against the face.
   [at *shaker* W3]

pan of ice: see **ice pan**

pan shovel noun; see **banjo**
a short-handled shovel with a large circular blade used to load and shovel coal
   1946 Beaton Institute MG 12 107, 13 Nov. n.p. There is a shortage of Pan Shovels in all the Coal Company's mines at present, and men are being forced to return home. 1979 CURRIE *Glace Bay Miner's Museum* 2 He had a huge hand. Pan shovel hands we used to call people with hands like that. We used to think you got them from loading coal with a pan shovel. 1988 Beaton Institute Tape 2371 They [coal trimmers] worked in the coal piers and they used to have these great big pan shovels ... [for] shovelling coal ... 1999a MIGLIORE and DIPIERRO eds. *Italian Lives* 330 The "loaders" then used large "pan shovels" to lift the coal by hand into "boxes" (small railcars). 2000 MACGILLIVRAY *Men of the Deeps* ix These men would take the coal from the "chutes" and unload it with their pan shovels at the homes of the miners who had earlier loaded this same coal into boxes deep out under the sea. 2008 *DCBE* Tape CURRIE 7 The pan shovel was the big shovel they used for loading coal because it was ... like a big pan. It would carry a lot of coal ...

Parade of Concern noun; also **March of Concern**; see **Black Friday**
a march and rally of an estimated 20,000 people on Nov. 19, 1967, to prevent the

announced closure by Hawker-Siddeley of the Sydney Steel Plant

1967 *CB Post* 20 Nov. 1 MARCH OF CONCERN – An estimated 20,000 persons paraded through city streets Sunday to express concern over the proposed closure of the Sydney Steel Plant. The parade climaxed in a giant rally at the Cape Breton Sports Centre addressed by Premier G. I. Smith and Federal Health Minister Allan MacEachen. 1967 *CB Post* 20 Nov. 2 THEY CAME FROM INVERNESS COUNTY – Students of Margaree Forks District High in Inverness County joined in Sunday's Parade of Concern. People from all parts of the island and parts of the mainland came to Sydney for the parade. 1991 *CB's Magazine* 58, 51 Some funny things happened (at the Parade of Concern). We never had a crowd like that before, so we had no experience – nobody. We were hoping that there would be no trouble. And people had told us there might be trouble. Because there was anger ... Charlie [MacKinnon] wrote that song, and he had the words written on the back of a MacDonald Export A cigarette package. And the darn thing took off. We had nothing else to do, anyway. And the crowd all got in on the chorus. And it really worked. You know, it was just a pure accident. 2003 SLAVEN sydneysteelmuseum.com/history/black-friday.htm What was the decisive factor in saving the Sydney plant in 1967? No doubt it was the Parade of Concern and the effect it had on the government officials. 2011 DOYLE *CB Facts and Folklore* 192-3 On Sunday, November 19, 1967, more than twenty thousand people marched in a Parade of Concern through the streets of Sydney to focus attention on the announced closure of the steel plant and the crisis it would cause ... Not long after, the province of Nova Scotia took over the steel plant and ran it as a Crown corporation.

parcel post noun; also spelled **Parcel Post**
a fundraising activity where people bid on wrapped packages without knowing their contents

1979 *Inverness Oran* 3 May 5 The Margaree members will hold a Pie Sale, the Mabou members a bake sale and the Port Hood members a "Parcel Post." 1985 *CB's Magazine* 40, 20 The Auxiliary raised $338.73 by card socials and Parcel Post sales and from lunches at the Auxiliary Meetings ... 2011 ST. CLAIR Email 21 June [Parcel post was] a popular feature at fund raising activities ... Within the wrapped up parcel was some item and people would bid on the item with the funds going to the charity whatever it was – and the highest bidder got the parcel – it might have a cup and saucer inside or two candy bars or an old shoe or a fine china platter – the fun was in the not knowing what you bid on.

parlour noun; also spelled **parlor**; also **jail, prison**; compare **head, double parlour**
a chamber in a lobster trap used to trap the lobster after it leaves the baited chamber (or kitchen)

1957 WILDER *Canada's Lobster Fishery* 15 A similar, single [mesh] funnel leads from the kitchen to the parlour from which escape is more difficult. 1972 STAEBLER *CB Harbour* 119 We ... takes lopsters out o' parlour ... 1987 Beaton Institute Tape 2324 [Tape 1] They call it the parlour and temple ... Nearly every one [lobster] you get is in there. 1992 *CB's Magazine* 61, 61 There were two blank ends, two entrance openings and one parlor head to each trap. Pilot Survey Inf. 2 Then there's another heading that they crawl up and they fall into the parlour and they can't get back out. Survey II Inf. 1 Parlour is used but mostly called the prison in this area. Survey II Inf. 6 Jail is the first choice, second choice parlour. Survey II Inf. 8 The parlour [is used] in Big Bras d'Or, but jail is used down North.

[*DNE, DPEIE* (1910); at *parlor DARE*]

*Parlour and *jail* are the two most popular names for the chamber that traps the lobster, but fishers also use *prison*, *temple* and *bedroom* for this.

parlour trap noun; compare **double parlour**
a lobster trap with at least two chambers: one with bait (the kitchen) and the second (the parlour) that traps the lobster
1910 CANADA, DEPARTMENT OF MARINE AND FISHERIES *Lobster Fishery: Evidence* 761 Q. What trap do you fish now? A. What they call the jail or parlour trap. 1910 CANADA, DEPARTMENT OF MARINE AND FISHERIES *Lobster Fishery: Evidence* 662 A. Well, the chief merit is that the lobsters when they get into the parlour trap stay there, although, of course, I suppose some of them get out. 1985 MACGILLIVRAY et al. *History of Fourchu* 17 After several experiments with lath traps, the "parlour" trap was developed and it is that which is used today.

[at *parlour DNE* (1964)]

**Although the document *Lobster Fishery: Evidence* examined fishers from Quebec and the Maritimes, citations used here and below are taken from Cape Breton informants.

pavement noun
the floor in a coal mine
1905 DAVIDSON and MACKENZIE *The Canadian Mining Review* 24 (3), 50 The surface in the vicinity [of the Phalen Seam] is 89 feet above sea-level, while the pavement is 68 feet below sea-level. 1972 Beaton Institute Tape 570 They had a vertical steel column that they screwed between the roof and the pavement. These are mining terms, of course, roof and pavement. 1993 *CB's Magazine* 62, 8–9 When the roof is working, you maybe hear a few pebbles falling, but actually what you hear is when the stone hits the pavement or the floor. If you don't hear that, then you're probably underneath it. 1995 *DCBE* Tape NICHOLSON 7 Why do they call it the pavement [interviewer]? We have stone on top and stone on the bottom.

[*OED3 Mining* (1672)]

peggy noun; also **tiddly, peacock**
a children's game with regionally varied rules played with two sticks: a peggy or tiddly (a short stick, pointed at each end) and a makeshift bat used to hit the airborne peggy into the outfield
n.d. Beaton Institute Tape 2003 Tiddly – that's a game that is played by the kids today. You get a stick, you point it on both ends and ... then you bat it. You find out how many feet the tiddly went so the winner scores. You have to sort of flip it [interviewer]? Oh yes you flip it [the tiddly]. 1991 CAMERON *Wind, Whales and Whisky* 53 *Peggy* is based on a children's game which used to be played on Isle Madame. It involves batting a six-inch wooden peg, pointed at both ends, out past a fielder. I thought it was an indigenous Acadian game ... Then I learned it had also been played in Toronto, New Hampshire, Saskatchewan and Scotland. It had a variety of other names – peacock, tiddley [*sic*], one-eyed Sally, piggy, one-a-cat. 2008 *DCBE* Tape CURRIE 1 You get that six inch piece of broom stick and sharpen it at both ends and that's the peggy, and then that's the equivalent of a ball in other games ... You make a circle as wide as you can ... The batter then ... stands in front of that circle and the pitcher throws the peggy. As in baseball or softball, it would be an underhanded throw, and the batter then has to bat the ball.

[*DARE* **chiefly Nth, esp NEast** (1958); at *tiddly DNE*; compare *piggy*: *EDD, OED3 Eng. regional* (*north.*) and *Irish English*

(*north.*) (1862), and *peg and stick EDD*
(1898)]

pick noun; often in the phrase **not a pick**
a small amount of anything, especially of
flesh or food, a bit
　　Survey I Inf. 14 A pick of food. Survey
I Inf. 23 Similar to a pinch – a pick of that
will do. You have a pick of paint on your
jacket. Survey I Inf. 28 Not a pick on his
bones. Survey I Inf. 34 Not a pick of flesh
on him. Survey I Inf. 41 Not a pick of meat
on that rabbit.
　　[*DNE, DPEIE, EDD, OED3* referring to
food Now *regional* (chiefly *Sc.* and *Irish
English*) and *colloq.* (1688); referring to a
small portion or amount Chiefly *Sc.* and
Irish English (*north.*) (1866), *DSL*, W3 *dial*]

*Compare the Scottish Gaelic, *pioc* "small
portion, pinch" *GED*.

picking arms verbal noun
an entry-level job at a lobster cannery,
removing the meat from the lobster's arm,
the portion between the claw and the
body
　　1972 Beaton Institute Tape 501 ...
picking arms at night – $2.50 a month.
1981 Beaton Institute Tape 2039 Picking
arms was hell on the hands but crank-
ing wasn't. 1985 MACGILLIVRAY et al.
History of Fourchu 22 Hector MacCormick
recalls his first job of "picking arms": It
wasn't a pleasant job taking the meat out
of the arms; it was hard on the hands.

piece-can noun; also spelled **piece can**;
also **pit can**
a lunch can, typically used by miners
　　1942 DENNIS *CB Over* 94 He had evi-
dently been just going to have his lunch
for he had his piece-can on his arm and
his flask of tea in his pocket. 1979 *Inverness
Oran* 8 Mar. 1 The three couples carried
a piece-can, a pit-helmet and a glennie to
the altar along with the bread and wine.

1980 *CB's Magazine* 25, 3 You know the
part of the mine that bothered me more
than anything else? To open my father's
pit can when we'd be doing the dishes.
And to smell it. 1991 NATIONAL FILM
BOARD *They Didn't Starve Us Out* When a
young fella would go in the mine, the old
fellas would show him how to carry his
piece-can, as they called it, you know ...
little round piece-can and a water-can.
1992 O'DONNELL *Coal Mining Songs* 51 ...
you dine / With your battered old piece-
can down deep in / the mine.
　　[Compare *piece* meaning a slice of bread
or snack: *FWCCD Dial., EDD Sc., OED3
Brit. regional* (chiefly *Sc., Irish English*, and
Eng. regional (*north.*)) and *U.S. regional*
(1619), *COED Scottish, DARE* **chiefly N
Midl, West** *old-fash*, W3]

pie social noun; compare **box social**
a fundraiser and dance where women
bring pies or cakes for auction and share
the food and evening with the successful
bidders
　　1906 Beaton Institute MB [Microfilm]
65, 17 May Attended pie social in the
Salvation Army hall in the evening. 1920
Beaton Institute MG 12 59 Box 1 n.p. Half
drunken crowd at the pie social at Westmount last night. [1991?] MACLEAN
Story of Canoe Lake, CB 55 The pie social
was an interesting event. The ladies
would bake a cake or other sweets and
make sandwiches and put it all in a decorated box ... The box would go to the highest bidder. Then the lady who made up
the box would have lunch with whoever
had bought it. There was much interest in
seeing who would get the boxes, especially if there was a guy who was bent on
having lunch with a certain girl. There
would always be a dance that would
continue until the morning. 1994 SAM-
SON *River Bourgeois* 222 Residents generated some income through events such as
Pie Socials. For the occasion, girls baked

pies or cakes which were placed out for auction. The highest bidder, hopefully a favourite young lad, would have the opportunity to walk the lassie home and share the tasty pie along the way. These Socials were very popular and many resulted in lasting relationships.

[*DPEIE* (1892), *GCD Cdn.*, *DARE*; compare *pie supper*: *OED3* U.S. (1887), *DARE*, *DA*]

pigeon hole: see **manhole**

pillar noun; often in the phrase **room and pillar**, **pillar and room**; compare **room**, **rob the pillar**
a solid block of coal (typically forty to sixty feet square) left to support the mine roof between areas (rooms) where the coal has been excavated

1889 GILPIN *Canadian Mining Review* 8 (6), 77 The shape and size of pillars varies with the depth of the seam, and the nature of the roof. 1893 ARCHIBALD *Canadian Mining & Mechanical Review* 12 (4), 59 The pillar and room system has been universally adopted at the coal mines in Cape Breton, until the Gardener mine very recently changed from that system to longwall. 1903 VERNON *CB Canada* 227 The system of working is the pillar and room. 1928 HAY *Coal Mining Operations in the Sydney Coal Field* 19 The system of mining is pillar and room. This is the only system feasible within present cover limits, where 56 percent of the coal is left to support the sea bottom. 1983 SHEDDEN et al. *Mining Photographs* 271 **Pillar** – A column or body of coal left unmined to support the roof. 1984 *CB's Magazine* 36, 61 ... [in 1885] it was not unusual to find the boards seven or eight yards, and the pillars only two or three yards, wide. As a natural consequence, the pillars, being too weak to bear the weight of the superincumbent strata, were crushed in and entirely lost ... 1999 FRANK *J. B.*

McLachlan 49 ... the miners worked in a small, isolated space – known as a "room" – seventeen feet square and divided from the next room by a sixty-foot block – or "pillar" – of coal. 2007 MACKENZIE *CB Coal Mine Disasters* 95 What we have now are two 10-foot-wide rooms, created by mining out the coal, and a 40-foot solid block of coal, or "pillar," that separates the two rooms and supports the roof.

[*COD*, *EDD*, *OED3 Mining* (chiefly *Coal Mining*) (1708), *W3*, *MWCD*]

pin head: see **head**

pint noun
a half bottle (approximately 375 ml or 13 oz.) of liquor, especially of rum; occasionally a bottle or drink of beer or ale

1975 *CB's Magazine* 11, 11 ... I met this fellow and we went to the bootlegger for a few pints of beer. 1990 MACDONALD *Assuming I'm Right* 67 Politics has changed. The Parish Hall and the handshake are gone ... halls full of people looking for 'spies' and 'fence jumpers' and a pint are a part of the past. 1990 *CB's Magazine* 55, 28 (He) suggests that we go out to the lake, pick up the bottle of rum – pint – and bring it back to my place. 2007b BARBER *Only in Canada* 136 **pint** (*Maritimes*) a mickey of liquor.

[*COD Cdn* (*Maritimes*); at *pint* meaning a drink of beer or ale: *OED3* (1613), *NOAD Brit. informal*, *W3 chiefly Brit*]

pit noun
a coal mine, occasionally a bootleg mine

1856 PROVINCE OF NOVA SCOTIA *Journal and Proceedings of Her Majesty's Legislative Council* 95 ... a Lot of Land was purchased at the Barrasois [now New Waterford] ... for the purpose of striking a Pit thereon ... 1910 in 1992 *CB's Magazine* 59, 43 [quoting *Eastern Labor News*] Some have been known likewise to have fainted in the pit from want of nourishment.

1976–7 Miners' Museum Tape 124 I started with my father in what we call the pit in the lane. It was used actually for to supplement the wages ... It was actually considered an illegal mine. 1979 FRANK "CB Coal Miners, 1917–1926" 104–5 The recitation of traditional stories, new tales, old songs and new songs, was a feature of many formal and informal social gatherings ... in the tavern, on street corners, the yards, the wash-house and the pit. 2006 MACISAAC *Better Life* 105 Out of economic necessity many boys left school at a young age to go to work "in the pit."

[Dictionaries specifically identifying a *pit* as a coal mine: *COD, OED3* (1447), *COED, W3, NOAD*]

pit boot noun, usually plural; also spelled **pit-boot**; see **pit shoe**
a work boot, not exclusively worn by miners

1905 *Sydney Mines Illustrated* n.p. If you want a good pair of Pit Boots or working boots of any kind, buy the "Amherst" make. 1939 in 1985 MOOGK *CB at 200* 152 ... we [the militia] were all going around with working boots on, pit boots and everything else. 1981 *CB's Magazine* 29, 45 And the man who was exhausted, with his huge big pit boots on, sitting alongside of him, felt he just had to get up and dance, the music was that good. 1991 *CB's Magazine* 57, 25 It's a terrible thing among children to create the jealousy. And I knew that. So if they wore pit boots, my children wore pit boots. And they were dressed exactly like the miners' kids. 1997 MACDONALD *Fall on Your Knees* 219 Now at dawn he turns homeward, listening for the sound of pit boots along Plummer Avenue, expecting to hear the mine whistle.

[*OED3* (1894); compare the more general understanding of *pitboots* "boots worn by miners when hewing coal" *EDD* (1894)]

pit bottom noun
in a coal mine, typically the bottom of a shaft or the lowest point of the slope into the mine

1890 Anon. *Canadian Mining Review* 9 (4), 46 At the Sydney mines the management are fitting up a new underground forcing pump of 36 in. cylinder and 5 ft. stroke to force the water from pit bottom in one lift of 700 feet to the surface ... 1969 Beaton Institute Tape 118 So Jack jumped in the empty tub [coal car], and here it wasn't an empty tub at all. There were a dead horse in it, and he had to keep with the dead horse for five minutes till he got to the pit bottom. 1974 *CB's Magazine* 8, 7 ... then if the mine knocked off they'd give you 6 raps from the pit bottom, bottom of the shaft – and you'd give 6 raps to the next fellow, and he'd give it – messages. 1979 Beaton Institute Tape 2421 [Tape 1] I remember working on that low side on the pit bottom. 2000 MACGIL-LIVRAY *Men of the Deeps* 144 *Then you'd get in the cage and go down to the pit bottom to report.*

[*EDD, OED3* (c1540)]

pit can: see **piece-can**

pit clothes noun
work clothes worn in a coal mine

1925 GOLD *Social Welfare* 7 (11), 223 The mine-worker must provide himself with pit clothes and other equipment ... 1995 *DCBE* Tape NICHOLSON 4 All you had was one hook. You pull it down, your pit clothes was all on to it ... every couple of weeks we'd wash them out. 2000 MACKENZIE *Cape Bretoner* 7 (6), 24 The wash house was a beehive of activity. Murmur of a hundred men or more. Everyone changing from street clothes to pit clothes getting ready for the shift. 2003 SAINT AGNES ELEMENTARY SCHOOL *Coal Miners' Stories* 78 You get to work, undress, put your pit clothes on and punch your card in to start your work day.

[*EDD*, *OED3* (1859)]

pit head noun; also spelled, **pit-head, pithead**; compare **bankhead**
the area around the entrance to a coal mine; the entrance itself

1917 in 1978 *CB's Magazine* 21, 6 [quoting *Sydney Daily Post* 26 July] ... the crowd had grouped themselves, discussing the disaster in low tones, and watching with worried, strained faces the wagons, ambulances and teams as they passed to and fro from the pit head. 1970 Beaton Institute Tape 165 There is more real adult education at the pit heads down in the mines ... 1983 MELLOR *Company Store* 89 Long before dawn, miners working the day shift left their company houses to report for work at pitheads all across Cape Breton. 1985 MACKENZIE *Tracks across the Maritimes* 41 The first track the company built ran from the pit head at Sydney Mines to the shipping piers at North Sydney. 2000 MACKENZIE *Cape Bretoner* 7 (6), 24 ... then another mad rush from this pithead memorial to the washhouse.

[at pithead: *COD*, *OED3* (1749), *COED*, *W3*]

pit horse: see **pit pony**

pit lamp noun; compare **clanny, stop a lamp**
a miner's safety light, either a clanny (also glanny) lamp or an electric light

1993 Beaton Institute Tape 3191 And we carried the "glannies" then – we didn't even have electric lights ... just called it a pit lamp. 1995 *DCBE* Tape SMITH 1 And then we used to wear a soft canvas cap with a leather peak, and the leather peak it was made in such a way that it would hold our pit lamp. 1996 MACMILLAN *Boy from Port Hood* 54 It [the explosion]

drove a pit lamp into the side of his head. 2000 MACGILLIVRAY *Men of the Deeps* 32 Plus, for this trip to Expo we borrowed real pit lamps.

[*OED3* (1860)]

pit pony noun; also **pit horse**
a sturdy pony, or small horse, used for hauling in a coal mine

1921 *Glace Bay Gazette* 2 July 6 A new day was ushered in at Dominion No.'s 2 and 9 collieries, when the Edison electric safety lamp was first used. All the men were delighted and the poor pit horses with their 'pit eyes' were dazzled, and puzzled to understand what strange happening had taken place. 1963 *Punching with Pemberton* Jan. 3 ... Roddie learned to drive a pit pony in the old Reserve French Slope Mine in 1911. 1964 ROBINSON *Canadian Geographical Journal* 69, 91 [Caption] Pit ponies have been replaced almost completely by machines in [the] town's mines. Only a small number are still in service. 1977 *Inverness Oran* 21 Apr. 14 The pit-horses were brought by the company on condition ... For obvious reasons, the universal qualification for a mine-horse was that he was low set. He also required strength, a sharp animal wisdom and quick reflexes ... Their work day was unionized, a horse worked the same shift hours as the crew, and there were horses assigned to each shift. 1990 [MACNEIL] *History of Sydney Mines* 29 [In] 1960 Last pit pony to work in Princess [Mine]. 2000 TENNYSON and SARTY *Guardian of the Gulf* 101 One inspecting officer was clearly impressed by how 'hardy and active' the pit ponies proved to be ... 2007 ST. CLAIR and LEVERT *Nancy's Wedding Feast* 150 Edward's older brothers were already experienced handlers of the pit ponies that pulled the carts full of coal through the mines.

[*OED3* (1876), *COED* Brit. historical, *W3* chiefly Brit; at *pit-horse OED3* (1798)]

pit prop noun; also **prop**; compare **pit timber, timber**
a trimmed log, six to eight feet long and approximately six inches in diameter, used as a vertical support for the mine roof; later, a steel post similarly used

1903 VERNON *CB Canada* 135 The most important uses to which it [timber] is put are for pit-props for the mines ... 1905 DAVIDSON and MACKENZIE *The Canadian Mining Review* 24 (3), 56 In some places where the roof was very heavy props were used in the centre of the boom. 1920 Beaton Institute MG 12 46 A9 n.p. Timber used in Mines year ending Sept. 30, 1919 ... Props ... 496,236. 1974 LOTZ and LOTZ *CB Island* 97 In 1969, Cape Breton produced a little over a million cubic feet of rough pit props ... 1986 *CB's Magazine* 41, 2 See, in the wintertime they cut timber for the mine-booms and pit props. Pit props were for Glace Bay. That was part of your farming. 1988 Beaton Institute Tape 2381 ... pit props would be piled ... and Dunlap's [a general store] would exchange the wood for groceries or merchandise or money. 1990 Beaton Institute Tape 3004 They used to ship car loads from River Denys, pit props they called them. They're sticks of wood eight feet long about six to eight inches in diameter, and they ship car loads of that down to the mines in Sydney. 1996 *CB Post* 1 June 3A When the lake ice was thick enough the pit props would be loaded on to a steel shod sleigh and hauled across to Boisdale.

[*EDD, OED3* (1794), W3; at *prop: EDD, OED3 Mining* (1613), W3]

pit shoe noun; see **pit boot**
a work boot, especially worn by miners

1972 Beaton Institute Tape 345 I told him I got no pit shoes, working boots ... 1979 FRANK "CB Coal Miners, 1917–1926" 390 Men's pit shoes, 6 pairs 16.50. 1984 Beaton Institute Tape 2159 We had to buy everything on our own, pit shoes, hat, lamp and everything. 1995 *DCBE* Tape SMITH 1 Back in 1936 when I started to work there were no safety boots. Our pit shoes – we used to call them tar paper, tar paper boots because they were made of rough leather and they were very soft.

pit sock noun, usually plural
a grey woolen work sock, whether worn by a miner or not

1976 CURTIS *Atlantic Advocate* 69 Mar. 42 With the coming of snow, out from the mothballs came the long johns, and the wool melton ski pants and breeches, then the heavy grey woolen "pit socks". 1990 MACDONALD *'Tis Me Again, B'y* 80 I pulled on three overcoats, one over the other, and grabbed a pair of discarded pit socks for mitts to face the arctic temperatures. 2007b BARBER *Only in Canada* 104 **pit socks** (*Cape Breton*) standard grey work socks, especially worn by miners. 2008 CREWE *Ava Comes Home* 176 They [two women] had on thick pit socks and both had terrible bedhead.

[*COD Cdn* (*Cape Breton*)]

pit talk noun
conversations about coal mining, the events, humour, technical details, and stories, shared in the mine and at social gatherings

1979 FRANK "CB Coal Miners, 1917–1926" 232 In the course of the day's work the men in a section gathered from time to time to exchange rounds of "pit talk", which ranged from serious discussions of mine operations, union affairs and politics to horseplay, practical jokes and ribald stories. 2000 MACGILLIVRAY *Men of the Deeps* xi "Pit talk" was really a celebration of the mining experience. It centered around the skills and the creativity and comradeship of the miners. Many of the stories had to do with feats of strength in times of crisis. They would tell and retell accounts of how powerful men had rescued injured "buddies" who had been trapped under the crushing weight of fallen stone. Other stories would tell of the contests between miners, where the raw strength of one collier was often bested by the ingenuity of a less-muscled competitor. 2001 SMITH-PIOVESAN *Sculptures from Jagged Ore* 184–5 Edna said that whenever her family gathered for any occasion the topic inevitably turned to "pit talk."

pit timber noun; compare **pit prop**, **timber**
a trimmed log, six to eight feet long and approximately six inches in diameter, used primarily as a vertical support for the mine roof
1916 RANKIN *Old Home Week. Grand Mira CB* n.p. This parish, I understand, has been for many years a veritable hive of industry, supplying pit timber for the coal mines ... 1961 Beaton Institute MG 12 43 D3 f10 Box 2, 107 ... pit timber, 5 in. diameter. 6 ft. long. 1970 Beaton Institute Tape 205 We could go to the woods and cut pit timber ... The most they wanted at that time would be six foot props and six foot eight caps ... the props were 50 cents a dozen. 1974 Beaton Institute Tape 1005 ... grandpa had no monthly income so for substitute he and Dan MacLean ... would cut pit timber amounting to two car loads yearly on grandpa's farm. 1994 *CB's Magazine* 66, 5 They used pit timber for going underground, to hold the land up (the roof of the mine). There was every length and dimension you could need. 1996 *CB's Magazine* 70, 6 I cut pit timbers for the mines and everything.
[*OED3* (1793)]

plaster noun
gypsum; also used in place names
1768 in 1935 HOLLAND *Description of the Island of CB* 60 In Plaster Cove is a large Clifft, with a Cavern that goes for some Distance under Ground, from which the French transported great Quantities of Plaster to Louisbourg, for sundry Uses; it is of a good Quality as appeared to me upon Tryal. 1878 in 1989 *CB's Magazine* 51, 51 We passed some plaster-cliffs, which furnish material for many of the best ceilings in our cities, and add a striking feature to the scenery. 1885 in 1987 *CB's Magazine* 44, 74 Aug. 8th – Speeding along on the back eddy of a strong tide, I kept close under the over-hanging cliffs of pure plaster, which literally forms the shore from Seal Island to Baddeck. 1894 BOLLES *From Blomidon to Smoky* 42 Gypsum, or "plaster," as Cape Breton calls it, occurs in many places on the Bras d'Or and along the north coast. 1899 WARNER *Baddeck and that Sort of Thing* 100 ... Port Hastings (as Plaster Cove now likes to be called) ... 1944 in 1995 *CB's Magazine* 68 Inside Front Cover FROM DUNCAN H. MacDONALD'S DIARY: May 2nd: Set nets. 5th: Two plaster boats. 1982 Beaton Institute Tape 2069 Way out back in the woods there is all big plaster holes there – ponds. And if you ever missed your step out there and go in they'd never find you. 1989 *CB's Magazine* 50, 110 I worked in the gypsum plant. Plaster quarry.

*As the citations indicate, the use of *gypsum* to mean the finished product *plaster* has a long history in Cape Breton and is reflected in some of the early descriptive place names.

pluck transitive verb
to deduct (money) unfairly from a worker's pay
1971 Beaton Institute Tape 217 ... you give your check number and it was deducted off your pay sheet, and the name became pluck-me as you'd pluck a chicken ... There was many of them never had drew a cent at all. It was plucked off their sheets. 1983 MELLOR *Company Store*

14 ... his sum total of earnings after deductions was nil, he turned to his mates and shouted "Christ, they've plucked me!" And the name stuck. 1999 CALABRESE *Cape Bretoner* 7 (4), 36 They used to call the store the 'pluck me'. I wasn't around at that time, but they plucked them alright.

[Compare *pluck* meaning to swindle or rob: FWCCD *Slang*, GCD *Slang*, OED3 (chiefly *slang* in later use) (*a*1500), W3]

pluck-me noun; also spelled **pluck me**, **Pluck-Me**, **Pluck Me**, **pluckme**; often used in the phrase **pluck-me store**; compare **company store**, **bobtail paysheet**
a disparaging term for the company store where workers purchased on credit

1902 BELL *The Canadian Mining Review* 21 (3), 46 It is rather a favorite pastime in some quarters to abuse and hold up to execration what are termed the "pluck me's", but we feel sure that any legislation directed against such stores as are run by the Dominion Coal Co. would be inimical to the best interests of the workmen. 1922 Beaton Institute MG 12 88 A1e f1, 4 ... a meeting was held one evening of the Retail Merchant's Association. It was for the purpose of devising some way to combat the unfair opposition of the Company "PLUCK-ME" Stores. 1967 MACDONALD *Atlantic Advocate* 57 Aug. 22 Even when those stores went down in 1925 there were men in debt to the Pluck-Me Store up to $1,000. 1981 HAMILTON *NS Traveller* 145 Meanwhile Besco played its trump card by eliminating all credit at company stores ... known locally as "pluck me's" (a phrase borrowed from Scottish miners who laboured under frighteningly similar conditions) ... 1986 PETRIE *Bay Boy* 52 MOTHER "Yes, that's what they're called, "Pluck Me." And for good reason. Miners get skinned in those places." 1988 BOUTILIER *New Waterford* 141 ... "The Pluck Me," [was] perhaps essential in early days but a bar to progress and independence

by 1925 when they were closed following the big strike which had actually started when management cut off credit at the company stores. 1992 O'DONNELL *Coal Mining Songs* 86 ["The Pluck Me Store"] But many a briny tear was shed / When the Pluck Me burned to the ground. 2006a MACADAM *Big Cy* 68 The miners bought on credit and purchases were deducted from their Friday night pay envelopes. The stores were known as "pluck-me's."

plum loaf noun
raisin bread

1990 *CB's Magazine* 55, 23 Like Mum would be making either raisin bread or plum loaf, whatever you want to call it ... 1990 MACQUEEN *Memory is My Diary* 28 ... raisin bread which we called "plum loaf." 2001 LEWIS *Sculptures from Jagged Ore* 114 Yet another time Marion recalls attempting to lock her prized plum loaf (raisin bread) in the dining room when she went out for the evening, confident that her ingenuity would result in the family having plum loaf to enjoy on Christmas morning. Survey I Inf. 17 Plum loaf [is used] for raisin bread. Survey I Inf. 23 Plum Loaf – spices – cinnamon or nutmeg, raisins.

[OED3 (1787); compare *plum bread* DA (1709)]

*The use of *plum* to indicate raisins (and occasionally currents) in cooking is widespread, but the compounds *plum loaf* and *plum bread* are rare as the dictionary list demonstrates. The OED3 notes at *plum* (4a) "The name was probably retained after the replacement of dried plums or prunes by raisins in certain recipes."

pogey noun
ground or cooked fish thrown overboard by commercial fishers to lure fish

1929b MCCAWLEY *CB Humour* 63 The politician scatters his promises as the

hand-liner scatters his "pogey," and the poor fish rise to the bait and get the hook. 1977 *CB's Magazine* 17, 1–2 When they're [mackerel] coming back in the fall, they don't school. You have to use what we call tollins or pogey – people often grind up mackerel and mix in salt. When it hits the water the salt'll take it down quicker. (That attracts mackerel.) 1993 Beaton Institute Tape 3229 A Well we used to call it tollins, but some called it pogey. It was mackerel; you chopped it up or cooked it on the stove ... and made it like soup, and when you throw it out to mackerel, they come to the boat for it.
[*DPEIE* (1980–1)]

*As T. K. Pratt notes about this meaning of *pogey*, "There appears to be no connection with the general Canadian slang sense of 'unemployment insurance'" (1988, 114).

pogy noun; also spelled **pogey, pogie**
menhaden (genus *Brevoortia*), fished seasonally by many Cape Bretoners off the New England coast
    1877 HALIFAX COMMISSION *Record of the Proceedings of the Halifax Fisheries Commission* 405 ... pogie is not necessarily an American bait, it is a deep-sea fish, as has been shown by different witnesses. 1920 SMITH and WIARD *CB Tales* 128 ... the pogeymen often did not put into port for weeks at a time ... 1992 *CB's Magazine* 61, 59 We finished pogy fishing in September 1915 and went back home for the winter. 1994 SAMSON *River Bourgeois* 86 In the 1940s, when Martin Pottie went to fish pogie each spring in Boston ... 1996 *CB's Magazine* 70, 2 My father was a fisherman in the States. They were pogy fishermen. Mostly all the settlers here [on Isle Madame], they were going pogy fishing in the spring. They'd fish for about eight months ... Pogy is a fish that they make fish meal with it. It's a fat, fat fish. And that's what the factories make fertilizer with.

[*OED3 U.S. regional* (1840), *DARE* (1840), *DAE, DA, W3, ML*]

poor man's fertilizer noun
a snowfall in late spring, thought to increase the fertility of the soil
    1997 MACLELLAN Oral Communication 22 Apr. My father used poor man's fertilizer and he lived in Benacadie. 1998 ST. CLAIR Oral Communication 11 May Late spring snow, believed to fertilize the field. Survey I.
    [*DPEIE, NCD Maritime Canada & New England, SSPB, DARE* **chiefly NEast** (1959); compare *robin snow ML*]

pork pie: see **Cape Breton pork pie**

pot: see **black pot**

pot noun
a rounded pot-shaped stone in a mine roof creating a risk to miners
    1990 PEACH *Memories of a CB Childhood* 119 ... one of these [risks] is the occurrence of "pots" in the roof. These are perfectly moulded cylinders of solid granite formed in the stone overlying the coal seam, weighing anywhere from two hundred pounds to tons. 1995 MACDONALD *Port Morien* 29 ... the [Gowerie] pit had a number of what were called pots. These deadly pots were rounded sections of the roof, about one to two feet in diameter, that protruded downwards. 1999 O'HANDLEY *Untold Stories of the Mine* 11–12 Another time a pot came out of the roof. It is a big round stone they can weight up to 100–500 pounds; it is just like a dome. My father told me to get out of the way and he wasn't even looking my way. I did and a big pot fell from the roof.
    [at *potstone EDD* (n.d.)]

potatoes and point noun
a meager meal of potatoes where those eating jokingly point at the little or no meat

1951 BRASSET *Doctor's Pilgrimage* 125 ... that evening we had a wonderful dinner of Potatoes and Point ... It means boiled potatoes served with nothing else but salt and pepper and imagination. It was invented, I believe, by an old sea cook who, when he found the pork barrel empty during an extra-long voyage, suspended the last tiny scrap of meat by a string from the ceiling of the galley so that each member of the crew could point to it between bites of boiled potato. Whether the story is true or not I do not know. Anyway, the term Potatoes and Point is commonly used in some parts of Cape Breton to designate a very skimpy meal. 1983 MELLOR *Company Store* 139–40 His [Wolvin's] sumptuous Christmas fare could hardly be compared with that of a Cape Breton miner or steel worker. Breast of turkey against "potato and point." With typical Cape Breton humour, miners made light of the cruel fact that they could no longer afford to buy meat for their daily sustenance. When a minuscule portion of meat was uncovered among the inevitable potato hash that comprised almost every evening meal, they would "point" at the precious speck as proof that their meal, often shared by eight or more children, was not totally devoid of meat! [*DPEIE*; at *point OED3* Chiefly *Irish English* (*humorous*) (1793); compare *bread and skip DARE*]

pound party noun
a party to which guests bring a pound typically of some food item as a donation, often followed by a dance; also, the admission fee for a dance
1976 MACDONALD *Bread & Molasses* 106 Pound parties were invented just at the proper time for us brothers as no money was involved. All you had to do was take a pound of anything from butter to tea to the home having the party and drop it in the wicker basket near the door on your arrival. Each donation was well wrapped, and no one knew what the other had given. This pound of whatever was your entry fee and entitled you to stay for the dance ... 1981 MACGILLIVRAY *CB Fiddler* 165 "They'd have 'pound parties' where everyone would bring a pound of something – soap, tea, butter – and there would be a fiddler sitting in the corner ..." 1984 CUMMING et al. *Story of Framboise* 163 Pound parties were held to assist a troubled family or as a house-warming party. Each person would bring a pound of something – groceries, for example – to help the family out. 1985 MACGILLIVRAY et al. *History of Fourchu* 62 An example of members of the community helping each other and having a good time in the bargain was the pound party ... They would take bread, flour, butter; it was all food they brought. The family the party was for didn't know anything about it. They would be surprised. 1992 BEATON and PEDERSEN *Maritime Music Greats* 96 ... a generation earlier, at the "pound parties" (admission followed upon payment of a pound of tea, butter or cheese) the musicians might have been paid with bartered goods.
[*DPEIE*, *OED3 U.S.* (1869), *DARE* **chiefly Midl, Cent**, *DAE*, *DA*, *W3 chiefly South & Midland*]

precent transitive and intransitive verb, and verbal noun; also spelled **present**
to lead the singing of psalms (typically in Gaelic) without musical accompaniment by singing a verse and then repeating it as the congregation sings along
1953 DUNN *Highland Settler* 140 There is North River, where many families still conduct their daily worship in Gaelic and where at least one family retains the custom of precenting and singing the Gaelic psalms each morning and evening at family worship. 1981 Beaton Institute Tape 2045 ... he'd precent, and all the

choir would sing those two lines, and then he'd precent the third line because they didn't have a book, and they'd listen very closely to him and when he'd start singing this third line [again], they'd sing along with him, and they would follow right through. 1984 CUMMING et al. *Story of Framboise* 121 In the early years, **precenting** made up for lack of musical accompaniment. The precentor intoned each verse of a psalm, one line at a time in a chant, using the Gaelic metrical version of the psalms. [1991?] MACLEAN *Story of Canoe Lake, CB* 46 They "presented" the psalms in Gaelic. The choir would select a particular tune and the presenter would sing a line at a time. The rest of the choir would repeat it in a long chant. 2001 MACGILLIVRAY *Cape Bretoner* 9 (1), 39 I was brought up in the Presbyterian Church and ... they would do "precenting" – and, of course, there was no organ. I remember the service being two hours long; could you imagine a child at that?

*Several dictionaries (*FWCCD, EDD* Sc., *OED3* (1639), *W3*) define this term generally as one who leads or directs congregational singing.

precentor noun
a person who leads the singing of psalms (typically in Gaelic) without musical accompaniment by singing a verse and then repeating it as the congregation sings along
   1878 HALL *Newfoundland Monthly Messenger* 5 (7), 1 I renewed my acquaintance with the old-time practice of lining the Psalms by the precentor ... 1891 in 1991 *CB's Magazine* 58, 81 They sang a Psalm with ever so many verses, the precentor leading off the first few words of each verse alone and the rest joining in all on the same note – there was no singing in parts ... The voices rose and fell in an almost unearthly sweetness and pathos ... 1913 CAMPBELL *CB Worthies* 19 He

was especially pleasing as a precentor in Gaelic. 1940 in 1986 *CB's Magazine* 42, 42 Seated within an enclosure at the foot of the elevated pulpit were the precentors – the leaders of the music. No pipe organs or gowned choirs were to be heard or seen in the days of which I write ... 1953 MACDONALD *CB Mirror* 2 Jan. 5 The "precentor" would sing a line of the psalm (no hymns were used then) and the people would join in as he repeated it a second time, for there were few books in the congregation. 1982 MERTZ "No Burden to Carry" 349 The main function of the precentor, 'reading out the line,' was adopted because texts were scarce and the vast majority of the Highland congregations were unlettered ... 2006 STANLEY-BLACKWELL *Tokens of Grace* 66 In the overall drama of Cape Breton's outdoor communications, the precentors were far from bit players ... they single-handedly controlled the musical part of public worship in the Presbyterian church for most of the 19th century.

*Several dictionaries define *precentor* as leader of congregational singing in general with the *OED3* having the earliest citation (1516).

prison: see **parlour**

prop: see **pit prop**

puck noun
a forceful blow, punch, and by extension an emotional blow
   1991 *CB's Magazine* 57, 90 ... the same kid who'd give anybody a puck on the mouth. 1993 *CB's Magazine* 64, 89 We had my sister Louise die with pleurisy ... then his father died before New Year's that same year. So, as they say in Sydney Mines, my father got a couple of tough pucks that year. 2005 KENDALL *Cape Bretoner* 13 (1), 7 ... a puck is a punch. 2009 ST. CLAIR Email 19 Mar. Steve

[Sutherland] grew up using the word "peuk" meaning a blow. Survey I Inf. 22 A puck in the face.

[*DNE, EDD, OED3* Chiefly *Irish English* (1855), *W3 dial chiefly Brit*]

puck transitive verb
to hit or strike (someone or something) forcefully, to punch

1996 GABRIEL Oral Communication 2 July Puck means to punch. 2002 COADY *Saints of Big Harbour* 324 Isadore would have pucked me on the head at this point ... 2006a MACADAM *Big Cy* 107 The windows in the principal's office at St. Anne's high school were routinely "pucked out" with stones and crab apples. Survey I Inf. 7 Often used jokingly, "I'll puck you if you do not smarten up." Survey I Inf. 55 Puck him in the mouth.

[*DNE, EDD, OED3* Chiefly *Irish English* (1861), *W3 dial chiefly Brit*]

puirt-a-beul ['puršta'biəl] noun; also spelled **puirt a beul**, **port-a-beul**, and rarely **porst a bhueil**; compare **canntaireachd, jigging, mouth music**
singing repeated Gaelic words or vocables (syllables that do not express words) to imitate bagpipe or fiddle music, frequently for dance music and often with less improvisation than jigging and mouth music

1970 MACPHAIL *Loch Bras d'Or* 95 Give us a porst a bhueil (pipe song of the mouth). 1992–3 SHAW *Scottish Language* 11–12, 44 ... but a more direct and productive channel between language and music has been the 'mouth music' (*puirt-a-beul*), consisting of words and vocables sung to a fiddle or pipe tune ... In Cape Breton it was common for people to step-dance to puirt-a-beul as well as instrumental music. 1996 PATTERSON *CB Post* 23 Mar. 10A She [Rosemary McCormack] says Ashley Mac Isaac's and Mary Jane Lamond's rendition of Sleepy Maggie

brings the traditions of fiddle-playing and puirt-a-beul (mouth music) to a younger audience nationally, who in turn, may become interested enough to learn more about the language and the culture. 2006 GRAHAM *CB Fiddle* 18 Cockburn seems to require fiddlers to have advanced fluency when he notes the connection between fiddle playing and *puirt-a-beul* (literally "tunes from the mouth" or "mouth music" – Gaelic words and vocables sung as tune melodies). 2013 SPARLING Email 8 Aug. 3 Where canntaireachd is most often associated with *ceòl mòr* (great or big music), the classical music of the pipes, jigging and puirt-a-beul are most often associated with *ceòl beag* (little music), instrumental dance tunes. 2014 SPARLING *Reeling Roosters and Dancing Ducks* 50 What makes puirt-a-beul different from the other types of mouth music discussed here is that, contrary to popular belief, they consist of actual words (rather than vocables) most of the time. Puirt-a-beul texts are also fixed, which means that they are deliberately composed and must be performed as learned ... Puirt-a-beul is not improvised as jigging is, nor is it a system like canntaireachd where particular consonant and vowel combinations are used to represent particular musical sounds.

*A loanword from Gaelic, *port-a-beul* "mouth music" *GED*. Compare the definition in the *OED3* for *port-a-beul*, "A fast-paced reel or dancing song consisting of a tune of Lowland Scottish origin to which repetitive, easily memorized Gaelic lyrics have been added, sung unaccompanied".

pulpit noun
an elevated platform in the steel mill used by a machine operator to control rolled steel such as rebar, rails, etc.

1990 Beaton Institute MG 14 206 Box 7 C. iii c) File 57, 4 I went to the Heavy

Mills and I had a choice to go up in the pulpit and operate the levers or go on the inspecting end ... When you're up in the pulpit operating levers, I couldn't handle that because you're in, like a cage, to me. 1990 Beaton Institute MG 14 206 BOX 6 C. iii c) File 23, 7 And by the time it [rebar] got to the bottom it was after turning grey so it was cooling off and this was done by a pulpit operator, a hot bed pulpit operator, he was called. And he did the watching of the steel coming up the bed and he pushed it over ... on the apron when he had so many pieces, and pushed it out on the roll line. 1992 *Making Steel* [Note on Jacket Cover] **pulpit** Station in the mill from which the rolling of steel is controlled.

[*FWCCD, NCD, OED3* (1880), *DAE* (1880), *DA* (1880), *W3*]

puncher noun; also **punching machine**, **puncher machine**; compare **undercutter**, **radial machine**, **mining**, **cut** noun
a pneumatic coal cutting machine with a sharpened bar or bit used to undermine (or cut) the coal face to allow room for the coal to break once blasted

1900 BELL *The Canadian Mining Review* 19 (9), 198 DOMINION No. 1 COLLIERY. Seam Phalen, 8 ft. thick, dip 1 in 14, *Mined*, pillar and room, with Puncher type mining machine, driven by compressed air. 1926 DUNCAN *Royal Commission ... Coal Mines of NS 1925* 34–5 In mines where radical [*sic*] or punching machines are in use ... we would advise the operators to change the two [*sic*] operations of cutting, shooting and loading ... to one tally embracing the three operations. 1979 FRANK "CB Coal Miners, 1917–1926" 223 Mounted astride his air-driven "puncher" machine, or manipulating the direction of his "radial" cutter, the machine miner and his helper drove a percussive pick or drill bit into the coal face in order to make the deep horizontal undercut. 1987

DEROCHE *Political Economy of Underdevelopment in CB* 118 ... the infamous "puncher" machine was used for much of the under cutting of the coal face, in the room-and-pillar system that prevailed in Cape Breton. Commonly labeled the "widow-maker" ... 1999a MIGLIORE and DIPIERRO eds. *Italian Lives* 330 The "punching machine" or "puncher" was massively heavy and hard to run. The operator rolled it, on its low trolley, up to the coal "face" at the end of the advancing tunnel ("room"), where he made a deep, narrow cut across the bottom of the face.

[at *punching machine DAE* (1850)]

pung sleigh noun; also **pung sled**
a horse-drawn sleigh with a box behind the driver, used for transportation and farm work

1984 CUMMING et al. *Story of Framboise* 172 The riding sleigh (sometimes called a "pung" or "goose neck") had a curl in front. 2002 MACKENZIE *Harvest Train* 28 It would keep me nice and warm when I'm taking long trips with the pung sleigh in the winter. 2005 MACKENZIE *Neighbours are Watching* 91 ... cow dung was manhandled out of the byre to be eventually loaded with sweat and swearing on dumpcart or pung sled and distributed by dung forks onto the field. 2008 ST. CLAIR Email 10 Feb. Pung sleigh was a common phrase for a horse-drawn sleigh with a box on the back – hereabouts the word seemed to be said as though it were spelled pong.

[*DPEIE, DC Maritimes, FWCCD U.S. Dial., NCD Maritimes & New England, GCD Maritimes* and *New England, OED3 N. Amer. regional* (chiefly *New England* and *Maritime Provinces*) Now chiefly *hist.* (1804), *DARE* chiefly **NEng, NY**, *DAE New Eng., DA* Chiefly *N. Eng., W3* New-Eng, *MWCD* NewEng, *ML*]

*Several dictionaries note that *pung* is derived from the Algonquian *tom-pung*.

purse transitive and intransitive verb;
compare **fish trap**
to draw up (the edges of a net or fish
trap)

1977 *CB's Magazine* 17, 3 You get that
up and tie it [door bar of the fish trap] in
the door boat. Then you're ready to purse
your trap. 1993 Beaton Institute Tape
3229 A And they used to purse, that's the
word they used then, it wasn't haul it,
it was purse it, two to three times a day.
1996 *CB's Magazine* 70, 86 They'd go with
the boat fishing, trapping. They'd have a
trap all around and they'd surround fish
and then they'd purse that underneath
and then they'd get a big bag of fish
and load the boat. 2004 CAPLAN and
GRACE *Acadian Lives in CB Island* 14 A
cent a pound, cent and a half, two cents a
pound. And we put in our mind to salt the
haddock. Well, we used to go and purse,
and then come ashore, dress those fish,
split it, and salted them.
[*OED3 N. Amer.* (1871), *W3*]

pussy in the corner noun
a children's game in which the player in
the centre of a room tries to occupy one
of the corners as the other four players
exchange corners

1978 *Inverness Oran* 16 Nov. 16 There
are people who never stood beside the
tracks counting freight cars or climbed
into a box car on a rainy day and played
"pussy in the corner." 1988 MANN *School
Days at Gabarus* 10 A favorite game was
"pussy in the corner" played by only five
pupils at one time, but we took turns.
Not everyone cared to play this rough
and tumble game, but it was great fun!
One participant stood in the center of the
porch and one in each corner. The two at
each end joined hands and when "pussy
in the corner" was shouted, they swung
each other around, so as to exchange
places, trying to do so before the one in
the center could slip into a vacant place.

[at *puss in the corner*: *OED3* ([1699]),
DARE, *W3*; at *pussy wants a corner*: *EDD*,
DARE, *W3* (as a variant)]

putting up song noun; compare **pairing
song**, **milling frolic**, **milling song**
a song performed at the end of a milling
frolic as the cloth was placed on forms
to set

1953 DUNN *Highland Settler* 40 After
the cloth was satisfactorily fulled – and
that might not be until five or six o'clock
in the morning – it was carefully wound
onto forms to set. This process also called
for a song, a "putting up" song, of different metre from the milling song. 1980
BENNETT *Folklore Studies ... Herbert
Halpert* 107 The rolling songs (sometimes
referred to as "clapping songs" in the
Outer Hebrides and "putting up songs"
in Cape Breton) were also of the chorus/
verse/chorus pattern, but were sung at
quicker tempo than the milling songs.
1991 LAVERY and LAVERY *Gabarus and
Vicinity* 79 After the cloth was milled it
was carefully wound onto forms to set.
This process called for a "putting up"
song, of a different meter from the milling
song.

Q

quatorze vieux, les noun; also spelled
Quatorze Vieux; variously translated as
fourteen elders, **old ones**, **old people,
old settlers**, **founding families**, **original
settlers**
the fourteen signatories of the 1790 land
grant for 7,000 acres in the Chéticamp
area, which they later divided among the
twenty-six Acadian families who first settled there

1986 CHIASSON and LE BLANC
trans. *History and Acadian Traditions of
Chéticamp* 261 Since that time, we call

them "les quatorze vieux" (the fourteen original settlers), and we honour them as the founders of Chéticamp. Their names are: Pierre Bois, Pierre Aucoin, Joseph Boudreau, Joseph Gaudet, Paul Chiasson, Basile Chiasson, Joseph Deveau, Gregoire Maillet, Jean Chiasson, Lazare Leblanc, Raymond Poirer, Anselme Aucoin, Joseph Aucoin and Justin Deveau. 1992 ROSS and DEVEAU *Acadians of NS* 105 The men mentioned in the land grant, named the "Charter of 1790," are considered to be the founders of Chéticamp and are referred to as *Les Quatorze Vieux* or the Fourteen Elders. 2008 ASSOCIATION TOURIS-TIQUE DE CHÉTICAMP www.cheti-camp.ca/en/ In 1790, five years after the arrival of the first settlers, fourteen heads of families from Chéticamp were given a charter in the names of all inhabitants granting them 7000 acres of land. They themselves divided these lands into the 26 families that inhabited Chéticamp ... Further generations always referred to these petitioners of the 1790 charte as the "Quatorze Vieux" (which translates to "Fourteen Elders", even though their average age was only 47). 2008 MORGAN *Story of CB Island Book One* 109 In 1790, a group of Acadians from Chéticamp, known as "Les Quatorze Vieux" – the fourteen original settlers – were granted a charter by Cape Breton's Lieutenant-Governor William Macarmick for 7,000 acres of land, which they in turn parceled out to their fellow settlers at Chéticamp.

queer thing noun; also **queer jigger**, **queermajigger**
an object for which the correct name is forgotten or not known, a what-d'you-call-it
   1978 *Oran Inbhirnis* 2 Feb. 16 We have more CB short hand for people, places and things than you can count ... How's about C.R.U.F.O.N.? Sounds like some of those dried up little queer jiggers you would toss into a salad. 1979 Beaton

Institute Tape 2421 [Tape 1] There's the coal conveyor there; well, over on the other side of it, there was a queer thing with cups on it. 1999 *CB's Magazine* 74, 90 They put that queer thing around the ship for submarine detecting. 2007 DCBE Tape SHERRINGTON 6 When you can't think of the name of it, you call it a queer thing. You know, that queer thing that he bought yesterday. 2009 HAYES Oral Communication 20 Sept. You often hear people say, "I've lost my queermajigger."

quenching car noun; also **hot car**, **quench car**
in steel making, a railway car that transfers hot coke from the coke ovens to be quickly cooled with water
   1980 *CB's Magazine* 27, 8 The coke is pushed into the quenching car. After it gets the charge of coke, it goes down to the quenching tower and we dump water on it. 1984 *CB's Magazine* 37, 6–7 On the coke side [of the ovens] they had the hot car. The coke just came out and fell into the hot car that was on tracks. 1989 Beaton Institute Tape 2600 A The hot car, they always called it the hot car – actually it's the quench car – the proper name for it. 2000 BARLOW and MAY *Frederick Street* 10 Once the coke was ready, the doors at either end of the oven opened and a giant steel ram scraped through the rectangular oven, pushing the molten mass of coke to the railcar below, known as the "quenching car."

*Compare *quench-coal* "Something which extinguishes burning coal. Chiefly *fig.*: an extinguisher, a deterrent" *OED3* (1615).

Question Day noun; also **Day of Questioning**; compare **ceist, open-air communion, men**
the second day (Friday) of a five-day Presbyterian communion service during which a question (or ceist) about a

scriptural passage was raised and the spiritual merits of the passage were discussed chiefly by the "men," the lay catechists and spiritual leaders 1884 in 1984 CUMMING et al. *Story of Framboise* 115 [quoting the *Presbyterian Witness*] Friday was duly observed as "Question Day." After the preliminaries of praise, prayer, and reading of the scriptures over, one of the communicants gave out a passage (Proverbs 9: 5) asking to prove the characteristics of those who truly come ... [to] eat of the bread of life and drink of the spiritual wine of the gospel feast, distinguished from those who came by profession only. 1896 Anon. *Presbyterian Record* 21 (11) 287 ... the communion services from Thursday to Monday, with the latter as "Thanksgiving" and Friday as "Question" day, still prevail. The latest reported was at Middle River, C.B., Sept. 24–8 ... 1921 MURRAY *History of Presbyterian Church in CB* 262 Friday was the "ceist" or question day. The ministers conducted the opening devotional exercises, but the speaking was chiefly by laymen, elders, catechists and others from far and near, who had a reputation for godliness and who were endowed with the power of speaking intelligently and experimentally. 1940 MORRISON *Dalhousie Review* 20, 186 Friday was known as "Question Day," "the Ceist." ... the minister called for the "Question." Immediately some old Christian enquirer stood up, read or quoted a Bible verse, and asked for its interpretation: the discussion following virtually involved a differential diagnosis between saints and sinners, and was so intended. The minister invariably led off in this discussion; and then, from a list of names, called upon those who were to address the assemblage. 2006 STANLEY-BLACKWELL *Tokens of Grace* 29 *Là na Ceist* (The Day of Questioning), often styled as "the Men's day," was regarded

in Cape Breton as "the greatest day of the five except the Sabbath day."

quintal noun
a variable unit of measure, typically for codfish, either salted and dried, or uncured; rarely, a measure of some other food item
1823 GREAT BRITAN COLONIAL OFFICE *Papers Relative to the Re-Annexation of the Island of Cape Breton to the Government of Nova Scotia* 179 The inhabitants of this island, by the union, derive immediate and great advantages; the participation in the Nova Scotia colonial bounty of 2 s. 6 d., a quintal on cured fish ... 1832 BOUCHETTE *British Dominions in North America* vol. 2, 86 The quantity of fish exported in 1828 amounted to 41,000 quintals of dried, and 18,000 barrels of pickled fish. 1846 in 1978 FERGUSSON *NS Historical Quarterly* 8 (4), 287 [quoting a diary] Cure about 50,000 Quintals of Cod Fish per year. 1885 in 1978 PATTERSON *History of Victoria County* 35 According to an official report sent to the Board of Trade in 1740 by Captain Smith ... Niganiche furnished 54 shallops and caught 13,500 quintals. 1972 STAEBLER *CB Harbour* 126–7 Fish wasn't any price; in those days the merchants treated us like heathens, they'd take two quintals – that's three hundred pounds fish – for a box o' raisins. 1981 *CB's Magazine* 29, 9 You've got 4 or 5 quintals of fish in the big dories. 1994 SAMSON *River Bourgeois* 23 Anthony Landry, who also did this work, recalls that the normal pay was 50 cents per quintal (220 lbs) of finished product. 1998 *CB's Magazine* 73, 100 Codfish – now, we pay seven dollars – (back then it was) six dollars a quintal, that's 112 pounds.
[*DNE* (1623), *DC Esp. Nfld*, COD, NCD *Newfoundland*, GCD *Cdn. Newfoundland*, *DARE* **coastal NEng**, *DAE, ML*; other dictionaries define *quintal* without reference to a measurement for fish]

R

rabbit job noun
a small job done at work for personal use
or for a co-worker

1991 Beaton Institute Tape 2659 And
there were little rabbit jobs; you know,
somebody always wanted something
made. 1992 *Making Steel* [Note on Jacket
Cover] **rabbit job** Making something
for personal use as a favour for a fellow
worker, using company time and materials. 1992 *Making Steel* n.p. Rabbit jobs, you
know what I mean? People wanted some
job done for their home, you know, something cut or made in the machine shop or
what have you.

racket: see **kitchen racket**

radial machine noun; compare **mining,
puncher**
a coal cutting machine with a drill bit
used to dig a narrow channel in the coal
being excavated (the coal face) to allow
the coal to break after the explosive
charge (the shot) is fired

1972 Beaton Institute Tape 570 They
went to the top of the wall with a radial
machine ... the machine took itself up the
wall on its cats and its teeth were set at
this part of the wall to be cut ... run by
electricity. 1974 Beaton Institute Tape 940
B There were 216 coal cutting machines
which were commonly called the radial
machines. 1999a MIGLIORE and DIP-
IERRO eds. *Italian Lives* 330 In the 1920s,
the "puncher" was replaced by the "radial
machine." 2007 MACKENZIE *CB Coal
Mine Disasters* 151 This meant that the
men working the room had to "cut" the
wall face with a radial machine. This put
a six-inch-wide, six-foot-deep cut into the
coal midway between the pavement and
roof of the seam.

raft intransitive verb
of sea ice, to pile in layers, typically at sea

Pilot Survey Inf. 3 We almost had a
bad train accident one time when the ice
was rafting. The wind was blowing from
southwest pretty well, and one clamper
would get in under the other and raise
it on the next. After a while there was a
whole lot of ice over the railway tracks.
Survey II Inf. 1 Ice piling up, one on top of
the other. Survey II Inf. 6 Pans of ice rafted
on top of each other. The ice behind will
raft it, build layers of ice.
[*DNE* (1843), *DPEIE, DC, COD, NCD
Canadian, GCD Cdn., OED3* (1843), *NOAD*]

rafting verbal noun; compare **barricade**
causing sea ice to pile in layers, typically
at sea

Survey I Inf. 22 Rafting is a barricades
of ice along the shore – come in with the
tide, and the ice is piled up. Survey II Inf.
2 Rafting occurs away from the shore.
Survey II Inf. 4 A barricade is rafting on
the shore. Survey II Inf. 6 Look at that
rafting! Survey II Inf. 8 Rafting occurs in
the ocean.
[*DNE* (1909), *OED3*; compare *rafting ice
DC* (1883)]

*Several of the commercial fishers interviewed
in Survey II (2, 3, 4, 7, 8) distinguished between
a *barricade,* layers of ice on shore, and *rafting*
that occurs at sea, but respondents to Survey I
did not make this distinction.

rake noun; also **man-rake, man(-)rake**;
compare **riding rake, travel, trip**
a number of coupled mine cars or boxes
travelling on rails, typically used to
transport miners into and out of the mine;
occasionally, a number of coupled mine
cars used to haul coal, a trip

1889 CANADA *Report ... Labor and
Capital in Canada: Evidence, NS* 291 A. I
do not think it would be any loss at all
to the company, for this reason that they

generally have to run down the rakes empty every morning but if you go in them as they are now you risk your life ... 1901 Anon. *The Canadian Mining Review* 20 (1), 17 The angle of the seam [of the Colliery at Port Hood] being fairly steep, the ordinary system of slope haulage will be employed. Eight fifteen to twenty hundred weight boxes will constitute a rake. 1934 *NS Miner* 4 (18), 4 The Caledonia rake runs in the air-course, and in winter it is a terrible place ... 1976 *Oran Inbhirnis* 6 Aug. 7 When five [coal] boxes were collected at the level they were formed into a 'rake' and pulled by horses to the 'slope.' 1985 FITZGERALD *Atlantic Advocate* 75 Apr. 46 I got on the man-rake, which consists of a series of small cable cars which lower men and supplies into the mine. Then for about one hour, we raced down the "deep" on this rake, which is the main tunnel into the mine. 1990 [MACNEIL] *History of Sydney Mines* 83 The twenty-six car man-rake, carrying over 200 men, travels a 10,000 foot long slope, with a grade slightly more then [*sic*] ten per cent. 1999a MIGLIORE and DIPIERRO eds. *Italian Lives* 330 The "rake" is a train of open railcars in which miners ride from the shaft bottom or from the mouth of a slope mine, down the main tunnel to their work areas. 2000 "Episode 1" *Pit Pony* n.p. The rake driver didn't see him and ran right over him. 2007 MACKENZIE *CB Coal Mine Disasters* 111 In Princess Colliery, however, the coal miners ... were lowered down the shaft in a cage for about 750 feet – and then they got on a rake that carried them down the slope and farther into the coal mine. 2011 DOYLE *CB Facts and Folklore* 179 To get down to where coal is mined, miners ride rakes, which are essentially boxes attached to wheels that ride on rails. Steel cables hauled rakes to the surface when they were filled with coal and lowered them for the return trip with miners aboard.

*The *OED3* has one definition for *rake* (noun 3) that is similar to the meaning given above: "6. orig. *Sc.* and *Eng. regional* (*north.*). A row, a series; *esp.* a string of railway carriages or coal trucks" (with 1901 with the first citation referring to cars carrying coal). Other definitions of *rake* as "journey" or "load" are found in the *OED3* (noun 3 II (7)), *EDD* substantive 2 (7), and *DSL* at *raik* (II n. 2(2)).

rear noun; also **rear land**; compare **backland, frontland**

rear noun; also **rear land**; compare **backland, frontland**
the land behind communities fronting on rivers or coastlines, backland; used in place names
1827 HORTON *Instructions under the Direction of the Secretary of State* 55 I have been disappointed in my Expectations of obtaining a Survey of the Cluster of Lakes in the Rear of the Red Island Lots ... 1885 in 1978 PATTERSON *History of Victoria County* 83 This autumn (1836) again the frost nipped the potatoes on the rivers and rear lands on the 6th and 7th of September ... 1967 PUBLIC ARCHIVES OF NS *Place Names of NS* 647 The name was changed in 1884 from Indian Rear to Stewartdale in honour of settlers. 1977 Beaton Institute Tape 900 ... the people in the rear had as much if not better land and living quarters and culture ... as those who were living in the front ... 1979 Beaton Institute Tape 1185 They lived out at the rear before we came here – three and a half miles back of here. 1990 *Inverness Oran* 6 June 26 Luke Severin (White) Leblanc was born in rear Belle Cote, or familiarly known as "the Backlands" ... 1994 MACLEOD and ST. CLAIR *Pride of Place* 28 John Peter MacKay from Rear Chimney Corner ... was hired to rebuild the house. 1996 HAMILTON *Place Names of Atlantic Canada* 391 Use of 'rear' as part of a place name is common in CAPE BRETON and the eastern Nova

Scotia mainland, and to a lesser extent on Prince Edward Island. 2005 MACINTYRE and WALLS *NS Book of Everything* 42 **Rear:** A meaning of this word unique to Nova Scotia, especially Cape Breton, is its usage to denote the back section of a community, sections of land often deemed less desirable. 2008 MORGAN *Story of Cape Breton Island Book One* 117 [The parents of Donald MacDonald] came from Moidart to Cape Breton and settled on a mountain top in what is known as "the rear" of South-West Margaree.

*As the citations indicate, many areas in the rear did not have good soil, but some did.

red ice noun; also **last ice**
reddish ice appearing along the Cape Breton coasts in early spring
  1885 CANADA *Sessional Papers of the Dominion of Canada: Vol. 6*, 9– 95 Consequently, these waters are at so low a temperature that lobsters do not make their appearance near the shores until some time after the last ice has passed away, so that in the most favorable seasons there is no catch of this fish before the lst of June, but frequently much later. 2001 *CB Post* 26 Apr. 25 ... sometimes the packs will be composed of red ice. Red ice is because it was formed in P.E.I. where the red soil comes out to sea in river estuaries. 2004 ELLISON *Cape Bretoner* 12 (2), 58 Folklore has it that when the "red ice" appears, spring is not far away. Maybe the "red ice" is simply pans of ice that have picked reddish sediments from the shores of Northumberland Straight and Prince Edward Island. Survey I Inf. 5 The last ice from PEI is drifting past Sydney Mines and Florence. It may also come from the shoreline of parts of Cape Breton. Survey I Inf. 7 Red ice is also called the last ice. Survey II Inf. 8 The red ice coming around Cape North in the spring signals the end of the ice.

red row noun, often plural; also spelled **Red Row**; compare **row**
a line of company-built attached houses, originally painted a rusty red
  1977 Beaton Institute Tape 236 The Red Rows were built and the miners went in them. 1986 LATREMOUILLE et al. *Pride of Home* 57 The early company houses were attached units ... Sydney Mines once boasted eleven rows, although only the last, the brick and timber Red Row is still standing. 1994 SAMSON *Contested Countryside* 131 Families living in the "Red Rows" had better housing, with improved services and a few perks such as access to small plots of land for growing vegetables. 2006 MACISAAC *Better Life* 99–100 In Pictou and Inverness, the row houses were called "red rows" because of their deep red paint. 2011 DOYLE *CB Fact and Folklore* 213 Residents of Inverness and Sydney Mines referred to them [company houses] as Red Rows because they were painted that colour.

refuse a lamp: see **stop a lamp**

reiteach ['rečʊx] noun; also spelled **Reiteach, reiteich, reiatch**
a formal betrothal and agreement on the terms of the marriage arranged between the bride's family, and the groom and his representative, followed by a celebration
  1970 MACPHAIL *Loch Bras d'Or* 64 Meantime the marriage of Donald Glic and Sarah took place the morning after the reiteach (betrothal) – a family dinner followed. 1973 *CB's Magazine* 5, 20 ... 1923 – the wedding a product of the last formal Reiteach on Cape Breton Island ... Malcom Angus MacLeod of Birch Plain remembered having seen only one Reiteach. He said the table was prepared for a little feast, and everyone except the young girl herself sat at the table. Her chair was left empty at the table. And the young man who wished to marry her had

brought an older man to speak for him, and this older man described the future groom's qualities and love for the girl and asked for her hand. And when all other arrangements were made, as the final act of agreement, the young girl would come to the table and sit – and strong drink was available, and the feast was served. 1978 CAMPBELL *Highland Community on the Bras d'Or* 43 Usually the time and place of the proposal was known in advance, and also whether the answer would be favourable, in which case a "Reiatch", or gathering celebrating the occasion, would ensue ... 1987 *Inverness Oran* 26 Aug. 20 ... they gathered with relatives and friends at the Smith Island home of the bride-to-be. This was the traditional Gaelic "reiteach" or "match-making ceremony" where the man stood in the midst of the revelry to state his qualifications and his earnest desire to have the girl's hand in marriage. Following this, it was the custom of the father to stand up, praise his daughter, congratulate the young man, and announce the dowry. 2000 CHISHOLM comp. *As True as I'm Sittin' Here* viii Now, Reiteach (pronounced "ray-tchuck") is a Gaelic word for making a clearing, as in cutting away small spruce, preparing the ground. It was used to mean a very formal way of asking a father for his daughter's hand in marriage.

*A loanword from Scottish Gaelic, see *rèiteach* "betrothal celebration" *GED*.

retarded cooling: see **MacKie Retarded Cooling**

retreat the pillar: see **rob the pillar**

rib noun
the side wall of an excavation in a coal mine
 1971 Beaton Institute MG 12 129, 10 ... [some miners] would dig trenches or

(minings) from the floor to the roof in the two ribs or (sides) of their working place. 1983 SHEDDEN et al. *Mining Photographs* 271 **Rib** – The side of an excavation. 2007 MACKENZIE *CB Coal Mine Disasters* 108 Bill Collier says that when he first walked in No.11 level, about three years after the accident, there were three lunch cans set in the rib halfway between the pavement and the roof, marking the spot where the miners were killed – a mute memorial to Nelson, Robert and Walter.
 [*W3*]

riding rake noun; also spelled **ridin' rake**; compare **rake**
a number of coupled mine cars travelling on rails, used to transport miners to and from their work places, as opposed to mine cars (or trips) used to carry coal or mine materials
 1974 Beaton Institute Tape 940 You see, there was no riding rakes then, my friend. 1984 Beaton Institute Tape 2137 We went down on riding rakes. That's mine boxes made for riding in. There'd be ten to each rake and there'd be about ten rakes. 1999 FRANK *J. B. McLachlan* 49 There they clambered into the wooden boxes of the riding rakes and coasted thousands of feet down sloping haulageways into the working sections of the mine. 2007 MACKENZIE *CB Mine Disasters* 131 Once at the bottom of the shaft, the miners got on a riding rake and traveled farther underground, riding down sloping tunnels called "deeps."

rig[1] noun
an eccentric, odd, or humorous person, a character
 1999 THURGOOD "Storytelling on the Gabarus-Framboise Coast" 280 At the wake ... there was a Mary Ferguson – she was an awful rig ... too – and there was John Ferguson. 2011 MUISE Email 15 Nov. Rig can also refer to a person "he

is quite a rig that fella," in this context meaning a character – usually humourous. 2012 HAYES Oral Communication 18 Feb. We were driving last week when my daughter saw an odd looking man and said "Look at that rig."

[Compare "RIG An amusing sort of chap, *cuss, joker*, etc: 'Oh that Newt! He's a *rig!'*" ML]

rig[2] noun; also spelled **rigg**
any vehicle, often a truck
1998 GILLIS *John R. and Son* 49 Many of the Roosters who were kin of Christina's and Molly's came back with Ronnie and John J. on the truck. The rest arrived in rigs of various descriptions. 1999 MAC-INTYRE *Long Stretch* 147 The mansion. It had a big carport for at least two or three rigs. 2000 CHISHOM comp. *As True as I'm Sittin' Here* 144 Finally, the bicycle got up close to them and it hit Sarah. Knocked her right in the ditch ... Flora said, "Some picnic! That queer fella came along, with that rig that he had between his legs, on top of Sarah in the ditch of the road. That was the picnic we had!" 2003 MUISE Email 3 July ... vehicle – "I saw his rig parked in the street".
[*OED3* "any vehicle (usually large)." Several dictionaries limit the meaning of *rig* to a large vehicle, a truck or a tractor trailer: *COD N Amer. & Austral., NCD, GCD, COED chiefly N Amer. & Austral./NZ, W3, NOAD, MWCD*]

rigger noun; also **crane chaser**
a worker who assists a crane operator by attaching slings, chains, etc. to items before they are lifted
1984 *CB's Magazine* 37, 15 A rigger is the man that does the knots and holds the slings and everything, gets everything ready for the lifts. All the knots and everything to hold all that heavy equipment. Of course, they're a climber, too, they have to climb. 1984 *CB's Magazine* 37, 17 Well, they

would have to have a crane-chaser take the straps off for them. They would have to follow the crane. 1988 Beaton Institute Tape 2381 He went to work training as a rigger, which is a very dangerous job. 1990 Beaton Institute MG 14 206 Box 7 C. iii c) File 62, 10 ... you'd have to watch out for your crane chaser and make sure he's well out of the way before you make your first pour [of the ladle filled with molten iron]. 1999 *CB's Magazine* 74, 89 I got back on the Steel Plant. I got down the docks where I was a rigger. I hung onto the job there, unloading ships.
[*FWCCD, W3*]

right adverb, especially modifying an adjective
very, fully, completely
1884 Anon. *Church Guardian* 6 (33) 26 Nov. 2 ... over half a hundred children sang with right good will ... 1920 Beaton Institute MG 12 59 3 Box 1, 13 May n.p. The church looked right empty as the organ was out. 1920 SMITH and WIARD *CB Tales* 65 ... I was right tongue-tied; ... 1972 STAEBLER *CB Harbour* 40 You're doin' right good. 1979 Beaton Institute Tape 2420 The Sloans lived right handy to our place. 2001 DOUCET *Codfish and Angels* 28 "You did right good," said Marianne à Sammy. 2007 DCBE Tape SHER-RINGTON 3 Something being "right nice," where I would have said very nice.
[*DNE, COD archaic, FWCCD* used dialectally or in some titles, *SSPB, EDD, OED3* "Now usu. in nonstandard and regional use, or *arch.* in **right royal**" (?c1200), *COED dialect or archaic, DARE* **chiefly Sth, S Midl**, *W3, NOAD dialect or archaic, MWCD*]

*One of the frequently used patterns of *right* in Cape Breton English is "right good," so it is interesting that one of the earliest citations for this phrase in the *OED3* is *rihht god inoh*, "right good enough" (*Orumulum* ?c1200).

rimrack transitive verb, usually used as a past particle; also spelled **rim-rack**, **rimwrack**

to wreck, spoil, ruin, vandalize (something)

1977 Beaton Institute Tape 896 It met the fate of most vacant houses. It was rimracked ... the plumbing was torn out, there were boards torn down. It was just wrecked inside. 1983 *CB's Magazine* 34, 17 ... they rim-racked every hut but the Salvation Army's. 1989 Beaton Institute Tape 2404 [Tape 1] And it was getting pretty well rimracked and torn apart, and we had the impression that it was haunted. 2007 *DCBE* Tape SHERRINGTON 33 John Mac-Eachern's summer house in Sydney was rimwracked. "Vandalized [interviewer]?" Yeah. Survey II Inf. 6 The ocean is rimracked, spoiled, torn to pieces, polluted.

[*SSPB*, *OED3* at *rim-rack* orig. and chiefly *N. Amer. regional* (1841), *DARE* (1841), *ML* at *rimwracked*]

road maker noun; also spelled **roadmaker**

a worker responsible for constructing, laying tracks, and maintaining haulage ways in a coal mine

1967 Beaton Institute Tape 28 William Davis was a man, who was a road maker by trade ... 1992 HORNSBY *Nineteenth-Century CB* 100 Timbering and throughways were maintained by road makers ... 1995 *DCBE* Tape NICHOLSON 13 We're loading coal; we gotta have a road maker to put a road on for us. 1997 *CB's Magazine* 72, 11–12 (But) you'd see all the roadmakers'd be going down ... supposedly necessary people.

[Compare *roadman* "in mining : one who has charge of the ways of a mine" *EDD* (1885)]

rob the pillar verb phrase; also **draw the pillar**, **retreat the pillar**

in room and pillar mining, to remove a block of coal (the pillar) that supports the mine roof between the areas where the coal has been excavated (the rooms), thereby allowing the roof to collapse

1889 GILPIN *Canadian Mining Review* 8 (6), 77 ... the drawing of the pillars when the rooms have gone their distance, should give a good pillar coal with little danger of creep. 1969 Beaton Institute Tape 118 ... they were drawing pillars in some areas. 1983 MELLOR *Company Store* 92 ... a pillar of coal was left between each pair of rooms to support the roof, but once a room had been worked out, miners had to start "retreating" or robbing the pillars to obtain as much coal as possible before the roof collapsed. 1990 [MAC-NEIL] *History of Sydney Mines* 74 The first attempt at successful pillar drawing at Princess Colliery was made in 1895 ... 1997 CAMPBELL *Banking on Coal* 39 But the death knell [of No. I Mine, Inverness] was sounded when, in 1915 ... management opted for a retreat operation whereby the large pillars of coal that helped keep the roof in place would be removed, "robbing the pillars" as it was called. 2007 MACKENZIE *CB Coal Mine Disasters* 96 To "rob" or take out the pillar, they had to go in the 250 feet to the inside face of the mined-out rooms, drive a crosscut through the pillar along the face of the rooms, then begin taking out the pillar from the inside out, or "retreating" it.

[at *rob*: *EDD*, *OED3* (1811), *W3*; compare *draw* in the sense of "raise ore to the surface": *EDD*, *OED3* (*a*1300)]

rolag ['rolæk] noun

a roll of carded wool prepared for spinning, typically used with a spinning wheel

1973 *CB's Magazine* 2, 8 To roll up the rolag ... draw the Right-hand Carder toward yourself in short, brushing motions. At this point ... some people would roll the rolag back and forth between the smooth sides of the carders.

1984 CUMMING et al. *Story of Framboise* 47–8 First the sheep were shorn, then the wool was washed, then the **rolag** or rolls were made, first with hand cards, then by 1864, taking them to carding mills at Loch Lomond. 1999 *CB's Magazine* 74, 24 She had a bag – she had gone to the carding mill – a bag of yellow rolls (*called* rolag *in Gaelic*).

[*OED3* (1932); compare *roller EDD* (1777)]

*A loanword from Scottish Gaelic, see *rolag* "small roll" *GED.*

roller noun
a log used to move a building or a large object

1983 *CB's Magazine* 35, 13 We pried it [a shed, twelve feet long] and put it on rollers and got it up on a high place on a hill, and got the truck down below, and slid it on. 1987 *CB's Magazine* 46 Inside Front Cover And we tried to put rollers under it [a sled, thirty feet long], to be ready to go. 2007 *DCBE* Tape SHERRINGTON 34 ... things I wanted to write down to remember, like moving a house on rollers ... logs.

roof noun
the rock or other material above an excavation or passage in a mine, the ceiling of a coal mine

1888 in 1987 *CB's Magazine* 46, 58 Q. Does the roof come down to a considerable extent? A. No; we have no difficulty overhead. On the eastern side of the pit, where they are working at pillars, the roof comes down. 1976 *Oran Inbhirnis* 6 Aug. 7 The 'Shot-firer' was called to inspect the 'shot' and the 'roof' and to connect the 'cable' to the shot. 1983 SHEDDEN et al. *Mining Photographs* 271 **Roof bolts** – Steel bolts which are commonly four to six feet in length, and are generally inserted at intervals of every four feet in a grid like pattern. 1980 MCINTYRE *Collier's Tattletale*

32 During "room and pillar" methods of mining, a shale roof may have problems for the miners and the operation ... 1997 *CB's Magazine* 72, 47 You'd be down in the mines and you'd see water coming through the roof and it was cold and very damp. I said, this life is not for me.

[*EDD*, *OED3* Mining and *Geol.* (1644), W3]

room noun; also **bord**; often in the phrase **room and pillar, pillar and room**; compare **pillar, level**
a nearly level excavation to remove coal, driven into the seam from a haulage way and leaving a block of coal (a pillar) to support the roof

1871 BROWN *Coal Trade of the Island of CB* 68 As the workings advanced from the shore in a westerly direction, new shafts were sunk at intervals of about 200 yards, so that the length of haulage from the faces of the bords to the bottom of the shaft never exceeded that distance. 1893 ARCHIBALD *Canadian Mining & Mechanical Review* 12 (4), 59 ... about twenty years ago the plan of driving the rooms ten yards wide and leaving the pillars the old width [six yards] was adopted and has continued successfully ever since. 1905 DAVIDSON and MACKENZIE *The Canadian Mining Review* 24 (3), 51 The plan of working [of the Phalen Seam] is the ordinary "room and pillar"; the deeps, headways and levels are driven 12 feet wide, and the rooms 22 feet wide. 1942 DENNIS *CB Over* 89 "Up to 1923 the method of mining in Cape Breton was all 'room and pillar.' The mines were laid off somewhat after the fashion of a checker-board with little rooms and pillars of coal between, and with cross cuts about every so many feet." 1992 HORNSBY *Nineteenth-Century CB* 16 Rooms or "bords" were cut into the coal, and "pillars" were left to support the roof. 1999 CALABRESE *Cape Bretoner* 7 (4), 36 There would be two men working in what we called a room, which would be an area about 14 to 16 feet wide, depending on the thickness of the seam. In the centre of the room would be a railroad. On either side of the railroad we had timbers to hold the stone up, spaced about four feet apart. 2007 MACKENZIE *CB Coal Mine Disasters* 98 Indeed, men who were working in other rooms about 300 feet away from the accident heard what they took to be a "bump" – an incident where the tunnel closes and the floor meets the ceiling, crushing everything between.

[at *room*: OED3 *Mining.* orig. *Sc.* (1670), *DSL, W3*; at *bord EDD* (1843); at *board*: OED3 (1708), *W3*]

*The *OED3* and *W3* state that the use of *board* or *bord* to describe the working space may have derived from the practice of using boards on the floor of the mine passage to assist the movement of the coal tubs or sledges before tracks and coal cars were used.

room, the noun; also **best room**
a living room or parlour

1974 CAMPBELL and MACLEAN *Beyond the Atlantic Roar* 218 Upon entering the home, he [a priest] would be ushered into "the room," usually cold and always damp, and opened only for special occasions. 1986 *Inverness Oran* 29 Oct. 11 Mary was in her bedroom preparing it seemed for the wedding ceremony which was to take place in 'the room.' 2005 MACKENZIE *Neighbours are Watching* 33 About nine o'clock most of the guests crowded into the "best room," normally reserved for wakes and other festive occasions.

[*DNE, EDD, OED3 Sc., Irish English, Eng. Regional* (*north.*) and *Newfoundland* (1795), *DSL, DARE*]

rope noun; compare **trip, rake**
a steel cable used to haul connected rail boxes (a trip or rake) in a coal mine

1889 CANADA *Report ... Labor and Capital in Canada: Evidence, NS* 260 Q. What kind of ropes are generally employed? A. Steel ropes I think. 1983 MELLOR *Company Store* 85 ... roadways for mined coal to be hauled in coal boxes ... attached to an endless steel rope for haulage to the surface. 1989 *CB's Magazine* 52, 2 And we were making wire rope used for the pits, for the cables. 1999a MIGLIORE and DIPIERRO eds. *Italian Lives* 330 Both rakes and "trips" (trains of coal boxes) were winched up and down on a steel cable. If this "rope" broke, the obvious end result was a "smash on the deep," often with loss of life. 2007 MACKENZIE *CB Coal Mine Disasters* 110 ... he began to talk about "the rope" – a miner's term for the heavy steel cable that lowered the man rake down the slope.

[The following dictionaries name wire as one of the materials used in making *rope: COD, OED3, W3, MWCD*]

round noun; typically in the phrase **in the round**
whole logs, limbed but not sawn lengthwise

Survey II Inf. 6 [Round means] unfinished timber. Survey II Inf. 8 Logs in the round along the edge of the road.

[*DNE, OED3* (1808); compare *round log* (1768), *round timber* (1656) *OED3*]

round adjective; often in the phrase **round fish**
of fish, not headed or cleaned, whole

1976 *CB's Magazine* 14, 4 They're [gaspereaux] salted as they come from the river – salted round – 100 pounds of salt to 200 pounds of fish. 1984 *CB's Magazine* 36, 66 These dories used to take 1000 pounds of fish, round fish – they could take more than that, but that's all you'd put in them. For safety. 1984 BALCOM *Cod Fishery of Isle Royale* 11 ... the whole or "round" cod was first "dressed," i.e. the

head and entrails were removed ... Survey
II Inf. 1 You could buy the fish round or
cleaned. Survey II Inf. 4 Round fish, whole
fish, that are not gutted. Survey II Inf. 6 If
they are too busy to gut them, [they] leave
them round.
   [*DNE, COD, OED3* (1865), *W3*; at *in the
round DPEIE*]

row noun; often modified with **red, bug,
miner's (-s')**, **company, monkey**, and with
one citation for **bog, mosquito, grey**; compare **bug row, miners' row, red row**
a line of company-built houses, either
attached or duplex; a street containing
such houses
   1940 WISDOM *Glace Bay Looks Ahead*
8 Acquaintance with the Town's early
history as a mining community will
account for the number of "miner's rows"
still in evidence in the colliery districts ...
1951 MACLENNAN *Each Man's Son* 8
Somewhere in the row was a door which
they called their own, but nothing distinguished it from the doors to right or left
of it ... The houses were divided in two by
a common wall between the doors ... 1969
Beaton Institute Tape 118 They started
to build the first houses in Bog Row in
1866 ... five double houses. 1990 DAVEY
Onomastica Canadiana 72 (2), 74 In Glace
Bay, the row houses are called either *The
Shacks* or *The Rows*. An informant from
Glace Bay explained these were the poorest of the company buildings and were
usually occupied by the newly arrived
immigrants or the poorest people. 1999a
MIGLIORE and DIPIERRO eds. *Italian
Lives* 106 *I remember the "Bug Row," and
the times we used to have there. It was a place
where they had entertainment, an accordion
player.* 1999 FRANK *J. B. McLachlan* 170
We lived in the Monkey Row, in two
rooms ... 2005 MACDONALD *Forest for
Calum* 13 Four summers earlier, when
we were ten, Duncan and I were walking
through the Company Rows on our way

to John Alex's barn when we heard the
screeching.
   [*EDD* (1866); compare "A number of
houses standing in a line; a street (esp.
a narrow one) with a continuous line of
houses along one or both sides" Chiefly
Sc., Eng. regional (north.), and *N. Amer.
OED3*]

rubber intransitive verb
to listen to a conversation on a telephone
party line without permission
   1991 MACLEOD *Place Called Donkin*
n.p. Probably the most common remarks
were – "get to h ... off the line," or "someone is rubbering" (listening to the conversation). This was not unusual, when 10 or
12 persons would try to contact the operator at the same time. 2007 *DCBE* Tape
SHERRINGTON 13 ... there were all these
party lines, and rubbering was of course
listening in on somebody else's phone
call. The one near us had twenty people,
twenty houses on the line. And as I said,
you could tell who was rubbering by their
clock chiming or somebody talking in the
background; you knew who was there.
   [*OED3 N. Amer. colloq.* (1905), *DARE*
esp wInland Nth; compare "To listen in
or eaves drop" *DA* (1896)]

rum row noun; also spelled **Rum Row**
during prohibition in Nova Scotia (c. 1910–
30) as legislated by the Nova Scotia Temperance Act, an area offshore beyond the
prohibited limit, where liquor was sold and
then illegally transported and resold ashore;
a street where illegal alcohol was sold
   1975 *CB's Magazine* 11, 5 And any Canadian boat – any boat registered in Canada – must stay outside the 12-mile limit
but any boat registered outside of Canada
can stay just outside of 3 miles – 3-mile
limit from any headland or coast – if
they're carrying liquor or any contra-
band ... they were all outside on Rum
Row we called it. And the big boats – the

Mother Ships – they generally would lay off 15–20 miles ... 1979 RIPLEY "Industrialization and Urbanization in CB County" 47 Bell Street [in Glace Bay] was known as "rum row" because it was situated along the harbour and many of the transporters of liquor as well as many of the "speak-easies" were there. 1980 MACINTYRE *Collier's Tattletale* 132 Three years after the first World War started in Europe, the Nova Scotia Temperance Act became law in Cape Breton, and "rum-row" was established off the Eastern Atlantic Coast. 1983 MELLOR *Company Store* 286 Rum Row, where scores of rumrunners lay outside the three-mile limit off the coast of Cape Breton, provided an income for many an unemployed Cape Breton miner during the 1925 strike. 1984 Beaton Institute Tape 2178 They used to [have] rum row here in Sydney Harbour ... They used to go out and get rum and be coming in with it. 1997 MACDONALD *Fall on Your Knees* 192 He goes to the mouth of a certain stream and meets the dories that row in from the boats anchored offshore on "rum row". These boats are en route from the British colony of Newfoundland, where liquor is legal, to points down the coast as far as New York City. 1999a MIGLIORE and DIPIERRO eds. *Italian Lives* 81 During rum-running days, the Dominion Beach was a popular site for landing liquor and rum that came from Rum Row, a twelve mile distance off shore.

[*OED3 U.S.* (now *hist.*) (1923), *DA* (1923)]

rum sick adjective phrase
hungover; sick to one's stomach because of excessive drinking

1975 Beaton Institute Tape 210 My brother and another fellow were rum sick at a telephone [booth]. 2008 DCBE Tape CURRIE 9 And then I got rum sick, a word for a hangover. Survey I Inf. 20 "Rum sick" for hungover.

run[1] noun, usually plural; compare **checkers**
in steel making, a tunnel-like structure below the open-hearth furnace that allows hot gasses to move and where soot and waste collect

1990 Beaton Institute Tape 2623 A I helped loading rails and in the open-hearth underneath the furnaces in the – what they call the runs – that was where the waste – just a tunnel actually, very small tunnels ... They [the runs] would build up with dust and heavy stuff that the draft couldn't take out with the smoke. 1990 Beaton Institute MG 14 206 Box 7 C. iii b) File 49, 4 We worked in the runs. This is kind of like the draft section of the open-hearth furnaces ... There was like an ash, kind of like a cinder box type thing, underneath the furnaces, and a person had to go down there with shovels and picks and dig this stuff out and haul it out and make sure the furnace had a proper draft. 1991 BEATON *Scientia Canadensis* 15, 63 Johnny Martell ... worked first in bricking the open hearth, and cleaning the open-hearth 'runs' or flues ...

run[2] noun; compare **tittle**
a narrow, saltwater channel, especially one leading into or from a harbour

Pilot Survey Inf. 5 I'd say an entrance to a harbour. Survey II.

[*DPEIE* (1979), *COD Cdn* (*Nfld & Maritimes*)]; compare "A narrow salt-water strait or extended navigable passage between the coast and an island or a series of islands; a passage between islands" *DNE* (1842), *DC* 5 *Nfld*]

runaway trip noun; also **runaway boxes**; compare **trip**
a number of coupled mine cars (a trip) travelling on rails that rolls out of control down a slope with increasing speed

1969 Beaton Institute Tape 118 Can you tell us something about the runaway trip in 1930? 1974 *CB's Magazine* 8, 9 There was horses got killed. Runaway boxes. 1984 FERGUSON and JOHNSTON *Carman Recollections* 16 ... on a bleak December morning, a run-away trip into the Princess mine took the lives of 21 men. 2003 SAINT AGNES ELEMENTARY SCHOOL *Coal Miners' Stories* 45 One other time I was walking along the tracks when over the intercom they announced there was a runaway trip. (Which is the train that carries the men and materials into the mine). When my buddy and I heard this we jumped in holes on either side of the track.
[W3; compare *runaway train OED3* (1848)]

runner noun
a spout or trough carrying molten metal from the furnace
1990 Beaton Institute MG 14 206 Box 5 C. iii b) File 10, 1 You saw how the iron came out. It just went down a runner and dropped. Previous to that it ran into a runner, all right, but it ran outside into ladles ... 1991 BEATON *Scientia Canadensis* 15, 63 They had a huge bar for what they called "bad stickers." You'd have three or four guys trying to stand on the end of it while somebody held it in place to try to wedge this thing out of the ground or maybe the runner. 2005 CAPLAN ed. *Views from the Steel Plant* 76 When the furnace was charging, the Second Helper and I would be over at the back of the furnace, cleaning out the runner. The runner would be a long spout at the back of the furnace from the tap hole.
[NCD Metall., OED3 (1799), W3]

running ice noun
broken ice being moved by wind, currents, or tides
1892 GILLIES *Canadian Mining & Mechanical Review* 11 (10), 173 ... the damage done to Sydney and Louisburg pier by impact of running ice during the winter of 1891. 2007b BARBER *Only in Canada* 20 **running ice** (*Atlantic Canada*) ice that is moving, carried by currents or the wind. Pilot Survey Inf. 3 [Running ice] Oh yeah, that's quite common. You see it in the lake ... The tide is going out, and the ice is breaking up. Survey II Inf. 7 [Running ice is] driven by wind.
[*DNE, DPEIE, DC, COD Cdn* (*Nfld* & *Maritimes*), *NCD, OED3 N. Amer.* (1804)]

S

Sàcramaid, the ['sæxkrəmɪč] noun; compare **open-air communion**
the sacrament of communion, typically at an open-air communion; the sacramental season of the early Presbyterian Church
2006 STANLEY-BLACKWELL *Tokens of Grace* 13 Between 1840 and 1890, the so-called "sacramental season" – the Sàcramaid – was a dominant symbol in the lives of Cape Breton's Presbyterians. 2006 STANLEY-BLACKWELL *Tokens of Grace* 44 Following an address to intending participants, communion tokens for admission to the Sàcramaid were handed out ... 2007 ST. CLAIR and LEVERT *Nancy's Wedding Feast* 128 *While the sacrament was the emotional high point of this communion, known in Gaelic as the Sàcramaid, only those finally deemed worthy by elders, and by themselves, were issued a communion token which permitted them to receive the bread and wine.*

*A loanword from Scottish Gaelic, see *Sàcramaid* "sacrament" *GED*.

salter noun
a crew member that salts fish to preserve it as a dried or pickled product
1760 PICHON *Genuine Letters ... CB* 109 The salter immediately draws it aside, and

places it with the skin undermost. Then he covers it with salt, but very slightly, and lays the fish regularly one upon another. 1765 ROGERS *Concise Account of North America* 21 ... then it is conveyed to the salter, who places it with the skin undermost in a barrel ... 1981 *CB's Magazine* 29, 10 Then when they get 6 or 7 quintal split and washed in tubs full with water, you fork it down the hold. The salter takes it then. You'd carry 30 to 40 tons of salt in the schooners. The salter has a little scoop and he spreads a layer of fish, then salts it, spreads another layer – the fish side up, not the skin. 1984 BALCOM *Cod Fishery of Isle Royale* 37 In this instance, the schooner crew probably consisted of the master and the companion fishermen, with one of the fishermen also acting as the salter. 1992 HORNSBY *Nineteenth-Century CB* 12 ... others were engaged on shore, either as ... salters ...

[*DNE* ([1663]), *DC*, *COD Cdn* (*Nfld*), *EDD*; other dictionaries define the word in a general sense]

saqmaw [sɑkɑmɑʊ] noun; also spelled **sagamaw, sakamow**; compare **kji**
a chief

1992 MANNETTE ed. *Elusive Justice* 11 We spoke of his father, the Kjisakamow (Grand Chief), who had died in August. 1996 PRINS *Mi'kmaq: Resistance, Accommodation, and Cultural Survival* 203 Like cardinals electing a distinguished peer as pontiff, keptins choose one of their own as *kji saqmaw* (grand chief). The kji saqmaw serves as the ceremonial head. 1996 MCMILLAN "Mi'kmaq Grand Council" 100 Gabriel Sylliboy ... won the election, thus becoming the first elected Kji Sagamaw in the history of the Grand Council. 1999 JOE *We Are the Dreamers* 3 With my Niskam, the Kji-saqmaw of all that is good. 2008 MORGAN *Story of Cape Breton Island Book One* 11 The larger seasonal groupings or "residential kin" were

headed by a *saqmaw*, a chief or war leader, whose authority was based on persuasion and/or family connections, though obedience to him was not obligatory. To keep peoples' respect such a man would have to show superior insight or wisdom. 2012 SABLE and FRANCIS *Language of this Land, Mi'kma'ki* 23 Specific resource-use areas would be determined annually by the *saqmaw* and adjusted to changing demographics and resources.

*A Mi'kmaw loanword, see *saqamaw* "chief; big shot; gentleman" *MD*.

Sassenach noun; also spelled **Sasunnach**
an English person, often derisive

1929a MCCAWLEY *CB Come-All-Ye* 67 In the same trench they fell, / The Sassenach by kilted Gael ... [from the song "The Cape Breton Highlander's Soliloquy"]. 1976 MACLEAN *God and the Devil* 107 In contrast, her sister, Aunt Mary, had spent many years in Boston, where she became so fluent in the "Sassenach" tongue ... 1987 MACEACHERN *George MacEachern* 94 The Scotch here, they didn't look on Lowlanders as being altogether Scotch. They included them among the Sassenach. 1992 DUCHARME *Archie Neil* 49 I'm a Sasunnach, from over to Boston.

[*COD Scot. & Irish, FWCCD Scot. & Irish, GCD Scottish and Irish, OED3* (1771), *COED Scottish & Irish, NOAD Scottish Irish derogatory, W3*]

*The variant *Sasannach* is found in Scottish Gaelic "Englishman" *GED*.

scat noun
a card game with two or more players, the objective of which is to obtain thirty-one points, or close to that, before other players

1952 Beaton Institute MG 12 112 n.p. Simon enjoys talking and usually has something to say, especially when he lost too many games of scat. 1976–7 Miners' Museum Tape 425 In the morning we play tarabish, and then in the afternoon, after the story, we play scat until four o'clock ... 1997 DOUCET *Parables from Big Pond* 68 They brought out cards and they played tarabish, scat or forty-fives ...

scoff noun
an abundant meal of delicious food; a feed of seasonal food

1985 Beaton Institute Tape 2328 They used to kill their own cattle ... and they'd cook a big – they used to call a scoff – you'd cook a big supper. 1991 *Inverness Oran* 30 Oct. 24 In the meantime, Gaelic fouragh is served – a mixture of cream and oatmeal – a traditional Gaelic scoff. 1998 *CB's Magazine* 73 Inside Front Cover The fox had just had a scoff of Cheesies [*sic*] and sandwiches and goodness knows what else from a crowd of tourists who seemed oblivious to a very large sign which forbade the feeding of wildlife. 2003 [O'NEIL] *Cape Bretoner* 11 (3), 46 We sincerely hope no one panicked and threw away a scoff of perfectly good lobsters this summer! 2007b BARBER *Only in Canada* 155 **scoff** *informal* (*Atlantic Canada*) a big meal, especially of seafood, served in conjunction with a party. Pilot Survey Inf. 1 Just a big meal is how we'd use it. A lot of food ... a scoff ... it wouldn't have to be at a party – any big meal. A lot of times we refer to it if there's something that's available for only certain times of the year. Survey I Inf. 26 If it's one type of food, I would say "a feed" of lobsters. A scoff can be any meal. Survey I Inf. 32 Quite a scoff, a great meal.

[*DNE, DPEIE, COD Cdn* (*Maritimes & Nfld*), *GCD slang, OED3 colloq.*, orig. *S. Afr.* (1846), *COED informal, W3*]

*In contrast to definitions in other dictionaries that emphasize that *scoff* is a meal at an

impromptu party, the majority of respondents to Survey I indicated that a *scoff* does not need to take place at a party.

scordatura noun
a non-standard tuning, usually of a fiddle/violin, to create a special effect, also called high bass tuning

1981 MACGILLIVRAY *CB Fiddler* 5 There exists a fairly large repertoire of tunes suitable for this scordatura tuning, but it is mostly the older violinists who seem to specialize in them. 1987 *CB's Magazine* 44, 55 **A Note on Scordatura (High Bass Tuning)** Paul Cranford: "Scordatura tunings were commonly used by solo unamplified musicians, just to get a fuller, more resonant sound. Part of it has to do with more volume, part of it has to do with more colour – colour, volume, resonance." 1992 DUCHARME *Archie Neil* 48 He re-tuned a fiddle to scordatura ...

[*OED3* (1876), *COED, W3, NOAD Music*]

Scottish concert noun
a public performance held annually in communities, featuring such things as Scottish music (fiddle, pipes, vocals in Gaelic and English) and Highland dancing

1975 Beaton Institute Tape 1026 ... seeing the family, going to Scottish concerts, which are part of the way of life here ... 1993 *Inverness Oran* 18 Aug. 22 On Saturday, August 7, the Nova Scotia Highland Village treated a crowd of thousands to one of the best Scottish Concerts on the Island this summer at the 32nd Annual Village Day celebrations. One of the largest crowds in years was in attendance and enjoyed a day-long program of piping, violin and vocal selections ... 1997 *CB's Magazine* 72, 23 Well, there are concerts from July 1 until September 1; there are Scottish concerts every weekend each year. As a matter of fact, certain halls have a certain weekend.

script noun
an abbreviation for a doctor's prescription
to purchase alcohol during Prohibition
Pilot Survey and Survey I.
   [DNE (1917), DPEIE; compare script
"Shortened form of prescription, esp. one
for narcotic drugs" OED3 slang (orig. U.S.)
(1951)]

*As would be expected, more respondents in-
dicated that they had heard script used in this
way than those who use the term.

Scottish Mod: see **Gaelic Mod**

sea egg: see **whore's egg**

sealer noun
a worker who solders lids onto cans containing lobster
   1910 CANADA, DEPARTMENT OF
MARINE AND FISHERIES Lobster Fishery:
Evidence 737 Q. What is the average price
paid to sealers? Those are the best paid
men in the factory? – A. Yes; they get
about $45. 1977 Beaton Institute Tape 712
The sealer sat at his bench ... with solder
in one hand and curved sealing iron in the
other. He'd seal the cans and they were
thrown in the case. 1978 CB's Magazine 20,
3 One man, the sealer, would be sealing
all the cans, soldering them as they came
from the packing room, full cases. In those
days the covers went down inside the can.
And there was no word those days about
a sealing machine. They'd have to do it by
hand. Seal the cover, put lead all around
the lid. They used a soldering iron.
   [DNE, FWCCD, OED3 (1928), W3]

second helper noun; compare **melter**
one of three workers on the open-hearth
furnace, second to the operator or melter
in responsibility
   1980 CB's Magazine 27, 12 I went in
there as third helper. There was a melter
and a second helper – three of us at the
open hearth. 1991 BEATON Scientia
Canadensis 15, 63 Martell took the recognized succession of jobs, from spare
man on the furnace to second helper. His
description of a second helper's typical
day indicates that manual labour could
still be very much a part of steelmaking
in this modern era. 1992 CB's Magazine
60, 32 That bull gang were people who
would fill positions on the furnace as First
Helper and Second Helper. And that was
a top job. Made big money, 'cause you got
tonnage.

seed beer noun; compare **bull beer**
a homemade beer brewed with seeds, a
sweetener such as molasses, and water
   1993 CB's Magazine 63, 37 We used to
make – they call that seed beer. You could
make that in 24 hours. But it wasn't good
till 48 hours, to drink. 1994 CB's Magazine
65, 15 There were seeds, and they'd multiply. You could put, say, a cupful into a gallon jar, and put some molasses. And after
a while you'd have about a half a gallon.
They'd multiply. In the Depression that's
what it was called, seed beer. 1999 CB's
Magazine 74, 59 Flora: Bull beer. Jimmy:
There was a seed and some grew it with a
California seed, did you ever hear of that?
You put it down and eight hours, they
used to say, you had a brew made.
   [DARE (1970); compare Californian beer
"A homemade, usu non-alcoholic drink"
DARE]

seid: see **field bed**

set transitive verb; also in the phrase **setting day**
to lower (a baited lobster trap) to the
ocean floor
   1957 WILDER Canada's Lobster Fishery 5
[Caption] Their boats loaded with traps,
lobster fishermen approach the grounds
on the opening of the season, the "setting day". 1973 CB's Magazine 5, 23 The

photograph ... Breton Cove, taken when they were setting traps the first of the season. 1979 *CB's Magazine* 23, 42 [Caption] They set the traps out in long straight lines running with the shore across the fishing grounds. 2001 *CB Post* 26 Apr. 25 "It will be a problem for setting traps if it [lolly ice] lingers" Curtis said. 2005 MAC-DONALD *Forest for Calum* 294 ... pulling traps, removing lobsters, re-baiting and re-setting the traps as the season wound down towards its end-of-June closure. Survey II Inf. 4 Setting day is the first day of the lobster season when we set the traps.

[at *setting day DPEIE* (1985)]

sgeulachd ['skiələxk] noun, plural form
sgeulachdan
a long Gaelic folk tale often recounting heroic and fantastic events

1931 FRASER *Folklore of NS* xiii Around newly-kindled hearth fires the old *sgéulachdan* (tales) were related at the *Célidh* (friendly visit) in the poetic language of the Gael. 1953 DUNN *Highland Settler* 45 Their chief delight at such a *ceilidh* (gathering) was to ... listen to *sgeulachdan*, the ancient folk-tales of the Gael. 1966 Beaton Institute Tape 202 What does the word sgeulachdan mean [interviewer]? It means a story, telling about some famous giant, or famous men, or warrior ... 1977a MOR-GAN *Archivaria* 4, 202 The wealth of material in *sgeulachdan* (folk tales) and music is our proudest possession for it deals with the roots of our Cape Breton identity. 1999 THURGOOD "Storytelling on the Gab-arus-Framboise Coast" 230 Also lacking were the lengthy *sgeulachdan* – the Scottish hero and wonder tales told by the Gaelic storyteller Joe Neil MacNeil (1987) from Big Pond, thirty kilometers away. 2000 SHAW and ORNSTEIN *Brìgh an Òrain: A Story in Every Song* 48 Lauchie was by universal agreement a gifted raconteur, but did not credit himself with being a

competent reciter of the full-length tales known in Gaelic as *sgeulachdan*.

*A loanword from Scottish Gaelic, see *sgeulachd* "fable, legend, story, tale, yarn" *GED*.

sgoth [skoh] noun
a boat with one or two masts and square sails

[1940] MACNEIL *History of Iona-Washabuck* 57 The boat in which they made the trip was of the type commonly known as a Barra Boat or "Sgoth" ... This boat was rigged with two square sails. 1960 MORLEY *Sacred Heart Parish: John-stown* 19 They built boats or "sgothan." 1969 Beaton Institute Tape 120 A ship referred to as a sgoth, a squared rigged [boat] ... 1978 CAMPBELL *Highland Community on the Bras d'Or* 21 They built boats, or "sgothan", loaded their families and their meager possessions and, follow-ing the coast line, rounded Cape George, passed through the Gut of Canso and entered St. Peters' [*sic*] Bay.

*A loanword from Scottish Gaelic, see *sgoth* "skiff" *GED*.

shack noun, usually plural
a large bunkhouse built for coal and steel workers, providing poor housing to newly arrived immigrants and Newfoundland workers; by extension, any substandard house for workers, rented from the com-pany or private owners

1926 DUNCAN *Royal Commission ... Coal Mines of NS 1925* 41 ... the latter [buildings] are little better than tempo-rary shelters and are known and properly described as "shacks." 1983 MELLOR *Company Store* 6 To given them shelter, large boarding houses or "shacks" as they were known locally, were hurriedly built, each accommodating a total of seventy-two men, with each bed shared by two men on a shift basis. 1985 *CB's Magazine*

39, 47 But the problems were still there in mid-1901: "It is the duty of any town to see that individuals are not allowed to put up shacks where human beings will have to live day after day paying enormous rent, and at the same time leaving their lives foreshortened ..." 1988 CRAWLEY *Acadiensis* 17 (2), 44 On the other hand, when a reporter for the Sydney *Daily Post* visited the Coke Ovens district of Sydney, he found the "Newfoundlanders' shacks reeking with filth" ... 1993 WHITNEY PIER HISTORICAL SOCIETY *From the Pier Dear* 22 The "shacks" were an alternate form of private accommodation for plant workers, mainly young single men of Newfoundland origin. The shacks were owned by private business interests ... 1995 BEATON *Acadiensis* 24 (2), 82 Shacks, or very basic bunk houses, were the most common shelter supplied by the steel company for unskilled workers. Foreign skilled workers, including the Italians and Hungarians, also found accommodation in company shacks. 2000 BARLOW and MAY *Frederick Street* 45 Whitney Pier had an infamous reputation in its early days. The workers were housed in company shacks or substandard houses they built themselves.

shaker pan: see **pan line**

shallop noun; also spelled **shallope;** compare **chaloupe**
1. a light boat, open or partly decked, powered by oars or sails and used in the inshore fishery or as a tender
1597 in 1962 HAKLUYT ed. *Voyages* vol. 6 107 [quoting M. Charles Leigh] And when we had dispatched our businesse, we gave him ... one shallop with mast, sailes and other furniture, and other things which belonged to the ship. 1629 in 1992 GRIFFITHS and REID *William and Mary Quarterly* 49 (3), 502 The second day we coasted for the Cape, and for Porte

Anglois, and seing some fishermen at sea afishing in there boats, we sent our Shallope to Speake with them they leaving there boats fled to the woods. 1761 in 1977 *CB's Magazine* 18, 15 We found a shallop on the north bank of the channel, apparently long since abandoned. 1765 ROGERS *Concise Account of North America* 20–1 The fish caught near the shore are observed to be by far the best; the vessels employed in this business are generally small shallops, which come to shore every day, where the fishermen throw the cod upon a stage prepared for that purpose. 1992 HORNSBY *Nineteenth-Century CB* 7 The shallop was an undecked or partially decked rowing boat with one or two masts that could be set up as necessary. 1999 MACLEOD *No Great Mischief* 26 ... 'shallop.' It's sort of a small open boat. You can row it or use sails. Sort of like a dory. 2007 ST. CLAIR and LEVERT *Nancy's Wedding Feast* 73 They secured a small boat, perhaps a shallop, a small boat with two sails.
2. a mid-sized, ocean going sailboat used for coastal transport
1782 in 1968 PRENTIES *Castaway on CB* 60 The rest of my fellow sufferers in the shipwreck soon after arrived at Halifax in a shallop from Spanish River. 1788 in 1869 BROWN *History of the Island of CB* 399 Those [seventy convicts] who reached Mainadieu in safety were sent to Sydney in a shallop belonging to one Luke Keegan, except twenty which the shallop could not take. 1815 in 1990 *CB's Magazine* 55, 42 However, as we neared *Scatari* Island ... you can see shallops of 18 to 20 tons, sometimes even barges, fishing during the entire day in this dangerous and disagreeable spot ... 1974 JACKSON *Windows on the Past* 42 In that year, Captain Jeremiah Allen (1726–1809) built the 28-ton shallop. 1992 HOWARD *Early CB Newspapers* 63 FOR SALE: The Shallop Alert, nearly 20 tons, lying at Mira

River, completely fitted with sails, rigging, ground tackle, etc.

[Sense 1: *COD, FWCCD, NCD Naut., OED3* (1590), *DAE, W3, NOAD chiefly historical, MWCD*. Sense 2: *DNE, OED3* (1578), *W3, NOAD chiefly historical, MWCD*]

Shanachie ['ʃɛnəçi, 'ʃɛnəki] noun; also spelled **Shenachie, shennachie, seanaichie**, and in Gaelic **seanachaidh, seanchaidh, seannachaidh**
a storyteller, oral historian, tradition bearer

1953 DUNN *Highland Settler* 48 The local story-reciter, or "shennachie" (spelt in Gaelic *seanachaidh*), could provide him with hours of entertainment, sometimes by reciting only one long story. 1976 MACGREGOR *Days That I Remember* 34 A good story teller was known as a Shenachie. 1979 *Inverness Oran* 11 Jan. 8 Most folk know that the name Shanachie comes from the Gaelic and means "storyteller." These individuals, and they were men always, traveled throughout the countryside weaving tales at each household that they happen to frequent ... As there were no modern means of communications in those days of yore, the Shanachie was an invaluable human being. Today, here in Inverness, I would stack Willie the Piper, John Alex MacKinnon, Corner Street, and Big Red up with the best Shanachie that ever traveled the Celtic soil. 1999 THURGOOD "Storytelling on the Gabarus-Framboise Coast" 37–8 ... Jimmy with his knowledge of genealogy would be described as a *seanchaidh* (shanachie) meaning a "tradition bearer" (personal communication). However, Catriona Parsons, originally of the island of Lewis in Scotland, uses the same word to describe a storyteller specifically (personal communication). 1999 MACLEOD *No Great Mischief* 65 And if the older

singers or storytellers of the *clann Chalum Ruaidh*, the *seanaichies*, as they were called, happened to be present they would "remember" events from a Scotland which they had never seen ...

*A loanword from Scottish Gaelic, see *seanchaidh* "historian, narrator, story-teller, tradition bearer" *GED*.

shank noun, often plural; also **moose-shank**
footwear, homemade from the hide taken from the lower legs of a large animal

1933 MACDONALD *Cape North and Vicinity* 153 What beautiful moose-shanks they often wore in those days, so suitable to protect the feet from snow, and so perfectly comfortable in the frostiest weather! 1942 DENNIS *CB Over* 165 Footwear was of home manufacture and consisted of moccasins, or more often, shanks. 1976 MACGREGOR *Days that I Remember* 14 When killing the winter's beef the hind legs had to be skinned in a certain way to allow the hide of the back joint to become the heel of the shank, a name given to this kind of foot wear.

[*DPEIE* Archaic [1890?]; compare the meaning of "stockings or leggings": *DC Esp. Maritimes, OED3* Sc. (*a*1547), *EDD, W3 Scot*]

shareman noun
a member of a fishing crew who works for a share of the profits instead of wages

1987 *CB's Magazine* 44, 21 ... they used to keep what they called a "shareman." (A fisherman would) hire somebody to fish with him. Well, (the shareman would) get a quarter of what they'd make. 1991 LAVERY and LAVERY *Gabarus and Vicinity* 95 Besides the regular fishermen there were the "sharesmen" from farming communities who helped out with the catch during June, July and August in Gabarus Lake and Grand Mira.

[*DNE*, *DC Esp. Nfld*, *OED3* (1687), *DAE* (1687), *DA* (1687); at *sharesman W3*; compare "A tenant farmer who pays a share of the crop as rent" *DARE*]

shearer noun; also **Anderton shearer**; compare **continuous miner**
a machine using tapered metal teeth on a rotating drum or blade that cuts the coal
   1983 SHEDDEN et al. *Mining Photographs* 269 **Anderton shearer** – A patented, long wall mechanical miner with blades or shearers for cutting into the coal. 1986 *CB's Magazine* 42, 24 (What took the Dosco Miner out of the mines?) Well, the present machine, which is called a "shearer" – a poor name – but it's simpler ... instead of the picks being on a chain, like on a chain saw, they're on a drum. That's the main difference. The drum turns, and it's much simpler. 1990 [MAC-NEIL] *History of Sydney Mines* 66 The first shearer for Princess Colliery was installed late in 1966 on a face 900 feet long, supported on wood chucks, props, and cap for roofing control. 1992 NEWTON *Where Coal is King* 51 The shearer which cuts the coal costs between $1.5 and $2.0 million. 2003 SAINT AGNES ELEMENTARY SCHOOL *Coal Miners' Stories* 69 The Shearer (the machine that cuts the coal) was at the bottom of the coalface ... He looked up the wall face and saw flames about four feet high between the drums (what cuts the coal also) of the shearer.
   [*OED3* (1956), *W3*]

sheep manure tea noun; also **sheep manure's tea**
a folk remedy made from sheep dung simmered in water
   1974 *CB's Magazine* 7, 24 We began to collect old cures after Dr. MacMillan of Baddeck told us about sheep manure tea, a cure once in general use on Cape Breton. 1975 MACMILLAN *Memoirs of a CB Doctor* 155 He had gone out into the pasture

and gathered up enough sheep manure to more than half fill the pot. Then he had added water to fill it up and put it on the back of the stove until it began to simmer. Every two hours Victor had to drink a glassful. I didn't tell them to stop using this special "tea," but perhaps the expression on my face conveyed the message. 1981 *CB's Magazine* 28, 19 And the old Scotch cures ... And for the measles, they used to give you sheep manure's tea.
   [Compare *sheep dung tea DPEIE* and *sheep tea DARE* ([1872])]

shell ice noun; also spelled **shelly ice**
a thin layer of ice covering an air pocket
   1978 *CB's Magazine* 19, 16 He asked me what the track was like, what the ice was like. And I said, "Very good, it's good and solid anyway – no shelly ice." 2004 BROWN Email 29 Mar. Shell ice, never shelly ice, is usually found in the fall or spring when there has been a quick freeze of puddles and the ice is always white, thin, opaque, brittle and sounds like breaking glass when little boys (or big boys) walk or jump on it. Shell ice is very distinctive. Oftentimes it can be found on thick, dark ice as a film in a small depression. Survey I Inf. 23 Shell ice along the edge of the pond for 2 or 3 feet.
   [*DPEIE*, *DC North*, *NCD*, *GCD Cdn. North*, *OED3 Canad.* (1875), *W3*; compare *shelly DPEIE*]

shift transitive verb
to change (one's own clothes)
   1979 THOMAS *Songs and Stories from Deep Cove* 12 All I had to do was shift my clothes and go out in the boat. 2007 *DCBE* Tape SHERRINGTON 21 Now shifting clothes ... I would have thought he was moving clothes from here to there, but no, he meant he was changing.
   [*DNE*, *COED chiefly N. Amer.*, *EDD*, *OED3 Now chiefly dial.* (c1400), *DARE*, *W3 chiefly dial*]

shine noun; compare **Cape Breton Silver**
distilled alcoholic liquor made illegally;
an abbreviation of moonshine

1982 *CB's Magazine* 32, 34 "I'll give you
so many trout for so much 'shine." We
made a bargain. I had got two bottles of
shine. 1983 Beaton Institute Tape 2116
What about the drink, would it be homemade shine or would they have store-
bought liquor [interviewer]? There was
a time when, during prohibition times,
when the stuff they used to get was, well
moonshine, but in earlier years than
that, they used to get a lot of rum. 1991
Beaton Institute Tape 2652 Do you know
anybody that makes Cape Breton shine
[interviewer]? Oh yes, I know all kinds of
people that make it. 2005 MACKENZIE
Neighbours are Watching 102 But "Silver
Dan" and some other manufacturers
turned out an acceptable product; "White
Lightening," "Shine" or whatever, it was
part of an old tradition.

[*COD* slang, *OED3*, *DARE* **scattered, but
chiefly S Atl** (1923), *W3*]

shoe-cork: see **cork**

shoot transitive verb; often in the phrases
shoot down and **cut, shoot, and load**;
compare **shotfirer, cut** verb
to detonate (an explosive charge) in holes
bored into a coal face (the area where the
coal is excavated) to break the coal so it
can be loaded

1934 *NS Miner* 4 (167), 4 The miners
working in rooms or narrow works are
compelled to load or clear away all the
duff or fine coal before the place is considered safe to shoot. 1974 Beaton Institute
Tape 878 ... you put the amount of powder that you thought was right for to open
out the center. Then you shoot your side
hole. 1974 *CB's Magazine* 8, 7 You didn't
have to call a shotfire – not then, when
they had the handpick like that. Shooting
your own coal. 1986 *CB's Magazine* 42, 18

When I came in, they undercut the coal,
the coal was blasted down – the mining
term is "shot down." 2007 MACKENZIE
CB Coal Mine Disasters 151 Once the holes
were bored, they had a shotfirer come
and "shoot" the holes, blasting the coal
and breaking it up in lumps from the
solid block face, so they could load it into
boxes.

[*NCD*, *OED3* (1830–1860), *EDD*,
MWCD; other dictionaries link *shoot* to
explosives in oil or gas wells: *GCD*, *DAE*,
DA; compare "To mine (coal) by blasting
without previous undercutting or shearing" *W3*]

shore ice noun; compare **big ice**
ice that is aground on the coast

Pilot Survey Inf. 2 [Shore ice] pushes
up on the beach. Survey II Inf. 3 Ice that is
aground, stuck along the shore. Survey II
Inf. 6 Ice on the shore and it stays – ice to
the water's edge.

[*DNE*, *DPEIE*, *DC Esp. North*, *COD N
Amer.*, *GCD Cdn.*, *esp. Northern*; at *shore-ice
OED3* (1752)]

shotfirer noun; also spelled **shotfire**,
short-fire(r), **shot fire(r)**; compare **shoot**
a miner certified to inspect for mine safety
and to detonate explosive charges (or
shoot) placed in holes bored into the coal
face (the area where the coal is excavated)

1942 DENNIS *CB Over* 90 "Explosives
will later be put in these holes by the
'shot-firer.'" 1976 *Oran Inbhirnis* 6 Aug.
7 The 'Shot-firer' was called to inspect
the 'shot' and the 'roof' and to connect
the 'cable' to the shot. After the room
was cleared the Shot-firer exploded the
charge. 1984 Beaton Institute Tape 2162
Is a shotfirer lower than an overman on
the totem pole [interviewer]? Yes, next to
an overman. 1995 *DCBE* Tape NICHOL-
SON 19–20 You're all done boring, your
shotfire will shoot it for you ... Now you
give him a plug of powder, he'd put the

cap into it, you'd fill up one hole. You just
moved out of the way; he'd shoot it for
you. Breaks it all up. 1999 KELLY *Cape
Bretoner* 7 (4), 36 ... an older fellow told me
I should go and get my shot-fire or mine
examiner's papers. Then I was qualified
to carry caps and detonators and blast
coal. 1999 MIGLIORORE and DIPIERRO
eds. *Italian Lives* 66 "Shotfirers" *were highly
experienced and specially certified people who
discharged explosives. A key responsibility
was first to inspect the place for explosive
gases, using a specifically designed flame
lamp.* 2008 *DCBE* Tape CURRIE 14 ... the
guy who ... blew the coal out of the face,
was called a shot-fire.

[at *shot-firer OED3* (1883), W3]

side head noun; also **side heading, pin
head**; compare **head, kitchen**
a funnel-shaped mesh entry on the side of
a lobster trap, giving access to the baited
chamber (the kitchen)

Pilot Survey Inf. 2 It's the sides of the
traps that have the two rings in it that the
lobster crawls through ... Glace Bayers call
it side heads and we [in Port Morien] call
it pin heads. I don't know why. Survey II
Inf. 1 Side head is where they enter the
kitchen. Survey II Inf. 2 Side head is the
same as the head, heading. Survey II Inf.
5 It [the side head] allows the lobster to
enter the trap, not the parlour.

[at *head DNE*; at *fishing head DPEIE*
(with *side head* as a variant) (1985)]

*The *pin head* mentioned by informant 2 of the
Pilot Survey may derive from the *bait pin* that
holds the bait that lures the lobster through
the side head into the trap's kitchen. The more
frequently used term in the dictionary files
for *bait pin* is *spindle* (see below). Some lobster
fishers use a *bait box* (see above) instead of
the pin or spindle as it holds the bait more
securely.

sill noun; compare **bow**

one of the four boards forming the rectangular base of a lobster trap and holding
the bows

1987 Beaton Institute Tape 2324 [Tape 1]
You get two sills in a length that we buy ...
I cut mine twenty-five inches and center
at twenty-one – that gives two inches
over into the bow where the bow is bent
down. 1993 Beaton Institute Tape 3229 B
Some people even cut their own sills but
not that many. They're what goes into the
bows.

[*DPEIE* (1985)]

silver thaw noun; also **glister**; compare
glitter storm
a layer of ice on exposed surfaces resulting from freezing rain; a storm of freezing
rain

1891 Beaton Institute MG 12 45, 22
Jan. 4 Thurs 22 this is the first fine day
we have had this week but the trees and
every thing are still covered thick with
Silver thaw. 1906 Beaton Institute MB 20
Apr. n.p. Silver thaw in the evening. 1935
Beaton Institute MG 12 59, 26 Feb. [37]
A silver thaw. Hard crust on the snow.
Slippery sidewalks. Trees crusted with
ice. 1950 Beaton Institute MG 6 23 9 Apr.
n.p. Easter Sunday nice but Silver Thaw –
could not stand on your feet. 1989 MLEC-
ZKO *My Book of Memories* [PART II] 73
And I'll never forget my first experience
in Canada of the silver thaw, the time
when rain freezes and everything every-
where is coated with a thick layer of ice.
2007 DANIELSON *CB Weather Watching*
160 The most beautiful and treacherous
precipitation of all is the freezing rain
storm, known widely throughout Cape
Breton as a silver thaw, a perfect name
for the spectacle. 2007b BARBER *Only in
Canada* 20 **silver thaw** (*Atlantic Canada*) a
slick glassy coating of ice formed on the
ground or an exposed surface, caused by
freezing rain or a sudden light frost. 2007
DCBE Tape SHERRINGTON 26 There's

a silver thaw and a glister storm. They're pretty much the same thing, those two.

[*DNE* ([1700]), *DC Esp. Atlantic Provinces and BC, COD Cdn (Maritimes & Nfld), FWCC Canadian, NCD, GCD Cdn., OED3* ([1700]), *COED, DARE* **esp. OR, WA**, *W3, NOAD*]

sinker (rock): see **dummy rock**

skiff noun
a thin layer, especially of snow
    1968 ROWE "Linguistic Study of Lake Ainslie Area" 46 Another vocabulary item with a great number of variations is skim, as "skim of ice." Six informants used skim, four used skum, and one each used shale, slib, skiff, skeem, and skale. Pilot Survey Inf. 3 Just a skiff [of snow], you might get during the winter. Well, today they call it a flurry. Survey I Inf. 5 A light even fall of snow. Survey I Inf. 23 A little skiff of snow, but it could be paint.
    [*DPEIE* (1821), *COD N Amer., OED3* Chiefly *Sc., DSL* (used as a verb); at *skift: DARE* **widespread exc NEast, Sth, SW** ([1808]), *W3 dial*; compare *skiff* "A slight or flying shower" *EDD*]

skooshin [skušən, skúšəŋ] verbal noun; also spelled **scushing, sqooshying**; compare **clamper**
moving quickly and nimbly on pans of ice to avoid falling in the water, jumping clampers
    1994 JONES *Cape Bretoner* 3 (1), 28 There was ocean skooshin and brook skooshin. In ocean skooshin one ran from clamper to clamper without (you hoped) getting wet ... Now brook skooshin was quite different. What you did was, ahem, "borrow" a clothes pole, find a good clamper (what the mainlanders call ice floes) and pole around the brook till all hours. 2000 MACDONALD Email 4 Jan. One would go sqooshying in the spring when the ice is breaking up. Sqooshying is to

jump from ice clamper to ice clamper as it moves out and along the shore. They still do it here [in the Ingonish area]. 2002 *DCBE* Tape *Information Morning* 27 Feb. 5 ... the word that we used for jumping on clampers when I was a kid was scushing not skooshing ... when we grew up in Glace Bay. 2002 MACISAAC *Cape Bretoner* 10 (3), 34 ... jumping from one piece of ice (called clampers) to another. The fun was called "skooshin" and its not surprising that this dangerous pastime was strictly forbidden. Survey II Inf. 6 I heard the word from a friend in Glace Bay – jumping clampers or scushing.
    [Compare *step clumpers* "in children's pastime, to jump from one pan of ice to another" *DNE*]

*The origin of this word is uncertain, but the *EDD* has *scoosh* "To rush to shelter," the *OED3* records *skoosh* "move rapidly, especially of vehicles ...," and *COD* has *scooch N Amer.* meaning "move quickly."

slag man: see **monkey man**

sleeveen noun; also spelled **sleeven**
a sly, deceitful person
    2003 MUISE Email 3 July "Sleeven bastard" – probably a derivative of "sleeveen" which I think is a Newfoundland word. Survey I Inf. 22 I heard this [sleeveen] from my mother who was born in Main-à-Dieu but was Irish. It characterizes [someone] as sly, foxy.
    [*DNE, COD Cdn (Nfld) & Irish, derogatory OED3 Irish* and *Newfoundland* (1834); at *slieveen EDD* (with *sleeveen* as a variant)]

slink[1] noun
a sneaky, dishonest, untrustworthy person
    1992 GILLIS *Promised Land* 41 "The slink!" Laughie grinned, then frowned. 2002 *DCBE* Tape *Information Morning* 27 Feb. 10 If there was a certain person in the area that she didn't particularly like, she

used to say "nothing but a slink." 2010
RANKIN Email 23 Mar. Do you know the
word "slink" about someone who is sly
or dishonourable? Survey I Inf. 11 A thief,
untrustworthy. Survey I Inf. 35 Sly – they
fib, do things behind your back.

[*EDD, OED3 dial.* or *colloq.* (1824), *W3
chiefly dial*]

slink[2] noun
1. a weak, undernourished salmon, cod,
and, less frequently, any weak fish

1974 *CB's Magazine* 9, 8 According to
the fish officer in Baddeck, they saw slink
salmon up to the falls. 2002 *DCBE* Tape
Information Morning 27 Feb. 10 Ian: "What
are those salmon that come up the river?"
Jim: "Slinks." Survey I Inf. 5 Any small
fish, not cod specifically – the river is full
of slinks, not suitable to eat. Survey I Inf.
16 A sick fish, salmon or cod. Survey I Inf.
34 Salmon in the springtime.
2. any person or thing undersized or
inferior

Survey I Inf. 5 The word is used for
objects – a slink of a tree or a slink of a car.
Survey I Inf. 22 A slink of a thing – very
thin. Survey I Inf. 37 A person who is thin.

[Sense 1: *DNE* ([1771]), *DC Esp. Nfld*
(1771), *EDD, OED3 dial.* and *U.S.*. Sense
2: *EDD, OED3 dial.* and *U.S.* (1863), *W3
chiefly dial*]

slobby adjective; compare **slob ice, lolly**
covered with floating fragments of sea ice
and snow, densely packed

Survey I and II.

[*DNE* (1973), *DPEIE, COD Cdn*]

*Only the *DNE* and *DPEIE* record the sense of
fragments of ice, but the *EDD, OED3,* and *W3*
define the word as "muddy," reflecting the
Irish origin.

slob ice noun; rarely **slob**; compare **lolly**
floating fragments of sea ice and snow,
densely packed

1919 *North Sydney Herald* 24 Dec. 4
Sydney was ice locked as a result of
Saturday's storm. The ferry boats found it
impossible to force their way through the
heavy slob ... 1970 Beaton Institute Tape
145 I remember one time there was slob ice
coming in the harbour. 1986 MACLEOD
As Birds Bring Forth the Sun 53 ... at other
times a sort of floating slush was formed
mingling with snow and "slob" ice which
was not yet solid. 2004 ELLISON *Cape
Bretoner* 12 (2), 56 Slob ice isn't much more
than a growth of slush on the surface of
the sea. 2011 DOYLE *CB Facts and Folklore*
45 When the heavy snows of winter come
in contact with the frigid salt water they
ooze into a slurry that can bog down the
ferry until it stops. In some places, this is
called slob ice. Survey I Inf. 16 Slob ice is
melting drift ice. Survey I Inf. 22 Lolly is
snow and ice, slush over the water; slob
ice is more substantial, broken ice fragments. Survey II Inf. 4 Slob ice forms in
the spring of year when the ice is smashed
ice. Survey II Inf. 8 Slob ice is old ice that
has broken or ground up, waves going
through it, loosely packed ice, unstable,
can't stand on it.

[*DNE, DPEIE, DC Orig. Nfld* (1835),
*COD Cdn, FWCCD Canadian, NCD Cana-
dian, GCD Cdn., OED3 orig. Canad.* (1835);
at *slob DNE* (1846), *OED3 Canad., W3*]

*Both *lolly* and *slob ice* are unstable masses of
ice and snow, but respondents to the Surveys
indicated that *slob ice* has more ice fragments
caused by the grinding of the sea ice.

slope noun; also **slope shaft**; compare
deep
an inclined entrance to an underground
coal mine; the inclination from horizontal of the coal seam and by extension the
haulage passage (or the deep) that follows
the incline

1815 in 1991 *CB's Magazine* 56, 52
Sometimes it [coal] is reached at 30 feet

from the surface, other times at 60 or
more, depending on the slope of the
coal seam, which is not always the same.
1976 *Oran Inbhirnis* 6 Aug. 6 The main
'slope' was run directly into the seam
in the direction of the ocean ... After a
few years the engineers angled the main
slope more to the east to follow the
'dip' of the seam more correctly. 1983
SHEDDEN et al. *Mining Photographs* 271
Slope – An entrance to a mine driven
down through an inclined coal seam ...
1983 MELLOR *Company Store* 83 ... workmen ... commenced work on the sinking
of slope shafts extending from the shore
towards the rich coal seams under the sea
– "towards the slope" as miners say. 1988
BOUTILIER *New Waterford* 160 Entrance
to the mines in the New Waterford area
was of the slope type rather than the
shaft method used elsewhere. 1996 *CB's
Magazine* 71, 70 We had to let the six god-
damn coal boxes go back into the mine
without a chain on them. Tore the slope
in for about 75 feet. The mine had to be
closed down a week to rebuild the slope.
2007 MACKENZIE *CB Coal Mine Disasters*
41 The men were working at the bottom
of the slope which was driven at an angle
about 200 feet down into the coal seam.
They were removing coal from the bottom end of the slope, "driving" the slope,
or deep, further into the coal mine.
[*OED3 Mining* (1863), *W3*]

sloven noun
a low, horse-drawn wagon, used to haul
heavy loads; rarely a low sled used for
hauling
1951 MACLENNAN *Each Man's Son* 41
The shops were now closed, the coal carts
and slovens were off the streets ... 1982
CB's Magazine 32, 38 And then Dr. Sullivan
had an ambulance made, over the yard
there. It was sloven, they call them; you
know, a low axle, drop axle, a low heavy
wooden structure. And it was drawn by

two horses. 1985 *CB's Magazine* 39, 32 ... he
had a double team of horses and a sloven.
It's an old sleigh that they used to haul
wood and what-have-you. It took 7 men
to haul that bear on[to] the sloven ... 2004
AYERS *Cape Bretoner* 12 (6), 26–7 Starting
in mid-April, McGuire's Ice used a horse
and sloven, a low wagon whose surface
was about a foot off the ground, to deliver
the ice to customers in Glace Bay, Sydney,
Sydney River, and Westmount.
[*DNE, DPEIE, DC Atlantic Provinces*
(1895), *COD Cdn* (*Maritimes & Nfld*),
GCD Cdn. "In Atlantic Provinces," *OED3*
Chiefly *Canad. regional* (*Newfoundland* and
the Maritimes) (1895), *DARE* (1895)]

smack noun; also **lobster smack, smack
boat, fishing smack**; compare **well boat**
a boat, powered by sail or motor, used
primarily to collect and transport live
lobsters from the fishers to a cannery or
merchant
1871 CANADA *Parliamentary Debates,
Dominion of Canada, Fourth Session, 33
Victoriae* 477 ... there were only Port Hood
and Mabou – not a single other port
where a fishing smack of 50 tons could
enter and lie securely. 1910 CANADA,
DEPARTMENT OF MARINE AND
FISHERIES *Lobster Fishery: Evidence* 650 Q.
Does Mr. Baker's boat come around and
collect them? – A. Yes, he collects them
in his smack. 1977 *CB's Magazine* 17, 48
They sold lobsters to the lobster smack, a
boat like a large sloop. 1984 CUMMING et
al. *Story of Framboise* 73 After the smaller
canneries closed, "smacks" (sail-boats
first, then motorboats) would travel up
and down the shore picking up lobsters
from the fisherman to take to the packers
at Fourchu. 1992 *CB's Magazine* 59, 82 You
know what a smack is – it's like a fishing
boat, but it's a bigger boat (used for gathering the catch from several fishing boats).
2006 STANLEY-BLACKWELL *Tokens of
Grace* 89 By the 1880s ... schooners and

fishing smacks, frequented its [Sydney's] harbours ...

[Several dictionaries define *smack* as fishing vessel with a well for keeping fish alive; only three emphasize collection and transportation of the catch: *DNE* (1895), *NCD*, *DARE* **scattered, but chiefly NEast** (1811)]

smack transitive and intransitive verb
to collect and transport (live lobsters) to a cannery or merchant

1910 CANADA, DEPARTMENT OF MARINE AND FISHERIES *Lobster Fishery: Evidence* 701 Q. Within what distance each side of Lingan do you run? A. I only smacked on one side. 1977 Beaton Institute Tape 903 The lobsters were smacked ... the fellows gathering them up. 1978 *CB's Magazine* 20, 8 When I was smacking, I had to stay out until the fishermen came to me. 1987 *CB's Magazine* 46, 10–11 Came home to White Point. I bought lobsters for a merchant down there, that's all. Smacking – called them smacking lobsters.

[*DAE* (1880), *DA* (1880)]

smackman noun; also spelled **smack man**; also **smacker**
a crew member aboard a boat who collects and transports live lobsters to a cannery or merchant

1910 CANADA, DEPARTMENT OF MARINE AND FISHERIES *Lobster Fishery: Evidence* 719 A. The union has discussed that matter for the past couple of years, and it was thought that if the smackman were a sworn officer for the lobster fishing season, and when the fisherman brought his lobsters to the smack the smackman would take an account of the number of berried lobsters and put them overboard, giving a check to the fisherman that he had put so many berried lobsters overboard. 1910 CANADA, DEPARTMENT OF MARINE AND FISHERIES *Lobster*

Fishery: Evidence 765 A. I think it is the smacker who takes the berried lobster who could check it. 1978 *CB's Magazine* 20, 10 [Caption] L'Archeveque cannery crew ... Dannie MacKillop (the smackman for many years) ... 1994 SAMSON *River Bourgeois* 26 The company used three smackers to purchase and transport lobster from fishermen in the plant areas.

[*W3*]

smart adjective; also in **smart on (my) feet**
agile, nimble

1919 in 1998 *CB's Magazine* 73, 50 They [survivors of a shipwreck] ware some scared. We had to land them on a rough place and be smart getting out of the boat but they wouldnt jump so we dragged some of them out and thrue some of them overboard. 1985 Beaton Institute Tape 960 Well, I was pretty smart on my feet when I was young. I was good to run. My feet were good and I was smart on my feet. 1989 *CB's Magazine* 50, 71 But I'm pretty careful. I'm not as smart on my feet as I used to be, but I'm thankful. Why should I complain at my age? 1994 *CB's Magazine* 65, 41 [She] could weave, smart with her hands and her mind. Survey I Inf. 26 To describe an old person who is agile. "She's right smart for her age."

*Several dictionaries define *smart* as "quick," "brisk," "lively," or "energetic," but the *OED3* seems closest to the Cape Breton sense with *deftly* in "Of an action, movement, etc.: quickly or deftly executed ..." (*a*1325).

snapper boat noun
a motorized boat used in the inshore fishery, especially for fishing for swordfish

1948 STAEBLER *Maclean's* 15 July 47 I pondered the gambling spirit of these men who follow the swordfish, the fishermen who come in their schooners and jacks, ketches and smacks, snapper boats and skiffs. 1983 Beaton Institute Tape

2048 The snapper boat also had a keel, but she was flat eh. She came down and she turned in, and of course much higher from the water to the top of the bow. This enabled them to put on a longer stand, a higher spar, a better lookout, and everything was better all around. This is what made fishing, sword fishing much better. 1985 MACGILLIVRAY and O'DONNELL *CB Song Collection* 19 Snapper: a small motorized boat used for in-shore fishing. 2005 DONOVAN *Molly Poems & Highland Elegies* 31 The clear moon's glow on the Jolson pit-faces, / The black buttons of water behind the snapper boats, / Cod to their gunnels.
[*DNE* (n.d.)]

snig transitive verb; often followed by **out** to drag (timber), especially from the woods, rather than using a sled or wagon

1986 MACLEOD *As Birds Bring Forth the Sun* 104 He and his twin brother had built it in "the old way" ... cutting all the logs themselves and "snigging" them out with their horses ... 2005 MACKENZIE *Neighbours Are Watching* 120 Johnny Callaghan, "snigging" – hauling out hardwood with a pair of Clyde horses – had his troubles one day. Pilot Survey Inf. 3 [To snig logs] you just tie a chain onto them and drag it out ... with a horse or an ox. Pilot Survey Inf. 5 My uncle who had a mill ... we'd snig the logs out, and he used horses.
[*DNE, DPEIE, EDD* (1790), *OED3 north. dial., Austral., N.Z.,* and *Canad. local* (1790), *COED Austral./NZ, W3 chiefly dial*; compare "To pull sharply, to jerk" *DSL*]

snood noun; compare **ganging, trawl, backline, haul-up**
1. in longline fishing, a light line of about eighteen inches that attaches the hook to the main line (trawl or backline) at regular intervals

1992 HORNSBY *Nineteenth-Century CB* 158 Consisting of a longline with numerous shorter hook-lines or "snoods" attached at regular intervals, the trawl was fixed to the seabed by anchors ... Pilot Survey Inf. 2 Trawl is a handline ... then every foot you'd have a snood and a hook on the snood. Survey II Inf. 2 A snood is an 18 inch line with a hook on it. A trawl would have a snood every six feet (one fathom). Survey II Inf. 4 The snood is attached to the backline of the trawl. Survey II Inf. 6 Snood is the most commonly used but also ganging.
2. in lobster fishing, the line that attaches the trap to the buoy; also the line that attaches the trap to the main line that connects a number of lobster traps (or string)

Survey II Inf. 3 The buoy has a snood that attaches to the bridle on the trap. That end of the trap is called the kitchen end or snood end. Survey II Inf. 4 I use a snood or haul-up to raise the trap. Survey II Inf. 8 The snood is the branch line [from the main line] to the trap.
[Sense 1: *EDD, OED3* (c1682), *COED, NOAD*. Sense 2: *DPEIE*]

*John Gould reports at *snood* that "Maine coastal people have extended it [snood] to the twine from which a net is made, usually as a noun *snoodin'* ..." ML.

soaking pit noun
an oven in the steel plant used to heat steel ingots to a uniform temperature before they are reshaped and rolled

1952 POWELL *CB Mirror* 1 June 13 Beyond the Open Hearth are the soaking pits – huge ovens where the ingots are kept red-hot while they await their turn at the mills, where tremendous rollers roll the ingots continuously thinner into rails, bars, rods, wire and nails. 1980 *CB's Magazine* 27, 17 Those ingots would be cold by the time they got up there. They would have to be put in what they call the soaking pits, to re-heat the ingots up to the proper temperature before they could

roll them. 1991 Beaton Institute MG 14
206 Box 5 C. iii b) File 45, 3 The soaking
pit actually takes the ingot from the Open
Hearth in those days, and there is twelve
of those ingots that go in a pit.
[at *soaking* noun *OED3* (1882)]

society bull noun; also spelled **Society
Bull**
a bull owned by an agricultural society for
breeding cows belonging to its members
1982 MACLELLAN *The Glen* 87–8 The
Glen Agricultural Society was instrumental in obtaining a pure-bred bull ...
The "Society Bull", on the other hand,
possessed not only a noble lineage with
authoritative documents to prove it, but
his awesome appearance put the lowly
scrub bull to shame. 1990 *CB's Magazine*
54, 49 In lots of districts they had what
they called a "society bull." The bull
would do probably from halfway between
here [Belle Côte] and Margaree Church,
and as far down again. They had a bull –
fellow kept it. And you'd have to take
the cows there to breed them. 2007 *DCBE*
Tape SHERRINGTON 28 They had society
bulls, which meant that the agricultural
society owned the bull and it was used by
a lot of people to breed their cows.

*The Agricultural Societies also brought in
rams for breeding as Ethridge and Munro note
in *The Nova Scotian Journal of Agriculture*, "a
Cotswold ram and two Leicester rams. These
animals safely arrived in Margaree" (1867, 229).

sook [sʊk] noun; also **sooky** adjective;
also spelled **sookie**
a person (adult or child), or animal, acting
like a baby, wimp, or sissy; acting in the
manner of a sook
2002 COADY *Saints of Big Harbour* 73
People clung to their clichés like sooky
blankets in this part of the world. 2007b
BARBER *Only in Canada* 9 **sook / sooky
baby** (*Atlantic Canada*) derogatory a person

acting childishly; a wimp, coward, or
sissy. Survey I Inf. 26 Sook can mean any
person or animal who likes to be babied.
"The dog is a real sook" or is "right
sookie." Sookie bird" is said jokingly
about a person.
[at *sook*: *DNE, DPEIE, COD* Austral., *NZ,*
& *Cdn* (*Maritimes* & *Nfld*) *derogatory, SSPB,
OED3* Austral. and *N.Z. slang* (1933),
*COED informal chiefly Austral. /NZ & Ca-
nadian, NOAD informal chiefly Austral./NZ
Canadian*]

sound bone noun; compare **split** verb
a part of a fish's backbone adjacent to air
bladder (or the sound)
1877 HALIFAX COMISSION *Halifax
Commission, Appendix G* 91 The American fishermen are always in the habit
of throwing overboard the offals of the
fish, and the sound bone which is thrown
overboard destroys great numbers of large
fish, this our fishermen never practice.
1981 *CB's Magazine* 29, 10 ... the gutter
will take the gut out and break the head
off, throw it overboard. The sound bone
is taken out, and the fish is flat. 1985
MACGILLIVRAY et al. *History of Fourchu*
15 On most boats there would be one person [the splitter] who was the most adept
at this task and he would remove the back
bone or sound bone from about one-half
of the length of the fish and slip it into the
soaking tub.
[*DNE* ([1663]), *W3*]

spawn noun; in the phrases **spawn lobster, spawn herring**
a herring or lobster bearing eggs
1891 CANADA *Sessional Papers of the
Dominion of Canada: Vol. 8*, 9–135 Victoria
County – No; many fishermen are known
to take spawn lobsters and remove berries before bringing them to factory. 1910
CANADA, DEPARTMENT OF MARINE
AND FISHERIES *Lobster Fishery: Evidence*
687 A ... where any fisherman can put a

trap in order to catch the spawn lobsters in the latter part of the season during the very fine days. 1979 *CB's Magazine* 23, 47 What helped the lobster stock was when we started shipping lobsters to Boston. Most of all the spawn lobsters, the berried lobsters – they're in the market size ... Everybody was scared of sending spawn lobsters. Pilot Survey Inf. 4 When the water's warming up, and they're starting to reproduce, people start making reference to lobster that are spawning or spawn. Pilot Survey Inf. 5 A lobster with eggs is always called a spawn. Survey II Inf. 6 Spawn herring or row fish. Survey II Inf. 8 Spawn herring and spawn lobsters.

[*DNE* for herring (1960), *DPEIE* for lobster (1979); compare *spawny herring OED3 rare* (1908 in a citation at *spawny*)]

spawny noun
a lobster with eggs
Survey II Inf. 4 Spawny lobsters are pregnant females. The eggs are on the underbelly of the females, seedies and spawnies. Survey II Inf. 6 Lobsters with eggs are spawnies or berried lobsters. Survey II Inf. 7 Spawn or spawnies for lobster.

[*DNE*]

*Berried, indicating a lobster with eggs, is widespread: *DPEIE, COD, NCD, GCD, OED3* (1868), *COED, NOAD, W3, MWCD.*

spill intransitive verb
to rain hard
Survey I Inf. 2 [Spilling is] pissin' rain. Survey II Inf. 8 Heavy rain. Survey I.

[*DNE* (n.d.); compare the noun "of rain: a heavy fall" *EDD* (1892)]

spindle noun; compare **bait box**
a sharpened metal or wooden rod to hold bait in a lobster trap
1957 WILDER *Canada's Lobster Fishery* 15 The trap is usually divided into two compartments, the "kitchen", where the bait is fastened to a cord or wooden spindle, and the "parlour" or "bedroom". 1972 STAEBLER *CB Harbour* 119 We visits 'em [lobster traps] every morning, hauls 'em up to boat, takes lopsters out o' parlour, puts bait on spindles and lowers 'em down again. 1979 *CB's Magazine* 23, 43 We take the bait off (the spindle, out of the trap) every second day and put complete new stuff on. Pilot Survey Inf. 2 ... during the tide it rips the bait off the spindle. Survey II Inf. 1 A spindle holds the bait, a hardwood or a galvanized spike, a six to eight inch spike.

[Compare *bait spear* Also *bait pin, bait spike, bait spindle DPEIE,* and *bait iron DARE* **ME, ML**]

splint noun
a hard, stony coal that splinters like shale, useful at high temperatures needed for commercial purposes but unsuitable for domestic burning
1897 Anon. *The Canadian Mining Review* 16 (6), 219 ... the coal is distributed over the belt area, giving the boys and men every opportunity to pick out the impurities of brass and splint which may be in the coal ... 1933 Beaton Institute MG 12 43 D2 f5 Box 2, 92 The splint dump from end to end would be about 300 ft. 1934 *NS Miner* 4 (188), 4 "**Sells Splint to Miners**" ... Dinn, Dinn, the dirty man, / Sends the splint where e'er he can; / Charges high for every load ... 1968 Beaton Institute Tape 57 That's where they pick the splint out of the coal.

[*EDD, OED3* (1789); at *splint coal: EDD, OED3, DAE* (1873)]

split noun, usually plural
1. a narrow piece of wood, typically used for kindling and occasionally for other purposes
1923 in 1985 *CB's Magazine* 40, 34 ... each piece [of birch bark] held stretched

out at the ends by splits of white maple.
1972 *CB's Magazine* 1, 5 Making a good
axe handle begins months in advance
when you select just the right tree to cut
and make splits. 1973 *CB's Magazine* 2, 3 ...
she has taught her daughter, Barbara ...
to make splits and from those splits[,]
baskets, just as her mother before her
taught her. 2000 WILLIAMS *Cape Bretoner*
8 (5), 29 ... chop wood and make sure
there was enough splits (kindling) for the
next day. Pilot Survey Inf. 1 We used to
refer to kindling as splits when we were
sawing. We'd have a bag of splits – we'd
get a nickel each. Survey I Inf. 22 Did you
get the splits ready? We dried them in the
oven for the next day – quite a mess if
they caught fire.
2. a thin strip of wood used as a match to
light a fire, candle, etc.
    1970 MACPHAIL *Loch Bras d'Or* 29 A
bunch of spills (wood splits) were hanging beside every fireplace or chimney to
be used for lighting candles or tobacco
pipes. Survey I Inf. 25 You would light the
fire with them. Get the splits ready for the
morning. Survey I.
    [Sense 1: *DNE* (1858), *DPEIE, COD
Cdn (Nfld), OED3 Canad.* (chiefly *Newfoundland*) (1858). Sense 2: *DPEIE* ([1959]);
compare "A piece of bogwood burned for
illumination" *OED3, EDD*]

*Split identifying a "split piece of firewood" is
widespread and is also found in Cape Breton
usage; see, for example, 1982 MACLELLAN
The Glen 60 During the winter, the lobby
would be piled high with large splits of wood
– really large since the square stove could hold
quite a supply of big splits and blocks.

split transitive verb; compare **sound bone**
to remove (the backbone or sound bone)
from a fish to allow the fish to be flattened
for salting, drying, and stacking
    1983 *CB's Magazine* 34 Inside Front
Cover I've seen me go, split fish till 11

o'clock at night down in the stage by
lantern light. 1984 BALCOM *Cod Fishery of Isle Royale* 41 All three men stood
at a splitting table and performed their
duties in sequence. 1991 JOHNSTON
18th-Century Louisbourg 88 [Caption] This
man is splitting cod that have been gutted
and headed by others at the same table.
1992 *CB's Magazine* 59, 65 We were getting a dollar for a hundred pounds of fish,
splitting. Fifty cents for the hake, split.
1994 *CB's Magazine* 66, 63 The heads and
gut out, and take the bone out. Split them
flat. (For drying.) 2005 LA MORANDIÈRE
French Cod Fishery 11 ... [the] splitters (who
split the fish and removed the backbone)
stationed around a table in the middle of
the deck.
    [*DNE* ([1663]), *W3*]

splitter noun
the person who removes the fish's backbone (or sound bone) to allow the fish to
be flattened for salting and drying
    1983 *CB's Magazine* 34, 31 The other
fellow'd take the gut out and knock the
head off, and shove it over to me, the splitter ... you've got to have a little curve into
it [the knife blade], so as to get under the
bone, to take the bone out. 1984 BALCOM
Cod Fishery of Isle Royale 37 The act of 1743
regulating the fishery specified a crew of
11 [on schooners] ... a *trancheur* (splitter),
and a boy. 1985 MACGILLIVRAY et al.
History of Fourchu 15 ... the fish was next
handed to the splitter ... He would remove
the back bone or sound bone from about
one-half of the length of the fish and slip it
into the soaking tub. 1991 *Inverness Oran* 3
July 3 Fish splitter Jim MacNeil noted that
there is little demand for his skill in Inverness. "There are not too many other plants
splitting fish," he pointed out. 2005 LA
MORANDIÈRE *French Cod Fishery* 11 ...
splitters (who split the fish and removed
the backbone) stationed around a table in
the middle of the deck.

[*DNE* (1612), *DC, COD Esp. Nfld, OED3, DAE*]

sprag transitive verb
to use (a bar or wedge – a sprag) as a brake on a vehicle, typically a coal box
  1961 *Punching with Pemberton* May 3 ... he suffered the loss of an arm while spragging a box in Caledonia mine. 1969 Beaton Institute Tape 118 ... working on the landing coupling boxes and spragging boxes. 1983 MELLOR *Company Store* 86 A boy then disconnected each coal box from the rope before "spragging" it to a halt on the weighing machine ... 2007 MACKEN-ZIE *CB Coal Mine Disasters* 106 Spragging means placing blocks of wood in front of the wheels so that they cannot roll ...
  [*EDD, OED3* (1878), *W3*]

*The noun *sprag*, meaning a wooden or metal bar used as a brake or mine prop, is well represented in dictionaries.

spring herring noun
Atlantic herring (*Clupea harengus*) that migrate inshore in the spring to spawn
  1891 CANADA *Sessional Papers of the Dominion of Canada: Vol.8*, 8– 99 Our spring herring have little commercial value ... some restrictive measure or regulation should be adopted to prevent the wholesale destruction of these fish, as is sometimes done when they "strike in" in large quantities and they are used for manuring land. Pilot Survey Inf. 3 Well, they're different animals – the herring and the gaspereau. The herring and the gaspereau look very much alike, but I'd say the biggest difference is the belly of the gaspereau is very sharp to grab it. Survey II Inf. 2 Spring herring come in April or May after the drift ice. At St. Anns, Jersey Cove, they trap the herring and sell it as bait. Survey II Inf. 3 [Spring herring] come in to spawn; fall herring have more flesh on them. Survey II Inf. 4 Spring herring run before the mackerel (mid to late April); fall herring come in December. Survey II Inf. 6 Spring herring come first and the gasperaux afterward.
  [*DNE* (1842)]

*While *DNE* uses the general term "herring schools" to identify *spring herring*, other dictionaries define *spring herring* as the alewife or gaspereau (*DPEIE, OED3 Obs.*) or simply as the alewife (*DC Maritimes, DARE, DAE, DA, W3*). C. Richard Robins, *Common and Scientific Names of Fishes from the United States and Canada* (1991, 18), however, states that the Atlantic herring (*Clupea harengus*) is a different species than the alewife and gaspereau (a French Canadian name for alewife), both of which he classifies as *Alosa pseudoharengus*. *OED3* makes a similar distinction between the herring (*a700*), and the alewife (1633) / gaspereau (1703). It would seem, however, that in general usage *herring* is used as a generic term to include different species since even the *OED* defines *alewife* and *gaspereau* as "shad or herring" (*Alosa pseudoharengus*).

spring skate noun, usually plural; compare **stock skate**
an ice-skate blade attached to a metal frame, which is fastened to a boot by a spring-loaded clamp
  1971 Beaton Institute Tape 306 There was another called spring skates and then they came into the hockey skate. 1973 *CB's Magazine* 3, 1 They were followed by the spring skates which clipped onto the shoe, fiercely gripping the heel and often ripping it off. 1982 Beaton Institute Tape 994 The spring skates came out, you know, and you'd clamp them on. 2001 LEWIS *Sculptures from Jagged Ore* 100 Later, they acquired "spring skates," metal-based skates that fastened to the boots with metal springs.
  [*DPEIE* (1979)]

*The *OED3* indicates that *skate* has a long history with the first citation dating from 1648.

squib noun; also spelled **squibb**, **squid**; compare **coal face, stemmer**³
a fuse made of gun powder wrapped in paper and used to ignite the explosive in holes drilled into the coal face (the area where coal is excavated)

1920 Beaton Institute MG 12 46 A9 n.p. Warehouse Prices Squibs – Blue Label – per case of 100 boxes – 13.75. 1974 *CB's Magazine* 8, 8 ... at that time you used what they called squibbs – powder done up in paper, you know? You'd open up the end of it and tear a little piece off and you'd stick that in the hole. It would go right in the hole where you pulled the needle out. And you'd light it – with your lamp. Then you'd take off. 1974 Beaton Institute Tape 878 ... you paid for your powder and your squibs. That was the thing that set off the powder. 1978 *Oran Inbhirnis* 5 Jan. 7 There was no caps as are used today. Instead squids were used (the squids were somewhat like the sparklers used by children at a fireworks). The squid was inserted [with] the home made sticks and were lit. 1993 Beaton Institute Tape 3191 The shotfirers didn't have caps [interviewer]? In the early days it was squibs ...

[*OED3 Mining* (1881), *DAE* (1881), *W3*]

squid jig noun
a sinker with twenty or more needle-sharp hooks, attached to a line that is jerked upwards (jigged) to catch small squid used for bait

1984 *CB's Magazine* 36, 64 You've seen squid jigs. All the little pins in it. You're liable to get as high as 4 and 5 on that jig at one time. 1997 WARNER *How Deep is the Ocean* 224 You used little lead weights – squid jigs, you called them – painted red and crowned at their bottoms with 20 or more tines, bent upward and needle-sharp. You jerked a string of these weights up and down, attracting the curious squid, and pretty soon, sure enough, you hooked one on the tines.

[*DNE* (1861), *OED3*, *DAE* (1861), *DA* (1861); compare *squid jigger: DNE, COD Cdn (Nfld), GCD Cdn., esp. Nfld., OED3* (1875), *DAE* (in a citation at *squid jig*), *DA, W3*]

stage noun; also **fishing stage, fish stage**
a raised platform frequently with a shed and tables to process fish (head, gut, split and salt), and often with a wharf extending into the water to receive the catch (a stagehead)

1765 ROGERS *Concise Account of North America* 20–1 ... small shallops, which come to shore every day, where the fishermen throw the cod upon a stage prepared for that purpose ... the Beheader, opens the fish with a two-edged knife, and cuts off his head; a second hands the fish on to the carver, who stands opposite to him at a table erected upon the stage. 1829 HALIBURTON *Historical and Statistical Account of N-S* vol. 2, 232 The rocks are high and steep, and the only mode of landing the fish is by erecting stages from the rocks into the sea. On to these the fish are thrown from the boats in which they were taken ... 1869 BROWN *History of the Island of CB* 150 Most of the fishermen settled in the small harbours near Louisbourg, but small parties found their way to more distant places along the coast, wherever safe and sheltered inlets invited them to erect their huts and stages. 1873 *North Sydney Herald* 10 Sept. n.p. I have lost in the last gale or hurricane, of Sunday night £1500 at the least ... all of the buildings at Point Canso, stages, fish house, etc. 1972 STAEBLER *CB Harbour* 15 Past the silver shingle shacks (the women called them stages) was a wooden wharf ... 1985 MACGILLIVRAY et al. *History of Fourchu* 15 After soaking, the fish would then be thrown onto the floor of the "stage" which was the building on the wharf used by the fishermen for salting and storing fish. 1992 *CB's Magazine* 61, 64 From the door of that shanty they build a platform; they call it a stage – you or I would call it a wharf. 1997 SAMSON *How Deep is the Ocean?* 109 The stage was a large building with a "stagehead" on stilts extending into the harbour. The fishing boats would draw up to the stagehead every day and unload their catch. The cod was then immediately dressed and split by a separate shore crew on the tables set up for this purpose on the stagehead. 2002 DONOVAN *Acadiensis* 32 (1), 3 The work associated with fishing properties seemed endless ... preparing stages, erecting flakes ... Survey II Inf. 2 Tie your boat to the stage.

[*DNE* ([1589]), *DPEIE, DC Esp. Nfld, COD Cdn* (esp. *Nfld*); compare "a platform for drying fish": *GCD, OED3* (1535), *DAE, W3*]

stand the gaff verb phrase
to survive severe hardship or privation
1925 *Sydney Post* 10 Mar. 1 "Getting better every day they stay out," was the comment made by J. E. McLurg, vice president of the British Empire Steel Corporation, when asked last night to express his opinion on the state of the tie-up throughout the coal fields of Nova Scotia ... Asked for the reasons upon which he based this statement, the vice president replied: "They can't stand the gaff". 1925 MCCAWLEY *Standing the Gaff!* 6 We are law abiding, and "standing the gaff" without showing any yellow streak. 1926 in 1976 FRASER *Echoes of Labor's War* 84 The Bosses couldn't stand the gaff – / Oh, let me write their epitaph! 1953 FARRELL *CB Mirror* 2 Apr. 21 "Cripes! You'd need lungs of iron to stand the gaff down there! 1981 AKERMAN *Black around the Eyes* 76 "Stand the Gaff" was to become a household phrase in Cape Breton for generations to come; a challenge to the stubborn spirit of our people. 1999 FRANK *J. B. McLachlan* 374

Crowning it all was a colloquial insult that became one of the most memorable statements in Cape Breton labour history: "They can't stand the gaff." ... McLurg's remark was regarded as an offensive slur on the character of the long-suffering people of the coalfields. The phrase "standing the gaff" became a rallying cry of the [1925] strike.

[at *gaff*: *COD* slang N Amer., *FWCCD U.S. Informal, GCD Slang, OED3* (1899), *DAE* (1899), *DA* (1899), *W3, NOAD, MWCD*]

*As the citations indicate, the phrase has become especially significant to the Cape Breton labour movement.

statute labour noun
formerly, legislated work on public roads in lieu of taxes, especially in rural areas
1845 PROVINCE OF NOVA SCOTIA *Journal and Votes of the House of Assembly* 266 Mr. DesBarres, pursuant to leave given, presented a Bill to amend the Act relative to the performance of Statute Labour on Highways ... 1972 Beaton Institute Tape 515 They had to go [for] what they call statute labour. You have to go if you owe taxes for so much. Say if you owe taxes for 15 or 20 dollars, well you'd have to work so many days to pay on that ... That is why the road today has so many curves. 1981 Beaton Institute Tape 2035 In order to repair the roads in those days, there was no money, and they had what they called statute labour ... Every farmer, he worked so many days according to his evaluation of property so to speak. If you were a big farmer you had to put in more time hauling gravel with a horse and cart and digging out ditches than a man with a small farm. 1988 *CB's Magazine* 47, 69 And in place of paying tax – that's how roads were maintained, with statute labour. And each farmer in the area that the road was going through,

had to work so many days to maintain the road. Whatever sluices – they'd call them sluices – were on the road, you had to put the lumber there for nothing.

[*DC Hist.*, *OED3* now *hist.* (1729); compare *statutework* "work done on the highway which occupiers of land in a parish are bound to render" *EDD* (n.d.)]

stemmer[1] noun
a boat varying in length from twelve to twenty-two feet with the bow and stern similarly shaped, often clinker built, and sailed or rowed in the inshore fishery
1972 STAEBLER *CB Harbour* 120 Some years ago we used to fish wi' two-stemmers; fine boats they was, bigger'n ours is now, but a storm smashed 'em to pieces, twenty six in one night. 1978 *CB's Magazine* 20, 22 It was what they called an oversized stemmer. She was the same in the build fore and aft, the same shape. And she'd have a beam about 8 or 9 feet. And she'd be 20, 22 feet long, with two spars – foresail and mainsail, no jib. And the rudder was removable. 1984 CUMMING et al. *Story of Framboise* 69 In the early days of the lobster fishery, fishing was done from small rowboats, sixteen to eighteen feet long, equipped with two sets of oars. These boats were laminated or lapped, and were called "clinker boats" or "stemmers" ... At one time, some of the row boats had a small sail on them. 1988 *CB's Magazine* 49, 60 ... they called them "stemmers." They were sharp bow and stern. But they were able boats. They were built [with] strong timbers in them and riveted strong – stronger than you'd get today. You could depend on them not going to pieces. They'd be about 4 feet, 5 feet across – about that width. And they'd be from probably 12 to 16 feet long. Clinker-built – what they call clinker-built. They'd lap the 3/4-inch board over. Some of them were seam-built too ... Rowboat and sail.

stemmer[2] noun
a street person, one asking for money from strangers
1986 HARRIS *Justice Denied* 228 At fifty-nine, he was a well known "stemmer" – what in other places would be less elegantly known as a wino. 1997 *CB Post* 12 May 1 Business is so bad "we don't have stemmers (street panhandlers) any more." 2004 MACKENZIE *Bloody CB Coal* 2 Also, stemmers [beggars] were all over the place, especially at the liquor store, and they could be more than a little abrasive if they were refused a "donation."
[W3]

*W3 states that the probable etymology is from *stem* (meaning "street") plus –er.

stemmer[3] noun; compare **coal face**, **squib**
in mining, a pole or bar used to create a small hole through the packing between the explosive charge and the coal face to allow space for a fuse (or squib); by extension, the miner doing the stemming
1974 Beaton Institute Tape 878 ... then you took the clay and a wooden stemmer. You roll up a ball of clay and you shove it in that hole. Then you stem it up, stem it right to the mouth of the hole and you pull your stemmer back. There was a hole there then. Then you put the pat and squib in there, and you waited for the shotfirer to come and he'd light it. 1974 *CB's Magazine* 8, 7 ... put it [gun powder] in with your stemmer they called it, piece of copper on the end of it – you'd push it back and then you'd stem it up ... 2005 SHAW Email 16 Feb. ... the stemmer who uses a "stem" to leave a hole for the shotfirer's fuse in a mine.
[*OED3* (1909), W3]

stench adjective
physically strong, sturdy
2007 ST. CLAIR Email 30 Jan. I have recently heard my 89 year old cousin use

the word "stench" to refer to a person who was sturdy in their ways – "he was quite stench" she used it recently to refer to her niece Geraldine Rankin who died suddenly in Calgary when she said that "Geraldine has never seemed as stench as some of her brothers and sisters – as strong I guess. 2008 ST. CLAIR Email 10 Feb. Without prompting she again used the word "stench" last evening – to refer to the strength of a photograph – "this picture is more stench than that," a stronger picture it would seem.

[*Stench* is a variant of *staunch* (adjective) in *OED3* and *EDD*]

step dance intransitive verb; also spelled **step-dance, stepdance**; compare **step it off, Judique on the floor**
to perform patterned foot movements to music, both traditional and free-style, either as part of a square set or as a solo performance
1966 Beaton Institute Tape 202 ... there'd be a group of friends or neighbors in there and they would start violin music and sing songs and tell stories, and some [would] step dance and we'd be there until 12 o'clock at night. 1977 Beaton Institute Tape 900 Inevitably there'd be somebody who knew how to step dance. 1979 *CB's Magazine* 23, 1 But my husband used to play the fiddle and the bagpipes and step dance and carry on like that. Step dance right there in the kitchen. 1992–3 SHAW *Scottish Language* 11–12, 44 In Cape Breton it was common for people to step-dance to *puirt-a-beul* as well as instrumental music ... 1999 DOUCET *Notes from Exile* 20 In my dreams, I am a great fiddle player, able, like Ashley MacIsaac, to step-dance and play at the same time.

[*step-dance DNE* (1964), *COD*]

step hole noun; also spelled **step-hole, stephole**
one of a series of holes left by a horse in deep snow
1975 MACMILLAN *Memoirs of a CB Doctor* 21 I remember a call to Iona one winter morning that meant driving across the ice to Washabuck and then over the mountain. The going was heavy, with just step-holes in places. 1980 *CB's Magazine* 26, 45 ... he was in South Haven that night – there were just step holes for the horse, just where another horse had stepped. 1993 *CB's Magazine* 62, 18 When I was younger ... the highway in wintertime, there was no plowing done, you know. And if you'd get out at nighttime [*sic*], and the stepholes where the horses went, would have the road broke down, you'd get stuck tumbling all over the place.

step it off verb phrase; also **step (h)er off**; compare **step dance**
to perform the patterned foot movements of step dancing with energy and skill
1972 Beaton Institute Tape 548 The mother would jig a tune for the children to dance. Sometimes she would step it off herself. 1986 *Inverness Oran* 29 Oct. 12 The old lady and the two magistrates and a fourth person whom they didn't recognize were "stepping it off" in a four-hand reel. 1988 MACGILLIVRAY and MACGIL-LIVRAY *CB Ceilidh* 88 They just made a circle around and they'd step it off – face each other and go at it! 1993 *Inverness Oran* 23 June 2 Did you go steppin' her off last night?

*Compare a similar meaning in the *DNE* at *step it out*: "to perform the variety of steps characteristic of a step-dance."

stepmother's breath noun; also **mother-in-law's breath**
a cold draught or cold weather
Pilot Survey Inf. 1 Mother-in-law is what we used to hear here. It's cold as

your mother-in-law's breath – weather, coldness. Pilot Survey Inf. 5 Cold as a mother-in-law's kiss and cold as a mother-in-law's breath. Survey I.

[*DNE, DPEIE, EDD*]

stick transitive verb
to harpoon (a large fish, typically a swordfish)

1973 *CB's Magazine* 4, 3 A mile, two miles out from the shore – and that was about where they thought all the sword-fish was. Somebody would stick some and everybody would hang around and by and by somebody else would stick some ... 1983 Beaton Institute Tape 2048 ... we called it sticking him, well that was har-pooning, and he was probably hunched over in this cage. 1985 MACGILLIVRAY et al. *History of Fourchu* 20 Malcolm Mac-Donald ... "stuck" the last swordfish taken off Fourchu. 1993 Beaton Institute Tape 3229 B George went up on the rig; he's an older man. He had stuck a few; he done the sticking.

[*OED3* (1820), *W3*]

sticker noun
harpooner on a boat fishing for swordfish

1948 STAEBLER *Maclean's* 15 July 46 ... he was the engineer and the "sticker" who, when a fish was sighted, would run out to the pulpit, untie the harpoon and make the fatal lunge. 1973 *CB's Magazine* 4, 24 The photograph on page 1 is of the sticker, Jack Strickland, on a calm day – "not a hair of wind" – just as he was striking a 565 pound swordfish ... It was the last of the season, about 1935 or 1936. 1993 Beaton Institute Tape 3229 B ... going up on the fish wondering if the sticker is going to hit him or miss him.

[*OED3* (n.d.)]

stock skate noun, usually plural; also **strap skate, wood-stock skate**; compare **spring skate**

an ice skate with a metal blade attached to a tapered wooden block (or stock) and fastened to footwear with straps

1971 Beaton Institute Tape 306 It was all stock skates at that time. 1973 *CB's Magazine* 3, 20 The blocks of stock skates are like a boat, the blades the keel. The blocks are much narrower than the foot that rides them, and continue to taper to the blade. They are made so that there is the least chance of wood touching the ice. 1976 PRINGLE *Pringle's Mountain* 104 Strap skates were iron or steel runners set in wood and curved at the front. The wood base was shaped like the sole of a shoe and through it holes were cut to allow straps to pass through. 1981 Beaton Institute Tape 2035 You fellows used to take your skates, the old fashioned stock skates with the wooden homemade top, and they were made out of a file, and the file was curved. 1982 Beaton Institute Tape 994 Well, they were the stock skates ... They were made by a blacksmith, you know – the iron [blades] were long ... there was a heel strap and a front strap and they went through rings you know and you tightened them on. 2001 LEWIS *Sculptures from Jagged Ore* 99–100 Marion happily recalls youthful pleasures like coasting on the hill or skating on the frozen pond in the field on homemade "wood-stock skates." These were simple devices, consisting of a blade attached to a boat-shaped piece of wood that attached to one's outdoor boots with leather straps.

[*DPEIE* (1973); compare *skate OED3* ([1648])]

stog transitive verb; also spelled **stug**; also **stog up**
1. to fill completely, often with food

Pilot Survey Inf. 2 My dad'll say, if he ate too much, he stogged himself. Pilot Survey Inf. 4 I haven't heard it very much, but if someone is going to get stogged up, they're going to fill up on food, stog themselves with food. Survey I Inf. 13 To

stog one's mouth. Survey I Inf. 22 "I'm stogged," meaning a full feeling. Survey I Inf. 23 Father would say, "We were stogged on deer meat."
2. to block (an opening), fill (a cavity)
1974 Beaton Institute Tape 878 [To make a brattice or temporary wall in a mine] you could stretch the canvas right along – do it quickly, and where there was any holes where the canvas couldn't get to, you'd stog that up with old wraps of canvas and made everything air tight. 1979 CURRIE *Glace Bay Miner's Museum* 106 He put the powder and cap in the hole and pushed it as far as it would go with a broom handle. Ok, now, Jimmie. You stug that hole with dirt. 2008 *DCBE* Tape CURRIE 19–20 Stog something; stog up that pipe with a rag … You'd stog up some kind of an opening, probably temporarily. Pilot Survey Inf. 1 You use it for stuff as well, stog the chicken. Survey I Inf. 3 Stog was used in the pit.
3. to fill (spaces) between logs of a building, chink
1983 *CB's Magazine* 33, 41 … the little log house stogged with moss got too cold for winter use. Pilot Survey Inf. 5 I've heard stog, putting moss in chinks of logs.
[Sense 1: *DNE, DPEIE, NCD Atlantic Canada, EDD, SSPB.* Sense 2: *DNE, DPEIE, NCD Atlantic Canada.* Sense 3: *DNE* (1836), *DC* (1835) *Esp. Nfld*]

stop a lamp verb phrase; also **refuse a lamp**; compare **pit lamp**
to prevent or suspend a miner from working by refusing to issue a pit lamp
1939 Beaton Institute MG 12 37, 9 May 39 One thousand four hundred men come out on strick [*sic*] when one of their number is Refused his Lamp … 1939 MCARTHUR commissioner "Inquiry into Conditions at Florence Colliery" 3 On the night shift of Wednesday, August 9th, those men's lamps were stopped, which, in mine practice, means that they

were suspended until the question of their guilt could be properly inquired into. 1979 FRANK "CB Coal Miners, 1917–1926" 129 A critic in the Sydney Post complained that ballplayers who left the pit early to prepare for a game ran the risk of having their lamp stopped. 1989 EARLE *Workers and the State* 135 On 27 August the officials at Caledonia mine began "refusing lamps" to some of the miners, turning them away when they reported for work.

stopping noun, often plural
a partition or wall in a mine excavation built to block or direct airflow
1905 DAVIDSON and MACKENZIE *The Canadian Mining Review* 24 (3), 51 It [the stopping] was composed of hemlock boards lined with brattice cloth: the average width of this particular cross-cut was 12 feet. 1922 Beaton Institute MG 12 88 A1e f2, 2 … possibly a few boards taken to build a garage could [be] charged up as so many stoppings. 1973 Beaton Institute Tape 795 We were in the process of building permanent stoppings, that was concrete stoppings. They had to be poured down through a borehole from the surface down to the deep. 1974 *CB's Magazine* 8, 9 … he opened a slide, a little trap slide in the stoppings and stuck his open light in and when he did she went up. 8 men killed. 1995 *DCBE* Tape NICHOLSON 17 Soon as we put a cross-cut through [there would] be a pair of men there on the stoppings. That's what they'd do, put a stopping there, close this off all together. 2004 MACKENZIE *Bloody CB Coal* 154–5 … they decided to build a barricade, or "stopping," about 500 feet out from the wall face to try to suffocate the fire.
[*EDD, OED3* (1708), *W3*]

strap skate: see **stock skate**

string: see **trawl**

stripper[1] noun
the crane with an apparatus to remove the molds or casings from cooled ingots

Anon. 1901 *The Canadian Mining Review* 20 (10), 246 ... it [molten metal] is poured into the moulds on cars and transferred to the stripper building where moulds are removed and ingots deposited in the pit furnaces. 1987 PEABODY et al. *Maritimes: Tradition, Challenge and Change* 59 The moulds themselves were brought in from the stripper yard on "stool" cars ... 1990 Beaton Institute MG 14 206 Box 6 C. iii c) File 37, 6 That [steel ingots in molds] would be taken up to the stripper and there stripped by two overhead cranes and pushed into the mill by the engine. 1990 Beaton Institute Tape 2623 A ... to pull the outer mold off, that was another piece of equipment ... one of the stripper cranes from the Sydney Mines steel plant. 1992 *Making Steel* [Note on jacket cover] **stripper** Machinery used to remove molds from steel ingots after solidification. 2005 CAPLAN ed. *Views from the Steel Plant* 6 He worked at the stripper, where they take those ingots that you saw poured yesterday, and take that casing off of them.
[*OED3* (1835)]

stripper[2] noun
a cow capable of producing milk throughout the winter

1984 CUMMING et al. *Story of Framboise* 40 Maggie MacQueen says that people would trade a cow with a calf for a "stripper" – an unbred cow which would produce milk all winter. 1994 *CB's Magazine* 67, 8 And then we'd probably have a cow, they called her "the stripper." She wasn't in calf and we'd milk her all year 'round. Probably the following year then she'd be bred.
[The *DCBE* citations indicate a different meaning than other dictionaries defining *stripper* as a cow that is "stripped,"

giving little or no milk: *DPEIE, EDD, OED3, DARE* (1779), **scattered, but more frequent Midl**, *W3*]

strupag ['strupæk] noun; also spelled **strupach**
a drink of tea alone or with a snack

1975 CALDER *Uncle Angus and the Causeway* 33 ... the good wife served us a strupag (Gaelic for tea and a snack) ... 1976 PILLAR *Aunt Peggy* 48 ... a *strupach* of hot strong tea! 1984 ROTHE *Barra Settlement* 36 "Highland hospitality" became not whiskey, but a simple "strupach", a lunch served with tea.
[at *strupac DPEIE* (1975); at *strupak* "drink of tea" *DSL*]

*Compare related forms: *stroupie* "teapot" (1897) *EDD; strùp* "spout" *GED; strupag* "little drop of spirits" *Dwelly's Illustrated Gaelic to English Dictionary* (2001).

study club noun
a group, meeting regularly to research and discuss mutual concerns such as housing, cooperatives, and credit unions, originally as part of the Cooperative or Antigonish Movement

1937 Beaton Institute MG 12 43 E3 Box 3, 27 ... something should be done to help the leaders of study clubs. 1940 ARNOLD *Story of Tompkinsville* 8 There are now 165 credit unions in Nova Scotia and each one grew out of a study club. 1977 *CB's Magazine* 16, 8 Nothing much happened here in Reserve Mines until the Extension Department through Dr. Coady and Dr. Tompkins started a program of adult education for economic action. They started study clubs in all these mining communities around here. In Reserve we had about 15 study clubs organized. 1982 *CB's Magazine* 32, 9 Fr. Jimmy Tompkins was the father of the Cooperative or the Antigonish Movement ... And there [in Sweden and Denmark] he found out their methods of

organizing study groups, study clubs, and their cooperative movement. 1994 *CB's Magazine* 67, 62 And then, we had what they called a study club around here. They had the schoolteacher ... And I asked her one day if she'd teach me how to read the pattern. So she did.
[at *study-club OED3* (1910)]

suête [suɛt] noun, usually plural; also spelled **suete(s)**, **sou'et**; also **les suêtes** derived from the French *sud-est*, a strong southeastern wind often reaching hurricane force and affecting the western and northern coastal areas bordering the Cape Breton Highlands, from Margaree Harbour to Bay St. Lawrence
1986 CHIASSON and LE BLANC trans. *History and Acadian Traditions of Chéticamp* 20 ... these hurricanes are caused by extreme southeast winds, the suêtes, as the people call them. 2000 BOUDREAU and CHIASSON *Chéticamp Memoirs* 152 In 1972, a strong *suête* (bad southeast wind) lifted this school up and moved it 75 feet away. 2002 *DCBE* Tape *Information Morning* 27 Feb. 1 There's a suete warning for the Highlands that's continued: winds very high, reaching possibly gusts of 130 km per hour tonight for Margaree Harbour to Bay St. Lawrence. 2005 MACINTYRE and WALLS *NS Book of Everything* 40 **Les Suetes:** They are created when warm air moves over cool water. This front inversion creates a "funneling effect" over elevations like the Cape Breton Highlands and the air is forced to speed up, creating strong gusts as it comes down the side of the elevation. 2007 DANIELSON *CB Weather Watching* 169 A December 2003 suête spun the anemometer at Grand Etang up to a speed of 183 km per hour – 7 km per hour stronger than the peak gust in Hurricane Juan which ravaged Halifax four months earlier – but the Grand Etang event was only a minor footnote in the day's news.

2007b BARBER *Only in Canada* 24 **suete** (*Cape Breton*) a very strong southeasterly wind in the west coastal areas of the Cape Breton Highlands.
[at *suete COD Cdn* (*Cape Breton*); from French, "SUÈTE ... Vent du sud-est" *DFA*]

*A loanword from French, see *suète* "Vent du sud-est" *DFA GÉNÉRAL*. Cormier's *DFA* gives two citations for *suète*: one by Fr. A. Chiasson, referring to Chéticamp, and the other by A. Maillet, *Les Cordes-de-Bois*, referring to New Brunswick. Thus, as an abbreviation of *sud-est*, the form *suête* or *suète* is not unique to Cape Breton, but, as a loanword that is widely understood in English to refer to the south-east winds in a particular locality, it is considered a Cape Bretonism.

sugar teat noun
a baby's soother made by tying some sugar in a cloth
1975 DUBBIN *40 Years A Nurse* 76 ... I came across something hard in a piece of rag which didn't look any too clean, tied around with a piece of string. "What on earth is this?" I asked the mother. "Oh, that's a sugar teat." 1983 MACKENZIE "Social Conditions in Sydney, N.S., 1900 to 1914" 59 Then, to keep a newborn baby quiet, the midwives would place a primitive form of an artificial nipple, known as a "sugar teat", in the baby's mouth. This was usually a large lump of sugar in a piece of rag, tied with a piece of string.
[at *sugar-teat OED3* (1847); at *sugar-tit*: *OED3* (1892), *DARE* (1831 for a citation with the variant *sugar teat*), *W3* (with *sugar-teat* as a variant); compare *sugar rag DA*]

summer complaint noun; also **summer sickness**
potentially lethal diarrhea, especially for children, prevalent during hot weather
1939 Beaton Institute MG 12 224 C1 Diary 3 July n.p. Baby has a touch of summer complaint, not feeling very well.

1975 DUBBIN *40 Years a Nurse* 74 "Why are so many children dying?" I asked a maternity patient. "It's either because of the White Mouth, or the Summer Complaint ..." 1981 *CB's Magazine* 30, 19–20 There was a terrible lot of deaths during my first summer, or take the second summer that I was there, from this "summer sickness" they called it, or enteritis. 1983 MACKENZIE "Social Conditions in Sydney 1900–1914" 33 In the summer there was often a high rate of "summer complaint" or diarrhea especially prevalent among young children.
[*DPEIE, OED3 U.S., DARE* (1819), *DAE, DA, ML*; at *summer diarrhea W3*]

summer kitchen noun; compare **back kitchen**
an additional kitchen, attached to the house or separate from it, used for cooking in the hot weather and for storage
1987 *CB's Magazine* 44, 17 On the sketch not shown here, the summer kitchen chimney is at the end ... 1994 MACLEOD and ST. CLAIR *Pride of Place* 151 In summer the heat from these [coal] stoves was almost unbearable. Contrary to many other houses in Cape Breton "summer kitchens" were not built onto #13–15 Ferris Street. 2007 MACDONALD *Lauchlin of the Bad Heart* 70 ... at the rear of the house a room once used as the summer kitchen but now the only kitchen ... Pilot Survey Inf. 2 I know someone in Loch Lomond that has two kitchens – a winter kitchen and a summer kitchen. Pilot Survey Inf. 3 Oh, summer kitchen, that's quite common ... they often have homes with the two kitchens. There's the summer kitchen and then in winter they move in. I have heard the term [back kitchen] but perhaps more so the summer kitchen.
[*OED3 N. Amer., DARE* **chiefly Nth, N Midl, exc NW** (1833), *DAE, DA, W3, MWCD*; at *back kitchen* with *summer kitchen* as a variant: *DNE, DPEIE*]

swinge transitive verb
to singe by burning or scalding (often the down and small feathers of a fowl)
Pilot Survey Inf. 5 [Swinge after] duck hunting. Survey I Inf. 22 Metal was heated in the stove to swinge the chicken, to get the fuzz off – an awful smell. Survey I Inf. 25 [Swinge means to] singe with a hot poker.
[*DNE, DPEIE, EDD, OED3* Now *dial.* and *U.S.* (1590), *DARE* **chiefly Sth, S Midl**, *W3 dial, MWCD dial*]

T

taibhs [taɪš] noun; also spelled **taibhse**; compare **droke, forerunner**
a spirit, vision, or sign foretelling an event, a forerunner
1931 FRASER *Folklore of NS* 45 "And what is a *taibhs*?" asked the younger girl. "It's a spirit. We're going to get some bad news." 1953 DUNN *Highland Settler* 47 Even those who were not normally endowed with this power might occasionally see a "forerunner" (*taibhs*) of something that would later come to pass – perhaps the spectre of a railroad engine thundering through the forest ... [1991?] MACLEAN *Story of Canoe Lake, CB* 75–6 They believed in forerunners or "taibhs." It is said that one of the young men of Canoe Lake experienced a strong tugging at his shoulders that he couldn't explain. Some time later as he was pulling the sleigh that carried the body of Mrs. Furlong he realized what the tugging had been about. It was a forerunner. 1996 *CB's Magazine* 70, 48 When you see "the bird," it's a sign that someone is going to die. It's called the Taibhse in Gaelic. The bird is (a messenger) from the other world.

*A loanword from Scottish Gaelic, see *taibhse* "apparition, ghost, spectre" *GED*.

taigh [taɪ] noun; often modified; also spelled **tigh**
a house

1977 SURRETTE *Maclean's* 30 May 28 Such places as Dundee, Glencoe Mills, Loch Lomond, Ben Eoin or Iona where Gaelic is still spoken and where post offices are sometimes marked Post Office/ Tigh Litrechean/Bureau de Poste. 1981 MACDONELL and SHAW eds. *Folktales from CB* xi There he built a log house (taigh logaichean). 1984 CUMMING et al. *Story of Framboise* 49 It was done by people gathered at a **tigh-laudhaidh** or **milling frolic** at someone's house. 1989 *CB's Magazine* 50, 102 Visit displays of early architecture, including the only known replica of a "Taigh Dubh" (Black House) in North America. 2000 SHAW and ORNSTEIN *Brìgh an Òrain: A Story in Every Song* 15 In each Gaelic settlement the *céilidh* houses (*taighean céilidh*), though not formally designated, were known to all.

*A loanword from Scottish Gaelic, see *taigh* "apartment, house" *GED* and the variant form *tigh* "a house" *GD*.

tail drag: see **drag**

tally noun
a metal tag with a number placed on a loaded coal box to give credit to the miner who loads it; also the number itself that the miner marks on the coal box

1889 in 1974 CROSS ed. *Workingman in the Nineteenth Century* 85 Q. For tally 30 cents [deduction]? ... That is for the man the miners employ to watch the tally? A. Yes. 1920 Beaton Institute MG 12 46 A9 n.p. Schedule of Datal rates ... 1918 ...Tally boy $2.18 [per day]. 1979 FRANK "CB Coal Miners, 1917–1926" 223 They loaded the fallen coal into a one or two ton car, marked it with their tally number ... 1984 Beaton Institute Tape 2152 I, as check-weighman, give you a number. Well, you use that number, what they call a tally, and you put it on every box you load. As that box comes up onto the bank on there ... a tally boy ... hollers in as the boxes go past him. He hollers in your number ... and I weigh that coal. 1995 *DCBE* Tape NICHOLSON 19 Before we load, all them tallies there [pointing to small metal tags hung from a nail on a pit prop by individual straps of thin leather], we take a bunch of tallies down with us. Put one tally on a box; we load it.
[*EDD, OED3* (1883), *W3*]

tap hole noun
a small hole in a blast furnace used to drain the liquid metal when the plug is removed

1975 *CB's Magazine* 12, 29 The temperature at the charging door is now about 900–1000 degrees, and at the tap hole 2500–3000 degrees F. 1989 *CB's Magazine* 52, 5 Make your tapping bars to punch the hole out. There was no such thing as oxygen then to burn out a tap hole, or bombs – you had to punch them out with a big steel bar. 1990 Beaton Institute MG 14 206 Box 7 C. iii c) File 67, 5 ... it was number three furnace, it broke out a tap hole. It got too hot or somebody didn't plug up that tap hole properly. I don't know what happened anyway, but it burned out and it wasn't steel, it was pure raw metal – iron – almost from the blast furnace.
[at *tap-hole OED3* (1825); at *taphole W3*]

tarabish [tar'bɪš] noun; also **bish**; compare **Bella**
a card game typically played by four players in two teams using thirty-six cards, the primary goal being to win as many of the 282 points as available in each hand (162 base points and 120 possible points from runs and Bella) and to accumulate 500 points to win the game

1976–7 Miners' Museum Tape 425 In the morning we play tarabish ... 1991

MACGILLIVRAY *Diamonds in the Rough* 139 If the rake isn't too crowded, you can play tarabish both going underground and coming back up ... A lot of guys learned to play tarabish in the pit. 1996 KENNEDY *Centre of the World* 62 Between each round, however, the silence is broken by what might be called "shoulda-been" bish or "after" bish – essentially an analysis of the playing or players of the round that has just passed. 1998 KEOUGH *Cape Bretoner* 6 (2), 39 Tournament organizers have seen this Tarabish adventure gain a foothold on the Cape Breton Winter Activity scene, and this tenth Tournament, like all the others, showed the fervour and dedication these "Bish" buffs have for their game. 2000 MACEACHERN *Tarabish* 44 **History of Tarabish** The origin of the game was possibly Germanic, Hungarian or Ukrainian and a two handed version of the game has been included in several editions of *Hoyle's Games* under the name of **Clob, Klob, Clabber, Calabrias**, and **Clubby**. The origin of the game in Cape Breton, Nova Scotia, can be traced to immigrants in the late **1800's and early 1900's**. 2007b BARBER *Only in Canada* 161 **tarabish** (*Cape Breton*) a card game based on bridge. 2009 MORGAN *Story of CB Island Book Two* 203 In the meantime, Cape Breton and Maritime Clubs in places like Boston, Kitchener, Brantford, and Detroit, flourished as venues to "keep the culture alive where [people] could get together" to hear traditional music and enjoy Cape Breton card games like Tarabish. Survey I Inf. 3 Tarabish is played all over the island in tournaments. Survey I Inf. 5 [Tarabish is] mainly played in Industrial Cape Breton, but it has expanded to the west side.
    [*COD Cdn* (*Cape Breton*)]

*The dictionary files contain several suggestions for the game's country of origin and the origin of the name *tarabish*, but it is difficult to verify which argument is most compelling. J. Y. MacEachern, *Tarabish: How the Game is Played* (2000, 44–7), gives an overview of the game's history and development in Cape Breton.

tar pond noun, usually plural
one of two collecting areas in the estuary of Muggah Creek, separated by a causeway and containing toxic waste from steelmaking, coke production, and processing coal tar (now remediated)
    1981 *CB Post* 15 Aug. 4 The gull was unable to fly because of oil and grease which soaked into its feathers, believed [to be] from the nearby "tar pond" in the city's Northend. 1986 *CB Post* 28 June 1 Ottawa has been adamant about not starting a cleanup while the coke operation continues to add to the mess in Muggah's Creek, the proper name of the harbor inlet known as the tar pond. 1996 CLARKE *Cape Bretoner* 4 (3), 28 So even if the sludge in the Tar ponds were removed, there will still be some sludge left covered by the huge slag pile and several developments. 1997 *CB Post* 23 May 1 ... the Sydney tar ponds contain 700,000 tonnes of toxic tar containing both PAHs and PCBs along with a host of other chemicals. 2000 BARLOW and MAY *Frederick Street* 70 Although the estuary was not a contained body of water, it was universally known as the tar ponds.
    [*COD Cdn*]

task work noun; see **contract work**
a specific job to be completed for a set rate of pay, piece work
    1972 Beaton Institute Tape 537 I was six months on task work. 1997 *CB's Magazine* 72, 88 Task work. That's a form of a bonus. That's incentive time off. Which means they can go down and work four hours and go home. (If they get their job done.) 2003 SAINT AGNES ELEMENTARY SCHOOL *Coal Miners' Stories* 19 If our jobs were finished early we could leave for the

surface and still receive a full day's pay. This was called task work.

[*EDD*, *OED3* (1486–1487), *W3*, *MWCD*]

tea noun; often in the phrase **tea and sale**, rarely **tea-meeting**
a fundraiser, often in the afternoon or early evening, with tea, a light meal, and frequently a sale
1889 *North Sydney Herald* 17 (2), n.p. A very successful tea-meeting was held in Temperance Hall, Sydney Mines, on Monday evening, by the Methodists of that place. A first-class tea was laid and there was a large number in attendance many from North Sydney being present. $105 was realized. 1929 *Glace Bay Gazette* 5 Sept. 5 St. Mary's W. A. will be holding an afternoon tea Sept. 28 from three to seven o'clock. 1979 *Inverness Oran* 3 May 5 During Hospital Week, the I.C.M.H. Auxiliary will hold a Tea & Sale. This will be held Friday May 11th in the Hospital Cafeteria from 7 to 9 p.m. The Inverness area members are asked to donate sweets for the tea. 1993 *Inverness Oran* 3 Nov. 32 Xmas tea and bake sale Dec. 4 from 2–4 pm at the Cameron Hall, Whycocomagh, sponsored by the Stewart United Church Women.

[*DNE* (1964); at *tea-meeting OED3* (1897), *DNE*]

tea bheag [ti vɛk] noun; also spelled **tea beag, teabheg, tea bheg, tea veck**; compare **beag**
literally, a small tea; tea with a snack taken between meals
1966 Beaton Institute Tape 202 ... true Cape Breton hospitality which did not and does not permit anyone who enters the home to leave without the tea bheag [interviewer]. 1970 MACPHAIL *Loch Bras d'Or* 18 Mrs. MacNab busied herself preparing 'Tea Bheg' (light refreshments) over the tea cups, oat cakes buttered and sugar biscuit. 1976 PILLAR *Aunt Peggy*

48 What would these ladies think of Margaret's *teabheg* (light lunch) ... 1982 MACLELLAN *The Glen* 47 The morning began with a cup of tea, then there was the small tea, or *tea bheag* at mid-morning, tea at dinner time, another *tea bheag* at mid-afternoon, tea for supper and often tea before bed. 1984 CUMMING et al. *Story of Framboise* 53 At ten o'clock, **tea bheag** was served. 1988 PRINGLE *Look to the Harbour* 79 We ate up our tea beag, and closed the drafts ...

*Compare the Scottish Gaelic, *beag* "light (of import), little, minor, petty, slender, slight, small, trifling, wee" *GED*.

tea can noun; also spelled **teacan**
a thermos-shaped metal container with a stopper used for carrying and heating tea
1951 BRASSET *Doctor's Pilgrimage* 20 Suspended from strong hooks in the ceiling were clumps of pit-boots, teacans – bottle-shaped tins with cork stoppers which the miners used to take into the pit ... 1969 Beaton Institute Tape 118 I remember I wasn't very tall ... we used to have long tea cans with handles on them, and if I'd tramped in a hole in the road, my tea can would scrape in the ground. 1992 MCLEOD *CB Captain* 17 ... it was customary for the lumpers and stevedores to warm their tea cans on the galley stove.

[at *tea-can OED3* (1890)]

tent noun; compare **open-air communion**
a shed-like pulpit with a window facing the congregation, typically used in a Presbyterian open-air communion service
1872 in 1940 MORRISON *Dalhousie Review* 20, 188 The ministers, being in a tent constructed like a large sentry-box, alone were protected from the weather. 1913 CAMPBELL *CB Worthies* 19 At the open air communion his place was in front of the "tent" and he was often the leading precentor ... 1942 DENNIS *CB*

Over 226 An arresting little structure, shaped very like a sentry box, stood among the daisies. It was here, I learned, the minister stood and preached in the days before the present church was built ... The people sat on the bank in the form of a semi-circle, around this "tent" of the minister. 1983 STANLEY *Well-Watered Garden* 140 They turned their faces towards the so-called "Tent," a protective wooden shelter with a window for the clergymen ... 1984 CUMMING et al. *Story of Framboise* 114 In Framboise, people sat on the slope between the Church and the Lake ... the ministers were in the "Tent," a small building from which they conducted the services. 2006 STANLEY-BLACKWELL *Tokens of Grace* 59 These served as a prelude to the all-important "Action Sermon," an animated address disclosing the central truths of redemption, delivered by one of the ministers in the tent.
   [*EDD, OED3 Sc.* (1678), *DAE*]

thick-a-fog adjective
so foggy as to prevent travel by sea
   1972 STAEBLER *CB Harbour* 148 We wanted to go back next day but thought we better wait till it was thick-a-fog and nobody'd see us. 1986 *CB's Magazine* 43, 80 And it was thick-a-fog – you could hardly see from the bow to the stern of the boat. 1988 *CB's Magazine* 49, 69 And he figured it right. 'Cause we were anchored all night. It was thick-a-fog. It was raining and a little thunder. But it wasn't stormy or nothing.
   [at *thick-o-fog: OED3* (1935), *ML*; at *thick of fog DARE* **ME coast** (1839)]

*Thick referring to foggy or misty weather is widespread with the earliest documented use around 1000 (*OED3*).

ticket of location noun; also **ticket, ticket of occupation**

formally, a permit allowing settlement on a lot of land and requiring the settler to clear a portion of the land and erect a dwelling prior to applying for a permanent grant
   1820 in1823 KEMPT *Papers Relative to the Re-Annexation of the Island of Cape Breton to the Government of Nova Scotia* 20–1 ... Captain Crawley [Surveyor General of Cape Breton] is authorized to grant tickets of location to such persons as upon a careful inquiry into their character and circumstances he shall consider as likely to make good settlers, and to be faithful and loyal subjects of His Majesty ... [settlers] will on no account be confirmed in the possession of the respective lots by grant, until they shall be fairly settled, and have erected houses thereon. 1839 BULLER et al. *Minutes of Evidence ... Enquiry for Crown Lands and Emigration* 14 ... on the payment of a moderate fee to the Surveyor General, they should receive tickets of location, and be considered as the future purchasers of the lots assigned to them ... 1893 GOW *CB Illustrated* 352 He [the Surveyor-General] was to lay off lots of 100 acres each to single men, and of 200 acres each to married men. "Settlers were permitted to occupy these lots, under tickets of location, until they were prepared to pay for grants, but no absolute title could be given except to *bona fide* settlers who had actually made improvements." 1974 LOTZ and LOTZ *CB Island* 55 In 1821, Boards of Land Commissioners were set up in various localities and the settler applied to one of these for a 'ticket of location'. Up to 1827 land was granted free to settlers. 1988 BATTISTE *Work, Ethnicity and Oral History* 66 Although knowing that they could not pass lawful land grants in Mi'kma'kik, Nova Scotia officials issued settlers unofficial "tickets of location" without any specific authority.
   [at *ticket (of location) DC Hist.* (1840); compare *location ticket DC*]

tickle: see **tittle**

tiddly: see **peggy**

tight adjective
close, humid; cloudy
  Pilot Survey Inf. 1 I've heard that, "it's very tight in here." Sometimes we use close as well. Survey I Inf. 37 I've heard clammy and humid meaning the same [as tight]. Survey I.
  [Compare "Of the air, close, stuffy" *DNE*, and" Of the sky, overcast, cloudy" *DPEIE*]

tilt noun
a teeter-totter or see-saw, often homemade
  1999 MACDONALD Oral Communication 26 Sept. "Tilt" was used in the Sydney area for teeter-totter but not on the west side of the island. Survey I Inf. 23 Dad would make a tilt. [We] grew up with it.
  [*DPEIE, DARE* esp **MA** (1917 for this form)]

timber transitive and intransitive verb; compare **pit prop, pit timber**
to use (pit props or timbers) to support the roof of a mine
  1889 CANADA *Report ... Labor and Capital in Canada: Evidence, NS* 255 Q. Do the men working those places have to timber them themselves? A. Those that are capable of doing so timber for themselves and those that are not accustomed to timber the company does the timbering for them. 1936 *NS Miner* 271, 2 The main orders given are, timber your place with large timber or up you go! 1971 Beaton Institute Tape 230 Now to timber ... a good miner would cut the timber – measure from the roof to the floor – cut his timber and leave enough for what they call a cap piece, that is a short block of wood over the top of the timber and pound it in with the maul to tighten it. 1984 Beaton Institute

Tape 2134 The only tools we had were axes, saws, and mauls for timbering. 1995 *DCBE* Tape SMITH 3 And he showed me how to timber the place, to set the timbers up strong to hold the roof up. 2004 MAC-KENZIE *Bloody CB Coal* 85 Sometimes he would be timbering behind the Miner – putting up straps ...
  [*EDD, OED3* (1702)]

time noun
a house party or community celebration at a hall
  1951 MACLENNAN *Each Man's Son* 107 On Friday night next week, my glory, but there will be a time! 1956 Beaton Institute MG 6 23 2B, 10 June n.p. Went to John Ban's and had a real time. 1972 STAEBLER *CB Harbour* 55 "You're goin' the wrong way, dear, there's a Time in the Hall tonight. Better not miss it." "I wasn't invited," I said. "Times is fer everybody. Tonight it's a send-off fer young men joined up for soldiering, can't make a livin' at fishin' no more." 1972 Beaton Institute Tape 501 Mowing frolic ... I suppose they'd have a time that evening again after the mowing [interviewer]. Sometimes they'd gather around, play cards, and sing songs and tell ghost stories. 2007b BARBER *Only in Canada* 156 **time** (*Atlantic Canada*) a festive gathering of friends and relatives, especially in celebration of an event, such as a wedding, or community event. Pilot Survey Inf. 4 They're going to have a time. It's used interchangeably as a party or a celebration, but it's more or less used with people who are in their thirties and upwards in age, not so much with the younger people now. Survey I Inf. 5 We had a time in the hall – a term of praise for a "good party." Survey I Inf. 7 [A time] could be a house party. Survey I Inf. 15 A time is any get together. Survey I Inf. 22 A time could be a family party, but more likely a community party.

[*DNE* (1878), *DPEIE*, *DC Esp. Atlantic Provinces*, *COD Cdn* (*Maritimes* & *Nfld*), *NCD Atlantic Canada*, *OED3 N. Amer. regional* (chiefly *New England* and *Newfoundland*) (1878); compare *on a time* "a drunken spree" *DAE*]

*The majority of respondents to Survey I indicated that a *time* could be any party, either a private or community gathering for such events as a wedding reception, a fundraiser, etc., whereas several of the dictionaries listed above emphasize the community celebration.

tittle noun; also **tickle**; compare **run**²
a narrow, dangerous saltwater passage, typically between an island and a larger land mass; also used in names of water features
1870 CANADA *Sessional Papers of the Dominion of Canada: Vol. 4*, 11–116 On the 19th left the port [of Arichat], and proceeded to the eastward, examining the shore. Passed through the "Tittle" passage, arriving at Cow Bay, 20th Sunday. 1973 *CB's Magazine* 5, 13 They used to call it The Tittle [on St. Pauls Island]. 1976 *CB's Magazine* 14, 32 Water gets an awful tide in the tittle, you know. Water'd be going through there sort of like white foam. 1993 CANADIAN PERMANENT COMMITTEE ON NAMES *Gazetteer of Canada: NS* xxix Tickle Narrow stretch of saltwater; usually with hazardous tides, currents and rocks. Tittle Swiftly flowing saltwater in a small narrow channel with rocks and reefs, which constitute a danger to navigation. 2001 RAYBURN *Naming Canada* 153 *Tickle* occurs ... in 7 names in Nova Scotia. It is a narrow, treacherous salt-water channel, often characterized by hazardous tidal currents and rocks, both submerged and exposed. 2007b BARBER *Only in Canada* 26 **tickle** (*Atlantic Canada*) **1** a narrow strait or channel between islands or between an island and the mainland, especially one that is difficult

to navigate. Survey II Inf. 6 A tittle is between the island and the shore in saltwater. Survey II Inf. 8 Tittle is the same as tickle: going through a tittle between Main-à-Dieu and Scatarie Island.
[*DC Maritimes* (1896); at *tickle*: *DNE* ([1770]), *DC Atlantic Provinces* (*esp. Nfld*) (1770), *COD Cdn* (*Nfld & Maritimes*), *FWCCD Canadian*, *NCD Atlantic Canada*, *GCD Cdn., esp. Nfld.*, *OED3* (1770)]

*Compare *tickle adj.* "Variable, uncertain, not to be relied on, used esp. of the weather" *EDD* (1795)]

token noun; also **communion token**; compare **fencing**, **open-air communion**
a coin-like metal disk signifying full membership in the Presbyterian church and showing eligibility to receive communion, especially during an open-air communion service
1927 ARCHIBALD *The Token* 32 The Token is given to you when the Elders decide that you are ready to be a full member of the Congregation. On Sacrament Sabbath you must hand it in before you are allowed to take Communion. 1940 MORRISON *Dalhousie Review* 20, 187 Those who were considered satisfactory became the happy recipients of the "token," which they were allowed to retain in their possession until the following day, when it was given up to one of the attending elders as the communicant took his or her place at the Lord's Table. 1983 STANLEY *Well-Watered Garden* 145 Following the practice of their Free Church counterparts in Scotland, the Cape Breton ministers exercised stiff fencing procedures, in contrast with the "Moderates" who had indiscriminately admitted all who applied for tokens. 2006 STANLEY-BLACKWELL *Tokens of Grace* 44 The small coin-like tokens, often impressed with the scriptural text "This do in Remembrance of Me," as well as

an image of a communion table, were the outward symbols signifying full fellowship with the Church and one's eligibility to sit at the "table" on the morrow. 2007 ST. CLAIR and LEVERT *Nancy's Wedding Feast* 128 *While the sacrament was the emotional high point of this communion, known in Gaelic as the Sàcramaid, only those finally deemed worthy by elders, and by themselves, were issued a communion token which permitted them to receive the bread and wine.*

[*EDD, OED3* (1534)]

ton timber noun; also spelled **ton-timber**
a measure of squared logs for shipping, estimated by weight or volume; the squared logs themselves

1810 NS ARCHIVES AND RECORDS MANAGEMENT http://novascotia.ca/archives/virtual/land/results.asp?Search=leaver%2C+tim&SearchList1=3&SearchButton=Search+Land+Petitions Cape Breton Number 590, Microfilm 15790, n.p. **Leaver Timothy** Petition to Nepean ... He asks an additional 1000 acres on the west end of Bouladerie [*sic*] Island. His was the first ton timber to be exported from the island since it came under the Crown of Great Britain. 1816 COGSWELL *The Statutes at Large Passed in the Several General Assemblies* 124 *Be it therefore enacted ... all hewed Timber, commonly called Ton Timber, which shall be exported from this Province, shall be strait lined, and well squared, without offsets* [*sic*] *or joints, and square butted at both ends ... that no Spruce or Pine Timber, shall be less than fifteen feet in length, nor any Birch or other Ton Timber, commonly called Hard Wood Ton Timber, less than ten feet in length ... the same shall square at least ten inches.* 1922 MACDOUGALL *History of Inverness County* 458 For quite a space of time the late Hon. John MacKinnon was engaged in the buying, selling and shipping, of timber commonly called "ton-timber" for use overseas. 1989 *CB's Magazine*

51, 21 At that time they were cutting timber. And these ships used to come, he'd load this ton timber. Survey I Inf. 51 [Ton timber was] cut up in certain shapes or size in order to ship and handle easier and prepare for delivering and shipping to customers.

[*DNE* (1876), *DPEIE, ML*; at *ton OED3* (1521), *W3*]

*The dictionaries cited vary in the method of determining the quantity of ton timber: linear feet, board feet, volume, or weight. For example, *OED3* gives two measurements for timber at *ton*: "usually equivalent to 40 cubic feet (or for hewn timber, 50)."

trap: see **fish trap**

trapper noun; also **trapper boy**
a boy in charge of a ventilation door (a trap) in a mine, opening it to allow coal boxes to pass and closing it to control air flow

1889 in 1974 CROSS ed. *Workingman in the Nineteenth Century* 84 Q. Do you know what the trappers get? A. I am not sure whether it is 40 or 50 cents [per day]. 1892 MADDEN *The Critic* 9 (22), 16 Another familiar form of accident is the "trapper boy" being either jammed by boxes, or trampled on by horses. 1973 *CB's Magazine* 3, 9 ... Allie [MacKenzie] was 9 years old and he had already worked three months as a Trapper Boy in Caledonia Colliery. 1983 SHEDDEN et al. *Mining Photographs* 271 **Trapper** – Trapper boy, a boy stationed at an underground door, to open and close it when boxes pass, and thus control the air current. 1983 MELLOR *Company Store* 89–90 ... those chosen to be trapper boys, opening and closing ventilation doors to allow horses and trips of coal cars to pass through, had an especially nerve racking task. 2007 MACKENZIE *CB Coal Mine Disasters* 38 Also trailing behind the other four was a

13-year-old trapper boy whose presence of mind saved his life.

[*EDD*, *OED3* (1815), *W3*]

travel intransitive verb; compare **rake**
to move in a mine by walking or riding in a rake (coupled mine cars used to transport miners)

1889 CANADA *Report ... Labor and Capital in Canada: Evidence, NS* 271 Q. How wide are these travelling roads? A. Some six feet and some ten feet. 1905 DAVIDSON and MACKENZIE *The Canadian Mining Review* 24 (3), 51 He gave the alarm to the underground manager, who, with an overman, immediately travelled directly towards the fire, through the smoke on the Back Deep. 1982 *CB's Magazine* 31, 53 We travelled into the mine – in the rake – we had to travel for about 45 minutes to get to our destination ... 5 miles underground, maybe 5 miles and a half. 1992 O'DONNELL *Coal Mining Songs* 176 A deputy was travellin' his section of the mine. 1999a MIGLIORE and DIPIERRO eds. *Italian Lives* 330 A "driver" travelled a section of mine with his "pit pony," collecting boxes into a short train, called a "trip," to be hauled out of the mine. 2007 MACKENZIE *CB Coal Mine Disasters* 131 Once at the bottom of the shaft, the miners got on a riding rake and traveled farther underground, riding down sloping tunnels called "deeps."

[*EDD* (n.d.); compare *travel* "to go on foot : WALK" *W3 dial*]

trawl noun; also **string**; compare **backline**
a group of lobster traps, connected to a main line (backline) with a buoy at each end

1891 CANADA *Sessional Papers of the Dominion of Canada: Vol. 8*, 8–19 ... (c) All boats and trawl buoys used in connection with the lobster fishery ... shall have a mark of identification ... 1957 WILDER *Canada's Lobster Fishery* 16 Some fishermen fish two or three traps from each buoy,

whereas others prefer a trawl of ten to fifteen traps fastened to a heavy ground-line. Pilot Survey Inf. 5 Now the trawl, I've heard it used for lobster traps – a string of traps, maybe twenty traps off one line. But the trawl is still used mostly for codfish. Survey II Inf. 3 Lobster fishing uses trawl or string ... called a trawl because the traps are dropped one after the other. Survey II Inf. 8 The whole group of traps is a trawl, ten traps in a trawl.

[at *dog trawl* Also *bull trawl, trawl DPEIE* (1975)]

*The understanding of a *trawl* as a longline with a series of hooks attached at regular intervals is widespread: *DNE* (used attributively), *COD N Amer., FWCCD, NCD, GCD, OED3 U.S., DAE* (1860), *DA* (1860), *W3*; at *trawl line COED N. Amer., NOAD, MWCD*.

trawl tub: see **tub**

trimmer: see **coal trimmer**

trip noun; compare **rake**, **runaway trip**
a number of coupled mine cars or boxes travelling on rails, used to transport miners, coal, or mine materials

1889 CANADA *Report ... Labor and Capital in Canada: Evidence, NS* 424 Q. You have to travel on the main road on which the engine hauls the trips? A. Yes. 1918 Beaton Institute MG 12 46 A9 n.p. Trip Riders [$3.34 per day]. 1928 HAY *Coal Mining Operations in the Sydney Coal Field* 20 Three headway trips, or fifty-one cares [*sic*], constitute a normal main haulage trip. 1983 MELLOR *Company Store* 89 Long "trips" of coal boxes were pulled by the ponies on narrow-gauge rails for long distances underground before hooking them onto the main deep haulage system to be brought to the surface. 1990 *Inverness Oran* 14 Mar. 9 A "trip" is the line of cars which takes the miners and the coal in and out of the mine. 2000 MACGILLIVRAY *Men of the Deeps* 149 Whenever I heard a trip coming, I'd just get down on my stomach, close to the wall, and I'd pray to God that it would stay on the tracks. 2007 MACKENZIE *CB Coal Mine Disasters* 104 Four tired men, they no doubt checked to see if a trip – boxes loaded with coal – would be going out about this time.

[*OED3* (1909), *W3*]

truck wagon noun; also spelled **truckwagon, truckwagon**; also **truck sleigh**
a horse-drawn vehicle for carrying heavy loads and occasionally passengers; a sled used in the winter for similar purposes
Anon. 1892 *Ladies' Pictorial Weekly* 3 (26), 25 June 412 In the year of 1879 Mr. Jerritt received a fall from a truck wagon, the wheel of which passed over the small of his back. 1897 MAC. *Outing: An Illustrated Monthly Magazine* July 352 As soon as we landed the next morning at Baddeck our camping outfit was packed upon a truck-wagon for transfer to the scene of our future exploits. 1975 MACMILLAN *Memoirs of a CB Doctor* 73 We had her on a cot in a box on a truck sleigh. 1978 *Oran Inbhirnis* 30 Mar. 11 We loaded the truck wagon with 500' of boards, 10 boxes of hops and 5 gallons of molasses, harnessed the horses and were ready to leave. 1994 *CB's Magazine* 67, 88 For instance, there is a forerunner ... of a lady who lived up at Blackstone. She would hear a truckwagon. She'd hear the sound of a truckwagon coming to the house at night. 1998 *CB's Magazine* 73, 18 We went over the next day to Mabou and we went on a horse-and-truck-wagon, it was.

[*DPEIE, DAE* (1805), *DA* (1805); at *truckwagon OED3* (1897)]

tub noun; often in the phrase **trawl tub, tub of trawl**
a container, typically a wooden flour barrel, modified to store baited hooks attached to longlines (a trawl) and used in dory fishing; a measure of the amount of trawl lines
n.d. Beaton Institute Tape 2354 You only got the boats that was fishing 25–30 tubs. The fellow that went back to 10 tubs and got 3300–3400 [pounds of fish] and proved it right there. 1981 *CB's Magazine* 29, 7 You set [the trawl] with a stick; it was something to toss the gear out of the tub. 1984 *CB's Magazine* 36, 66 You'd get a load of fish to every tub – probably you'd have 5 loads of fish to each dory – that'd be around 10 thousand pounds. 1996 CAPLAN ed. *CB Works* 251 See, your trawl – seven lines of gear – was down into a flour barrel. The flour barrel had a piece of it cut off, and you made a "trawl tub," we called it. 1997 *CB's Magazine* 61, 64–5 So he made a couple of tubs of trawls, took two fishing lines, spliced them together, fastened 500 fish hooks to each tub. 1999 *CB's Magazine* 74, 3 They would just jig it, or hand-line it, whatever you want to call it, over the side of the boat. We fellas – we had six tubs of trawl (to) a dory.

[*DNE* (1952), *ML*]

*The *DAE* records *tub* in a citation at *trawl*; this is the earliest documented evidence (1884) for the above meaning of *tub*.

tub of gear noun; also **tub, trawl tub**; compare **backline**
in dory fishing with a trawl, a modified barrel or plastic container holding coiled backlines with hooks attached; also a measure of the backlines, or the amount of fish caught by a tub of trawl
n.d. Beaton Institute Tape 2354 They didn't have to pay six dollars a tub to make the 15 tubs of extra gear or 12 tubs of extra gear. 1983 *CB's Magazine* 34, 34 There were two tubs of gear, and the two buoys, the two anchors, everything, were all afloat. And there was a shark on; he was as long as a horse. 1984 *CB's Magazine*

36, 66 It takes you an hour to haul a tub of gear in good fishing. (And one tub of gear might give you a dory load?) It could. In good fishing, it would. 1996 CAPLAN ed. *CB Works* 251 See, your trawl – seven lines of gear – was down into a flour barrel. The flour barrel had a piece of it cut off, and you made a "trawl tub," we called it. Survey II Inf. 1 A trawl line is two coils to a tub of gear. Survey II Inf. 3 A trawl line used in cod fishing could be five miles long (usually two to three miles), varies with the number of tubs of gear.
[at *tub*: DNE (1952), W3, ML]

tuckamore noun
low growing, matted evergreen trees, stunted by the coastal weather
1977 *CB's Magazine* 16, 14 ... so they had to walk for three miles ... fighting their way through over a mile of tuckamore, the prostrate spruce forest that grows on headlands where the wind off the sea is so fierce that the trees are unable to grow upright. This stuff is much like walking on a wire bedspring with holes in it. It both supports and impedes the person trying to cross it. 1977 *CB's Magazine* 16, 16 Wet and ragged the crew were led and helped over the tuckamore thicket, along the cliff edge, down the slope to Ezra Bailey's solitary house at the edge of Schooner Pond ... Survey I.
[DNE (1863), DC Nfld, COD Cdn (Nfld), NCD Newfoundland, OED3 Canad. (1863)]

tucker[1] noun
a dancing game in which a lone dancer seeks a partner already engaged in the dance
1979 RIGBY *St. Paul Island* 3 Very often the dancing broke off early in the evening to be followed by a game of Tucker for which the music was provided by the Northeast Lightkeeper and his violin. 1990 PEACH *Memories of a CB Childhood* 97 The chief recreation at such affairs had

always been a pairing-off game called Tucker; which involved certain innocent convolutions around the floor to a musical accompaniment.
[DARE (1881), DAE (1881), DA (1881), W3; compare *tucker party* DPEIE]

tucker[2] noun; compare **milling frolic**
a participant in the milling or fulling of homespun
1927 ARCHIBALD *Token* n.p. The web of cloth thus folded is then presented to the mistress of the family by the chief of the "Tuckers," with a formal good wish that is much like a blessing ... In some instances the measuring of the yards of cloth have been known to be attended by the giving and taking of a *kiss* as the "tuckers" come together with outstretched arms at the end of each yard. 1933 MORRISON *Collections of the NS Historical Society* 22, 78 The process [a milling or tucking frolic] in question was merely the beating of the cloth on a low table made for the purpose, at which the tuckers sat, and which operation they accompanied with the singing of all the known Gaelic songs.
[EDD, OED3 Obs. exc. dial. ([1273])]

tucking verbal adjective and noun; used to modify **frolic**, **party**, **song**; compare **milling frolic**
formerly, milling or thickening homespun cloth by beating it on a board to the rhythm of Gaelic milling songs; now, milling in a public venue that re-enacts the traditional actions and songs
1927 ARCHIBALD *The Token* n.p. At these "Milling" or "Tucking Parties" as they were called, certain songs peculiar to the occasion were always sung, and even to the present day they still survive, although homespun as the general wear has passed into oblivion. 1933 MORRISON *Collections of the NS Historical Society* 22, 78 Before the cloth was ready to be made into garments it was subjected to

more or less severe manipulation known as the "Louah" or the "tucking" and the occasion was called the "tucking frolic." 1975 Beaton Institute Tape 1022 They had tucking songs – they used to put on tucking frolics. 1988 MACGILLIVRAY and MACGILLIVRAY *CB Ceilidh* 130 There were regular events at the Boisdale Hall – like "tucking (milling) frolics" and variety concerts ... 1992 HORNSBY *Nineteenth-Century CB* 78 There were also "spinning" and "tucking" frolics, where women met to spin thread, beat cloth, and swap gossip ... 2004 MACKINNON *Silent Observer* 6 At spinning bees and tucking parties, Grandma was forever talking and working in a hurry ...

[at *tucking* noun *OED3 Obs.* (1467–1488); compare *tuck* verb: *EDD, OED3* Now *local* (1273)]

twine needle noun; also **knitting needle**; compare **knit**
a flat, oblong implement with one rounded end, made of bone, wood, or plastic and used to make mesh for lobster traps or to mend nets

Pilot Survey Inf. 2 That's [twine needle] what's used for mending nets or knitting heads ... they used to all be wood [when] they'd make them themselves, but now a lot of them are plastic. Survey II Inf. 2 The knitting needle could be made of wood, whale bone, but plastic now.

[*DNE*; at *knitting needle DNE* (1885); at *heading needle DPEIE* (with *twine needle* as a variant)]

U

uisge ['uškə] noun; often in phrases; compare **water of life**
water

Anon. 1889 *Dominion Illustrated* 2 (39), 30 Mar. 198 "Uisge Bau [*sic*]" (whose

name, meaning "White Water," bears testimony to the race of the early settlers) is a waterfall about nine miles from the town [of Baddeck]. 1933 MACDONALD *Cape North and Vicinity* 27 All kinds of strong drink were often included under the term, "*Uisge beatha*" *water of life*. 1999 HAYNES *Hiking Trails of CB* 118–19 Uisge (pronounced *ush-ka*) Ban, is Gaelic for "white water," and if you walk to the base of this 15-m (50-ft) waterfall after a heavy rain, you will understand why it received that name. 2007 MACDONALD *Lauchlin of the Bad Heart* 167 "And whisky?" "Lead the way, my son, they don't call it *uisge beagh* for nothing."

*A loanword from Scottish Gaelic, see *uisge* "water" *GED*.

ulnoo: see **l'nu**

Unama'ki [unəmɑːgi] noun; also spelled **Unama'kik, Onamagi, Oonamaagik, Wunama'kik**
foggy land, designating Cape Breton Island, one of seven Mi'kmaw districts

1873 RAND *A Short Account of the Lord's Work among the Micmac Indians* 4 ... Cape Breton is called *Oonumahghee*, Land of the *Oonumacks*; *ghee* (the same as in Greek,) meaning land, but what the other part of the word means, is uncertain. 1996 PRINS *Mi'kmaq: Resistance, Accommodation, and Cultural Survival* 177 Because the grand chief of Cape Breton ranked above his peers, his district, called *Unama'kik*, was recognized as the head district. 1996 MCMILLAN "Mi'kmaq Grand Council" 30 Cape Breton Island made up the district of Onamagi or "foggy land." This area was heavily populated because of abundant resources, particularly its fishery. 1997 *CB's Magazine* 72, 20 Chief Lindsay Marshall "Visitors" A white cloud appears on the blue horizon off the shore of Unama'ki. / Strangers are coming in strange vessels. 2008 MORGAN *Story of CB Island Book One* 10 They [early Mi'kmaw people] called their sea-girt land – so different from their earlier home in the continental interior – "Unama'ki," the foggy land, and they likened the island to a head, with the mainland of today's Nova Scotia its torso. 2012 SABLE and FRANCIS *Language of this Land, Mi'kma'ki* 21 **Unama'kik** (a variation of the word Mi'kma'kik, meaning "Mi'kmaw territory") Cape Breton Island.

*A Mi'kmaw loanword, see *Unama'ki* "land of the fog, one of the seven districts (Cape Breton Island)" MEL. The suffix *k*, as in *Unama'kik*, indicates a locative case meaning "in the place of Unama'ki" (Oral Communication, Stephanie Inglis, 8 May 2014).

undercut: see **mining**

undercutter noun; compare **cut** verb, **mining**, **puncher**
a machine that cuts or punches a narrow channel along the bottom or sides of the coal being excavated (the coal face), to allow the coal to break after the explosive charge (the shot) is fired
  1894 Anon. *The Canadian Mining Review* 13 (12), 250 New bank head and pit frame have been erected and new screening machinery put in operation [at the Old Bridgeport Colliery]. 1983 SHEDDEN et al. *Mining Photographs* 271 **Undercutter** – A machine equipped with a movable cutter bar that resembles a chain saw. 1986 *CB's Magazine* 42, 19 The company I represented supplied the undercut, made by Samson Undercutters. 1992 NEWTON *Where Coal is King* 17 There was a bull wheel, a Samson undercutter, a Dosco Miner ...
  [*OED3* (1891); compare *undercutter* "a mine worker who operates a machine for cutting the bottom or side of the working face of coal ..." *W3*]

undermining: see **mining**

up-and-down saw noun; also **web saw**
a two handled saw, used to cut boards from a log by two sawyers (one above, the other below) moving the saw upward and downward, as opposed to a circular blade
  1973 BEATON comp. *Glencoe: An Historical Sketch* 13 Every parishioner contributed in his own way to the labor involved in constructing the church. Every board was hand-planed. Up-and-down saws were used. 1984 CUMMING et al. *Story of Framboise* 25 (Whip saws – or "up and down" saws – were two-man saws for cutting boards. With the log on a frame, one man sawed from above, while the other pulled the saw down from below.) 1985 MACKENZIE *Tracks across the Maritimes* 55 The only other alternative was the 'web' saw, in a specially-made frame or pit where one man above and another man below would slowly saw a log into boards or scantling with a fairly heavy saw.
  [at *pitman ML*; at *up and down mill SSPB*; *web saw OED3* (1875), *DAE, DA, W3*]

up south prepositional phrase; compare **down north**
in a southerly direction, down south
  1932 in 1991 *CB's Magazine* 56, 67 **Aug 3rd**. Saw Tuna inside sandbar ... he rested to get his second wind – then off up South shore to the point ... 1976 *CB's Magazine* 15, 25 She [a boat] used to go up south through St. Peter's Canal and around to Margaree Harbour and Grand Etang and Cheticamp. 1983 *CB's Magazine* 33, 18 See, we were way up south, way down there. We'd get fish, and there'd be maggots in it, you know. 1987 Beaton Institute Tape 2324 [Tape 1] "Where's that at, now, the Westers?" "Up South West Nova." 2007 *DCBE* Tape SHERRINGTON 7 And, of course, *up* being south, and that's not just here.
  [*DNE, EDD, DAE* (1935–37), *DA* (1835–37)]

V

Valley: see **Kolonia**

var noun
the balsam fir; the resin from this tree
    1885 Beaton Institute MG 12 17, 14 June
19 Constantly on the bed ... Have to drink
nothing but flax and water (var water) ...
1984 CUMMING et al. *Story of Framboise*
2 Native trees included ... balsam fir (or
"var") ... 1995 *CB's Magazine* 69, 54 ... my
mother in the fall of the year, used to go in
the woods. Used to take the (var) balsam –
you know the fir, balsam on the fir – take
that. Pilot Survey Inf. 3 [Var] that's common enough.
    [*DNE, DPEIE, DC Atlantic Provinces*
(1793), *OED3 Canad.* (1793)]

*The dictionaries noted above state that *var* is a
variant pronunciation of *fir*.

W

wagon house noun; also spelled **wagon-
house**
a building to shelter a wagon
    1985 *CB's Magazine* 39, 79 ... he used
to have a wagon house on the mainland.
1988 *CB's Magazine* 48, 41 We used to play
hide-and-seek. I remember hiding in the
wagon house ... 1994 MACLEOD and ST.
CLAIR *Pride of Place* 45 For many years,
a wagon-house was attached to an entry
porch which led to the door on the side of
the house.
    [*DARE* **scattered, but esp NEast, eN
Midl,** *DAE*; at *wagon-house OED3* (1648)]

wall face noun; also spelled **wall-face;**
also **wall, face;** compare **coal face**

the vertical surface of the coal seam where
miners excavate coal, often in reference to
longwall mining
    1969 Beaton Institute Tape 78 I was
transferred back to Sydney Mines in 1955.
By this time we were starting mechanization on the wall faces – Dosco Miners.
1985 CALDER *Coal in NS* 43 The production of coal takes place along a face, or
"wall," ... 1991 MACGILLIVRAY *Diamonds in the Rough* 143 I'm a wall-face
cutter. I work four or five miles out under
the sea. 2003 SAINT AGNES ELEMEN-
TARY SCHOOL *Coal Miners' Stories* 69
The machine started to go up the wall to
cut more coal when he heard the shearer
operator scream fire. He looked up the
wall face and saw flames about four feet
high between the drums (what cuts the
coal also) of the shearer. 2007 MACKEN-
ZIE *CB Coal Mine Disasters* 151 It was "cut,
shoot and load" for those working room
and pillar. This meant that the men working the room had to "cut" the wall face
with a radial machine.
    [at *wallface EDD*; at *wall-face OED3*
(1839)]

Waltes [wɑltəs] noun; also spelled **waltes**
an ancient Mi'kmaw game played by
bumping a shallow wooden bowl (or burl)
on a flat surface to raise and overturn
six coin-shaped disks (called dice, typically with one side blank and the other
marked with dots around a cross) to score
points according to the face value of the
dice, with points being recorded using an
elaborate arrangement of counting sticks
    1923 in 1985 *CB's Magazine* 40, 35 The
most constant pastime of all was the
women's game of dish-dice (Waltes ...).
In one wigwam or another a game was
usually on of the afternoon or evening
[during the St. Ann's Day Mission]. 1962
HOWARD *Museum News* 26 (3–4), 10 We
were told that the people would probably remain encamped on the island for a

couple more days, visiting, feasting, and playing Waltes, the Micmac bowl game ... 1973 *CB's Magazine* 6, 12 In Waltes there is no final score, except that one player has everything and the other has nothing. There are some people with real skill at it, who can slam the bowl with such control they can get point-making combinations several times in a row ... In old times it was never played without stakes; today gambling at Waltes would be very rare. 1976b JOE *Tawow* 5 (2), 24 There is much activity on the island during Mission time – dancing, story-telling, waltes and other traditional games. 1988 JOE *Song of Eskasoni* 12 And in the same room / A folded blanket there lay / With two people on their knees playing waltes / While two more kept count. / The ancient game of the Micmac / Known throughout the pages of time. / It is just a game of bone dice and burl plate / To the poor, this is no crime. 2001 HUNTER *Sculptures from Jagged Ore* 47 Waltes is an ancient game employing a large shallow dish and two-sided die made from bone.

*A Mi'kmaw loanword, see *waltes* "an ancient traditional Mi'kmaq game played with bowl, six dice, and counting sticks" MEL. A detailed discussion of the game and scoring is found at www.cbu.ca/mrc/waltes.

wash house noun; also spelled **wash-house**
a building used primarily by miners to shower after work and store their work and street clothes
   1952 TERRY *CB Mirror* 1 Oct. 20 We saw the wash-house where the men's surface clothes are hoisted high on pulleys. 1987 *CB's Magazine* 44, 42 There was no wash house then. And no bathtubs [in company houses]. You'd come home [from the coal piers] black from head to foot ... The wash house was built the week I got married! I was married in 1937, in

October. 1988 MACDONALD *Eyestone* 138 Our weekly showers (company houses had no bathrooms) we took at the colliers' wash house, a huge place empty of miners that time of night, their street clothing, to keep it from dust, tied on the ends of ropes and clustered high up against the ceiling as if it had risen there on its own. 1989 MLECZKO *My Book of Memories* [PART II] 78 ... [he] went down to the pit, to the wash house, where the men hung their pit clothes and showered before coming home. 2007 MACKENZIE *CB Coal Mine Disasters* 111 In Princess Colliery, however, the coal miners left the wash house, walked over to a shaft, were lowered down the shaft in a cage for about 750 feet ...

*The earliest known citation for *wash house* meaning a building for people to bathe or wash is found in the *OED3 Obs. rare* (c1000). The more frequent meaning of *wash house* is to cleanse objects such as laundry (*COD, FWCCD, DARE, DAE, W3*), cod (*DNE*), or wool (*EDD*).

wash plant noun
see quotation at 1983
   1952 TERRY *CB Mirror* 1 Nov. 14 A wash plant is for washing the coal, grading it into sizes, and sorting it ... automatically ... or as automatically as possible. 1983 SHEDDEN et al. *Mining Photographs* 271 **Wash plant** – An enclosed area of the surface works where many types of machines clean, wash, and break the coal as it comes from the mines.

water of life noun; compare **uisge**
distilled alcohol, especially moonshine or whisky, from Gaelic *uisge beatha* and the Latin *aqua vitae*
   1933 MACDONALD *Cape North and Vicinity* 27 All kinds of strong drink were often included under the term, "Uisge beatha" *water of life*. 2005 MACKENZIE *Neighbours Are Watching* 102 After a

couple of ill-starred experiments, Jay quit
trying to manufacture the water of life –
not patient enough to wait until it was fit
to drink. 2006 MACISAAC *Better Life* 65
Their use of liquor, which the Highland
men lovingly called "the water of life,"
had a long and noble tradition as a mark
of hospitality, and therefore drinking was
a custom that was hard to curb.
  [*OED3* (1576); at *water COED, W3*]

*The Cape Breton usage of the *water of life* may
be influenced by the popular Gaelic phrase
uisge beatha (from *uisge* "water" and *beatha*
"life, existence" *GED*) more so than the Latin
equivalent. Compare *usquebaugh* "whisky"
OED3 (1581).

waulking [wɑkɪŋ] verbal noun and adjective; compare **milling frolic**
formerly, milling or thickening homespun cloth by beating it on a board to the
rhythm of Gaelic milling songs; now, milling in a public venue that re-enacts the
traditional actions and songs, or milling
done by machine
  1926 MACKENZIE *Travel* June 42 The
process of milling, also called in the Highlands *waulking*, is the treatment of cloth
to thicken and strengthen it after it comes
from the loom, and is a highly skilled
performance accompanied by its special
movements and special songs. 1975 *CB's
Magazine* 12, 14 ... in association with that
[the dyeing mill] there had to be a mill
where woven material was put through
a process of thickening – they call that
"fulling" or "milling" or "waulking." 1984
CUMMING et al. *Story of Framboise* 49
Milling (or **waulking** or **fulling**) thickened and softened the blanket cloth and
shrunk it just enough, but not too much.
2006 GRAY *Alexander Graham Bell* 238
Long-established Gaelic customs, such
as "waulking" or milling the cloth, were
occasions for singing old Gaelic songs and
composing new ones. 2006 MACISAAC

Better Life 39 The *waulking* songs that
accompanied the milling of the cloth contain a wealth of information about traditional life in the Highlands.
  [*DPEIE, OED3* Chiefly *Sc.* in later use.
Now *hist.* (*c*1300); compare *waulk*: *EDD*,
OED3 (*c*1300), *DSL, W3 Scot*]

web saw: see **up-and-down saw**

wedding reel noun; also spelled **Wedding
Reel**
a four handed reel danced by the bridal
party (the bride, groom, maid of honour,
and best man) at a wedding reception; at
one time, a dance performed by the bridal
party and may have been an informal
marriage ceremony
  1964 RHODES *Traditional Dancing in
Scotland* 275 As in Scotland, with the
change in the fashion of dancing the wedding Reel became in some places just a set
of Quadrilles ... 1976 PRINGLE *Pringle's
Mountain* 42 That evening [following the
wedding] the other neighbours gathered,
and a fiddle player. We danced the four
hand reels, or, *wedding reels*, as some
called them. 1988 MACGILLIVRAY and
MACGILLIVRAY *CB Ceilidh* 133 Before
Fr. Dan E. MacDonald died in 1960, he
got interested when he heard that this
Wedding Reel *was* once the ceremony of
marriage ... Well, when they went through
this Wedding Reel, they could live
together until a priest would happen to
come by and bless the marriage ... Still, Fr.
MacLeod was saying that this ceremony
was perfect: the publication was there, the
wish of the parents, and the idea of "mar-
rying into the family". 1994 *CB's Magazine*
66, 29 He put on his wedding shoes, and
he was moving around as light as a bird.
And the wedding reel commenced. 2012
RANKIN *Wedding Reels* 50 ... there are
couples before them, and behind, / corner
partners are part of the figure, "John of
Badenyon," / and the couple starts and

ends together their first wedding reel. /
The faces are intent, all are wordless, only
the music is speaking.

*The wedding reel originated in the region
from which many Cape Breton settlers emi-
grated. As Flett and Flett, *Traditional Dancing in
Scotland*, note: "In the West Highlands and the
Western Isles the first dance after the wedding
supper was a Scotch Reel called the 'Wedding
Reel' or 'Ruidhleadh na Banais'. This was
danced by the bride and groom, best man, and
bridesmaid, and was watched by the rest of the
company" (1964, 46).

wee darg noun
a small day's work, a deliberate slowing
of coal production to reduce the daily
output
   1979 FRANK "CB Coal Miners, 1917–
1926" 254 ... in protest the miners loaded
"the wee darg". A Scottish immigrant,
McLachlan ... played an important part
in popularizing the tactic in Cape Breton,
where it usually was known as "striking
on the job". 1983 MELLOR *Company Store*
146 Remembering the "Wee Darg" (the
small day's work) slow-down strike ... to
reduce coal output by at least the same
percentage that miners' wages had been
reduced. 1999 FRANK *J. B. McLachlan*
242 ... in the case of disputes it was not
unusual to see the normal "master's darg"
replaced by the "wee darg." McLachlan
was familiar with this practice from
his days in the Lanarkshire mines, and
when the necessity arose he seized the
opportunity to apply the old tactic to new
circumstances.

Darg, meaning a day's work, was mainly used
in the north of England and Scotland: *EDD*,
OED3 Sc. and *north. dial.* (c1489), *DSL*, and *W3*
chiefly Scot.

well boat noun; also spelled **wellboat**;
also **well-smack boat**; compare **smack**

a boat having a tank with seawater circu-
lating through it, used to transport live
lobsters
   1978 *CB's Magazine* 20, 11 A wellboat is
a boat that the bottom was bored full of
holes. It had watertight compartments.
And you could put possibly 20 to 25,000
pounds of lobsters in that hold. And
when she moved, that circulated the
water, aerated it – and the lobsters would
go down [to] the States. 1984 CUMMING
et al. *Story of Framboise* 74 New methods
of transporting lobsters came in – "well
boats" that pumped ocean water in and
out to keep lobsters well and alive ...
[1996] BRAY *Our CB Lobster* 24 Fifty
years ago, smacks or well boats transported market lobsters from Port Morien
to Boston. The reason that they were
called "well boats" was because they
had a well in the mid-section with holes
bored in the planking for the circulation
of sea water.
   [*W3*; at *well-boat OED3* (c1600); at *wet
smack ML*]

whack noun; often in the phrase **a whack
of** ...
a lot of (something), a surprisingly large
number or amount of (something)
   1989 *CB's Magazine* 50, 26 And I
worked with a couple of other girls –
whack of them, really – there were about
10 of us from GI [General Instruments].
1995 *CB's Magazine* 68, 89 But what if you
had to play [music] to somebody other
than Maritimers? Because that's who we
were getting – a whack of Cape Bretoners there and Maritimers there. 1999 *CB's
Magazine* 74, 79 He learned all the older
songs. Boy, he had an awful whack of
them.
   [*COD*, *EDD* (n.d.), *COED N. Amer.*;
compare *whacker* "anything abnormally
large of its kind ..." *OED3*, *W3*]

wet fishery: see **green fishery**

whiff transitive verb; compare **biff**
to throw (something)

2002 COADY *Saints of Big Harbour* 278
Howard had whiffed a beer bottle at
them, and Hugh squealed away. Survey
I Inf. 2 Whiff means biff with a purpose,
"She whiffed a shoe at me." Survey I
Inf. 35 Whiff is a harder throw like a
whipped-in ball. Survey I Inf. 38 You
would say, "I whiffed it" when throwing
something without an intended target.

[*DPEIE*]

white mouth noun
a children's disease characterized by
white sores in the mouth and throat,
thrush

1975 DUBBIN *40 Years a Nurse* 73 But
there were infants who needed treatment.
They had an aggravated form of Thrush,
which the mothers called "White Mouth."
I had seen minute ulcers in a baby's
mouth, but nothing like these large bleeding ones which had spread to the throat.
1983 MACKENZIE "Social Conditions
in Sydney 1900 to 1914" 60 Diphtheria or
"White Mouth" was present at the Pier at
this time. The mothers would try to cure
the large bleeding ulcers in the mouth by
feeding the babies a potion of honey and
Borax.

[*DARE* (1990)]

white pudding noun, often plural; compare **marag**
a sausage made with suet, oatmeal,
onions, and seasoning, traditionally
encased in intestines

1976 MACGREGOR *Days That I
Remember* 15 ... the marrick was a far cry
from the so called white puddings sold
now at the stores ... 2000b MACDON-
ALD *Cape Bretoner* 8 (5), 19 Marag, that
tube of suet and oatmeal also known as
white pudding, has a following, as does
its ugly brother, the blood pudding. 2006
MACISAAC *Better Life* 78 Climaxing

the achievement of the old farm kitchen
were black and white puddings (*maragan*) ...

[*EDD, OED3* (1776), *COED, W3*]

whore's egg noun; also **sea egg**
a spherical shellfish with sharp spines, a
sea urchin

1829 HALIBURTON *Historical and
Statistical Account of N-S* vol. 2, 405 SHELL
FISH ... Whore's egg. 1972 STAEBLER
CB Harbour 85 ... you be careful when
you's swimming that you don't step on a
whoore's egg, they sea urchins is full o'
prickles will give you a fester. Pilot Survey Inf. 2 Whore's eggs, yes, that's what
we call them. Survey II Inf. 3 Sea egg is
also used. They are fished off Main-à-Dieu
and sold overseas.

[*DPEIE, OED3* N. Amer. (chiefly *Newfoundland*), *DARE* **ME** (1674), *ML*; at *ose
egg DNE* (with *whore's egg* as a variant)]

widow man noun
a widower

Pilot Survey Inf. 1 We use that [widow
man]. Survey I Inf. 23 One of the old
widow men called me up looking for
companionship.

[*DNE, DPEIE*; at *widowman: EDD,
DARE* **scattered, but chiefly Sth, S. Midl**
(1688), *W3 chiefly dial*; at *widow-man: OED3
dial., DSL*;]

widow woman noun
a widow

1989 *CB's Magazine* 50 Inside Front
Cover ... he married a widow woman
who was well-off, and she had two sons.
1995 *CB's Magazine* 69, 7 And there was a
widow woman ... and her two sons.

[*DNE, DPEIE, OED3* (1382), *DARE*
formerly widespread, now esp Midl, Sth,
W3 chiefly dial; at *widowwoman EDD*; at
widow-woman DSL]

wood-stock skate: see **stock skate**

working intransitive verb and verbal noun; compare **pillar**
of a mine roof or pillar (a block of coal left to support the roof), slowly moving, cracking, threatening to collapse

1978 *Oran Inbhirnis* 9 Feb. 18 The pillar they were sent to pull had been "working" a couple of times in previous days – giving small bumps and cracks. Even the rats had abandoned the area, lack of rats in any portion of the mine was a natural safety warning. 1979 FRANK "CB Coal Miners, 1917–1926" 224 Because the coal cutting machines were cumbersome to move and their noise drowned out the ominous "working" of the roof, this task required the traditional talents of the handpick miner. 1993 *CB's Magazine* 62, 8 But the area was still working very heavy. The roof material was falling around us. There were pieces of roof material that were hanging over our heads. By working, I mean that the roof, being unsupported, is still continuing to collapse.

[*EDD* (1849); at *work* W3]

Y

Yahie miner noun; also spelled **Ya-he**, **yakie**
a non-unionized miner, frequently a Gaelic speaker known for mentioning home, *dhachaigh*; strike-breaking miner

1929a MCCAWLEY *CB Come-All-Ye* 20 Join the Union right away, / Don't you wait until after pay, / Join the Union right away, / You dirty Yahie miners. 1992 O'DONNELL *Coal Mining Songs* 116–17 The term 'Yahie' is sometimes taken as a corruption of 'Yankee,' referring to seasonal workers from the USA, but a more acceptable explanation popular in Cape Breton is that it actually derives from the Gaelic word for homeward: 'dhachaidh'

(home = 'dachaidh'), pronounced (g) ackey – the 'g' being softened to a somewhat guttural 'y'! Because many of the immigrants constantly spoke of home and the better life there, they were castigated as the '(g)ackey' or 'Yahie' Miners. 1999 FRANK *J. B. McLachlan* 50 "The Yahie Miners," a local industrial folk song directed at strikebreakers, dated from this period and was based on a similar north of England song, "The Blackleg Miners." 2011 DOYLE *CB Facts and Folklore* 226 yakie miners: Gaelic-speaking coal miners who went home for the winter, the usual down time for Cape Breton coal mines. The Gaelic term for home sounded like "yakie."

*The Gaelic noun for *home* is *dachaigh*, giving the derivative adverb *dhachaigh* "home, home(wards)" *GED*, which in turn was pronounced by English speakers as *yahie*.

Z

zombie noun; also spelled **Zombie**
a conscripted soldier during WWII who avoided active service overseas

1985 MOOGK *CB at 200* 177 The conscripts were scornfully nicknamed "Zombies" after the corpses animated by Voodoo magic who were a feature of current horror movies ... One reaction on the part of the voluntary soldiers was to put distance between themselves and the despised "Zombies". This was easily done since half of the conscripts came from Western Canada and over half had German, Slavic, Italian and French surnames. 1988 BOUTILIER *New Waterford* 9 The community was naturally none too enthusiastic about soldiers who didn't volunteer for overseas service and there was more than one lively tussle between the "zombies" sent here for home defence, and locals, particularly local boys home on leave. 1993 *CB's Magazine* 63, 87 They didn't want to learn, see? They were all "zombies," as we'd call them. They didn't join the active service, they were just corralled and dragged in. And they didn't want to do anything. They figured if they didn't learn anything they'd be sent home or something.

[*DC Slang, Derog., Hist.,* COD *Cdn slang,* FWCCD *Canadian Slang,* GCD *Cdn. Slang,* OED3 *Canad. Mil. Slang* (1943), W3 *Canada*]

*The regional labels indicate that this sense is Canadian, but it is useful to know that it was also current on Cape Breton Island, particularly in the Cape Breton County.

Works Consulted

PUBLISHED WORKS AND DISSERTATIONS, THESES, AND SENIOR PAPERS

Abbot, C. G. 1905. "Novella Souvenir Edition." *Sydney Mines Illustrated*, July 17–22, 4–15. Beaton Institute, Cape Breton University, Sydney, NS: Pamphlet 1564.

Acadiensis. 1971–2007.

Adam, Margaret I. 1920. "The Causes of the Highland Emigrations of 1783–1803." *The Scottish Historical Review* 17 (66): 73–89.

Adams, George Matthew. 1931. *Glimpses of Nova Scotia*. Halifax: Bureau of Information.

Adlam, Robert G. 2003. "Indigenous Rights, the Marshall Decision and Cultural Restoration." *Acadiensis* 33 (1): 108–13.

Akerman, Jeremy. 1981. *Black Around the Eyes: A Novel*. Toronto: McClelland & Stewart.

– 1984. "Wakeup Coaltown." In *The Cape Breton Collection*, edited by Lesley Choyce, 8–26. Porters Lake, NS: Pottersfield.

Alexander, Henry. 1982. "Linguistic Geography." *Journal of the Atlantic Provinces Linguistic Association* 4:3–8.

Alexander, Sir William. 1885. *The Earl of Stirling's Register of Royal Letters Relative to the Affairs of Scotland and Nova Scotia from 1615 to 1635*. Edited by C. Rogers. Edinburgh: Burness.

Allaby, Eric. 1973. *"The August Gale": A List of Atlantic Shipping Losses in the Gale of August 24, 1873*. Saint John, NB: New Brunswick Museum.

Allen, Francis H. 1891. "Summer Birds of the Bras d'Or Region of Cape Breton Island, NS." *Auk* 8 (2): 164–6.

– 1895. "Some Notes on Cape Breton Summer Birds." *Auk* 12 (1): 89–90.

Almon, Albert. 1920. *Souvenir of Louisbourg 1731*. Glace Bay, NS: Brodie.

– 1940. *Rochefort Point, a Silent City in Louisbourg: A Booklet Dealing with the Old French Fortress in Cape Breton – The Unveiling of Monuments, the Hospital and Cemeteries, and Other Historical Matter Connected with Louisbourg*. Glace Bay, NS: MacDonald.

– 1952. "Famous Shipwrecks," *Cape Breton Mirror*, June 4.

Amos, Janet. *Down North*. 1982. [screenplay adapted for the book of the same name]. S.l.: s.n.

Anderson, Eleanor L. 1999. *Broughton: Cape Breton's Ghost Town*. [Sydney, NS]: Icon Communications.

Anderson, Isabel Harriet. 1885. *Inverness Before Railways*. Inverness, NS: A. and W. MacKenzie.

Anglin, Gerald. 1966. "The Great Cape Breton Treasure Caper." *Star Weekly*, May 14, 8–15.

Anon. n.d. *Ship Building Industry of St. Ann's 1845–1860*. Beaton Institute, Cape Breton University, Sydney, NS: Pamphlet 3662.

– n.d. *The Sixth Regiment Cape Breton Militia 1866–70: The Volunteers of Gabarus and of the Surrounding Districts*. S.l.: s.n. Beaton Institute, Cape Breton University, Sydney, NS: Pamphlet 3679.

– 1874. "Reform in Ocean Passenger Travel." *The Canadian Monthly and National Review*, 5 (2), 97–101. http://eco.canadiana.ca/

– 1875. "Everything." *The Canadian Gentleman's Journal and Sporting Times*, 4 (202), 3. http://eco.canadiana.ca/

– 1884. "News from the Home Field: Diocese of Nova Scotia." *The Church Guardian*, 6 (33), 2–5. http://eco.canadiana.ca/

– 1889. "The 'Uisge Bau [*sic*]' and 'Star Falls,' Baddeck, Victoria County, Cape Breton, N.S." *The Dominion Illustrated*, 2 (39), 198. http://eco.canadiana.ca/

– 1890. "Mining Notes." *Canadian Mining Review* 9 (4): 45–6. http://eco.canadiana.ca/

– 1891. "Mining Notes from our Correspondents: Cape Breton." *Canadian Mining & Mechanical Review* 10 (5): 130–1. http://eco.canadiana.ca/

– 1892. "A Cape Breton Miracle." *Ladies' Pictorial Weekly*, 3 (26), 412. http://eco.canadiana.ca/

– 1892. "Nova Scotia Coal Mining in 1891." *Canadian Mining & Mechanical Review* 11 (1): 1. http://eco.canadiana.ca/

– 1893. "Mining Notes From Our Correspondents." *Canadian Mining & Mechanical Review* 12 (1): 9–10. http://eco.canadiana.ca/

– 1894. "Copper Mining in Cape Breton." *Canadian Mining Review* 13 (8): 134–5.

– 1894. "Dominion Coal Co.: A New Record for Canada – One Million Dollars Spent on Improvements and a Million Tons Shipped in the Twelve Months." *The Canadian Mining Review* 13 (12): 249–50. http://eco.canadiana.ca/

– 1896. "Our Home Work." *Presbyterian Record*, 21 (11), 287. http://eco.canadiana.ca/

– 1897. " Mining Notes, Nova Scotia." *The Canadian Mining Review* 16 (6): 218–19. http://eco.canadiana.ca/

– 1899. "Hints of Butter Making." *The Journal of Agriculture and Horticulture* 3 (7): 166–7. http://eco.canadiana.ca/

– 1900. "Haulage Plant." *The Canadian Mining Review* 19 (9): 206. http://eco.canadiana.ca/

– 1901. "Coal Mining and Trade." *The Canadian Mining Review* 20 (10): 246–8. http://eco.canadiana.ca/

– 1901. "Company Notes." *The Canadian Mining Review* 20 (1): 15–18. http://eco.canadiana.ca/

– 1901. "New Furnaces at Sydney, Cape Breton, of the Dominion Iron and Steel Company." *The Canadian Mining Review* 20 (10): 240–6. http://eco.canadiana.ca/

– 1905. "Cape Breton in the Early Days." *Blue Banner* 3 (4): 3–4.

– 1905. "Cape Breton in the Early Days II." *Blue Banner* 3 (6): 3–4.

– 1914. "Louisbourg on Cape Breton." *Saturday Night*, July 18, 12.

– 1932. *The Cape Breton Historical Society: Some Papers and Records of the Society 1928 to 1932*. North Sydney, NS: M. A. McInnis.

– 1959. "Cape Breton's Value to Great Britain." *Royal Magazine*, July n.p.

– 1970. *Cape Breton's Deserted Mining Town, Broughton*. Glace Bay, NS: Brodie.

- 1979. "The Sudden Boom in Atlantic Fish." *Saturday Night*, May 89–90.
- 1988. "Cape Breton's 'Grand Hotel.'" *Update Cape Breton*, July 36–7.
- 1996a. *Festival de l'Escaouette*. [Advertising Pamphlet] S.l.: s.n.
- 1996b. "Les Masques du Moine." [Advertising Pamphlet]. S.l.: s.n.
- 1998. "Celtic Colours International Festival." *The Cape Bretoner*, 6 (1), 8–10.
- 2000. "Christmas Island: What's in a Name?" 2000. *The Cape Bretoner*, 8 (6), 19–20.
Appleby, Bill. 1998. "Load of Wood (and Load of Hay) New and Used Performers." *The Cape Bretoner*, 6 (4), 38.
Archibald, Charles. 1893. "Gowrie Colliery, Cape Breton." *Canadian Mining &Mechanical Review* 12 (4): 59. http://eco.canadiana.ca/
- 1897. "Patent Fuel and its Manufacture." *The Canadian Mining Review* 16 (10): 292–3. http://eco.canadiana.ca/
Archibald, Mrs. Charles. 1914. "Early Scottish Settlers in Cape Breton." *Nova Scotia Historical Society* 18:69–100.
Archibald, Edith J. 1927. *The Token: A Play in Three Acts of Old Days in Cape Breton*. Halifax: privately printed.
Armour, Elizabeth P. 1994. *Our Legacy of Love*. Hantsport, NS: Lancelot.
Arnold, Mary Ellicott. 1940. *The Story of Tompkinsville*. New York: The Cooperative League.
Arts Cape Breton News. 1990 Fall.
Asch, Timothy, and Douglas A. Harper. 1994. *Cape Breton 1952: The Photographic Vision of Timothy Asch*. Louisville, KY: International Visual Sociology Association; Ethnographics Press.
Association Touristique de Chéticamp. n.d. "History." http://www.cheticamp.ca/en/ [This revised website no longer has the information quoted in the dictionary]
Atkins, B. T. Sue, and Michael Rundell. 2008. *The Oxford Guide to Practical Lexicography*. New York: Oxford University Press.
The Atlantic Advocate. 1956–1991.
Atlantic Insight. 1979–1989.
Aucoin, Alexander J. 1977. "The Cellophane Dinner." *The Inverness Oran*, May 5, 15–16.
Aucoin, Clarence R. n.d. *History of Cheticamp*. Cheticamp, NS: privately printed.
Aucoin, Réjean. 1985. *Cap Rouge : Sur les Traces des Habitants*. Cheticamp, NS: Les Amies Du Plein Air.
Ayers, Tom. 2004. "Cool in Cape Breton." *The Cape Bretoner*, 12 (6), 24–7.
- 2006. "Sinking In: Part 2 – The Legacy Continues." *The Cape Bretoner*, 13 (6), 20–4.
Ayto, John. 2003. *The Oxford Dictionary of Slang*. Oxford: Oxford University Press.
Babitch, Rose Mary. 1996. *Le Vocabulaire des pêches aux îsles Lamèque et Miscou*. Moncton: Éditions d'Acadie.
Baddeck: A Search for Yesterday. n.d. Baddeck: privately printed.
Bagnell, Kenneth. 1974. "Tom Kent's Real Work is Fighting Defeatism." *Financial Post*, February 23, 7.
- 1982. "In Closing." *The Review* 4 (3): 30–1.
- 1988. "A Cape Breton Contribution to Literature in Canada." *Update Cape Breton*, July 10–11.
Balawyder, Margurite Martha. 1973. "The Influence of Interest Groups on the Settlement of the Trawlermen's Strike in Petit de Grat in 1970." MA thesis, St. Francis Xavier University.

Balcom, B. A. 1984. *The Cod Fishery of Isle Royale, 1713–58*. Studies in Archaeology, Architecture, and History. Ottawa: Parks Canada, National Historic Parks and Sites Branch.

Bannon, R. V. 1937. *Eastland Echoes*. Toronto: Macmillan.

Barber, Katherine. 2007a. "Canadian English: A Real Mouthful." *Tabaret Magazine*, March 3.

– 2007b. *Only in Canada, You Say: A Treasury of Canadian Language*. Don Mills, ON: Oxford University Press.

Barkhouse, Joyce, and Henry Van der Linde. 1990. *Pit Pony*. Toronto: Gage.

Barlow, Maude, and Elizabeth May. 2000. *Frederick Street: Life and Death on Canada's Love Canal*. Toronto: HarperCollins.

Barrett, Harold. 2000. *August Prelude: Essays and Reflections*. Sydney, NS: University College of Cape Breton Press.

Barrie, Glenn David. 1970. *The Tragic Hero*. North Sydney, NS: G. D. Barrie.

Barrington, Bey. 1930. *The Lady Rosemary Ann: A Romance*. Sydney, NS: Don Mackinnon.

Barss, Peter, and Joleen Gordon. 1980. *Older Ways: Traditional Nova Scotian Craftsmen*. Toronto: Van Nostrand Reinhold.

Bartels, Dennis A., and Olaf Janzen. 1990. "Micmac Migration to Western Newfoundland." *Canadian Journal of Native Studies* 10 (1): 71–96.

Bartlett, George. 2005. "Mystery Guest: The Man in Black." *The Cape Bretoner*, 13 (5), 16–17.

Bartlett, Richard H. 1986. *Indian Reserves in the Atlantic Provinces of Canada, Studies in Aboriginal Rights*. Saskatoon: University of Saskatchewan Native Law Centre.

Bartlett, Ted. 1998. *A Century of Service: The Newfoundland Ferry Story*. S.l.: Marine Atlantic.

Bate, Edgar. 1958. *History of Modern Louisbourg, 1758–1958*. [Louisbourg, NS]: Publication Committee of the Louisbourg Branch of the Women's Institute of Nova Scotia.

Battiste, Marie Ann. 1983. "An Historical Investigation of the Social and Cultural Consequences of Micmac Literacy." EdD diss., Stanford University.

– 1988. "Different Worlds of Work: The Mi'kmaq Experience." In *Work, Ethnicity and Oral History*, edited by Dorothy E. Moore and James H. Morrison, 63–70. Halifax: Saint Mary's University.

Battiste, Marie Ann, and Jim Watson. 1989. "A Conversation on Cape Breton Minority Cultures: Fighting to Stay Alive." *New Maritimes*, July/August 16–19.

Bauer, Marie. 1995. *Cape Breton's True Paranormal Mysteries*. S.l.: s.n.

Bayfield, H. W. 1860. *The St. Lawrence Pilot: Comprising Sailing Directions for the Gulf and River*. London: Printed for the Hydrographic Office, Admiralty. http://eco.canadiana.ca/

Beaton, Elizabeth. 1980. "Sorcery Beliefs and Oral Tradition in Cheticamp, Cape Breton." MA thesis, Memorial University.

– 1988–9. "The Beaton Institute's Steel Project." *Archivaria* 27:194–8.

– 1991. "Making Steel: Understanding the Lived Experience." *Scientia Canadensis* 15 (1): 58–72.

– 1995. "An African-American Community in Cape Breton, 1901–1904." *Acadiensis* 24 (2): 65–97.

– 1996a. "Housing, People and Place: A Case Study of Whitney Pier." PhD diss., University of Manitoba.

– 1996b. "Slag Houses in a Steel City." *Material History Review* 44:45–65.

– 1999. "Thomas Cozzolino: An Introduction." In *Italian Lives: Cape Breton Memories*, edited by Sam Migliore and A. Evo DiPierro, 40–4. Sydney, NS: University College of Cape Breton Press.

Beaton Planetta, Elizabeth. 1983. "Stone Houses Built by Highland Scottish Immigrants in Cape Breton." In *Dimensions of Canadian Architecture: Society for the Study of Architecture in Canada Selected Papers 6*, edited by Shane O'Dea and Gerald L. Pocius, 1–7.

– 1984. "A Tale of Three Churches: Ethnic Architecture in Sydney, Nova Scotia." *Canadian Ethnic Studies* 16:89–110.

– 1988. "Religious Affiliation and Ethnic Identity of West Indians in Whitney Pier." *Canadian Ethnic Studies* 20:112–31.

Beaton, Josephine, comp. 1973. *Glencoe: An Historical Sketch, 100th Anniversary of St. Joseph's Parish*. S.l.: s.n. Beaton Institute, Cape Breton University, Sydney, NS: Pamphlet 1981.

Beaton, Kenneth J. 2005. "The Change I've Seen." *The Cape Bretoner*, 13 (1), 8.

Beaton, Kevin. 1978. "Alexander Munro, Early Schoolmaster." *Cape Breton's Magazine*, 20:17–21.

Beaton, Virginia, and Stephen Pedersen. 1992. *Maritime Music Greats: Fifty Years of Hits and Heartbreak*. Halifax: Nimbus.

Beautiful Cape Breton the Place to Spend a Summer Holiday: Great Resources, Great Industries, Great Field for Investment. [c1900]. Sydney, NS: Albert M. MacLeod.

Beazley, C. Raymond. 1898. *John and Sebastian Cabot: The Discovery of North America*. Burt Franklin Research and Source Works Series. New York: B. Franklin.

Bedford, Jay. 1996. "On the Risers." *The Cape Bretoner*, 4 (3), 11–12.

– 1998 "Three Dollars at the Door." *The Cape Bretoner*, 6 (1), 26.

Béjoint, Henri. 2000. *Modern Lexicography: An Introduction*. Oxford: Oxford University Press.

– 2010. *The Lexicography of English from Origins to Present*. Oxford: Oxford University Press.

Bell, Mrs. Alexander Graham. 1913. *Just an Incident: Being a Story Founded on Fact*. [A Series of Tableaux Vivants Performed by the Young Ladies' Club of Baddeck at Beinn Bhreagh]. S.l.: s.n.

Bell-Aliant. 2008–9. *Bell-Aliant: Cape Breton Phone Book*. S.l.: s.n.

Bell, B. T. A. 1899. "The Dominion Coal Company in 1898." *The Canadian Mining Review* 18 (1): 5–7. http://eco.canadiana.ca/

– 1900. "Visit to Canada of the American Institute of Mining Engineers." *The Canadian Mining Review* 19 (9): 193–200. http://eco.canadiana.ca/

– 1902. "Dominion Coal and Dominion Iron and Steel." *The Canadian Mining Review* 21 (3): 45–6. http://eco.canadiana.ca/

– ed 1894. *The Canadian Mining Review* 12 (8): 131–68. http://eco.canadiana.ca/

Belliveau, John Edward, Silver Donald Cameron, and Michael Harrington. 1991. *Iceboats to Super Ferries: An Illustrated History of Marine Atlantic*. St John's: Breakwater.

Benjamin, S. G. W. 1878. *The Atlantic Islands as Resorts of Health and Pleasure*. New York: Harper.

– 1884. "Cruising Around Cape Breton." *Century Magazine*, July 352–64.

Bennett, Margaret. 1980. "A Codroy Valley Milling Frolic." In *Folklore Studies in Honour of Herbert Halpert: A Festschrift*, edited by Kenneth S. Goldstein and Neil V.

Rosenberg, 99–110. Folklore and Language Publication Series. St. John's: Memorial University of Newfoundland.

Bentley, P. A., and E. C. Smith. 1956. "The Forests of Cape Breton in the Seventeenth and Eighteenth Centuries." *Proceedings of the Nova Scotia Institute of Science* 24 (1): 1–15.

– 1999. "To Australia, Colombia, and Cape Breton: Biagi Family Migrations." In *Italian Lives: Cape Breton Memories*, edited by Sam Migliore and A. Evo DiPierro, 289–92. Sydney, NS: University College of Cape Breton Press.

Bethune, Jocelyn. 2005. "Tarbot: Our own Little Woodstock." *The Cape Bretoner*, 13 (1), 14–17.

Biagi, Susan, and Norman Munroe. 1997. *Louisbourg: A Living History Colourguide*. Halifax: Formac.

Biddle, Richard. 1831. *A Memoir of Sebastian Cabot: With a Review of the History of Maritime Discovery: Illustrated by Documents from the Rolls, Now First Published*. London: Hurst, Chance.

Biggar, Henry Percival. 1903. *The Voyages of the Cabots and of the Corte-Reals to North America and Greenland, 1497–1503*. Paris: s.n.

Billard, Lynn, and John Giovannetti. 1999. "Early Settlement: The Giovannetti Family in Port Morien." In *Italian Lives: Cape Breton Memories*, edited by Sam Migliore and A. Evo DiPierro, 33–4. Sydney, NS: University College of Cape Breton Press.

Binkley, Marian. 1994. *Voices from Off Shore: Narratives of Risk and Danger in the Nova Scotian Deep-Sea Fishery, Social and Economic Studies*. St. John's: Institute of Social and Economic Research, Memorial University of Newfoundland.

Bird, Lilah Smith. 1975. "My Island Home." *Nova Scotia Historical Quarterly* 5 (4): 32–40.

Bird, Will R. 1949. "Nova Scotia's Highland Cape Breton." *Canadian Geographical Journal* 38 (2): 78–91.

– 1950. *This is Nova Scotia*. Toronto: Ryerson.

– 1956. *Off-Trail in Nova Scotia*. Toronto: Ryerson.

– ed. 1959a *Atlantic Anthology*. Toronto: McClelland & Stewart.

– 1959b. *These Are the Maritimes*. Toronto: Ryerson.

Bishop, Elizabeth. 1969. "Cape Breton: A Poem." In *The Complete Poems*, 75–7. New York: Farrar, Straus and Giroux.

Bishop, Joan. 1990. "Sydney, NS Steel: Public Ownership and the Welfare State, 1967–1975." In *The Island: New Perspectives on Cape Breton History 1713–1990*, edited by Kenneth Donovan, 165–86. Fredericton and Sydney: Acadiensis Press and University College of Cape Breton Press.

Bittermann, Rusty. 1987. "Middle River: The Social Structure of Agriculture in a Nineteenth-Century Cape Breton Community." MA thesis, University of New Brunswick.

– 1988. "The Hierarchy of the Soil: Land and Labour in a 19th Century Cape Breton Community." *Acadiensis* 18 (1): 33–55.

– 1990. "Economic Stratification and Agrarian Settlement: Middle River in the Early Nineteenth Century." In *The Island: New Perspectives on Cape Breton History 1713–1990*, edited by Kenneth Donovan, 71–88. Fredericton and Sydney: Acadiensis Press and University College of Cape Breton Press.

Black, Mary. 1975. "Cape Breton's Early Roads." *Nova Scotia Historical Quarterly* 5 (3): 277–95.

Blakeley, Phyllis R. 1970. *Nova Scotia's Two Remarkable Giants*. Windsor, NS: Lancelot.

Blakemore, W. 1894. "The Introduction of Endless Haulage into Cape Breton." The *Canadian Mining Review* 13 (8): 151–4. http://eco.canadiana.ca/

– 1897. "Coal Cutting by Machinery." *The Canadian Mining Review* 16 (1): 9–11. http://eco.canadiana.ca/

Bloomer, Ramona. 2000. "Memories of the Pier." *The Cape Bretoner*, 8 (1), 54–5.

Bolles, Frank. 1894. *From Blomidon to Smoky, and Other Papers*. Boston: Houghton, Mifflin.

Bond, Jess. 2001. *Oatcakes and Other Cape Breton Stories*. Belleville, ON: Epic Press.

– 2006. *Maggie*. Picton, ON: Wilkinson.

Bond, Nancy. 1988. *Another Shore*. New York: Margaret K. McElderry Books.

Boone, Laurel. 1980. "Each Man's Son: A Romance in Disguise." *Journal of Canadian Fiction* 28 (9): 147–56.

Boone, Margaret I. 1956. *Golden Jubilee 1906–1956: Our 50th Anniversary, Town of Dominion, Nova Scotia, July 29–Aug 4th, 1956*. S.l.: s.n.

Booth, Gwen Pearson. 1961. *Twilight Tales*. New York: Vantage.

Borrett, William Coates. 1945. *Down East: Another Cargo of Tales Told Under the Old Town Clock*. Halifax: Imperial.

Bouchette, Joseph. 1832. *The British Dominions in North America, or, A Topographical and Statistical Description of the Provinces of Lower and Upper Canada, New Brunswick, Nova Scotia, the Islands of Newfoundland, Prince Edward, and Cape Breton: Including Considerations on Land-Granting and Emigration to Which are Annexed Statistical Tables and Tables of Distances*. 2 vols. London: Longman, Rees, Orme, Brown, and Green.

Boudreau, Anselme, and Anselme Chiasson. 2000. *Chéticamp: Memoirs*. Moncton, NB: G. Boudreau.

Boudreau, Bernice. 2005. "Personal Stories from the Causeway." *The Cape Bretoner*, 13 (3), 14–15.

Bourinot, John George. 1892. *Historical and Descriptive Account of the Island of Cape Breton, and of its Memorials of the French Régime*. Montreal: W. F. Brown.

Bourinot, Marshall J. 1978. *St. John's Anglican Church of Isle Madame, 1828–1978*. S.l.: s.n.

Boutilier, Ted. 1962. *Our Lady of Mount Carmel Parish: Golden Jubilee 1912–1962*. S.l.: s.n.

– 1963. *The New Waterford Story, 1913–1963: A Souvenir of New Waterford's Golden Jubilee, August 4–8, 1963*. S.l.: s.n.

– 1973. *New Waterford Sixty: The Story of New Waterford, the Town, its Organizations and its People, 1913–1973*. S.l.: s.n.

– 1983. *New Waterford, Three Score & Ten: Seventy Years of Civic History*. Sydney, NS: Aim Print and Design.

– 1988. *Three Generations – New Waterford, 1913–1988*. New Waterford, NS: Town of New Waterford.

Boyle, Doris. 1967. "Comments." *Cape Breton Highlander*, October 18, 2.

Braddock, John. 1968. "The Remarkable Progress of Port Hawkesbury." *The Atlantic Advocate*, August 18–23.

Brasset, Edmund A. 1951. *A Doctor's Pilgrimage*. Philadelphia: Lippincott.

Bray, Thomas E. [1970]. *Port Morien 1720–1970: Come Home Week*. Port Morien, NS: Community Development Association.

– [1996]. *Our Cape Breton Lobster*. Port Morien: privately printed.

Brinley, Gordon. 1936. *Away to Cape Breton*. Toronto: McClelland & Stewart.

Brisbane, R. M. 1957. "Sidney Smith: From College to Cabinet." *Saturday Night*, September 28, 14–15, 47.

Britt, Eddie. 1996. *Rhymes of a Faith Tryer: The Collected Works of Eddie Britt, Sr.* Sydney, NS: Capers Aweigh.

Broadfoot, Barry. 1975. *Ten Lost Years, 1929–1939: Memories of Canadians Who Survived the Depression*. Don Mills, ON: Paper Jacks.

Brown, Andrew H. 1940. "Salty Nova Scotia: In Friendly New Scotland Gaelic Songs Still Answer the Skirling Bagpipes." *National Geographic*, May 575–624.

Brown, Cassie. 1996. *The Caribou Disaster and Other Short Stories*. St. John's: Flanker.

Brown, Douglas Arthur. 1999. *A Deadly Harvest*. Sydney, NS: Solus.

Brown, Keith G. 1994. *Cape Breton County Economic Development Authority Strategic Economic Action Plan, August 12, 1994*. S.l.: Cape Breton County Economic Development Authority.

– 1998. "Enterprise Cape Breton Corporation: Where Top Down Meets Bottom Up." In *Perspectives on Communities: A Community Economic Development Roundtable*, edited by Gertrude Anne Macintyre, 135–56. Sydney, NS: University College of Cape Breton Press.

Brown, Lesley. 2000. "Leaving." *The Cape Bretoner*, 8 (5), 23.

– 2001. "What's for Supper?" *The Cape Bretoner*, 9 (2), 10.

Brown, Richard. 1869. *A History of the Island of Cape Breton: With Some Account of the Discovery and Settlement of Canada, Nova Scotia, and Newfoundland*. London: Sampson, Low, Son, and Marston.

– 1871. *The Coal Fields and Coal Trade of the Island of Cape Breton*. London: S. Low, Marston, Low, and Searle.

– 1899. *The Coal Fields of Cape Breton*. Stellarton, NS: Maritime Mining Record Office.

– 1904. "The First Settlement of Cape Breton." *Cape Breton Illustrated* 1:11. Beaton Institute, Cape Breton University, Sydney, NS: Pamphlet 291.

Browne, Joan A. 1982. "A Comparative Study of Socio-Economic Patterns in Black Nova Scotian Communities." MA thesis, Dalhousie University.

Bruce, Harry. 1974. "The Politics of Cape Breton Cockfighting." *Maclean's*, July 74, 76.

– 1976. "Allan MacEachern: At Home with New Zealand's 'Bluenosers'." *Axiom*, December 10–13, 25.

– 1977. *Lifeline: The Story of the Atlantic Ferries and Coastal Boats*. Toronto: Macmillan.

Bruce, Marion. 1988. "Unknown Cape Breton." *Cities*, July/August 36–8.

Bruneau, Carol. 1995. *After the Angel Mill*. Dunvegan, ON: Cormorant Books.

Brunton, R., J. Overton, and J. Sacouman. 1994. "Uneven Development and Song: Culture and Development in the Maritimes." In *Canadian Music: Issues of Hegemony and Identity*, edited by Beverly Diamond and Robert Witmer, 459–89. Toronto: Canadian Scholar's Press.

Buchloh, H. D., and Robert Wilkie, eds. 1983. *Mining Photographs and Other Pictures 1948–1968*. Halifax: Press of the Nova Scotia College of Art and Design.

Buckingham, James Silk. 1843. *Canada, Nova Scotia, New Brunswick and the Other British Provinces in North America, with a Plan of National Colonization*. London: Fisher, Son.

Buker, Russell. 1984. "Poetry." In *The Cape Breton Collection*, edited by Lesley Choyce, 28–30. Porters Lake, NS: Pottersfield.

Buller, Charles, Richard Davies Hanson, Charles Franklin Head, Henry Petre. 1839. *Minutes of Evidence Taken Under the Direction of a General Commission of Enquiry for Crown*

Lands and Emigration: Appointed on the 21st June, 1838 by His Excellency the Right Honorable the Earl of Durham, High Commissioner and Governor General of Her Majesty's Colonies in North America. Quebec: J. C. Fisher and W. Kemble. http://eco.canadiana.ca/

Burnham, Harold B. 1972. "The Textile Arts." *Canadian Antiques Collector* 7 (1): 51–3.

Butler, Gary R. 1991. "The Lutin Tradition in French-Newfoundland Culture: Discourse and Belief." In *The Good People: New Fairylore Essays,* edited by Peter Narvaez, 5–21. New York: Garland.

Byers, Mary, and Margaret McBurney. 1994. *Atlantic Hearth: Early Homes and Families of Nova Scotia.* Toronto: University of Toronto Press.

Byrne, Cyril. 1977. "The Maritime Visits of Joseph-Octave Plessis, Bishop of Quebec." *Nova Scotia Historical Society* 39:22–57.

Calabrese, Hinson. 1999. "The Hobo Train and the Pluck-Me Store." *The Cape Bretoner,* 7 (4), 36.

Calder, John H. 1985. *Coal in Nova Scotia.* Halifax: Nova Scotia Department of Mines and Energy.

Calder, J. William. 1974. *All Aboard.* Antigonish, NS: Formac.

– 1975. *Uncle Angus and the Canso Causeway.* Antigonish, NS: Formac.

– 1977. *Booze and a Buck.* Antigonish, NS: Formac.

Calkin, John B. 1864. *The Geography and History of Nova Scotia with a General Outline of Geography and a Sketch of the British Possession in North America.* Halifax: A. and W. MacKinlay.

Call, Frank Oliver. 1930a. "History of Louisbourg." In *The Spell of Acadia,* edited by Frank Oliver Call, 210–43. Boston: LC Page.

– 1930b. "The Lilac Trail to Louisbourg." In *The Spell of Acadia,* edited by Frank Oliver Call, 244–317. Boston: LC Page.

Cameron, Ella Hunt. 1952. "A Study of Imperial Policy in Cape Breton, 1785–1795." MA thesis, Acadia University.

– 1957. "Imperial Policy in Cape Breton, 1784–1795." *Nova Scotia Historical Society* 31:38–63.

Cameron, Donald, ed. 1974. *Voices Down East.* Halifax: The 4th Estate.

Cameron, Silver Donald. 1976a. "Behind the Rising Sun." *Weekend Magazine,* November 29, 8–10, 14.

– 1976b. "A Tale of Two Chinas." *Weekend Magazine,* December 4, 8–11.

– 1977. *The Education of Everett Richardson: The Nova Scotia Fishermen's Strike, 1970–71.* Toronto: McClelland & Stewart.

– 1980. *Dragon Lady.* Toronto: McClelland & Stewart.

– 1981. "The People of D'Escousse." *Quest,* December 22–36.

– 1982a. *The Baitchopper.* Toronto: James Lorimer.

– 1982b. "Louisbourg, NS." *Atlantic Insight,* June 38–40.

– 1983. "Lewis of Louisbourg: A Mayor with a Mission and a Town in Transformation." *En Route,* May 38–40, 66, 68, 70.

– 1984. "Snapshot: The Third Drunk." In *The Cape Breton Collection,* edited by Lesley Choyce, 32–43. Porters Lake, NS: Pottersfield.

– 1985. "Bell and Baddeck: Cape Breton was his Summer Home and the Setting for Many of his Most Fascinating Experiments." *Canadian Geographic,* August/September 10–19.

– 1991. *Wind, Whales and Whisky: A Cape Breton Voyage.* Toronto: Macmillan.

– 1992. "Salt, Wind, and Song." *Canadian Living,* April 142–5.

– 1994. *Sterling Silver: Rants, Raves and Revelations.* Edited by Ronald Caplan. Wreck Cove, NS: Breton Books.

– 1996a. "Re-Gaeling Cape Breton." *Canadian Geographic*, January–February 62–71.

– 1996b. "The World Which Is At Us." In *The Centre of the World at the Edge of a Continent: Cultural Studies of Cape Breton*, edited by Carol Corbin and Judith A. Rolls, 213–20. Sydney, NS: University College of Cape Breton Press.

– 1998a. "Island Passages." *Imperial Oil Review*, Autumn, 2–5.

– 1998b. "Reelin' & Readin'." *Canadian Living*, May 40–3.

– 2009. "Northern and Eastern Restaurants." *Mytown.* http://www.mytown.ca.

Campbell, Angus. 1990–1. "A First Hand Account of Pioneering Life from a Highland Gael." *Clansman*, December 17, 19.

Campbell, Brian. 1995. *Tracks Across the Landscape: The S & L Commemorative History.* Sydney, NS: University College of Cape Breton Press.

Campbell, Delores. 2005. "Irish Cove: Small Community, Big History." *The Cape Bretoner*, 13 (3), 21–4.

– 2006. "Music and Machines." *The Cape Bretoner*, 13 (6), 32–4.

Campbell, Douglas F. 1997. *Banking on Coal: Perspectives on a Cape Breton Community within an International Context.* Sydney, NS: University College of Cape Breton Press.

Campbell, Dugal, and Raymond A. MacLean. 1974. *Beyond the Atlantic Roar: A Study of the Nova Scotia Scots.* Toronto: McClelland & Stewart.

Campbell, Frank. 1975. "Sail Cape Breton." *The Atlantic Advocate*, February 19–20.

Campbell, Gray. 1960. "Cape Breton Cowboy." *Family Herald*, Aug. 4, 20–3.

Campbell, John Lorne. 1936. "Scottish Gaelic in Canada." *American Speech* 11:128–36.

– 1938. "A Visit to Cape Breton." *The Scots Magazine*, October 17–27.

Campbell, John L. and Seamus Ennis. 1990. *Songs Remembered in Exile: Traditional Gaelic Songs from Nova Scotia Recorded in Cape Breton and Antigonish County in 1937, with an Account of the Causes of Hebridean Emigration, 1790–1835.* Aberdeen: Aberdeen University Press.

Campbell, Malcolm. 1913. *Cape Breton Worthies: Life Sketches of Notable Men in the Early Presbyterian Church, Eminent for Piety and Talent.* Sydney, NS: Don. Mackinnon.

Campbell, Patricia. 1991. *As Worlds Collide: Mature Students Speak Out.* Sydney, NS: Extension and Community Affairs, University College of Cape Breton.

– 1991. *No Going Back: Older Women as University Students.* Sydney, NS: University College of Cape Breton.

Campbell, Peter J. MacKenzie. 1957. *The Story of Co-operative Wholesaling in Cape Breton.* Sydney NS: Cape Breton Co-operative Services.

– 1969a. "The Struggle for Survival in Eastern Nova Scotia." *Canadian Co-operative Digest*, Summer, 25–9.

– 1969b. "Thirty Years of Service." *Canadian Co-operative Digest*, 12 (3), 11–17.

– 1977. *Among the Gaels: Being an Account of the 1974 Tour of the Highlands and Islands of Scotland by the Gaelic Society of Cape Breton.* Sydney, NS: Highlander.

– 1978. *Highland Community on the Bras d'Or.* Antigonish, NS: Casket.

Canada. 1889. *Report of the Royal Commission on the Relations of Labor and Capital in Canada: Evidence, Nova Scotia.* Ottawa: A. Senecal. http://eco.canadiana.ca/

– 1932. *Report of the Royal Commission Respecting the Coal Mines of Nova Scotia, 1932.* Halifax: Minister of Public Works and Mines.

– 1983. *Royal Commission on Forestry.* S.l.: s.n.

Canada, Department of Agriculture. 1970. *Food – à la Canadienne*. Ottawa: Department of Agriculture.

Canada, Department of Marine and Fisheries. 1910. *Lobster Fishery: Evidence Taken before Commander William Wakeham, M.D., Officer in Charge of the Gulf Fisheries Division, in Quebec and the Maritime Provinces, pursuant to Order in Council dated June 21, 1909*. Ottawa: King's Printer.

Canada, Environment Canada Parks Service. 1977. *Le Buttereau Trail*. Informational Pamphlet: 1–5.

Canada, Natural and Historic Resources Branch. [1965]. *Alexander Graham Bell Museum, Baddeck, Cape Breton Island, Nova Scotia*. [Ottawa]: Department of Northern Affairs and Natural Resources.

Canada, Parliament. 1870. *Sessional Papers of the Dominion of Canada: Volume 4, Third Session of the First Parliament 1870*. Ottawa: I. B. Taylor. http://eco.canadiana.ca/

– 1871. *Parliamentary Debates, Dominion of Canada, Fourth Session, 33 Victoriae*. Ottawa: Ottawa Times Print. & Pub. Co. http://eco.canadiana.ca/

– 1873. *Sessional Papers of the Dominion of Canada: Volume 4, First Session of the Second Parliament, Session 1873*. Ottawa: I. B. Taylor. http://eco.canadiana.ca/

– 1884. *Sessional Papers of the Dominion of Canada: Volume 5, Second Session of the Fifth Parliament, Session 1884*. Ottawa: MacLean, Roger. http://eco.canadiana.ca/

– 1885. *Sessional Papers of the Dominion of Canada: Volume 6, Third Session of the Fifth Parliament, Session 1885*. Ottawa: MacLean, Roger. http://eco.canadiana.ca/

– 1886. *Official Report of the Debates of the House of Commons of the Dominion of Canada: Fourth Session, Fifth Parliament ... Comprising the Period from the Twentieth Day of April to the Second Day of June, 1886*. Ottawa: MacLean, Roger. http://eco.canadiana.ca/

– 1891. *Sessional Papers of the Dominion of Canada: Volume 8, First Session of the Seventh Parliament, Session 1891*. Ottawa: B. Chamberlin. http://eco.canadiana.ca/

– 1892. *Sessional Papers of the Dominion of Canada: Volume 9, Second Session of the Seventh Parliament, Session 1892*. Ottawa: S. E. Dawson. http://eco.canadiana.ca/

– 1894. *Sessional Papers of the Dominion of Canada: Volume 9, Fourth Session of the Seventh Parliament, Session 1894*. Ottawa: S. E. Dawson. http://eco.canadiana.ca/

– 1899. *Sessional Papers of the Dominion of Canada: Volume 9, Fourth Session of the Eighth Parliament, Session 1899*. Ottawa: S. E. Dawson. http://eco.canadiana.ca/

– 1899. *Sessional Papers of the Dominion of Canada: Volume 11, Fourth Session of the Eighth Parliament, Session 1899*. Ottawa: S. E. Dawson. http://eco.canadiana.ca/

– 1899. *Official Report of the Debates of the House of Commons of the Dominion of Canada: Fourth Session, Eighth Parliament Comprising the Period from the Eighteenth Day of May to the Sixth Day of July Inclusive*. Ottawa: S. E. Dawson. http://eco.canadiana.ca/

– 1900. *Official Report of the Debates of the House of Commons of the Dominion of Canada: Fifth Session, Eighth Parliament Comprising the Period from the First Day of February to the Fifth Day of April Inclusive*. Ottawa: S. E. Dawson. http://eco.canadiana.ca/

The Canadian-American Gael: Clanna nan Gaidheal ri Guaillibh a Cheile. 1943–8. St. Anns, NS: The Gaelic College.

Canadian Permanent Committee on Names. 1993. *Gazetteer of Canada: Nova Scotia / Répertoire Géographique du Canada*. Ottawa: Energy, Mines, and Resources.

The Canadian Trade Review [Cape Breton Illustrated Edition]. 1900. April 13, n.p.

Candow, James E., and Carol Corbin, eds. 1997. *How Deep is the Ocean? Historical Essays on Canada's Atlantic Fishery*. Sydney, NS: University College of Cape Breton Press.

Cape Breton A Special Place. 1983. [Sydney, NS]: Cape Breton Development Corporation.

Cape Breton By The Sea. 1977. Sydney, NS: Industrial Cape Breton Board of Trade and the Girl Guides of the Industrial Area.

Cape Breton Community Fairs. 1938. [Calendar of events for a fair organized by the Cape Breton Dairymen's Society]. S.l.: s.n.

Cape Breton Connection. 1993. *Retiring to Cape Breton.* Sydney, NS: Cape Breton Connection.

Cape Breton County-Cape Breton Island. 1968. Sydney, NS: Cape Breton Tourist Association.

Cape Breton Craft News. 1990–2.

The Cape Bretoner. 1992–2006.

Cape Breton Genealogical Society Newsletter. 1983–92, 1993.

Cape Breton Highlander. 1967. October 18, 2.

Cape Breton Mirror. 1951–3.

Cape Breton, Nova Scotia. The Unspoiled Summerland of America. [Tourist Brochure]. 1928. S.l.: s.n.

Cape Breton Post [Selected Articles].

Cape Breton Times. 1983.

Cape Breton's Magazine. 1972–99. Edited by Ronald Caplan. http://www. capebretonsmagazine.com.

Caplan, Ronald, ed. 1980. *Down North: The Book of Cape Breton's Magazine.* Toronto: Doubleday.

– ed. 1988. *Cape Breton Lives: A Book from Cape Breton's Magazine.* Canada's Atlantic Folklore / Folklife Series. St. John's: Breakwater Books.

– 1989. "The Function of Narrative Obituary Verse in Northern Cape Breton, 1894–1902." MA thesis, Saint Mary's University.

– ed. 1991. *Cape Breton Book of the Night: Stories of Tenderness & Terror.* Wreck Cove, NS: Breton Books.

– ed. 1995. *Another Night: Cape Breton Stories True and Short and Tall.* Wreck Cove, NS: Breton Books.

– ed. 1996. *Cape Breton Works: More Lives from Cape Breton's Magazine.* Canada's Atlantic Folklore / Folklife Series. Wreck Cove, NS: Breton Books.

– ed. 1999a. *Cape Breton Shipwreck Stories.* Wreck Cove, NS: Breton Books.

– ed. 1999b. *The Day the Men Went to Town: 16 Stories.* Wreck Cove, NS: Breton Books.

– ed. 2005. *Views from the Steel Plant: Voices and Photographs From 100 Years of Making Steel in Cape Breton Island.* Wreck Cove, NS: Breton Books.

– ed. 2006. *Talking Cape Breton Music: Conversations with People Who Love and Make the Music.* Wreck Cove, NS: Breton Books.

Caplan, Ronald, and Rosie Aucoin Grace. 2004. *Acadian Lives in Cape Breton Island.* Wreck Cove, NS: Breton Books.

Carmichael, Isobel. 1975. "Boularderie Island." *Nova Scotia Historical Quarterly* [Special Supplement] 121–30.

Casselman, Bill. 1998. "The Joy of Lex." *Canadian Geographic*, January/February 61–4.

Cassidy, Frederic G. 1973. "Of Matters Lexicographical: The Meaning of 'Regional' in DARE." *American Speech* 48:282–9.

– 1985. "Introduction." Vol. 1 of *Dictionary of American Regional English*, edited by Frederic G. Cassidy. Cambridge, MA: Belknap Press of Harvard University Press.

Catholic Women's League. 1992. *Serving Family and Friends Cookbook*. Sydney, NS: St. Theresa's Parish.

Challoner, S. P., ed. 1895. *The Louisbourg Monument*. Sydney, NS: S. P. Challoner.

Chambers, Robert W. 1931. *War Paint and Rouge*. New York: D. Appleton.

Chard, Donald F. 1977. "Canso, 1710–1721: Focal Point of New England – Cape Breton Rivalry." *Nova Scotia Historical Society* 39:49–72.

Chard, Richard. 1980. "The Price and Profits of Accommodation: Massachusetts-Louisbourg Trade, 1713–1744." *Seafaring in Colonial Massachusetts: A Conference Held by the Colonial Society of Massachusetts*. Boston: Publications of the Colonial Society of Massachusetts 52:131–51. Rpt. 1995. In *Aspects of Louisbourg: Essays on the History of an Eighteenth-Century French Community in North America*, edited by Eric Krause, Carol Corbin, and William, O'Shea, 209–27. Sydney, NS: University College of Cape Breton Press.

Charlevoix, Pierre-François-Xavier de. 1763. *Letters to the Dutchess of Lesdiguieres: Giving an Account of a Voyage to Canada, and Travels Through That Vast Country, and Louisiana, to the Gulf of Mexico: Undertaken by Order of the Present King of France; Being a More Full and Accurate Description of Canada, and the Neighbouring Countries Than has Been Before Published*. London: Printed for R. Goadby, and sold by R. Baldwin. http://eco.canadiana.ca/

Chartrand, René. 1973. "The Independent Company of Saint-Pierre and Miquelon 1763–1793." *Military Collector & Historian* 25 (1): 32–3.

Chiasson, Anseleme. 1986. *History and Acadian Traditions of Chéticamp*. Translated by Jean Doris Le Blanc from 3rd ed. St. John's: Breakwater.

– ed. 1988. *The History of the Hooked Rugs of Cheticamp and their Artisans*. Researched by Annie-Rose Deveau. Yarmouth, NS: Lescarbot Publications.

– 1996. *The Seven-headed Beast and Other Acadian Tales From Cape Breton Island*. Translated by Rosie Aucoin Grace. Wreck Cove, NS: Breton Books.

– ed. 2006. *The Story of the Hooked Rugs of Cheticamp and their Artisans*. Revised ed. Researched by Annie-Rose Deveau. Wreck Cove, NS: Breton Books, 2006.

The Chicago Manual of Style. 2010. 16th Ed. Chicago: University of Chicago Press.

Chisholm, Archie Neil, collector. 2000. *As True as I'm Sittin' Here*. Edited by Brian Sutcliffe and Ronald Caplan with folklore motifs by Michael Taft. Wreck Cove, NS: Breton Books.

Cogswell, Henry H. 1816. *The Statutes at Large Passed in the Several General Assemblies Held in His Majesty's Province of Nova-Scotia: From the Sixth Session of the Eighth General Assembly, Which Met at Halifax, the Twenty-Eighth Day of November, in the Forty-Sixth Year of His Majesty's Reign, A.D. 1805, Being the Fifty-Fifth Session of the General Assembly, to the Fifty-Sixth Year of His Majesty's Reign, Inclusive; With an Index*. Halifax: Printed by John Howe. http://eco.canadiana.ca/

Choyce, Lesley, ed. 1984. *The Cape Breton Collection*. Porters Lake, NS: Pottersfield.

– ed. 2001. *Atlantica: Stories from the Maritimes and Newfoundland*. Fredericton: Goose Lane.

– ed. 2005. *Nova Scotia: A Traveller's Companion: Over 300 Years of Travel Writing*. East Lawrencetown, NS: Pottersfield.

Chronicle Herald. 1967. October 16, 1.

Chute, Janet. 1992. "Ceremony, Social Revitalization and Change: Micmac Leadership and the Annual Festival of St. Ann." In *Papers of the Twenty-Third Algonquian Conference*, edited by William Cowan, 45–61. Ottawa: Carleton University Press.

Clark, Andrew Hill. 1968. *Acadia: The Geography of Early Nova Scotia to 1760*. Madison, WI: University of Wisconsin Press.

– 1980. "New England's Role in the Underdevelopment of Cape Breton Island during the French Regime 1713–1758." In *Cape Breton Historical Essays*, edited by Don MacGillivray and Brian Tennyson, 1–10. Sydney, NS: College of Cape Breton Press.

Clarke, David. 1996. "Tar Ponds Complex Problem." *The Cape Bretoner*, 4 (3), 28.

Clarke, Henriette Burchill. 1934. *Little Towns*. Philadelphia: Poetry Publishers.

– 1951. *Unseen Blossoms and Other Poems*. New York: Exposition Press.

Clarke, Sandra. 2010. *Newfoundland and Labrador English*. Edinburgh: Edinburgh University Press.

– 2012. "From Ireland to Newfoundland. What's the perfect after doing?" In *New Perspectives on Irish English*, edited by Bettina Migge and Máire Ní Chiosáin, 101–30. Amsterdam / Philadelphia: John Benjamins Publishing.

Clark, Joan. 1982. *From a High Thin Wire*. Edmonton: NeWest Press.

Clark, Reg. 1997. *A Night on Kelly's Mountain*. Sydney, NS: Flint Books.

Coady, Lynn. 1994a. "Batter My Heart." *Fiddlehead* 181, 87–99.

– 1994b. "A Great Man's Passing." *Antigonish Review* 97:13–32.

– 1998. *Strange Heaven*. Fredericton: Goose Lane.

– 2000. *Play the Monster Blind: Stories*. Toronto: Doubleday.

– 2002. *Saints of Big Harbour*. Toronto: Doubleday.

– ed. 2003. *Victory Meat: New Fiction from Atlantic Canada*. Toronto: Anchor.

Coady, Moses. 1971. *The Man from Margaree: Writings and Speeches of M. M. Coady, Educator/ Reformer/Priest*. Edited by Alexander F. Laidlaw. Toronto: McClelland & Stewart.

Cockburn, Robert H. 1970. *The Novels of Hugh MacLennan*. Montreal: Harvest House.

Connor, Ralph. 1932. *The Arm of Gold*. Toronto: McClelland & Stewart.

Conrad, Margaret, Toni Ann Laidlaw, and Donna E. Smyth. 1988. *No Place Like Home: Diaries and Letters of Nova Scotia Women, 1771–1938*. Halifax: Formac.

Cook, Mathew Patrick. 1996. *The Night in the Kitchen: Collection of Music for Piano, Fiddle, Guitar, Flute, Highland and Lowland Bagpipes, and Voice*. Dominion, NS: Vanmarkin Publications.

Corbin, Carol. 1996. "Introduction: Communication, Culture, and Cape Breton Island." In *The Centre of the World at the Edge of a Continent: Cultural Studies of Cape Breton*, edited by Carol Corbin and Judith A. Rolls, 11–16. Sydney, NS: University College of Cape Breton Press.

Corbin, Carol, and Judith A. Rolls, eds. 1996. *The Centre of the World at the Edge of a Continent*. Sydney, NS: University College of Cape Breton Press.

Corbin, Carol, and Eileen Smith-Piovesan. 2001. *Sculptures from Jagged Ore: Essays about Cape Breton Women*. Sydney, NS: University College of Cape Breton Press.

Cormier, Jim. 1993. "Brothers of the Deep: Working the Perilous Black Seam in the `City Under the Sea', Cape Breton Coal Miners Discover Resilience in Numbers." *Equinox*, June 55–65.

County of Cape Breton 1979 Centennial. 1979. [Sydney, NS]: County of Cape Breton.

Cowan, Gordon. 1968. Human Rights. Cape Breton Lecture Series. 5 May. Beaton Institute, Cape Breton University, Sydney, NS: Pamphlet 1768.

Cox, Carolyn. 1938. "The Rugs of Cheticamp." *Canadian Homes and Gardens*, 15, 64, 66, 68.

Cox, Lori Vitale. 1991. "Meat Cove Revisited." *New Maritimes*, May/June 11–13.

- 1997. "Engineered Consent: The Relocation of Black Point, a Small Gaelic Fishing Community in Northern Cape Breton." MA thesis, Dalhousie University.

Coxon, June. 2004. "Faces of the Deeps." *The Cape Bretoner*, 12 (2), 46–9.

Cozzens, Frederic S. 1859. *Acadia; or, A Month with the Blue Noses*. New York: Derby & Jackson.

Crawley, Ron. 1990. "Class Conflict and the Establishment of the Sydney Steel Industry, 1899–1904." In *The Island: New Perspectives on Cape Breton History 1713–1990*, edited by Kenneth Donovan, 145–64. Fredericton: Acadiensis Press.

- 1998. "Off to Sydney: Newfoundlanders Emigrate to Industrial Cape Breton, 1890–1914." *Acadiensis* 17 (2): 27–51.

Creighton, Helen. 1957. *Bluenose Ghosts*. Toronto: McGraw Hill Ryerson.

- 1962. "Cape Breton Nicknames and Tales." In *Folklore in Action: Essays for Discussion in Honor of MacEdward Leach*, edited by Horace P. Beck, 71–6. Philadelphia: The American Folklore Society.

- 1966. *Songs and Ballads from Nova Scotia*. Toronto: Dover.

- 1968. *Bluenose Magic: Popular Beliefs and Superstitions in Nova Scotia*. Toronto: Ryerson.

- 1975. *Helen Creighton: A Life in Folklore*. Toronto: McGraw-Hill Ryerson.

- ed. 1979. *Maritime Folk Songs*. Canada's Atlantic Folklore / Folklife Series. St. John's: Breakwater.

- 1993. *A Folk Tale Journey through the Maritimes*. Edited with an introduction by Michael Taft and Ronald Caplan. Wreck Cove, NS: Breton Books.

Creighton, Helen, and Calum MacLeod. 1964. *Gaelic Songs in Nova Scotia*. Anthropological Series, No. 66. Ottawa: National Museum of Canada.

Creighton, Helen, and Ronald Labelle. 1988. *La Fleur du Rosier: Chansons Folkloriques d'Acadie*. Sydney, NS.: University College of Cape Breton Press.

Cremo, Lee. 1990. "Lee Cremo." In *Sound of the Drum: A Resource Guide*, 59–63. Brantford, ON: Woodland Cultural Center.

Crocks, Pots and What-Nots. 1973. S.l.: Women's Institute of NS.

Crook, Esperanza, and Maria Razzolini. 1999. "All Our Fathers: The North Italian Colony in Industrial Cape Breton." In *Italian Lives: Cape Breton Memories*, edited by Sam Migliore and A. Evo DiPierro, 16–23. Sydney, NS: University College of Cape Breton Press.

Crewe, Lesley. 2005. *Relative Happiness*. Halifax: Vagrant.

- 2008. *Ava Comes Home*. Halifax: Vagrant.

Cross, Michael S., ed. 1974. "A Coal Miner Testifies. Canada, *Royal Commission on the Relations of Labor and Capital in Canada, 1889 Evidence – Nova Scotia*." In *The Workingman in the Nineteenth Century*, 81–7. Toronto: Oxford University Press.

Crystal, David. 1991. *Making Sense of English Usage*. Edinburgh: Chambers.

Cumming, Peter, Heather MacLeod, and Linda Strachan. 1984. *The Story of Framboise: An Eachdraidh air Flambois*. Framboise, NS: St. Andrew's Presbyterian Church.

Currie, Michael D. n.d. "Pioneer Days in Cape Breton." *Teachdaire nan Gaidheal [Gaelic Herald]*. Beaton Institute, Cape Breton University, Sydney, NS: Pamphlet 3418.

Currie, Sheldon. 1976. "Glace Bay Miner's Museum." *Antigonish Review* 24:35–53.

- 1979. *The Glace Bay Miner's Museum*. Ste. Anne de Bellevue, QC: Deluge.

- 1988. *The Company Store: A Novel*. Ottawa: Oberon.

- 1997. *The Story So Far*. Wreck Cove, NS: Breton Books.

– 2001. "Tessie Gillis: Prophetic Storyteller." In *Sculptures from Jagged Ore: Essays about Cape Breton Women*, edited by Carol Corbin and Eileen Smith-Piovesan, 49–63. Sydney, NS: University College of Cape Breton Press.

– 2002. *Down the Coaltown Road: A Novel*. Toronto: Key Porter Books.

– 2004. *Lauchie, Liza & Rory*. Winnipeg: J. Gordon Shillingford Publishing.

Cursio, Lucia. 2001. "Stitching Conversations." In *Sculptures from Jagged Ore: Essays about Cape Breton Women*, edited by Carol Corbin and Eileen Smith-Piovesan, 195–217. Sydney, NS: University College of Cape Breton Press.

Curtis, J. Redmond. 1976. "Pit Socks and Gum Boots." *The Atlantic Advocate*, March 42–4.

Cuthbertson, Brian. 1994. *Johnny Bluenose*. Halifax: Formac.

– 1996. "Voyages to North America before John Cabot: Separating Fact from Fiction." *Collections of the Royal Nova Scotia Historical Society* 44:121–44.

– 1998. "John Cabot and his Historians: Five Hundred Years of Controversy." *Royal Nova Scotia Historical Society Journal* 1:16–35.

D'Amour, Antonio. 2000. "The Wreck of the Alice May." *The Cape Bretoner*, 8 (3), 42–3.

D'Amour, Donna. 2001. "In the Ancient Tradition: The Reading Ceilidh." *Reading Today*, June/July 6.

Danard, J. 1977. "Cape Breton's Cure for Big-City Doldrums." *Financial Post*, July 2, 29.

Danielson, Bill. 2007. *Cape Breton Weather Watching for the Naturally Curious*. Sydney, NS: Cape Breton University Press.

Davey, William. 1990. "Informal Names for Places in Cape Breton: Nicknames, Local Usage, and a Brief Comparison with Personal Nicknames." *Onomastica Canadiana* 72 (2): 69–81.

– 1993. "European Naming Patterns on Cape Breton Island: The Early Period." *Onomastica Canadiana* 75 (1): 11–26.

– 1995. "European Naming Patterns on Cape Breton Island: 1758–1820." *Onomastica Canadiana* 77 (1): 35–59.

– 1998. "Naming Patterns on Cape Breton Island: 1820–1890." *Onomastica Canadiana* 80 (1): 1–25.

Davey, William, and Richard MacKinnon. 1993. "A Plan for the Dictionary of Cape Breton English." *Papers from the Seventeenth Annual Meeting of the Atlantic Provinces Linguistic Association*. Halifax: Mount Saint Vincent University. 1–10.

– 1995. "A Report on the Dictionary of Cape Breton English." *Papers from the Nineteenth Annual Meeting of the Atlantic Provinces Linguistic Association*. Charlottetown: University of Prince Edward Island. 21–34.

– 1996. "The Use of Nicknames in Cape Breton." In *The Centre of the World at the Edge of a Continent: Cultural Studies of Cape Breton*, edited by Carol Corbin and Judith A. Rolls, 197–220. Sydney, NS: University College of Cape Breton Press.

– 2001. "Nicknaming Patterns and Traditions among Cape Breton Coal Miners." *Acadiensis* 30 (2): 71–83.

– 2002. "Atlantic Lexicon." *Proceedings of the 26th Annual Meeting of the Atlantic Provinces Linguistic Association*. St. John's: Memorial University of Newfoundland. 157–69.

– 2007. "Making a Regional Dictionary: The Defining Process." *Proceedings of the 31st Annual Meeting of the Atlantic Provinces Linguistic Association*. Fredericton: St. Thomas University and the University of New Brunswick: 2007. 3–13.

– 2010. "Dictionary of Cape Breton English: Regional Vocabulary." In *Canadian English: A Linguistic Reader*, edited by Elaine Gold and Janice McAlpine, 162–75. Occasional Papers, Number 6, Strathy Language Unit. Kingston, ON: Strathy Language Unit, Queens University.

Davidson, Shirley, and Norman MacKenzie. 1905. "The Mine Fire at Dominion No. 1 Colliery." *The Canadian Mining Review* 24 (3): 50–6. http://eco.canadiana.ca/

Davies, Gwendolyn. 1982. "William Charles M'Kinnon: Cape Breton's Sir Walter Scott." *Collections of the Royal Nova Scotia Historical Society* 41:21–46.

– 1977. "William Charles M'Kinnon." In *The Oxford Companion to Canadian Literature*, edited by Eugene Benson and William Toye, 704. Toronto: Oxford University Press.

– 1986. "Discussions on the K-Mart Bus: Teaching Maritime Literature." In *Teaching Maritime Studies*, edited by Phillip Buckner, 209–15. Fredericton: Acadiensis Press.

– 1987. "The Song Fishermen: A Regional Poetry Celebration" In *People And Place: Studies of Small Town Life in the Maritimes*, edited by Larry McCann, 137–52. Fredericton: Acadiensis Press.

Davis, A. J., ed. 1954. *Souvenir of the 50th Anniversary of the Town of Inverness, 1904–1954. Old Home Week, July 25–31*. S.l.: s.n.

Davis, Edith A. 1933. "Cape Breton Island." *Canadian Geographic Journal* 6 (3): 134–44.

Dawson, Samuel Edward. 1894. "The Voyages of the Cabots in 1497 and 1498; With an Attempt to Determine Their Landfall and to Identify Their Island of St. John." *Transactions of the Royal Society of Canada*. 1st Series, 12:51–112.

– 1896. "The Voyages of the Cabots in 1497 and 1498 – A Sequel to a Paper in the 'Transactions' of 1894." *Transactions of the Royal Society of Canada*, 2nd Series, 2:3–30.

– 1897. "The Voyages of the Cabots – Latest Phases of the Controversy." *Transactions of the Royal Society of Canada*, 2nd Series, 3:139–267.

Deacon, William Arthur. 1953. "James D. Gillis: A Man of Parts." In *The Four James*, 85–109. Toronto: Ryerson.

Deane, Charles. 1884. "The Voyages of the Cabots." In *Narrative and Critical History of America*, edited by Justin Windsor, 31–58. Boston: Houghton Mifflin.

Dembling, Jonathan. 1997. "Joe Jimmy Alec Visits the Gaelic Mod and Escapes Unscathed: The Nova Scotia Gaelic Revivals." MA thesis, Saint Mary's University.

DeMont, John. 1993. "The Gaelic Revival in Song, Dance and Language: Cape Breton is Rediscovering its Old-country Celtic Roots." *Maclean's*, December 6, 58–9, 62.

– 1994. "Fiddler on the Hoof." *Maclean's*, May 4, 62–3.

– 1995. "Manhattan, NS." *Maclean's*, August 14, 50–1.

– 1999a. "Bringing Back 'The Gaelic.'" *Maclean's*, September 13, 22–3.

– 1999b. "Cape Breton Farewell." *Maclean's*, January 31, 2000, 39.

– 2000a. "Anger from the Deeps." *Maclean's*, January 24, 16–17.

– 2000b. "Sweetness and Light on a Fiddle." *Maclean's*, March 6, 58–9.

– 2001a. "Beating the Odds." *Maclean's*, October 29, 54–6.

– 2001b. "One Last Whistle." *Maclean's*, August 6, 16–19.

Dennis, Clara. 1942. *Cape Breton Over*. Toronto: Ryerson.

Dennys, Nicholas Belfield. 1862. *An Account of the Cruise of the St. George on the North American and West Indian Station During the Years 1861–1862*. London: Saunders Olley.

Denys, Nicolas. 1908. *The Description and Natural History of the Coasts of North America (Acadia)*. Translated and edited by William Francis Ganong. Toronto: The Champlain Society.

deRoche, Constance. 1999. "Rice Salad." In *Italian Lives: Cape Breton Memories*, edited by Sam Migliore and A. Evo DiPierro, 210. Sydney, NS: University College of Cape Breton Press.

– 2001. "Women's Work in an Acadian Village." *Sculptures from Jagged Ore: Essays about Cape Breton Women*, edited by Carol Corbin and Eileen Smith-Piovesan, 161–77. Sydney, NS: University College of Cape Breton Press.

deRoche, Constance and Assunta Mascioli Mahar. 1999. "Italian Voyages." In *Italian Lives: Cape Breton Memories*, edited by Sam Migliore and A. Evo DiPierro, 313–21. Sydney, NS: University College of Cape Breton Press.

deRoche, Constance P. and John E. deRoche, eds. 1987. *"Rock in a Stream": Living with the Political Economy of Underdevelopment in Cape Breton*. St. John's: Institute of Social and Economic Research, Memorial University of Newfoundland.

deRoche, Constance and Margaret Dorazio-Migliore. 1999. "A Second Generation Italian American of Cape Breton." In *Italian Lives: Cape Breton Memories*, edited by Sam Migliore and A. Evo DiPierro, 308–12. Sydney, NS: University College of Cape Breton Press.

deRoche, John. 1987. "Class Politics of Management and Technology in Cape Breton Mines." In *"Rock in a Stream": Living with the Political Economy of Underdevelopment in Cape Breton*, edited by Constance P. deRoche, and John E. deRoche, 105–42. St. John's: Institute of Social and Economic Research, Memorial University of Newfoundland.

– 1999a. "Dominic and James Nemis of New Waterford." In *Italian Lives: Cape Breton Memories*, edited by Sam Migliore and A. Evo DiPierro, 63–7. Sydney, NS: University College of Cape Breton Press.

– 1999b. "One's Weed, Another's Salad: The Cultural Perils of Dandelions." In *Italian Lives: Cape Breton Memories*, edited by Sam Migliore and A. Evo DiPierro, 191–2. Sydney, NS: University College of Cape Breton Press.

– 1999c. "In Others' Eyes: Pit Talk About Italians." In *Italian Lives: Cape Breton Memories*, edited by Sam Migliore and A. Evo DiPierro, 71–7. Sydney, NS: University College of Cape Breton Press.

– 1999d. "Remembering the Pain of 1940." In *Italian Lives: Cape Breton Memories*, edited by Sam Migliore and A. Evo DiPierro, 98–104. Sydney, NS: University College of Cape Breton Press.

– 1999e. "Three Men of Dominion." In *Italian Lives: Cape Breton Memories*, edited by Sam Migliore and A. Evo DiPierro, 68–70. Sydney, NS: University College of Cape Breton Press.

DesBarres, A. W. [1818]. *A Description of the Island of Cape Breton, in North America; Including a Brief and Accurate Account of its Constitution, Laws and Government*. London and Sherwood: Neely & Jones.

DesBarres, J. F. W. 1795. *A Statement Submitted by Colonel DesBarres, for Consideration Respecting his Services, From the Year 1755, to the Present Time – in the Capacity of an Officer and Engineer During the War of 1756 – the Utility of his Surveys and Publications of the Coasts and Harbours of North America, Entitled The Atlantic Neptune – and his Proceedings and Conduct as Lieutenant Governor and Commander in Chief of his Majesty's Colony of Cape Breton*. London: s.n.

– 1804. *Letters to Lord **** on a Caveat Against Emigration to America with the State of the Island of Cape Breton, from the Year 1784 to the Present Year; and Suggestions for the Benefit of the British Settlements in America, Lately Published by William Smith, Esq.* London: T. Bentley.

- n.d. *Recapitulation of a Statement Submitted by Lieutenant Colonel DesBarres for Consideration* S.l.: s.n.
De Vries, Pieter J., and Georgina MacNab-de Vries. 1983. *They Farmed, Among Other Things: Three Cape Breton Case Studies*. Sydney, NS: University College of Cape Breton Press.
Dickason, Olive Patricia. 1986. "Amerindians between French and English in Nova Scotia, 1713–1763." *American Indian Culture and Research Journal* 10 (4): 31–56.
Dickason, Olive Patricia, and Linda Hoad. 1976. *Louisbourg and the Indians: A Study in Imperial Race Relations, 1713–1760*. Ottawa: National Historic Parks and Sites Branch, Parks Canada, Dept. of Indian and Northern Affairs.
Dimock, Celia C. n.d. *Children of the Sheiling*. S.l.: Lynk.
DiPierro, A. Evo. 1999a. "The Cape Breton Italian Cultural Association." In *Italian Lives: Cape Breton Memories*, edited by Sam Migliore and A. Evo DiPierro, 269–73. Sydney, NS: University College of Cape Breton Press.
- 1999b. "Halls of Fun and Fame: The Amadiaos of Cape Breton." In *Italian Lives: Cape Breton Memories*, edited by Sam Migliore and A. Evo DiPierro, 243–8. Sydney, NS: University College of Cape Breton Press.
Discover Your Own Special Place: Cape Breton. 1996. [Sydney, NS]: Cape Breton Development Corporation.
Doherty, Elizabeth Anne. 1996. "The Paradox of the Periphery: Evolution of the Cape Breton Fiddle Tradition c1928–1995." PhD diss., University of Limerick.
Dollinger, Stefan, Laurel J. Brinton, and Margery Fee. 2012. "Revising *The Dictionary of Canadianism on Historical Principles*: A Progress Report, 2006 – (April) 2012." *Dictionaries: Journal of the Dictionary Society of North America* 33:164–78.
Domanski, Don. 1975. *The Cape Breton Book of the Dead*. Toronto: House of Anansi.
- 1978. *Heaven*. Toronto: House of Anansi.
- 1982. *War in an Empty House*. Toronto: House of Anansi.
- 1986. *Hammerstroke*. Toronto: House of Anansi.
- 1991. *Wolf-Ladder*. Toronto: Coach House.
- 1994. *Stations of the Left Hand*. Toronto: Coach House.
- 1998. *Parish of the Physic Moon*. Toronto: McClelland & Stewart.
Donald, James Richardson. 1966. *The Cape Breton Coal Problem*. Ottawa: Queen's Printer.
Donaldson, Gordon. 1966. *The Scots Overseas*. London: Hale.
Doncaster, Viola. 1992. *So Tiny and Trusting and Other Poems for You*. East Bay, NS: East Bay Creations.
Donham, Parker Barss. 1981. "Baddeck: Cape Breton Charm." *Atlantic Insight*, August/ September 60.
- 2000. "Industrial Warfare, Caper Style." *Canadian Dimension*, March–April 7.
- 2001. "Sysco Plant Euthanasia Overdue." *Canadian Dimension*, March–April 7.
Donovan, Kenneth, ed. 1985a. *Cape Breton at 200: Historical Essays in Honour of the Island's Bicentennial, 1785–1985*. Sydney, NS: University College of Cape Breton.
- 1985b. "Tattered Clothes and Powdered Wigs: Case Studies of the Poor and Well-To-Do in Eighteenth-Century Louisbourg." In *Cape Breton at 200: Historical Essays in Honour of the Island's Bicentennial, 1785–1985*, edited by Kenneth Donovan, 1–20. Sydney, NS: University College of Cape Breton.
- ed. 1990a. *The Island: New Perspectives on Cape Breton History 1713–1990*. Fredericton: Acadiensis Press.

- 1990b. "'May Learning Flourish': The Beginnings of a Cultural Awakening in Cape Breton During the 1840's." In *The Island: New Perspectives on Cape Breton History 1713–1990*, edited by Kenneth Donovan, 89–112. Fredericton: Acadiensis Press.
- 1990c. "Reflections on Cape Breton Culture: An Introduction." In *The Island: New Perspectives on Cape Breton History 1713–1990*, edited by Kenneth Donovan, 1–30. Fredericton: Acadiensis Press.
- 2002. "After Midnight We Danced Until Daylight: Music, Song and Dance in Cape Breton 1713–1758." *Acadiensis* 32 (1): 3–28.

Donovan, Rita. 1990. *Dark Jewels: A Novel*. Charlottetown: Ragweed.

Donovan, Stewart L. 1994. *Cape Breton Quarry*. Wreck Cove, NS: Breton Books.
- 2005. *The Molly Poems and Highland Elegies*. Wreck Cove, NS: Breton Books.

Dorazio-Migliore, Margaret. 1999. "La Mamma: Italian Canadian Mothers of Cape Breton." In *Italian Lives: Cape Breton Memories*, edited by Sam Migliore and A. Evo DiPierro, 160–2. Sydney, NS: University College of Cape Breton Press.

Dornadic, Hal. 2001."The True Cape Bretoner." *The Cape Bretoner*, 9 (2), 63.

Doucet, Clive. 1980. *My Grandfather's Cape Breton*. Toronto: McGraw-Hill Ryerson.
- 1984. "Stan Goes to the Doctor." In *The Cape Breton Collection*, edited by Lesley Choyce, 56–61. Porters Lake, NS: Pottersfield.
- 1992. *The Priest's Boy*. Windsor, ON: Black Moss.
- 1999. *Notes from Exile: On Being Acadian*. Toronto: McClelland & Stewart.

Doucet, Clive, and Ramsay Derry. 1999. *Looking for Henry: A Poem*. Saskatoon, SK: Thistledown.

Doucet, Daniel. 1999. *Fiddles and Flowers: The Lady of Guadalupe in Cape Breton*. Sydney, NS: New View Productions.
- 2000. "Rory's Rooster." *The Cape Bretoner*, 8 (4), 47–9.
- 2001. *Codfish and Angels*. Sydney, NS: Sea-Cape.

Doucet, Daniel, and James O. Taylor. 1997. *Parables from Big Pond*. Sydney, NS: Solus.

Doucette, David. 2001. *Strong at the Broken Places: A Novel*. Halifax: Nimbus.
- 2007. *North of Smokey: A Novel*. Sydney, NS: Cape Breton University Press.

Doucette, Mary Ellen. 1958. *Notes of Ingonish and its People*. Edited by Tom Brewer. Ingonish, NS: privately printed.

Doull, John. 1945. "The First Five Attorney-Generals of Nova Scotia." *Collections of the Nova Scotia Historical Society* 26:33–48.

Dow, David Stuart. 1978. *The Cliff Hanger House*. Antigonish, NS: Formac.

Doyle, Bill. 1975. "Devco's Island in the Sun." *The Atlantic Advocate*, June 37–39.
- 2011. *Cape Breton Facts and Folklore*. Halifax: Nimbus.

Doyle, Donna. 1984. "The Feast of Christ the King." In *The Cape Breton Collection*, edited by Lesley Choyce, 63–5. Porters Lake, NS: Pottersfield.

Dubbin, Mabel Louise. 1975. *40 Years a Nurse, Thirty-Two a V.O.N.* Sydney, NS: Martin Equipment.

Ducharme, Mary Anne. 1992. *Archie Neil: From the Life and Stories of Archie Neil Chisholm of Margaree Forks, Cape Breton*. Edited by Ronald Caplan. Wreck Cove, NS: Breton Books.

Duncan, Andrew Rae. 1926. *Report on the Royal Commission Respecting the Coal Mines of the Province of Nova Scotia, 1925*. Halifax: Minister of Public Works and Mines.

Duncan, Dorothy. 1946. *Bluenose: A Portrait of Nova Scotia*. Toronto: Collins.

Dunkly, Nancy Rose. 1984. "Studies in the Scottish Gaelic Folk-Song Tradition in Canada: A Thesis." PhD diss., Harvard University.

Dunlay, Kate. 1989a. "A Cape Breton Primer, Canada's Old World Music." *Sing Out! The FolkSong Magazine*, Fall, 24–32.

– 1989b. "The Playing of Traditional Scottish Dance Music: Old and New World Styles and Practices." In *Celtic Languages and Celtic Peoples: Proceedings of the Second North American Congress of Celtic Studies*, edited by Cyril J. Byrne, Margaret Harry, and Padraig O Siadhail, 173–91. Halifax: D'Arcy McGee Chair of Irish Studies, Saint Mary's University.

– 2001. "Snapshot: The Celtic Revival in Cape Breton." Vol. 3 of *The Garland Encyclopedia Of World Music*, edited by Ellen Koskoff. New York: Garland.

Dunlay, Kate E., and David Greenberg. 1996. *Traditional Celtic Violin Music of Cape Breton: Containing Strathspeys, Reels, Jigs, etc. Transcribed From the Playing of Some Outstanding Exponents of the Traditional Style of Highland Scottish Fiddling as Cultivated in Cape Breton, Nova Scotia*. Toronto: DunGreen Music.

Dunn, Charles W. 1948. "Gaelic in Cape Breton." *An Gaidheal* 43 (12): 143–5.

– 1953. *Highland Settler: A Portrait of the Scottish Gael in Nova Scotia*. Toronto: University of Toronto Press.

– 1959. "Gaelic Proverbs in Nova Scotia." *Journal of American Folklore* 72:30–5.

Dunton, Hope, and A. J. B. Johnston. 1986. *From the Hearth: Recipes from the World of 18th-Century Louisbourg*. Sydney, NS: University College of Cape Breton Press.

Dwelly, Edward. 2001. *Faclair Gaidhlig Gu Beurla Le Dealbhan, Dwelly's Illustrated Gaelic to English Dictionary*. 12th ed.. Glasgow: Gairm.

Earle, Michael, ed. 1989. *Workers and the State in the Twentieth Century Nova Scotia*. Fredericton: Acadiensis Press; Halifax: Gorsebrook Institute for Atlantic Canada Studies.

Early Canadiana Online. 1998–2013. http://eco.canadiana.ca/

Easthouse, Katherine. 1975. *Settlers of Southside: An Historical Account*. St. George's Channel, NS: s.n.

Eber, Dorothy. 1991. *Genius at Work: Images of Alexander Graham Bell*. Halifax: Nimbus.

Edwards, Joseph Primsoll. 1893–5. "Louisbourg: An Historical Sketch, 1894." *Nova Scotia Historical Society* 9:137–96.

Elliot, Shirley B. 1970. "A Nineteenth Century Tourist in Cape Breton." *Journal of Education* 19 (4): 37–40.

Ellison, Wally. 2003. "Seacoasts of Cape Breton." *The Cape Bretoner*, 11 (3), 8–11.

– 2004. "The 'Big Ice' Will it ever leave?" *The Cape Bretoner*, 12 (2), 56–8.

– 2005a. "Eden: A Brick Maker's Paradise." *The Cape Bretoner*, 13 (3), 37–8.

– 2005b. "Hey Canada, Welcome to Cape Breton." *The Cape Bretoner*, 13 (3), 9–11, 13.

Elmsly, Robert. [1969]. *Elmsly: Diary and Historical Papers, 1855–1889*. Edited by Willard Lyman Elmsly. S.l.: s.n.

Emmerson, George S. 1972. *A Social History of Scottish Dance and Celestial Recreation*. Montreal: McGill-Queen's University Press.

Endlice, R. M. 1888. "Cape Breton Island." *The American Magazine*, January 259–76.

Erskine, John S. 1970. "Early Cultures of Nova Scotia." *Journal of Education* 19 (4): 34–6.

Ethridge, Thomas, and John Munro. 1867. "North-East Margaree Agricultural Society." *The Nova Scotian Journal of Agriculture* 1 (26): 229–30. http://eco.canadiana.ca/

Evans, Geraint Nantglyn Davies. 1969. *Uncommon Obdurate: The Several Public Careers of J. F. W. DesBarres*. Toronto: University of Toronto Press.

Evans, R. D. 1938. "Stage Coaches in Nova Scotia, 1815–1867." *Collections of the Nova Scotia Historical Society* 24:107–35.

Falk, Lillian. 1990. "Between Emphasis and Exaggeration: Verbal Emphasis in the English of Cape Breton Island." *Papers from the Annual Meeting of the Atlantic Provinces Linguistic Association.* 14:39–50.

Farnham, C[harles] H. 1886. "Cape Breton Folk." *Harper's New Monthly Magazine,* March 607–25.

Farrell, John Charles. 1953. "Explosion." *Cape Breton Mirror,* April 20–1.

Farrell, Rita Hauser. 1993. *Our Mountains and Glens: The History of River Denys, Big Brook and Lime Hill (North Side), Cape Breton, Nova Scotia.* Truro, NS: Rita Hauser Farrell.

Fauteux, Aegidius. 1929. "La Baie de Cabbarrus." *Bulletin des recherches historiques,* 35 (2): 72–4.

Ferguson, Audrey, and Nettie Johnston. 1984. *Carman Recollections: A Brief History of Carman United Church, Sydney Mines, NS.* Hantsport, NS: Lancelot.

Ferguson, Max. 1970. "At Neil's Harbour." *Maclean's,* April 66–7.

Ferguson, Wilma, Sandra Gillis, and Mary MacDougall eds. 1993. *Pride in the Past, Faith in the Future.* Pictou, NS: Advocate.

Fergusson, Charles Bruce. 1953a. "Cabot and Cape Breton Island." *Maritime Advocate & Busy East,* May 23–5.

– 1953b. "Cabot's Landfall." *Dalhousie Review* 33 (4): 257–76.

– ed. 1958. *Uniacke's Sketches and Other Papers Relating to Cape Breton Island.* The Nova Scotia Series. Halifax: Public Archives of Nova Scotia.

– 1966. "Sir James Stewart." Vol. 1 of *Dictionary of Canadian Biography.* Toronto: University of Toronto Press.

– 1969–70. "Ambrose F. Church and his County Maps." *Dalhousie Review* 49 (4): 505–16.

– 1978. "Charles Rogers Ward, Editor of the *Cape Bretonian.*" *Nova Scotia Historical Quarterly* 8 (4): 273–88.

Field, Richard Henning, and Michael S. Cross. 1985. *Spirit of Nova Scotia: Traditional Decorative Folk Art, 1780–1930.* Halifax and Toronto: Art Gallery of Nova Scotia and Dundurn.

50 Years 1906–1956: Town of Dominion, NS. 1956. Dominion, NS: s.n.

"Findings and Recommendations re Investigation into Dispute between the Men and Management of Princess and Florence Collieries." 1939. Beaton Institute, Cape Breton University, Sydney, NS: BI MG 12. 43. Crawley Collection.

Finlayson, Ann. 1988. "The Sweet Sound of Success." *Maclean's,* November 64–5.

Finlayson, R. D. 1956. *Journey to Cape Breton Island.* Whangarei, NZ: Clark & Matheson.

Finney, Sherry. 2001. "Creative by Design: Cape Breton Artisans Take Their Crafts to Market." In *Sculptures from Jagged Ore: Essays about Cape Breton Women,* edited by Carol Corbin and Eileen Smith-Piovesan, 141–60. Sydney, NS: University College of Cape Breton Press.

Firstbrook, Peter. 1997. *The Voyage of the Matthew: John Cabot and the Discovery of North America.* Toronto: McClelland & Stewart for BBC Books.

Fitzgerald, Owen. 1978. *Cape Breton: Photographs by Owen Fitzgerald.* Toronto: Oxford University Press.

– 1985. "Photography Under the Atlantic." *The Atlantic Advocate,* April 45–7.

– 1986. *Cape Breton, a Changing Scene: A Collection of Cape Breton Photographs, 1860–1935.* Sydney, NS: University College of Cape Breton Press.

Flett, J. F., and T. M. Flett. 1964. *Traditional Dancing in Scotland*. London: Routledge and Kegan Paul.

Flewwelling, R. G. 1949. "Immigration to and Emigration from Nova Scotia, 1839–1851." *Collections of the Nova Scotia Historical Society* 28:75–106.

Forristal, Linda Joyce. 1999. "The Spirit of the Highlands." *The World and I*, May 134–43.

Fortier, Mark. 1986. "Alistair MacLeod." *Books in Canada*, August/September 38–40.

Foster, Douglas B. 1985. "DesBarres the Town Planner." *Nova Scotia Historical Review* 5 (2): 29–39.

4-H Heritage Leaders Resource Manual http://www.novascotia.ca/agri/documents/4h/manuals/RGheritage.pdf

Fowke, Edith. 1969. "Labour and Industrial Protest Songs in Canada." *Journal of American Folklore* 82 (323): 34–50.

– ed. 1973. *The Penguin Book of Canadian Folk Songs*. Harmondsworth, UK: Penguin.

Frame, Elizabeth. 1892. *A List of Micmac Names of Places, Rivers, Etc., in Nova Scotia*. Cambridge, MA: J. Wilson. http://eco.canadiana.ca/

Frank, David. 1974. "Coal Masters and Coal Miners: The 1922 Strike and the Roots of Class Conflict in the Cape Breton Coal Industry." MA thesis, Dalhousie University.

– 1977a. "The Cape Breton Coal Industry and the Rise and Fall of the British Empire Steel Corporation." *Acadiensis* 7 (1): 3–34.

– 1977b. "Organizing against Unemployment." *Canadian Dimension* 12 (6): 13–14.

– 1979. "The Cape Breton Coal Miners, 1917–1926." PhD diss., Dalhousie University.

– 1980. "Report on Sydney Coal." *Canadian Dimension* 14 (4–5): 33–52.

– 1983. "The Miner's Financier: Women in the Cape Breton Coal Towns, 1917." *Atlantis* 8 (2): 137–43.

– 1985a. "Tradition and Culture in the Cape Breton Mining Community in the Early Twentieth Century." In *Cape Breton at 200: Historical Essays in Honour of the Island's Bicentennial, 1785–1985*, edited by Kenneth Donovan, 203–18. Sydney, NS: University College of Cape Breton Press.

– 1985b. "Workers in Atlantic Canada." In *Lectures in Canadian Labour and Working-Class History*, edited by W. J. C. Cherwinski and Gregory S. Kealey, 135–48. Toronto: Committee on Canadian Labour History and New Hogtown Press.

– 1986a. "Coal Wars." *Horizon Canada*, 4 (44), 1046–51.

– 1986b. "Contested Terrain: Workers' Control in the Cape Breton Coal Mines in the 1920s." In *On the Job: Confronting the Labour Process in Canada*, edited by Craig Heron and Robert Storey, 102–23. Montreal and Kingston: McGill-Queen's University Press.

– 1986c. "The Industrial Folk Song in Cape Breton." *Canadian Folklore Canadien* 8 (1–2): 21–42.

– 1987. "Company Town/Labour Town: Local Government in the Cape Breton Coal Towns, 1917–1926." In *Canadian Labour History*, edited by David Bercusson, 138–55. Toronto: Copp Clark Pittman.

– 1988. "A Note on Cape Breton Nicknames." *Journal of the Atlantic Provinces Linguistic Association* 10:54–63.

– 1990. "The Election of J. B. McLachlan: Labour Politics in Cape Breton, 1916–1935." In *The Island: New Perspectives on Cape Breton History 1713–1990*, edited by Kenneth Donovan, 187–220. Fredericton: Acadiensis Press.

– 1992. "Class Conflict in the Coal Industry: Cape Breton 1922." In *Essays in Working Class History: Selected Readings*, edited by Peter Warrian and Gregory Kealey, 161–85. Toronto: Canadian Scholar's Press.

– 1995. "The Trial of J. B. McLachlan." *Canadian Historical Association Papers 1983*. In *Labour and Working Class History in Atlantic Canada: A Reader*, edited by David Frank and Gregory Kealey, 279–97. St. John's: Memorial University, Institute for Social and Economic Research.

– 1996. "Industrial Democracy and Industrial Legality: The UMWA in Nova Scotia, 1908–1927." In *The United Mine Workers of America: A Model of Industrial Solidarity*, edited by John H. M. Laslett, 438–55. University Park, PA: Pennsylvania State University Press in Association with Pennsylvania State University Libraries.

– 1999. *J. B. McLachlan: A Biography*. Toronto: James Lorimer.

Frank, David, and John Manley. 1992. "The Sad March to the Right: J. B. McLachlan's Resignation from the Communist Party of Canada, 1936." *Labour/Le Travail* 30: 115–34.

Frank, David, and Nolan Reilly. 1979. "The Emergence of the Socialist Movement in the Maritimes, 1899–1916." In *Under-Development and Social Movements in Atlantic Canada*, edited by Robert J. Brym and R. James Sacouman, 81–106. Toronto: New Hogtown Press.

Fraser, Dawn. 1976. *Echoes From Labor's Wars: Industrial Cape Breton in the 1920s: Narrative Verse by Dawn Fraser*. Introduction by David Frank and Donald MacGillivray. Toronto: New Hogtown Press.

– 1992. *Echoes from Labor's Wars: Industrial Cape Breton in the 1920's, Echoes of World War One, Autobiography and Other Writings*. Expanded edition by David Frank and Donald MacGillivray. Wreck Cove, NS: Breton Books.

– n.d. *The Crime of Johnny Kyle and Other Stuff*. Glace Bay, NS: Eastern Publishing.

Fraser, Mary L. [1931]. *Folklore of Nova Scotia*. Toronto: Catholic Truth Society.

Fraser, James. 1948. "Boularderie: An Island Within an Island." *Canadian-American Gael*, 2:6–7.

Frenette, Yves. 1996. *The Anglo-Normans in Eastern Canada*. Translated by Carole Dolan. Ottawa: Canadian Historical Association.

Friends Forever. 1991–9, 2001, 2004.

Friesen, Gerald. 2001. "A Cape Breton Hampden." *Acadiensis* 30 (2): 160–3.

From the Highlands and the Sea. 1974. Ingonish, NS: McCurdy Printing Company.

Furlong, Pauline, ed. 2004. "Cape Breton Pork Pies." In *Times & Transcript,* edited by Pauline Furlong. http://www.canadaeast.com.

Ganong, W. F. 1928. "The Origin of the East-Canadian Place-names Gaspé, Blomidon, and Bras d'Or." *Transactions of the Royal Society of Canada*, 3rd Series, 22 (2): 249–70.

Gardner, Jo Ann. 1990. "Restoring Heritage Flowers ...The Highland Village Plant Project." *The Atlantic Advocate*, June 9–12.

Gates, R. Ruggles. 1938. "The Blood Groups and Other Features of the Micmac Indians." *Journal of the Royal Anthropological Institute of Great Britain and Ireland* 68:283–98.

Gaum, Lawrence I. 1996. *From Belarus to Cape Breton and Beyond: My Family, My Roots*. Toronto: Rainbow Recording and Publishing.

Gesner, Claribel. 1971. *Cape Breton Anthology*. Windsor, NS: Lancelot.

– 1974a. *Cape Breton Vignettes*. Windsor, NS: Lancelot.

– 1974b. "Cape Breton Heritage." *The Atlantic Advocate*, September 35.

– 1988. "Sir John Bourinot: An Illustrious Son." In *The Huguenot Heritage of Some Families of Nova Scotia*, edited by Donald Wetmore and Leone Cousins, 21–5. Kingston, NS: Falcon.

Gibson Palermo, Sharon. "Almonds and War." In *Italian Lives: Cape Breton Memories*, edited by Sam Migliore and A. Evo DiPierro, 87–9. Sydney, NS: University College of Cape Breton Press.

Gillies, D. M. 1928. *Zigzags of a Cape Breton Clergyman*. Whycocomagh, NS: s.n.

Gillies, J. A. 1892. "The Sydney and Louisbourg Coal and Railway Company: That 'Impact of Ice' Flatly Contradicted from an Official Source [in a letter to B. T. A. Bell]." *Canadian Mining & Mechanical Review* 11 (10): 173. http://eco.canadiana.ca/

Gillis, Francine. 1994. *A Rose in November: True Stories for Overcoming Adversity and Following Your Dreams*. Port Hood, NS: Daily Bread.

Gillis, James D. n.d. *A Little Sketch of My Life*. Halifax: T. C. Allen.

– n.d. *The Pie Social, A Modern Romance*. S.l.: s.n.

– 1890. *The Great Election*. Halifax NS: T. C. Allen.

– 1899. *The Cape Breton Giant*. Montreal: Printed for the author by J. Lovell.

Gillis, Rannie. 1994. *Travels in the Celtic World*. Halifax: Nimbus.

– 2000. *This is not the Mainland Either: A Bard's Tour of Cape Breton*. Halifax: Nimbus.

Gillis, Tessie. 1992. *The Promised Land: Stories of Cape Breton*. Tribute and Introduction by James O. Taylor. West Bay, NS: Medicine Label.

– 1996. *Stories From the Woman From Away*. Wreck Cove, NS: Breton Books.

– 1998. *John R. and Son and Other Stories*. With Afterword by Ronald Caplan. Wreck Cove, NS: Breton Books.

Gilpin, E., Jr. 1889. "Coal Mining in Nova Scotia." *Canadian Mining Review* 8 (6): 75–78. http://eco.canadiana.ca/

Gilson, Clive H. J. 1988. *The State of Industrial Labour Relations in Cape Breton*. Sydney, NS: Enterprise Cape Breton.

Glabay, Margaret. 1987. "Turning Idle Time into Industry." *The Atlantic Advocate*, October 37–8.

Glace Bay Gazette. Selections from 1916 to 1948.

Glencoe: An Historical Sketch. n.d. Sydney, NS: Lynk.

Gobineau, Arthur. (1861) 1993. *A Gentleman in the Outports: Gobineau and Newfoundland*. Translated and edited by Michael Wilkshire. Ottawa: Carleton University Press.

Godwin, Catherine A. 1994. *Angus McKinnon, Pioneer Settler of Northside East Bay*. Dominion, NS: C. A. Godwin.

Goin' Down the Road. [A Review]. 1970. http://www.imdb.com/title/tt0065788/.

Gold, Sara M. 1925. "A Social Worker Visits Cape Breton." *Social Welfare* 7 (11): 219–24. Rpt. "A Social Worker Visits Cape Breton, 1925." 1985. *Cape Breton's Magazine*, 38, 22–5, 47–50. Citations refer to *Social Welfare*.

Golden Gleanings: Fiftieth Anniversary of St. Joseph's Hospital, 1902–1952, and its School of Nursing, 1905–1955, Glace Bay, Nova Scotia. 1955. Sydney, NS: Lewis R. Macdonald Printer.

Gordon [of Lochinvar]. 1886–7. "Copy of Journal kept by Gordon, one of the Officers Engaged in the Siege of Louisbourg under Boscawen and Amherst, in 1758." *Nova Scotia Historical Society* 5:97–153.

Gordon, Robert. 1625. *Encouragements for Such as Shall Have Intention to Bee Under-Takers in the New Plantation of Cape Briton, Now New Galloway in America, by mee Lochinvar*. Edinburgh: John Wreittoun.

Gordon, Warren. 1985. *Cape Breton: Island of Islands*. Sydney, NS: Steel Town Publishing.

Gow, John M. 1893. *Cape Breton Illustrated: Historic, Picturesque and Descriptive*. Toronto: William Briggs.

Goya, Miren Egana. 1992. "Basque Toponymy in Canada." *Onomastica Canadiana* 74 (2): 53–74.

Graham, Glenn. 2006. *The Cape Breton Fiddle: Making and Maintaining Tradition*. Sydney, NS: Cape Breton University Press.

Grant, Elizabeth. 1952. "Handcrafts: The Story of Weaving." *Cape Breton Mirror*, January 9.

Grant, W. L. 1919–20. "Cape Breton Past and Present." *Canadian Magazine*, 54, 434–2. Beaton Institute, Cape Breton University: Pamphlet 2035.

Gray, Charles. 1968. "The Fishermen That Walk upon the Beach." *The Atlantic Advocate*, March 46–56.

Gray, Charlotte. 2006. *Reluctant Genius: Alexander Graham Bell and the Passion for Invention*. New York: Arcade.

Gray, Glen. 2005. *Da Mudder Tung: A Cape Breton Slang Dictionary*. Sydney, NS: Microtext Publishing.

Gray, Viviane. 1976. "The Personal Views of Today's Micmac People." *Tawow* 5 (2): 44–6.

Great Britain, Colonial Office. 1823. *Papers Relative to the Re-annexation of the Island of Cape Breton to the Government of Nova Scotia*. London: s.n. http://eco.canadiana.ca/

– 1852. *Papers Relative to the Fisheries of British North America*. London: G. E. Eyre and W. Spottiswood. http://eco.canadiana.ca/

Grey, James T. 1987. *Handbook for the Margaree: A Guide to the Salmon Pools of the Margaree River System*. 3rd ed. Yardley, PA: J. T. Grey.

Griffiths, N. E. S., and John Reid. 1992. "New Evidence on New Scotland, 1629." *William & Mary Quarterly* 49 (3): 492–508.

Grosvenor, Edwin S., and Morgan Wesson. 1997. *Alexander Graham Bell: The Life and Times of the Man who Invented the Telephone*. New York: Harry Abrams.

Grosvenor, Lillian. 1950. "My Grandfather Bell." *New Yorker*, November 44–8.

Gunn, Christina. 1998. *Lily*. Lockeport, NS: Roseway.

Hakluyt, Richard. 1906, rpt. 1962. "The Voyage of M. Charles Leigh, and Divers Others, to Cape Briton and the Isle of Ramea, 1597." Vol. 6 in *Voyages in Eight Volumes*, 100–14. London: Dent.

Haliburton, Gordon M. 1979a. "Clement Henry MacLeod (1851–1917)." In *Clansmen of Nova Scotia*, edited by Gordon M. Haliburton, 79–81. Halifax: Petheric.

– 1979b. "Hon. Geo Henry Murray (1861–1929)." In *Clansmen of Nova Scotia*, edited by Gordon M. Haliburton, 83–7. Halifax: Petheric.

– 1980. *For their God – Education, Religion and the Scots in Nova Scotia*. Ethnic Heritage Series, Vol. 1. Halifax: [Halifax International Center].

Haliburton, Thomas Chandler. 1829. *An Historical and Statistical Account of Nova-Scotia in Two Volumes, Illustrated by a Map of the Province and Several Engravings*. Halifax, NS: Joseph Howe.

Hall, Joan Houston. 2010. "*DARE*: The View from the Letter Z." *Dictionaries: Journal of the Dictionary Society of North America* 31:98–106.

Hall, Rev. T. 1878. "The Editor on His Travels." *Newfoundland Monthly Messenger*, 5 (7), 1–2. http://eco.canadiana.ca/

Halifax Commission. 1877. *Halifax Commission, Appendix G Affidavits Produced in Support of the Case of Her Majesty's Government*. London: s.n. http://eco.canadiana.ca/

– 1877. *Halifax Commission, Appendix L United States Evidence*. London: s.n. http://eco. canadiana.ca/

– 1877. *Halifax Fisheries Commission, Appendix M Affidavits Produced on Behalf of the United States*. London: s.n. http://eco.canadiana.ca/

– 1877. *Record of the Proceedings of the Halifax Fisheries Commission*. S.l.: s.n. http://eco. canadiana.ca/

Hamilton, Pierce Stevens. 1858. *Nova-Scotia Considered as a Field for Emigration*. London: J. Weale. http://eco.canadiana.ca/

Hamilton, William B. 1981. *The Nova Scotia Traveller: A Maritimer's Guide to his Home Province*. Toronto: Macmillan.

– 1996. *Place Names of Atlantic Canada*. Toronto: University of Toronto Press.

Hamilton, William D. 1986. *The Federal Indian Day Schools of the Maritimes*. Fredericton: Micmac-Maliseet Institute, University of New Brunswick.

Hannigan, George L. n.d. *Cape Breton Island: The Switzerland of America Scenery Unsurpassed Anywhere in the World*. S.l., s.n.

Harder, Sandra. 1988. "Bed and Breakfast in a Brave New World." *New Maritimes*, August 8–10.

Harley, David. 1989. "Cheticamp Charms Tourists." *The Atlantic Advocate*, April 40–1.

– 1993. "Going Down the Road." *Leisure World*, February 21–2.

Harper, Douglas, ed. 1994. *Cape Breton 1952: The Photographic Vision of Timothy Asch*. Louisville, KY: International Visual Sociology Association, Department of Sociology, University of Kentucky; California: Ethnographics Press, Department of Anthropology, University of California.

Harris, Michael. 1986. *Justice Denied: The Law Versus Donald Marshall*. Toronto: Macmillan.

Harrisse, Henry. 1898. "The Cabots." *Transactions of the Royal Society of Canada*, 2nd Series, 4 (2): 103–6.

Hart, John Franklin. 1963. *History of Northeast Margaree*. Margaree Centre, NS: s.n.

Hartmann, R. R. K., and Gregory James. 1998. *Dictionary of Lexicography*. London and New York: Routledge.

Harvey, D. C. 1935. "Educational Activities in Cape Breton, 1758–1850." *Journal of Education* 6 (5): 518–32.

– 1941. "The Wreck of the Astraea." *Dalhousie Review* 21 (1): 7–14.

– 1951. *Report on the Board of Trustees of the Public Archives of Nova Scotia for the Year 1950*. Halifax: s.n.

– 1967. "Sir William Alexander." Vol. 1 of *Dictionary of Canadian Biography*. Toronto: University of Toronto Press.

– 1980. "Scottish Immigration to Cape Breton." In *Cape Breton Historical Essays*, edited by Don MacGillivray and Brian Tennyson, 31–40. Sydney, NS: College of Cape Breton Press, 1980.

Harvey, James. 1935. "Sydney Celebrates." *Saturday Night*, July 11, 15.

Harvey, M. 1893–5 "The Voyages and Discoveries of the Cabots." *Collections of the Nova Scotia Historical Society* 9:17–37.

Hawkins, John. 1969. *The Life & Times of Angus L*. Windsor, NS: Lancelot.

Hay, Alexander L. 1928. *Coal Mining Operations in the Sydney Coal Field*. S.l.: s.n.

Hayes, Albert Orion, and W. A. Bell. 1923. *The Southern Part of the Sydney Coal Field, Nova Scotia, Geological Series / Geological Survey of Canada*. Ottawa: F. A. Acland.

Haynes, Michael. 1999. *Hiking Trails of Cape Breton*. Fredericton: Goose Lane.

Headlum, Bruce. 1995. "The Devil Went Down to Cape Breton." *Saturday Night*, September 54–8.

Higgins, Benjamin Howard. 1994. *Cape Breton and its University College: Symbiotic Development*. Sydney, NS: University College of Cape Breton Press.

Highlander. November 1980–January 1982.

Highlander. 1974. *Cape Breton's Historical Calendar 1974*. Sydney, NS: Highlander.

Highlander. 1978. *Cape Breton's Historical Calendar 1978*. Sydney, NS: Highlander.

Highland Village Museum. 2005. Sign. Iona, NS: Highland Village Museum.

History of Louisbourg 1958–1982. n.d. Sydney, NS: City Printers.

History of Modern Louisbourg, 1758–1958. 1958. [Louisbourg, NS]: Publication Committee of the Louisbourg Branch of the Women's Institute of Nova Scotia.

Hitsman, J. MacKay and C. C. J. Bond. 1980. "Louisbourg: A Foredoomed Fortress." In *Cape Breton Historical Essays*, edited by Don MacGillivray and Brian Tennyson, 11–17. Sydney, NS: College of Cape Breton Press.

Hogeboom, Amy. 1941. *Gay Kilties of Cape Breton*. New York: E. P. Dutton.

Hogg, Elaine Ingalls. 2005. *When Canada Joined Cape Breton: Celebrating Fifty Years of the Canso Causeway*. Halifax: Nimbus.

[Holland, Samuel]. 1794. "Miscellaneous Remarks and Observations on Nova Scotia, New Brunswick and Cape Breton." *Collections of the Massachusetts Historical Society* 3:94–101.

Holland, Samuel. 1935. *Holland's Description of Cape Breton Island and Other Documents*. Compiled with Introduction by D. C. Harvey. Halifax: Board of Trustees of the Public Archives of Nova Scotia.

Holmes, Samuel MacEwan. 1953. "The Baptists of Cape Breton." MA thesis, Acadia University.

Hooper, Neil Albert. 1988. "The History of the Caledonia Amateur Athletic Club of Glace Bay, Nova Scotia." MA PE thesis, University of New Brunswick.

Hornsby, Stephen J. 1988. "Migration and Settlement: The Scots of Cape Breton." In *Geographical Perspectives on the Maritime Provinces*, edited by Douglas Day, 15–24. Halifax: Saint Mary's University.

– 1989. "Staple Trades, Subsistence Agriculture, and Nineteenth-Century Cape Breton Island." *Annals of the Association of American Geographers* 79 (3): 411–34.

– 1990. "Scottish Emigration and Settlement in Early Nineteenth-Century Cape Breton." In *The Island: New Perspectives on Cape Breton History 1713–1990*, edited by Kenneth Donovan, 49–69. Fredericton: Acadiensis Press.

– 1992. *Nineteenth-Century Cape Breton: A Historical Geography*. Montréal: McGill-Queen's University Press.

Horton, Robert Wilmot, and Francis Cockburn. 1827. *Instructions under the Direction of the Secretary of State for the Colonial Department: Communicated to Lieut. Col. Cockburn by the Rt. Hon*ble *R. W. Horton in a Letter Dated 26th January 1827, With a Letter and Appendix Addressed to the Rt. Hon*ble *R. W. Horton by Lieut. Col. Cockburn, Detailing the Execution of These Instructions*. S.l.: s.n. http://eco.canadiana.ca/

How, Douglas. 1990. "The Voice of Cape Breton." *Canadian Geographic*, April/May 60–8.

Howard, James H. 1962. "The St. Anne's Day Celebration of the Micmac Indians." *Museum News* 26 (3–4): 5–14.

Howard, Mildred, ed. 1992. *Early Cape Breton Newspapers*. S.l.: [Mildred Howard].

Huk, John. 1986. *Strangers in the Land: The Ukrainian Presence in Cape Breton.* Sydney, NS: City Printers.

Hunter, Mike. 2000. "The Winds of Change." *The Cape Bretoner,* 8 (4), 6–7.

– 2001. "Murdena Marshall, Mi'kmawi'skw: Mi'kmaw Woman." In *Sculptures from Jagged Ore: Essays about Cape Breton Women,* edited by Carol Corbin and Eileen Smith-Piovesan, 35–47. Sydney, NS: University College of Cape Breton Press.

Huntington, Eleanor. n.d. *Huntington Heritage.* Sydney, NS: privately printed.

– 1977. *Cape Breton by the Sea: Being a Collection of Some of Our Favorite People, Places and Things.* S.l.: s.n.

– [1986?]. *Looking Around.* Sydney, NS: privately printed.

Hutchison, Rosemary. 1973. "Emigration from South Uist to Cape Breton." In *Essays in Cape Breton History,* edited by Brian Tennyson, 9–24. Windsor, NS: Lancelot.

Hutt, Ann, et al. 1995. *Old Town Reunion.* Louisbourg, NS: Louisbourg Heritage Society.

Hutton, Elizabeth Ann. 1961. "The Micmac Indians of Nova Scotia to 1834." MA thesis, Dalhousie University.

Hyde, Susan Ann, and Michael S. Bird. 1995. *Hallowed Timbers: The Wooden Churches of Cape Breton.* Erin, ON: Boston Mills Press.

Ile Madame. [1973]. Arichat: privately printed.

Industrial Cape Breton Clubs and Organizations. 1979. Sydney, NS: Cape Breton Regional Library.

Innis, Harold A. 1954. *The Cod Fisheries: The History of an International Economy.* Rev. ed,. Toronto: University of Toronto Press.

Inshe, George Pratt. 1922. *Scottish Colonial Schemes 1620–1686.* Glasgow: Maclehouse, Jackson & Co.

Inverness County, Cape Breton County, Richmond County, Victoria County. n.d. Sydney, NS: Cape Breton Tourist Association.

Inverness Oran [Oran Inbhirnis] 1976–9; 1986–8; 1990–3.

The Islands of the Gulf – Cape Breton and Prince Edward. [1900]. Toronto: Canada Railway News.

Jackson, Elva E. 1971. *Cape Breton and the Jackson Kith and Kin.* Windsor, NS: Lancelot.

– 1974. *Windows on the Past: North Sydney, Nova Scotia.* Windsor, NS: Lancelot.

– 1988. "The True Story of the Legendary Granny Ross." *Nova Scotia Historical Review* 8 (1): 42–61.

– 1989. *Fivescore and More.* North Sydney, NS: Dr. Milford R. Jackson.

Jackson, Howard. 2002. *Lexicography: An Introduction.* London: Routledge.

Jenkins, H. P. 1938. *Nova Scotia at Work.* Toronto: Ryerson.

Jessome, Bill. 1999. *Maritime Mysteries and the Ghosts Who Surround Us.* Halifax: Nimbus.

Jessome, Phonse. 1994. *Murder at McDonald's: The Killers Next Door.* Halifax: Nimbus.

Jewell, Marianne. 1997. "A Visit with Mi'kmaq Fiddler Wilfred Prosper." *Am Bràighe,* Summer, 17.

Jobb, Dean. 1988. "Between Old Friends: The King v. MacLean, 1950." In *Shades of Justice: Seven Nova Scotia Murder Cases,* edited by Dean Jobb, 115–34. Halifax: Nimbus.

Joe, Rita. 1976a. "Key Qua Joo." *Tawow* 5 (2): 29.

– 1976b. "The Micmac People of Nova Scotia." *Tawow* 5 (2): 22–4.

– 1976c. "A Story." *Tawow* 5 (2): 30.

– 1978. *Poems of Rita Joe.* Halifax: Abanaki.

– 1979. "We Make Baskets." In *Nearly an Island: A Nova Scotia Anthology*, edited by Alice Hall and Sheila Brooks, 175. St John's: Breakwater.

– 1984. " Poetry." In *The Cape Breton Collection*, edited by Lesley Choyce, 67–70. Porters Lake, NS: Pottersfield.

– 1988. *Song of Eskasoni: More Poems of Rita Joe*. Charlottetown: Ragweed.

– 1991. *Lnu and Indians We're Called*. Charlottetown: Ragweed.

– 1996. *Song of Rita Joe Autobiography of a Mi'kmaq Poet*. Charlottetown: Ragweed.

– 1999. *We are the Dreamers: Recent and Early Poetry*. Wreck Cove, NS: Breton Books.

Johansen, Michael F. 1989. "Fighting a 250-year-old Fight." *Atlantic Insight*, April 54–6.

Johnson, Eleanor V. 1992. "Mi'kmaq." MA thesis, Saint Mary's University.

Johnson, Ralph. 1986. *Forests of Nova Scotia: A History*. Halifax: Nova Scotia Dept. of Lands and Forests: Four East Publications.

Johnston, A. A. 1960. *Sacred Heart Parish, Johnstown, Nova Scotia, 1860–1960, Centenary Anniversary*. S.l.: s.n.

Johnston, A. J. B. 1985. "A Vanished Era: The Petersfield Estate of J. S. McLennan, 1900–1942." In *Cape Breton at 200: Historical Essays in Honour of the Island's Bicentennial, 1785–1985*, edited by Kenneth Donovan, 85–106. Sydney, NS: University College of Cape Breton Press.

– 1989. "The Fishermen of Eighteenth-Century Cape Breton: Numbers and Origins." *Nova Scotia Historical Review* 9 (1): 62–72.

– 1990. "Into the Great War: Katharine MacLennan Goes Overseas, 1915–1919." In *The Island: New Perspectives on Cape Breton History 1713–1990*, edited by Kenneth Donovan, 129–44. Fredericton: Acadiensis Press.

– 1991. *The Summer of 1744: A Portrait of Life in 18th-Century Louisbourg*. Studies in Archaeology, Architecture and History. Ottawa: National Historic Sites, Parks Service, Environment Canada.

– 2001. *Control and Order in French Colonial Louisbourg, 1713–1758*. East Lansing, MI: Michigan State University Press.

– 2004. *Storied Shores: St. Peter's, Isle Madame, and Chapel Island in the 17th and 18th Centuries*. Sydney, NS: University College of Cape Breton Press.

Johnston, Beth. 2006. "A Mabou Musical Pedigree." *The Cape Bretoner*, 13 (6), 35–6.

Johnstone, Caroline Biscoe. 1931. *Memories*. Sydney Mines, NS: s.n.

Johnstone, Hope Hart. 1973. "The Contribution of the Scottish Teachers to Early Cape Breton Education (1802–1865)." MA thesis, Dalhousie University.

J.A.G. [Joint Action Group for Tarponds Clean-up] Vision of Promise for the Muggah Creek Watershed. 1997. Newspaper Clippings File, Ecology: Pollution, Beaton Institute, Cape Breton University, Sydney, NS.

Jones, David G. 1994. "Games and Phrases My Mother Never Taught Me." *Cape Bretoner*, 3 (1), 28.

Jones, Frank. 1981. *Trail of Blood: A Canadian Murder Odyssey*. Toronto: Seal Books.

Juricek, John T. 1968. "John Cabot's First Voyage." *Smithsonian Journal of History* 2 (4): 1–22.

Kavanagh, Afra. "Beatrice MacNeil and Her Writing Ceilidhs." In *Sculptures from Jagged Ore: Essays about Cape Breton Women*, edited by Carol Corbin and Eileen Smith-Piovesan, 89–95. Sydney, NS: University College of Cape Breton Press.

Kavanagh, Peter. 1985. "Pollution Cleanup Plan Creates Jobs, Costs Little." *Globe and Mail*, October 8, 1.

Kawi, Shirley Kiju. 1993. *Sons of Membertou*. Sydney, NS: Capers Aweigh.

Keeling, Corrine Tubetti. 1999. "Giacomo Tubetti: His Life and Times." In *Italian Lives: Cape Breton Memories*, edited by Sam Migliore and A. Evo DiPierro, 78–80. Sydney, NS: University College of Cape Breton Press.

Kelly, John. 1999. "From Miner, to Overman, to Manager." *The Cape Bretoner*, 7 (4), 36–7.

Kempt, James. 1823. "No. 16 – Extract of a Letter from Lieutenant General Sir James Kempt. G. C. B. to Earl Bathurst, K. G. Dated Halifax, 10th November 1820." *Papers Relative to the Re-Annexation of the Island of Cape Breton to the Government of Nova Scotia*. London: Parliament of Great Britain.

Kendall, A. S. 1936. "Reminiscences." *Nova Scotia Medical Bulletin* 15 (3): 180–4.

Kendall, Peter. 2005. "Just Words: A Poem about Cape Breton by a Cape Bretoner," *The Cape Bretoner*, 13 (1), 7.

Kennedy, Ida Mara. 1929. *Touring Quebec and the Maritimes*. Toronto: Armac.

Kennedy, Joanne. 1996. "'You Couldn't Do that in a Hall': The Social Institution of Tarabish." In *The Centre of the World at the Edge of a Continent: Cultural Studies of Cape Breton*, edited by Carol Corbin and Judith A. Rolls, 57–63. Sydney, NS: University College of Cape Breton Press.

Kent, Phyllida, ed. 1987. *Windrow Anthology: New Writing from Inverness County*. Inverness, NS: Inscribe.

Keough, Ron. 1983. *Cape Breton Passport*. S.l.: s.n.

– 1998. "Tarabish: Tenth Annual World Tarabish Tournament." *The Cape Bretoner*, 6 (2), 39.

– 2000. "Theatres of Old." *The Cape Bretoner*, 8 (2), 29–30.

Kernaghan, Lois K. 1981. "A Man and his Mistress: J. F. W. DesBarres and Mary Cannon." *Acadiensis* 11 (1): 23–42.

– 1985. "A Most Eccentric Genius: The Private Life of J. F. W. DesBarres." *Nova Scotia Historical Review* 5 (2): 41–59.

Kincaid, Barbara. 1964. "Scottish Immigration to Cape Breton, 1758–1838." MA thesis, Dalhousie University.

King, Conor. 2003. "Hitting the Streets." *The Cape Bretoner*, 11 (3), 18, 20.

King, Helen (Fritz). 2000. "Virgin Mother." *The Cape Bretoner*, 8 (5), 51–3.

King, Jo-Ann and W. L. Johnson. 1982. *Cape Breton Hospital and Braemore Home: A Historical Perspective*. Sydney, NS: s.n.

Kirwin, William J. 2006. "Standardization of Spelling in the Editing of the *Dictionary of Newfoundland English*." *Regional Language Studies ... Newfoundland* 19:19–25.

– 2011. "*Barachois* in Newfoundland and Labrador." *Regional Language Studies ... Newfoundland* 22:25–8.

Kitchen Karnival of Kooking. 1956. Kansas City, MO: North American Press.

Knight, John T. P. 1913. "Cape Breton Lakes." *Incidentally*. Montreal: Westmount News, 101–8.

Korson, George Gershon. 1965. *Coal Dust on the Fiddle*. Hatboro, PA: Folklore Associates.

Krause, Eric, Carol Corbin, and William O'Shea, eds. 1995. *Aspects of Louisbourg: Essays On the History of an Eighteenth-Century French Community in North America*. Sydney, NS: University College of Cape Breton Press.

Kyte, Hugh. 2000. "All on a Halloween Night." *The Cape Bretoner*, 8 (5), 64.

– 2005. "Fishing for Lobsters and Dreaming of Sunken Treasure." *The Cape Bretoner*, 13 (1), 51–2.

Labour Day Celebrations, Cape Breton Labour Council. 1953. Glace Bay, NS: Brodie.

Labour Journal. 1956–7.

Lamb, James Barrett. 1975. *The Hidden Heritage: Buried Romance at St. Ann's, N. S.* Windsor, NS: Lancelot.

– 1988. *A Place Apart: The Cape Breton Story.* Hantsport, NS: Lancelot.

La Morandière, Charles de. 2005. *The French Cod Fishery in Newfoundland from the 16th Century to the Present: Its Economic, Social and Political Significance.* Translated by Aspi Balsar. St. John's: Centre for Newfoundland Studies, Memorial University of Newfoundland.

Landau, Sidney I. 2001. *Dictionaries: The Art and Craft of Lexicography.* 2nd ed. Cambridge, UK: Cambridge University Press.

Langhout, Rosemarie. 1985. "Alternative Opportunities: The Development of Shipping at Sydney, NS Harbour 1842–1889." In *Cape Breton at 200: Historical Essays in Honour of the Island's Bicentennial, 1785–1985,* edited by Kenneth Donovan, 53–70. Sydney, NS: University College of Cape Breton Press.

Langille, Jacqueline. 1990. *Giants Angus McAskill and Anna Swan.* Tantallon, NS: Four East Publications.

Latremouille, Joann, Kathleen Flanagan, and Joan Rentoul. 1986. *Pride of Home: The Working Class Housing Tradition in Nova Scotia, 1749–1949.* Hantsport, NS: Lancelot.

Lavery, Mary, and George Lavery. 1991. *Tides and Times: Life on the Cape Breton Coast at Gabarus and Vicinity, 1713–1990.* Scarborough, ON: M. and G. Lavery.

Lawley, David. 1994. *A Nature and Hiking Guide to Cape Breton's Cabot Trail.* Halifax: Nimbus.

Leavitt, Robert M., ed. 1986. *A'tukwqnn: Micmac Stories.* Fredericton: Micmac-Maliseet Institute.

LeBlanc, Alfred. 1994. "The Reel Thin." *Equinox,* September/October 60–5.

LeBlanc, Alice B. 1988. *History of Margaree.* Cape Breton, NS: s.n.

LeBlanc, Larry. 2001. "Canada's Jimmy Rankin Steps out Solo." *Billboard* 12:119–33.

LeBlanc, U. and H. M. Tead Jr. 1952. *The Rehabilitation of a Nova Scotia Fishing Village: A Case Study (Grand Étang).* S.l.: Haverford College.

Ledrew, Bob. 1988. "Capitalizing on Popularity of Wood Heat Boosts Morale." *Atlantic Insight,* April 42.

Lee, Illa. n.d. *Cape Breton Isle.* S.l.: Normaway Handcrafts.

Legge, James H. 1970. *St. George's, Sydney, Cape Breton, N. S.: A Layman's Study: Gleanings from Historical Notes.* Sydney, NS: NS Highlander.

LeLievre, Annie Jane. 1992. *The Belle Côte Story.* S.l.: s.n.

Lenhart, John. 1969. *History Relating to Manual of Prayers, Instructions, Psalms and Hymns in Micmac Ideograms used by Micmac Indians of Eastern Canada and Newfoundland.* Sydney, NS: Lynk Printing.

– 1976. *History of Micmac Ideographic Manual.* Sydney, NS: Nova Scotia Native Communications Society.

LesCarbot, Marc. 1609. "Figvre de la Terre Nevve, Grand Rivière de Canada, et Côtes de l'Océan en la Novvelle France." *Histoire de la Nouvelle-France ...* Paris: Adrian Perier.

Let's Explore Cape Breton. [1941]. S.l.: s.n.

LeVert, Yvonne, and Warren Gordon. 1993. *Cape Breton Pictorial Cookbook.* Sydney, NS: Steel Town Publishing.

Lewis, Diane. 2000. "*Cape Breton Mirror:* Revisited." *The Cape Bretoner,* 8 (4), 21–3.

Lewis, Emma. 1980. "Grandmother's Old Fashioned Garden." *The Atlantic Advocate,* June 86–7.

Lewis, Jane. 2001. "Marion MacKinnon: The Girl from Main-a-Dieu." In *Sculptures from Jagged Ore: Essays about Cape Breton Women,* edited by Carol Corbin and Eileen Smith-Piovesan, 97–103. Sydney, NS: University College of Cape Breton Press.

Lewis, Ruth. 1980. "Why Did You Say That?" *Nova Scotia Historical Quarterly* 10 (1): 273–8.

L'Indienne and Lingan-Missing Chalice. n.d. S.l.: s.n.

Lismer, Arthur. 1945. "Killick Anchor, Cape Breton Island." [A painting] http://www.lochgallery.com.

Livingston, Neal. 1991. "Inside Outside: The Meat Cove Mystery." *New Maritimes,* May/June 18–23.

Livesay, Dorothy. 1927. "The Tenth Province: Cape Breton the Home of a Quaint and Distinctive Community." *Saturday Night,* November 11, 5.

Lockett, Edwin, ed. 1889. *Cape Breton Hand-Book and Tourist Guide.* Sydney, NS: s.n.

Lockyer, J. S. 1953. "An Appreciation of Two of Glace Bay's Pioneers." *Cape Breton Mirror,* October 2, 19. Rpt. from *The Glace Bay Daily Gazette* 19 March 1906.

Long, P. J. 2001. "Sister Rose is Missing." *The Cape Bretoner,* 9 (2), 58–61.

Longstreth, Thomas Morris. 1935. *To Nova Scotia: The Sunrise Province of Canada.* New York: Appleton-Century.

Loring, Augustus P. 1980. "The Atlantic Neptune." In *Seafaring in Colonial Massachusetts: Proceedings of the Colonial Society of Massachusetts,* 119–30. Vol. 52. Boston: Colonial Society of Massachusetts.

Lotz, Jim. 1972. *Insiders and Outsiders.* Antigonish, NS: privately printed.

– 1986. *Head, Heart and Hands: Craftspeople in Nova Scotia.* Halifax: Braemar Publishing.

– 1998. *The Lichen Factor: The Quest for Community Development in Canada.* Sydney, NS: University College of Cape Breton Press.

Lotz, Jim, and Pat Lotz. 1974. *Cape Breton Island.* Vancouver: Douglas, David & Charles.

Lotz, Jim, and Michael Robert Welton. 1997. *Father Jimmy: The Life and Times of Father Jimmy Tompkins.* Wreck Cove, NS: Breton Books.

Louisbourg High School Homecoming, July 1992. 1992. Louisbourg, NS: Louisbourg Heritage Society.

Lucas, Rex A. 1971. *Minetown, Milltown, Railtown: Life in Canadian Communities of Single Industry.* Toronto: University of Toronto Press.

Luce, John. 1812. *Narrative of a Passage from the Island of Cape Breton Across the Atlantic Ocean with Other Interesting Occurrences, in a Letter to a Friend.* London: Printed by Charles Squire for James Forsyth.

Mac., W. H. 1897. "Salmon Fishing in Cape Breton." *Outing: An Illustrated Monthly Magazine of Sport, Travel and Recreation,* July 352–4.

MacAdam, Pat. 2000a. "A. B. MacGillvray: Courtroom Legend." *The Cape Bretoner,* 8 (4), 26–7.

– 2000b. "Travels with the Chief." *The Cape Bretoner,* 8 (5), 36–7.

– 2001. "Savoy Flashback: 12¢ Matinee, and Worth Every Penny." *The Cape Bretoner,* 9 (2), 26–7.

– 2002. "MacAdam's Ribs: Family Trees." *The Cape Bretoner,* 10 (3), 52–3.

– 2005a. "God's Ambassador." *The Cape Bretoner,* 13 (2), 36–7.

– 2005b. "Grandfather of Health Care Plans Was Made for Cape Breton Miners." *The Cape Bretoner,* 13 (4), 36–7.

– 2005c. "Hub Beaudry's Islanders Were the Scourge of the Maritime Majors." *The Cape Bretoner*, 13 (1), 38–9.
– 2006a. *"Big Cy" and Other Characters: Pat MacAdam's Cape Breton*. Sydney, NS: Cape Breton University Press.
– 2006b. "A Cape Bretoner in Wolf's Clothing." *The Cape Bretoner*, 8 (3), 30–2.
– 2006c. "Glace Bay Legend Joe Smith." *The Cape Bretoner*, 13 (6), 46–7.
MacAulay, John A. 1977. "Sydney in the 1880's." In *More Essays in Cape Breton History*, edited by Robert J. Morgan, 5–11. Windsor, NS: Lancelot.
MacBean, Allister W. D. 1987. *The Inverness and Richmond Railway*. Halifax: Tennant Publishing House.
MacDonald, Alphonse, comp. 1935. *Cape Breton Songster: A Book of Favorite English and Gaelic Songs*. Sydney, NS: s.n.
MacDonald, Andy. 1976. *Bread & Molasses*. Don Mills, ON: Musson.
– 1978. *Don't Slip on the Soap*. Don Mills, ON: Musson.
– 1986. *Tell Pa I'm Dead*. Toronto: Doubleday.
– 1990. *'Tis Me Again, B'y*. St. John's: Breakwater.
– 1997. *Don't Be Funny, Daddy!* Sackville, NB: MediaNet Communications.
MacDonald, Angus J. [1980]. *From Forest and Stream*. S.l.: Loch Lomond Heritage Association.
– 1982. *Tales from the Glen*. S.l.: privately printed.
MacDonald, Ann-Marie. 1995. *The Arab's Mouth*. Winnipeg: Blizzard Publishing.
– 1997. *Fall on Your Knees*. Toronto: Vintage Canada.
MacDonald, Ann-Marie, and Bev Cooper. 1985. *Clue in the Fast Lane: A Mystery in Three Episodes*. Toronto: Playwrights Canada Press.
MacDonald, Allan the Ridge, and Effie Rankin. 2004. *As a'Bhràighe Beyond the Braes: The Gaelic Songs of Allan the Ridge MacDonald (1794–1868)*. Sydney, NS: University College of Cape Breton Press.
MacDonald, C. S. 1951. *50 Years: Fiftieth Anniversary, 1901–1951, Town of Glace Bay, Nova Scotia*. S.l.: s.n.
MacDonald, Dan. 2005. "The Godfather of Cape Breton Celtic." *The Cape Bretoner*, 13 (4), 12–15.
MacDonald, David. 1954. "A Coal Town Fights for Its Life." *Maclean's*, March 15, 24–5, 58, 60, 63.
MacDonald, Dan A. n.d. *Folklore and Folks of Cape Breton: With Family Trees*. Sydney, NS: Cameron Print.
MacDonald, Dan J. 1967. "Farewell to Coal: Into the Mines as a Child." *The Atlantic Advocate*, August 21–3.
MacDonald, Donald. 1933. *Cape North and Vicinity: Pioneer Families, History and Chronicle Including Pleasant Bay, Bay St. Lawrence, Aspy Bay, White Point, New Haven and Neil's Harbour*. S.l.: s.n.
MacDonald, Donalda. [1988]. *Echoes of the Past*. S.l.: s.n.
MacDonald, D. R. 1988. *Eyestone: Stories*. Wainscott, NY: Pushcart Press.
– 1994. "Green Grow the Rushes O." In *An Underlying Reverence: Stories of Cape Breton*, edited by James O. Taylor, 9–23. Sydney, NS: University College of Cape Breton Press.
– 2000. *Cape Breton Road*. New York: Harcourt.
– 2002. *All the Men are Sleeping: Selected Fiction*. Toronto: Doubleday.

– 2007. *Lauchlin of the Bad Heart*. Toronto: HarperCollins.

Macdonald, Frank. 1990. *Assuming I'm Right*. Inverness, NS: Cecibu.

– 1991. "Cairn Protects Resting Place of Early MacIsaac Settlers." *Clansman*, October/ November 18–19.

– 2000a. "From the Other Side: Learning to Live with Someone from Ontario." *The Cape Bretoner*, 8 (2), 15.

– 2000b. "From the Other Side: The National Dish." *The Cape Bretoner*, 8 (5), 19.

– 2005. *A Forest for Calum*. Sydney, NS: Cape Breton University Press.

– 2012. *A Possible Madness*. Sydney, NS: Cape Breton University Press.

– 2014. *Tinker and Blue*. Sydney: Cape Breton University Press.

MacDonald, G. Frederick. 1963. *North Sydney Past and Present*. North Sydney, NS: privately printed.

MacDonald, Helen, and Eleanor Anderson. 1994. *Treasured Memories and Recipes from a Coal Mining Town, Glace Bay*. Glace Bay, NS: Miners' Village Restaurant.

MacDonald, Helen C. 1953. "The Old Church at Mira Ferry." *Cape Breton Mirror*, January 5, 24.

– 1978. *A Brief History of Albert Bridge (Mira Ferry)*. S.l.: privately printed.

– 1979. *Margaret Macleod: The Story of the Cape Breton-New Zealanders*. Hantsport, NS: Lancelot.

MacDonald, Hugh. 1996. "Talent Shows in Cape Breton." In *The Centre of the World at the Edge of a Continent: Cultural Studies of Cape Breton*, edited by Carol Corbin and Judith A. Rolls, 49–50. Sydney, NS: University College of Cape Breton Press.

MacDonald, Hugh Martin. 1967. "The Vikings of Dingwall." In *Our Storied Past: The Ceilidh and Other Tales of Nova Scotia*, edited by Hugh Martin MacDonald, 89–98. Antigonish, NS: Casket.

MacDonald, J. P. 1977. *Cape Breton Island: A Few Words and Pictures*. Sydney, NS: Cape Breton Publications.

MacDonald, Janette. 1968. "The Historical & Social Development of Judique." BA thesis, St. Francis Xavier University.

MacDonald, John E. C. 1984. "Junk." In *The Cape Breton Collection*, edited by Lesley Choyce, 72–80. Porters Lake, NS: Pottersfield.

MacDonald, John Gordon. 1980. "Urban Kinship in Cape Breton: A Study of the Conjugal Family System." MA thesis, University of New Brunswick.

MacDonald, Johnny Allan. 1993–4. "How the North Uist People Came to Cape Breton." *Am Bràighe*, Winter, 8–9.

MacDonald, Ken. 1994."My Youthful Memories of Cape Breton." *The Cape Bretoner*, 3 (1), 6.

MacDonald, Kenneth James. 1995. *Port Morien: Pages from the Past*. Sydney, NS: University College of Cape Breton Press.

MacDonald, M. Elizabeth, ed. 1981. *To the Old and New Scotland*. Sydney, NS: City Printers.

MacDonald, Martha. 1988. "The Cape Breton Ceilidh." *Culture and Tradition* 12:76–85.

MacDonald, Ned. 1979. *The Broken Ground: A History of Inverness Town, 1803–1954*. S.l.: s.n.

MacDonald, Paul. 2000. "Wilfred Prosper: A Mi'kmaq Fiddler." *Fiddler Magazine, Cape Breton Edition*, 27–30.

MacDonald, Peter V. 1985. *Court Jesters*. Toronto: Methuen.

MacDonald, W. James, and Bonnie Thornhill. 1999. *In the Morning: Biographical Sketches of the Veterans of Victoria County, Cape Breton that Served in Both World Wars*. Sydney, NS: University College of Cape Breton Press.

MacDonell, Jim. 1995. "A Born Cape Bretoner." *The Cape Bretoner*, 3 (7), 5.

MacDonell, Margaret. 1982. *The Emigrant Experience: Songs of Highland Emigrants in North America*. Toronto: University of Toronto Press.

MacDonell, Margaret, and John Shaw, eds. 1981. *Luirgean Eachainn Nill. Folktales from Cape Breton [A Collection of Folktales Told by Hector Campbell]*. Trans. Margaret MacDonell and John Shaw. Stornoway, Scotland: Acair.

MacDonnell, Kevin. 1993. "Cape Bretoners in Halifax's North End." *The Cape Bretoner*, 1 (3), 6, 36.

MacDougall, John L.1910. "The County of Inverness, Cape Breton." In *Melinda Maxwell an Interesting Story of Scotland in the Olden Day*s. Inverness, NS: Inverness News.

– 1922. *History of Inverness County, Nova Scotia*. Truro, NS: News Publishing.

MacEachen, Frances. 1996. "Micmac Teacher Instills Pride in Students." *Am Bràighe*, Spring, 10.

MacEachern, George. 1987. *George MacEachern: An Autobiography: The Story of a Cape Breton Labour Radical*. Edited by David Frank and Donald MacGillivray. Sydney, NS: University College of Cape Breton Press.

MacEachern, J. Y. 2000. *Tarabish: How the Game is Played*. Sydney, NS: Sea-Cape Music.

MacEwan, Paul. 1976. *Miners and Steelworkers: Labour in Cape Breton*. Toronto: S. Stevens.

MacFarlane, Walter Scott. 1984. *Songs of the Valley*. Edited by Kay MacDonald and Pat MacFarlane. [Westville, NS: P. MacFarlane].

MacGillivray, Allister. 1979. *Song for Mira and Other Compositions by Allister MacGillivray*. Piano Arrangements by Alan Feeney. Introduction by John Allan Cameron. Sydney, NS: New Dawn Enterprises.

– 1981. *The Cape Breton Fiddler*. Sydney, NS: College of Cape Breton Press.

– 1991. *Diamonds in the Rough: 25 Years with the Men of the Deeps*. Glace Bay, NS: The Men of the Deeps Music.

– 2000. *The Men of the Deeps: The Continuing Saga*. New Waterford, NS: The Men of the Deeps Music.

– 2001. "Mae Cameron." *The Cape Bretoner*, 9 (1), 38–9.

MacGillivray, Allister, and Beverly MacGillivray. 1988. *A Cape Breton Ceilidh*. Sydney, NS: Sea-Cape Music.

MacGillivray, Allister, and John C. O'Donnell. 1985. *The Cape Breton Song Collection*. Sydney, NS: Sea-Cape Music.

– 1989. *The Nova Scotia Song Collection*. Sydney, NS: Sea-Cape Music.

MacGillivray, Beverly, Annabel MacLeod, and Marie Jaarsma. 1985. *A History of Fourchu*. Fourchu, NS: Fourchu Framboise Fire Department.

MacGillivray, Don. 1971. "Industrial Unrest in Cape Breton 1919–1925." MA thesis, University of New Brunswick.

– 1980. "Military Aid to the Civil Power: The Cape Breton Experience." In *Cape Breton Historical Essays*, edited by Don MacGillivray and Brian Tennyson, 95–109. Sydney, NS: College of Cape Breton Press.

– 1983. "Cultural Strip-Mining in Cape Breton." *New Maritimes*, September 15.

– 1993. "George MacEachern, 1904–1993." *New Maritimes*, July/August 2.

– 1993–4. "Jack London's *Sea Wolf*: Cape Breton's Gael Alex MacLean." *Am Bràighe*, Winter, 10.

– 1994a. "The MacLeans and Cape Breton Emigration." *Am Bràighe*, Autumn, 10.

– 1994b. "Sibling Rivalry – Part II of the 'Sea Wolf' MacLeans." *Am Bràighe*, Spring, 22.
– 1994c. "A Victorian Evening with Alex MacLean – the Seawolf Part III." *Am Bràighe*, Summer, 9.
– 1998a. "Alexander MacLean." Vol. 14 of *Dictionary of Canadian Biography*. Toronto: University of Toronto Press.
– 1998b. "David MacKeen." Vol. 14 of *Dictionary of Canadian Biography*. Toronto: University of Toronto Press.
MacGillivray, Don, and Brian Douglas Tennyson, eds. 1980. *Cape Breton Historical Essays*. Sydney, N.S: College of Cape Breton Press.
MacGregor, Francis. 1976. *Days that I Remember: Stories with a Scottish Accent*. Windsor, NS: Lancelot.
MacGregor, John. 1828. *Historical and Descriptive Sketches of the Maritime Colonies of British America*. London: Longman, Rees, Orme, Brown, and Green.
MacInnes, Daniel William. 1972. "What Can Be Said of Those Who Remained Behind? A Historic, Cultural and Situational Perspective of the Popular Grove Scot." MA thesis, Memorial University of Newfoundland.
MacInnes, Sheldon. 1977. "Cape Bretoners in Windsor: A Folk Society in an Urban Setting." MA thesis, Merrill Palmer Institute.
– 1996. "Stepdancing: Gach taobh dhe'n Uisge 'Both Sides of the Water'." In *The Centre of the World at the Edge of a Continent: Cultural Studies of Cape Breton*, edited by Carol Corbin and Judith A. Rolls, 111–17. Sydney, NS: University College of Cape Breton Press.
– 1997. *A Journey in Celtic Music: Cape Breton Style*. Sydney, NS: University College of Cape Breton Press.
– 2007. *Buddy MacMaster: The Judique Fiddler*. Lawrencetown Beach, NS: Pottersfield.
MacIntyre, John, and Martha Walls. 2005. *Nova Scotia Book of Everything*. Lunenburg, NS: MacIntyre Purcell Publishing.
MacIntyre, Linden. 1999. *The Long Stretch: A Novel*. Toronto: Stoddart.
– 2006. *Causeway: A Passage from Innocence*. Toronto: HarperCollins.
MacIntyre, Ronald. 1953. "The 'Pluck-Me' Store." *Cape Breton Mirror*, May 9.
MacIsaac, John Lorne. 2002. "Thanks for the Memories: Gone Skooshin'!" *The Cape Bretoner*, 10 (3), 34–5.
MacIsaac, Teresa. 2006. *A Better Life: A Portrait of Highland Women in Nova Scotia*. Sydney, NS: Cape Breton University Press.
MacIsaac, Virginia. 2003. "Joyce Rankin – A Bard in Her Own Right." *The Cape Bretoner*, 11 (1), 29–31.
– 2005a. "O s'alainn an t-aite: Fair is the Place." *The Cape Bretoner*, 13 (2), 32–5.
– 2005b."Richmond Raconteur." *The Cape Bretoner*, 13 (1), 44–6.
MacIvor, Daniel. 1990. *See Bob Run and Wild Abandon*. Toronto: Playwrights Canada Press.
– 1992. *2 Plays: Never Swim Alone and This is a Play*. Toronto: Playwrights Canada Press.
– 1999. *Marion Bridge*. Vancouver: Talonbooks.
MacKay, A. H. 1899. "Phenological Observations in Canada." *The Canadian Record of Science* 8 (2): 71–84. http://eco.canadiana.ca/
MacKay, H. B. 1966. "Those Who Go Down." *The Atlantic Advocate*, December 45–8.
MacKeen, R. D., ed. 1974. *Cruise Cape Breton*. [Sydney, NS]: Cape Breton Development Corporation.

MacKenzie, A. A. 1979. *The Irish in Cape Breton*. Antigonish, NS: Formac.

– 1985. "Cape Breton and The Western Harvest Excursions 1890–1928." In *Cape Breton at 200: Historical Essays in Honour of the Island's Bicentennial, 1785–1985*, edited by Kenneth Donovan, 71–84. Sydney, NS: University College of Cape Breton.

– 2002. *The Harvest Train: When Maritimers Worked in the Canadian West, 1890–1928*. Wreck Cove, NS: Breton Books.

– 2003. *Scottish Lights: Robust Reflections on Celtic Nova Scotia*. Wreck Cove, NS: Breton Books.

– 2005. *The Neighbours are Watching: An Extraordinary Entertainment*. Wreck Cove, NS: Breton Books.

MacKenzie, Archibald A. 1984. *The MacKenzies' History of Christmas Island Parish*. Sudbury, ON: Mackenzie Rothe.

MacKenzie, Catherine Dunlop. 1920. "The Charm of Cape Breton Island: The Most Picturesque Portion of Canada's Maritime Provinces. A Land Rich in Historic Geographical Associations, National Resources and Appeal." *National Geographic*, July 34–60.

– 1926. "Creating a New Scotland in Canada." *Travel*, 47, 16–19, 42, 44.

– 1928. *Alexander Graham Bell: The Man Who Contracted Space*. Cambridge: Riverside.

MacKenzie, James. 1970. "Out of Ga-ba-roose and after the Lobster." *Globe Magazine*, July 25, 8–9, 12.

MacKenzie, John. 1996. "East Bay, Cape Breton: People and Priests." BA thesis, St. Francis Xavier University.

MacKenzie, Kathleen Michelle. 1983. "Social Conditions in Sydney, N.S., 1900 to 1914." BA thesis, Dalhousie University.

MacKenzie, Michael. 1978. *Reflections of Yesteryear: True Stories, Old and New*. Grand Falls, NL: Robinson-Blackmore.

– 1981. *Remember the Time: True Stories, Old and New*. Christmas Island, NS: MacKenzie Books.

– 1984. *Glimpses of the Past: True Stories, Old and New*. Christmas Island, NS: MacKenzie Books.

– 1985. *Tracks Across the Maritimes: True Stories, Old and New*. Christmas Island, NS: MacKenzie Books.

– 1992. *Memories Recalled: True Stories, Old and New, From the Atlantic Provinces*. Christmas Island, NS: MacKenzie Books.

MacKenzie, Renford. 2000. "Memories from Underground." *The Cape Bretoner*, 7 (6), 24–6.

MacKenzie, Rennie. 2001. *In the Pit: A Cape Breton Coal Miner*. Wreck Cove, NS: Breton Books.

– 2003. "Bootlegging the Black Gold." *The Cape Bretoner*, 11 (5), 13–16.

– 2004. *That Bloody Cape Breton Coal: Stories of Mining Disasters in Everyday Life*. Wreck Cove, NS: Breton Books.

– 2007. *Blast! Cape Breton Coal Mine Disasters*. Wreck Cove, NS: Breton Books.

MacKinnon, Christy. 1993. *Silent Observer*. Wreck Cove, NS: Breton Books.

MacKinnon, Daniel B. 2000. "A Most Memorable Adventure." *The Cape Bretoner*, 8 (1), 52–3.

MacKinnon, Don, and Peter McGahan. 2001. "Sailor Don MacKinnon." *The Cape Bretoner*, 9 (2), 42–3.

MacKinnon, Francis Ian. 1989. "Fiddling to Fortune: The Role of Commercial Recordings Made by Cape Breton Fiddlers in the Fiddle Music Tradition of Cape Breton Island." MA thesis, Memorial University of Newfoundland.

MacKinnon, Jonathan G. 1989. *Old Sydney: Sketches of the Town and its People in Days Gone By*. Sydney, NS: Old Sydney Society.

MacKinnon, Kenneth. 1980. *Cape Breton Gaeldom in Cross-Cultural Context: The Transmission of Ethnic Language*. Hatfield, UK: Hatfield Polytechnic School of Business & Social Sciences.

MacKinnon, Richard. 1990. "Cape Breton Tradition: Public Image and Private Reality." *Forerunner*, Spring, 28–31.

– 1996a. "Cooperativism and Vernacular Architecture in Tompkinsville." In *The Centre of the World at the Edge of a Continent: Cultural Studies of Cape Breton*, edited by Carol Corbin and Judith A. Rolls, 145–62. Sydney, NS: University College of Cape Breton Press.

– 1996b. "Tompkinsville, Cape Breton Island: Cooperatavism and Vernacular Architecture." *Material History Review* 44:45–63.

– 2009. *Discovering Cape Breton Folklore*. Sydney, NS: Cape Breton University Press.

MacKinnon, Robert Alexander. 1991. "The Historical Geography of Agriculture in Nova Scotia, 1851–1951." PhD diss., University of British Columbia.

MacKinnon, Robert and Graeme Wynn. 1988. "Nova Scotian Agriculture in the 'Golden Age': A New Look." In *Geographical Perspectives on the Maritime Provinces*, edited by Douglas Day, 15–24. Halifax: Saint Mary's University.

MacKinnon, Walter. 2001. "Good and Remarkable Men." *The Cape Bretoner*, 9 (2), 14–15.

MacLean, Angus Hector. 1976. *God and the Devil at Seal Cove*. Halifax: Petheric.

MacLean, Annie Munroe. [1991]. *Only a Memory: The Story of Canoe Lake, Cape Breton*. S.l.: s.n.

MacLean, Don. 2004/05. "A Trip to the Big Lake." *The Cape Bretoner*, 12 (6), 42–5.

MacLean, George J. 1960. *In the Remembrance of the 75th Anniversary: Immaculate Conception Parish, Bridgeport, Nova Scotia, 1885–1960*. S.l.: s.n.

MacLean, M. C. 1939. "Cape Breton A Half Century Ago." *Public Affairs* 2 (4): 184–192.

MacLean, R. A. 1992. *A State of Mind: The Scots in Nova Scotia*. Hantsport, NS: Lancelot.

MacLean, Terrence D. 1985. "Historical Research at Louisbourg: A Case Study in Museum Research and Development." In *Cape Breton at 200: Historical Essays in Honour of the Island's Bicentennial, 1785–1985*, edited by Kenneth Donovan, 21–40. Sydney, NS: University College of Cape Breton.

– 1993. *Westmount, Cape Breton: An Illustrated Community History*. Sydney, NS: Westmount District 8 Community Council.

– 1996. *Asylum: A History of the Cape Breton Hospital 1906–1995*. Sydney, NS: Cape Breton Mental Health Services Charitable Foundation.

MacLean, Terry, and Judy McMaster, eds. 1992. *The Cabot Trail 1932–1992*. Sydney, NS: University College of Cape Breton Press.

MacLellan, Malcolm. 1982. *The Glen: "An Gleann's an robh mi og"*. Antigonish, NS: Casket.

– 1985. *Coady Remembered*. Antigonish, NS: St. Francis Xavier University Press.

MacLennan, Hugh. 1951. *Each Man's Son*. Toronto: Macmillan Company of Canada.

– 1951. "Cape Breton: The Legendary Island." *Saturday Night*, July 10–11, 15–16.

– 1965. "The Cabot Trail." *Maclean's*, June 5, 13–5, 22, 24.

– 1984. "*Each Man's Son*: Chapter Two." In *The Cape Breton Collection*, edited by Lesley Choyce, 82–91. Porters Lake, NS: Pottersfield.

MacLeod, Alistair. 1976. *The Lost Salt Gift of Blood*. Toronto: McClelland & Stewart.

– 1984. "The Tuning of Perfection." In *The Cape Breton Collection*, edited by Lesley Choyce, 93–120. Porters Lake, NS: Pottersfield.

– 1986. *As Birds Bring Forth the Sun and Other Stories*. Toronto: McClelland & Stewart.

– 1991–2. "Recollecting R. J. MacSween." *Antigonish Review* 87 (8): 299–305.

– 1999. *No Great Mischief*. Toronto: McClelland & Stewart.

– 2000. *Island: The Collected Stories*. Toronto: McClelland & Stewart.

MacLeod, C. I. N. 1952. "Ceol Mor: The Classical Music of the Bagpipes." *Cape Breton Mirror*, July 5, 20.

– 1974. *Stories from Nova Scotia*. Antigonish, NS: Formac.

MacLeod, David R. 1991. *A Place Called Donkin*. Donkin, NS: Donkin Elementary Parent Teacher Group.

MacLeod, Don. 2005. "Growing up on Gritton Avenue." *The Cape Bretoner*, 13 (3), 45–7.

MacLeod, Erna. 1996. "Bungalows and Barbecues." In *The Centre of the World at the Edge of a Continent: Cultural Studies of Cape Breton*, edited by Carol Corbin and Judith A. Rolls, 27–35. Sydney, NS: University College of Cape Breton Press.

MacLeod, Jea. 1924. "Lord Ochiltree's Colony." *Dalhousie Review* 4 (3): 308–16.

MacLeod, Mary K. 1985. "Whisper in the Air, Marconi: The Cape Breton Years, 1901–1945." In *Cape Breton at 200: Historical Essays in Honour of the Island's Bicentennial, 1785–1985*, edited by Kenneth Donovan, 107–26. Sydney, NS: University College of Cape Breton.

MacLeod, Mary K., and James O. St. Clair. 1992. *No Place Like Home: The Life and Times of Cape Breton Heritage Houses*. Sydney, NS: University College of Cape Breton Press.

– 1994. *Pride of Place: The Life and Times of Heritage Homes in Cape Breton*. Sydney, NS: University College of Cape Breton Press.

MacKley, M. Florence. 1967. *Handweaving in Cape Breton*. Sydney, NS: privately printed.

MacMechan, Archibald. 1924. "Tonge at Petit de Grat." In *Old Province Tales*, 123–40. Toronto: McClelland & Stewart.

MacMillan, Carrie, and L. D. McCann. 1992. *The Sea and Culture of Atlantic Canada: A Multidisciplinary Sampler*. Sackville, NB: Centre for Canadian Studies, Mount Allison University

MacMillan, Carleton Lamont. 1975. *Memoirs of a Cape Breton Doctor*. Toronto: McGraw-Hill Ryerson.

MacMillan, Lofty, Emery Hyslop, and Peter McGahan. 1996. *The Boy from Port Hood: The Autobiography of John Francis "Lofty" MacMillan*. Fredericton: New Ireland Press.

MacNeil, Beatrice. 1993. *The Moonlight Skater: 9 Cape Breton Stories and the Dream*. Edited by Ron Caplan. Wreck Cove, NS: Breton Books.

– 2002. *Butterflies Dance in the Dark*. Toronto: Key Porter Books.

MacNeil, Glen B. 2001. "Go Down Below No More (a Song)." *The Cape Bretoner*, 9 (2), 22.

[MacNeil, Jack]. *History of Sydney Mines: A Centennial Project*. 1990. Sydney Mines, NS: Town of Sydney Mines.

MacNeil, James Hugh. [1940]. *History of Iona–Washabuckt Area, Victoria County*. Halifax: Vincent J. MacLean.

MacNeil, Jeannine L. 1996. "What Comes Around, Goes Around: Bingo as a Cape Breton Subculture." In *The Centre of the World at the Edge of a Continent: Cultural*

Studies of Cape Breton, edited by Carol Corbin and Judith A. Rolls, 51–6. Sydney, NS: University College of Cape Breton Press.

MacNeil, Joe Neil, and John William Shaw. 1987. *Tales Until Dawn: The World of a Cape Breton Gaelic Story-teller*. Montréal: McGill-Queen's University Press.

MacNeil, John, ed. 1992. *Capers Aweigh Magazine*. Issues 1, 2.

MacNeil, Mickey. 1993. "A Pioneer Thanksgiving." *Am Bràighe*, Summer, 12–13.

MacNeil, Neil. 1948. *The Highland Heart in Nova Scotia*. New York: Scribner's.

MacNeil, Rita with Anne Simpson. 1998. *On a Personal Note*. Toronto: Key Porter Books.

MacNeil, Roddie C., et al. 1994. *The Story of St. Columba Parish, Iona, Cape Breton*. Sydney, NS: City Printers.

MacNeil, S. R. 1979. *All Call Iona Home: 1800–1950*. Antigonish, NS: Formac.

MacNeil, T. R. 1960. *Twenty-fifth Anniversary 1935–1960: Sydney, NS Credit Union Ltd*. S.l.: s.n.

MacPhail, Margaret. 1970. *Loch Bras d'Or*. Windsor, NS: Lancelot.

– 1973. *The Girl from Loch Bras d'Or*. Windsor, NS: Lancelot.

– 1974. *The Bride of Loch Bras d'Or*. Windsor, NS: Lancelot.

MacQueen, Angus J. 1990. *Memory is My Diary Vol. I The First Thirty, 1912–1942*. Hantsport, NS: Lancelot.

MacSween, R. J. 1984. "Poetry." In *The Cape Breton Collection*, edited by Lesley Choyce, 121–4. Porters Lake, NS: Pottersfield.

Mac-Talla [Selected Articles in Translation].

Madden, W. 1892. "Mining: Coal Trade." *The Critic*, 9 (22), 16. http://eco.canadiana.ca/

Maillard, Antoine Simon Abbé. 1758. *An Account of the Customs and Manners of the Micmakis and Maricheets Savage Nations, Now Dependent on the Government of Cape-Breton from an Original French Manuscript-letter, Never Published, Written by a French Abbot, who Resided Many Years, in Quality of Missionary, Among Them to which are Annexed, Several Pieces, Relative to the Savages, to Nova-Scotia, and to North-America in General*. London: Printed for S. Hooper and A. Morley.

Mahalik, David. 1996. "Music as a Living Tradition." In *The Centre of the World at the Edge of a Continent: Cultural Studies of Cape Breton*, edited by Carol Corbin and Judith A. Rolls, 101–4. Sydney, NS: University College of Cape Breton Press.

Manley, John. 1992. "Preaching the Red Stuff: J. B. McLachlan, Communism and the Cape Breton Miners, 1922–1935." *Labour/Le Travail* 30:65–114.

Mann, Mrs. G. Frederick. 1987. *Memories of the Harbour Point, 1878–1917*. Sydney, NS: s.n.

Mann, Stella. 1968. Village Life, Gabarus, Cape Breton, WW1 – The Great War 1914–1918. Diary. Beaton Institute, Cape Breton University: Pamphlet 3529.

Mann, Stella Catherine. 1988. *School Days at Gabarus, Cape Breton, Nova Scotia, 1878–1917*. Sydney, NS: S. C. Mann.

Mannette, Joy, ed. 1992. *Elusive Justice: Beyond the Marshall Inquiry*. Halifax: Fernwood Publishing.

Marchand, Richard, ed. 1997. *Eastern Horizons: New Writing from Cape Breton*. Sydney, NS: University College of Cape Breton Press.

Marconi-MacAskill, Bella. 2003. "The Big Cheque." *The Cape Bretoner*, 11 (3), 17.

Marshall, Lindsay. 1997. *Clay Pots and Bones*. Sydney, NS: Solus.

Martell, Debbie. 2004. "Winter in the Highlands." *The Cape Bretoner*, 12 (6), 13–15.

Martell, J. S. 1942. *Immigration to and Emigration from Nova Scotia 1815–1838*. Halifax: Public Archives of Nova Scotia.

– 1980. "Early Coal Mining in Nova Scotia." In *Cape Breton Historical Essays*, edited by Don MacGillivray and Brian Tennyson, 41–53. Sydney, NS: College of Cape Breton Press.

Martijn, Charles A. 1989. "An Eastern Micmac Domain of Islands." In *Actes du Vingtième Congrès des Alogonquistes*, edited by William Cowan, 208–31. Ottawa: Carleton University Press.

Martin, Calvin. 1974. "The European Impact on the Culture of a North-Eastern Algonquian Tribe: An Ecological Interpretation." *William and Mary Quarterly* 31 (1): 3–26.

– 1975. "The Four Lives of a Micmac Copper Pot." *Ethnohistory* 22 (2): 111–33.

Martin, R. Montgomery. 1837. *History of Nova Scotia, Cape Breton, the Sable Islands, New Brunswick, Prince Edward Island, the Bermudas, Newfoundland, etc. etc.* London: Whittacker.

Masson, Dr. [s.n.] 1873–4. "The Gael in the Far West." *Transactions of the Gaelic Society of Inverness* 3–4: 26–44.

Mathieson, Robert. 1989. "Health, Disease and Medicine in a Nineteenth Century Highland Emigrant Community: A Case Study in Cape Breton Island." MA thesis, University of Guelph.

Maurer, David W. 1930. "Schoonerisms: Some Speech-Peculiarities of the North-Atlantic Fishermen." *American Speech* 5 (5): 387–95.

McArthur, R. N. 1939. "Inquiry into Conditions at Florence Colliery, Sydney Mines before his Honour Judge McArthur." Beaton Institute, Cape Breton University, Sydney, NS: MG 12. 43. Crawley Collection.

McArthur, Tom, ed. 1992. *The Oxford Companion to the English Language*. Oxford: Oxford University Press.

McCann, Larry, and Carrie MacMillan. 1992. *The Sea and Culture of Atlantic Canada: A Multidisciplinary Sampler*. Sackville, NB: Centre for Canadian Studies.

McCawley, Stuart. 1925. *Standing the Gaff! The Cape Breton Mines and Miners*. Glace Bay, NS: privately printed.

– 1929a. *A Book of Songs and "Come-all-Ye" of Cape Breton and Newfoundland*. Glace Bay, NS: Brodie.

– 1929b. *Cape Breton Humour*. S.l.: s.n.

– 1936. "Cape Breton Tales." *Sydney Post Record*, October 13, 4.

McCharles, Aeneas. 1908. *Bemocked of Destiny: The Actual Struggles and Experiences of a Canadian Pioneer, and the Recollections of a Lifetime*. Toronto: W. Briggs.

McConnell, Ruth E. 1979. *Our Own Voice: Canadian English and How it is Studied*. Toronto: Gage.

McCulloch, Ian. 2000. "Mechanic Street Memories." *The Cape Bretoner*, 8 (3), 60.

McDonald, James. 1935. *Sydney, NS's 150th Anniversary, July 29th to August 4th, 1935, July 29th to August 4th, 1935. Official Souvenir Program*. Sydney, NS: Sydney, NS's 150th Anniversary Association.

McEachern, Gordon. 2000. "Christmas on the Battlefield." *The Cape Bretoner*, 8 (6), 32–3.

McGrail, Thomas H. 1940. *Sir William Alexander, First Earl of Stirling: A Biographical Study*. Edinburgh: Oliver & Boyd.

McGuire, Stephen. 1944. "Electric Lines." *Railroad Magazine*, July 126–9.

McIntyre, John E. 1986. *Cape Toons*. Sydney, NS: J. E. McIntyre.

McIntyre, Ronald H. 1980. *The Collier's Tattletale*. Antigonish, NS: Formac.

McKay, David Wayne. 1999. *A Cast of Characters: Five Cape Breton Mon[o]logues*. Sydney, NS: University College of Cape Breton Press.

McKay, Ian. 1988. "The Crisis of Dependent Development: Class, Conflict in Nova Scotia Coalfields, 1872–1876." In *Class, Gender, and Region: Essays in Canadian Historical Sociology*, edited by Gregory S. Kealey, 9–48. St. John's: Committee on Canadian Labour History.

McKay, Ian, and Scott Milsom, eds. 1992. *Toward A New Maritimes: A Selection from Ten Years of New Maritimes*. Charlottetown: Ragweed.

McKinnon, William Charles. 1844. *The Battle of the Nile a Poem in Four Cantos*. Sydney, NS: s.n.

– 1850. *St. Castine: A Legend of Cape-Breton*, Sydney, NS: s.n.

– 1851. *Frances, or, Pirate Cove: A Legend of Cape-Breton*. Halifax: s.n.

– 1852. *St. George, or, The Canadian League*. Halifax: E. G. Fuller.

McKinnon, William Charles, Gwendolyn Davies, and Jonathan G. MacKinnon. 2002. *The Midnight Murder: A Novel From Early Cape Breton*. Wreck Cove, NS: Breton Books.

McLeod, David A., and Ronald Caplan. 1992. *Cape Breton Captain: Reminiscences from 50 Years Afloat & Ashore*. Wreck Cove, NS: Breton Books.

McLeod, Joseph. 1977. *Cleaning the Bones*. Erin, ON; Don Mills, ON: Press Porcepic; distributed by Musson Book Co.

McLeod, Dr. William McK. n.d. *Memoirs of Dr. William McK. MacLeod, Sydney, Nova Scotia*. S.l. s.n.

McMahon, Wendy. 2004. "Baffle'em with Gaffle." *The Cape Bretoner*, 12 (3), 39.

McMillan, Donald. 1905. *History of Presbyterianism in Cape Breton: With Brief Memorial Sketches of the Lives of Rev. Hugh McLeod, D. D., Rev. Matthew Wilson, Rev. Alexander Farquharson and Other Pioneer Ministers of Cape Breton*. Inverness, NS: Inverness News.

McMillan, Leslie Jane. 1996. "Mi'kmawey Mawio'mi Changing Roles of the Mi'kmaq Grand Council from the Early Seventeenth Century to the Present." MA thesis, Dalhousie University.

McMullin, Allan. 1939. Letter to Mary Arnold. Radcliffe College Archives, Boston, MA. A 122–7. Arnold, Mary. E. Collection.

McNabb, Debra, Lewis Parker, and Old Sydney Society. 1986. *Old Sydney Town: Historic Buildings of the North End, 1785–1938*. Sydney, NS: Old Sydney Society.

McNeil, Bill. 1978. *Voice of the Pioneer*. Toronto: Macmillan of Canada.

– 1988. *Bill McNeil Presents Voice of the Pioneer*. Toronto: Doubleday Canada.

McNeil, Ian. 2010. *Pit Talk: The Legacy of Cape Breton's Coal Miners*. [Sydney, NS]: ICON Communication and Research.

McNeil, Jean. 1996. *Hunting Down Home*. London: Phoenix House.

McNeill, F. Marian. 1973. *Recipes from Scotland*. Edinburgh: Albyn.

McPherson, Flora McGregor. 1962. *Watchman Against the World: The Story of Norman McLeod and his People*. Toronto: Ryerson.

Mellor, John. 1983. *The Company Store: James Bryson McLachlan and the Cape Breton Coal Miners, 1900–1925*. Toronto: Doubleday.

Melski, Michael. 1996. *Blood on Steel*. Sydney, NS: University College of Cape Breton Press.

– 2001. *Hockey Mom, Hockey Dad: A Play in Two Acts*. Wreck Cove, NS: Breton Books.

Mertz, Elizabeth. 1982. "No Burden to Carry: Cape Breton Pragmatics and Metapragmatics." PhD diss., Duke University.

Metropolitan Alliance for Development. 1972. *Studies in the History of Cape Breton Island.* S.l.: s.n.

Micmac News. January 1965–November 1984.

Migliore, Sam, and A. Evo DiPierro, eds. 1999. *Italian Lives: Cape Breton Memories.* Sydney, NS: University College of Cape Breton Press.

Migliore, Sam. 1999a. "Alvise Casagrande: A 'Scoop' for the *Cape Breton Post.*" In *Italian Lives: Cape Breton Memories,* edited by Sam Migliore and A. Evo DiPierro, 224–7. Sydney, NS: University College of Cape Breton Press.

– 1999b. "Angela Giacomantonio: Memories of Whitney Pier." In *Italian Lives: Cape Breton Memories,* edited by Sam Migliore and A. Evo DiPierro, 23–9. Sydney, NS: University College of Cape Breton Press.

– 1999c. "Benny DeLorenzo: Work in the Steel Plant." In *Italian Lives: Cape Breton Memories,* edited by Sam Migliore and A. Evo DiPierro, 152–4. Sydney, NS: University College of Cape Breton Press.

– 1999d. "Country Living: DiVito and Marinelli: Family Memories." In *Italian Lives: Cape Breton Memories,* edited by Sam Migliore and A. Evo DiPierro, 155–9. Sydney, NS: University College of Cape Breton Press.

– 1999e. "The Early Years: A Talk with Tony Bruno (1902–1979)." In *Italian Lives: Cape Breton Memories,* edited by Sam Migliore and A. Evo DiPierro, 59–61. Sydney, NS: University College of Cape Breton Press.

– 1999f. "Family Disruption, Hard Work, and Success: A Talk with Frank and Marty Martinello." In *Italian Lives: Cape Breton Memories,* edited by Sam Migliore and A. Evo DiPierro, 122–30. Sydney, NS: University College of Cape Breton Press.

– 1999g. "From Internment to Military Service: An Historical Paradox." In *Italian Lives: Cape Breton Memories,* edited by Sam Migliore and A. Evo DiPierro, 108–22. Sydney, NS: University College of Cape Breton Press.

– 1999h. "Introduction." In *Italian Lives: Cape Breton Memories,* edited by Sam Migliore and A. Evo DiPierro, 11–15. Sydney, NS: University College of Cape Breton Press.

– 1999i. "*La Sala Italiana* in Dominion." In *Italian Lives: Cape Breton Memories,* edited by Sam Migliore and A. Evo DiPierro, 263–9. Sydney, NS: University College of Cape Breton Press.

– 1999j. "Learning 'English' at Barachois Mountain: A Talk with Romeo Sylvester." In *Italian Lives: Cape Breton Memories,* edited by Sam Migliore and A. Evo DiPierro, 62–3. Sydney, NS: University College of Cape Breton Press.

– 1999k. "The Mancini Family of St. Peter's." In *Italian Lives: Cape Breton Memories,* edited by Sam Migliore and A. Evo DiPierro, 166–71. Sydney, NS: University College of Cape Breton Press.

– 1999l. "Memories of an Annual Ritual in Dominion." In *Italian Lives: Cape Breton Memories,* edited by Sam Migliore and A. Evo DiPierro, 193–4. Sydney, NS: University College of Cape Breton Press.

– 1999m. "Memories of Papa Jimmy: The Tubetti Family of Inverness." In *Italian Lives: Cape Breton Memories,* edited by Sam Migliore and A. Evo DiPierro, 172–5. Sydney, NS: University College of Cape Breton Press.

– 1999n. "Memories of Thomas Cozzolino." In *Italian Lives: Cape Breton Memories,* edited by Sam Migliore and A. Evo DiPierro, 44–59. University College of Cape Breton Press.

- 1999o. "Secondina DiPersio: A Son's Tribute to his Mother." In *Italian Lives: Cape Breton Memories*, edited by Sam Migliore and A. Evo DiPierro, 133–8. Sydney, NS: University College of Cape Breton Press.
- 1999p. "Three Women from Dominion." In *Italian Lives: Cape Breton Memories*, edited by Sam Migliore and A. Evo DiPierro, 104–7. Sydney, NS: University College of Cape Breton Press.

Mi'kmaq Fisheries: Netukulimk. 1993. Truro, NS: Native Council of Nova Scotia Language Program.

Mi'kma'ki. 1994. *Aboriginal Self Government for the Mi'kma'ki People of Nova Scotia.* Truro, NS: Native Council of Nova Scotia, Language Program.

Millward, C. M. 1996. *A Biography of the English Language.* Fort Worth: Harcourt Brace.

Millward, Hugh. 1985. "Mine Locations and the Sequence of Coal Exploitation on the Sydney Coalfield, 1720–1980." In *Cape Breton at 200: Historical Essays in Honour of the Island's Bicentennial, 1785–1985*, edited by Ken Donovan, 183–202. Sydney, NS: University College of Cape Breton Press.
- 1988. "Mining and Landscape Modification on the Sydney Coalfield." In *Geographical Perspectives on the Maritime Provinces*, edited by Douglas Day, 76–92. Halifax: Saint Mary's University.

Mitcham, Allison. 1989. *Island Keepers.* Hantsport, NS: Lancelot.

Mleczko, Hilda. 1989. *My Book of Memories [and] Picking up the Pieces.* Glace Bay, NS: H. Mleczko.

Molloy, Maureen. 1986. "'No Inclination to Mix with Strangers': Marriage Patterns Among Highland Scots Migrants to Cape Breton and New Zealand, 1800–1916." *Journal of Family History* 11(3): 221–43.

Molloy, M. P. 1991. *Those Who Speak to the Heart: The Nova Scotian Scots at Waipu 1854–1920.* Palmerston North, New Zealand: Dunmore.

Monro, Alexander. 1855. *New Brunswick, with a Brief Outline of Nova Scotia and Prince Edward Island: Their History, Civil Divisions, Geography, and Productions With Statistics of the Several Counties, Affording Views of the Resources and Capabilities of the Provinces, and Intended to Convey Useful Information, as Well to their Inhabitants, as to Emigrants, Strangers, and Travellers, and for the use of Schools.* Halifax: s.n.

Moogk, Peter. 1985. "From Fortress Louisbourg to Fortress Sydney, NS: Artillery and Gunners on Cape Breton, 1743–1980." In *Cape Breton at 200: Historical Essays in Honour of the Island's Bicentennial, 1785–1985*, edited by Kenneth Donovan, 127–82. Sydney, NS: University College of Cape Breton.

Moore, Christopher. 1990. "Cape Breton and the North Atlantic World in the Eighteenth Century." In *The Island: New Perspectives on Cape Breton History 1713–1990*, edited by Kenneth Donovan, 31–48. Fredericton: Acadiensis Press.

Moore, Kathleen. 2000. "Bishop's Cape Breton." *The Explicator*, Spring, 161–3.

Morgan, Robert J. 1969. "Joseph Frederick Wallet DesBarres and the Founding of Cape Breton Colony." *Revue d'Université d'Ottawa* 39:212–27.
- 1972. "Orphan Outpost: Cape Breton Colony, 1784–1820." PhD diss., University of Ottawa.
- 1975. *A History of Block 16, Louisbourg: 1731–1768, Fortress of Louisbourg.* Ottawa: Parks Canada.
- 1976. "Louisbourg: Key to a Continent." *Journal of the Council on Abandoned Military Posts* 8 (2): 3–14.

- 1977a. "Focus: Beaton Institute of Cape Breton Studies." *Archivaria* 4:202–4.
- ed. 1977b. *More Essays in Cape Breton History.* Windsor, NS: Lancelot.
- 1979. "David Mathews." Vol. 4 of *Dictionary of Canadian Biography.* Toronto: University of Toronto Press.
- 1980. "The Loyalists of Cape Breton." In *Cape Breton Historical Essays,* edited by Don MacGillivray and Brian Tennyson, 18–30. Sydney, NS: College of Cape Breton Press.
- 1982. "Ranna Cossit: The Loyalist Rector of St. George's, Sydney, Cape Breton Island." In *Eleven Exiles: Accounts of the Loyalists of the American Revolution,* edited by Phylllis R. Blakeley and John N. Grant, 226–43. Toronto: Dandurn.
- 1983a. "Ingram Ball." Vol. 5 of *Dictionary of Canadian Biography.* Toronto: University of Toronto Press.
- 1983b. "John Despard." Vol. 6 of *Dictionary of Canadian Biography.* Toronto: University of Toronto Press.
- 1983c. "John Murray." Vol. 6 of *Dictionary of Canadian Biography.* Toronto: University of Toronto Press.
- 1983d. "Ranna (Rene) Cossit (Cossitt)." Vol. 5 of *Dictionary of Canadian Biography.* Toronto: University of Toronto Press.
- 1983e. "Richard Stout." Vol. 5 of *Dictionary of Canadian Biography.* Toronto: University of Toronto Press.
- 1983f. "William Macarmik." Vol. 5 of *Dictionary of Canadian Biography.* Toronto: University of Toronto Press.
- 1983g. "William McKinnon." Vol. 5 of *Dictionary of Canadian Biography.* Toronto: University of Toronto Press.
- 1983h. "William Smith." Vol. 5 of *Dictionary of Canadian Biography.* Toronto: University of Toronto Press.
- 1984. "Past and Present Sources and Uses of Oral History." In *Proceedings of Atlantic Oral History Association Conference Glace Bay 1981,* edited by Elizabeth Beaton Planetta, 1–8. Sydney, NS: University College of Cape Breton Press.
- 1985. "Separatism in Cape Breton 1820–1845." In *Cape Breton at 200: Historical Essays In Honour of the Island's Bicentennial, 1785–1985,* edited by Kenneth Donovan, 41–52. Sydney, NS: University College of Cape Breton.
- 1987a. "Cape Breton By Itself." *Horizon Canada* 9 (100): 2390–5.
- 1987b. "Joseph Frederick Wallet DesBarres." Vol. 6 of *Dictionary of Canadian Biography.* Toronto: University of Toronto Press.
- 1987c. "Laurence Kavanaugh." Vol. 6 of *Dictionary of Canadian Biography.* Toronto: University of Toronto Press.
- 1988a. "George Robert Ainslie." Vol. 7 of *Dictionary of Canadian Biography.* Toronto: University of Toronto Press.
- 1988b. "The Heritage Movement in Cape Breton: Cultural Integrity Must Not Be Lost in Scramble to Lure Tourist Dollars." *The Forerunner,* Spring, 5–8.
- 2000. *Early Cape Breton: From Founding to Famine, 1784–1851: Essays, Talks and Conversations.* Wreck Cove, NS: Breton Books.
- 2004. *Perseverance: The Story of Cape Breton's University College, 1952–2002.* Sydney, NS: University College of Cape Breton Press.
- 2008. *Rise Again! The Story of Cape Breton Island* Book One. Wreck Cove, NS: Breton Books.

– 2009. *Rise Again! The Story of Cape Breton Island* Book Two. Wreck Cove, NS: Breton Books.

Morgan, Robert, Adriana Cavaliere, and Jeanne Russell. 1994. *University College of Cape Breton Alumni Directory 1994*. Edited by Dave Reynolds. Sydney, NS: University College of Cape Breton Press.

Morgan, Robert J. and Robert Lochiel Fraser. 1987. "Sir William Campbell." Vol. 6 of *Dictionary of Canadian Biography*. Toronto: University of Toronto Press.

Morgan, Robert J., and Terrence D. MacLean. 1974. "Social Structure & Life in Louisbourg." *Canada, an Historical Magazine*, June 60–75.

Morely, F. A. 1960. *Sacred Heart Parish*. Johnstown, NS: s.n.

Morien Memories. 1985. Port Morien, NS: privately printed.

Morley, Margaret W. 1900. *Down-North and Up Along*. New York: Dodd.

Morrison, Murdoch D. 1933. "The Migration of Scottish Settlers from St. Ann's Nova Scotia to New Zealand, 1851–1860." *Collections of the Nova Scotia Historical Society* 22:72–95.

Morrison, M. D. 1940. "Religion in Old Cape Breton." *Dalhousie Review* 20:181–96.

Morse, Susan L. 1946. "Immigration to Nova Scotia, 1839–1851." MA thesis, Dalhousie University.

Mowat, Farley. 1984. "Snow." In *The Cape Breton Collection*, edited by Lesley Choyce, 126–32. Porters Lake, NS: Pottersfield.

MRC [Mi'maq Resource Centre], Cape Breton University. http://www.cbu.ca/mrc/waltes.

Muise, Del. 1980. "The Making of an Industrial Community: Cape Breton Coal Towns 1867–1900." In *Cape Breton Historical Essays*, edited by Don MacGillivray and Brian Tennyson, 76–94. Sydney, NS: College of Cape Breton Press.

Mullaly, John. 1855. *A Trip to Newfoundland: Its Scenery and Fisheries, with an Account of the Laying of the Submarine Telegraph Cable*. New York: T.W. Strong.

Murphy, Peter. 2000. "Buddy MacMaster on the Fiddle." *The Cape Bretoner*, 8 (4), 36–8.

Murphy, Thomas Redmond. 1962. "A History of the Scottish on Cape Breton Island." BA thesis, St. Francis Xavier University.

Murray, James A. H. 1900. *The Evolution of English Lexicography*. Oxford: Clarendon.

Murray, John. 1921. *The History of the Presbyterian Church in Cape Breton*. Truro, NS: Printed by News Publishing.

Musial, Charlotte. 2002. "St. Joseph's School of Nursing, Class of '62: A Look Back." *The Cape Bretoner*, 10 (2), 39–41.

Nash, Ronald J. 1978. "Prehistory and Cultural Ecology – Cape Breton Island, Nova Scotia." In *Canadian Ethnology Society, Papers from the Fourth Annual Congress, 1977*. Mercury Series, edited by Richard J. Preston, 131–55. Ottawa: National Museum of Man.

New Waterford Gaelic Society [Cookbook]. n.d. New Waterford, NS: New Waterford Gaelic Society.

Newton, David. 1973. "What is Happening in Cape Breton?" *Canadian Geographical Journal* 87 (5): 25–31.

Newton, David. 1995. *Tainted Justice 1914*. Sydney, NS: University College of Cape Breton Press.

Newton, David, and Cape Breton Miners' Foundation. 1992. *Where Coal is King: The Story of the Cape Breton Miners' Museum*. Glace Bay, NS: Cape Breton Miners' Foundation.

Newton, Pamela, ed. 1985. *Sydney 1785 – 1985*. Sydney, NS: privately printed.
- 2005. "Three Writers from Away." *The Cape Bretoner*, 13 (3), 25–8.
Newton, Pamela George Van Nostrand. 1984. *The Cape Breton Book of Days: A Daily Journal of the Life and Times of an Island*. Sydney, NS: University College of Cape Breton Press.
Nicholls, Andrew D. 2005. "'The purpois is honorabill, and may conduce to the good of our service': Lord Ochiltree and the Cape Breton Colony, 1629–1631." *Acadiensis* 43 (2): 109–123.
Nicholson, Alexander. 1994. "A Stick and a Peg and Place to Play." *Cape Bretoner*, 3 (2), 18.
Nicholson, John A., and Middle River Area Historical Society. 1985. *Middle River: Past and Present History of a Cape Breton Community, 1806–1985*. Sydney, NS: Printed by City Printers for the Middle River Area Historical Society.
Nicoletti, Livio. "Memories of Mushroom Picking." In *Italian Lives: Cape Breton Memories*, edited by Sam Migliore and A. Evo DiPierro, 192–3. Sydney, NS: University College of Cape Breton Press.
Nightingale, Marie. 1989. *Out of Old Nova Scotia Kitchens*, 164. Halifax: Nimbus.
Noble, William J. 1948. "The British and Cape Breton." *The Dalhousie Review* 28 (2): 173–6.
Norman, Stefan. 2001. "Cruising Cape Breton Culture." *Canadian Geographic*, March/April 9–10.
North Sydney Herald. February 1873–February 1929.
Nova Scotia Archives and Records Management. 1810. Microfilm 15790. http://novascotia.ca/archives/virtual/land/results.asp?Search=leaver%2C+tim&SearchList1=3&SearchButton=Search+Land+Petitions
Nova Scotia Historical Review. 1981–1994.
Nova Scotia Historical Society. 1878–1980.
Nova Scotia Miner August 1932–March 1936.
O'Brien, Archbishop Cornelius. 1897. "Presidential Address on Cabot's Land Fall. *Transactions of the Royal Society of Canada*, 2nd Series, 3:105–39.
O'Dell, C.M. 1922. "Men and Methods of the Early Days of Mining in Cape Breton." *Transactions of the Canadian Institute of Mining and Metallurgy*. 25:503–29.
O'Donnell, John C. 1975. *The Men of the Deeps*. Waterloo, ON: Waterloo Music Co.
- 1992. *"And Now the Fields are Green": A Collection of Coal Mining Songs in Canada*. Sydney, NS: University College of Cape Breton Press.
Official Programme, Sydney 150th Anniversary 1785– 1935. 1935. Sydney, NS: 150th Anniversary Association.
Official Programme, Sydney's 175th Anniversary Week, July 24 to 30, 1960. 1960. Sydney, NS: City of Sydney.
150th Anniversary Sydney Academy 1841–1991. 1960. Sydney, NS: City of Sydney.
O'Handley, Ann Marie. 1999. The Untold Stories of the Mine. Paper Submitted for Folklore 113. Folklore Reports, Beaton Institute, Cape Breton University. 1999. 1–17.
O'Leary, Bill. 2001. "Rescued." *The Cape Bretoner*, 4 (2), 19–21.
Oleson, Tryggui J. 1963. *Early Voyages and Northern Approaches*. Toronto: McClelland & Stewart.
O'Neil, Pat. 1994. *Explore Cape Breton: A Field Guide to Adventure*. Halifax: Nimbus.

– 2000a. "Camp Rankin: A World of Its Own on the Shore of Bras d'Or." *The Cape Bretoner*, 8 (4), 58–60.
– 2000b."Cote de Bras d'Or: The Vineyards (and the Wine!) of Marble Mountain." *The Cape Bretoner*, 8 (5), 16–18.
– 2000c. "Natalie of Troy Music in the Blood." *The Cape Bretoner*, 8 (2), 31–4.
– 2000d. "O Give Me a Home: Where the Buffalo Roam." *The Cape Bretoner*, 8 (6), 12–14.
– 2000e. "Rita." *The Cape Bretoner*, 8 (6), 21–3.
– 2000f. "Tainted Cargo." *The Cape Bretoner*, 8 (5), 8–9, 11.
– 2000g. "A Train Called 'Bras d'Or.'" *The Cape Bretoner*, 8 (3), 24–6.
– 2000h. "Treasures of the Wild: Standing over Cape Breton's Disappearing Lynx and Pine Marten." *The Cape Bretoner*, 8 (4), 16–18.
– 2001a. "Blaise MacLeod." *The Cape Bretoner*, 9 (1), 31–3.
– 2001b. "The Tarponds and Other Legacies." *The Cape Bretoner*, 9 (1), 11–13, 18.
– 2002a. "Dancing the Night Away." *The Cape Bretoner*, 10 (4), 34–7, 51.
– 2002b. "Thanks for the Memories." *The Cape Bretoner*, 10 (1), 36–7.
– 2002/03. "The Baille Ard Nature Trail: Cape Breton's Best Kept Secret." *The Cape Bretoner*, 10 (6), 11–14.
– 2003. "A Day in the Life: Kevin Bond, Lobster Fisher." *The Cape Bretoner*, 11 (2), 17–21.
[O'Neil, Pat]. 2003 "Big Lobster Oops." *The Cape Bretoner*, 11 (3), 46.
Oran Inbhirnis [Inverness Oran] 1976–8; 1986–7; 1990–3.
Ormond, Douglas Somers. 1985. *A Century Ago at Arichat and Antigonish and other Familiar Surroundings: Reminiscences of Mary Belle Grant Ormond (1860–1947).* Hantsport, NS: Lancelot.
Orr, Clifford. 1994. *Where Morien Meets the Sea: The Memoirs of a Transplanted Cape Bretoner.* Port Morien, NS: Peach Tree.
Orton, David and SEPOHG [Socialist Environmental Protection and Occupational Health Group]. 1983–4. *Pulpwood Industry in Nova Scotia and the Environmental Question.* Halifax: Gorsebrook Research Institute.
O'Shea, William, and Helen O'Shea. 1993. *Stella Maris Roman Catholic Church, Louisbourg, Nova Scotia.* Louisbourg, NS: Louisbourg Heritage Society.
Owen, Michael. 1990. "Making Decent Law-Abiding Canadian Citizens: Presbyterian Missions to Cape Breton's Foreigners, 1900–1915." In *The Island: New Perspectives on Cape Breton History 1713–1990,* edited by Kenneth Donovan, 113–28. Fredericton: Acadiensis Press.
Palango, Paul. 1999. "This Christmas's Gift to Everyone is the Joy of Having Lived to 100." In *Italian Lives: Cape Breton Memories,* edited by Sam Migliore and A. Evo DiPierro, 298–300. Sydney, NS: University College of Cape Breton Press.
Palmater, Marcia. 1996. "Crossing the Causeway: Forgetting the Great Ones." *The Cape Bretoner*, 4 (5), 6.
Parker, John P. 1967. *Cape Breton Ships and Men.* Toronto: McGraw-Hill Ryerson.
Parsons, Elsie Clews. 1926a. "Micmac Folk-lore." *Journal of American Folklore* 39 (154): 55–133.
– 1926b. "Micmac Notes." *Journal of American Folklore* 39 (154): 460–85.
Partici-Paper 1991. 12:6.
Patterson, G. G. (1885) 1978. *George Geddie Patterson's History of Victoria County, Cape Breton, NS.* Sydney, NS: College of Cape Breton Press.

Patterson, Lisa Lynne. 1986. "Indian Affairs and the Nova Scotia Centralization Policy." MA thesis, Dalhousie University.

Patterson, Rev. George. 1890. "The Portuguese on the north-east coast of America, and the first European attempt at the colonization there, a lost chapter in American history." *Transactions of the Royal Society of Canada*, 2nd Series, 8:127–73.

– 1892. "Sir William Alexander and the Scottish attempt to colonize Acadia." *Transactions of the Royal Society of Canada*, 2nd Series, 10:79–107.

Patterson, Stephen E. 1998. "Historians and the Courts." *Acadiensis* 28 (1): 18–23.

Patton, W. W., and LeRoy Peach. 1995. *Lost Village: When Louisbourg Was a Walled City*. Port Morien, NS: Peach Tree.

Payne, Ed. 1969. "From Rags to Riches? An Industrial Revolution for Cape Breton." *The Atlantic Advocate*, September 29–33.

– 1972. "The Cabot Trail." *The Atlantic Advocate*, May 19–20.

– 1978. "An In-Depth Look at Cape Breton." *The Atlantic Advocate*, June 32–35.

Peabody, George, ed. 1988. *Best Maritime Short Stories*. Halifax: Formac Publishing.

Peabody, George, Carolyn MacGregor, and Richard Thorne, eds. 1987. *The Maritimes: Tradition, Challenge and Change*. Halifax: Maritext Limited.

Peach, Earle. 1990. *Memories of a Cape Breton Childhood*. Halifax: Nimbus.

Peach, Leroy. 1981. *Heartreign*. Hantsport, NS: Lancelot.

– 1990. *Pilgrims on this Shore: The Anglican Parish of Port Morien, 1786–1990*. Port Morien, NS: Peach Tree.

– 1991. *Cape Breton, My Cape Breton*. Port Morien, NS: Peach Tree.

– 1998. *Inlets of the Heart*. Sydney, NS: University College of Cape Breton Press.

Pearson, Norman. 1966. *Town of Glace Bay, Nova Scotia, Urban Renewal Study*. Glace Bay, NS: s.n.

Peck, Mary Biggar. 1989. *A Nova Scotia Album: Glimpses of the Way We Were*. Willowdale, ON: Hounslow.

Perrault, Rev. Julien. 1636. "Relation of Certain Details Regarding the Island of Cape Breton and its Inhabitants." translated from *Realtion de ce qui s'est passé en la Nouvelle France en l'année 1635*. Paris: Sebastien Cramoisy.

Petit De Grat. [1989]. S.l: privately printed.

Petrie, Daniel. 1986. *The Bay Boy*. Porters Lake, NS: Pottersfield.

Pichon, Thomas. 1760. *Genuine Letters and Memoirs, Relating to the Natural, Civil, and Commercial History of the Islands of Cape Breton, and Saint John, from the First Settlement There, to the Taking of Louisburg by the English, in 1758. In which ... the Causes and Previous Events of the Present War are Explained*. London: J. Nourse.

Pickup, Douglas. 1972. "The Development of Sydney, NS (1900–1914)." BA thesis, St. Francis Xavier University.

Piers, Harry. 1900. "The Cabots and their Voyages." In *Canadian History Readings*, edited by George U. Hays, 31–37. Saint John, NB: Barnes.

Pillar, Mabel MacPhail. 1976. *Aunt Peggy from Loch Bras d'Or*. Windsor, NS: Lancelot.

Poirier, Michel. 1984. *Les Acadiens aux îles Saint-Pierre et Miquelon 1758–1828: 3 déportations, 30 années d'exil*. Moncton: Editions d'Acadie.

Pope, Joseph. 1896. "The Cabot Celebration." *Canadian Magazine*, December 158–64.

Pope, Peter Edward. 1997. *The Many Landfalls of John Cabot*. Toronto: University of Toronto Press.

Pope, William. 1981. *Clarence Mackinnon Nicholson: An Intimate Profile of his Achievement, Thought and Spiritual Leadership*. Hantsport, NS: Lancelot.

Poteet, Lewis J. 1984. "Elizabethan English on Nova Scotia's South Shore." *Nova Scotia Historical Review* 4 (1): 57–63.

The Pottersfield Portfolio. 1979–1996.

Powell, John. 1952. "Industrial Cape Breton: Steel in Our Midst." *Cape Breton Mirror*, June 12–14.

Power, T. P. 1991. *The Irish in Atlantic Canada, 1780–1900*. Fredericton: New Ireland Press.

Prenties, Samuel Waller. 1968. *Ensign Prenties's Narrative: A Castaway on Cape Breton*. Edited by G. G. Campbell. Toronto: Ryerson.

Prince, Wendy. 2003. "Caper Away: Caper or Newfie." *The Cape Bretoner*, 11 (1), 64.

Pringle, Will. 1976. *Pringle's Mountain*. Windsor, NS: Lancelot.

– 1988. *Look to the Harbour*. New York: Carlton.

Prins, Harald E. L. 1996. *The Mi'kmaq: Resistance, Accommodation, and Cultural Survival, Case Studies in Cultural Anthropology*. Fort Worth: Harcourt Brace College Publishing.

Protheroe, Winnifred Mitchell. 1971. *Cape Breton Memories in Verse*. Windsor, NS: Lancelot.

Province of Nova Scotia. 1837. *Journal and Votes of the House of Assembly for the Province of Nova Scotia*. Halifax, N.S.: s.n. http://eco.canadiana.ca/

– 1843. *Journal and Votes of the House of Assembly for the Province of Nova Scotia*. Halifax: s.n. http://eco.canadiana.ca/

– 1845. *Journal and Votes of the House of Assembly for the Province of Nova Scotia*. Halifax: s.n. http://eco.canadiana.ca/

– 1848. *Journal and Votes of the House of Assembly for the Province of Nova Scotia*. Halifax: Queen's Printer. http://eco.canadiana.ca/

– 1856. *Journal and Proceedings of Her Majesty's Legislative Council of the Province of Nova-Scotia*. Halifax: King's Printer [*sic*]. http://eco.canadiana.ca/

– 1860. *Journal and Votes of the House of Assembly for the Province of Nova Scotia*. Halifax: W. Compton. http://eco.canadiana.ca/

– 1867. *The Statutes of Nova-Scotia Being the Fourth Session of the Twenty-Third General Assembly Convened in the Said Province*. Halifax: J. S. Thompson. http://eco.canadiana.ca/

Public Archives of Nova Scotia. 1967. *Place Names of Nova Scotia*. Halifax: Public Archives of Nova Scotia.

Punch, Terrence M. 1980. "Laurence Kavanagh (1764–1830), First Catholic Assemblyman." In *Some Sons of Erin in Nova Scotia*, edited by Terrence M. Punch, 25–29. Halifax: Petheric.

Punching with Pemberton October 1960–December 1965.

Raddall, Thomas. 1965. "The Road to Fortune." *The Atlantic Advocate*, December 39–48.

Radikowski, Angela V. 1973. *The History of the Polish Community in Sydney, NS*. Antigonish, NS: St. Francis Xavier University.

Raine Reilly, Norman. 1925. "Toilers Under the Sea." *Maclean's*, January 15, 20, 38–40.

Rand, Silas Tertius. 1873. *A Short Account of the Lord's Work Among the Micmac Indians*. Halifax: W. McNab. http://eco.canadiana.ca/

– 1875. *A First Reading Book in the Micmac Language: Comprising the Micmac Numerals, and the Names of the Different Kinds of Beasts, Birds, Fishes, Trees, &c. of the Maritime*

Provinces of Canada. Also, Some of the Indian Names of Places, and Many Familiar Words and Phrases, Translated Literally Into English. Halifax, N.S.: Nova Scotia Printing. http://eco.canadiana.ca/

– 1888. *English Micmac Dictionary: Dictionary of the Language of the Micmac Indians who Reside in Nova Scotia, New Brunswick, Price Edward Island, Cape Breton and Newfoundland.* Halifax: Nova Scotia Printing.

Rankin, Duncan Joseph. 1916. *Old Home Week: Grand Mira, Cape Breton.* S.l.: s.n.

– 1930. *Our Ain Folks and Others.* Toronto: Macmillan.

– 1941. *Laurence Kavanagh.* Hull, QC: Canadian Catholic Historical Association.

Rankin, Effie. 2004. *As a' Bhràighe Beyond the Braes: The Gaelic Songs of Allan The Ridge MacDonald, 1794–1868.* Sydney, NS: University College of Cape Breton Press.

Rankin, Joyce. 2002. *At My Mother's Door.* Sydney, NS: Sea-Cape Publishing.

– 2012. *The Wedding Reels.* Wreck Cove, NS: Breton Books.

Rayburn, Alan. 2001. *Naming Canada: Stories About Canadian Place Names.* Toronto; Buffalo: University of Toronto Press.

– 2010. *Place Names of Canada.* Toronto: Oxford University Press.

Raymond, C. W. 1965. *The Cape Breton Island's Tourist Industry: 1964.* St. John's: s.n.

Razzolini, Esperanza Maria, and Saint Mary's University International Education Centre. 1983. *All our Fathers: The North Italian Colony in Industrial Cape Breton.* Halifax: International Education Centre, Saint Mary's University.

Record Guide Book and Business Directory for Sydney, NS, 1901. n.d. S.l.: s.n.

Reid, John G. 1981. *Acadia, Maine, and New Scotland: Marginal Colonies in the Seventeenth Century.* Toronto; Buffalo: Published in Association with Huronia Historical Parks, Ontario Ministry of Culture and Recreation by University of Toronto Press.

– 1987. "Henry May: An Early English Admirer of the Maritime Landscape." In *The Red Jeep and Other Landscapes: A Collection in Honour of Douglas Lochhead,* edited by Peter Thomas, 15–19. Sackville; Fredericton: Mount Allison University Centre for Canadian Studies; Goose Lane.

– 1990. *Sir William Alexander and North American Colonization: A Reappraisal.* Edinburgh: Centre of Canadian Studies, University of Edinburgh.

Rendall, Barbara. 1996. "A Sense of Family." In *The Centre of the World at the Edge of a Continent: Cultural Studies of Cape Breton,* edited by Carol Corbin and Judith A. Rolls, 191–94. Sydney, NS: University College of Cape Breton Press, 1996.

Retson, Don. 1975. "John Allan Cameron ... Cape Breton's Troubadour." *The Atlantic Advocate,* February 19–20.

Rhodes, Curry & Co., Ltd. 1908. *Sydney Branch Price List.* Amherst, NS: Rhodes, Curry and Co., Head Office and Main Works.

Rhodes, Frank. 1964. "Dancing in Cape Breton Island, Nova Scotia." In *Traditional Dancing in Scotland,* edited by J. F. Flett and T. M Flett, 267–85. London: Routledge and Kegan Paul.

– 1996. "Step-Dancing in Cape Breton Island." In *Traditional Step-Dancing in Scotland,* edited by J. F. Flett and T. M Flett, 185–214. Edinburgh: Scottish Cultural Press.

Rigby, Carle A. 1979. *St. Paul Island, "the Graveyard of the Gulf": The Story of a Little Known Nova Scotian Island.* Hartland, NB: Rigby.

Ripley, Ralph Wayne. 1979. "Social and Cultural Implications of Industrialization and Urbanization in Cape Breton County, 1893–1914." BA thesis, St. Francis Xavier University.

Roach, Thomas E. 1997. *Arn? Narn! Faces and Voices of Atlantic Inshore Fishers*. Sydney, NS: University College of Cape Breton Press.

Robertson, Barbara R. 1986. *Sawpower: Making Lumber in the Sawmills of Nova Scotia*. Halifax: Nimbus Publishing and Nova Scotia Museum.

Robertson, Ellison. 1981. *Cape Breton Island Sketchbook*. Tantallon, NS: Four East Publications.

– 1985. *Cranberry Heul: Stories and Paintings*. Sydney, NS: University College of Cape Breton Press.

– 1992. *In Love With Then*. Fredericton: Goose Lane.

– 1997. *The Last Gael and Other Stories*. Wreck Cove, NS: Breton Books.

Robertson, Frank. 1992. *Birds on a Rock*. Sydney, NS: University College of Cape Breton Press.

– 1994. *The Humble Bowl, and Other Poems: With Prose Commentaries*. Sydney, NS: University College of Cape Breton Press.

Robertson, Marion. 1969. *Red Earth: Tales of the Micmacs with an Introduction to the Customs and Beliefs of the Micmac Indians*. Halifax: Nova Scotia Museum.

Robin Hood. n.d. http://www.robinhood.ca/recipe.details.

Robins, C. Richard, Chairman, and Reeve M. Bailey, Carl E. Bond, James R. Brooker, Ernest A. Lachner, Robert M. Lea, and W. B. Scott. 1991. *Common and Scientific Names from the United States and Canada*. American Fishers Society Special Publication 20. Bethesda, Maryland.

Robinson, Cyril. 1964. "Glace Bay." *Canadian Geographical Journal* 69 (3): 89–95.

Roche, Rev. Edmund J. 1968. The Future of the Church's Involvement in Higher Education. Cape Breton Lecture Series. 9 June. Beaton Institute, Cape Breton University, Sydney, NS: Pamphlet 1770.

Rogers, Robert. 1765. *A Concise Account of North America Containing a Description of the Several British Colonies on that Continent, Including the Islands of Newfoundland, Cape Breton, &c. ... By Major Robert Rogers*. London: printed for the author, and sold by J. Millan.

The Romantic Cape Breton Highlands: The Cradle of Celtic Culture in North America. 1964. Sydney, NS: privately printed.

Ross, Moira. 1996. "The Irish of Rock Bay." In *The Centre of the World at the Edge of a Continent: Cultural Studies of Cape Breton*, edited by Carol Corbin and Judith A. Rolls, 171–76. Sydney, NS: University College of Cape Breton Press.

Ross, Sally, and J. Alphonse Deveau. 1992. *The Acadians of Nova Scotia Past and Present*. Halifax: Nimbus.

Rothe, Marian. 1984. "The Barra in Grand Narrows, Cape Breton: 1804–1904." BA thesis, Laurentian University, 1984.

Rowe, Nora Alice. 1968. "A Linguistic Study of the Lake Ainslie Area of Inverness County, Nova Scotia." PhD diss., University of New Orleans.

Russell, Henry Harrison. 1926. "Cape Breton Island: The Land and the People." PhD diss. Clark University.

Ryan, Judith Hoegg. 1984. *The Mine, Growth of a Nation Series*. Markham, ON: Fitzhenry & Whiteside.

Ryan, Patrick G. 2002. "Miner's Day Picnic: The Great Race of '49." *The Cape Bretoner*, 10 (4), 19–20.

Sabattis. [T. M. Gill]. 1929. *The Lure of the City*. Sackville, NB: Tribune.

Sable, Trudy, and Bernard Francis. 2012. *The Language of This Land, Mi'kma'ki.* Sydney, NS: Cape Breton University Press.

Saint Agnes Elementary School. 2003. *A Collection of Coal Miners' Stories.* New Waterford, NS: Saint Agnes Elementary School.

St. John the Parish, *Glace Bay.* n.d. S.l.: s.n.

Sacouman, R. James. 1978. "Cooperative Community Development Among Nova Scotian Primary Producers, 1861–1940: A Critical Comparison of Three Cases." In *Issues in Regional/Urban Development of Atlantic Canada,* edited by Neil B. Ridler, 11–26. Saint John: University of New Brunswick at Saint John, Division of Social Science.

Sacred Heart Parish: Johnstown, Nova Scotia. 1960. S.l.: MacKenzie Campbell.

Sampson, Gordon H., and Donna Anderson Currie. 1985. *North Bar Remembered: North Sydney's Centennial and Bicentennial.* Sydney, NS: [City Printers].

Sampson, Gordon H., and Emerson Allen. 1988. *Northside Tourism Complex.* S.l.: Tourism Subcommittee Northside Community Futures.

Samson, Daniel. 1994. "Dependency and Rural Industry: Inverness, NS, 1899–1910." In *Contested Countryside: Rural Workers and Modern Society in Atlantic Canada, 1800–1950,* edited by Daniel Samson, 105–49. Fredericton: Acadiensis Press.

– 1999. "Industrial Colonization: The Colonial Context of the General Mining Association, Nova Scotia, 1825–1842." *Acadiensis* 29 (1): 3–28.

Samson, David Lloyd, and Reed Wooby. 1992. *When the Doctor Couldn't Come: Folk Medicine.* Hantsport, NS: Lancelot.

Samson, David Lloyd, Reed Wooby, and Warren Gordon. 1992. *Island of Ghosts: Folklore and Strange Tales of the Supernatural from Cape Breton.* Hantsport, NS: Lancelot.

Samson, Garvie. 1994. *The River that Isn't: A Tale of Survival and Prosperity: River Bourgeois, Cape Breton, 1714–1994.* Dartmouth, NS: G. Samson.

Samson, Roch. 1997. "Good Debts and Bad Debts: Gaspe Fishers in the 19th Century." In *Historical Essays on Canada's Atlantic Fishery,* edited by James E. Candow and Carol Corbin, 107–20. Louisbourg, NS: Louisbourg Institute; Sydney, NS: University College of Cape Breton Press.

Sawlor, Elaine. 2003. "Home Children of Kennington Cove." http://canadianbritishhomechildren.weebly.com/kennington-cove.html.

Schmidt, David. 1996. "Kaqietaq 'All Gone': Honouring the Dying and Deceased in Eskasoni." In *The Centre of the World at the Edge of a Continent: Cultural Studies of Cape Breton,* edited by Carol Corbin and Judith A. Rolls, 163–70. Sydney, NS: University College of Cape Breton Press.

Schmidt, David L., and B. A. Balcom. 1993. "The Reglements of 1739: A Note on Micmac Literacy." *Acadiensis* 23 (1): 110–27.

Schmidt, David L., and Murdena Marshall. 1995. *Mi'kmaq Hieroglyphic Prayers: Readings in North America's First Indigenous Script.* Halifax: Nimbus.

Schneider, Aaron L. 1998. *Wild Honey.* Wreck Cove, NS: Breton Books.

Schneider, Phyllis Worgan. 1979. *Ferndell, Sydney, Cape Breton.* Sydney, NS: City Printers.

Schneider, Ruth Morris. 1984. *A Woods Home: The Story of a Canadian Homestead.* New York: McGraw-Hill.

Scribners, A.M. 1882. *Lumber and Log Book.* S.l.: s.n.

Senior Writers' Guild of Nova Scotia. 1995. *Yarns Worth the Telling.* Halifax: Department Of Supply and Services, Publishing Section.

Senior, Doreen H., and Helen Creighton. 1950. *Traditional Songs from Nova Scotia*. Toronto: Ryerson Press.

Seward, Alice. 1984. *This is Cape Breton: Verses*. New York: Vantage.

Shaw, John William. 1982. "A Cape Breton Gaelic Story-Teller (Vols. I and II)." PhD diss., Harvard University.

– 1992–93. "Language, Music and Local Aesthetics: Views from Gaeldon and Beyond." *Scottish Language* 11–12:37–61.

Shaw, John William, and Lisa Ornstein. 2000. *Brìgh an Òrain A Story in Every Song: The Songs and Tales of Lauchie MacLellan*. McGill-Queen's University Studies in Ethnic History. Montreal: McGill-Queen's University Press.

Shea, Ammon. 2012. "That Most Ill-Defined Book: Problems with Labeling the Dictionary in Educated Writing." *Dictionaries: Journal of the Dictionary Society of North America* 33:103–12.

Shedden, Leslie, B. H. D. Buchloh, Robert Wilkie, Don MacGillivray, Allan Sekula, and Shedden Studio. 1983. *Mining Photographs and Other Pictures, 1948–1968: A Selection From the Negative Archives of Shedden Studio, Glace Bay, Cape Breton*. Halifax: Press of the Nova Scotia College of Art and Design and the University College of Cape Breton Press.

Sherwood, Roland H. 1972. "First Transatlantic Cable." In *Atlantic Harbours*, 103–08. Windsor, NS: Lancelot.

– 1984. *Legends, Oddities, and Facts From the Maritime Provinces*. Hantsport, NS: Lancelot.

Silver, Marietta. 1971. "Mrs. Alexander Graham Bell, Founder of the Canadian Parent-Teacher Federation, and Much Besides." *The Atlantic Advocate*, September 32–36, 39.

Sinclair, Lister. 1956. *The Blood is Strong: A Drama of Early Scottish Settlement in Cape Breton*. Agincourt, ON: Book Society of Canada.

Skelton, R. A. 1966. "John (Giovanni) Cabot (Caboto)." Vol. 1 of *Dictionary of Canadian Biography*. Toronto: University of Toronto Press.

Slafter, Rev. Edmund F. 1873. *Sir William Alexander and American Colonization*. Burt Franklin Research and Source Works Series 131. American Classics in History and Social Sciences 2. Boston: The Prince Society.

Slaven, Sid. 2003 http://sydneysteelmuseum.com/history/blackfriday.htm.

Sleigh, Burrows Willcocks Arthur. 1853. *Pine Forests and Hacmatack Clearings: or, Travel, Life and Adventure, in the British North American Provinces*. London: R. Bentley.

Smith, Gordon E. 1994. "Lee Cremo: Narratives about a Micmac Fiddler." In *Canadian Music: Issues of Hegemony and Identity*, edited by Beverley Diamond and Robert Witmer, 541–56. Toronto: Canadian Scholars' Press.

Smith, Gordon E., and Kevin Alstrup. 1995. "Words and Music by Rita Joe: Dialogic Ethnomusicology." *Canadian Journal for Traditional Music*. 23:35–53.

Smith, Harry James, and Oliver M. Wiard. 1920. *Cape Breton Tales*. Boston: The Atlantic Monthly Press.

Smith, J. T. 1965. "Timber-framed Buildings in England: Its Development and Regional Differences." *Archaeological Journal* 122:133–58.

Smith, Perley W. 1967. *History of Port Hood and Port Hood Island with Genealogy of the Smith Family, 1610–1967*. Port Hood, NS: Perley W. Smith.

Smith, Ray. 1969. *Cape Breton is the Thought Control Centre of Canada*. Toronto: Anansi.

– 1984. "The Dwarf in his Valley Ate Codfish." In *The Cape Breton Collection*, edited by Lesley Choyce, 152–60. Porters Lake, NS: Pottersfield.

Smith-Piovesan, Eileen. 2001. "Agents of Change: Examining Cape Breton Women's Involvement in the Devco Mine Closures." In *Sculptures from Jagged Ore: Essays about Cape Breton Women*, edited by Carol Corbin and Eileen Smith-Piovesan, 181–93. Sydney, NS: University College of Cape Breton Press.

Smith-Piovesan, Eileen and Carol Corbin, eds. 2001. *Sculptures from a Jagged Ore: Essays about Cape Breton Women*. Sydney, NS: University College of Cape Breton Press.

[Smith, William]. 1803. *A Caveat Against Emigration to America: With the State of the Island of Cape Breton From the Year 1784 to the Present Year*. London: Betham & Warde.

Southwell, Robert, and Tompkins Institute for Human Values and Technology. 1987. *The Self-Esteem of Employed and Unemployed Cape Bretoners, Occasional Paper*. Tompkins Institute for Human Values and Technology. Sydney, NS: University College of Cape Breton Press.

Souvenir of the 50th Anniversary of the Town of Inverness 1904 - 1954. 1954. Inverness, NS: s.n.

Sparling, Heather Lee. 1999. "Puirt-a-Beul: An Ethnographic Study of Gaelic Mouth Music in Cape Breton." MA thesis, York University.

– 2014. *Reeling Roosters and Dancing Ducks: Celtic Mouth Music*. Sydney, NS: Cape Breton University Press.

Spencer, Sharon. 2001."Tribute to Tommy Gun Spencer." *The Cape Bretoner*, 9 (1), 47–48.

St. Clair, James O. 2009. "Year of the British Home Child." *Information Morning*. CBC Radio 14 October.

St. Clair, James O., Yvonne LeVert, and Peter Rankin. 2007. *Nancy's Wedding Feast and Other Tasty Tales*. Sydney, NS: Cape Breton University Press and CBC Radio.

Spettigue, D. O. 1983. "Hugh MacLennan." In *The Oxford Companion to Canadian Literature*, edited by Eugene Benson and William Toye, 705–07. Toronto, Oxford and New York: Oxford University Press.

The Spirit of the Times. December 1843; 6 September 1844; April 1845.

Staebler, Edna. 1948. "Duellists of the Deep." *Maclean's*, July 15, 18, 46–48.

– 1972. *Cape Breton Harbour*. Toronto: McClelland & Stewart.

Stanley, Laurie. 1983. *The Well-Watered Garden: The Presbyterian Church in Cape Breton, 1798–1860*. Cape Breton, NS: University College of Cape Breton Press.

Stanley-Blackwell, Laurie C. 2006. *Tokens of Grace: Cape Breton's Open-Air Communion Tradition*. Sydney, NS: Cape Breton University Press.

Steelworker and Miner. 19 August 1944; 26 August 1944; 9 September 1944; 23 September 1944; 29 January 1945.

Steele, Charlotte Musial. 1991. "A Special Christmas Ceilidh." *The Atlantic Advocate*, December 33–35.

Steele, Joseph. 1960. "The Big Strike, 1909–1910." MA thesis, Saint Francis Xavier University.

Stephenson, Len. 1981. *Dominion, Nova Scotia: A Brief History of the Town of Dominion and Its Early Development*. Dominion, NS: Town of Dominion.

– 1999. "A Brief Note on Rum-Running." In *Italian Lives: Cape Breton Memories*, edited by Sam Migliore and A. Evo DiPierro, 81–82. Sydney, NS: University College of Cape Breton Press.

Sterkenburg, Piet van, ed. 2003. *A Practical Guide to Lexicography*. Philadelphia: Bejamins.

Stewart, Anita. 2008. *Anita Stewart's Canada: The Food, The Recipes, The Stories*. Toronto: Harper Collins Publishing.

Stirling, Lilla. 1981. *Anne of St. Ann's*. Antigonish, NS: Formac Publishing Company.

Stirling, William Alexander. 1885. *The Earl of Stirling's Register of Royal Letters Relative to the Affairs of Scotland and Nova Scotia from 1615 to 1635*. Edinburgh: s.n.

Stone, Arthur J. 1991. *Journey through a Cape Breton County*. Sydney, NS: University College of Cape Breton Press.

Storm, Alex. 1990. "Seaweed and Gold: The Discovery of the Ill-Fated *Chameau*, 1961–1971." In *The Island: New Perspectives on Cape Breton History 1713–1990*, edited by Kenneth Donovan, 221–44. Fredericton: Acadiensis Press.

Story, Norah. 1967a. "Burrows Willcocks Arthur Sleigh." *The Oxford Companion to Canadian History and Literature*. Toronto: Oxford University Press.

– 1967b. "John Cabot." *The Oxford Companion to Canadian History and Literature*. Toronto: Oxford University Press.

– 1967c. "Lord Ochiltree." *The Oxford Companion to Canadian History and Literature*. Toronto: Oxford University Press.

Street, David. 1979. *The Cabot Trail*. Toronto: Gage Publishing.

Souvenir of Louisbourg 1731. n.d. Glace Bay, NS: Brodie.

Sunderland, Terry. 1980. *Still Standing: Cape Breton Buildings From Days Gone By*. Sydney, NS: College of Cape Breton Press.

Surrette, R. 1977. "Cape Breton Blues." *Maclean's*, May 30, 24, 28–30, 32.

Sydney Mines: 100 Years and More. [1989]. Sydney Mines, NS: D.U. Mac Donald.

Sydney Summer Carnival and Old Home Week. 1905. Sydney, NS: privately printed.

Tarducci, Francesco, and Henry F. Brownson. 1893. *John and Sebastian Cabot: Biographical Notice with Documents*. Detroit: H. F. Brownson.

Taylor, James O., ed. 1994. *An Underlying Reverence: Stories of Cape Breton*. Sydney, NS: University College of Cape Breton Press.

Tennyson, Brian Douglas, ed. 1973a. *Essays in Cape Breton History*. Windsor, NS: Lancelot.

– 1973b. "John George Bourinot: MHA and Senator." In *Essays in Cape Breton History*, edited by Brian Tennyson. 35–48. Windsor, NS: Lancelot.

– 1980. "Economic Nationalism and Confederation: A Case Study in Cape Breton." In *Cape Breton Historical Essays*, edited by Don MacGillivray and Brian Tennyson, 54–65. Sydney, NS: College of Cape Breton Press.

– ed. 1986. *Impressions of Cape Breton*. Sydney, NS: University College of Cape Breton Press.

– 1990. "Economic Nationalism, Confederation and Nova Scotia." In *The Causes of Canadian Confederation*, edited by Ged Martin, 130–41. Fredericton: Acadiensis Press.

– comp. 2005. *Cape Bretoniana: An Annotated Bibliography*. Toronto: University of Toronto Press.

Tennyson, Brian Douglas, and Roger Flynn Sarty. 2000. *Guardian of the Gulf: Sydney, Cape Breton, and the Atlantic Wars*. Toronto: University of Toronto Press.

Terry, Ann. 1952. "The Women's World." *Cape Breton Mirror*, October 5, 20.

– 1952. "The Women's World." *Cape Breton Mirror*, November 14–15.

Thomas, Amby. 1979. *Songs and Stories from Deep Cove, Cape Breton*, edited by Ron MacEachern. Sydney, NS: College of Cape Breton Press.

Thomas, George C., Lynn Zimmerman, and Richard Lyons. 1980. *Margaree*. Margaree Harbour, NS: Harbour Lights.

Thompson, Alice W. n.d. *The Story of Springfields, Part One*. [Westmount]: s.n. Beaton Institute, Cape Breton University, Sydney, NS: Pamphlet 2223.

Thornhill, Bonnie, and W. James MacDonald, eds. 1999. *In the Morning: Veterans of Victoria County, Cape Breton*. Sydney, NS: University College of Cape Breton Press.

Thurgood, Ronald. 1999. "Storytelling on the Gabarus–Framboise Coast of Cape Breton: Oral Narrative Repertoire Analysis in a Folk Community." PhD diss., Memorial University of Newfoundland.

Tornøe, Johannes Kristoffer. 1965. *Norsemen Before Columbus: Early American History*. London: Allen & Unwin.

Toward, Lilias M. 1951. "The Influence of Scottish Clergy on Early Education in Cape Breton." *Nova Scotia Historical Society* 29:153–77.

– 1960. *The Silver Dart Motel Presents Baddeck and Cape Breton Island, Nova Scotia*. Sydney, NS: Commercial Printers.

Toward, Lilias M., and Mabel Gardiner Hubbard Bell. 1984. *Mabel Bell: Alexander's Silent Partner*. Toronto: Methuen.

Trichoche, G. R. 1930. "Caribou Hunting in Cape Breton." In *Rambles Through the Maritime Provinces: A Neglected Part of the British Empire*, 22–39. London: Stockwell.

Trottier, Maxine, Dozay Christmas, and Helen Sylliboy. 1996. *Loon Rock: Pkwimu Wkuntem*. Sydney, NS: University College of Cape Breton Press.

Trottier, Maxine, Patsy MacAulay-MacKinnon, and Rosemary McCormack. 1997. *Heartsong: Ceòl Cridhe*. Sydney, NS: University College of Cape Breton Press.

True, David O. 1956. "Cabot Exploration in North America." *Imago Mundi* 13:11–24.

Tryggvi, J. Oleson. 1963. *Early Voyages and Northern Approaches, 1000–1632*. Canadian Centenary Series. Toronto: McClelland & Stewart.

Tuck, Clyde Edwin. 1916. *History of Nova Scotia*. Halifax: A. W. Bowen. http://eco. canadiana.ca/

Tucker, Brian. 2007. *Big White Knuckles*. Halifax: Vagrant.

Uniacke, Richard John. 1958. *Uniacke's Sketches and Other Papers Relating to Cape Breton Island*, edited by Bruce C. Fergusson. The Nova Scotia Series. Halifax: Public Archives of Nova Scotia.

Upton, Leslie F. S. 1979. *Micmacs and Colonists: Indian-White Relations in the Maritimes, 1713–1867*. Vancouver: University of British Columbia Press.

[Varenne, M de la]. 1980. "A Letter from Louisbourg, 1756." *Acadiensis* 10 (1): 113–30.

Vernon, C. W. 1903. *Cape Breton, Canada at the Beginning of the Twentieth Century: A Treatise of Natural Resources and Development*. Nation Building Series. Toronto: Nation Publishing.

[Viator]. 1970. " A Nineteenth Century Tourist in Cape Breton." *Journal of Education* 5th Series 19 (4): 37–40.

Vigneras, L. A. 1956. "New Light on the 1497 Cabot Voyage to America." *Hispanic American Historical Review* 36 (4): 503–9.

– 1957. "The Cape Breton Landfall: 1494 or 1497?" *Canadian Historical Review* 38 (3): 219–28.

Waite, Helen Elmira. 1961. *Make a Joyful Sound: The Romance of Mabel Hubbard and Alexander Graham Bell, an Authorized Biography*. Philadelphia: Macrae Smith.

Walker, Archie. 1980. *Letters from the Outports*. Markham, ON: Initiative Publishing House.

Walsh, Lillian Crewe. 1950a. *Calling Cape Breton*. Glace Bay, NS: Brodie.

– 1950b. *Greetings from Cape Breton, the Pride of the Maritimes: A Collection of Verse*. Glace Bay, NS: Brodie.

– 2006. *Cape Breton's Lillian Crewe Walsh: A Treasury of Ballads and Poems; With a Conversation about Lillian Crewe Walsh*, edited by Ronald Caplan. Wreck Cove, NS: Breton Books.

Walsh, Noel. 1968a. Love and Rebellion. Cape Breton Lecture Series. 10 March. Beaton Institute, Cape Breton University, Sydney, NS: Pamphlet 1764.

– 1968b. The Psychology of Emigration. Cape Breton Lecture Series. 10 March. Beaton Institute, Cape Breton University, Sydney, NS: Pamphlet 1766.

Walworth, Arthur. 1948. *Cape Breton, Isle of Romance.* Toronto: Longmans, Green.

Wanamaker, Murray Gorham. 1983. "The Language of King's County, Nova Scotia." PhD diss., University of Michigan.

Ward, Don. 2000. "A Youngster's View of the Coke Ovens." *The Cape Bretoner,* 8 (3), 61.

Warner, Charles Dudley. 1899. *Baddeck, and that Sort of Thing.* Boston: Houghton, Mifflin.

Warner, William W. 1997. "The Fish Killers." In *Historical Essays on Canada's Atlantic Fishery,* edited by James E. Candow and Carol Corbin, 223–42. Louisbourg, NS: Louisbourg Institute; Sydney, NS: University College of Cape Breton.

Watson, Duika Burges. 2007. "Public Health and Carrageenan Regulation: A Review and Analysis." *Nineteenth International Seaweed Symposium: Proceedings of the Nineteenth International Seaweed Symposium held in Kobe, Japan.* S.l.: Springer.

Watson, James, and Ellison Robertson. 1987. *Sealladh Gu Taobh: Oral Tradition and Reminiscences by Cape Breton Gaels.* Sydney, NS: University College of Cape Breton Press and University College of Cape Breton Art Gallery.

Watson, Jim. (1894) 1994. "From the Isle of Coll to Inverness County: A Pioneer's Account." edited and translated by Jim Watson. *Am Bràighe,* Spring, 20.

Webb, Jeff A. 2012. "Cullers of Words: Writing the *Dictionary of Newfoundland English.*" *Dictionaries: Journal of the Dictionary Society of North America* 33:58–82.

Webster, Noah, ed. 1828. *An American Dictionary of the English Language.* New York: S. Converse.

Wheeldon, Emily Kendall. 1935. "Where East Begins." *Canadian Geographical Journal* 10 (6): 299–306.

White, William John. 1978. "Left Wing Politics and Community: A Study of Glace Bay, 1930–1940." MA thesis, Dalhousie University.

Whitehead, Ruth Holmes. 1987. "I Have Lived Here Since the World Began: Atlantic Coast Artistic Tradition." *The Spirit Sings: Artistic Traditions of Canada's First People,* 17–50. Toronto and Calgary: McClelland & Stewart and the Glenbow Museum.

– 1991. *The Old Man Told Us: Excerpts From Micmac History, 1500–1950.* Halifax: Nimbus Publishing.

Whitehead, Ruth Holmes, and Ronald Merrick. 1980. *Elitekey Micmac Material Culture from 1600 A.D. to the Present.* Halifax: Nova Scotia Museum.

Whitman, James. 1874. "Seven Weeks on Sable Island." *The New Dominion Monthly,* March, 129–35. http://eco.canadiana.ca/

Whitney Pier Historical Society. 1993. *From the Pier Dear! Images of a Multicultural Community.* Sydney, NS: Whitney Pier Historical Society.

Wicken, William C. 1994. "Encounters with Tall Sails and Tall Tales: Mi'kmaq Society, 1500–1760." PhD diss., McGill University.

– 1998. "R. v. Donald Marshall Jr., 1993-1996." *Acadiensis* 28 (1): 8–17.

Wilcox, Mae. 1978. *Memoirs.* Sydney, NS: City Printers.

Wilder, D. G. 1957. *Canada's Lobster Fishery*. Ottawa: Department of Fisheries of Canada.

Williams, Fred. n.d. *Keep the Light: A History of St. John's and Its People*. S.l.: s.n. Beaton Institute, Cape Breton University, Sydney, NS: Pamphlet 2965.

Williams, Fred, and Ken Murray. 1993. *To Heal Sometimes, to Comfort Always: A History of the Care of the Sick North of Smokey*. Ingonish, NS: s.n.

Williams, Jobe. 2000. "The Rabbit Man of Pool's Cove and North Sydney." *The Cape Bretoner*, 8 (5), 29–30.

Williams, Mary "Pixie." 1985. "Angelica of Louisbourg." *The Occasional*, 9 (3), 21–28.

Williams, Scott. 2000. "Piper John Alexander: 'Black Jack.'" *The Cape Bretoner*, 8 (4), 30–31.

Williams, Trevor. 1988. "The Williams Lobster Factory at Neil's Harbour, 1901–1935." *Nova Scotia Historical Review* 8 (1): 77–83.

Williamson, James Alexander. 1962. *The Cabot Voyages and Bristol Discovery Under Henry VII, Works Issued by the Hakluyt Society*. Cambridge: Published for the Hakluyt Society at the University Press.

Williston, Floyd. 1990. *Johnny Miles: Nova Scotia's Marathon King*. Halifax: Nimbus.

– 2001. "Johnny Miles: Still Going Strong at 95." *The Cape Bretoner*, 9 (1), 43.

Wilson, John H. 1895. "St. Ann's Day Among the Micmacs." *Donahoe's Magazine*, July 754–58.

Winterbotham, W. 1795. *An Historical, Geographical, Commercial, and Philosophical View of the American United States, and of the European Settlements in America and the West-Indies*. London : Printed for the Editors, J. Ridgway, H.D. Symonds, and D. Holt. http://eco.canadiana.ca/

Wisdom, Jane B. 1940. *Glace Bay Looks Ahead*. Ottawa: Canadian Welfare Council.

Wisdom, Jane. 1952. "When Everybody Played the Game." *Cape Breton Mirror*, April 5, 21.

Women's Institutes of Nova Scotia. 1973. *Crocks, Pots and What-Nots*. Truro, NS: Women's Institutes of Nova Scotia.

Wood, Kenneth Scott, and Harold F. Verge. 1966. *A Study of the Problems of Certain Cape Breton Communities*. Halifax: Institute of Public Affairs, Dalhousie University.

Wright, Nancy. "Fishing, Farming, Forestry." 1980. *The Scotia Sun*, April 16.

Wuorio, Eva-Lis. 1950. "Cape Breton: Into the Land of Mod." *Maclean's*, July 16–17.

Yipp, Roy. 2005. "The Final Refrain of a Culture That Was?" *The Cape Bretoner*, 13 (1), 18–21.

Young, George. 1977. *Ghosts in Nova Scotia: Tales of the Supernatural*. Queensland, NS: G. Young.

Zimmeran, Lynn. 1978. "People of Margaree: Portrait of a Good Place." *Harrowsmith*, 15 (3), 74–83.

Zinck, John R. 1998. *The East Coast Ceilidh: A Look at Atlantic Canada's Music Scene*. Dominion, NS: Vanmarkin Publications.

Zgusta, Ladislav. 1971. *Manual of Lexicography*. Prague: Academia; The Hague: Mouton.

FILMS

ATV Reflections. Directed by Evan Scott. Beaton Institute Video FT 3(2), 1981.

Age of The Rivers. Directed by Albert Kish. NFB, 1986. Videocassette (VHS), 52 min 02 s.

The Bay Boy. Directed by Dan Petrie. Bay Boy Productions, 1984. Videocassette (VHS), 107 min.

Buddy MacMaster: The Master of the Cape Breton Fiddle. Directed by Peter Murphy. 1992. Videocassette (VHS), 48 min.

Cape Breton Bras d'Or Lakes, A Sailing Tour with Silver Donald Cameron. Directed by Silver Donald Cameron. 1993. Videocassette (VHS).

Cape Breton Highlands Park. Directed by Peter Trueman. Toronto: Good Earth Productions, 1996. Videocassette (VHS), 20 min.

Cape Breton Scottish Fiddling Today. Directed by Mary Larsen and Rob Roberts. Fiddler Magazine, 1996. Videocassette (VHS), 90 min.

Celtic Spirits. Directed by James Littleton. NFB, 1978. Videocassette (VHS), 57 min 48 s.

Children of Canada 3. NFB, 1987. Videocassette (VHS), 51 min 15 s.

Crimson Flower of Battle. Directed by Silver Donald Cameron. 1994. Videocassette (VHS), 44 min 39 s.

The Fairy Faith. Directed by John Walker. NFB, 2000. Videocassette (VHS), 77 min 02 s.

Fortress of Louisbourg: The Phoenix of the New World. Toronto: Good Earth Productions, 1998. Videocassette (VHS), 23 min.

Going Down the Road. Directed by Donald Shebib. 1972. Seville, DVD, 90 min.

Herbicide Trials. Directed by Neal Livingston. NFB, 1984. Videocassette (VHS), 48 min 16 s.

It's Just Better. NFB, 1982. Videocassette (VHS), 15 min 23 s.

The Fortress of Louisbourg: Making History. Directed by Joan Weeks. Folkus Atlantic, 1995. Videocassette (VHS), 45 min.

Making Steel: Technology, History, Culture of Work. Directed by Elizabeth Beaton. NFB and The University College of Cape Breton, 1992. DVD, 59 min 30 s.

Margaret's Museum. Directed by Mort Ranson. Malofilm Video, 1995. Videocassette (VHS), 114 min.

Marion Bridge. Directed by Wiebke von Carolsfeld. Idlewild Films, 2003. Videocassette (VHS), 90 min.

New Waterford Girl. Directed by Allan Moyle. Alliance Atlantis Video, 2001. Videocassette (VHS), 97 min.

On Assignment: Cape Breton History Series. Directed by Ralph Ripley. Beaton Institute Video FT (3a), 1980.Videocassette (VHS).

On Assignment: Cape Breton History Series. Directed by Ralph Ripley. Beaton Institute Video FT 3 (3b). 1980. Videocassette (VHS).

The Pipes, The Pipes are Calling. Directed by Peter Murphy. Seabright Video Productions, 1996. Videocassette (VHS), 90 min.

Pit Pony, Directed by Eric Till. Cochran Entertainment Inc., 1997. DVD, 92 min.

Pit Pony. Television Series, Episodes 1–10, Cochran Entertainment, 2001.

Pleasant Bay, House Raising. CBC Television, 9 April 1987. Beaton Institute Video FT (33)

Scoggie. NFB, 1975. Videocassette (VHS), 26 min 08 s.

Something About Love. NFB, 1988. Videocassette (VHS), 93 min 14 s.

Song of Eskasoni. NFB, 1993. Videocassette (VHS), 28 min 50 s.

They Didn't Starve Us Out: Industrial Cape Breton in the 1920s. Directed by Patricia Kipping. NFB, 1991. Videocassette (VHS), 21 min 04 s.

12,000 Men. Directed by Martin Duckworth. NFB, 1978. Videocassette (VHS), 34 min 27 s.

Write Canada. East Coast Post & Duplication, 1991.

AUDIOTAPES

Beaton Institute Tape 5. 1973. Murphy, Peter J. New Waterford, Rural History.

Beaton Institute Tape 7. Kennedy, Dan. 1963. Early Life in [Inverness] Cape Breton.

Beaton Institute Tape 8. 1 July 1976. Chisholm, Willy D. Margaree Forks.

Beaton Institute Tape 28. Akerman, Jeremy. 31 July 1967. Documentary on the Labor Strike in the Cape Breton Coal Fields during the years 1924 and 1925 ... CHER Radio.

Beaton Institute Tape 37. 1967. Day, Rev. Joseph, and W.G. Fraser. Reminiscences of Ingonish.

Beaton Institute Tape 40. 1966. Campbell, Joseph. Pioneers of Big Pond.

Beaton Institute Tape 49. 1976. Forgeron, Dave, Alice Maude Bain, and Flora May Humber. CBC Radio, Sydney, Souvenirs.

Beaton Institute Tape 57. 1968. Fergusson, John, and Donald Fergusson. Broughton History.

Beaton Institute Tape 73. 1978. MacKenzie, Joseph. Mira Gut History.

Beaton Institute Tape 74. 1968. Ferguson, Dan, and John MacLellan. Reminiscences of Mira.

Beaton Institute Tape 77. 13 January 1969. MacDonald, Angus R. Cape Breton Stories in English and Gaelic.

Beaton Institute Tape 78. 1969. MacDonald, Archie. Coal Mining in Cape Breton.

Beaton Institute Tape 97. 1976. Chaisson, Mary Ellen. Autobiography.

Beaton Institute Tape 99. 1969. Lynch, Dr. J. G. B. Medical Service in DOSCO Since 1910. Names of Managers and Officials.

Beaton Institute Tape 111. 1976. Beaton, John. The Beatons of Mabou Coal Mines.

Beaton Institute Tape 118. 1969. Stewart, Billy, and Fred Guy. Early Coal Mining on the North Side.

Beaton Institute Tape 120. 1969. MacLean, Alex. Reminiscences of Early Days in Washabuck.

Beaton Institute Tape 123. 1969. MacLellan, John. History of Brickyard Road.

Beaton Institute Tape 129. 1969. MacPhee, Russell. Stories of Cape Breton.

Beaton Institute Tape 132. 14 December 1976, 4 January 1977. Cann, Arthur, Bill Fraser, Grace Carmichael, John D. MacDonald, Ethel MacDonald, J. J. Chaisson, Rebecca Collier, Harry Muldoon, Harriet MacLean, and Archie MacKinnon. Biographical Sketches. CBC Radio Sydney, Souvenirs.

Beaton Institute Tape 133. 1968. MacNeil, Hector. Songs and Anecdotes.

Beaton Institute Tape 139. 1969. Morrison, Daniel. Marble Mountain History.

Beaton Institute Tape 145. 1970. Anderson, Dan. Reminiscences of Sydney.

Beaton Institute Tape 160. 1969. MacDonald, Billy S. Early Mining Methods.

Beaton Institute Tape 165. 1970. Topshee, Rev. George. Sayings of Dr. Jimmy Tompkins: Reading of the Poem, Bocan Bridge of Canso.

Beaton Institute Tape 171. 30 July 1969. MacNeil, Lewis, and Lizzie MacNeil. History of Grand Narrows.

Beaton Institute Tape 175. 1976. MacNeil, Gussie. History of New Waterford.

Beaton Institute Tape 175. 1976. MacNeil, Michael. Co-op and Credit Union.

Beaton Institute Tape 182. 1970. MacKinnon, J. D. [Northside East Bay]. History of Northside East Bay and East Bay Church. By Sr. Margaret Beaton and Mrs. A. C. Day.

Beaton Institute Tape 183. 1970. MacKinnon, John Angus. Reminiscences of St. Rose. By Sr. Margaret Beaton and Mrs. A. C. Day.

Beaton Institute Tape 202. 1966. MacNeil, J. C. Reminiscences of Life in Cape Breton in the Early 1900's.

Beaton Institute Tape 203. 1970. MacLean, Alex D. Reminiscences of Baddeck.

Beaton Institute Tape 205 A. 1970. MacDonald, Dan R. History of Barachois.

Beaton Institute Tape 207. 1972. Burke, Minnie. Biographical Sketch, Lingan and Victoria Mines History.

Beaton Institute Tape 210. 1975. Timmons, Sid. Remember the Miner.

Beaton Institute Tape 212. 1971. MacInnis, Ron. The Vanishing Cape Breton Fiddler. Stories and History of Cape Breton. CBC Radio, Halifax.

Beaton Institute Tape 213. January 1971. MacPhail, Colin. Reminiscences of South Bar. By Hilda Day.

Beaton Institute Tape 217. 1971. MacPhee, Russell, Dan J. MacDonald, Joseph MacDonald, Peter MacIntyre, Stanley Appleton. History of Coal Mining in Glace Bay.

Beaton Institute Tape 223. 1971. MacDonald, Dan J. Coal and Steel Strikes.

Beaton Institute Tape 226. 1971. Steele, Allan. Ceilidh at his Home [in Boisdale].

Beaton Institute Tape 229. 1971. MacGregor, Gordon. History of Coal Mining in Cape Breton.

Beaton Institute Tape 230. 1971. MacPhee, Russell. Coal Mining in Cape Breton.

Beaton Institute Tape 234. 1977. MacDonald, Terry, and Phonse Chisholm. History of Inverness Town.

Beaton Institute Tape 235. 1977. MacIsaac, Mr., George Poirier, Joseph LeFort, Mrs. J. LeFort, and John Edward MacKay. History of Inverness Town and Coal Mines.

Beaton Institute Tape 236. 1972. MacIsaac, Mrs. and John Angus MacNeil. History of Inverness Town and Mines.

Beaton Institute Tape 239. 1978. Aucoin, Pat, and Joe Delaney. Cheticamp History and Folklore.

Beaton Institute Tape 242. 1971. MacKenzie, Hugh. Humorous Stories.

Beaton Institute Tape 255. 1976. Campbell, Malcom. Folklore.

Beaton Institute Tape 261. 1971. MacQueen, Neil. Pioneer Days.

Beaton Institute Tape 267. 1971. Fahey, Fred. Sydney Mines.

Beaton Institute Tape 275. 1971. Ferguson, Archie. Stories.

Beaton Institute Tape 277. 1971. MacNeil, Jim Charles. Miscellaneous: Cape Breton Railroad, Gaelic Readings, Songs, and Stories.

Beaton Institute Tape 280. 1971. Carmichael, Harry. Georges River History.

Beaton Institute Tape 282. 1971. MacNeil, Jim. Talks and Stories.

Beaton Institute Tape 293. 1971. MacNeil, Donald. Reminiscences of Bras d'Or.

Beaton Institute Tape 306. 1971. Pendergast, Florence. Bras d'Or History: Social Life, Ferry Service, Mining, Genealogy.

Beaton Institute Tape 308. 10 August 1976. MacDonald, Dan. Old Times in Cape Breton.

Beaton Institute Tape 316. 1972. MacDonald, Eugene. Local Industry, Songs and Stories.

Beaton Institute Tape 326. 1972. MacDonald, Joseph Lawrence. Early Settlers in Boisdale.

Beaton Institute Tape 331. 17 February 1972. MacDonald, J. L. History of Boisdale Area and Biographical Sketches.

Beaton Institute Tape 335. 1972. Campbell, Finlay. Finlay Campbell Discusses Malcom Gillis of Margaree.
Beaton Institute Tape 342. 1972. Timmons, Irene. Education in New Waterford.
Beaton Institute Tape 344. 1972. Ratchtford, Guy. Low Point.
Beaton Institute Tape 345. 1972. Lamey, Tom. New Waterford.
Beaton Institute Tape 346. 1972. MacDonald, Angus F. New Waterford Coal Mining.
Beaton Institute Tape 351. 1972. Ruck, Winston. Social Life, Sydney.
Beaton Institute Tape 366. 1972. MacDonald, Joseph. Witchcraft, Humour, and Satire.
Beaton Institute Tape 367. 1972. Matheson, John. Native Stories and Songs.
Beaton Institute Tape 369. 1972. Delorenzo, Benny. History of Sydney Steel.
Beaton Institute Tape 373. 1972. Anderson, Mrs. Rod. Salvation Army, Glace Bay.
Beaton Institute Tape 383. 1972. Gaelic Songs and Stories from Glencoe. By Elizabeth MacEachern.
Beaton Institute Tape 385. 1972. MacDonald, Archie Alex. Coal Mining, New Waterford.
Beaton Institute Tape 393. 1972. Anderson, Mrs. Rod. History of Sight Point.
Beaton Institute Tape 394. 1965. MacNeil, Margaret. History of Low Point.
Beaton Institute Tape 396. 1972. MacLeod, Murdock. Baddeck: Social Life, Education and Stories. By Mrs. A. C. Day.
Beaton Institute Tape 396. 1971. Pendergast, Florence. Reminiscences of Bras d'Or.
Beaton Institute Tape 398. 1972. Currie, Lauchie. History of Grand Mira.
Beaton Institute Tape 406. 1972. MacDonald, Joseph. Ghost Stories.
Beaton Institute Tape 412. 1972. MacPherson, Duncan. History of Cape Breton.
Beaton Institute Tape 415. 11 April 1972. Rudderham, Gordon. Biography of the Rudderham Family.
Beaton Institute Tape 421. 1972. MacIsaac, John. Number 6 Colliery, Donkin.
Beaton Institute Tape 422. 1972. MacIntyre [unknown name] and Joe Coady. Piping and Stories.
Beaton Institute Tape 427. 1972. MacKinnon, Joseph, Joseph MacDonald, Neil Campbell, Stephen R. MacNeil. Biography and Social Life in Christmas Island, Boisdale, MacKinnon's Harbour, Iona. By Joseph Lawrence MacDonald.
Beaton Institute Tape 458. 1972. MacKenzie, M. B., and Joseph L. MacDonald. Boisdale and Christmas Island Stories.
Beaton Institute Tape 459. 1972. MacDonald, Joseph Lawrence. History: Big Pond, Iona, Barra Glen, and Ottawa Brook.
Beaton Institute Tape 460. 1972. Various Biographies. By Joseph Lawrence.
Beaton Institute Tape 466. 1968. MacNeil, Jim Charles. History of Scottish Catholic Society: Stories of Cape Breton.
Beaton Institute Tape 467. 1972. MacIsaac, Alex, Sandy MacFarlane, and John A. MacIsaac. Biographies, Songs, and Stories.
Beaton Institute Tape 471. 1976.Williams, Buck, Anne Williams, and Pat Pentecost. The 1929 Earthquake.
Beaton Institute Tape 500. 1972. MacLeod, Norman, John A. MacIsaac, Mrs. James MacNeil, and Jim McEvoy. Descriptions and Stories.
Beaton Institute Tape 501. 1972. MacKinnon, Charlie, Mrs. John E. MacNeil, and John E. MacNeil. Giant MacAskill, Picnics and Customs, Fishing, History of Giant MacAskill and Bay St. Lawrence. By Mary Elizabeth MacNeil.
Beaton Institute Tape 503. 1972. MacKeen, Rankin. History of Sydney.

Beaton Institute Tape 515. 1972. Burke, Alice, Henry Campbell, and Martin Sampson. Biography, Homes, and Stories: Lower L'Ardoise, Early Acadians. By Ileana Barrett.

Beaton Institute Tape 526. 1972. Yazer, Jack. Biography.

Beaton Institute Tape 535. 1976. MacPherson, Abby, and Archie MacIntyre. History of the Company Stores.

Beaton Institute Tape 537. 1972. White, Murdock. Biography, Retired Miner.

Beaton Institute Tape 538. 1972. MacDougall, Mabel. Early Days in New Waterford: 1925 Strike.

Beaton Institute Tape 541. 1992. Leudy, Patricia. Early Days in New Waterford.

Beaton Institute Tape 548. 1972. MacKinnon, Mrs. D. V., and E. MacKinnon. Biographical Sketch and the Life of Stephen MacKinnon.

Beaton Institute Tape 551. 1972. Burke, Minnie. History of Lingan.

Beaton Institute Tape 562. 1972. Sampson, A. L'Ardoise History.

Beaton Institute Tape 563. 1972. Campbell, Henry, Martin Sampson, Mr. Wincey, and Peter S. Clannen. L'Ardoise History. By Ileana M. Barrett.

Beaton Institute Tape 570. MacKenzie, William. 1972. Early Mining Days in Glace Bay: The Union Struggle in the Area, Strikes.

Beaton Institute Tape 605. 12 January 1973. Poirier, Joseph. Early Days in Sydney. By Mrs. A. C. Day.

Beaton Institute Tape 623. December 1972. MacNeil, Mrs. John R. Biography and History of Hay Cove. By John Campbell.

Beaton Institute Tape 632. 1977. MacPhee, Annie, *et al.* Interviews on Cape Breton History. By Ron Caplan.

Beaton Institute Tape 671. 1977. Jackson, Hubert. History of Howie Center.

Beaton Institute Tape 672. 1977. Mullins, Bernard. History of Bateston.

Beaton Institute Tape 708. 1973. MacKay, Neil. Baddeck History.

Beaton Institute Tape 711. 1977. MacKeigan, Irene. History of Coxheath.

Beaton Institute Tape 712. 1977. Murant, Henry. History of Port Morien.

Beaton Institute Tape 723. 1977. Holm, Dick. New Waterford History.

Beaton Institute Tape 762. 14 June 1978. Lynch, Sadie. Biography and Sydney History. CBC Radio, Sydney, Souvenirs.

Beaton Institute Tape 763. 16 August 1980. Gallant, Henry. Coal Mining in New Waterford. By Doug MacPhee at Maple Hill Manor, New Waterford.

Beaton Institute Tape 795. 1973. Moran, Daniel. Number 12 Colliery, New Waterford.

Beaton Institute Tape 796. 1972. Beaton, Peggy. Glencoe Mills.

Beaton Institute Tape 809. 1973. Billaway, Glen. North of Smokey. CBC Documentary. CBC Radio, Sydney.

Beaton Institute Tape 812. 15 October 1973. "Black Friday Review." CBC Radio, Sydney.

Beaton Institute Tape 844. 10 June 1977. MacNeil, Josie, et al. Scottish Culture in Cape Breton.

Beaton Institute Tape 854. 16 January 1978. Peters, James B., and Mary Margaret Peters. Violin Making and Other Crafts. CBC Radio, Sydney, Souvenirs.

Beaton Institute Tape 855. 17 June 1977. Dubbin, Mabel. Biography. CBC Radio, Sydney, Souvenirs.

Beaton Institute Tape 856. 8 February 1979. Campbell, Malcolm. Folklore. By Daphne MacKay. CBC Radio, Sydney, Souvenirs.

Beaton Institute Tape 861. 3 June 1977. Boutilier, William, and Minnie Boutilier. History of Waddens Cove. By Daphne MacKay. CBC Radio, Sydney, Souvenirs.

Beaton Institute Tape 870 A. 1977. MacDonald, Joseph L., Rev. John Hillborn, John Nicholson, Harvey Webber, Robert Morgan, Tom Kent, Rev. John Capstick, Rev. Andy Hogan, Rev. Greg MacLeod, John Allan Cameron, Hugh MacKenzie, and Allan MacDonald. Documentary on Cape Breton Economy. CBC Radio, Sydney.

Beaton Institute Tape 870 B. 1977. Boyd, Sandy, Tony Basso, Archie Neil Chisholm et al. Cape Breton: The Hidden Identity. CBC Radio, Sydney.

Beaton Institute Tape 878. 1974. McGowan, Thomas. Early Days of Mining [late 1800s to 1900s].

Beaton Institute Tape 894. 1980. MacAskill, John A. Giant MacAskill. CBC Radio, Sydney, Souvenirs.

Beaton Institute Tape 895. 1980. Fraser, William. His Career in the RCMP. CBC Radio, Sydney, Souvenirs.

Beaton Institute Tape 896. 1977. Huntington, Eleanor. Mira History. CBC Radio, Sydney, Souvenirs.

Beaton Institute Tape 898. 1977. MacNeil, Steve. History of Big Pond. By Neil MacNeil.

Beaton Institute Tape 899. 1977. Matheson, Murdock, Ronald Murphy, Joe MacNeil, and Mr. and Mrs. Isaac Batten. History and Biography of New Aberdeen.

Beaton Institute Tape 900. 1977. Chafe, Winnifred. Ceilidhs.

Beaton Institute Tape 903. 1977. Clarke, Charles. Fishing at Gabarus.

Beaton Institute Tape 904. 1977. Kelly, Herman. History of Lingan.

Beaton Institute Tape 905. 1976. MacDonald, Olive. History of the Royal Theatre Dominion.

Beaton Institute Tape 906. 14 November 1976. Gouthro, Dan J. The Old Gouthro Homestead at Frenchvale.

Beaton Institute Tape 934. Dickson, Hugh, and Archie MacDonald. 1980. Company Houses in Sydney Mines.

Beaton Institute Tape 939. 1974. MacMillan, Dr. C. L. Address to Old Sydney Society: Early Days in Medical Practice and Early Doctors in Cape Breton.

Beaton Institute Tape 940. 1974. MacIntyre, Archie. Strikes, 1909, 1925; Mine Explosion, 1909 [On Side A]. Early Days in Mining, Caledonia #4 [On Side B].

Beaton Institute Tape 960. 1984. MacLeod, Rachael, et al. Alderwood Guest Home, Baddeck. CBC Radio, Sydney, Fresh Air.

Beaton Institute Tape 983. 20 February 1978. A Look at Ourselves, Heritage Day. CJCB Radio, Sydney.

Beaton Institute Tape 992. 1973. Murphy, Rory. Moonshine in Cape Breton.

Beaton Institute Tape 993. 1977. Matheson, Murdock. Early Days in Glace Bay: Coal Mines and Mining.

Beaton Institute Tape 994. 1982. History of Loch Lomond. CBC Radio, Sydney, Fresh Air.

Beaton Institute Tape 1005. 10 December 1974. Steele, Sarah. History of Agriculture and Social Life in Boisdale.

Beaton Institute Tape 1017. 1975. MacLeod, Dan. Agriculture in Grand Mira. By Blair MacKinnon.

Beaton Institute Tape 1019. 1975. MacNeil, John Hector. Agriculture in Shenacadie.

Beaton Institute Tape 1022. 1975. Campbell, John Neil. Agriculture and Early Life in Boisdale, Parts 1 and Part 2. By Brian MacKinnon.

Beaton Institute Tape 1026. 1975. Doyle, Bill. CBC Documentary on Cape Breton: A
   Culture, An Epic, and a Cowboy Economy.
Beaton Institute Tape 1037. 1978. MacKenzie, Hughie, and Allan MacDougall. Hughie
   and Allan: Cape Breton Humour.
Beaton Institute Tape 1051. 1975. Grant, Mary. Biography.
Beaton Institute Tape 1052. 1975. MacPhail, Margaret. Biography.
Beaton Institute Tape 1077. 1978. Deveaux, Marie. Cheticamp History and Folklore.
Beaton Institute Tape 1095. 1975. Cantwell, Bernie. History of Agriculture in Bras d'Or.
   By Blair MacKinnon.
Beaton Institute Tape 1107. 1975. Burke, Mary. [100 years old] Life in the Early Days.
Beaton Institute Tape 1144. June 1978. Deveaux, J. J., and Mrs. Deveaux. Witchcraft in
   Cheticamp. By Elizabeth Beaton.
Beaton Institute Tape 1146. 1978. LeLievre, Ulysses, and Henrietta Aucoin.
   Superstitions in Cheticamp.
Beaton Institute Tape 1154. November 1978. Cloak, Mrs. John W., and Janet (MacInnes)
   Spray. Port Hawkesbury History.
Beaton Institute Tape 1155. 1978. Rum Running in Cape Breton. By Tony Tierney.
Beaton Institute Tape 1157. December 1978. Chiasson, J. J. Cheticamp History and
   Folklore. By Betty Beaton.
Beaton Institute Tape 1159. 1979. Murphy, John. Margaree, Museum of Musical
   Instruments.
Beaton Institute Tape 1166. 1979. Deveaux, Denise, and Marie Deveaux. Cheticamp
   Folklore and French Folk Songs.
Beaton Institute Tape 1170. 1979. MacDonald, John Alex. Margaree Ghost Stories.
Beaton Institute Tape 1175. 1979. MacNeil, Lewis. History of Grand Narrows.
Beaton Institute Tape 1183. 1979. Brennan, Lorraine. Inverness History.
Beaton Institute Tape 1185. 1979. MacDonnell, Alex. Judique.
Beaton Institute Tape 1194. 1980. Deveaux, J. J., and Mrs. Deveaux. Cheticamp Folklore
   and History. By Betty Planetta.
Beaton Institute Tape 1199. 9 August 1982. MacKillop, Jim. Justice and the Penal
   System.
Beaton Institute Tape 1416. 2 January 1980. Chisholm, Archie Neil, Host and Storyteller
   with Alex John MacIsaac. CBC Radio, Sydney, Archie Neil's Cape Breton.
Beaton Institute Tape 1417. n.d. Chisholm, Archie Neil, Host and Storyteller with
   Paddy MacDonald and Alex John MacIsaac. CBC Radio, Sydney, Archie Neil's Cape
   Breton.
Beaton Institute Tape 1418. 16 January 1980. Chisholm, Archie Neil, Host and
   Storyteller with Rev. John Angus Rankin and Buddy MacDonald. CBC Radio,
   Sydney, Archie Neil's Cape Breton.
Beaton Institute Tape 1419. 23 January 1980. Chisholm, Archie Neil, Host and
   Storyteller with Malcolm MacDonald. CBC Radio, Sydney, Archie Neil's Cape
   Breton.
Beaton Institute Tape 1420. 30 January 1980. Chisholm, Archie Neil, Host and
   Storyteller with Paddy MacDonald. CBC Radio, Sydney, Archie Neil's Cape Breton.
Beaton Institute Tape 1421. 6 February 1980. Chisholm, Archie Neil, Host and
   Storyteller with Rev. John Angus Rankin. CBC Radio, Sydney, Archie Neil's Cape
   Breton.

Beaton Institute Tape 1428. 26 March 1980. Chisholm, Archie Neil, Host and Storyteller with Malcolm MacDonald. CBC Radio, Sydney, Archie Neil's Cape Breton.

Beaton Institute Tape 1660. 20 November 1983. MacNeil, Kyle, and Shamus MacNeil. Donnie Campbell's Home, Sydney. CBC Radio, Sydney.

Beaton Institute Tape 1923. August 1980. French Milling Frolic in Cheticamp.

Beaton Institute Tape 2003. n.d. MacNeil, Mike. His Childhood, Reared by his Grandparents at Christmas Island. CBC Radio, Sydney, Souvenirs.

Beaton Institute Tape 2008. 1990. Nathanson, Dr. Dan, Rose Schwartz, James P. MacNeil, and Margaret MacPhee. Interviews from New Waterford. CBC Radio, Sydney, Fresh Air.

Beaton Institute Tape 2009. 10 November 1980. Buffett, Betty. Biography, Retired School Teacher. CBC Radio, Sydney, Fresh Air.

Beaton Institute Tape 2031. 1980. Aucoin, Mrs. On Hooking Rugs, Cheticamp.

Beaton Institute Tape 2034. 1982. MacDonald, Angus J. Interview. By Wilma J. Macdonald.

Beaton Institute Tape 2035. 1981. Chisholm, Archie Neil, Host and Storyteller with Roddie MacNeil. Reminiscences of Life in the Early Days, Margaree. CBC Radio, Sydney, Archie Neil's Cape Breton.

Beaton Institute Tape 2037. 1981. Hicks, Thomas. History of Glace Bay Pensioner's Club; History of Early Mining.

Beaton Institute Tape 2039 [Tape 1]. December 1981. Campbell, Angus B., Chuen Guddang, Danny Graham, Flora MacMillan, and Buddy MacMaster. Judique. CBC Radio Sydney, Fresh Air.

Beaton Institute Tape 2041. 1982. Haye, Elizabeth. Rich Town, Poor Town: A Comparison of Sydney, Cape Breton, to Markham, Ontario. CBC Radio, Sydney.

Beaton Institute Tape 2045. 11 April 1981. MacKeigan, Christine, Mary Ann MacDonald, Roddy Monroe, Helen MacDonald, G. Weisner, John Ewen MacKenzie. Mira History. CBC Radio, Sydney, Fresh Air.

Beaton Institute Tape 2046. 7 March 1981. Burke, Charlie, et al. Fresh Air Visits Baleine and Washabuck. CBC Radio, Sydney, Fresh Air.

Beaton Institute Tape 2047. n.d. MacKay, Dan, Dolly MacKay, Lloyd Grant, Jessie MacKay, and Andrew MacDonald. Fresh Air Programme on Boularderie. CBC Radio, Sydney, Fresh Air.

Beaton Institute Tape 2048. 1983. Kennedy, Vince, Mary Rice, and Kate Burke. Fresh Air from Little Lorraine. Radio, Sydney, Fresh Air.

Beaton Institute Tape 2063. n.d. Fresh Air on Sydney River. CBC Radio, Sydney, Fresh Air.

Beaton Institute Tape 2067. 16 January 1982. Williams, Fred, Lloyd Lamey, Don Ingraham, Frank Dowling, Frances Digout. Fresh Air Visits Neils Harbour. CBC Radio, Sydney, Fresh Air.

Beaton Institute Tape 2068. 1982. Fresh Air Visits Middle River and Benacadie. CBC Radio, Sydney, Fresh Air.

Beaton Institute Tape 2069. 1982. MacKenzie, Carl, Charlie MacKenzie, Malcolm MacDonald, Josie MacLean, and Joe MacLean. Fresh Air Visits Washabuck. CBC Radio, Sydney, Fresh Air.

Beaton Institute Tape 2071. 1982. Fresh Air Visits Pleasant Bay and Port Hastings. CBC Radio, Sydney, Fresh Air.

Beaton Institute Tape 2073. 10 March 1986. MacLean, Mary [Nicholson]. MacRae-Bitterman House, Middle River.

Beaton Institute Tape 2079. 11 April 1983. Evans, Dean. Coal Mining at St. Rose.

Beaton Institute Tape 2100. December 1983. MacDonald, Betty, Sid Murray, John Campbell, Hughie MacDonald, Jacqueline MacDonald, Don Rudderham, et al. Fresh Air from Away. CBC Radio, Sydney, Fresh Air.

Beaton Institute Tape 2101 [Tape 1]. 1980. Baggio, Condo. Dominion History.

Beaton Institute Tape 2101 [Tape 2]. 1980. Stephenson, Len. Italians in Dominion.

Beaton Institute Tape 2101 [Tape 3]. 1979. Hawkins, Mrs. George. Life in Dominion.

Beaton Institute Tape 2101 [Tape 4]. 28 April 1981. Gaetan, Fred. New Waterford History.

Beaton Institute Tape 2101 [Tape 5]. 1980. Gatto, Ralph. Dominion History.

Beaton Institute Tape 2101 [Tape 6]. 1980. Baggio, Condo. Dominion History.

Beaton Institute Tape 2101 [Tape 7]. 1981. Gatto, Bert. New Waterford History.

Beaton Institute Tape 2101 [Tape 8]. 28 April 1981. Gatto, Gordon. New Waterford History.

Beaton Institute Tape 2108. 1984. MacDonald, Mrs. J. Folklore 100. By Michael Gerard MacDonald.

Beaton Institute Tape 2109. 5 April 1984. MacDonald, Genny. Farm Life. Folklore 100.

Beaton Institute Tape 2110. 5 December 1983. MacLellan, John A. Cape Breton Horse Racing on Ice. By Ken MacLean.

Beaton Institute Tape 2111. 1984. MacDonald, Amy. Polish Christmas.

Beaton Institute Tape 2112. 1983. Children's Folk Games. By Mary MacSween.

Beaton Institute Tape 2113 [Tape 1]. 1983. MacDonald, Alice. Boisdale History.

Beaton Institute Tape 2113 [Tape 2]. 1983. MacDonald, Joseph L. Boisdale History.

Beaton Institute Tape 2113 [Tape 3]. 1984. MacIntyre, Hughie. Boisdale History.

Beaton Institute Tape 2113 [Tape 4]. 1984. MacDonald, Mary and Hector. Boisdale History.

Beaton Institute Tape 2113 [Tape 5]. 1984. MacKinnon, Martin. Boisdale History.

Beaton Institute Tape 2114. 1983. MacDonald, Charles. East Lake Ainslie History.

Beaton Institute Tape 2116. Campbell, Peter MacKenzie. 1983. Johnstown History, Folklore 100.

Beaton Institute Tape 2121. 22 December 1984. Caulfield, Georgina, George MacNeil, Bernie Morrison, Arthur Morrison, Annie Duncan, et al. Fresh Air Christmas Messages. CBC Radio, Sydney, Fresh Air.

Beaton Institute Tape 2122. 29 December 1984. MacLellan, Donald, Marie MacLellan, Roy McKeen, Myrtle McKeen, Bessie Edwards, et al. Christmas Messages From Away. By Daphne MacKay. CBC Radio, Sydney, Fresh Air.

Beaton Institute Tape 2133. 7 June 1969. MacDonald, Dan R. Cape Breton Violinist and Composer. By Jim Carroll.

Beaton Institute Tape 2134. 1984. Porter, Harry. New Waterford Coal Mining.

Beaton Institute Tape 2135. 1984. Morrison, William. Coal Mining, New Waterford.

Beaton Institute Tape 2136. 1984. Ling, Bert. Coal Mining, New Waterford.

Beaton Institute Tape 2137. 1984. MacNeil, Gussie [with Michael MacNeil]. Coal Mining, New Waterford.

Beaton Institute Tape 2138. 1984. MacKay, Henry. Coal Mining, New Waterford.

Beaton Institute Tape 2139. 1984. Pastuck, Barney. Coal Mining, New Waterford.

Beaton Institute Tape 2140. 1984. Aucoin, Leo L. Coal Mining, New Waterford.

Beaton Institute Tape 2141. 1984. Chaisson, John Joseph. New Waterford Coal Mining. By Marie Brann.

Beaton Institute Tape 2142. 1984. Connors, Jack. New Waterford Coal Mining.

Beaton Institute Tape 2143. 1984. Mullins, Mickey. New Waterford Coal Mining. By Marie Brann.

Beaton Institute Tape 2144. 1984. Bruce, Nathan. New Waterford Coal Mining.

Beaton Institute Tape 2145. 1984. White, Julia. New Waterford Coal Mining.

Beaton Institute Tape 2146. 1984. MacNeil, John J. Super[intendant]. New Waterford Coal Mining.

Beaton Institute Tape 2148. 22 August 1984. Boudreau, Leo, and Rose Schwartz. Biography.

Beaton Institute Tape 2150. 1984. MacMullin, Mrs. Roddy. New Waterford History.

Beaton Institute Tape 2151. 1984. MacKenzie, Cecil. Town of New Waterford [coal mining]. By Leslie MacLean.

Beaton Institute Tape 2152. 14 August 1984. MacNeil, Jimmy P. New Waterford and Coal Mining

Beaton Institute Tape 2153. 1984. MacNeil, Michael. New Waterford Coal Mining.

Beaton Institute Tape 2154. 1984. Chaisson, Joe. New Waterford History.

Beaton Institute Tape 2155. 1984. MacMullin, Mr. Coal Mining in New Waterford.

Beaton Institute Tape 2156. 1984. Sicky, John. New Waterford Coal Mining. By Leslie MacLean.

Beaton Institute Tape 2159. 1984. Muise, Herbert and Spouse. New Waterford Coal Mining.

Beaton Institute Tape 2161. 1984. Nathanson, Dr. Dan. Town of New Waterford. By Leslie MacLean.

Beaton Institute Tape 2162. 1984. Berger, J. Coal Mining in New Waterford. By Leslie MacLean.

Beaton Institute Tape 2164. 1984. MacKinnon, Waldo. New Waterford Coal Mines.

Beaton Institute Tape 2167. June 1981. Nathanson, Dr. Dan. Town of New Waterford. Talk Back. [CJCB Radio, Sydney].

Beaton Institute Tape 2172. 7 August 1978. MacDonald, Nancy, Donnie MacDonald, and George Grant. West Side Middle River. By Debbie MacIvor.

Beaton Institute Tape 2173. 5 May 1978. MacDonald, Donnie Neil. West Side Middle River, History.

Beaton Institute Tape 2174. 12 March 1978. MacKenzie, Mrs. George. History of West Side Middle River.

Beaton Institute Tape 2176. 2 March 1978. MacLeod, Clarence. West Side Middle River History.

Beaton Institute Tape 2178. 10 March 1984. Evans, Norma, Ward MacLellan, Louise MacLellan, Merit Richardson, Ethel Dingwall, and Sarah Murphy. Fresh Air on South Bar. CBC Radio, Sydney, Fresh Air.

Beaton Institute Tape 2186. 1984. Corbett, Molly. Reserve History. By Ed Kyte.

Beaton Institute Tape 2189. 31 May 1985. Wowk, Fred. Biography.

Beaton Institute Tape 2210. 18 April 1986. Morrison, Malcolm. Local Cape Breton History.

Beaton Institute Tape 2212. 1986. Rosenblum, C. M. Biography. By Pam Newton.

Beaton Institute Tape 2217. 1986. MacDonald, Gus. Port Morien, Time of our Lives.

Beaton Institute Tape 2241. 23 January 1985. MacKay, Jessie. Jessie MacKay Celebrates her 100th Birthday. CBC Radio, Sydney.

Beaton Institute Tape 2242. 1984. MacKay, Jessie. Early Days and Christmas in
 Boularderie.
Beaton Institute Tape 2249. 17 February 1977. Hinkley, Jack Sam, U. LeLievre, and D.
 Fraser. History of Pleasant Bay.
Beaton Institute Tape 2251. 2 November 1986. MacNeil, Mary Ann, and Georgie Beaton.
 Cures and Remedies.
Beaton Institute Tape 2253. 1988. DeYoung, Terra, and Ellen MacKinnon. Folklore and
 Skipping Songs.
Beaton Institute Tape 2259. n.d. Gilmet, Walter. CMU Card Signer and Miner.
Beaton Institute Tape 2270. May 1989. Day, Hilda. History and Genealogy of Cape
 Breton. By Robert Morgan.
Beaton Institute Tape 2276. May 1991. Merner, Martin. Trade Unions.
Beaton Institute Tape 2300. 1987. Harley, Dave [General John Cabot Trail]. Comedy.
Beaton Institute Tape 2302. 1988. Lovelace, James. Memories. CHER Radio, Sydney.
Beaton Institute Tape 2311. 28 May 1986. MacDonald, Olive. Royal Theatre, Dominion.
Beaton Institute Tape 2313. 1986. Barratt, Wanda. Tales of Ghosts and the Supernatural.
Beaton Institute Tape 2315. n.d. Myers, Chrissie, and Charlie Myers. Glace Bay History.
Beaton Institute Tape 2317. 1986. Dow, David. Folklore Medicine.
Beaton Institute Tape 2324 [Tape 1]. 1 April 1987. Burke, Joe. Trap Making.
Beaton Institute Tape 2324 [Tape 2]. 1987. Goyetche, Gerry. Trap Making.
Beaton Institute Tape 2328. 8 April 1985. Slade, Wilemina. Traditions and Customs.
Beaton Institute Tape 2331 [Tape 1]. 1987. MacNeil, Phyllis. Forerunners.
Beaton Institute Tape 2331 [Tape 2]. 1987. Brown, Mildred. Forerunners.
Beaton Institute Tape 2333 [Tape 1]. April 1987. MacMullin, Patsy. Weaving.
Beaton Institute Tape 2333 [Tape 2]. April 1987. MacDonald, Eleanor. Weaving.
Beaton Institute Tape 2336. n.d. MacLellan, John A. A History of Riverside, Inverness
 County.
Beaton Institute Tape 2337. 14 May 1980. MacLeod, Dave, Parker Barss Donham, Joe
 Legg, Pepe Salzo, Wilfred Chaisson, Micky Hayes, Benny O'Neil, Don Holahan,
 George Clarke, Bernadette Salzo, Betty Clarke, Enez Holahan, Winston Parkhill,
 Murray Hanaham, and Clarence Keller. CBC Radio Morningside Documentary on
 the victims of the August 25, 1977 Coke Ovens Explosion. Morningside.
Beaton Institute Tape 2338. n.d. MacDonald, Hugh Gillis. History of Riverside,
 Inverness County.
Beaton Institute Tape 2339. n.d. MacLellan, Marie, and Theresa MacLellan. Biographies.
Beaton Institute Tape 2342. 1970. Hart, Ernest. Stories about North East Margaree.
Beaton Institute Tape 2347. 31 August 1989. Caume, Blair. Steel Plant.
Beaton Institute Tape 2354. n.d. Keough, John, and Cameron MacKenzie. Fishing in
 Cape Breton. By Mary K. MacLeod.
Beaton Institute Tape 2370 [Tape 2]. 7 June 1988. Aitken, Stella, Vernie Aitken, Mel
 Aitken. Historic Research on Westmount. By Lisa Campbell.
Beaton Institute Tape 2371. 9 June 1988. Bain, Russell and Clara Russell. Historic
 Research on Westmount.
Beaton Institute Tape 2372. 10 June 1988. Whitty, Sophie. Historic Research on
 Westmount.
Beaton Institute Tape 2373. 16 June 1988. McLellan, Daniel. Historic Research on
 Westmount.

Beaton Institute Tape 2374. 15 July 1988. Rudderham, Ouida. Historic Research on Westmount.

Beaton Institute Tape 2375. July 1988. Youden, Annie. Historic Research on Westmount.

Beaton Institute Tape 2378 A. 1989. MacDonald, Agnes. History of Point Edward.

Beaton Institute Tape 2378 B. 1989. Fraser, Robert. History of Point Edward.

Beaton Institute Tape 2380. July 1989. Fraser, Lloyd, and Gilbert Lewis. History of Point Edward and Westmount.

Beaton Institute Tape 2381. 1988. Gillis, Rita, and Vera Ratchford. Cape Breton Women Working at the Sydney Steel Plant.

Beaton Institute Tape 2390. 1986. Richards, Robert, Ward MacLennan, Johnston MacKinnon, and Hughie MacKinnon. Dairy Farming in South Bar.

Beaton Institute Tape 2399. 25 January 1989. Fitzgerald, John Robb. Sugar Loaf.

Beaton Institute Tape 2400 A. March 1989. Gillis, B. J. Bochan Stories.

Beaton Institute Tape 2400 B. 21 March 1989. Rankin, Sally. Prayer Line.

Beaton Institute Tape 2401. 1989. Skinner, Basil. Model Railroading. By Steven Lewis.

Beaton Institute Tape 2403 [Tape 1]. 2 February 1989. Greenwell, Mary. Ice Cream Making.

Beaton Institute Tape 2403 [Tape 2]. 27 February 1989. Aspinall, Evelyn. Ice Cream Making.

Beaton Institute Tape 2404 [Tapes 1 and 2]. 1989. Lewis, Brian. Personal History.

Beaton Institute Tape 2406. 26 March 1989. MacDonald, Cora Lee. Step Dancing.

Beaton Institute Tape 2409. 1989. Hart, Mrs. Toots. Humor and Stories.

Beaton Institute Tape 2411 [Tapes 1 and 2]. 1985. MacDougall, Margaret. Stories and Folklore.

Beaton Institute Tape 2420. September 1979. Scott, Eric. Dominion, Bridgeport and Area History. By Lennie Stephenson.

Beaton Institute Tape 2421 [Tapes 1 and 2]. 1979. MacVicar, Fred. Dominion History. By Len Stephenson.

Beaton Institute Tape 2424. 1988. Hest, Theresa, and Gerald Spencer. History of the Bottom Lake Road.

Beaton Institute Tape 2425 [Tape 1]. 9 April 1987. MacDonald, Charles. History of Cape Breton Chorale. By Katherine Godwin.

Beaton Institute Tape 2425. [Tape 2]. 1987. Clare, Sr. Rita. History of the Cape Breton Chorale. By Katherine Godwin.

Beaton Institute Tape 2428 [Tape 1]. 13 July 1989. Cechetto, Angello. Life Story of Angelo Cechetto: Canadian/Italian Shoemaker in Dominion, and 18 July 1989. Chronis, Themis. Life Story of Themis Chronis Markodonis Shoe Repair, Glace Bay.

Beaton Institute Tape 2429. 1988. MacNeil, Capt. Angus. Iona-Grand Narrows Ferry.

Beaton Institute Tape 2431. Dec 1981. MacKenzie, Harvey, and Harvey MacEwan. W. R. MacAskill and Family, St. Peters.

Beaton Institute Tape 2501. 18 May 1990. Anderson, Charles. Steel Project: Pattern Shop, Mechanical Design, Sketch Shop.

Beaton Institute Tape 2502 B. September 1990. Aucoin, Shelly. Steel Project: His Career at Steel Plant.

Beaton Institute Tape 2503. 28 March 1990. Bonnell, Owen. Steel Project: Roll Mills.

Beaton Institute Tape 2508. 20 September 1990. Cadden, Alfreo. Steel Project: Baghouse Operator.

Beaton Institute Tape 2513 A. 25 November 1989. Caume, Brian. Steel Project: Blast Furnace Slide Identification.

Beaton Institute Tape 2531. 21 November 1990. Ellis, Wayne. Steel Project: Concast.

Beaton Institute Tape 2600 A. 26 September 1989. Miles, John. Steel Project: Coke Ovens.

Beaton Institute Tape 2600 B. 3 October 1989. Miles, John. Steel Project: Coke Ovens.

Beaton Institute Tape 2600 E. 30 March 1990. Miles, John. Steel Plant: Coke Ovens.

Beaton Institute Tape 2615. September 1990. O'Neil, Ben. Steel Project: Welder and Union Activist.

Beaton Institute Tape 2622. 30 October 1990. Phillipo, Donald. Steel Making: Millwright.

Beaton Institute Tape 2623 A. 15 May 1990. Pickles, Walter. Steel Making.

Beaton Institute Tape 2623 B. 15 May 1990. Pickles, Walter. Steel Making.

Beaton Institute Tape 2623 C. 15 May 1990. Pickles, Walter. Steel Making.

Beaton Institute Tape 2624. 26 October 1990. Pierre, Archie. Steel Making.

Beaton Institute Tape 2631. 29 January 1990. Ruck, Winston. Steel Project: General Yard Electrician and Union Affairs.

Beaton Institute Tape 2639. 1990. Sprackling, Garfield. Steel Project: Planning Scales.

Beaton Institute Tape 2652. 1991. Young, Rose Grant. Steel Project.

Beaton Institute Tape 2657. 9 June 1989. Closing of the Open Hearth. By Joella Foulds. CBC Radio, Sydney, Information Morning.

Beaton Institute Tape 2659. 17 April 1991. Henrich, Kay. Steel Project: Women in the Steel Mill, WW II.

Beaton Institute Tape 2670. June 1992. Delorenzo, Benny, and Dan Yakimchuk. Steel Plant Safety. By Joyce Ruck.

Beaton Institute Tape 3000. 1992. Robertson, Robbie. History of Radio Station CJCB.

Beaton Institute Tape 3001. 18 April 1992. Holloran, Toby. History of Radio Station CJCB.

Beaton Institute Tape 3002. February 1992. Muggah, Sander, and Victor Coffin. Jack MacLean [Mayor of Sydney]: Alleged Murder of Joseph MacKinnon.

Beaton Institute Tape 3003. 2 February 1990. Rankin, Fr. John Angus. [Glendale]. St. Margaret of Scotland, River Denys Mountain.

Beaton Institute Tape 3004. 1 March 1990. MacIsaac, Hughie [Port Hawkesbury]. St. Margaret of Scotland Church, River Denys Mountain.

Beaton Institute Tape 3005. 23 February 1990. MacLeod, Mrs. Dan [Glendale]. St. Margaret of Scotland Church, River Denys Mountain.

Beaton Institute Tape 3006. 22 March 1990. MacDonald, Jessie. St. Margaret of Scotland Church, River Denys Mountain.

Beaton Institute Tape 3007. 9 January 1990. White, Fred. Concerts and Festivals. By Anne Hollohan.

Beaton Institute Tape 3008. 22 January 1990. MacPhee, Doug. Concerts and Festivals. By Anne Hollohan.

Beaton Institute Tape 3009. 5 February 1990. MacNeil, Joe Neil. Concerts and Festivals. By Anne Hollohan.

Beaton Institute Tape 3010. 5 February 1990. MacNeil, Joe. Concerts and Festivals. By Anne Hollohan.

Beaton Institute Tape 3011. 9 February 1990. MacNeil, Jackie. Concerts and Festivals.

Beaton Institute Tape 3012. 13 February 1990. MacInnis, Dan Joe. Concerts and Festivals. By Anne Hollohan.

Beaton Institute Tape 3013. 16 February 1990. MacEachern, Fr. John Hugh. Concerts and Festivals.

Beaton Institute Tape 3014. 17 February 1990. MacInnes, Sheldon. Concerts and Festivals.

Beaton Institute Tape 3015. 17 February 1990. MacInnes, Sheldon. Concerts and Festivals.

Beaton Institute Tape 3016. 12 January 1990. Kyte, John. Blacksmithing and Harness Racing, Sydney.

Beaton Institute Tape 3017. 3 January 1990. Moffatt, James. Harness Racing: Owner, Trainer and Driver [Sydney].

Beaton Institute Tape 3018. April 1990. Bernard, Darrell. Native War Veterans.

Beaton Institute Tape 3080. 1985. MacRury, Isabelle et al. Baddeck History.

Beaton Institute Tape 3089. 1970. Horton, Greg. Legends and Forerunners.

Beaton Institute Tape 3129. 1990. Haley, Jim. Glace Bay.

Beaton Institute Tape 3145. 1968. Milling Frolic [Gaelic only]. North River.

Beaton Institute Tape 3184. 21 January 1991. Campbell, Alan. Folklore 100: Broughton. By Eleanor Anderson.

Beaton Institute Tape 3185. 11 February 1992. Caplan, Ronald. Twenty Years of Oral History. By Dawn Morrison.

Beaton Institute Tape 3186. 11 February 1992. St. Clair, Jim. Folklore. By Dawn Morrison.

Beaton Institute Tape 3187. 18 March 1992. Chafe, Winnifred. Life History. By Mary Ferguson.

Beaton Institute Tape 3191 A. 1993. [Side B a duplicate]. Chaisson, Joe, Bill Hefferman, and Alex MacDonald. 1925 Miners' Strike.

Beaton Institute Tape 3205. 1986. Welcome to Cape Breton, Summer 1986.

Beaton Institute Tape 3215. 23 March 1993. Denny, Sarah. Native Folk Medicine.

Beaton Institute Tape 3216. February 1993. Fagan, Theresa. World War II Experiences. By Margie McMullin.

Beaton Institute Tape 3217. 1989. Rice, George S. Modern Music and Folklore.

Beaton Institute Tape 3219. 21 September 1993. Rankin, Fr. John Angus. Devil Legends. By Don Bonnar.

Beaton Institute Tape 3219 A. 9 February 1993. St. Clair, Jim. Devil Legends. By Don Bonnar.

Beaton Institute Tape 3219 B. 10 February 1993. MacLellan, Leonard. Devil Legends.

Beaton Institute Tape 3219 C. 28 March 1993. Helena Bonnar and Gertie Bonnar. Devil Legends. By Don Bonnar.

Beaton Institute Tape 3219 E. 21 September 1993. Chisholm, Archie Neil, Host and Storyteller. Devil Legends. CBC Radio, Sydney, Archie Neil's Cape Breton.

Beaton Institute Tape 3229 A. 20 March 1993. Roper, Keith. Fishing in Ingonish. By Kim Stockley.

Beaton Institute Tape 3229 B. 21 May. 1993. Stockley, Earl. Fishing in Ingonish. By Kim Stockley.

Beaton Institute Tape 3230. 30 March 1993. Edwards, Kelly. Witchcraft. By Heather MacIsaac.

Beaton Institute Tape 3231. n.d. Riggs, Stewart. Railroads in Cape Breton. By G. Nightingale.

Beaton Institute Tape 5928. 1986. Lahey, M. Steel Project: Voices. Open Hearth.

Beaton Institute Tape [no number, side 2]. July 1976. Beaton, Joey. Biography.

Beaton Institute Tape [no number]. 1987. Brown [two brothers]. Washabuck, Cape Breton.

Beaton Institute Tape [no number]. n.d. Ceilidh.

Beaton Institute Tape [no number, side one]. 28 July 1976. Chisholm, Archie Neil. Margaree Forks.

Beaton Institute Tape [no number, side one]. 29 June 1976. MacDonald, Dan R. Biography.

Beaton Institute Tape [no number, side one]. July 1976. MacEachern, Dan Hughie. Biography.

Beaton Institute Tape [no number, side two]. 1977. MacKillop, Angus. Easter Customs in Creignish.

Beaton Institute Tape [no number]. July 1977. MacNeil, Steven R. Proverbs and Life in Barra.

Beaton Institute Tape [no number]. 3 April 1991. Milling Frolics.

Beaton Institute Tape [no number, side 2]. 12 July 1976. Rankin, The Family. Biography.

Dictionary of Cape Breton English Tapes

1995 *DCBE* Tape. Dan Nicholson, Glace Bay Miners' Museum.

1995 *DCBE* Tape. Jim Smith, Glace Bay Miners' Museum.

2002 *DCBE* Tape. *Information Morning*, CBC Radio, Sydney (27 February).

2007 *DCBE* Tape. Ann Sherrington, St. Ninian.

2008 *DCBE* Tape. Sheldon Currie, formerly of Reserve Mines, now Antigonish.

Miners' Museum Tapes

Miners' Museum Tape 1. 1976–1977. Scott Collection. Professionals.

Miners' Museum Tape 2. 1976–1977. Scott Collection. Teacher and Husband.

Miners' Museum Tape 3. 1976–1977. Scott Collection. Salesman.

Miners' Museum Tape 5. 1976–1977. Scott Collection. Train Engineer.

Miners' Museum Tape 6. 1976–1977. Scott Collection. Deputy Fire Marshal and Spouse.

Miners' Museum Tape 7. 1976–1977. Scott Collection. Factory Worker and Coal Miner from New Waterford.

Miners' Museum Tape 8. 1976–1977. Scott Collection. Coal Miner, New Waterford.

Miners' Museum Tape 9. 1976–1977. Scott Collection. Coal Miner, Hoisting Engineer, New Waterford.

Miners' Museum Tape 10. 1976–1977. Scott Collection. Coal Miner, Scotchtown.

Miners' Museum Tape 11. 1976–1977. Scott Collection. Coal Miner, Pumps Man, New Waterford.

Miners' Museum Tape 12. 1976–1977. Scott Collection. Coal Miner and Dairy Operator.

Miners' Museum Tape 13. 1976–1977. Scott Collection. Telegraph Operator.

Miners' Museum Tape 14. 1976–1977. Scott Collection. Coal Miner, Drillman, and Steel Worker.

Miners' Museum Tape 15. 1976–1977. Scott Collection. Retirement.

Miners' Museum Tape 16. 1976–1977. Scott Collection. Coal Miner.

Miners' Museum Tape 17. 1976–1977. Scott Collection. Coal Miner, Mechanic.

Miners' Museum Tape 18. 1976–1977. Scott Collection. Coal Miner, Underground Supervisor.

Miners' Museum Tape 19. 1976–1977. Scott Collection. Spouse of Retiree.

Miners' Museum Tape 20. 1976–1977. Scott Collection. General Manager, Eastern Light and Power.

Miners' Museum Tape 24. 1976–1977. Scott Collection. Steel Worker, Boiler Worker, Former Mayor.

Miners' Museum Tape 25. 1976–1977. Scott Collection. Worker at Department of Revenue, Sydney.

Miners' Museum Tape 26. 1976–1977. Scott Collection. Coal Miner, Number 12, New Waterford.

Miners' Museum Tape 27. 1976–1977. Scott Collection. Coal Miner, New Waterford.

Miners' Museum Tape 28. 1976–1977. Scott Collection. O. R. Nurse, New Waterford.

Miners' Museum Tape 29. 1976–1977. Scott Collection. House Cleaner, New Waterford.

Miners' Museum Tape 30. 1976–1977. Scott Collection. Coal Miner, Glace Bay.

Miners' Museum Tape 31. 1976–1977. Scott Collection. Spouse of Coal Miner, Glace Bay.

Miners' Museum Tape 32. 1976–1977. Scott Collection. Coal Miner, Glace Bay.

Miners' Museum Tape 33. 1976–1977. Scott Collection. Steel Worker, Sydney.

Miners' Museum Tape 34. 1976–1977. Scott Collection. Steel Worker, Sydney.

Miners' Museum Tape 35. 1976–1977. Scott Collection. Steel Worker, Sydney.

Miners' Museum Tape 36. 1976–1977. Scott Collection. Carpenter, Self-employed.

Miners' Museum Tape 37. 1976–1977. Scott Collection. Construction Worker, Sydney.

Miners' Museum Tape 45. 1976–1977. Scott Collection. Coal Miner.

Miners' Museum Tape 46. 1976–1977. Scott Collection. Coal Miner.

Miners' Museum Tape 48 [Tapes 1–3]. 1976–1977. Scott Collection. Trade Union Worker, Sydney

Miners' Museum Tape 49. 1976–1977. Scott Collection. Coal Miner and Spouse, Dominion.

Miners' Museum Tape 50 [Tapes 1–3]. 1976–1977. Scott Collection. Doctor, Glace Bay.

Miners' Museum Tape 60 [Tapes 1 and 2]. 1976–1977. Scott Collection. Steel Worker.

Miners' Museum Tape 61[A]. 1976–1977. Scott Collection. Railroad Worker, Sydney.

Miners' Museum Tape 61[B]. 1976–1977. Scott Collection. Spouse of Steel Worker.

Miners' Museum Tape 62. 1976–1977. Scott Collection. Auto Mechanic, Sydney.

Miners' Museum Tape 63 [Tapes 1 and 2]. 1976–1977. Scott Collection. Millwright, Sydney.

Miners' Museum Tape 64. 1976–1977. Scott Collection. Retired Post Master, Sydney.

Miners' Museum Tape 71 [Tapes 1 and 2]. 1976–1977. Scott Collection. General Foreman, Power Commission, and Coal Miner.

Miners' Museum Tape 72. 1976–1977. Scott Collection. Steel Worker and Coal Company.

Miners' Museum Tape 73. 1976–1977. Scott Collection. Teacher.

Miners' Museum Tape 75. 1976–1977. Scott Collection. Post Master.

Miners' Museum Tape 124. 1976–1977. Scott Collection. Coal Miner.

Miners' Museum Tape 125. 1976–1977. Scott Collection. Female Youth Camp Worker.

Miners' Museum Tape 128. 1976–1977. Scott Collection. Post Office Clerk.
Miners' Museum Tape 415. 1976–1977. Scott Collection. Senior Woman.
Miners' Museum Tape 425. 1976–1977. Scott Collection. Senior Woman.
Miners' Museum Tape 745. 1976–1977. Scott Collection. Housewife.
Miners' Museum Tape 785. 1976–1977. Scott Collection. Housewife.
Miners' Museum Tape [no number]. 25 October 1976. Scott Collection. Open State
    Project.
Miners' Museum Tape [no number]. October 1976. Scott Collection. Various Newscasts
    from CBC Radio and TV and CJCB Radio and Interview with Evan Scott on CBC
    Radio and TV.

Sydney and Louisbourg Railway Tapes

Sydney and Louisbourg Railway Tape [no number.] 24 January 1989. Lewis, Harvey.
Sydney and Louisbourg Railway Tape [no number]. 26 January 1989. Matias, Joas
    [John].
Sydney and Louisbourg Railway Tape [no number]. 24 January 1989. Pope, Mary.
Sydney and Louisbourg Railway Tape [no number]. 25 January 1989. Thomas, Dan Joe.
Sydney and Louisbourg Railway Tape [no number]. 26 January 1989. Trim, Joey.
Sydney and Louisbourg Railway Tape [no number]. 25 January 1989. Wilcox, Mary
    May [Poet].

MANUSCRIPTS

MB [Microfilm] 65. Huntington, Melvin S. Diaries, 1905–1996. Beaton Institute, Cape
    Breton University, Sydney, NS.
MG 1, Box 1840, Folder 7. Elmsley, Robert. Historical Baddeck, 1840–1889. Nova Scotia
    Archives and Records Management, Halifax, NS.
MG 3, 34. Kearny, Ann. Diary, 1802. Beaton Institute, Cape Breton University, Sydney, NS.
MG 6, 23. MacKenzie Mrs. Hugh (nee Mary Ann MacNeil). Diaries, 1950–1955. Hugh
    Francis MacKenzie, Papers 1905–1986. Beaton Institute, Cape Breton University,
    Sydney, NS.
MG 12, 1. Smith, James Mariner. Correspondence and Papers, 1813–1961. Beaton
    Institute, Cape Breton University, Sydney, NS.
MG 12, 2. Cash, Colin. Diary, 1882–1970. Beaton Institute, Cape Breton University,
    Sydney, NS.
MG 12, 17. Boyle, Dougald Robert. Diary, 1886–1887. Beaton Institute, Cape Breton
    University, Sydney, NS.
MG 12, 18. Brodie, Douglas Neil. Papers, 1940–1954. Beaton Institute, Cape Breton
    University, Sydney, NS.
MG 12, 29. Chapman, Emily. Papers and Notes, 1969. Beaton Institute, Cape Breton
    University, Sydney, NS.
MG 12, 30. Carey, John. Papers, 1888–1938. Beaton Institute, Cape Breton University,
    Sydney, NS.

MG 12, 32. Livingston, Joe. Diaries, 1870–1913. Beaton Institute, Cape Breton University, Sydney, NS.

MG 12, 35. Day, Angus Cyprian. Collection, 1933–1973. Beaton Institute, Cape Breton University, Sydney, NS.

MG 12, 37. Kelly, Michael. Diary, 1918–1952. Beaton Institute, Cape Breton University, Sydney, NS.

MG 12, 40. Dwyer, Michael. Papers, 1871–1971. Beaton Institute, Cape Breton University, Sydney, NS.

MG 12, 43. Crawley, Ann Leslie (Bown). Collection, 1767–1978. Beaton Institute, Cape Breton University, Sydney, NS.

MG 12, 45. Hart, John S. Collection, 1842–1946, and Mary Elizabeth Smith. Diaries, 1890–1891. Beaton Institute, Cape Breton University, Sydney, NS.

MG 12, 46. Morrison, Duncan Seward. Diaries and Papers, 1847–1953. Beaton Institute, Cape Breton University, Sydney, NS.

MG 12, 50. Parker, John. Correspondence, 1954–60. Beaton Institute, Cape Breton University, Sydney, NS.

MG 12, 51. MacDonald, Eugene Daniel. Papers, 1891–1955. Beaton Institute, Cape Breton University, Sydney, NS.

MG 12, 53. Howie, Rev. John William. Papers, 1835–1875. Beaton Institute, Cape Breton University, Sydney, NS.

MG 12, 58. Marsh, Flora Hallie. Memoirs, 1882–1968, and Mary Killam MacQuarrie. Genealogies in the Florie Hallie MacQuarrie Marsh, Papers, 1882–1968. Beaton Institute, Cape Breton University, Sydney, NS.

MG 12, 59. Liscombe, Ella. Liscombe Family Papers, 1860–1940. Beaton Institute, Cape Breton University, Sydney, NS.

MG 12, 75. Chappell, Melbourne Russell. Papers, 1894–1979. Beaton Institute, Cape Breton University, Sydney, NS.

MG 12, 76. Lynch, John George Brooks. Papers, 1885–1973. Printed Works 1870,1902, 1931 and undated. Beaton Institute, Cape Breton University, Sydney, NS.

MG 12, 77. Bethune, Clarence. Correspondence, 1865–1964. Beaton Institute, Cape Breton University, Sydney, NS.

MG 12, 78. Stevenson, L. B. [Bricky]. Correspondence and Papers, 1928–1949. Beaton Institute, Cape Breton University, Sydney, NS.

MG 12, 79. Morrison, Donald Neil. 1965. History of Some of the Families who Lived at Loch Lomond, Cape Breton, One Hundred Years Ago. Beaton Institute, Cape Breton University, Sydney, NS.

MG 12, 80. Maddin, James W. Papers, 1905–1961. Beaton Institute, Cape Breton University, Sydney, NS.

MG 12, 81. Hay, Alexander Lauder. Speeches, 1929–1938. Beaton Institute, Cape Breton University, Sydney, NS.

MG 12, 86. Newton, David. Radio Scripts, 1969. Beaton Institute, Cape Breton University, Sydney, NS.

MG 12, 88. MacDonald, William "Billy Senator." MacDonald Papers, 1899–1959. Beaton Institute, Cape Breton University, Sydney, NS.

MG 12, 91. Sutherland, Hester. Letter, 1875. Beaton Institute, Cape Breton University, Sydney, NS.

MG 12, 93. MacDonald, David. Diary, 1905–1920. Beaton Institute, Cape Breton
University, Sydney, NS.

MG 12, 100. MacDonald, Effie. Diaries, 1941–1962. Beaton Institute, Cape Breton
University, Sydney, NS.

MG 12, 101. Spencer Family Papers, 1845–1975. Beaton Institute, Cape Breton
University, Sydney, NS.

MG 12, 103. MacEachern, Elizabeth. Collection, 1817–1972. Beaton Institute, Cape
Breton University, Sydney, NS.

MG 12, 104. Howatson Family, Little Bras' d'Or. Papers, 1837–1897. Beaton Institute,
Cape Breton University, Sydney, NS.

MG 12, 105. Willing, Capt. John W. Correspondence, 1903. Beaton Institute, Cape
Breton University, Sydney, NS.

MG 12, 107. Anonymous Diary of Daily Events in Dominion in 1946. Beaton Institute,
Cape Breton University Sydney, NS.

MG 12, 108. MacKenzie, Dan. Diary, 1940–1950. Beaton Institute, Cape Breton
University, Sydney, NS.

MG 12, 109. McKeen, William. Correspondence, 1820–1852. Beaton Institute, Cape
Breton University, Sydney, NS.

MG 12, 112. Rigby, Charles. Personal Papers, 1827–1952. Beaton Institute, Cape Breton
University, Sydney, NS.

MG 12, 118. Johnston, Roderick, A. Papers, Diaries and Genealogies, 1858–1896. Beaton
Institute, Cape Breton University, Sydney, NS.

MG 12, 121. Andrew, Edmund. History of Coxheath, n.d. Beaton Institute, Cape Breton
University, Sydney, NS.

MG 12, 122. MacDonald, Angus. Tributes, 1945–1950. Beaton Institute, Cape Breton
University, Sydney, NS.

MG 12, 123. Crowdis, Edward. Papers, 1883–1949. Beaton Institute, Cape Breton
University, Sydney, NS.

MG 12, 127. MacDonald, John Archy. Diary and Papers, 1834–1967. Beaton Institute,
Cape Breton University, Sydney, NS.

MG 12, 129. MacGregor, Gordon. 1971. History of Coal Mines and Mining in Cape
Breton. Beaton Institute, Cape Breton University, Sydney, NS.

MG 12, 130. MacIntyre, Archie. Correspondence and Papers, 1896–1969. Beaton
Institute, Cape Breton University, Sydney, NS.

MG 12, 131. MacDonald, Angus J. Papers and Correspondence, 1885–1952. Beaton
Institute, Cape Breton University, Sydney, NS.

MG 12, 132. MacLean, Alexander D. Papers, 1878–1974. Beaton Institute, Cape Breton
University, Sydney, NS.

MG 12, 133. MacDonald, Kay. Papers, 1929–1976. Beaton Institute, Cape Breton
University, Sydney, NS.

MG 12, 134. MacLeod, Malcolm A. Papers, 1908–1950. Beaton Institute, Cape Breton
University, Sydney, NS.

MG 12, 137. MacKinnon, John A. M. Diaries, 1916–1934 in John J. MacKinnon Family
Papers. Beaton Institute, Cape Breton University, Sydney, NS.

MG 12, 146. MacNeil, John. Diary, 1919–1940. Beaton Institute, Cape Breton University,
Sydney, NS.

MG 12, 147. MacMillan, Cecilia. Diaries, 1917–1969, and E. McPherson, Diaries, 1935–1959 in the James MacMillan Papers. Beaton Institute, Cape Breton University, Sydney, NS.

MG 12, 148. MacDonald, Malcolm. Correspondence, 1900–1956. Beaton Institute, Cape Breton University, Sydney, NS.

MG 12, 150. MacNeil, James Hector. Correspondence and Papers, 1888–1918. Beaton Institute, Cape Breton University, Sydney, NS.

MG 12, 151. Kimber, Hettie. Correspondence and Papers, 1882–1903. Beaton Institute, Cape Breton University, Sydney, NS.

MG 12, 152. MacNeil, Angus D. [Captain]. Papers, 1895–1958. Beaton Institute, Cape Breton University, Sydney, NS.

MG 12, 153. Worgan, Philip H. Papers, 1859– 1969. Beaton Institute, Cape Breton University, Sydney, NS.

MG 12, 155. MacKenzie, Donald J. Some Community Landmarks and Events, 1869–1962. Beaton Institute, Cape Breton University, Sydney, NS.

MG 12, 156. Matheson, Roderick. Correspondence, 1915–1925. Beaton Institute, Cape Breton University, Sydney, NS.

MG 12, 158. Cleary, Fred. Correspondence and Clippings, 1929–1948. Beaton Institute, Cape Breton University, Sydney, NS.

MG 12, 159. Moran, Walter. Papers, 1870–1935. Beaton Institute, Cape Breton University, Sydney, NS.

MG 12, 161. Randall, W. Albert. Family Papers, 1875–1904. Beaton Institute, Cape Breton University, Sydney, NS.

MG 12, 167. Winton, Mary [Townsend]. Diary, 1892–1893. Beaton Institute, Cape Breton University, Sydney, NS.

MG 12, 174. MacDonald, Murdoch. Diary, 1940–1942. Beaton Institute, Cape Breton University, Sydney, NS.

MG 12, 178. Diary of the Lightkeeper at Clarke's Cove, Inverness County, 1900–1901 in the Joseph Matheson Papers. Beaton Institute, Cape Breton University, Sydney, NS.

MG 12, 185. MacDonald, David [of Cape North]. Diary, 1879–1895. Beaton Institute, Cape Breton University, Sydney, NS.

MG 12, 186. Nicoll, David Edward. Diary, 1893–1910. Beaton Institute, Cape Breton University, Sydney, NS.

MG 12, 192. Calder, Alvinus. Papers, 1962. Beaton Institute, Cape Breton University, Sydney, NS.

MG 12, 220. MacNeil, Theodore. MacNeil Diary, 1939–1948. Beaton Institute, Cape Breton University, NS.

MG 12, 224. Mann, Stella. Papers, 1858–1987. Beaton Institute, Cape Breton University, Sydney, NS.

MG 12, 238. Toward, Lilias M. 1985. Cape Breton: Those Who Came Before Us. Beaton Institute, Cape Breton University, Sydney, NS.

MG 12, 243. MacKinnon, Ed and Harriet MacKinnon. Diary, Trip around the Cabot Trail, 1943. Beaton Institute, Cape Breton University, Sydney, NS.

MG 12, 246. Davis, Donna, et al. 1976. History and Folklore of Inverness County. Beaton Institute, Cape Breton University, Sydney, NS.

MG 12, 247. MacRae, Martha, and Jessie MacRae MacKay. Letters, 1857–1889. Beaton Institute, Cape Breton University, Sydney, NS.

MG 14, 52. ARDA [Agricultural Redevelopment Areas]. Minutes of Meetings held in Little Judique Ponds, 1965. Beaton Institute, Cape Breton University, Sydney, NS.

MG 14, 63. Anderson, Eleanor L. et al. 1993. The Silent City: The History of Hardwood Hill Cemetery. Sydney, NS: UCCB Heritage Studies Group, Beaton Institute, Cape Breton University, Sydney, NS.

MG 14, 79. *BESCO Bulletin* 10 July 1926 to 14 February 1925. Beaton Institute, Cape Breton University, Sydney, NS.

MG 14, 116. Boys of Old Sydney Record Book, 1905–1925. Beaton Institute, Cape Breton University, Sydney, NS.

MG 14, 117. Lyceum Papers, 1903–1906. Beaton Institute, Cape Breton University, Sydney, NS.

MG 14, 118. Inverness County Temperance League. Correspondence and Minutes, 1910–1911. Beaton Institute, Cape Breton University, Sydney, NS.

MG 14, 158. North Highland Museum Collection, 1811–1940. Beaton Institute, Cape Breton University, Sydney, NS.

MG 14, 206. Cameron, Russell. Steel Project, File 5, 1990. Beaton Institute, Cape Breton University, NS.

MG 14, 206. Caume, Blair. Steel Project, File 10, 1989. Beaton Institute, Cape Breton University, NS.

MG 14, 206. Davis, Gerald. Steel Project, File 10, 1990. Beaton Institute, Cape Breton University, NS.

MG 14, 206. Flynn, Edward. Steel Project, File 19, 1990. Beaton Institute, Cape Breton University, NS.

MG 14, 206. Green, Frank. Steel Project, File 22, 1990. Beaton Institute, Cape Breton University, NS.

MG 14, 206. Gillis, Francis. Steel Project, File 23, 1990. Beaton Institute, Cape Breton University, NS.

MG 14, 206. MacAdam, John. Steel Project, File 36, 1990. Beaton Institute, Cape Breton University, NS.

MG 14, 206. MacAskill, Daniel. Steel Project, File 37, 1990. Beaton Institute, Cape Breton University, NS.

MG 14, 206. MacCormack, Gerald. Steel Project, File 38, 1990. Beaton Institute, Cape Breton University, NS.

MG 14, 206. Martheleur, Ray. Steel Project, File 45, 1991. Beaton Institute, Cape Breton University, NS.

MG 14, 206. MacNeil, Harvey. Steel Project, File 49, 1990. Beaton Institute, Cape Breton University, NS.

MG 14, 206. Muise, Nelson. Steel Project, File 55, 1990. Beaton Institute, Cape Breton University, NS.

MG 14, 206. Murphy, John. Steel Project, File 57, 1990. Beaton Institute, Cape Breton University, NS.

MG 14, 206. Orychuk, Don. Steel Project, File 60, 1990. Beaton Institute, Cape Breton University, NS.

MG 14, 206. Parris, Eddie. Steel Project, File 62, 1990. Beaton Institute, Cape Breton University, NS.

MG 14, 206. Sokol, Steve. Steel Project, File 67. 1990. Beaton Institute, Cape Breton University, NS.

MG 14, 206. Stevens, Michael. Steel Project, File 79, 1990. Beaton Institute, Cape Breton University, NS.

MG 14, 206. Whalen, Harold. Steel Project, File 84, 1990. Beaton Institute, Cape Breton University, NS.

MG 14 206. Young, Rose Grant. Steel Project, File 87, 1991. Beaton Institute, Cape Breton University, NS.

MG 20, 25. Murphy, Lt. James A. Private Papers, 1915–1972. Beaton Institute, Cape Breton University, Sydney, NS.

Scrapbooks 122, 122. Ecology: Pollution. 1981–1997. *Cape Breton Post* Newspaper Clippings File. Institute, Cape Breton University, Sydney, NS.

Scrapbook 139. Forestry. Beaton Institute, Cape Scrapbook of the King Edward Division and Hall of the Sons of Temperance, 1936. In private collection of Francis Butler, Sydney, NS [to be donated at a later date to the Beaton Institute, Cape Breton University, Sydney, N.S].

SURVEY PARTICIPANTS

Participants in the Pilot Survey (1996)

Informant 1 Kevin Kearney (New Waterford)
Informant 2 Nancy Wadden (Port Morien)
Informant 3 Roddy C. MacNeil (Barra Glen)
Informant 4 Patrick O'Shea (Louisbourg)
Informant 5 Gerald Donovan (Sydney)

Participants in Survey I (2002–4)

Informant 1 Tammy MacNeil (Sydney)
Informant 2 David Muise (Sydney)
Informant 3 David Gardiner (New Waterford)
Informant 4 Shirley Gardiner (New Waterford)
Informant 5 James St. Clair (Mull River)
Informant 6 Barry Gabriel (South Bar)
Informant 7 Robin Gillis (RR1 Inverness)
Informant 8 Katherine MacDonald (Port Morien)
Informant 9 Richard Marchand (Louisdale)
Informant 10 Silver Donald Cameron (D'Escousse)
Informant 11 Darlene Gillis (RR1, Ingonish)
Informant 12 Rannie Gillis (Broad Cove)
Informant 13 Carrie MacLean (Rankinville Road)
Informant 14 Mary Gillis (RR1 Inverness)
Informant 15 Geraldine Doucette (Ingonish)
Informant 16 David MacLean (Ingonish)
Informant 17 Harris Stubbert (Millville)

Informant 18 Diane Toomey (Sydney Mines)
Informant 19 Charlie MacLean (North Sydney)
Informant 20 Ann Marie MacNeil (Big Pond)
Informant 21 Karen MacIsaac (Sydney)
Informant 22 Mary Price (Little Lorraine)
Informant 23 Kay Mills (Main-à-Dieu)
Informant 24 Mike MacIsaac (Glace Bay)
Informant 25 Ellen Bugden (Sydney)
Informant 26 Bob Morgan (Sydney)
Informant 27 Redmond Curtis (Sydney)
Informant 28 Josephine Hopkins (Port Morien)
Informant 29 Terry Butts (Birch Grove)
Informant 30 Jason Boudrot (Arichat)
Informant 31 Kevin Kearney (New Waterford)
Informant 32 Ken MacDonald (Port Morien)
Informant 33 Hugh and Patricia McDonald (Port Morien)
Informant 34 Ron Dingwall (New Waterford)
Informant 35 Clara Kearney (New Waterford)
Informant 36 Shirley MacDonald (New Waterford)
Informant 37 Louisa Ranson (New Waterford)
Informant 38 Michael William Vickers (North Sydney)
Informant 39 Brian Targett (Sydney)
Informant 40 Bill Targett (Sydney)
Informant 41 Lisa Johnstone (Leitches Creek)
Informant 42 Michelle Bennett (Coxheath)
Informant 43 Patricia Campbell (North Sydney)
Informant 44 Robert Campbell (North Sydney)
Informant 45 Nancy MacDonald (Coxheath)
Informant 46 Mary MacDonald (Coxheath)
Informant 47 Eric Angus Whyte (Boularderie)
Informant 48 Ashley Marie Dunn (Catalone)
Informant 49 David Woodland (New Waterford)
Informant 50 Murray Morrison (North Sydney)
Informant 51 Beth MacNeil (Beaver Cove)
Informant 52 Shari Archibald (Sydney)
Informant 53 Kerry Gouthro (North Sydney)
Informant 54 Joe Gouthro (Sydney Mines)
Informant 55 Wallace Ellison (West Bay Road)

Participants in Survey II (2002)

Informant 1 Durant Cooke (Port Caledonia)
Informant 2 James MacQueen (Round Island)
Informant 3 Russell Spencer (Main-à-Dieu)
Informant 4 Kevin Spencer (Main-à-Dieu)
Informant 5 Ross Ingraham (Ingonish and Neils Harbour)

Informant 6 Brian Timmins (Big Bras d'Or)
Informant 7 Gerald Gallant (Little Lorraine)
Informant 8 Ralph Trenholm (Big Bras d'Or)

Oral Communications to Editors

Campbell, Terry. Oral Communication. 22 November 1999.
Curtis, Redmond. Oral Communication. 17 May 1998.
Gabriel, Barry. Oral Communication. 2 July 1996.
Gabriel, Barry. Oral Communication. 16 July 1997.
Hayes, Derrick. Oral Communication. 20 September 2009.
Hayes, Derrick. Oral Communication. 18 February 2012.
Inglis, Stephanie, Oral Communication. 8 May 2014.
MacArthur, Carmen. Oral Communication. 12 November 2014.
MacDonald, Charles. Oral Communication. 26 September 1999.
MacDonald, Greg. Oral Communication. 27 January 2000.
MacNeil, Ann Marie. Oral Communication. 20. September 1999.
MacLellan, Philip. Oral Communication. 22 April 1997.
St. Clair, Jim. Oral Communication. 11 May 1998.

EMAILS CITED IN DICTIONARY

Brown, Keith. Email to Bill Davey. 29 Mar. 2004.
Crane, Deborah. Email to Jennifer Gardiner. 23 Feb. 2003.
Doherty, Liz. Email to Richard MacKinnon. 23 Oct. 2013.
Frank, David. Email to Richard MacKinnon. 9 Aug. 2013.
Gabriel, Barry. Email to Bill Davey. 15 Jan. 2003.
Inglis, Stephanie. Email to Bill Davey. 24 February 2014.
Inglis, Stephanie. Email to Bill Davey. 11 May 2016.
Kerfoot, Helen. Email to Bill Davey. 20 Aug. 2009.
MacDonald, Marilyn. Email to Richard MacKinnon. 4 Jan. 2000.
McNeil, J. P. Email to Jennifer Gardiner. 12 Mar. 2004.
Muise, Dave. Email to Bill Davey. 1 Mar. 2002.
Muise, Dave. Email to Bill Davey. 25 Mar. 2002.
Muise, Dave. Email to Bill Davey. 2 Apr. 2002.
Muise, Dave. Email to Bill Davey. 26 Aug. 2002.
Muise, Dave. Email to Bill Davey. 3 July 2003.
Muise, Dave. Email to Bill Davey. 21 June 2008.
Muise, Dave. Email to Bill Davey. 15 Nov. 2011.
Rankin, Joyce. Email to Bill Davey. 23 Mar. 2010.
St. Clair, Jim. Email to Bill Davey. 6 Mar. 2005.
St. Clair, Jim. Email to Bill Davey. 30 Jan. 2007.
St. Clair, Jim. Email to Bill Davey. 15 Mar. 2007.
St. Clair, Jim. Email to Bill Davey. 19 May 2007.

St. Clair, Jim. Email to Bill Davey. 24 Mar. 2007.

St. Clair, Jim. Email to Bill Davey. 10 Feb. 2008.

St. Clair, Jim. Email to Bill Davey. 19 Mar. 2009.

St. Clair, Jim. Email to Bill Davey. 23 May 2010.

St. Clair, Jim. Email to Bill Davey. 27 Oct. 2010.

St. Clair, Jim. Email to Bill Davey. 21 June 2011.

St. Clair, Jim. Email to Bill Davey. 28 June 2011.

Shaw, John. Email to Richard MacKinnon. 16 Feb. 2005.

Sparling, Heather. Email to Richard Mackinnon. 8 Aug. 2013.

Sparling, Heather. Email to Bill Davey and Richard Mackinnon. 18 March 2014.

Sherrington, Ann. Email to Bill Davey. 4 Sept. 2007.

Syms, Laura. Email to Bill Davey. 24 Feb. 2006.

Lightning Source UK Ltd.
Milton Keynes UK
UKOW05f1000090418

320676UK00013B/948/P

9 781442 615991